LEISURE, SPORT AND TOURISM, POLITICS, POLICY AND PLANNING, 3RD EDITION

CABI TOURISM TEXTS are an essential resource for students of academic tourism, leisure studies, hospitality, entertainment, and events management. The series reflects the growth of tourism related studies at an academic level and responds to the changes and developments in these rapidly evolving industries; providing up-to-date practical guidance, discussion of the latest theories and concepts, and analysis by world experts. The series is intended to guide students through their academic programmes and remain an essential reference throughout their careers in the tourism sector.

Readers will find the books within the CABI TOURISM TEXTS series to have a uniquely wide scope; covering important elements in leisure and tourism, including management-led topics, practical subject matter and development of conceptual themes and debates. Useful textbook features are employed throughout the series such as case studies, bullet point summaries and helpful diagrams to aid study and encourage understanding of the subject.

Students at all levels of study, workers within tourism and leisure industries, researchers, academics, policy makers and others interested in the field of academic and practical tourism will find these books an invaluable and authoritative resource, useful for academic reference and real world tourism applications.

Titles available
Ecotourism: Principles and Practices
Ralph Buckley

Contemporary Tourist Behaviour: Yourself and Others as Tourists
David Bowen and Jackie Clarke

The Entertainment Industry: an Introduction
Edited by Stuart Moss

Practical Tourism Research
Stephen L.J. Smith

Leisure, Sport and Tourism, Politics, Policy and Planning, 3rd Edition
A.J. Veal

LEISURE, SPORT AND TOURISM, POLITICS, POLICY AND PLANNING, 3RD EDITION

A.J. Veal

School of Leisure, Sport and Tourism
University of Technology, Sydney
Australia

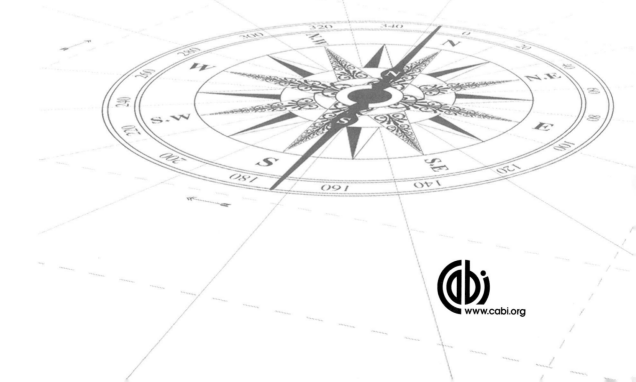

cabi
www.cabi.org

Loughborough
COLLEGE est 1909

CABI is a trading name of CAB International

CABI Head Office
Nosworthy Way
Wallingford
Oxfordshire OX10 8DE
UK

Tel: +44 (0)1491 832111
Fax: +44 (0)1491 833508
E-mail: cabi@cabi.org
Website: www.cabi.org

CABI North American Office
875 Massachusetts Avenue
7th Floor
Cambridge, MA 02139
USA

Tel: +1 617 395 4056
Fax: +1 617 354 6875
E-mail: cabi-nao@cabi.org

A catalogue record for this book is available from the British Library, London, UK.

Library of Congress Cataloging-in-Publication Data

Veal, Anthony James.
   Leisure, sport and tourism : politics, policy and planning / A. J. Veal. – 3rd ed.
      p. cm.
   Rev. ed. of: Leisure and tourism policy and planning. c2002.
   Includes bibliographical references and index.
   ISBN 978-1-84593-523-8 (alk. paper)

   1. Leisure--Government policy--Great Britain. 2. Tourism--Government policy--Great Britain. 3. Recreation--Great Britain--Planning. I. Title.
   GV75.V399 2010
   790.0941--dc22

                                    2010000124

First edition published in 1994 by Longman. ISBN 978 0 58223 820 6
Second edition published in 2002 by CAB International. ISBN: 978 0 85199 546 5

ISBN-13: 978 1 84593 523 8

Commissioning editor: Sarah Hulbert
Production editor: Kate Hill

Typeset by SPi, Pondicherry, India.
Printed and bound in the UK by Cambridge University Press, Cambridge.

CONTENTS

Preface   vii

PART I: Society, Politics, Policy and Planning   1

01   Introduction   3

02   Political Ideologies   18

03   Wants, Needs, Obligations, Demands, Benefits and Participation   44

04   Human Rights and Citizenship Rights   80

05   The Market Versus the State   100

PART II: Planning Frameworks   123

06   Public Policymaking   125

07   Plans and Planning for Leisure, Sport and Tourism   146

08   A Participation-based Approach to Planning for Leisure, Sport and Tourism   181

PART III: Planning Tools   215

09   Planning Tools 1: Consultative   217

10   Planning Tools 2: Facility/Service Audit   242

11   Planning Tools 3: Forecasting   287

PART IV: Evaluation   317

12 Economic Evaluation   319

13 Performance Evaluation   347

PART V: Sectors and Groups   379

14 Policy and Planning in Particular Sectors   381

15 Policy and Planning for Particular Groups   402

    References   417

    Subject Index   445

    Author Index   453

Lists of tables, figures and boxes and a detailed list of contents may be found on the book's website at http://www.leisuresource.net

PREFACE

This is the third edition of a book first published in 1994 by Longman. The evolution of the title from *Leisure Policy and Planning*, via *Leisure and Tourism Policy and Planning* to the current *Leisure, Sport and Tourism, Politics, Policy and Planning* is partly a reflection of a gradual widening of scope of the book and partly a response to the increasing specialization in fields of academic study, academic departments and courses. Thus sport has always been included within the scope of the book as a significant component of leisure, but there is a chance that potential readers involved exclusively with sport might see a book with just the word 'leisure' in its title as not being for them. Similarly, from the beginning, the book has included a chapter on political ideology and has recognized the political nature of policymaking and planning but, for some potential readers, this might not have been apparent from the title. In theory this process could be extended further, with the inclusion of terms such as recreation, exercise, play, events, culture and the arts, and management, decision-making and evaluation, but there are some practical limitations to the length of a book title!

Apart from a change of title, the book has been updated, in terms of reference material and political events. The new Chapter 8 presents a summary of the U-Plan System, a specific approach to planning for leisure that has been developed over the last few years at the University of Technology, Sydney (UTS). It arose from a critical review of some 50 sets of official and academic guidelines on planning for leisure, sport, tourism and culture that identified the many limitations in the currently available advice (Veal, 2009b). The addition of U-Plan has resulted in considerable restructuring of the chapters now included in Part III of the book, including a chapter on public consultation and one on facility/service auditing, which addresses topics such as capacity, usage and catchment areas.

In conducting the review of existing planning guidelines, I also noted that, while textbooks on policymaking and planning in the field invariably and appropriately included in their chapter-by-chapter statements of learning goals such terms as 'understand', 'appreciate' and 'critically evaluate', they rarely included words such as 'conduct', 'undertake' or 'apply'. The declared aim of this book has always been to bridge the gap between theory and practice and, while past editions did included some 'how to do it' sections, such as the conducting of some economic analytical processes, it seemed incumbent on me to do more in this direction. The U-Plan System is a *practical* guide to planning, developed in the first place for practitioners, and backed by a system of spreadsheets available online. Chapters 9–13 also include more applied content.

The supporting website material promised for the last edition has now been made available and comprises a set of PowerPoint slides including all the graphics and tables in the book and a number of the dot-point lists, and material related to the U-Plan System. This can be found at http://www.leisuresource.net.

In an effort to enhance the readability of the book, the amount of in-text referencing to the literature has been reduced, but references to literature related to topics covered in each chapter are provided in the 'resources' sections at the end of each chapter.

Over the years the gap between theory and practice seems to have widened in the leisure, sport and tourism studies areas, partly as a result of the increased specialization among scholars arising from growth in the scale of academic teaching and research. Thus, for example, there are specialists – and associated books, journals and conferences – in critical theory and separate groups of specialists, books, journals and conferences in applied planning and marketing. It is my belief that students should be familiar with as wide a range of social and political theory as possible, but should also be able to reconcile that knowledge and awareness with their own current and future roles as competent practising professionals, deploying practical, constructive, analytical skills. So the book includes theoretical and critical material as well as 'how to do it' sections, particularly in the second half of the book. The aim is therefore to contribute in a modest way to the development of a critically aware and technically competent leisure, sport and tourism planning and management profession.

The book arises from my teaching of public policy since the 1970s, at Birmingham University, the then Polytechnic of North London and the University of Technology, Sydney. Thus, while the intention is for much of the book to be general in nature, it relates particularly to the institutional setting and experiences of the UK and Australia.

While this book was in production, there was a change of government in Britain from Labour, under the Prime Ministership of Gordon Brown, to a Conservative–Liberal Democrat coalition, under the Prime Ministership of David Cameron. In Australia, there was a change of Prime Minister, from Kevin Rudd to Julia Gillard, but not of party. These changes are partly reflected in the text, but not fully. In particular, it has not been possible to amend the discussion of British policy documents in Chapter 13. Updates will be provided on the book's website in due course.

I am grateful to the many cohorts of students who have inspired me to develop this text. I would like to acknowledge the contribution of my colleague at UTS, Simon Darcy, who, as my colleague over a number of years, and now the leader in teaching and developing the unit 'Leisure, Sport and Tourism and Public Policy' at UTS, has provided much encouragement and many valuable insights. I am also grateful to Dr Ken Marriott of HM Leisure Planning, Melbourne, Sally Jeavons of @leisure consultancy, Melbourne, and other colleagues in Parks and Leisure Australia for help and encouragement in the development of the U-Plan system.

Tony Veal
Sydney, August 2010

Society, Politics, Policy and Planning

This part of the book provides a theoretical underpinning for the more applied chapters which follow. It comprises five chapters:

- Chapter 1, *Introduction*, presents some definitions, introduces the idea of government involvement in leisure, sport and tourism, outlines the broad philosophical/political perspective adopted in the book and provides an overview of the book's structure.
- Chapter 2, *Political Ideologies*, summarizes eight different political ideologies: conservatism, neo-liberalism, Marxism, democratic socialism, social democracy and 'Third way' politics, feminism, environmentalism and anti-globalism, and discusses their implications for leisure, sport and tourism policy.
- Chapter 3, *Wants, Needs, Obligations, Demands, Benefits and Participation*, discusses the six concepts in the title and their relationship to public policy in the context of leisure, sport and tourism.
- Chapter 4, *Human Rights and Citizenship Rights*, explores the concept of human rights and the numerous international declarations of rights concerning leisure/free time, children's play, sport and tourism and considers how rights to certain public services have become associated with the status of citizen.
- Chapter 5, *The Market Versus the State*, summarizes the welfare economics arguments for state involvement in a primarily market economy.

chapter 1

Introduction

INTRODUCTION

This book is concerned with the activities of policymaking and planning as carried out by governments and associated agencies in the field of leisure, sport and tourism. Governments are distinguished from organizations in the *private/commercial* and *voluntary/not-for-profit* sectors in that they are generally democratically elected and therefore accountable to the public at large and exercise considerable power over citizens and other institutions, within a framework of law. Government, together with a plethora of appointed and elected agencies and an independent judiciary, is referred to as the *state* or the *public sector*. In a number of Western countries, the distinction between the public and non-public sectors has, however, become less clear in many fields in recent years as more services traditionally provided by public bodies have been sold off, leased or contracted out to private and not-for-profit operators or developed in multi-sector partnerships. Such arrangements have, however, been commonplace in the field of leisure, sport and tourism for many years. Public sector services in this area have often been provided in whole or in part through contract arrangements or through partnerships in which public bodies have leased buildings or provided grant aid to other organizations.

It is hard to think of any type of leisure, sport or tourism facility or service which is not provided by public, commercial *and* not-for-profit organizations. For example: (i) golf courses are provided by local councils, by commercial companies and by not-for-profit clubs; (ii) theatres are owned and operated by governments at all levels, by commercial organizations and by not-for-profit trusts; and (iii) tourist attractions, such as heritage sites, are owned and managed by all three sectors.

Public bodies have for a long time contracted various leisure, sport and tourism functions to commercial and non-profit organizations, including the operation of catering outlets and seasonal swimming pools, and have leased out buildings, such as theatres and heritage sites, sometimes on a commercial basis and sometimes for a 'peppercorn' rent. And many commercial and not-for-profit organizations in sport, tourism, entertainment and the arts make use of public buildings and lands. There has always been a 'mixed economy' of leisure, sport and tourism. However, the scale of change in recent decades has been substantial, bringing a marked shift away from direct public sector management and giving rise to much soul-searching as to the appropriate role of the public and private sectors in leisure, sport and tourism, as in many other sectors.

DEFINING LEISURE, SPORT AND TOURISM

This book deals with leisure, sport and tourism, sometimes referring to them separately and sometimes together. Each of these is a form of human non-work activity, but also an industry and an area of government policy. Each has been subject to continuing debate over the question of definition, but for the purposes of this book we adopt three relatively simple definitions from the many available:

- *Leisure* is 'relatively freely undertaken non-work activity' (Roberts, 1978: 3).
- *Sport* is 'a recreational activity requiring bodily exertion and carried on according to a set of rules' (*Oxford Pocket English Dictionary*).
- *Tourism* is the 'temporary movement of people to destinations outside their normal places of work and residence' (Mathieson and Wall, 1982: 1).

Thus the three phenomena overlap, as shown in Fig. 1.1. Sport is entirely a form of leisure, except for the relatively small number of professional sports people, but in the case of tourism, travel for non-leisure purposes is often included in tourism, for example business and conference travel – but even these travellers generally make use of leisure facilities at their destination, often mixing business and pleasure. The industries associated with these phenomena provide many people with jobs, not only in management and service support, but also in engaging professionally in activities which they see as *work* – for example, professional artists and sports people – but which, when engaged in by the rest of us on an unpaid basis, are seen as *leisure*.

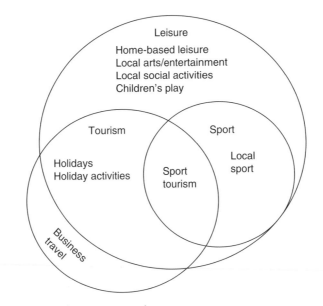

Fig. 1.1. Leisure, sport and tourism: overlaps.

The overlaps and relationships can also be viewed in spatial terms, as illustrated in Fig. 1.2. While leisure and sporting facilities are generally planned primarily to meet the needs of the residents of the local communities in which they are located, many cater both for tourists and locals. Thus the patrons of a restaurant or the visitors to a museum, a beach or a sports stadium are likely to be a mixture of local residents and tourists. The overlap can also be seen in the phenomenon of the day-tripper or excursionist who does not stay overnight in a destination, and is therefore excluded from many definitions of tourism, but who clearly acts like, and has many of the same demands as, the tourist. This intermingling of locals and tourists at leisure may not apply in some situations, or may only apply to a limited extent, where the bulk of local residents are generally much poorer than the tourists and/or when facilities for tourists are deliberately planned in relatively high-priced enclaves.

The geography of leisure, sport and tourism results in five different planning environments of which we are mindful throughout the book, as illustrated in Fig. 1.3.

1. *Single site*: eventually, all planning culminates in consideration of single sites, such as a single park or stadium. In this book we are mostly concerned with the other four scenarios, reflecting the principle that any one facility should be planned within a strategic context, taking account of other similar and/or competing facilities. However, even when planned in a strategic context, major facilities are invariably subject to more detailed individual study, often referred to as a *feasibility study*. Furthermore, we should be aware that much relevant research, particularly in relation to natural areas, has arisen from single-site planning contexts, where the policy focus is on internal management of the site rather than consideration of the strategic context, although there has been some discussion of the limitations of such an approach in the literature (e.g. Jubenville and Becker, 1983).

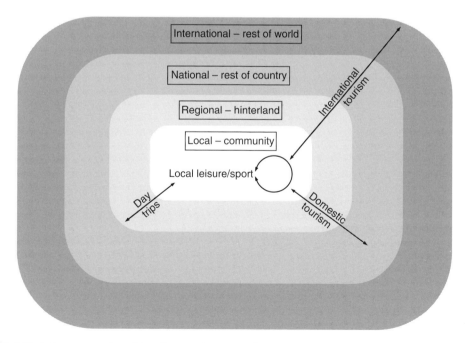

Fig. 1.2. Leisure, sport and tourism and geography.

2. *Urban planning environment*: the residential population is distributed throughout the planning area, as are the existing or projected leisure facilities.

3. *Urban–rural region type A*: the major population centre and a number of lesser population centres are located inside an otherwise rural or semi-rural planning area.

4. *Urban–rural region type B*: the major population centre is located outside the planning area and so a major source, possibly *the* major source, of certain types of leisure participation comes from outside the planning area, probably mainly in the form of day-trippers.

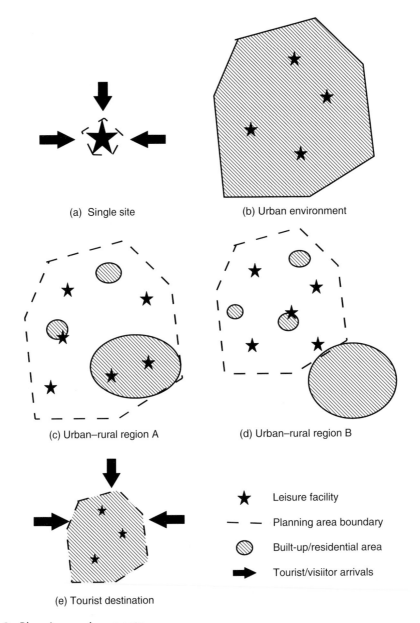

(a) Single site   (b) Urban environment

(c) Urban–rural region A   (d) Urban–rural region B

★   Leisure facility

— —   Planning area boundary

◯   Built-up/residential area

➤   Tourist/visiitor arrivals

(e) Tourist destination

Fig. 1.3. Planning environments.

5. *Tourism destination*: the major focus is on visitors who arrive from outside the region via a number of access points, such as airports or major highways. This can be an additional feature of any of the other three environments.

GOVERNMENTS AND LEISURE, SPORT AND TOURISM

Despite the importance of the commercial and non-profit sectors, substantial parts of the leisure industries nevertheless continue to lie wholly or partly within the public domain, including: (i) urban and national parks; (ii) many sports facilities and events; (iii) arts facilities, organizations and events; (iv) public broadcasting; (v) natural and cultural heritage; and (vi) tourism promotion.

Even when private or voluntary sector management is involved, public agencies generally retain overall responsibility or provide operating funds and/or land and capital. Local councils in particular have a wide-ranging responsibility and concern for the economic vitality of their local economies and for the overall quality of life of members of their communities. This involves a broad concern for the level and quality of available leisure services and facilities and for tourism as a sector of economic activity.

In a Western-style liberal democracy, governments provide and administer the law which controls, or places limits on, individual and collective behaviour, but are also involved in the economic activity of delivering goods and services. While most economic activity takes place in the market or non-government sector, typically about 30 per cent is accounted for by government activity. The rationale for this activity, particularly as it applies to leisure, sport and tourism, is discussed in some detail in Chapter 5; here we consider the range and types of government activity in general terms. The types of involvement of governments in these areas are indicated in Table 1.1. At one extreme this involves promotion of certain activities, such as sport and the arts, via subsidy or direct provision of facilities. At the other extreme some activities are prohibited, such as the use of certain recreational drugs and cruel sports. In between, legislation and taxation can be used to support or regulate leisure activities in a variety of ways.

It should be noted that the rationale for governmental involvement with tourism is different from that applying to the other forms of leisure. At the local level, a local council becomes involved with residents' leisure activity because of its implications for their well-being; but tourism, by definition, involves the leisure activity of *non*-residents. The council may become involved because it generates benefits for the local community primarily through its economic impacts, in the form of incomes and jobs, or it may be involved in order to control the industry and prevent it from damaging the environment. At national level, the same considerations apply to *international tourism*: it is promoted by governments largely because of its economic impacts. Nevertheless, even in the case of *domestic* tourism involving residents of the country, national governments are generally concerned with the economic implications of tourism, not with holiday-making as a leisure activity (except for the low-profile phenomenon of social tourism, discussed in Chapter 14).

The state and public policy activity associated with leisure, sport and tourism has a spatial or geographical dimension, as shown in Table 1.2. There is considerable overlap in responsibilities at the various levels of government but, in general, as we move up the geographical hierarchy the facilities and services provided have a more extensive physical catchment area and the policymaking is – or should be – more strategic.

In economically developed countries governments at various levels spend substantial sums each year on leisure, sport and tourism services and also garner substantial sums in the form of duties and taxes on leisure, sport and tourism services. Table 1.3 provides some

Table 1.1. The range of government involvement in leisure, sport and tourism.

Sector	Types of government involvement	
	Promotion/provision	**Regulation/control/prohibition**
Sport	Subsidy/funding to sporting bodies; direct provision of sport facilities/ services (usually subsidized)	Sports drug-testing; animal treatment regulations; banning of cruel sports; prohibition of performance-enhancing drugs
Outdoor/environment/heritage	Provision of parks and playgrounds; ownership and conservation of natural and historic assets	Protective conservation and planning law; protection of rare species; export bans on species/heritage
Arts/broadcasting	Subsidy/funding to arts bodies/artists; direct provision of cultural facilities/services (usually subsidized); public broadcasting	Copyright and moral rights laws and regulations; licensing of broadcasters; export bans on art heritage; censorship of literature, films/videos
Social activities	Some direct provision (e.g. sea-fronts, picnic sites, community centres)	Alcohol licensing/taxation; prohibition of recreational drugs; gambling licensing/taxation; prostitution/brothels control
Tourism	Funding of tourism marketing; ownership/conservation/provision/marketing of natural, heritage, arts facilities/services	Government trade missions/embassies; airline/air-traffic regulation; immigration/passports; anti-sex tourism legislation
All sectors	Training/education; research funding; charitable status; general enabling legislation for local councils	Safety regulations individual/crowd/venues; town/country planning; noise regulations

indication of the economic scale of public expenditure. Of particular note is the distribution of expenditure at various levels. Quite often analysis and commentary on leisure, sport or tourism policy is offered without taking all levels into account: in particular, national governments are sometimes criticized for concentrating funding on the *elite* level of sport or the arts, ignoring the fact that substantial funding of *grassroots* participation may be provided by other levels of government.

In a primarily capitalist society, what is the *rationale* for the particular patterns of state involvement that have evolved? What are the competing philosophies concerning the appropriate role of the state? Why do some fields of leisure apparently merit government involvement while others do not? Who benefits and who loses from the institutions and practices that have emerged? Why should the community as a whole – the ratepayers and taxpayers – provide for and subsidize some leisure-time activities but tax and regulate others? Why should taxpayers pay for the promotion and market research costs of a largely privately owned industry

Table 1.2. The state and leisure, sport and tourism: geographic dimensions.

Level	Examples of areas of activity	Examples of organizations
1. International	International airline regulation	International Air Transport Association (IATA)
	Hosting international sporting contests	International Olympic Committee (IOC)
	Environmental/heritage agreements	International Union for the Conservation of Nature (IUCN)
2. National	Tourism promotion/marketing	National tourism commissions
	Support of elite sports	National sports councils/commissions
	Licensing of broadcasting	Broadcasting regulatory bodies
	Provision of national parks	National parks departments/commissions
3. Regional	Planning and provision of regionally significant parks, sporting and arts facilities	States/provinces (in federal systems); counties; ad hoc regions
4. Local	Planning and provision of parks and sporting and arts facilities	Local councils and boards/committees
5. Single facility	Development and operation of a single leisure facility/programme	Any of levels 2–4 above, Trusts

like tourism? If these government activities are justifiable in principle, on what *scale* should they be conducted and what is the appropriate *distribution* of subsidies, facilities and services? And how are decisions made on these matters? These are among the issues we address in this book.

The role of governments in leisure, sport and tourism, as in other fields, has evolved over time, and continues to evolve. Sometimes change comes about gradually, for example by means of Acts of Parliament authorizing additional government expenditure or establishing a new government agency. At other times change is dramatic, as in the dismantling of the communist regimes and the establishment of market systems in Eastern Europe and the Soviet Union during 1989/90. But even when change is gradual, it is rarely achieved without controversy. Some groups gain desired services while others lose, because they are required to pay additional rates or taxes for services from which they feel they do not benefit, or because a facility is closed down. Some see particular instances of change as the fulfilment of political promises, others as a betrayal.

The role of governments in democratic societies is invariably contentious, and their role in relation to leisure, sport and tourism is not immune to this contention. Philosophy, political ideology and group interests come into play in the debate, as well as technical arguments about what the market and governments are and are not capable of doing. These philosophical, political and technical issues are also among the issues addressed in this book.

Table 1.3. Public expenditure on leisure: England and Australia.

	National	State	Local	Total
England 2007–08 (£'000s)				
Broadcasting[a]	120		0	120
Heritage	174		60	234
Libraries	142		1002	1144
Museums and galleries	413		246	659
Other arts	496		349	845
Sport	177		1023	1200
Parks	20		906	926
Tourism	56		128	184
Other	58		100	158
Total	1656		3814	5470
Australia 2006–07 (AU$'000s)				
Broadcasting and film[a]	1168	74	0	1242
Libraries	130	386	620	1136
Museums and galleries	257	498	464	1219
Other arts	264	442	0[b]	706
Sport[c]	229	781	532	1542
Parks[c]	82	1337	675	2094
Other recreation[c]	306	0	828	1134
Tourism[d]	62	544	106	712
Total	2498	4062	3225	9785

Sources: England: Dept of Communities and Local Government (available at: http://www.local. communities.gov.uk/finance/stats/index.htm); Australia: arts data from Australian Bureau of Statistics (ABS) (2008b), Cat. No. 4183.0.
[a] Australian figure includes total cost of public broadcasters, but UK equivalents are funded from licence fees, not included; at time of writing, AU$1 = £0.50.
[b] Local museums and galleries figure included in 'Other arts'.
[c] Sport and local government parks data from ABS (2002) Cat. No. 4147.0 (latest available) inflated by 2% per year.
[d] Lynch and Veal (2006: 173), 2003–2004 figures inflated by 2% per year.

FRAMEWORK

An overall framework for viewing the leisure, sport and tourism service delivery 'system' is presented in Fig. 1.4. The framework consists of five elements:

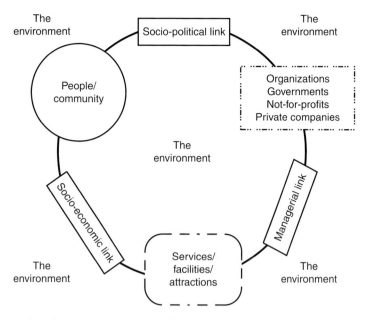

Fig. 1.4. A social, political and managerial framework for viewing leisure, sport and tourism service delivery processes.

1. *The People/Community* – individuals/households/communities.
2. *Organizations* – public and private sector organizations involved in the provision of leisure, sport and tourism facilities and services, including voluntary organizations, commercial companies and governments and their agencies, including elected and appointed members and senior and strategic management personnel.
3. *Leisure, Sport and Tourism Facilities/Services* – including their complement of line managers and 'frontline' staff.
4. *The Environment* – the natural and man-made physical environment.
5. *The Processes* – which link these various elements, including planning, marketing, political processes and the use, purchase and consumption of services, and which take place along the three links labelled *Socio-political, Managerial* and *Socio-economic*.

The essence of the framework lies in the linkages between the elements. Between any two elements there is a two-way flow of influence and activity. The nature of the processes, or at least their names, varies, depending on whether they relate to the public or private sector.

For the socio-political link, between *The Public* and *Organizations*, the flows are as follows:

• *Commercial sector*: (i) from the organization *to* the public: commercial organizations engage in the processes of market research, gathering information about markets, and public relations, designed to influence the public's views about the firm; (ii) from the public *to* organizations: the provision of market research information about preferences; and (iii), in some cases, campaigning against commercial activities.
• *Public sector*: the political process, including political campaigning, voting, lobbying and public participation in decision-making.
• *Non-profit sector*: combines features of the commercial and public sectors.

For the managerial link, between *Organizations* and the *Leisure Facilities/Services*, the flows are:

- From *Organizations* to *Leisure Facilities/Services*: the processes of planning, developing and managing.
- To *Organizations* from *Leisure Facilities/Services*: income and profits (or losses).

For the socio-economic link, between *The Public* and *Leisure Facilities/Services*:

- Here, the process of selling and promotion takes place, and the process of using or not using the facility or service provided.

The (physical) *Environment* is represented as a background, but all-pervasive, element of the system and includes the urban, rural and natural environment. It exists as an entity in its own right and is the object of policy, a constraint on activity and a resource which is used for leisure, sport and tourism. When a part of the environment gets taken over and managed for leisure or tourism it becomes part of the *Facilities/Services* element.

The framework demonstrates that leisure, sport and tourism facilities and services are not just 'there': they arise as a result of interaction between the public, as both users and political/social groups, and organizations and their activities. The framework also illustrates the idea that both public and private sector provision exists within the same basic framework, although the relationships between the elements vary. Finally, the framework shows the interconnectedness of the elements in the system and places various processes – politics, planning, design, marketing, market research, management – in context.

The emphasis of the book is therefore on the socio-political link, where the activities of policy-making and planning are mostly to be found. However, much of the book is concerned with generating and analysing information from the other links, concerning people's demands and behaviour, and management practices.

In this context, therefore, *policy* is concerned with ongoing principles and broad goals that guide the actions of a government body. Thus, a government might have policies concerning equity among social groups, or a policy to support mass participation in sport rather than elite sports, or to promote long-stay visitors rather than day-trippers. *Planning*, while in practice overlapping considerably with policy-making, is seen here as the process by which decisions are made as to the optimum way to implement policies and achieve goals. The term planning is used in a wide range of day-to-day contexts, but here it is intended to refer to a formal activity. Henry Mintzberg (1994: 12) defines such planning as 'a formalised procedure to produce an articulated result, in the form of an integrated system of decisions'. By 'articulated' he means that the results of the exercise must be communicated to interested parties – generally in the form of a written report. An 'integrated system of decisions' indicates that we are dealing with complex matters, usually involving a number of stakeholders and contingent decisions and action.

PERSPECTIVE

The framework outlined above is *functionalist* in nature; in an informal way it uses the *metaphor* of a biological system or machine to represent society, which suggests that society can function more or less smoothly when the various interacting elements behave in certain ways. This does not, of course, imply that smooth operation is guaranteed or automatic: the system will malfunction if the various elements fail to interact in certain ways; and smooth functioning to one group may be seen as malfunctioning to another. Chronic malfunctioning of the system results in unsustainability, an issue which has become particularly prominent in discussion of tourism in recent years. It should, however, be stressed that the framework is just a metaphor, an aid to thinking. It is illustrative of certain features of society only: it clearly cannot represent *all* aspects of society and their operation. Such a functionalist approach has been unfashionable among some theorists and commentators in the field of leisure studies in recent years and is roundly condemned in a number of texts (e.g. Jarvie and Maguire, 1994: 5–28; Wearing, 1998: 1–21). A number of theoretical positions in the social sciences see contemporary society as being chronically dysfunctional, and rife with conflict and division. This view reflects emancipatory philosophies, such as Marxism and some radical forms of feminism, which call for fundamental changes in the way society is organized – in particular the wholesale replacement of capitalism or the mixed economy by some alternative socio-political or economic system. Such perspectives see little point in the development of practices which seek to improve the operation of the existing, fundamentally flawed, system.

It is a premise of this book, however, that contemporary Western society is, on balance, more functional than dysfunctional. Clearly it does not function anywhere near perfectly and it does not function automatically, but only as a result of the considerable efforts of many people and organizations. It must also be recognized that the system involves a number of tensions and mixed blessings. For example, the extraordinary productive power of capitalism produces considerable threats to the environment; and the very basis of the system – private investment, risk and reward – produces great disparities in income and wealth which welfare and income redistribution policies only go some way towards ameliorating. A *functional* world is therefore not the same as a *perfect* world. In this book, it is assumed that governments have a legitimate role in seeking to improve an imperfect system and that part of that role involves a concern for the provision of leisure, sport and tourism services and the provision of a regulatory framework for the delivery of many of these services.

Another theoretical perspective that would raise doubts about the value of many of the practices advocated in this book is postmodernism, a view of contemporary society which rejects a consensus idea of social progress. In this book, it is assumed that society can indeed progress and improve through incremental change, even though views may differ about what constitutes progress and improvement. Furthermore, there are institutional structures which, while far from perfect, are capable of achieving and accommodating such change or can be reformed to do so. Any other position would, arguably, be hypocritical, since there would be no point in developing public policy and planning procedures for a society which was seen as requiring radical or fundamental change or where the ideas of progress or improvement were meaningless. The 'reformist' stance should not, however, be interpreted as being complacent or simply supportive of the status quo. There is a continuum between, at one extreme, a conservatism which envisages very little change of any sort and, at the other extreme, a radicalism which wishes to see the system completely dismantled and replaced. This book occupies the middle ground; it presents analytical tools designed to achieve improvement in the well-being of communities, in terms of supporting human rights, improving health and well-being and achieving greater equity as well as efficiency.

In Chapter 5, a wide range of differing views is explored concerning the appropriate role of the state, from complete state control to a minimalist, 'roll back the state', view. This book is predicated on a middle-road perspective. While not necessarily accepting the rhetoric of recent Third Way politics, as discussed in Chapter 2, the stance is broadly consistent with traditional social democratic ideals, of which Third Way ideas are one version (Veal, 1999). The environment in which leisure professionals in the Western world work is a basically capitalist one, but a strong and essential role is played by the state, and part of that role is legitimately concerned with the provision of leisure, sport and tourism services. That role can be enhanced, and society benefited, by the exercise of certain analytical skills which are directed at a better understanding of community leisure, sport and tourism demands and behaviour and their more effective and efficient satisfaction and facilitation.

The development of the public sector of leisure, sport and tourism has not been the result only of the actions of elected governments. Professionals involved directly in the area have also been influential. Professionals work as public servants at international, national, regional and local level – sometimes referred to as *the state bureaucracy* – and for the private and not-for-profit sectors, and in academe. There is also a substantial involvement of professional consultants in the field, who are often engaged by public bodies to conduct policy and planning studies, and who may be former public sector employees or academics and may be either small, one- or two-person operations or large, multi-disciplinary, possibly international, organizations. These professionals conduct the research and establish the terms of discourse in the field and they produce the reports and policy recommendations which are generally the basis of political decisions. Some of them are responsible for implementing the decisions and managing the facilities and services, or imposing the regulations that ensue, or, in the case of academics in particular, evaluating and critiquing the outcomes. Considerable power is therefore exercised by such professionals. This text is concerned with the knowledge and skills they bring to their tasks.

Hemingway and Parr (2000) argue that there are three types of relationship between knowledge and professional practice. In the *traditional* relationship, knowledge is generated by the science/research community and transmitted to practitioners to provide the basis for practice. In the *personal* relationship the professional develops his or her own body of knowledge from practical experience. In the *critical* relationship the value of knowledge and practice is evaluated against key normative criteria, such as development or emancipation. The field of leisure, sport and tourism policymaking and planning could be said to involve all three of these relationships and this book seeks to draw on and relate to all three.

Finally, we should be clear about the use of the term 'practice' in this book. A number of texts exist which are concerned with leisure *management* – where the emphasis is primarily on the efficient and effective operation of facilities and services once they are established – this text is concerned with the prior stage of formulating policies and plans, and evaluating their implementation as an input to further policy and plan formulation. It is of course recognized that it is not always easy to draw a precise line between these components of practice, especially when discussing services as opposed to facilities.

CONTENT AND STRUCTURE OF THE BOOK

Two topics of importance to public policy are *not* covered in this book, partly for reasons of space and partly because they are adequately covered elsewhere. The first of these is the question of history. There is no doubt that the current patterns of public, commercial and non-profit, leisure, sport and tourism services, and the values and practices that surround them, are the result of particular patterns of historical evolution, particularly dating from the Industrial Revolution.

This history has been well documented in a number of texts, as indicated in the Resources section. The historical perspective alerts us to the fact that public policy has been as much about *controlling* leisure, sport and tourism, through laws and regulation, as it has been about *providing* facilities and services, and that decisions on what to provide and what not to provide, and what to regulate and what not to regulate, reflect the relative power of various interests and classes in the political decision-making process. This historical legacy has ongoing consequences in terms of which groups have access to facilities and services of their choice and which do not.

Secondly, the book does not consider political *behaviour* in any detail. While political ideology, 'urban growth regimes', public participation and community consultation are considered, the role of pressure groups and parties, the relative powers of national, regional and local government, and the processes by which political decisions are made, are acknowledged but not analysed in detail. For coverage of these important topics, the reader is referred to other sources noted in the Resources section at the end of the chapter.

The contents of the rest of the book can be summarized as follows:

Part I: Society, Politics, Policy and Planning

In Chapter 2, competing ideas about the right and proper role of the state in society, and in relation to leisure, sport and tourism in particular, are examined from the point of view of various political ideologies.

Chapter 3 examines a number of basic concepts, such as wants, needs, demand, benefits and participation, which are widely used – and misused – in discussions of leisure, sport and tourism.

Among the most widely accepted roles of governments are the duty to uphold and protect the rights of their citizens. In Chapter 4, therefore, the status of leisure as a human right and a right of citizenship is examined.

In Chapter 5 the ideas of *mainstream economics* are examined, since they underpin much of the thinking from the centre-left to right of political thought, and provide the basis for economics-based analysis of state activities.

Part II: Planning Frameworks

Chapter 6 provides an introduction to government processes and public decision-making processes. Chapter 7 critically examines the various models of policymaking and planning for leisure, sport and tourism, related in particular to the concepts discussed in Chapter 3. Chapter 8 presents one particular leisure planning model – the U-Plan System – which is based on the key concept of participation.

Part III: Planning Tools

Chapter 9 discusses consultative methods and processes concerned with stakeholders in the policymaking and planning process. Chapter 10 features the facility/service audit, which involves methods for examining and evaluating existing facilities and services. Chapter 11 examines demand estimation and forecasting techniques.

Part IV: Evaluation

Chapter 12 presents an introduction to two economics-based techniques, namely cost–benefit analysis and economic impact analysis. Chapter 13, on performance appraisal, is concerned with evaluation of policies and plans once implemented, and how the information generated from such a process is utilized in further rounds of policy formulation and plan-making.

Part V: Sectors and Groups

Throughout the book there is a tendency to deal with leisure, sport and tourism as a whole and with the public or the community as a whole whereas, in fact, these sectors consist of a number of very different activities and industries with numerous disparate social groups of differing resource needs and tastes. The final two chapters give specific attention to sectors and groups. Chapter 14 discusses particular leisure sectors: sport and physical recreation; the arts; outdoor recreation in natural areas; urban outdoor recreation; and tourism. Chapter 15 features particular social groups defined by: gender; ethnicity; disability; income; and age – children, youth and the elderly.

CHANGES FROM THE SECOND EDITION

Readers familiar with earlier editions of the book will note major differences in this edition. The main difference lies in the introduction of the U-Plan System in Chapter 8. This has had implications for the 11 approaches to planning discussed in Chapter 7 of the 2nd edition. These 11 approaches are now dealt with as follows:

- standards: see Chapter 7;
- resource-based planning: see Chapter 7;
- gross demand/market share (GDMS) approach: essentially, the U-Plan System (Chapter 8) is an elaboration of the GDMS approach;
- spatial approaches: see Chapter 10;
- hierarchies of facilities: this approach is no longer covered; it can be seen as substantially historical, relating to the era of new town building in the UK;
- priority social area analysis: see Chapter 10, under spatial approaches;
- Recreation Opportunity Spectrum: see Chapter 7, under resource-based approaches;
- matrix approach: a fully developed U-Plan spreadsheet is, in effect, a version of the matrix approach;
- organic approach: see Chapter 8, under U-Plan Task 14, facility audit;
- community development approach: see Chapter 9;
- issues approach: see Chapter 9.

SUMMARY

In this chapter it is noted that, while sport and tourism can be seen conceptually as primarily forms of leisure, there are significant differences between leisure, sport and tourism and between leisure studies and tourism studies.

While marked changes took place in the balance between the public and private sectors in the last couple of decades of the 20th century, the public sector remains a significant force in the planning and provision of leisure, sport and tourism services in most Western countries.

A framework is presented for viewing government activity in a systems context, involving: (i) the public as consumers, clients and members of the political system; (ii) public, commercial and non-profit sector organizations; and (iii) facilities and services planned and managed by organizations.

While recognizing the need for critical analysis of the rationale for government activity, the book is premised on the belief that public sector activity to ensure certain leisure, sport and tourism services in the context of a market economy is legitimate.

RESOURCES

Political behaviour, leisure and sport: Limb (1986); Coalter (1988); Bramham *et al.* (1993); Henry (1993, 2001); political behaviour and tourism: Hall (1994).

Leisure/sport as a social service: Coalter (1988, 1998, 2000).

Sport as a business: Noll and Zimbalist (1997); Jeanrenaud and Késenne (2006); Nazareth (2007).

History of leisure/sport/tourism policy: Bailey (1979); Cunningham (1980); Henry (1993, 2001); Dredge and Jenkins (2007: 69–111).

Professions in leisure, sport and tourism: Coalter (1988: 177–180); Bacon (1989); Henry (1993: 110–137).

chapter 2

Political Ideologies

INTRODUCTION

A substantial part of public policymaking and planning is technical in nature, but underlying the overall process are *values*. Even when the process is driven purely by the self-interests of participants, this implies a certain set of values concerning the relative importance of sectional as opposed to broader community interests, whether the participants are aware of this or not. Values can be based on philosophical, religious or political systems of thought. While philosophical and religious dimensions are not unimportant, and are often closely related to political beliefs, they are beyond the scope of this text, but references to writings on those themes are provided in the list of Resources at the end of the chapter. The aim here is to outline major political ideological perspectives and discuss their implications for public policy in relation to leisure, sport and tourism in Western capitalist societies. First, the nature of ideology is discussed and this is followed by outlines of the basic ideas involved in six ideological positions and consideration of their implications for the role of the state in regard to leisure, sport and tourism policy.

THE NATURE OF IDEOLOGY

The *Shorter Oxford English Dictionary* defines ideology as: 'A system of ideas concerning phenomena, especially those of social life; the manner of thinking of a class or an individual'. Generally then, political ideology consists of internally consistent sets of ideas about how society should be run. People may agree with or support an ideology because of intellectual conviction or self-interest, or a combination of both. Self-interest arises when individuals believe that the achievement of the sort of society envisaged by the ideology would be to their benefit. Since people in similar social or economic situations, such as social classes, are likely to have similar views on which ideologies best serve their interests, ideologies are often class-based, as suggested in the definition.

In *Ideology and Modern Culture*, John Thompson points out that, while the term ideology can be used in the fairly neutral, descriptive sense that is used in this chapter, it is also used in a broader evaluative, and often pejorative, sense: 'Few people today would proudly proclaim themselves to be 'ideologists', whereas many would not hesitate to declare that they were conservatives or socialists, liberals or democrats, feminists or ecologists. Ideology is the thought of the *other*, the thought of someone other than oneself. To characterize a view as ideological is, it seems, already implicitly to criticize it, for the concept of ideology seems to convey a negative, critical sense' (Thompson, 1990: 5).

Thus 'ideology' and 'ideological' have a poor image, so that politicians are often *accused* of pursuing policies for 'ideological reasons' yet equally often, particularly during election campaigns, there are calls for them to convey to the electorate 'what they stand for'. This ambiguous situation should be borne in mind in reading and applying what follows.

The fact that political ideology is concerned with how society should be run means that it is closely involved with the political process. People may act or may not act in the political arena to achieve a society run along the lines of their preferred ideology. In some cases the ideology is fully and consciously developed, while in others it may be just a set of attitudes, perhaps even subconsciously held. Some have individual power to implement their ideology because of their occupation or other position of influence. Thus, for example, Jean Yule (1997a), in a study of gender and ideology in British local government leisure services, interviewed 30 councillors and council officers and identified nine distinct ideologies among them: three were variations on feminism of the sort discussed below, while six were 'not feminist', including four which were anti-feminist. Non-political organizations and movements are sometimes said to have ideologies: for example, what many would call the *philosophy* of the Olympic Games, or the *ideals* of Olympism, have been referred to as an ideology (Magdalinski *et al.*, 2005: 39).

Our focus in this chapter is on situations where like-minded groups of individuals organize themselves into political parties, or at least a recognizable *movement*, to advance their cause. Hence a political party is generally associated with a particular ideology and/or set of group interests. The party which gains governmental power attempts to mould society to operate in accordance with its ideology and in the interests of its supporters.

It can be argued that political ideology is less relevant to the real world of contemporary politics than it was in the past. One explanation for this is the shift from a 'modern' to a 'postmodern' society:

- *Pre-modern* societies tend to be guided primarily by spiritual values and goals, often in the context of hereditary class and status systems with an aristocracy and monarchy, and often a theocracy.
- *Modern* societies, as seen since about the 18th century in the West, while not abandoning religion and hereditary class systems, have been ostensibly guided by humanitarian values and ideals and the notion of human progress towards a better society – which political ideologies seek to define. Such all-encompassing ideologies are sometimes referred to in modern/postmodern discourse as a form of 'grand narrative'.

One feature claimed for *postmodern* societies has been the demise of such 'grand narratives' of both the right and left, marked particularly by the collapse of communism in the former Soviet Union and Eastern Europe in the late 1980s and subsequent loss of confidence in this ideology by leftist groups in the West.

The other explanation for the reduced relevance of political ideology is more prosaic: as Western societies have become more affluent, with higher levels of education and a growing preponderance of services and white collar occupations, the old class divides, which traditionally provided a basis for ideological differences, have become blurred politically. There has been a shift to the 'middle ground'. To gain power political parties must capture the support of 'floating voters' who have no particular class-based allegiance to any particular party. In order to do this parties have abandoned long-held policies and beliefs when they were seen to be unattractive to such voters. Thus ideology has been abandoned in favour of pragmatic seeking after power. Since all major parties are generally competing for the same 'middle ground' and are subject to the same national and international political, social and economic pressures, they often tend to adopt remarkably similar platforms. Thus it has been suggested that the political process is from time to time overlain with particular *political rationalities* which transcend ideology. For example, it has been argued that *neo-liberalism* (discussed below) is one such political rationality which dominated Australian politics from the early 1980s, regardless of the party in power (Beeson and Firth, 1998).

While these arguments are plausible, it is too early to ignore political ideology – for at least two reasons. First, while certain ideological creeds may be fading – for example socialism – others can be growing in influence – for example anti-globalism. Secondly, many of the debates in recent contemporary politics – such as 'Third Way' politics or 'Compassionate Conservatism' – have involved reshaping of traditional political parties and their philosophies, often amid considerable controversy. And it has been argued that the 2008–2009 global financial crisis was caused by the excesses of neo-liberalism and can only be corrected by a re-embracing of social democracy (Rudd, 2009) or a reform of conservative thinking (Blond, 2009). Thus it is necessary to be informed about the traditional political ideologies if one is to understand the debates about their reform or abandonment: to understand what 'all the fuss is about'.

There is a tendency to think that many of the elements of leisure – particularly sport and the arts – are 'above politics' and that they are not a factor in competing ideologies and so are not, or should not be, affected by party politics. This is far from true, as this chapter seeks to demonstrate.

In one short chapter it is not, of course, possible to provide a definitive account of even the leading political ideologies, but an attempt is made to outline key features of eight significant ideologies, or ideological positions, namely:

- conservatism;
- liberalism/neo-liberalism;
- Marxism;
- democratic socialism;
- social democracy/the 'Third Way'/communitarianism;
- feminism;
- environmentalism;
- anti-globalism.

Conservatism and liberalism are on the *right* of politics while the next three in the list are generally considered to be on the *left*, as illustrated in Fig, 2.1. The origin of this left/right designation dates back to where politicians physically sat in the parliament following the French Revolution in the late 18th century. In most Western democracies the 'mainstream'

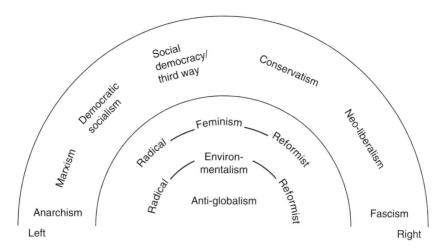

Fig. 2.1. The political spectrum.

ideologies of conservatism, neo-liberalism, social democracy and democratic socialism compete for power, but they are influenced by, and in many cases have incorporated ideas from, the other ideological movements listed. Communitarianism, feminism, environmentalism (or 'green' politics) and anti-globalism do not necessarily fit neatly into the 'left–right' spectrum of politics, although they each encompass both radical, left-leaning wings and reformist, right-leaning wings. Other ideologies, such as fascism on the extreme right and anarchism on the extreme left, are not considered here because of lack of space (but see Resources for further reading).

In the overviews that follow, the broad principles of each ideology are outlined, followed by discussion of how these relate to particular political parties and recent national governments in the Western world and how the ideas relate, in broad terms, to leisure, sport and tourism policy. Table 2.1 provides a summary of the political parties and governments referred to, while Table 2.2 provides a synopsis of the various ideologies discussed.

CONSERVATISM

Conservatism is, as its name implies, an ideology which places emphasis on *conserving* what exists, that is on *not* changing things, in contrast to all the other ideologies outlined, which stand for social and economic *change* in one form or another. The roots of conservatism predate the period of the Industrial Revolution in Europe, but it emerged as a political force in the 18th and 19th centuries in opposition to the rise of liberalism and socialism, which both sought radical change in society. At that time conservatives represented the landed classes, rural interests and 'old money', and they defended the right of the monarchy and the aristocracy to rule and resisted the democratic demands and the rising power of industrialists and professions and, later, the labour movement. While modern conservative parties maintain their traditional links with landed and rural interests, and sometimes with conservative religions, in contemporary political life they draw support from conservative sentiment across a wide spectrum of society.

Table 2.1. Parties, governments and ideologies: the UK and Australia, 1950–2010.

Ideology	The UK			Australia		
	Party	Government/PM	Dates	Party	Government/PM	Dates
Conservatism	Conservative Party	Winston Churchill Anthony Eden Harold Macmillan Alec Douglas-Home Edward Heath David Cameron	1951–1955 1955–1957 1957–1963 1963–1964 1970–1974 2010–	Liberal Party National Party	Robert Menzies Harold Holt/John McEwen/ John Gorton/William McMahon Malcolm Fraser Junior coalition partner with Liberal Party	1949–1961 1966–1972 1975–1983
Liberalism/Neo-liberalism	Conservative Party	Margaret Thatcher John Major	1979–1990 1990–1997	Liberal Party	John Howard	1996–2007
Marxism/communism	Communist Party	Not in government		Communist Party	Not in government	
Democratic socialism	Labour Party	Clement Attlee	1945–1951	Australian Labor Party	Gough Whitlam	1972–1975
Social democracy	Labour Party Social/Liberal Democrats	Harold Wilson James Callaghan In coalition	1964–1970 & 1974–1976 1976–1979 2010–	Australian Labor Party Australian Democrats	Bob Hawke Paul Keating Not in government	1983–1991 1991–1996
Third Way	Labour Party	Tony Blair Gordon Brown	1997–2007 2007–2010	Australian Labor Party	Kevin Rudd Julia Gillard	2007–present 2010–
Environmentalism	Social/Liberal Democrats	Not in government		Greens Australian Democrats	Not in government Not in government	

Table 2.2. Ideologies summarized.[a]

	Change	Economic growth	The capitalist market system	Role of the state	Social equality	Elitism
Conservatism	Against	For	For	Limited	Against	For
Liberalism	For	For	For	Against	Against	For – as symbol of individual success
Marxism/communism	For – by revolution if necessary	For	Against	For – total control	Against	Against (although regimes use it)
Democratic socialism	For – by democratic means	For	For	For – extensive role	For	Against
Social democracy/Third Way	For	For	For	For – but limited	For	Ambivalent
Communitarianism	For	Ambivalent	Ambivalent	Reduced	For	Against
Radical feminism	For – by revolution if necessary	For	Against	For	For – between men and women	Against
Reformist feminism	For – by democratic/legislative means	For	For	Ambivalent	For – between men and women	Ambivalent
Environmentalism	For	Against	For	For – as regulator	Ambivalent	Ambivalent
Anti-globalism	For	Ambivalent	Against	For	Against	Ambivalent

[a]This table inevitably presents information in highly simplified, 'black and white', form. More details and qualifications are provided in the main body of the chapter.

Principles

The principles of conservatism can be summarized as:

- a belief in stability and tradition rather than change;
- acceptance of a certain amount of inequality as part of the natural order of things;
- respect for 'traditional' institutions and values, such as the monarchy and the family;
- a pragmatic acceptance of the role of government in supporting all of the above;
- support for voluntary effort and organizations.

An important feature of conservatism, which distinguishes it from leftist ideologies, is the defence of *inequality* in society; the belief that inequality is part of the natural order of things and that, for example, wealth is part of the reward system that maintains society as we know it. Generally, the conservative outlook favours elitism as a concept, but in the guise of such concepts as 'quality' and 'excellence'. Conservative doctrine applies not only to economics and politics but also to social and moral matters, such as defence of 'the family', traditional religion and 'traditional values'; and it also tends to favour higher levels of public expenditure on military defence and a 'tough' approach to crime and punishment.

Conservatism is, however, nothing if not pragmatic, so that, over the years, the status quo which it has sought to defend has changed. So when conservatives have regained power following a period of socialist or social democratic rule, they have not necessarily dismantled the 'welfare state', reduced levels of personal taxation or privatized government-owned industries. They have been in favour of stability and 'not rocking the boat'. They defend capitalism, but not with the ideological fervour of neo-liberals. Their attitude can often be viewed as paternalistic towards the working classes rather than confrontational – evoking the idea that 'we know best how to look after the country and will take care of you – trust us'.

Parties

- In the *UK*, the Conservative Party was basically conservative in nature before the rise of the 'New Right'/neo-liberal thinkers under Margaret Thatcher in the 1980s. After some years in opposition, following the rise of Labour in the mid-1990s under Tony Blair, there have been attempts to move away from neo-liberalism back to the party's conservative roots. Thus, for example, the global financial crisis of 2008–2009 has spawned the Progressive Conservatism Project, which seeks to 'build a new economic and capital base that decentralises power and extends wealth and also makes a final break with the logic of monopoly and debt-financed capitalism' (Blond, 2009). Its manifesto is characterized by *communitarian* ideas, which are discussed below under social democracy. The success of these changes is partly reflected in the 2010 electoral success of the Conservatives under David Cameron.
- In *Australia* the National Party, previously called the Country Party, is the main conservative force, along with the left wing of the Liberal Party, the party with which it operates in coalition.
- In the *USA* the Republican Party is the more conservative of the two major parties, but it also incorporates much 'New Right' neo-liberal philosophy, as discussed below. Members of the radical right groups who are said to have influenced the presidency of George W. Bush (2001–2008) were referred to as 'neo-conservatives' or 'neo-cons', although in many ways they can be seen as indistinguishable from the 'neo-liberals' discussed below.

- In *Europe* conservative parties are often associated with the Catholic Church, using the label 'Christian Democrat'.

Leisure, sport and tourism

Conservatives can be expected to support those public services which are seen to have worked well in the past, and to seek to strengthen services that uphold traditional values and elitism. On the other hand, they would be reluctant to see the state take on new areas of public responsibility unless seen as necessary in relation to its traditional values, such as defence, rural interests and so on. In relation to leisure, sport and tourism and the role of the state therefore, the use of public funds to support elite activity and 'excellence' presents no problem to conservatives. Indeed, the provision of high-profile, prestige facilities and the fostering of winning national athletes and teams is consistent with the paternalistic approach to government. Similarly, support for excellence and prestigious organizations in the arts is consistent with conservative values, with preference being given to artistic activities which are themselves conservative. The gradual growth of public spending to provide community leisure facilities is consistent with the paternalistic dimension of conservatism, but support for voluntary sector activity would be favoured. Because conservatives do not adopt a hard ideological line on market economics, they frequently find themselves supporting government aid to industries such as tourism. As far as environmental issues are concerned however, conservatives are likely to be on the side of the exploiters of the environment rather than the conservationists, even though their links with the land lead them to see themselves as custodians of rural values.

LIBERALISM/NEO-LIBERALISM

The word *liberalism* shares the same Latin root as liberation and liberty: hence its basic tenet is the idea of freedom – of the individual. Its origins lie in the late 18th and 19th centuries in Europe among the newly emerging capitalist and middle-class interests that were trying to throw off the shackles of feudalism – the system under which monarchs ruled by divine right, hand in hand with the entrenched privileges of the aristocracy, the landed classes and the church, and everyone from monarch to peasant knew their place. Liberals, building on philosophers such as Adam Smith, believed in the power of the emerging market system and so wanted all restraints on trade, investment and commerce removed. Government control, linked as it then was to tradition and privilege, was to be dismantled and economic success was to be achieved by hard work, industry and trade. The cry of the French Revolution was 'Liberty, Equality and Fraternity' – the liberals placed the emphasis on *liberty*. As with conservatives, inequality was not seen in a bad light. But whereas conservative inequality was based on class privilege and heredity, liberal inequality was seen as a positive and dynamic force for change in society, providing incentives and material rewards for effort.

The term 'liberal' is a confusing one because it is used differently in different parts of the world. Thus in the USA it is often used to refer to left-leaning rather than right-leaning political positions. This can be seen as partly a reflection of history, when, as discussed above, liberals were the champions of change based on ideas of personal freedom in opposition to conservatives, partly a reflection of the fact that the American spectrum is considerably to the right of that of European countries and partly a genuinely different use of the word. For this reason, in recent years the label generally used for right-wing liberals is 'neo-liberal' or *New Right*.

Rather than accepting, and even encouraging, the growth of the state as previous social democratic and conservative governments had done during the 1960s and 1970s, neo-liberals sought to reverse the tide of 'creeping socialism' and restore the free rein of the market. Since much of the distinctiveness of the ideology is focused on economic policy, it is often referred to as *economic rationalism* – a link with economic theory that is explored in Chapter 5.

Principles

The policies advocated by neo-liberals/economic rationalists involve:

- reductions in personal and corporate taxation, since taxation is seen as a disincentive to work and an infringement of the freedom of individuals to spend their money as they see fit;
- minimization of state regulation of private sector organizations;
- reductions in industry protection, such as tariffs and subsidies, to encourage efficiency, competition and international competitiveness;
- privatization of state assets, because it is believed they will be more efficiently run by private enterprise;
- reduction in welfare spending, because of its cost and because it is seen as a disincentive to work and as encouraging a 'handout' mentality among recipients;
- reduction of government spending generally, to enable taxes to be reduced and to shift economic resources away from the public sector, which is regarded as inefficient and bureaucratic, to the private sector, which is regarded as efficient and responsive to people's needs.

Services run by the public sector are generally seen by neo-liberals as less efficient (costing more per unit of output) and less effective (failing to deliver what is intended) than those run by the private sector. These failings arise, it is argued, because public services are often monopolies (with no competitors seeking to provide better services or lower prices) and they do not have the incentive of profit and reward for good performance or the discipline of losses or going out of business if performance is poor.

Parties

- In the *UK* neo-liberalism or *New Right* ideology emerged in the Conservative Party under the leadership of Margaret Thatcher – hence 'Thatcherism' – in the late 1970s and into the 1980s and 1990s. In the UK, the Liberal Party had its origins in the 19th century as a radical opposition to the conservative Tories (forebears of the Conservatives), espousing free trade and the interests of commerce – thus it was originally 'liberal' in philosophy, as discussed above. Later, however, with the rise of the Labour Party on the left and the Conservative Party on the right, the Liberals came to occupy the middle ground in British politics and shifted their ideological focus, espousing largely social democratic policies (see below); this was confirmed when, in the 1980s, it combined with a dissident wing of the Labour Party, the Social Democrats, to form the Liberal Democrats.

- In *Australia,* neo-liberalism emerged in the Australian Liberal Party of John Howard (1996–2007) although, as noted above, many economic rationalist policies were adopted by the Australian Labor Party governments of Bob Hawke and Paul Keating in the 1980s.
- In the *USA* neo-liberalism is associated with the presidency of Ronald Reagan (1981–1988) – hence 'Reaganomics' – and to some extent with George W. Bush (2001–2008).

Leisure, sport and tourism

The neo-liberal philosophy espouses a private enterprise solution to leisure, sport and tourism services. Even where it is accepted that government should be involved in leisure provision, for example in the case of urban parks, the neo-liberal approach is for such services to be operated where possible by private enterprise under contract. The flexibility and responsiveness of the market is seen as making it an ideal mechanism for providing for people's leisure demands (Roberts, 1978: 155–164): hence the extensive programme of privatization of public services under New Right/neo-liberal governments in the recent past.

The neo-liberal perspective tends to see leisure, sport and tourism as *industries.* While this is unexceptionable in the case of tourism, which is largely a private sector phenomenon, it marks a break with tradition for areas such as parks, sport and the arts which, from a public policy perspective, have been seen as non-profit community services. One of the early statements of neo-liberal principles in this area came from the British Conservative Party: '... new jobs can be created by the commercial provision of pleasure and recreation to foreign tourists and Britons in their leisure time. The key is to understand the need for commercial provision. Too often, people expect their leisure to be subsidized. There are no jobs to be had there – only higher taxes. When people pay for their own pleasure they create a job for someone else' (Banks, 1985: 1).

The recommendations of this party document were endorsed by an official government policy statement in 1986 (Cabinet Office Enterprise Unit, 1986). In similar vein, a policy document on sport from the Australian Liberal–National coalition government in the 1990s stated:

Australia's reputation as an active nation and its record of high performance in sporting arenas around the world will be supported by a sport and recreation industry known for its:

- innovation in design and intellectual property;
- quality of sporting goods and services;
- ability to anticipate and lead the markets of the world;
- brand and design presence throughout the world;
- skill in adding value to our sporting and recreational resources;
- use of technology to achieve a competitive edge;
- quality and range of sports tourism products.

(Department of Industry, Science and Resources, 1999: 5)

Purist neo-liberals see no need for organizations which assist or usurp private enterprise roles, such as government-funded tourism promotion agencies or government-owned airlines or airports. This is in contrast to some of their supporters, including voters in electorates affected by such government enterprises, those with a more conservative philosophy and even industry itself, all of which are often happy to see governments provide subsidized infrastructure to ensure the viability of enterprises. Neo-liberal principles suggest that many services which have traditionally been publicly provided can be operated more efficiently and effectively on a commercial, 'user pays', basis. Hence, neo-liberal governments have overseen the privatization of, for example, airports, docks, railways and airlines – all key elements of the tourism industry infrastructure. Whether privatization in these and other industry sectors can be judged a success is a matter for debate (Hodge, 2000).

In the UK in the 1980s and early 1990s, the New Right government under Margaret Thatcher and John Major sought to impose privatization and the 'discipline of the market' on local government, including leisure services, by introducing Compulsory Competitive Tendering (CCT), by which councils were required to offer management contracts by competitive tender for public services – for example for parks maintenance and leisure centre management – with the possibility that the contract would be won by a commercial company. Similar measures were taken in Australia in the early 1990s by the Liberal government of Victoria under the premiership of Jeff Kennet. The CCT phenomenon is discussed in more detail in Chapter 5.

In the interests of smaller government, neo-liberalism encourages involvement of the voluntary sector in leisure provision. As with conservatism, support for excellence and elitism – for instance in sport or the arts – is welcomed, but even here the preference is for private sector sponsorship. It can be argued from a neo-liberal perspective that the very idea of leisure as freedom of choice is reflected in the free play of market forces, which seek to meet the expressed demands of the consumer. Thus some neo-liberal groups, following the logic of their basic philosophy, have advocated the legalization of recreational drugs, a cause usually associated with the left, but on the grounds of the upholding of individual freedom of choice.

MARXISM

Principles

Marxism can also be termed *revolutionary socialism*, *'scientific' socialism* (Henry, 1984a) or *communism*. The ideology is based on the ideas of Karl Marx who, with his collaborator Friedrich Engels, set out his ideas in a number of key works in the middle and second half of the 19th century, notably *The Communist Manifesto* and *Das Kapital*. Marx's thesis can be summarized very briefly as follows:

- Capitalist society is characterized by the irreconcilable clash of interests between: (i) the *capitalists* (or *bourgeoisie*), who own the 'means of production'; and (ii) the *workers* (or *proletariat*), who own nothing but their labour power.
- The relationship between capitalists and workers is an exploitative one – capitalists minimizing the wages they pay and retaining maximum profits for themselves.
- The state in capitalist countries merely plays the role of propping up the exploitative system by curbing and regulating some of the worst excesses of capitalism and providing it with a 'human face'.
- Because opportunities for further investment will eventually be exhausted and maintenance of profit levels will be achievable only by increased levels of exploitation and 'immiseration' of the workers, capitalism will eventually collapse under the stress of its own internal 'contradictions'.

- The workers should hasten this process by combining to overthrow capitalism (revolution) and transform society into a socialist state controlled by a working class party ('dictatorship of the proletariat'). In the final stage of transformation – the communist society – the state would no longer be required.

With the communist revolution in Russia in 1917 and wars and depression in the West, followed by the triumph of communism in Eastern Europe and China in the 1940s, it appeared that Marx's predictions were coming true. But capitalism survived, and later Marxist theorists, referred to as 'neo-Marxists', sought to explain its continued existence in a number of ways:

- For example, the institution of *colonialism*, or imperialism, by Western capitalist powers provided expanded, international scope for capitalist investment and exploitation, thus delaying the fall in profits which Marx had predicted. Later, *neo-colonialism*, in which capitalism extended its global reach via economic means, without the aid of colonial armies (e.g. the 'Coca Cola-ization' of the world), was seen to achieve the same economic effects as colonialism.
- It was further argued that the capitalist *ruling class* achieved *hegemony*, a sort of control over the generally accepted view of the world achieved through the engendering of *false consciousness* and *false needs*. This was achieved by such means as control over the media and advertising, thus subliminally persuading society at large, and the workers in particular, that life under capitalism is *the norm*, that there is no realistic alternative, that they need the products and services which capitalism has to offer, and must work to obtain them.
- A third approach has been to analyse the adaptability of the capitalist system by an historical analysis of *accumulation regimes*, that is the particular forms of arrangement between the state and capital, or forms of *regulation* (regimes) which have emerged to ensure the continued survival and growth (accumulation) of capital at particular times. Thus the *social democratic consensus* supported by Keynesian economic management, which held sway in the West in the 1950s and 1960s, is seen through Marxist eyes as one type of accumulation regime, which, when it was no longer successful, was replaced by the Thatcherist New Right era of the 1980s, which, in turn has been replaced by a *flexible regime of accumulation*, consistent with the move to a *post-Fordist* environment (Allen, 1992: 194; Henry, 2001: 199 ff).

Parties

- In the Soviet Union from 1917 and in the '*Eastern Bloc*' countries after the Second World War, Marxist or communist regimes created 'one-party states' and vested virtually all industrial and economic power in the state. International politics was dominated by the 'Cold War' between the communist East and the capitalist West from the 1950s until the end of the1980s and the collapse of these communist regimes, symbolized by the fall of the Berlin Wall in 1989.
- Within the *Western democracies* during this period Marxism was, with a few exceptions (e.g. Italy), minimal, being largely confined to some left-leaning trade unions and the left wings of democratic socialist parties. Its influence was, however, quite marked in some academic disciplines, notably sociology and cultural studies. The demise of the Soviet

Union and the Eastern Bloc communist states produced a crisis of confidence among Western Marxists. David Harvey refers to the collapse of the Wall as:

> ... the last nail in the coffin of any sort of Marxist credibility ... To pretend there was anything interesting about Marx after 1989 was to sound more and more like an all-but extinct dinosaur whimpering its own last rites. Free-market capitalism rode triumphantly across the globe, slaying all such old dinosaurs in its path. 'Marx talk' was increasingly confined to what might best be described as an increasingly geriatric 'New left' ... By the early 1990s the intellectual heft of Marxian theory seemed to be terminally in decline.

(Harvey, 2000: 5)

- Admitting that Marx's ideas were difficult to relate to everyday life in the 1970s and 1980s, Harvey argued that, with the changed international economic environment of the 1990s and beyond, Marx's writing 'teems with ideas as to how to explain our current state', but that it remained unfashionable among social scientists. Cassidy (1997) has noted that even some business people in the West were beginning to suggest that Marx's portrayal of capitalism was surprisingly relevant to the globalized system emerging at the end of the 20th century, with its massive international flows of speculative money, substantial and disruptive changes affecting ordinary people's lives and huge fortunes won and lost on the stock exchanges of the world. The global financial crisis which started in late 2008 would seem to support this view.
- While communist parties remain in power in a number of smaller states (such as *Cuba*, *North Korea* and *Vietnam*), the main survivor is in *China*. None the less, most would see the Chinese Communist Party as communist in political terms only since, while it maintains the one-party state system, it now presides over a largely privatized economy.

Leisure, sport and tourism

The relevance of Marxism to the study of leisure, sport and tourism lies not so much in the proposals for leisure provision in a future communist society, but in its critical analysis of contemporary capitalist societies. The idea of 'false needs' is particularly pertinent to leisure, since many of the goods and services that people in Western societies seek, once basic necessities have been acquired, are leisure goods and services, including such consumer goods and services as home entertainment equipment, leisure footwear and clothing, photographic and video equipment, swimming pools and boats, and such services as restaurant meals, concerts and holidays. Marxist analysis would suggest that it is the clever marketing activity of capitalism that keeps people on the materialist treadmill, working and striving to achieve these products of the market system, and thereby perpetuating the capitalist system. One view is that modern technology could release the masses from the burden of constant labour if capitalism were replaced by a socialist society (Gorz, 1980a).

Leisure is also seen as a medium of 'resistance' to the forces of capitalism: thus certain youth groups and subcultures and art and music forms, the historical struggle for increased leisure through reduced working hours, the phenomenon of 'dropping out', and institutions such as workers' clubs (Alt, 1979) are all means by which ordinary people are seen to attempt to 'do their own thing' rather than conform to the dictates of the capitalist system.

Additional Marxist analysis would point to the divisiveness, elitism and competitiveness of leisure institutions, particularly in sport, which perpetuate and reinforce the class divisions in society (see Clarke and Critcher, 1985: 147–150).

The Marxist critique also applies to the role of the state in leisure provision. It argues that by providing those leisure services which the market is often incapable of delivering – such as parks, sports facilities, children's play facilities, quality arts output and conservation of the natural and historic heritage – the state provides capitalism with a civilized face. Left to the market system, the leisure scene would be significantly depleted, and people might begin to question the efficacy of the market as a system for meeting needs. Not only does the state provide capitalism with a 'human face' but, the argument goes, it provides a basic infrastructure at the public expense upon which the private sector builds profitable enterprises. For example the public underpinning of sport enables the private sector to profit from the sale of sporting equipment and clothing and the subsidized arts underpin profits in the commercial music, film and television industry.

One of the ways in which communist regimes of the past sought to demonstrate the superiority of their system over the Western capitalist alternative was through international sporting success, notably in the Olympic Games. Hence Ritchie's (1984) inclusion of 'ideology' in his schema of topics to be addressed in assessing the impact of hallmark events. There is a considerable literature on this phenomenon, particularly in relation to the Soviet Union and East Germany, and China's hosting of the Olympic Games in 2008 saw a substantial burst of publications on sport in China. Examples of this literature are indicated in the Resources section.

DEMOCRATIC SOCIALISM

Democratic socialism, or *utopian* or *reformist socialism* as Ian Henry (2001: 49) terms it, can trace its roots back to before the Industrial Revolution in Europe, in the form of various workers' and peasants' protest and reform movements. However, it emerged as a reformist political movement under 19th century capitalism, reflecting the interests of the working classes as against the liberal industrialists and middle classes and the conservative aristocracy.

Principles

The essential tenets of democratic socialism can be summarized as:

- an emphasis on equality and fraternity rather than liberty;
- defence of the interests of the working class as against those of the middle and ruling classes;
- belief in the power of the state to control capitalism through state ownership and control of key industries;
- belief in the power of the state to create more equality and provide welfare for the community through progressive taxation and the establishment of a 'welfare state';
- belief that change can be brought about by democratic means, via parliamentary methods;
- a belief that capitalism can be 'tamed' and controlled and perhaps gradually replaced by socialism and does not have to be overthrown by force.

Social democracy, which is discussed separately below, is a related ideology which does not envisage the replacement of capitalism by socialism, but accepts the continued existence of capitalism alongside a strong welfare state. There is, therefore, considerable overlap between the ideas of democratic socialism and those of social democracy. Major state organizations, such as the institutions of the welfare state, public health care systems and state utilities and enterprises, have generally been established by democratic socialist or social democratic governments.

Democratic socialism therefore tolerates capitalism, at least in the medium term: a 'socialist society' is a long-term aim. Meanwhile the state is embraced as the main vehicle for the achievement of socialist goals – which is the exact opposite of the liberal position, which is to tolerate the state and embrace the market.

As with each of the political philosophies discussed in this chapter, democratic socialism embraces a range of beliefs. A left-wing democratic socialist would accept much of Marxism, seeking fundamental change to the capitalist system, but generally via democratic processes. Right-wing democratic socialists, however, would reject most of Marx, and may be indistinguishable from others who see themselves as 'social democrats'.

Parties

- In the *UK* the Labour Party, historically the political arm of the labour/trade union movement, has in the past been a democratic socialist party but more recently, from the 1970s, it would be more appropriate to designate it as a social democratic party. In its struggle to gain electoral support over the years, it faced a great deal of soul-searching over which of its long-standing socialist tenets to retain and which to abandon.
- The Australian Labor Party (always spelled the American way) reflects the British pattern.
- In the *USA* such socialist parties as exist are fringe groups which play an insignificant role in American politics.

Leisure, sport and tourism

Democratic socialist beliefs translate into a very active role for the state in leisure provision in all its forms. The arguments of mainstream economics concerning market failure, as discussed in Chapter 6, are accepted and used to support and justify state activity where necessary, but concerns for equality and democracy are probably the stronger motivators. Thus democratic socialists see a major role for governments to play in supporting sport, the arts, community recreation and outdoor recreation in natural areas. While excellence and elitism are viewed with suspicion by some democratic socialists, for others they are supported as a celebration of the success of state activity. At the same time, however, access to mass participation and democratization of institutions are stressed. At the local level, access to leisure facilities is seen as a right and the provision of such services as a part of social welfare, a means by which the standard of living and quality of life of disadvantaged groups can be improved. Even though tourism is a largely private sector industry, democratic socialists generally have no qualms about using government funds to promote tourism or to finance tourism enterprises – since they believe in government involvement in economic development and in the efficacy of state enterprise.

SOCIAL DEMOCRACY AND THE THIRD WAY

Social democracy is a left-leaning philosophy which supports the welfare state and public services and greater social equality. It differs from democratic socialism, however, in being generally more tolerant of private enterprise, believing that capitalism, suitably regulated, is here to stay;

it does not therefore envisage, even in the long term, a transformation into a socialist society. Because it occupies a position somewhere between socialism and neo-liberalism, social democracy might be treated – as it is by Ian Henry (2001: 32) – not as an ideology in its own right, but as a compromise between competing ideologies. In this section we also discuss 'Third Way' politics, which is a movement that developed in the 1990s to reshape social democracy in challenging the political success of neo-liberalism. The related phenomenon of *communitarianism* is also discussed.

Principles

The main principles of social democracy can be summarized as:

- a belief in social equality;
- support for a strong, interventionist state;
- promotion of welfare services, including social security, education and health services;
- acceptance of a basically capitalist economy, suitably regulated.

Parties

- In the *UK* social democrats have traditionally formed the centre to right wing of the Labour Party, with the left wing of the party consisting of democratic socialists. In the 1980s, a dissident group of social democrats broke away from the Labour Party to form the Social Democratic Party, but it gained little electoral support. As noted above, during the latter half of the 20th century the Liberal Party had, confusingly, become a social democratic party and, in the late 1980s, it joined together with the Social Democrats to form the Liberal Democrats, who came to power in 2010 as the junior partner in a Conservative-led coalition.
- In *Australia* a similar pattern of events occurred but in a different time frame, with the Australian Democrats being formed by a breakaway group of the Australian Labor Party in the 1960s. This party became a 'third force' in Australian politics but went into decline in the 21st century. The Australian Labor Party has a similar social democratic stance to the Labour Party in the UK.
- In the *USA* the Democratic Party is generally seen as being social democratic in philosophy, although a more right-wing electorate prevents the development of the sorts of welfare state that have emerged under other social democratic parties.
- In *Europe* social democratic parties occupy a similar position to the Labour Party in the UK, with the Scandinavian parties being particularly strong and electorally successful.

In most of the above cases, social democratic parties have evolved from parties which would previously have been described as democratic socialist. A distinctive indicator of the difference between the two ideologies is the attitude to government ownership of enterprises. In the past, democratic socialist governments have established, or nationalized existing, enterprises, such as railways, airlines, power companies, banks and telecommunications companies. The trend in the last 30 years has been to sell these enterprises to the private sector – to *privatize* them. This move has been led by neo-liberal governments, but some social democratic governments have followed suit. The strong resistance to privatization among sections of social democratic parties, notably trades unions, is evidence of the persistence of socialist ideals in such parties. In the leisure sector, transport enterprises are, of course, of significance to tourism and the process of Compulsory Competitive Tendering, as discussed in Chapter 6, resulted in the privatization of the *management* of public leisure facilities, even if the facilities themselves remained in public hands.

Leisure, sport and tourism

A social democratic perspective would see leisure services, including provision for recreational sport, as a social service. The emphasis is on access for all at minimum cost, preferably free, to the user. In the arts area there is clutch of terms associated with such a view, including *community arts* (a community-based, participatory alternative to professional, elite arts), *democratization of the arts* (making traditional arts accessible to all) and *cultural democracy* (widening the scope of what constitutes 'art' and 'culture'). The comparable term used in sport is *sport for all*. In the tourism sector, there is a concept known as *social tourism*, which is concerned with developing policies to enable less well-off groups in society to take a holiday away from home, with an element of public subsidy.

The Third Way

Social democracy was given a 'new spin' in the second half of the 1990s by the Blair Labour government in Britain, using the terms 'New Labour' and the 'Third Way', and by the Clinton government in the USA, using the terms 'new progressivism', 'New Democrats' and later 'Third Way'. Anthony Giddens, a sociologist adviser to Tony Blair who has written extensively on third way politics, states that it is 'above all an endeavour to respond to change' (Giddens, 2000: 27). The major changes which the Third Way seeks to respond to are: globalization, the declining relevance of class conflict and the growing importance of the information/knowledge economy. Giddens identifies the main principles of Third Way politics as:

- a focus on the 'centre' of politics rather than a class-based left/right divide;
- keeping a balance between government, the market and 'civil society';
- adopting the principle of 'no rights without responsibilities' as a feature of citizenship;
- fostering a 'diversified society based on egalitarian principles' – equality of opportunity rather than equality of outcomes;
- taking 'globalization seriously' – exploiting the opportunities it offers rather than opposing it (summary of Giddens, 2000: 50–54).

In the context of the spectrum shown in Fig. 2.1, Third Way proponents seek to insert a new ideology between social democracy and neo-liberalism. In putting forward their thesis, however, proponents often tend to oversimplify the existing political spectrum, ignoring conservatism, implying that it has been displaced entirely by neo-liberalism, and failing to distinguish between democratic socialism and social democracy.

Third Way politics has been subject to widespread criticism, from both left and right. For some, it is seen as just a mish-mash of policies designed to appeal to the 'middle ground' and get the Labour Party elected to government in the UK and therefore, in practice, regardless of the rhetoric, it adopts many of the policies of its liberal/'New Right' opponents. Thus the first principles listed above could be seen as indicating a desertion of Labour's working-class roots; the second and fifth policies downplay the role of the state and embrace the market as enthusiastically as the Conservatives; the third policy can be seen as abandoning the principles of the welfare state; and the fourth policy can be seen as basically abandoning the quest for equality as 'too hard' and adopting the same supposed 'level playing field' philosophy as the Conservatives.

- In the *UK*, Third Way principles became the official policy for the Labour Party from the 1990s.
- In *Australia* it is arguable that, to all intents and purposes, Third Way policies were followed by the Hawke/Keating Labor governments of 1982–1996, but without the terminology. As right-wing Labor administrations, they adopted many of the policies which later came to be called 'Third Way'. When the Australian Labor Party was in opposition, Third Way ideas were espoused by its leading figures, notably Mark Latham, who was leader for a short while. With its return to power in 2007, under the leadership of Kevin Rudd, Third Way ideas, such as the idea of reciprocal responsibility, were very much to the fore, but again, the term 'Third Way' has not been prominent in party rhetoric.
- In the *USA*, the movement appeared to have died with the end of the Clinton administration.
- In *Europe* the situation is mixed, with some labour parties adopting Third Way ideas, some being opposed and some claiming to have been practising them for years (Giddens, 2000: 14–21).

A related idea is the concept of 'civil society', mentioned by Giddens as a feature of Third Way thinking, which gives emphasis to non-economic features of public life. Many believe that technological, economic and social change during much of the 20th century resulted in a 'loss of community'. For a range of reasons, it is believed that people have become more self-centred or inward-looking, to the family unit and immediate acquaintances: thus there is less neighbourliness and increasing alienation from the wider society. This results in rising levels of such social ills as crime, family breakdown and suicide. An emphasis on 'civil society' is intended to counter these trends: the idea is to take account of 'social capital' as well as economic capital (Cox, 1995). This is clearly relevant to leisure, since many leisure-based organizations can be seen as part of a society's 'social capital'. However, apart from an increased role for the voluntary sector, it is not clear exactly how this is to come about.

Given that Third Way politics represents a 'shift to the centre', it can be expected that leisure, sport and tourism policies would move away from heavy state involvement and towards a greater involvement of the private sector. In the *UK*, the Conservative Party was basically conservative in nature before the rise of the 'Right'/neo-liberal thinkers under Margaret Thatcher in the 1980s. In the mid-1990s the Conservatives lost power to New Labour under Tony Blair, a change which moved the centre of gravity of British politics towards the centre-left; the Conservative Party has subsequently moved away from neo-liberalism back towards its more centrist conservative roots. In fact, probably because leisure is rarely a high priority for governments, particularly in a first term, there was little sign of this happening with the Blair government in the UK in the late 1990s. The Compulsory Competitive Tendering of local government services introduced by the Conservatives has ended, although the emphasis on efficiency and cost-cutting remains, through such programmes as 'Best Value' and customer service *charters*, as discussed in Chapters 4 and 6.

Communitarianism

Communitarianism is a movement associated with social theorists such as Amitai Etzioni (1995) and Micahel Walzer (2005). On the one hand communitarianism is linked to the Third Way and can therefore be seen as founded on a critique of social democracy located in the centre-left of politics, but on the other it is also founded on a critique of neo-liberalism on the right of politics. The main criticism which communitarianism levels at neo-liberalism is the latter's excessive focus on the isolated, self-interested individual and a non-interfering state: the communitarian view is that, as individuals, people live in, and are dependent on, communities and therefore have a set of reciprocal relationships, rights and obligations in regard to the collective community and that the state should reinforce these collective relationships. It is also critical of the left for over-emphasizing the role of the state, but the inclusion of the idea of *obligations* in Third Way and communitarian thinking has been criticised by the left, since it appears to undermine people's unqualified right to welfare.

The confusion created by the crowded nature of the 'centre of politics' is added to by the fact that communitarianism has also been put forward as a reformed version of neo-liberalism, as a replacement for Thatcherism in the UK in the forms of *communitarian liberalism* (Gray, 1996) and *progressive conservatism* (Blond, 2009).

FEMINISM

While the struggle for women's rights dates back at least to the campaigns for women's voting rights in the early part of the 20th century, modern feminism dates from the 1960s. Whether feminism can be described as a political ideology or a movement or a network of pressure groups is open to debate. A number of writers point out that feminism is not a single ideology, but exists in various forms, reflecting the mainstream ideologies discussed above.

Principles

At the core of most feminist analyses of society is the idea of *patriarchy* – that is that *men* organize and control society in their own interests, to the exclusion and disadvantage of women. Essentially the argument is that men wield excessive power in society and that historically, institutions and customs have developed to perpetuate this situation. Where various feminists disagree is over what should be done about it.

Reformist feminists believe that, through campaigns within the mainstream political process, a range of reforms, such as equal pay, anti-discrimination legislation and improvements in child care provision, can be instituted, which will eventually achieve equality between men and women in society. Marxist, or radical, feminists, on the other hand, argue that patriarchy is as fundamental to capitalism as the struggle between the classes; the exploitation of women as a group is as endemic to the system as the exploitation of workers as a group. So the only solution is a socialist revolution. Under a socialist or communist society the conditions for the domination and exploitation of women would be removed.

Parties

In party terms feminists have generally aligned themselves with the forces of the left; in general there have not been separate feminist political parties.

Leisure, sport and tourism

There is a substantial literature relating feminist ideas and analysis to leisure (see Resources). This literature points out that, because they continue to bear the bulk of child and home care responsibilities while being increasingly involved in the labour market, women have much less leisure time than men, and their leisure is often subservient to the leisure of others, for example in home-based socializing, going out on a family picnic or a self-catering holiday, or in accompanying children or partners to *their* sporting or other leisure events. Furthermore, social customs, frequently reinforced by commercial media and marketing, limit the range of activities considered to be 'suitable' for women. And the *institutions* and *infrastructure* of leisure – especially sport – are dominated by men and orientated to men's needs and ways of doing things (Mowbray, 1992, 1993). Thus the whole pattern of leisure reinforces the patriarchal system of society. However, as with the Marxist critique, it has also been pointed out that such leisure as women do enjoy can be used as a medium for *resistance* to the patriarchal forces in society (Wearing, 1990).

Insofar as past state practices have supported the development of the current institutions (e.g. grants to men-only or male-dominated sports clubs), they have reinforced and perpetuated the inequality of women. The reformist feminist solution, as far as leisure provision is concerned, is to use the state to correct the balance by, for example, greatly increasing child care provision at leisure venues, and providing more support for traditional women's activities, such as women's sports, and paying attention to such issues as transport access to leisure venues, and safety.

ENVIRONMENTALISM

As with feminism, the status of the environmental, or 'green', movement as a political ideology alongside the mainstream ideologies discussed above is open to debate, given that, as with feminism, a variety of green perspectives exists, often reflecting the mainstream political ideologies.

Principles

The fundamental environmentalist argument is that, while the mainstream political ideologies differ on how society should be organized and which interest groups should dominate, in fact they all share the same misguided aim, which is the pursuit of materialist economic growth. The greens argue that this should *not* be the goal of society because unlimited economic growth, of a conventional kind, is incompatible with the continued survival of 'planet earth'. Existing damage to the environment, in terms of pollution and excessive exploitation of non-renewable natural resources, such as old-growth forests, demonstrates the long-term unsustainability of current practices (Porritt, 1984).

As with feminism, there are leftist and a rightist sets of 'green' solutions. Greens of a right-wing or centrist tendency would argue that capitalist industry and commerce can and must be controlled and reformed through legislation requiring it to reduce pollution and environmentally exploitative practices, and that private citizens must be encouraged and required by the state to recycle waste and change consumption patterns. More radical greens would argue that the inexorable search for profit by capitalism makes attempts at such reforms futile and therefore the only way to save the environment is to bring about a fundamental change through the replacement of capitalism altogether. As André Gorz put it: '. . . the ecological movement is not an end in itself, but a stage in the larger struggle . . . what are we really after? A capitalism adapted to ecological constraints; or a social, economic, and cultural revolution that abolishes the constraints of capitalism and, in so doing, establishes a new relationship between the individual and society and between people and nature? Reform or revolution?' (Gorz, 1980b: 4).

Parties

The green movement has been divided on whether it should campaign independently as a pressure group to bring about change, whether it should seek to infiltrate and change mainstream party policies or whether it should form 'green' parties to operate independently. All three solutions continue to be pursued.

Leisure, sport and tourism

The environmental argument relates to leisure in a fundamental way. Leisure can be seen as a major offender in the 'consumer society': insofar as people 'want more', it is often leisure goods and services which they want more of. Of course it could be argued that all leisure activity does not depend on material props – much of it involves simple social interaction or the consumption of *services*, such as going to a show or a sports match or to a restaurant, which make relatively few demands on material resources. Further, it could be argued that more leisure *time* means less work, which means less material production. However, many leisure services do involve the use of material resources, such as fuel to travel (particularly air travel) and the range of leisure 'hardware' on which consumers spend massive amounts every year. Thus in most capitalist societies, in practice, more leisure entails more material consumption.

Much leisure, sport and tourism activity makes direct use of the natural environment. If it is not conserved then it will not be available for the enjoyment of current or future generations. Conservation is generally achieved through the intervention of the state, either directly through such mechanisms as the designation of National Parks and Wilderness Areas, or indirectly through planning and pollution controls.

The idea of *sustainability* has become the catchword of the environmental movement in recent years, as a result, in particular, of the publication in 1990 of the report of the World Commission on Environment and Development, *Our Common Future* (The 'Brundtland Report', WCED, 1990) and the publication in 1992 of an action plan, 'Agenda 21', following the United Nations 'Earth Summit' in Rio de Janeiro (Robinson, N.A., 1993). Sustainable development is that which does not 'compromise the ability of future generations to meet their needs'. Because of its attraction to unspoilt natural environments, this issue has loomed particularly large in relation to tourism development. The forcefulness of 'Agenda 21' and international debate about such issues as 'global warming' have added considerably to the momentum behind the environmental movement. The result is frequent opposition to many tourism developments in natural areas, arising from a consortium of local residents and politically active environmentalists.

ANTI-GLOBALISM

Whether or not the opposition to globalization that emerged in the 1990s can be called an *ideology* or just a *movement* is debatable, but it is discussed here because it has achieved such a high profile, eclipsing many more traditional political movements, at least in terms of media attention. The reason for the uncertainty is that, not surprisingly given its relative youth, the ideas and ideals of the movement have not been as fully spelled out or subject to such detailed examination and analysis as longer-established perspectives. As Zygmunt Bauman (1998: 1) has said: ' "Globalization" is on everybody's lips; a fad word fast turning into a shibboleth, a magic incantation, a pass-key meant to unlock the gates to all present and future mysteries'.

Principles

Particular features of a 'globalized world' are:

- the international reach of multinational enterprises (MNEs), such as Sony, Time–Warner–AOL, McDonald's, Nike and News Limited;
- the speeding up, massively increased capacity and reduced cost of international telecommunications facilitated by satellite technology;
- the consequent massive and instantaneous electronic movement of capital funds between the world's financial centres;
- the spread of the Internet;
- the worldwide spread of cultural 'product', such as film, television programmes, music and sporting events and their influence on national cultures;
- the internationalization of moral–political–lifestyle debates and movements (such as women's movements, environmentalism and, indeed, anti-globalism);
- deregulation of international trade established through the General Agreement on Tariffs and Trade (GATT) and its successor World Trade Organization (WTO);
- the advent of mass tourism.

While undoubtedly developing rapidly in the last three decades, globalization is not a totally new concept. Langhorne (2001) traces the basis of globalization to the speed-up of international communication brought about by steam trains and steam ships and the electric telegraph in the 19th century, with its full development emerging through the advent of computers, satellite communications and the Internet in the last quarter of the 20th century. However, even ignoring earlier phenomena such as the Alexandrian, Roman and Mogul empires, the Roman Catholic Church had reached truly global proportions by the 17th century, with a universal 'product' and even a globally recognized 'logo'. The British Empire, 'on which the sun never set', had extended into five continents by the 19th century. Hollywood established its worldwide reach in the 1930s and companies such as Ford, Shell, BP and Hoover had developed into multinational companies by the middle of the 20th century.

The focus of the anti-globalization movement has been the activities of multinational or transglobal companies, which have emerged along with the new communications technologies. As a result of all these changes, and changes in management practices, there has been a shift of jobs in some industries, notably clothing and footwear manufacture and lightweight assembly, such as electronics, from high-wage Western countries to low-wage developing countries in South America and Asia.

The number and sheer size of the MNEs makes them a significant economic force in the world, with the ability to locate their activities wherever they wish, in order to minimize wages and taxation and maximize access to markets. This, together with the free trade protocols put in place under GATT and WTO agreements, is seen as threatening the powers of individual governments, involving a shift of sovereignty from democratic governments to unaccountable commercial entities.

A further criticism of globalization lies in the cultural area: large, multifunctional, predominantly American-based communications organizations, such as News Ltd. and Time–Warner–AOL, are believed to be potentially dangerous for free speech and, together with MNEs involved in areas such as fashion and music, threaten a worldwide homogenization of culture and consequent loss of local culture and diversity (Barnet and Cavanagh, 1996). The MNEs, the WTO and the international financial system, including special international financial agencies such as the International Monetary Fund (IMF) and the World Bank – collectively referred to as 'global capital' – have become the target of attack by a loose collection of groups of activists, largely from Western countries and themselves organized mainly via the Internet. In particular the movement has targeted high profile meetings of such bodies, where mass demonstrations have been organized and widely publicized.

One of the most well-known representatives of the movement is Canadian journalist Naomi Klein, who presented the anti-globalization case in her book *No Logo: Taking Aim at the Brand Bullies* (Klein, 1999). The book concentrates on the growth of the *brand* in the North American economy and consumer culture, particularly consumer brands, such as *Nike* sports footwear, *Gap* clothing, *Marlboro* cigarettes and *Starbucks* coffee. A particular focus is on the trend for clothing companies in particular to 'downsize' their labour forces in Western countries and to contract all or most of their manufacturing to low-wage 'sweatshops' in developing countries. One of the strategies of the various anti-globalization groups which grew up around these issues in the 1990s has been to seek to embarrass companies like Nike by publicizing the sweatshop phenomenon and leading boycotts of their products until they undertake to ensure improved conditions for their contracted workers. But, as Klein points out, this strategy, even if successful, simply sanitizes and reinforces the position of these organizations and does not attack the broader agenda of the movement, which is outright opposition to 'global capital'. Klein's solution is a very traditional one, that the solution will come about only through a self-directed struggle for rights and decent conditions by the workers in the sweatshops themselves.

As a protest movement, anti-globalism overlaps with other movements, as illustrated by the collection of papers entitled *The Case Against the Global Economy and a Turn Toward the Local*, published by the California-based environmental organization the Sierra Club (Mander and Goldsmith, 1996), and papers on feminism and globalization in Sassen's *Globalization and its Discontents* (1998).

Opposition to the anti-globalization movement – or defence of globalization – is likely to come primarily from those who subscribe to a neo-liberal ideology. Rugman (2000), for example, argues that globalization trends have been exaggerated and very few companies are genuinely global. He notes that most international trade takes place *within* regions (the EU, Asia, the Americas) rather than between them and that most MNEs are regionally focused and concludes: 'No credible evidence can be found to support the viewpoint that a system of global capitalism exists' (Rugman, 2000: 218).

There are also alternative academic perspectives on some of the globalization themes. For example, it is suggested that alongside, and possibly countering, the cultural homogenization tendency of globalization is a tendency towards cultural diversity and affirmation of national cultural identities (Maguire, 1999: 21). Featherstone (1990) argues that 'global culture' may not involve homogenization or annihilation of national cultures but may represent a separate, additional cultural phenomenon arising from international exchange. There is also the suggestion that, while globalization may tend to marginalize certain disadvantaged groups, it can provide a platform for some groups to internationalize their cause – for example indigenous land rights. And the fact that centres for international capital must locate *somewhere*, notably in international cities (New York, Paris, London, Hong Kong, Sydney), provides a network of globalized platforms for political organization and campaigns by disadvantaged groups (Sassen, 1998).

Leisure, sport and tourism

The globalization debate clearly has implications for leisure, sport and tourism. Many 'global' products are leisure-related, including sports (Maguire, 1999), music and associated hardware, film, fashion and eating fast food and drinking coffee, beer and spirits. Tourism is quintessentially a global industry, although, while airlines and some hotel groups are among the major multinational corporations, tourism companies are rarely the target of anti-globalist protest. Much tourism research in recent years has focused on the type of tourism that involves seeking out the strange and exotic – hence the use of the term the 'tourist gaze' (Urry, 2002). The threatened homogenization of culture might, therefore, be considered a threat to tourism. In fact, however, this type of tourism is far outweighed in volume by domestic tourism generally, 'non-gazing' domestic and international tourism, such as: (i) the Blackpool/Southend phenomenon in the UK and the Gold Coast in Australia; (ii) the European Spanish 'Costa' tourism; and (iii) pilgrimages to the 'headquarters' of world popular culture – Disneyland, Disney World and Hollywood. On this evidence, it would appear that tourism could survive global homogenization.

SUMMARY

- Ideologies can be characterized by their attitudes towards a range of issues, including: social change, economic growth, social inequality, elitism, the market system and the role of the state. These characteristics are summarized in Table 2.2.
- Generally, only the conservative ideology is *not* in favour of changing the status quo. This is, however, to some extent a reflection of the particular historical situation in the Western democracies. Where non-conservatives hold power for a long period of time, sufficient to bring about radical change, then what were previously conservative forces wish to 'turn back the clock'. Thus they become supporters of change and the previous radicals become the conservatives. Hence the confusing terminology in the former communist states of Eastern Europe.
- Environmentalism is notable for being the only ideology having a clearly negative attitude towards conventional *economic growth*, with anti-globalism somewhat ambivalent on this issue. While some proponents and governments of other ideological persuasions may be more or less 'green' in outlook, in general they seek to show that they have a superior approach to achieving, and distributing the product of, economic growth.
- Attitudes towards the *market system* vary significantly, with Marxists committed to its abolition and neo-liberals being its main champion, while others wish to see it modified by the

activities of the state and the voluntary sector. The corollary to this is attitudes towards the role of the state, with neo-liberals being most suspicious and Marxist and democratic socialists most accepting.

- The ideologies reviewed differ in their approach to *social inequality*. Neo-liberals see inequality as the other side of the coin of incentive and freedom – the very mechanism that drives the successful market economy. At the other extreme, the left see the inequalities of the capitalist system as its worst fault, and feminism focuses on the inequality between men and women.
- It cannot be said that leisure, sport or tourism are the *focus* of any of the ideologies discussed above, but it can be shown that they each provide a distinctive perspective for viewing the role of these phenomena in contemporary society, and the role of the state in relation to their provision and regulation.

RESOURCES

Philosophical and religious aspects of leisure: Pieper (1965); Dare *et al.* (1987); Fain (1991); Cooper (1999); Sylvester (1999).

Political ideology and leisure generally: Henry (1984a, b, 1985, 1993, 2001); Bramham and Henry (1985); Coalter (1988, 1990); Wilson (1988); Henry and Spink (1990a).

Marxist and other discussion of 'false needs': Veal (2009e).

Sport and politics: Houlihan (1997).

Marxist/neo-Marxist views of sport: Brohm (1978); Gruneau (1999).

Sport and communist regimes: Riordan (1980); Price and Dayan (2008).

Tourism and politics: Hall (1994); Burns and Novelli (2007).

Social democracy: Dow (1993); and leisure: Veal (1998).

Third Way politics: Touraine (1991); Gray (1996); Blair (1998); Giddens (1998, 2000); Hale *et al.* (2004); Latham (1998).

Third Way politics – critics: Giddens (2000: 1–26); Callinicos (2001); Hale *et al.* (2004).

Communitarianism: Etzioni (1995); Rushton (1999); Walzer (2005); communitarian liberalism: Gray (1996).

Tourism, politics and the role of government: Hughes (1984); Richter (1989); Jeffries (2001).

Fascism and anarchism: Wilson (1988); Leach (1993).

Feminism: Deem (1986a, b); Wimbush and Talbot (1988); Henderson *et al.* (1989); Green, E. *et al.* (1990); Kenway (1992); Wearing (1998).

Environmentalism: Gorz (1980b); Porritt (1984); Spretnak and Capra (1985); WCED (1990); Papadakis (1993); Robinson, N.A. (1993); Doyle (2000).

Anti-globalism: Mander and Goldsmith (1996); Klein (1999); Held and McGrew (2000); Hertz (2001).

QUESTIONS/EXERCISES

1. Consider how the public funding of: (i) elite sport; and (ii) tourism promotion might be viewed from the perspective of each of the political ideologies outlined in this chapter.

2. Why is Marxism relevant today?

3. What are the differences between democratic socialism and social democracy?

4. What are the differences between conservatism and (neo-)liberalism?

5. Discuss ways in which the leisure, sport and tourism perspectives arising from feminism differ from those of the mainstream political ideologies.

6. Discuss ways in which the leisure, sport and tourism policies arising from environmentalism differ from those of the mainstream political ideologies.

7. What part do leisure, sport and tourism play in globalization and why might these features be subject to criticism by anti-globalists?

8. Examine any national or local government leisure or tourism policy document (they are often available on official websites) and suggest what is the implicit political philosophy behind it.

9. Via the Internet, explore the possibility of discovering the leisure, sport and tourism policies of one of the major political parties.

10. Discuss the place of equality and inequality in leisure, sport and tourism as seen from different political perspectives.

chapter 3

Wants, Needs, Obligations, Demands, Benefits and Participation

INTRODUCTION

The focus of concern for planning and management of a commercial organization is generally the share price or the level of profit, which is often expressed as the rate of return on capital employed. Profit is related to sales and costs. What is the comparable focus in the public sector? Public sector policymaking and planning have been based on a variety of concepts, which have often been poorly defined, if they have been defined at all. Here we explore six such concepts, as follows:

- *Wants*: interpreted in this book as those desires not classified as needs.
- *Needs*: used in leisure planning contexts to indicate necessities but, in the context of tourism market, seen as the basis of all wants/desires.
- *Obligations*: participation which takes place primarily as a result of social obligations, rather then individual desire.
- *Demand*: an economics-based concept indicating the amounts of a good or service which people will buy at various prices.
- *Benefits*: the (net) positive effects which result from participation.
- *Participation*: taking part in an activity or type of activity.

These are the definitions that are generally adopted in this chapter and subsequently in the rest of the book, but are elaborated upon in the rest of the chapter. Some additional concepts that have featured in leisure policymaking and planning are discussed briefly at the end of the chapter, including collective consumption, quality-of-life and well-being, while human rights and citizenship rights are discussed in Chapter 4.

Each concept offers a different perspective on human behaviour in leisure, sport and tourism and has different implications for the public policy response. These are discussed in turn in this chapter. The policymaking and planning relevance of each concept is discussed briefly here and followed up in more detail in Chapter 7.

WANTS AND NEEDS

Introduction

In general usage *want* is equivalent to *desire*: I want what I desire and I desire what I want. Need can be seen as a special type of want, but in some cases an individual may not actually want what someone else believes he or she actually needs: for example, children often do not want to eat the vegetables which their parents know they need as a source of vitamins. Because of its special nature we discuss the concept of need first, drawing a distinction between want and need at various points in the discussion and returning to the distinction at the end of the discussion. In leisure research and policy discourses, the concept of need has been used in two ways:

- *normatively*: to classify participation in leisure activity as a need so that leisure service provision is seen as a form of social service requiring government support;
- *analytically*: in the process of seeking insights into participants' motivations, as in consumer theory.

Both uses appear in the leisure policy context generally, including discourse related to sport and physical exercise, but in the tourism context the second use is dominant, particularly in the context of tourism marketing. Later in this chapter we consider these two uses of the concept, but first we examine briefly a range of theoretical conceptualizations of need. There is an enormous literature on the concept of need, from a wide range of disciplines; here we examine seven contributions:

- Maslow's hierarchy of need: humanistic psychology;
- optimal arousal and incongruity: social psychology;
- leisure satisfaction scales: social psychology;
- the Bradshaw/Mercer typology of need: social welfare;
- universal needs: sociology/socio-economic development;
- false needs: neo-Marxism;
- socio-economic deprivation.

The basic characteristics of these conceptualizations are summarized in Table 3.1.

Maslow's hierarchy of needs

The hierarchy of needs theory developed by Abraham Maslow in the 1940s and 1950s is the most well-known of all the theories on need. It divides human needs into five types arranged in a hierarchy of increasing prepotency, as shown in Table 3.1. As needs lower down the hierarchy are satisfied, the theory states, so the higher needs become salient and the individual is motivated to concentrate on satisfying them. The theory has been criticized for positing that all needs lower down the hierarchy must be fully met before an individual moves on to pursuing higher-level needs, and for suggesting that the particular hierarchical sequence will be strictly followed by everyone, but in fact Maslow did not insist that the theory would be so hard and fast on either of these points.

Table 3.1. Conceptualizations of need.

Theory	Main aspects	Categories	Category explanations	Sources
Maslow's hierarchy of need	'Basically important needs' are arranged in a hierarchy of prepotency; individuals tend to seek to satisfy needs in the order of the hierarchy, but this is not hard and fast; denial of 'basically important needs' produces psycho-pathological consequences	Physiological Safety Affiliation Esteem Self-actualization	Food, clothing, shelter Physical/financial security Love, relatedness Self-esteem, social esteem Achieving potential	Maslow (1954/1987)
Optimal arousal and incongruity	Too little mental stimulation results in boredom, too much results in stress: both are harmful to the individual	n/a	n/a	Iso-Ahola (1980)
Leisure satisfaction scales	Survey respondents indicate the extent to which participation in leisure activities results in the satisfaction of various types of 'need'	Various, typically 40–50 categories, e.g. excitement, relaxation, physical health	Likert scales indicating levels of satisfaction or of importance	Beard and Ragheb (1980); Driver et al. (1991b)

Bradshaw/Mercer typology	Need can be measured in four ways	Felt need	Individual expression, e.g. in response to a survey question	Bradshaw (1972); Mercer (1973)
		Expressed need	Current participation or indication of desire to do so, e.g. joining a waiting list	
		Comparative	Comparison between individuals or groups	
		Normative	As assessed by experts and/or other groups in society	
Universal needs	A set of needs can be identified that are common to all human beings and which, if denied, would result in serious harm to the individual	Various, depending on author	n/a	Doyal and Gough (1991); Max-Neef (1992)
False needs	'Needs' are shaped by capitalism (e.g. via advertising), but true needs will only be known when society is transformed	n/a	n/a	Marcuse (1964)
Socio-economic deprivation	People who are assessed as relatively deprived in general socio-economic terms are deemed to be in need in regard to leisure	n/a	n/a	Department of the Environment (1977)

However, a feature generally ignored in references to the theory is that it does not apply to *all* needs but only to 'basically important needs', which Maslow defined as follows: 'Thwarting of *unimportant desires* produces no psychopathological results: thwarting of *basically important needs* does produce such results' (Maslow, 1954/1987: 30, emphasis added). This principle, that 'need' refers only to those desires which, if thwarted, produce pathological consequences, can be seen as a version of the *harm prevention* conceptualization of need, discussed further below. It sets up a distinction between needs, the denial of which results in harm, and 'unimportant desires', the denial of which does not result in harm. The practice in this book will be to refer to such unimportant desires as *wants*.

The challenge, in applying Maslow's theory, is therefore to determine when a particular desire is a *need* (denial will cause harm) and when it is just a *want* (denial will not cause harm). This requires the adoption of a normative position on what is and is not harmful. Maslow was working in the context of clinical psychology, where desires, needs, wants and their underlying bases are explored on a one-to-one basis. Something approaching this may be achieved in small-scale leisure/sport programmes, particularly in the context of *therapeutic recreation* as practised in North America. But this is not generally possible in most social/managerial settings where, if it is necessary to decide whether something that leisure activity might prevent is or is not harmful, the assessment would be reliant on professional and, ultimately, political values.

It should be noted that, in a number of tourism marketing texts (e.g. Kotler *et al.*, 2006: 14; Mill and Morrison, 2006: 279–281), even when the definition of need is apparently based on Maslow, the above distinction between needs and wants is not made: all wants are seen as the conscious expression of Maslovian-type underlying needs and the harm prevention dimension of Maslow's theory is generally ignored. The distinction between the Maslow approach and this tourism marketing approach is illustrated in Fig. 3.1.

Optimal arousal and incongruity

Optimal arousal and incongruity refers to the amount of mental stimulation people require in their lives and has been identified by social psychologists, such as Seppo Iso-Ahola (1980), as a *need* and one which can be met through leisure participation. While Iso-Ahola rejects Maslow's hierarchy, he uses a similar criterion for distinguishing need, that is in terms of the negative consequences of denial, stating: 'too little or too much stimulation is *damaging to an individual, physiologically and psychologically*' (Iso-Ahola, 1980: 229, emphasis added). Optimal arousal and incongruity can be seen as similar to the concept of *flow*, as developed by Csikszentmihalyi

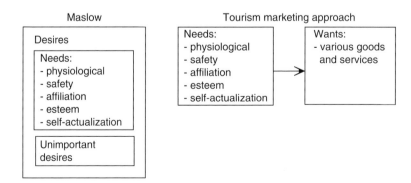

Fig. 3.1. Distinctions between the Maslow and tourism marketing approaches.

(1990), involving a feeling of timelessness and intense engagement with the moment. Of course leisure activity is not the only medium through which optimal arousal and incongruity or flow may be experienced – family life and work are other possibilities. For those individuals or groups not experiencing optimal arousal and incongruity by these other means, leisure activity may well meet a need, in that it may, in Iso-Ahola's terms, prevent physiological or psychological damage.

It might appear that applying the optimal arousal and incongruity idea to leisure contexts is more straightforward than applying the Maslow hierarchy, but deciding what is optimal and how suboptimal the situation has to be to cause physiological or psychological damage to the individual is likely to be as challenging as any Maslow-related appraisal.

Leisure satisfaction scales

Leisure satisfaction scales involve asking survey respondents to indicate the level of satisfaction they receive from different types of leisure experience using Likert-type scales. Here, need is equated with satisfaction, there being no distinction between needs and 'unimportant desires': all desires are classified as needs. In some cases the scales relate to the importance of various factors instead of, or in addition to, satisfaction, but this refers not to the importance of the factors to the individual in general but to the importance of the factor in relation to a particular activity (e.g. How important is relaxation in relation to a visit to a national park?). Iso-Ahola (1980: 229) sees such responses as mere surface indicators of underlying need for optimal arousal and incongruity, as indicated above. Leisure satisfaction scales have a strong tradition in North America, including:

- Beard and Ragheb's (1980) Leisure Satisfaction Scale (LSS);
- the Paragraphs about Leisure (PAL) scale developed by Howard Tinsley and his associates (1977);
- the Recreation Experience Preference (REP) scale developed by Bev Driver and his associates (PAL and REP are described in Driver *et al.*, 1991b).

In typical surveys using leisure satisfaction scales, fairly long lists of factors are involved – as many as 40 or 50. While statistical analysis of the results can provide insights into the motivations of different participant groups, the data do not distinguish between wants and needs in the sense discussed above.

The Bradshaw/Mercer typology of need

The Bradshaw/Mercer typology of need was developed by British social scientist Jonathan Bradshaw (1972) in relation to British social services, and then applied to leisure by Australian geographer David Mercer (1973). As indicated in Table 3.1, it comprises four types of need, or ways of measuring need: *expressed, felt, comparative* and *normative*. This typology has not generally been applied in tourism, but aspects of it have been widely used in local council leisure/recreation needs studies which often follow government advice to assess 'community needs', as indicated in the governmental quotations in Box 3.1.

In seeking to apply the Bradshaw/Mercer typology in the leisure/sport planning context we are faced with two major limitations. First, it does not indicate what a need *is*, only that it can be assessed in four different ways:

- *Expressed needs* are what people currently *do* or would like to do and so must include activity arising from wants and obligations as well as needs.
- *Felt needs* indicate what people say they need although, invariably, in practice they are an indication of wants. Surveys of so-called 'leisure needs' rarely actually ask respondents

---

Box 3.1. Governmental statements on leisure and need.

UK, 1973: House of Lords Select Committee on Sport and Leisure

'… the needs of leisure have been seriously underestimated in this country, and the significance of recreational provision has not been appreciated. Too often recreational facilities are treated as an optional extra. The Committee reject this idea and consider that the greatest impediment of all to the development of recreational facilities in this country is the belief that those facilities are not essential. They repeat the view expressed in the First Report that the provision of the opportunity for the enjoyment of leisure is part of the general fabric of the social services. Until Parliament, government, planners and educators accept the place of leisure as an essential ingredient of life, there will be no satisfactory provision of recreational facilities, and the well-being of the community will suffer. Society ought to regard sport and leisure not as a slightly eccentric form of indulgence but as one of the community's everyday needs' (House of Lords Select Committee on Sport and Leisure, 1973: xxvi; endorsed in the 1975 White Paper *Sport & Recreation* (Department of Environment, 1975: 1)).

Australia, 1974: Frank Stewart, Minister for Tourism and Recreation

'… the paradox is that the higher the standard of living and the greater the prosperity and well-being of the people, the more acute is the need for recreation, a regenerative process which can assume an almost unlimited number of manifestations' (Stewart, 1975: 3).

New South Wales, Australia, 1992: Department of Planning, Outdoor Recreation and Open Space Planning Guidelines for Local Government

'… this document moves away from rigid standards which have been adopted by many councils, to a needs based open space planning approach. For too long standards bearing no relationship to local community needs have been used to decide the amount of open space. A needs based approach offers councils and developers the opportunity to take into account local circumstances and to negotiate a solution that suits the area and population in question' (Department of Planning, 1992: i).

Australia, 1994: Creative Nation

'Because culture reflects and serves both the collective and the individual need, because it at once assures us of who we are and inspires us with intimations of the heights we might reach, this cultural policy pursues the twin goals of democracy and excellence' (Commonwealth of Australia, 1994: 5).

UK, 1999: Department of Culture, Media and Sport, Local Cultural Strategies guidelines

Local cultural strategies are to be based on 'the needs of local communities' (p. 5). One of the benefits of developing such strategies is their focus on the 'needs, demands and aspirations' of communities (DCMS, 1999a: 13). No explanation is offered regarding the difference between 'need', 'demand' and 'aspiration'.

UK, 1999: Department of Culture, Media and Sport, Policy Action Team Report 10

'Principles which help to exploit the potential of arts/sport in regenerating communities are: (a) valuing diversity; (b) embedding local control; (c) supporting local commitment;

(Continued)

Box 3.1. Continued.

(d) promoting equitable partnerships; (e) defining common objectives in relation to actual needs …' (Department for Culture, Media and Sport, 1999b: 8).

New South Wales, Australia, 2003: State Premier, Cultural Planning Guidelines

'… cultural amenities can be seen not as something remote or apart from everyday life but fundamental to people's needs'. (NSW Ministry for the Arts and Department of Local Government, 2004: 2).

UK, 2002: PPG 17: Planning for Open Space, Sport and Recreation

'To ensure effective planning for open space, sport and recreation it is essential that the needs of local communities are known. Local authorities should undertake robust assessments of the existing and future needs of their communities for open space, sports and recreational facilities. … As a minimum, assessments of need should cover the differing and distinctive needs of the population for open space and built sports and recreational facilities. … The needs of those working in and visiting areas, as well as residents, should also be included' (Office of the Deputy Prime Minister, 2002: 2).

UK, 2006: DCMS, Time for Play

'… the Government recognises that play is of fundamental importance for children and young people's health, well-being and learning' (Department for Culture, Media and Sport, 2006: 7).

---

about *needs* as such, they tend to ask people what they *want* or would 'like to participate in'. Thus the lists of so-called needs compiled from such surveys are in fact lists of people's wants or desires.

- *Comparative needs* involve comparing people on the basis of some criterion, which must be one of the other need categories.
- *Normative needs* indicate what experts, a political body, an organized group or the public at large consider to be needs, which begs the question as to the criteria used to make those assessments. The designation of a particular service, such as health or housing, as a need was not a problem for Bradshaw because he was dealing with mainstream social services, the status of which as needs was not in question, although the issue is discussed at length in the social policy literature. But, as Mercer (1973) observes, despite numerous statements by interested parties and academics, the status of leisure as a need was, and is, far from clear.

The second limitation is that, while Bradshaw and Mercer both recommend that in policymaking or planning exercises all four measures should be used, they are vague about just how any differences in the four measures should be reconciled or evaluated to provide a single measure of need to form the basis of policy.

Universal needs

Universal needs have been put forward by a number of theorists to counter the idea that all needs are entirely *relative*: that is that different groups of people have different needs which only they can identify. The concept of felt need as discussed above is an example of a relative conceptualization of need. Maslow's five needs are one example of a list of universal needs, but others have developed different lists and typically have rejected the hierarchy idea. Thus, for example, Les Doyal and Ian Gough (1991) reject Maslow's hierarchy but use a similar 'negative consequences of denial' criterion for defining a need, describing it as something which, if denied to the individual, produces 'serious harm'. Doyal and Gough do not explicitly include leisure in their list of needs, but other proponents of universal needs do so. For example, Manfred Max-Neef lists leisure as one of nine 'axiological' categories of 'fundamental human needs' developed in the context of economic and social development. Furthermore, he defines a need as something which, if denied would produce 'progressive, and sometimes irreversible, human malfunctions', while wants, if unsatisfied, 'lead to little worse than frustration' (Max-Neef, 1992: 181).

False needs

False needs is a concept developed by neo-Marxist theorists and others to explain how the capitalist market system survives, despite its inability to meet people's 'real needs'. An example is Herbert Marcuse, who defines false needs as: '… those which are superimposed upon the individual by particular social interests in his repression: the needs which perpetuate toil, aggressiveness, misery, and injustice … Most of the prevailing needs to relax, to have fun, to behave and consume in accordance with the advertisements, to love and hate what others love and hate, belong in this category of false needs' (Marcuse, 1964: 5).

According to Marcuse, under the conditions of capitalism, it is impossible to discover which needs are true and which are false. True needs, it is argued, will emerge only when society is transformed and people are free to be themselves: 'In the last analysis, the question of what are true and false needs must be answered by the individuals themselves, but only in the last analysis; that is, if and when they are free to give their own answer. As long as they are kept incapable of being autonomous, as long as they are indoctrinated and manipulated … their answer to this question cannot be taken as their own. By the same token, however, no tribunal can justly arrogate to itself the right to decide which needs should be developed and satisfied' (Marcuse, 1964: 22–23).

Clearly, to accept this perspective in full would involve embracing neo-Marxist political ideology, as discussed in Chapter 2, which would raise doubts about the usefulness of any sort of planning under capitalist conditions. But a partial acceptance might see public sector provision of leisure services within a capitalist or mixed economy as providing a counter to the power of commercial marketing.

A word of caution should be noted in relation to Marxist and neo-Marxist writing on need since, as it is heavily influenced not only by the work of Marx himself but also by other German and French theorists, anglophone readers are dependent on translations. In this regard Macpherson points out: '… neither the French or German languages use different words for needs and wants: in French, both are *besoins*; in German, *Bedürfnisse*. English translators of French and German texts commonly use 'wants' or 'needs' as seems to them appropriate in the context. This is proper enough, but the reader of English translations of, for example, Rousseau and Marx should not assume that the author made the same distinction the translator makes' (Macpherson, 1977: 27).

Socio-economic deprivation

In some policy documents leisure as a need is not assessed directly but is *inferred* from a person's general level of socio-economic deprivation. In most developed economies specific programmes of material and financial assistance are available for individuals and groups of people who suffer from such situations as very low income, inadequate job opportunities and housing, poor health or a physical or mental disability. Individuals and groups who suffer from a number of these indicators of deprivation, and residential areas or ethnic communities containing high proportions of such individuals, may be classified as socio-economically deprived in general. Governments at all levels then seek to orientate services to countering such incidences of deprivation. This may include leisure services. Although the census and health data sets typically used initially to classify areas as deprived do not generally include leisure indicators, it is often the case that they are lacking in leisure services – for example, poor areas of cities are often characterized by high-density housing and a lack of public open space and, due to low income, they often lack certain categories of commercial leisure services. Whether or not this is the case, as a result of being classified as being in need of housing, economic development, health services, etc., the populations of deprived areas will generally be classified as being in need of leisure services. This is explored further in the discussion below of leisure as a social service and the discussion of *priority social area analysis* in Chapter 10.

Implications of different conceptualizations of need for public policy

These various conceptualizations of need have different implications for public policy. If a need is something which, if denied to the individual, results in serious harm to the individual (Maslow, Iso-Ahola, Doyal and Gough, Max-Neef) then, arguably, this places an obligation on others, possibly society at large, to seek to ensure that such needs are met, thus providing justification for public support for provision. But it also means that there are other desires – namely wants or, to use Maslow's term, 'unimportant desires' – which do not trigger any such public obligation. A needs-based policy must therefore distinguish between leisure activities that satisfy needs and those that satisfy only wants.

The public sector response does, however, depend on who is assessing the condition of serious harm. If *individuals* consider an activity to be needs-satisfying, in this harm-prevention sense, for themselves, it does not automatically follow that society is obliged to support that particular activity. Thus, for example, many societies deny individual citizens the right to own firearms to satisfy what they may see as their own *safety needs*, and generally take a negative view of the use of mind-altering drugs as a means of *self-actualization*. Often individuals with common views form lobby groups to persuade the rest of the community of their views – hence gun lobbies and campaigns for legalization of the use of recreational drugs such as marijuana. In the end, if the responsible body, such as a local council or a government, is to implement a needs-based policy it must itself be persuaded that failure to provide the service in question will result in levels of harm to the individuals and/or the community at large which are significant enough to justify public action. Thus it cannot avoid normative decisions on which activities to support and which not to support.

The leisure satisfaction scales and the tourism marketing perspective discussed above see needs as the basis of *all wants/desires*, or as the object of *all satisfactions*, so this conceptualization of need does not of itself assist in making decisions on what should or should not be the object of public policy, although it may play a role in understanding consumer motivation as discussed further below.

Finally, the Bradshaw/Mercer typology may be a useful reminder of the variety of ways in which levels of needs and wants might be assessed but it does not, of itself, assist in determining whether leisure is a need in the mainstream social service sense.

Need and leisure/sport as a social service

In the 1970s, moves were made to classify leisure as a need and therefore as an essential social service. As Australian sociologist Robert Paddick put it: 'The inclination to call a great many things 'needs' is not difficult to appreciate. At least part of the answer is that 'need' is a particularly powerful planning concept, because we are much more likely to gain acceptance for giving people what they need, than for giving them what they want' (Paddick, 1982: 41).

The first Australia Minister for Tourism and Recreation stated: '… the higher the standard of living and the greater the prosperity and well-being of the people, the more acute is the need for recreation' (Stewart, 1975: 3). In the UK, a 1975 government policy paper on *Sport and Recreation* declared that recreation should be regarded as 'one of the community's everyday needs' and therefore that provision for it should be seen as 'part of the general fabric of the social services' (Department of the Environment, 1975: 1). The rationale for this designation and for the resultant assertion of government support for recreation included a significant emphasis on the value of sport – or at least physical exercise – as the following quotation indicates:

> The Government's concern with recreation stems basically from their recognition of its importance for the general welfare of the community. In a society which enjoys substantial leisure time, the Government has a responsibility to examine the contribution which leisure can make to a full life. For many people physical activity makes an important contribution to physical and mental well-being. There is some evidence to suggest that vigorous physical exercise can reduce the incidence of coronary heart disease … By reducing boredom and urban frustration, participation in active recreation contributes to the reduction of hooliganism and delinquency among young people. Equally, success in international sport has great value for the community not only in terms of raising morale but also by inspiring young people to take an active part in sport. The objectives of the Government range from a determination to improve the lot of the socially deprived in our city centres, through a broader concern for the enrichment of people's lives generally, to an overall responsibility for ensuring that, while people are encouraged to get out and about, a proper balance is kept in the use of the countryside between the demands of agriculture, conservation and recreation. [pp. 3–4] … Where the community neglects its responsibilities for providing the individual with opportunities and choice in the provision of sports and recreational facilities, it will rarely escape the long-term consequences of this neglect [p. 19].

(Department of the Environment, 1975)

Participation in certain forms of leisure activity were therefore classified by the government of the time as a need requiring public support, because these forms of activity were seen as a means to achieving certain highly desirable social goals, namely: (i) inspiration and raising of public morale through international sporting success and 'enrichment of people's lives generally'; or (ii) the prevention of individual or social ills, namely physical and mental illness and juvenile delinquency.

The second of these goals conforms to the harm prevention conception of need as discussed above, but the first goal raises the issue of positive net *benefits*, which is not the same as need. The concept of benefits is discussed later in the chapter.

It should be noted that the above statements were made by UK Labour governments. By contrast, the neo-liberal Conservative view of leisure was reflected in the statement from the 1985 Conservative Party report quoted in Chapter 2 (p. 27), which presented a view of leisure as primarily a commercial industry providing services which people who wanted to use them should pay for, rather than social services to be provided for all. It is also notable that the concept of need is much less prominent in discussions of leisure policy emanating from North America, where the political consensus is considerably to the right of that in both Europe and Australia. As indicated by the quotations in Box 3.1, in the UK, the wheel had come full circle some years later, in 2002, with the New Labour government under Tony Blair issuing guidelines for local 'cultural planning' based on assessment of the community's needs, and in Australia, the New South Wales state labour premier also endorsed the idea of cultural needs.

Thus, in the UK and Australia at least, planning based on the idea of leisure as a need has become the norm in certain political environments. However, it is difficult to find any policy documents in which the concept of need is defined. This raises the question of whether the governments involved are adopting the view that *all* leisure behaviour meets people's needs and that they are therefore prepared to make provision for all kinds of leisure activity. Clearly not: as we have seen, there are some leisure activities, such as the consumption of alcohol and gambling, which governments seek to limit by licensing and high taxation. And some activities, such as recreational drug consumption and blood sports, are illegal. For people wishing to participate in these activities, they might be seen as 'wants' or 'unimportant desires'. So what distinguishes need-based leisure activity from want-based activity? One solution to this conundrum lies in the UK's House of Lords statement above, which suggests that activity resulting in 'desirable social outcomes' is classified as meeting a need. If this is accepted then, in order to decide which activities to support, governments must indicate which activities produce which sorts of outcomes and which outcomes are to be judged as *desirable* or *beneficial*. Or, if the negative perspective is adopted, it is necessary to determine which activities are capable of preventing which undesirable social outcomes. In practice, of course, governments at all levels do make these assessments and choices, since only certain activities are planned for and supported, but the rationale for these decisions is not always explicit.

Need and the understanding of leisure/tourism motivation

In tourism marketing and the leisure satisfaction scales method, the term 'need' is used in a different way. There are generally no grand statements in the literature about tourism being a need, in the sense of a harm-preventing necessity, although the concept of *social tourism*, in which the state facilitates holidays for deprived groups and supports the right of employees to paid annual leave, as discussed in the next chapter, indicates some official recognition in that direction. It is notable that the leisure satisfaction scales have generally been developed in North American outdoor recreation contexts, involving trips to natural areas, such as national parks and forests. In fact, a substantial proportion of the users of such areas are tourists, either day trippers or people staying overnight, typically camping, and thus the scales have been substantially developed in a tourism-influenced context. *Planning* for tourism, and this type of outdoor recreation, is based primarily on the concept of *demand*, as discussed later in this chapter, but this is apparently underpinned by a conception of need, since, according to tourism marketing and consumer motivation theory, all tourist behaviour arises from needs.

Often, links are made with the Maslow hierarchy, as the following quotation from a tourism marketing textbook by Philip Kotler and his colleagues indicates: 'The most basic concept underlying marketing is that of human needs. Human needs are states of felt deprivation.

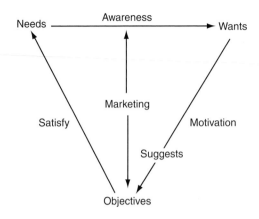

Fig. 3.2. Mill and Morrison's model of travel 'needs, wants and motives' (Mill and Morrison, 2006).

They include basic *physical* needs for food, clothing, shelter, and safety, *social* needs for belonging and affection, and *individual* needs for knowledge and self-expression. These needs are not invented by marketers; they are a basic part of human makeup' (Kotler *et al.*, 2006: 14).

No reference is, however, made to the harm-prevention dimension of Maslow's conception. This all-purpose need concept and the Maslow hierarchy is widely accepted among tourism scholars, albeit sometimes in adapted form. Phillip Pearce (2005) has suggested that people progress up the Maslow hierarchy during the course of their lives as they accumulate tourist experiences and become increasingly sophisticated in their requirements, but he modifies the hierarchy to form a 'travel career ladder'. A more pragmatic approach is put forward by Robert Mill and Alastair Morrison (2006: 280). In their model of motivation to travel, wants result from people becoming aware of unmet needs, as shown in Fig. 3.2. Marketing may be involved in stimulating or raising awareness of such needs, thus activating conscious associated wants. Marketing may then indicate to the potential consumer how the want can be satisfied. When the want has been satisfied the underlying need has been satisfied. Knowledge of the nature of the underlying needs assists marketers in devising their message for the potential consumer. Thus need is not used to give special status to certain forms of activity, as in its use in the leisure/sport context discussed above: it is simply a component in understanding all forms of demand.

The leisure satisfaction scales play a similar role in relation to the outdoor recreation contexts where they have generally been deployed: they are based on the proposition that the more service producers know about the motivations of consumers and potential consumers, the better placed they will be to match their product/service offerings to people's preferences, and even to influence those preferences.

Wants

The relationship between wants and needs can therefore be seen in three alternative ways:

- needs as a subset of wants;
- needs and wants as separate and different;
- needs and wants as the same, and therefore interchangeable.

All three can be found in the academic and policy literature and this variety of uses cannot be ignored in this book, but we can at least do two things:

- draw attention to these varying uses by other authors and discuss their implications;
- adopt an explicit and consistent use of the two words in this book.

In this book, therefore, while accepting that the first of the three approaches is the most valid, for practical reasons the second approach has been adopted: that is, the unqualified word *wants* is used to refer to those *desires* which are not classified as *needs*.

OBLIGATIONS

A leisure obligation is the phenomenon of participating in a leisure activity primarily because of an obligation to other persons. The individual may take some enjoyment from participation in the activity or no enjoyment at all; but he or she would be unlikely to participate in the absence of the obligation. The most common occurrence of leisure obligations occurs within families, particularly parents fulfilling obligations to children, but also among partners and extended family. It also occurs among friends, intimate or otherwise, and among work colleagues and in institutional settings.

Parents might classify obligated leisure involving children as childcare when completing a time diary, but in leisure participation surveys it is perhaps more likely to be counted as participation in specific leisure activities. In some cases the activity of the parent is the same as that of the child (for example cycling or going to the movies together), in other cases it is different (for example the parent is an audience member at a school concert while the child is a performer), indeed, as has long been observed by researchers on women's leisure, obligated leisure may even have work components attached to it – for example, preparing refreshments at a sports match (e.g. Dempsey, 1989).

Obligatory leisure in the literature

Various conceptions of obligatory leisure have appeared in the literature, for example, the idea of *semi-leisure* put forward by Dumazedier (1967: 19), *institutional leisure* by Gunter and Gunter (1980: 370), *externally motivated* (as opposed to intrinsically motivated) leisure by Iso-Ahola (1980: 236), *non-work obligations* by Parker (1983: 9), *complementary leisure* by Kelly (1983: 13) and *anti-leisure* by Godbey. The last of these is defined as: '… activity which is undertaken compulsively, as a means to an end, from a perception of necessity, with a high degree of externally imposed constraints, with considerable anxiety, with a high degree of time consciousness, with a minimum of personal autonomy, and which avoids self-actualization, authentication and finitude' (Godbey, 1989/1975: 75).

In the 1960s Anthony Giddens made the following observations:

> Basic to the definition of work is that it consists in (a) instrumental activity, undertaken (b) within a framework of direct or indirect economic obligation. However, a large number of leisure activities also have strong instrumental characteristics. Very often these take the form of an obligation or duty to perform a particular activity. The frequent use of the terms 'free' time or 'spare' time as synonyms for leisure suggests that such time is free of social or economic obligation. But much leisure is neither 'free' time, nor 'spare' time: various sorts of obligation and commitment extend far into leisure time. In many kinds of leisure activity there exists a fairly well-defined system of obligation or reciprocity which in part determines the use of leisure. Such is the case, for example, with the widespread activity of 'visiting' relatives among certain strata of the population. In other cases there are structured forms of obligation to participate in certain activities because of their association with social status in the group. An example might be church-going in certain middle-class groups.
>
> (Giddens, 1964: 81–82)

Quite why the qualifiers 'certain strata of the population' and 'certain middle-class groups' are required is not clear.

These theorists raise the question as to whether, if leisure activity is defined as being freely chosen, participation which does not arise from personal volition is leisure at all. From the leisure facility/programme provider's point of view, however, when the reluctant participants arrive at the pub, theatre, playing field or swimming pool they cannot be distinguished from the keen, freely choosing participants (apart, perhaps, from their glum expressions or forced smiles!).

With the exception of Kelly's work, which dates from 30 years ago and was conducted in new towns only, the phenomenon of obligated leisure is generally not identified as such in leisure participation surveys, so its quantity and attitudes towards it – for example the extent to which it is seen as leisure-like or non-leisure-like – are not known. A partial exception is the Australian Bureau of Statistics which, in its 1997 time-use survey, asked respondents to indicate 'for whom' activities were undertaken (ABS, 1977: 49–50).

Obligatory leisure and policymaking and planning

To a large extent, the importance of obligatory leisure for public policymaking depends on how significant it is in quantitative terms and how variable it is across leisure forms. If it is a very small proportion of all leisure participation it can be ignored. Where it is quantitatively significant it should ideally be taken account of in planning, otherwise demand would be underestimated. Thus, whether demand estimates are based on needs or wants, it may be necessary in some cases to apply a multiplier for a component arising from obligations.

Whether obligatory, or externally motivated, leisure activity is more or less highly valued than other forms of leisure, it raises questions as to the extent to which leisure behaviour and aspirations should be analysed as individual, group or collective phenomena and the implications of this for policymaking and planning. This cannot be pursued here, but the issue of collective consumption is discussed below.

DEMAND

Definition

It has been widely recognized for some time that, in the context of policymaking and planning in leisure, sport and tourism, *demand* is a concept drawn from the discipline of economics, indicating the amounts of a service which consumers are willing and able to purchase at various prices: typically, the lower the price the more people will buy. As economists Marion Clawson and Jack Knetsch (1966: 41) put it: 'Demand, … to the economist, … means a schedule of volume (visits, user-days, etc.) in relation to a price (cost of the recreation experience)'. Two points should be made about this definition:

- While price is a major focus in the economic theory of demand, in practice it is just one of a number of variables considered in demand analysis, as discussed further below.
- In using the term *recreation*, Clawson and Knetsch were referring primarily to trips to natural areas, such as national parks, lakes and rivers, which included informal recreation but also sporting activities, such as canoeing and rock climbing, and also, since many of such trips included overnight stays, tourism.

The economic concept of demand indicates a *relationship* between prices (and other variables) and quantities. This is a simple idea, based partly on empirical evidence and partly on a theoretical model of consumer choice and the behaviour of firms. Upon it has been built a body of economic theory which has considerable relevance to understanding the provision and consumption of goods and services in mixed/market economies, whether provided by the private sector or the public sector.

The following section provides a brief, and therefore simplified, outline of aspects of this theory. It might be helpful for the reader to have in mind a particular product or service – for example, trips to the movies, holiday trips by air or a gym membership – so that the ideas can be applied to a familiar situation as reading progresses.

Demand/supply theory

We concentrate on price initially, because that is the variable which has been used in traditional expositions of demand theory, but the relationship between price and consumption illustrates how the relationship between any relevant variable and consumption of leisure goods and serv-ices might be studied. Other variables are discussed later. The price/demand relationship can be repre-sented by a two-dimensional diagram in the form of a *demand curve*, as shown in Fig. 3.3. This is a theoretical indication of how demand, the amount people from a particular population are prepared to buy in particular circumstances, would change in response to different prices: typically, as the price falls the amount people are prepared to buy increases. For some products which are relatively expensive, such as wide-screen TV sets, the increase in purchases which takes place as the price falls is due to more people buying the product, while for lower-priced items, such as tickets to movies, as prices fall the increase in demand also involves the same people buying larger quantities of the item (e.g. going to the movies more often).

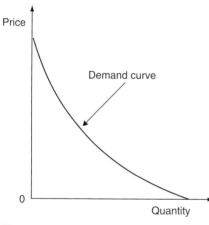

Fig. 3.3. Demand curve.

The downward-sloping demand curve immediately demonstrates a number of points that are important for both the public and private sectors:

- If the price to buyers or potential buyers is *reduced* consumption will *increase*, and vice versa – a key feature of the public sector is that it is able to subsidize a service to reduce the price of entry – even to zero – to encourage demand.
- Some demand curves might have a relatively *flat slope*, as shown in Fig. 3.4, so demand responds significantly in response to changes in prices (e.g. cheap air tickets) – such products are described as *price-elastic*; demand curves for other products have a *steep slope*, where price changes result in comparatively little change in the amount pur-chased (e.g. bread in relatively rich societies) – in this case the product is described as *price-inelastic*.
- If the price is set at any point above zero there will inevitably be some *unmet demand* that would only be satisfied at a lower price.
- At the maximum price indicated demand is zero, and at a point immediately below this there would be a very small level of demand, but at any point below this some people *would have been prepared to pay more* for the product or for a proportion of what they purchase at that price: the difference between what they actually have to pay and what they would

have been prepared to pay is referred to as the *consumer surplus* – see Fig. 3.5 – and is one measure of the value which current consumers of a product place on the product, over and above what they have been required to pay.

- Some of the consumer surplus can be captured by the supplier by offering higher-priced versions of a product (e.g. business class on planes).
- A *zero price* indicates the *maximum level of consumption* for that product/service in the given circumstances (e.g. level of population, incomes, distance to travel for a service).

A particular combination of price and quantity purchased at any one time is the level of *consumption* or *effective demand* at that time. This is shown by point A in Fig. 3.6, and is determined by the intersection of the *demand curve* with the *supply curve*, a theoretical indication of what *suppliers* would offer in different price situations. This curve is *upward sloping* because the higher the price, the more existing suppliers are willing to offer and the more additional suppliers are attracted to the market.

Demand and the public sector

It might be concluded that the demand/supply market concept is irrelevant to freely provided public services, but this is not the case. The statements in Box 3.2 indicate that leisure demand

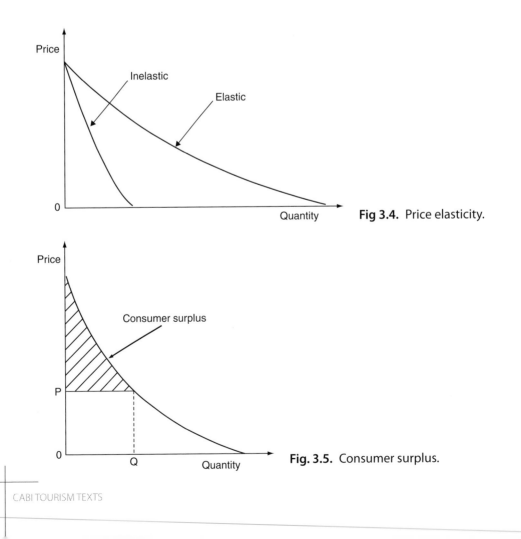

Fig 3.4. Price elasticity.

Fig. 3.5. Consumer surplus.

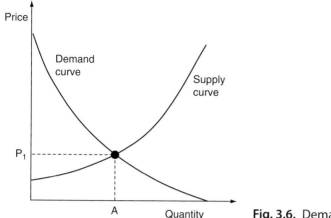

Price

Demand
curve

Supply
curve

P₁

A   Quantity   **Fig. 3.6.** Demand/supply interaction.

has often been a concern of governments, although sometimes the difference between demand and need is not always fully clear.

Box 3.2. Government statements on leisure demand.

USA, 1962: Outdoor Recreation for America

'The demand is surging. Whatever the measuring rod … it is clear that Americans are seeking the outdoors as never before. And this is only a foretaste of things to come. Not only will there be many more people, they will want to do more, and they will have more money and time to do it with. By 2000 the population should double; the demand for recreation should triple. This order of magnitude, in essence, is the heart of the problem' (ORRRC, 1962: 25).

UK, 1968: Planning for Sport

'… we have indicated that there is evidence of substantial demand, both existing and latent, for recreational facilities. With growing leisure and affluence this demand is likely to increase' (Sports Council, 1968: 77).

USA, 1979: Third Nationwide Outdoor Recreation Plan

'The demand for recreation, especially close to home, will continue to grow during the next five years. … Serious consideration must be given to the possibility that existing resources may have to be directed to meet these needs' (Heritage Conservation and Recreation Service, 1979: Assessment: 234).

NSW, Australia, 1992: Outdoor Recreation and Open Space Guidelines for Local Government

'A number of techniques are available for the collection of recreation demand information. The aim of these techniques is to understand the community demand for different recreational opportunities. The subsequent open space plan simply matches supply with demand to identify areas of need. … Resident recreation surveys are household based data collection exercises that attempt to understand the demand for recreation opportunities in any area and to identify needs' (NSW Department of Planning, 1992: 13).

Economic demand theory was developed in a market context, but the bulk of theoretical and applied research on the economics of leisure has been devoted to application of this and other economic concepts and processes to public policy contexts. After all, in the mixed economies of Western capitalism the public sector operates alongside the market: goods and services required to deliver public leisure services must be purchased in the marketplace and, for individual consumers, publicly provided services stand alongside commercially provided services in the mixed public/private 'supermarket' of leisure. Furthermore, public sector planning has a certain amount of control over private sector investment decisions because of their potential positive and negative wider community impacts – for example, the size and location of theme parks or pubs – so some understanding by planners of the demand processes underlying commercial enterprises is desirable.

Public sector suppliers offer a number of types of leisure facility where the price of admission is zero, for example urban parks and many galleries and museums, so consumption or effective demand (number of visits) for those particular facilities is at the maximum, as indicated by point Q_1 in Fig. 3.7. There is no conventional supply curve in these situations, since, in practice, the public sector supplier will not vary the amount of park, gallery or museum space in response to varying admission prices; in effect, the supply curve is a single point at the capacity of the facility. The capacity is unlikely to be exactly Q_1, but will either be a lesser figure, say C_2, in which case there will be queuing or overcrowding, or a larger figure, say C_1, in which case there will be spare capacity. Of course, measuring capacity exactly is difficult for some types of facility, as discussed in Chapter 10.

There are at least three points of relevance here:

1. If the shape of the demand curve were known, it would be possible to predict the likely effect of the introduction of an entrance price at various levels – entrance prices are changed significantly from time to time: for example charges were introduced for many previously free museums and galleries in the 1980s and 1990s, and this sometimes happens indirectly through the introduction of parking charges at otherwise free facilities.
2. If the shape of the demand curve is known it is possible to estimate the *consumer surplus* as mentioned above, and this can be used in cost–benefit analysis of public projects, as discussed further below and in Chapter 11.
3. While price of entry may be zero, other cost factors and influences on demand, which may be studied in a multivariate situation as discussed below, may be more complex.

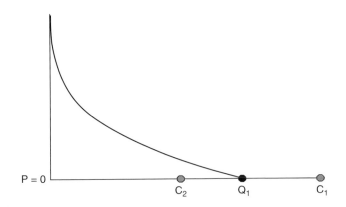

Fig. 3.7. Demand curve with zero price.

Researching demand/supply in leisure/sport/tourism contexts

In a typical real demand/supply situation, all that is known is the current price, and effective demand, which are P_1 and A, respectively, in Fig. 3.6 and zero and Q_1, respectively, in Fig. 3.7. The rest of the demand and supply curves are theoretical, and they are not known unless specific research is undertaken to identify them empirically in any given market situation. This a challenge in most cases because of the difficulty in finding situations in which a range of variations in prices and quantities purchased can be studied. The emphasis in research on public leisure facilities has been on the demand curve, given the unconventional nature of the supply curve, as noted above. As discussed in more detail in Chapter 11, a demand curve can be established from research, using one of two methods:

1. The *willingness-to-pay method* involves questioning potential users directly about their likely level of purchases of a service or visits to a facility at various prices.

2. The *travel–cost method* (also referred to as the *Clawson method*, after the economist who originally applied the method to outdoor recreation/tourism) is based on the observation that users travelling different distances face differing travel costs (including transport costs and the value of time) and they react to this in a similar way that they might to varying admission prices. Thus a demand curve can be established by studying the pattern of demand for existing facilities related to distance travelled. This is potentially useful in planning, because any increase in the supply of suitably located facilities will tend to reduce the average distance people have to travel, thus reducing their costs, which has an effect similar to a reduction in admission price. So, knowing the demand curve makes it possible to predict the response of demand to increases in supply.

Modelling

The simple two-dimensional price/quantity demand curve is widely known from 'Economics 101' but, while this simple model explains the underlying principles of a market, it is little used in practice. The two-dimensional model is a simple version of a more comprehensive model in which price becomes just one of a number of variables – and not necessarily the most important one. Such *multivariate models* may include variables such as: (i) characteristics of actual and potential participants, such as age and income; and (ii) *supply conditions*, which include the characteristics of the range of facilities available, including, in addition to entry prices, location, transport access, size and quality.

Supply conditions are the variables which are open to influence by policymakers: a plan may include proposals to increase the number of facilities or increase the size or quality of existing facilities. Among supply conditions a key variable of particular relevance to leisure, sport and tourism is *location*, which determines the distance the potential user has to travel and therefore the cost, in time and money, to use a facility. Much of economic theory is based on the idea of the production and consumption of goods which are purchased in a store and consumed elsewhere. There are plenty of leisure goods available, but one of the distinctive features of leisure, sport and tourism is that they are dominated by *services consumed at the point of sale*: people must travel to a particular location to consume them. Thus the distance people have to travel to consume a leisure service, and in particular the time and cost of doing so, is likely to have an influence on patterns of demand. Consequently planning decisions on the numbers, quality and locations of facilities will affect the overall level of effective demand.

Multivariate models are constructed mathematically, and the details cannot be presented graphically because each additional variable represents an additional dimension. A full set of data on the population from which potential participants are drawn and on the range of competing facilities available can be used to develop quantitative models which simulate the current pattern of demand, and can be used to predict the effects of changes in: (i) the size and distribution of population; (ii) the characteristics of the existing set of facilities (size, quality, etc.); (iii) the number facilities in the system; and/or (iv) the transport network (new/upgraded roads, airports, etc.).

Such modelling is most commonly used in tourism forecasting, where the facilities are individual *destinations*, which could be individual facilities such as ski resorts or theme parks, or whole regions or even countries. It is also used in research on outdoor, largely non-urban, recreation which includes a mixture of day tripper and tourist demand. Modelling is discussed further in Chapter 10 (under spatial methods) and Chapter 11 (Clawson method), and references to relevant literature are indicated in the Resources section of this chapter.

Critics

There is a certain amount of criticism of the demand concept in the leisure policy literature, although, arguably, much of it can be put down to misunderstanding and misrepresentation of the concept. This has, arguably, led to a decline in demand-based leisure planning in favour of methodologies based on the concept of *need*. A number of these criticisms can be briefly summarized as follows:

- Because demand has traditionally been defined in relation to price, it is claimed that demand is unable to deal with services which are free to the customer – clearly this is not the case since, as the above discussion indicates, demand theory encompasses the idea of a zero price.
- Use of the term demand is said to imply the exclusive operation of the free market – this is not so: nearly the whole of the literature on the economics of leisure is concerned with public sector leisure services that are subsidized or free to the user (see Veal, 2006a).
- It has been asserted that demand deals only with the existing pattern of participation and fails to take account of unmet demand – this is not the case: in the simple demand/quantity model discussed above, *unmet* demand is indicated by that part of the demand curve to the right of the consumption point and demand studies are invariably concerned with predicting the effects of measures such as reduced prices or increased supply on demand – that is, the process of turning unmet demand into met demand.
- Demand-based planning, it has been argued, implies 'more of the same', thus ignoring people's preferences or demands for different services in different locations, but demand-based analysis does not preclude the introduction of all sorts of additional market research and spatial modelling designed to detect trends in consumer behaviour in different conditions.
- Demand, it is claimed, does not indicate users' underlying motivations – this is true, but this does not mean that evidence on how people actually behave (*revealed preference* in economic terms) cannot provide insight into preferences.
- It is asserted that demand fails to take account of the demands/needs of underprivileged groups – this is simply not the case: demand studies invariably include information on user/non-user incomes and other socio-economic characteristics, and it is up to policy-makers to demand this type of information and to take account of it.
- Finally, some have argued that demand analysis does not deal with variation in the quality of facilities/services – again, this is not the case, as the above discussion on modelling indicates.

These critiques are discussed in more detail in Veal (2009e).

BENEFITS

Individuals engage in leisure behaviour because of the anticipated benefits it will bring to them and those close to them, and society supports certain types of leisure activity, through direct provision, grant-aid and subsidy, because of the anticipated social benefits which they generate. It is immediately apparent, therefore, that the concept of benefits involves normative judgements: if something is considered to be a benefit, or dis-benefit, then someone must make a judgement regarding its beneficial, or harmful, effects. As we shall see, such judgements may be made by the users, potential users and non-users of facilities/services, by managers and other professionals involved in the field, by pressure groups, by the general public and/or by governments. Some examples of governmental statements on the benefits of leisure are shown in Box 3.3.

Box 3.3. Governmental statements on the benefits of leisure.

1979: USA: Third Nationwide Outdoor Recreation Plan

'The great variety of recreation experiences available to Americans provides numerous benefits to society, including relief from daily stress, increased worker productivity, greater family solidarity, physical and mental fitness, and increased economic activity' (HCRS, 1979: 7).

1985: Australia: Towards the Development of a Commonwealth Policy on Recreation

'Over recent years, the health benefits resulting from participation in regular physical activity have been well documented' (Brown, 1985: 2).

1986: USA: President's Commission on Americans Outdoors

'Outdoor recreation helps us accomplish personal goals – fitness and longer life, family togetherness, friendship, personal reflection, and appreciation of nature and beauty. As the outdoors leads to the attainment of personal goals, it becomes a stimulant or catalyst for the achievement of the nation's social goals: health, education, employment, family cohesion, economic vitality, environmental quality' (President's Commission on Americans Outdoors, 1986: 13).

1989: Australia: What Price Heritage?

'The main justification for government intervention in areas such as national cultural heritage is the presence of … 'public good' benefits. These are benefits which accrue to the population generally whether or not individuals participate first hand as consumers of heritage activity …' (Department of Finance, 1989: 26).

1996: USA: Surgeon General's Report on Physical Activity and Health

Major conclusions (first three of eight):
1. People of all ages, both male and female, benefit from regular physical activity.
2. Significant health benefits can be obtained by including a moderate amount of physical activity (e.g., 30 minutes of brisk walking or raking leaves, 15 minutes of running, or 45 minutes of playing volleyball) on most, if not all, days of the week. Through a modest increase in daily activity, most Americans can improve their health and quality of life.

(Continued)

Box 3.3. Continued.

3. Additional health benefits can be gained through greater amounts of physical activity. People who can maintain a regular regimen of activity that is of longer duration or of more vigorous intensity are likely to derive greater benefit' (Surgeon General, 1996: 4).

1998: Australia: Developing an Active Australia

'The health benefits of physical activity have achieved recent prominence in Australia and internationally, following the publication and dissemination of the US Surgeon General's Report: Physical Activity and Health, and at the state level in Australia, by the dissemination of Physical Activity and Health, a special communication from the Chief Health Officer (1996). Recent reports strongly emphasise the preventive health benefits gained by the accumulation of 30 minutes of moderate-intensity physical activity on most or all days of the week' (Commonwealth Department of Health and Family Services, 1998: 12).

2002: UK: Game Plan

From Chapter 2: Why do we Care? Benefits and the Role for Government:

- 'Why should government invest in sport and physical activity? Because they have a major part to play in promoting health, and as part of a basket of measures, can contribute to improved educational outcomes, reduced crime and greater social inclusion.
- The benefits of physical activity on health are clear, well evidenced and widely accepted. . . . there is some evidence that sport and physical activity can benefit education . . .
- The role of sport in generating a 'feelgood factor' through international sporting success also appears to be significant (if difficult to quantify) . . .
- The existence of benefits to society does not mean government should necessarily intervene in sport and physical activity. Intervention is justified when it corrects 'inefficiencies' in provision by the private or voluntary sectors . . .; or it addresses inequality of access or opportunity . . .' (DCMS/Strategy Unit, 2002: 42–43).

Two major perspectives on the concept of benefits as applied to leisure, sport and tourism are considered here: (i) the benefits approach to leisure, developed by Bev Driver and his associates in North America; and (ii) the economics perspective.

Benefits approach

Moves have been made in North America over the last couple of decades to make *benefits* the focus of leisure management and policymaking. The approach began under the title Benefits-Based Management (BBM) but then, to widen its scope beyond management and link it explicitly with leisure, the title was changed to Benefits Approach to Leisure (BAL); however, in its most recent manifestation, Outcomes-Focused Management (OFM), the word 'management' has been reinstated and the word 'leisure' has been dropped. This label is clearly a potential source of confusion since, if we were to refer to the approach as Outcomes-Focussed Management (OFM) it could be confused with other outcomes-orientated systems, for example those described in Chapter 12. But if we were to refer to it as Benefits-Based Management

(BBM) it could be confused with earlier versions of the benefits approach. To avoid confusion, the current version of the benefits approach is referred to below as Outcomes-Focused Management/Benefits-Based Management, or OFM/BBM.

The leader of the 'benefits movement' has been Bev Driver, a research officer with the US Forest Service, now retired. He is editor of two books on the benefit phenomenon and author of numerous papers on the subject (see Resources section). The approach was supported by the main US professional body, the National Parks and Recreation Association (NRPA) and the Canadian equivalent, the Canadian Park and Recreation Association (CPRA), but seems to be less prominent in their current programmes. While some attempts have been made to apply the approach in urban leisure contexts, the available literature relates primarily to outdoor recreation in natural areas, such as national parks and forests. As discussed above, in relation to need, this means that tourism is included, because often the bulk of visitors to such sites are non-locals. With regard to sport, the literature relates to sporting and physical recreation activities undertaken in such settings, such as fishing, hunting, canoeing, whitewater rafting and hiking.

The OFM/BBM system is presented as a *recreation production process*, summarized in Fig. 3.8, where:

- *Inputs* are land and management resources.
- *Facilitating outputs and settings* relates to the planning process, *outputs* being specific facilities (e.g. a trail) and *settings* the environments in which they are located.
- *Recreation and other outcome opportunities* are the facilities and services established.
- *Outcomes* are the direct and indirect benefits and dis-benefits experienced by users and affected non-users of the facility/service and impacts on the environment.

The direct link between boxes B and D indicates that benefits may arise even if a facility/service/opportunity is not used, for example, conservation benefits.

The key principle of the approach is that provision of facilities for leisure should be determined by consideration of the benefits, or 'beneficial outcomes' which will result from such provision. This therefore requires the benefits generated by particular activities in particular settings to be identified and measured. Driver and his colleagues have devoted considerable efforts to this task, partly through the development of the Recreation Experience Preference (REP) scale, one of the leisure satisfaction scales discussed above. The REP scale, however, includes only personal satisfactions which people enjoy from the use of recreation facilities. Other types of benefit are considered in the OFM/BBM system, including those enjoyed by communities within the region where the park/forest is located, positive effects on the environment, economic dimensions and a number of negative effects. Examples of benefits identified in these categories are presented in Table 3.2.

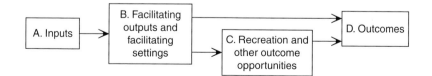

Fig. 3.8. OFM/BBM: recreation opportunity production process (from Driver and Bruns, 2008: 42).

Table 3.2. Benefits/outcomes: examples from OFM/BBM checklists (from Driver and Bruns, 2008: 68–73).

Categories/examples

Experiential benefits to recreation participants – from Recreation Experience Preference Scales

• Develop skills and abilities

• Enjoy the closeness of friends and family

• Enjoy getting some needed physical exercise

Benefits to community residents

• Just knowing the attraction is here, in or near my community

• Sharing our cultural heritage with new people

• Liking change and new growth here

Other and related benefits

1. To individuals

• better mental health and health maintenance

• closer relationship with the natural world

• improved physical fitness and health maintenance

2. To households and communities

• heightened sense of community satisfaction

• increased community sense of place

• less juvenile delinquency

3. Economic benefits

• reduced health maintenance costs

• increased local job opportunities

• increased property values

4. Environmental benefits

• improved maintenance of physical facilities

• increased awareness and protection of natural landscapes

• conservation of sustainable ecosystems

Negative outcomes checklist

• Increased personal stress

• Increased crime

• Increased pollution, litter and traffic noise

In the OFM/BBM system a unique set of benefits is seen as arising from:

• a given *activity* (e.g. hiking, whitewater rafting);
• utilizing *facilities* (e.g. signposted trails, boats and launching facilities);

- taking place in a *setting* (e.g. wilderness area, natural watercourse);
- located in a *management zone* (e.g. remote area of a national park preserved as wilderness, ravine stretch of a river).

Application of the OFM/BBM system involves measuring the range of the benefits listed in Table 3.2 in relation to each existing activity/facility/setting/zone. In the literature on OFM/ BBM the method used to measure personal experiential benefits is relatively clear: questionnaire surveys of participants involving Likert-type scales are used, as discussed in relation to leisure satisfaction scales above. For the other categories of benefit the intended measurement approaches are not clear. It is possible that similar scaling methods might be used – for example, suitable samples of members of local communities, facility/service managers, experts or members of councils/boards might be asked to scale the various factors on relative importance or significance. Alternatively, many of the factors could be measured directly – for example, savings in health costs could be measured in money terms and pollution could be measured in terms of the level of pollutants in water or the air. Whatever approach is used, the quantity of data to be collected for every activity/facility/setting/zone is clearly a challenge.

Once the data have been collected on the current situation for each activity/facility/setting/zone, the question arises as to how to use the information for policymaking or planning of new facilities/services. This is discussed in Chapter 7.

The economic perspective on benefits

In Chapter 5, the economic perspective on benefits is discussed in detail: here we present a brief summary of the essentials. In a conventional market situation, the economic perspective is that the value people place on the benefits they receive from the products or services they buy is at least equal to the price they pay – otherwise they would not buy. In fact, the downward-sloping demand curve, as shown in Fig. 3.3, suggests that only the last unit bought is valued at *exactly* the price paid, all the others being valued at varying amounts above the purchase price. The sum of all these extra valuations is known as the *consumer surplus*. Thus, even when the price paid is zero, as in Fig. 3.4, there is a consumer surplus represented by the triangle above the x-axis and below the demand curve. Once the shape of the demand curve is known, it is possible to estimate the consumer surplus and therefore place a value on the benefits enjoyed by the service users.

However, many leisure provision situations are not 'normal' in the above sense. We have already noted that some leisure services are provided free of charge. In addition, many are provided at a subsidized rate – for example, admission to public swimming pools. The detailed rationale for this is discussed in Chapter 5 but, in essence, justifications fall into three groups:

- *Public goods*: where it is difficult if not impossible to charge an admission fee – for example, most public parks.
- *Equity*: the principle that everyone has a right to enjoy certain basic services and so the less well-off groups in the community should not be excluded on grounds of price (this idea of 'rights' is discussed in Chapter 4).
- *Externalities*: where benefits are enjoyed not only by the users of the service, but also by other parties or the community at large – for example, the view of a park enjoyed by users of surrounding properties or the public health service cost savings arising from a physically active population.

Public goods are generally provided at zero price, and we have already seen how user benefits from such services can be evaluated. Services provided on the grounds of equity may be free of charge or subsidized for all, or for certain target groups, such as children, the elderly or low-income groups. Either way, the user benefits can be assessed as discussed above.

Externalities can be valued in a variety of ways, as discussed in Chapter 5. Considering the two examples used above, the scenic value of a view of a public park may be evaluated in terms of real estate values of properties with park views compared with those without – thus John Crompton (1995) reviewed a range of, mainly North American, studies and found that properties within 335 m of a park boundary enjoyed a boost in values of between 5% (for an 'average' park) and 15% (for a 'top-class' park). Health cost savings can be assessed by studies of the incidence of and cost of treating illness among those who take exercise compared with those who do not – thus an Australian government study in the 1980s found that savings in health costs and reduced absenteeism costs, arising from prevention of heart disease associated with regular physical activity, net of sports injury costs, amounted to US$417 per annum per active person (at 2009 prices) (DASETT, 1988b).

Thus, using economic analysis, it is possible to place a money value on a wide range of benefits arising from leisure, sport and tourism participation.

However, the cost of gathering and analysing the necessary data for such evaluations is quite high – too high to be used in everyday local planning exercises. Ideally, a database of sets of values from a wide range of studies should be available that could be utilized in local studies as, for example, is done in evaluating transport investment proposals. This technique is known as *value transfer*, but the necessary basic research has not been conducted for its adoption in the leisure, sport and tourism sector. Some work has been done for non-urban outdoor recreation in the USA, where details have been compiled on 760 benefit valuations for 20 activities from 163 identified studies (Rosenberger and Loomis, 2001). This topic is discussed further in Chapter 12.

PARTICIPATION

Participation is perhaps the least problematical of the concepts discussed in this chapter. People participate in an activity if they take part in it. Statistics on levels of participation are typically expressed as a percentage of a specific national, regional or local population participating in a given time period, such as a year or a month, but other measures are also used, as discussed below. Participation has the following characteristics:

- It may be motivated by wants, needs or obligations.
- It measures the same thing as demand – that is, the number of people taking part in an activity or visiting a facility, but it is not associated with the economic theory implicit in the demand concept, so it is clear that a participation measure relates to a specific time and place and price/supply context.
- Like demand, it does not of itself incorporate a 'benefits' dimension.

The concept of participation is used less when discussing leisure activity that takes place outside the community in which participants live – as in the case of day trips or tourism. In these circumstances, planners and policymakers in the host or destination community tend to conceptualize visits in terms of demand (Coppock and Duffield, 1975: 4).

Government and leisure participation

Box 3.4 presents some examples of governmental statements on leisure participation. Some statements express a general intent to promote participation, but more recent statements set specific targets arising from performance appraisal as discussed in Chapters 7 and 13. Of particular interest are the targets for participation in sports and physical activity that can be related to health outcomes. These targets can be given more specificity by referring to research-based recommendations from health experts stating that individuals should engage in at least moderate physical activity for at least 30 min/day on most, if not all, days. This is a measurable participation target which a number of governments have adopted as a component of policy. It should be noted that the assessment of health benefits is a separate research exercise, but it influences the way participation is measured.

Measuring participation

Participation levels of a given population in a given activity or group of activities can be measured in a number of ways, as set out in Table 3.3. Since participation is the same as demand in a given time, place and price/supply context, the same measures are used to measure demand. Each of these measures can apply to the whole of a population or to segments of it. While the measures are related, they can also vary independently, and can measure different dimensions of participation. Policy should of course be explicit about which measures are the focus of policy and why.

There are technical and administrative challenges in measuring leisure participation, for example:

- How long should the 'reference period' be over which survey respondents are asked to recall their leisure behaviour (e.g. a week, a month or a year)?
- How should participation patterns for young children, who may not be able to respond reliably to survey questions, be established?
- Which government agencies should be responsible for the conduct of participation surveys at national, regional and local levels?
- How often should they be conducted?
- What should be the scope of leisure covered in such surveys?

It is not proposed to canvass these issues in detail here, since they have been extensively discussed elsewhere (e.g. Veal, 2003; Cushman *et al.*, 2005).

Participation and policy

A feature of public policy in the leisure domain is that some national, and to some extent state/provincial, governments adopt participation targets as a policy focus while local councils generally do not. The planning approach presented in Chapter 8 is, however, based on the idea of participation becoming the basis of local policymaking and planning.

A notable feature of the statements in Box 3.4 is the emergence of leisure *participation targets* as the object of government policy. However, the targets tend to relate not to individual activities but to groupings of activities, such as sporting/physical activity or arts/cultural activity. The question then arises as to how broad targets are translated into participation in particular activities. This is the subject of the discussions of planning methods in Chapters 7 and 8.

Box 3.4. Governmental statements on leisure participation.

1985: Australia: Towards the Development of a Commonwealth Policy on Recreation

Objective three (of six): '… to encourage all Australians to appreciate the contribution which participation in satisfying recreation activities can make to a healthy lifestyle; and to encourage regular participation in satisfying recreation activities' (Brown, 1985: 11).

2001: Australia: Australian Government: Backing Australia's Sporting Ability

'Together, we will aim to:

- significantly increase the number of people participating in sport right across Australia, including in rural and regional communities;
- markedly increase youth participation in organised sport;
- boost the active membership and reach of sporting organisations and local sporting clubs' (Australian Government, 2001: 6).

2002: The UK: DCMS/Strategy Unit: Game Plan

'Our vision is … to increase significantly levels of sport and physical activity, particularly among disadvantaged groups (p. 82) … Participation levels need to be raised for the whole population; but interventions should focus on the most economically disadvantaged groups, and within those especially on young people, women and older people (p. 89). … The Government's overall objective is to increase the participation levels of *all* people, to ensure that society generally achieves the minimum levels of physical activity necessary for maintaining health' (p. 90) (DCMS/Strategy Unit, 2002).

2007: Australia: NSW Department of the Arts, Sport and Recreation, Corporate Plan

Corporate Result 2 relates to improved health and wellbeing. Performance measures are as follows:

- '1% increase per annum in adult participation in individual and organised cultural activities;
- 1% increase per annum in adults attending cultural venues;
- 1% increase per annum in number of children involved in organised arts and cultural activities;
- 0.5% increase per annum in participation of indigenous people in creative arts;
- 1% increase per annum in general participation of adults in sport and physical activity;
- 1% increase per annum in participation of adults in sport/active recreation 3 or more times a week;
- 3% increase per annum in participation of children in organised sports;
- 0.5% increase per annum in participation of adults in sport/active recreation for under-represented or disadvantaged groups;
- 1% increase per annum in participation of women in organised sport' (NSW Department of the Arts, Sport and Recreation, 2007: 2).

Table 3.3. Measuring leisure and tourism participation/demand.

	Leisure/sport		
Measure	Definition*	Relationships	Examples
A. Participation rate: (a) General (b) Conforming	(a) population engaging in an activity (%) (b) population engaging at a specified level (health-related) (%)		(a) 6% of the adult pop. went swimming at least once a week in 2009 (b) 40% of the adult pop. engaged in moderate-intensity physical activity for 30 min, 4+ days/week
B. Market/Participants	Number of people who engage in an activity	A × pop. or C ÷ mean frequency[a]	20,000 of the residents of Area X went swimming at least once a week in 2009
C. Visits (volume)	The number of engagements[b] in an activity in a defined area	B × mean frequency	There were 1.2 million visits to swimming pools in Area X (1 million by residents) in 2009
D. Time spent	Time spent on an activity/group of activities	C × time per visit	The average person spends 2.5 h/day watching television
E. Money spent	Money spent in total, per head or per household on a leisure activities, goods/services	C × spend per visit	Consumer expenditure on leisure in the UK is £50 billion/year.

(Continued)

Table 3.3. Continued.

Tourism

Measure	Definition*	Relationships	Examples
Visit rate	The proportion of the population of a TGR that visits a TDR[a]		5% of the adult population of region Y visited region X in the year 2001
Trips	(a) The number of departures from a TGR to a TDR, or (b) the total number of arrivals in a TDR	(a) A × population of Region Y by frequency of visit (b) Aggregate of (a) across all TGRs	(a) 100,000 tourist departures from region Y to region X in 2009 (b) 1.2 million tourist arrivals in Region X in 2009
Visits	Number of visits to particular attractions or destinations by tourists	(a) – (b) B(a) × visits per trip	(a) 50,000 tourist visits to Theme Park X in 2009 (b) Tourists from Region Y made 300,000 visits to Region X in 2009
Visitor-nights	Number of visitors to a TDR × average length of stay in nights	C × length of stay (nights)	Tourists spent 3 million visitor-nights in Region X in 2009
Expenditure	Expenditure by tourists in a TDR	C × expenditure per visit per head, or: D × expenditure per day per visitor	Tourists spent £50 million in Region X in 2009

TGR, Tourist Generating Region; TDR, Tourist Destination Region.
[a]Number of engagements in a given time period, e.g. twice a week.
[b]One episode devoted to an activity, e.g. a visit to a facility, a game played.
*All relate to a given population, place and time period.

OTHER RELEVANT CONCEPTS

Opportunities

Many governmental policy statements and official guidelines for leisure planning use the term *opportunities*, as shown in Box 3.5. In general, opportunity refers to available facilities or services. As some of the quotations suggest, the use of this term reflects a desire on the part of governments not to 'tell people what to do'. Typically, the policy is expressed as aiming to provide a *range* of opportunities, so it can be seen as transferring the concept of *market segmentation* to the public sector. However, in the private sector, market segmentation is a means to an end. The process involves matching products or product variations more closely with the tastes of identified segments of the market in order to increase overall sales and/or profits. Thus the success of the market segmentation exercise is judged by any resultant increase in sales or profit. But when used in public sector leisure planning, 'providing opportunity' is often portrayed as an end in itself, with no apparent criterion for judging the success of the outcome beyond the provision of the facilities or services. The implications for policymaking and planning are discussed in Chapter 7.

Collective consumption

Manuel Castells, in his seminal study *The Urban Question* (1977), drew attention to the role of cities as centres for *collective consumption* – an idea closely allied to the concept of public goods discussed above. Such collective consumption includes transport and other infrastructure, education, health and retail services, leisure and sports services and tourist attractions. The term collective consumption has not been widely used in the leisure literature. One exception is David Whitson (1987), who promoted the concept as an antidote to the tendencies towards commodification and privatization of public leisure services being experienced in the 1980s.

Quality of life

It is often argued that governments have a responsibility for the quality of life (QoL) of their citizens. The difficulties in defining some of the above concepts, such as need, are sometimes avoided by subsuming them under the broader concept of QoL. Leisure and sport are then deemed to be appropriate concerns for government because of their contribution to QoL. Geoffrey Godbey is critical of this practice, stating that: '… it is a cop-out to argue that leisure or recreation should be concerned with 'the quality of life', because no specific values are enunciated in such a statement. All human activities affect the quality of life. Additionally, the statement assumes that what constitutes superior quality can be readily agreed upon' (Godbey, 2008: 398).

The literature on QoL is extensive: numerous writers, both independently and under the auspices of organizations, notably the United Nations, have wrestled with the complex issues of definition and measurement. The fact that leisure contributes to the quality of life may suggest that governments should include leisure in the range of services they provide, but this does not help in deciding which forms of leisure should be publicly provided, in what quantities and in which circumstances, nor does it help in deciding the relative priority to be attached to leisure as opposed to other factors which contribute to QoL, such as

Box 3.5. Governmental and other statements on leisure opportunity.

1971: The Urban Institute, USA

'Recreation services should provide for all citizens, to the extent practicable, a variety of adequate, year-round leisure opportunities which are accessible, safe, physically attractive, and provide enjoyable experiences. They should, to the maximum extent, contribute to the mental and physical health of the community, to its economic and social well-being and permit outlets that will help decrease incidents of antisocial behaviour such as crime and delinquency' (Hatry and Dunn, 1971: 13).

1975: White Paper on Sport and Recreation, UK

'It is not for the Government to seek to control or direct the diverse activities of people's leisure time' (Dept. of the Environment, 1975: 4).

1985: Towards the Development of a Commonwealth Policy on Recreation, Australia

'Governments are not concerned with telling people how to spend their time but rather with ensuring that opportunities exist and that individuals have the knowledge to make informed choices' (Brown, 1985: 8).

1990: South Australian recreation planning guidelines, Australia

Example of a goal statement for local government: 'To ensure a diverse, safe, conveniently accessible leisure environment which provides opportunities for the satisfaction of a range of recreation pursuits for all sections of the community' (Marriott, 1990: 123).

2001: A Sporting Future for All, UK

'Government cannot and should not dictate. But Government can and should ensure that the opportunities are there for those who wish to seize them' (British Government, 2001: 37).

2002: Game Plan, UK

'While the government cannot, and should not, compel people to participate in sporting activities, it might wish to intervene to help remove the barriers that lead to inequality of opportunity' (DCMS/Policy Unit, 2002: 78).

2002: Game Plan, UK

'… government has a role to play in widening opportunities to participate …' (DCMS/Strategy Unit, 2002: 12).

2007: NSW Dept of Arts, Sport and Recreation: Corporate Plan, Australia

As part of 'Corporate Result 2: Improved health and wellbeing', among six 'strategic directions': 'Create opportunities for participation and enjoyment of arts, sport and recreation and leisure activities, particularly for under-represented or disadvantaged groups and people in regional areas' (NSW DASR, 2007: 2).

2008: Sport England Strategy 2008–2011, UK

'Creating opportunity for all: There is a need for new thinking in this area. All young people in particular should get a range of opportunities' (Sport England, 2008: 4).

nutrition, housing, health services, and so on. To do this, it would be necessary to place QoL at the centre of the policymaking process, covering all the services and environmental factors, whether or not directly provided by government, which government considers contribute to the QoL. Measurement of leisure outcomes would then be just one domain among many.

Of interest is the paper by Sirgy (1986), who seeks to provide a theoretical basis for QoL research based on Maslow's hierarchy, an approach which is further developed in Sirgy *et al.* (1995).

Well-being

Well-being is a concept similar to quality of life. It is associated with a 'movement' to reduce the emphasis given to economic indicators as goals and measures of the success of societies. Sources such as Diener and Seligman (2004) and the Australia Institute (undated) place particular emphasis on research which shows a lack of correlation between income/wealth and measures of happiness. Thus Diener and Seligman discuss an approach to assessing well-being focused on:

- society: governance, etc.;
- income: but also including issues such as inequality;
- work: including quality of working life;
- physical health;
- mental health;
- social relationships.

It is not proposed to pursue this concept here, but clearly assessments of the quality of people's leisure lives can be expected to feature in any complete picture of well-being.

SUMMARY

- This chapter reviews a number of concepts relating to policymaking and planning in leisure, sport and tourism, including: wants and needs, obligations, demand, benefits, participation and, in less detail, opportunity, collective consumption, quality of life and well-being.
- A variety of conceptualizations of the phenomenon of need is examined, including: (i) Maslow's hierarchy of need; (ii) the idea of optimal arousal and incongruity; (iii) leisure satisfaction scales; (iv) the Bradshaw/Mercer typology of need; (v) universal needs; and (vi) false needs. A number of these conceptualizations incorporate the idea that needs are distinguished from wants in that the satisfaction of needs prevents harm to the individual, as opposed to wants, where denial to satisfy does not result in harm. This would imply that focusing on the concept of need in a policy context requires this distinction to be made and the avoided harmful effects to be identified. In other conceptualizations – notably as used in tourism marketing and leisure satisfaction scales – either no distinction is made between needs and wants or needs are seen as the basis of all wants/desires.
- Obligatory leisure is activity undertaken because of an obligation to others, an aspect of leisure which is often neglected.

- Demand is analysed using two perspectives: (i) the Outcomes-Focussed Management or Benefits-Based Management (OFM/BBM) approach; and (ii) economics-based approaches. Both approaches require the measurement of a range of benefits resulting from leisure, sport or tourism projects, including those accruing to users, non-users, local communities and the environment. In economics-based approaches these measurements are, where possible, expressed in money terms, as discussed in Chapter 12, while in the OFM/BBM approach a variety of economic and non-economic measures is used. In both cases, the amount of data to be collected is substantial, raising questions about the practicability of their application in many policymaking/planning environments.
- Participation is seen as the simplest of the concepts examined, although a range of measures of participation exists.
- Finally, the concepts of opportunity, collective consumption, quality of life and well-being, which all appear in the leisure policy literature, are briefly discussed.

RESOURCES

Need: Springborg (1981); Veal (2009d)[a].
Maslow's hierarchy of need: Maslow (1954/1987); Fitzgerald (1977).
Bradshaw/Mercer typology: Bradshaw (1972); Mercer (1973); Paddick (1982).
Leisure satisfaction scales: Beard and Ragheb (1980); Driver *et al.* (1991b); Veal (2009d)[a].
Optimal arousal and incongruity: Iso-Ahola (1989).
Universal needs: Doyal and Gough (1991); Max-Neef (1992).
Social tourism: Haulot (1981); Minnaert *et al.* (2009); McCabe (2009).
Wants: Veal (2009c)[a].
Obligations: Veal (2009c)[a].
Demand: Veal (2009e)[a].
Demand modelling: outdoor recreation demand, Hanley *et al.* (2003); tourism demand, Smith (1995).
Benefits: Driver *et al.* (1991b); Driver and Bruns (1999, 2008); Driver (2008); Veal (2009f)[a].
Value transfer: Rosenberger and Loomis (2001).
Participation: Veal (2009c)[a].
Participation surveys: Cushman *et al.* (2005).
Opportunity: Veal (2009c)[a].
Market segmentation: Horner and Swarbrooke (2005: 39–42).
Collective consumption: Castells (1977); Whitson (1987).
Quality of life: Sirgy (1986); Sirgy *et al.* (1995); Iwasaki (2006).
Well-being: Australia Institute (undated); Diener and Seligman (2004).

[a] These items are online sources which review the literature on the concepts discussed in this chapter in more detail than is possible here; they can be found at: http://www.leisuresource.net

QUESTIONS/EXERCISES

1. Why is the idea of 'need' political?
2. What is the difference between a need and a want?

3. How are the concepts of need and want conceptualized in the context of tourism marketing?

4. What is obligatory leisure?

5. How does the economics approach to demand account for unmet demands?

6. How does the Outcome-Focussed Management/Benefits-Based Management approach differ from the economics-based approach to assessing benefits?

7. Identify three different ways of measuring participation.

8. Examine three examples of a public leisure/tourism service and suggest in what way, if at all, the service can be said to be meeting a 'need'.

9. Rank the leisure/sport/tourism activities you have engaged in over the last month (or ask a willing subject to do so) and rank them in order of importance. Draw a line dividing the activities into 'needs' and 'others' and explain the rationale for this.

10. Nominate one leisure/sport/tourism activity and suggest one benefit and one dis-benefit which a facility for such an activity might generate for: (i) users; (ii) members of the neighbourhood/community in which it is located; and (iii) the environment.

chapter 4

Human Rights and Citizenship Rights

INTRODUCTION

It could be argued, philosophically, that one of the reasons why governments should be involved in leisure, sport and tourism is that people have a *right* to enjoy leisure, to participation in sport and to travel for pleasure and it is the job of governments to protect the rights of its citizens. If these activities are seen as human rights it might be thought that this would provide powerful support for government involvement to ensure adequate levels of provision and minimization of constraints. As indicated in the rest of the book, however, public policymaking is generally a very pragmatic matter, influenced by 'practical politics', power relationships, availability of resources and technical considerations. But this does not mean that principles and values are irrelevant or should be ignored: hence the discussion of rights in this chapter, political ideology in Chapter 2 and needs and related concepts in Chapter 3.

In this chapter we examine the complex and contested nature of human rights and their implications for public policy, particularly governments' leisure, sport and tourism policies. The chapter is divided into the following sections:

- definitions: what do we mean by rights?
- history: the historical origins and evolution of the idea of rights;
- human rights declarations, in the area of: leisure generally; sports; the arts/culture; and tourism/travel;
- group, as opposed to individual, rights;
- the meaningfulness of rights declarations;
- rights and freedoms;
- rights other than human rights;
- citizens' rights.

DEFINITIONS

The *Shorter Oxford English Dictionary* defines a *right* as a 'justifiable claim, on legal or moral grounds, to have or obtain something, or to act in a certain way'. Thus a right is seen as something which must be claimed by an individual or group and, in turn, be recognized by others as legitimate. *Human rights* are those rights which *all* human beings are deemed to be entitled to on the basis of their humanity alone (Donnelly, 1989: 12). Statements of human rights are statements of belief or commitment; they are therefore political and moral in nature. In the 20th century a range of human rights came to be widely recognized, particularly by governments, through various national and international legal instruments.

HISTORY

An early exemplification of the idea that people might have rights in the area of leisure can be seen in 16th century England, where Queen Elizabeth I, while herself a Protestant, disapproved of attempts by extreme Protestants, later known as Puritans, using their influence on city councils and the Parliament, to restrict public leisure activity according to the Puritan moral code. In 1585 the Queen:

> . . . quashed a Puritan Bill aimed at banning all sports and entertainments on Sundays. The Queen felt that her people *had a right* to spend their only day of rest enjoying themselves as they pleased, without interference from killjoys. . . . The Puritan authorities in several cities, especially London, held the theatre in special odium, and made strenuous efforts to suppress play-going, as it drew people away from the churches. The Queen sympathised with the theatre-goers . . . When, in 1575, she discovered that the renowned Coventry cycle of mystery plays had been banned by the Puritan authorities in that city, she ordered them to be restored. The Puritans in London then began complaining that theatre-goers in the City helped spread the plague that was endemic each summer. In 1583, the Corporation of London closed the theatres on the Surrey shore, but Elizabeth retaliated by forming her own company of players, who became known as The Queen's Men. The civic authorities backed down, but in 1597 they eventually persuaded the Council to agree to close down the theatres on the grounds that they were hotbeds of subversive propaganda against the government. When Elizabeth heard, she was furious, and the Council hastily rescinded the order. There were no further threats to the theatre in her reign.

> (Weir, 1999: 56–57, emphasis added)

These 16th century events can be interpreted as involving a conflict between the supporters of the idea of people's leisure *rights* as opposed to the morally based views and interests of particular groups. Such rights were, however, at the discretion of the monarch and had to be reasserted by Elizabeth's successor, James I who, in 1618, issued what became known as the *Book of Sports*, which permitted the playing of specified sports on Sundays, after attendance at church. But in the reign of James' son, Charles I, the Puritans resumed their efforts to suppress such activities and he reissued the declaration in 1633. But in 1640, the Puritan-dominated Parliament ordered the *Book of Sports* to be publicly burned (Dulles, 1965: 10–12) and in 1642 closed all theatres (Armitage, 1977: 70).

The 18th century produced one of the most famous declarations of human rights, in the 1776 American Declaration of Independence, which stated: 'We hold these truths to be self-evident: that all men are created equal; that they are endowed by their Creator with certain inalienable rights; that among these are life, liberty and the pursuit of happiness'. While leisure is only one means by which people might 'pursue happiness', this can be seen as a formal recognition of leisure as a human right.

Europe in the 19th century saw a clash between industry and labour over campaigns for shorter working hours (first for a 10-hour working day, then for an 8-hour day), which arose in response to the inordinately long working hours demanded by factory owners. While concerns for health, self-improvement and family life, rather than leisure per se, were often advanced as justification for reductions in working hours, eventually, Gary Cross (1990: 83) notes: '… workers no longer felt the need to justify their leisure on family or moral grounds. The American slogan 'Eight Hours for What We Will' expressed this attitude clearly. Leisure was a right that required no rationale'. Cross further notes that 'short-hour activists' often linked their demands to the rights of 'free born Englishmen' and to the proposition that 'all citizens had an equal right to personal liberty' (Cross, 1990: 77). In a pamphlet entitled *The Right to be Lazy*, originally published in France in 1848, Paul Lafargue stated:

> …if the working class were to rise up in its terrible strength, not to demand the Rights of Man, which are but the rights of capitalist exploitation, not to demand the Right to Work, which is but the right to misery, but to forge a brazen law forbidding any man to work more than three hours a day, the earth, the old earth, trembling with joy would feel a new universe leaping within her.

(Lafargue, 1958: 114)

Almost 40 years ago, French leisure sociologist Joffre Dumazedier stated:

> In the Renaissance the individual achieved the right to choose his own God or his own ideal without risking being burnt at the stake. With the coming of democratic society in the eighteenth century, the individual achieved civil rights, i.e., protection from arbitrary will of political power (habeas corpus). The trade-union movement was a struggle against the arbitrary will of owners and management. The worker ultimately achieved the right to organize. All these rights have been achieved over the last four centuries. This conquest has reached a point of no return. In the new society the fact of leisure corresponds to a new social right for the individual, i.e., the right to have for his own use an increasing part of free time, leisure time.

(Dumazedier, 1971: 203)

HUMAN RIGHTS DECLARATIONS

The contemporary successor to the ideals of the American Declaration of Independence is the Universal Declaration of Human Rights, adopted by the United Nations in 1948. Leisure received explicit recognition in Articles 24 and 27 of the Declaration, and the right to travel was recognized in Article 13. The 1966 International Covenant on Economic, Social and Cultural Rights made specific reference to holidays with pay, and the 1989 UN Convention of the Rights of the Child specifically recognized children's right to play. These references are presented in Box 4.1.

Since all members of the United Nations are signatories to these declarations, it might reasonably be assumed that all national governments recognize leisure, travel and play as rights and accept a responsibility to uphold those rights. However, as Donnelly (1989: 42) states, 'The sad fact is that in the contemporary world virtually all internationally recognized human rights are regularly and systematically violated'.

Box 4.1. UN declarations on human rights and leisure (from http:// www. un.org/rights/).

1948: The Universal Declaration of Human Rights

Article 24: Everyone has the right to rest and leisure, including reasonable limitation of working hours and periodic holidays with pay.

Article 27: Everyone has the right freely to participate in the cultural life of the community, to enjoy the arts and to share in scientific advancement and its benefits.

1966: International Covenant on Economic, Social and Cultural Rights

Article 7: . . . the 'right of everyone to the enjoyment of just and favourable conditions of work' includes the right to: 'Rest, leisure, reasonable limitation of working hours and periodic holidays with pay, as well as remuneration for public holidays'.

1975: Declaration on the Rights of Disabled Persons

Article 3: Disabled persons have the inherent right to respect for their human dignity. Disabled persons, whatever the origin, nature and seriousness of their handicaps and disabilities, have the same fundamental rights as their fellow-citizens of the same age, which implies first and foremost the right to enjoy a decent life, as normal and full as possible.

Article 8: Disabled persons are entitled to have their special needs taken into consideration at all stages of economic and social planning.

1979: Convention on the Elimination of All Forms of Discrimination against Women

Article 3: States Parties shall take in all fields, in particular in the political, social, economic and cultural fields, all appropriate measures, including legislation, to ensure the full development and advancement of women, for the purpose of guaranteeing them the exercise and enjoyment of human rights and fundamental freedoms on a basis of equality with men.

Article 5: States Parties shall take all appropriate measures … to modify the social and cultural patterns of conduct of men and women, with a view to achieving the elimination of prejudices and customary and all other practices which are based on the idea of the inferiority or the superiority of either of the sexes or on stereotyped roles for men and women.

Article 10: States Parties shall take all appropriate measures to eliminate discrimination against women in order to ensure to them equal rights with men in the field of education and in particular to ensure, on a basis of equality of men and women … the same opportunities to participate actively in sports and physical education.

Article 13: States Parties shall take all appropriate measures to eliminate discrimination against women in other areas of economic and social life in order to ensure, on a basis of equality of men and women, the same rights, in particular … The right to participate in recreational activities, sports and all aspects of cultural life.

1989: Convention on the Rights of the Child

Article 31:

1. States Parties recognize the right of the child to rest and leisure, to engage in play and recreational activities appropriate to the age of the child and to participate freely in cultural life and the arts.

(Continued)

Box 4.1. Continued.

2. States Parties shall respect and promote the right of the child to participate fully in cultural and artistic life and shall encourage the provision of appropriate and equal opportunities for cultural, artistic, recreational and leisure activity.

1989: Convention Concerning Indigenous and Tribal Peoples in Independent Countries

Article 2:

1. Governments shall have the responsibility for developing, with the participation of the peoples concerned, co-ordinated and systematic action to protect the rights of these peoples and to guarantee respect for their integrity.

2. Such action shall include measures for:

(a) ensuring that members of these peoples benefit on an equal footing from the rights and opportunities which national laws and regulations grant to other members of the population;

(b) promoting the full realisation of the social, economic and cultural rights of these peoples with respect for their social and cultural identity, their customs and traditions and their institutions.

Article 5: In applying the provisions of this Convention:

1. The social, cultural, religious and spiritual values and practices of these peoples shall be recognised and protected, and due account shall be taken of the nature of the problems which face them both as groups and as individuals.

2. The integrity of the values, practices and institutions of these peoples shall be respected.

1999: Declaration on the Rights of Persons Belonging to National or Ethnic, Religious or Linguistic Minorities

Article 2: Persons belonging to national or ethnic, religious and linguistic minorities have the right to:

1. Enjoy their own culture, to profess and practise their own religion, and to use their own language, in private and in public, freely and without interference or any form of discrimination.

2. Participate effectively in cultural, religious, social, economic and public life.

3. Establish and maintain their own associations.

Article 24 is one of a group of four in the Universal Declaration dealing with 'economic' rights, including social security, the right to work under acceptable conditions, equal pay for equal work, 'just and favourable remuneration' and a decent standard of living, including 'food, clothing, housing and medical care and necessary social services, and the right to security in the event of unemployment, sickness, disability, widowhood, old age or other lack of livelihood'. In considering this group of declared rights in contrast to the more familiar political and civil rights, David Harvey comments as follows:

> What is striking about these articles … is the degree to which hardly any attention has been paid over the last fifty years to their implementation or application and how almost all countries that were signatories to the Universal Declaration are in gross violation of these articles. Strict enforcement of such rights would entail massive and in some senses revolutionary transformations in the political-economy of capitalism. Neoliberalism could easily be cast, for example, as a gross violation of human rights. (Harvey, 2000: 89–90)

This conclusion is perhaps ironic given the origins of the idea of human rights in Western liberal philosophy, as mentioned above.

Rights can be divided into *positive* rights, which are enshrined in national law, and *moral* rights, which are not so enshrined. Cranston uses the example of Article 13 of the Universal Declaration, relating to freedom of travel, which was consistently violated by the USA and the then Soviet Union during the Cold War and by South Africa during the apartheid era, to make the distinction: 'Clearly, therefore, the right to leave any country, which the United Nations Declaration says 'everyone' has, is not a positive right. The intention of the sponsors of that declaration was to specify something that everyone *ought* to have. In other words the rights they named were moral rights' (Cranston, 1973: 6).

The declarations on leisure and culture could similarly be termed *moral* rights, since they do not specify the *amount* of leisure time which is considered acceptable, or what constitutes *reasonable* limitation of working hours, or the *amount* of paid holidays or public holidays. Only some of these matters are codified in the laws of some countries and the details vary from country to country. Indeed, some critics have suggested that such declarations are not in fact universal in application, but relate primarily to developed countries with the resources to implement them.

More detailed declarations exist in relation to leisure in general and to different aspects of leisure, including sport, the arts and travel, and these are discussed briefly below.

LEISURE RIGHTS

The *Charter for Leisure* (Box 4.2), drawn up by the World Leisure Organization (WLO) in 1970 and revised in 2000, declares leisure to be a right, extols the virtues of leisure and exhorts governments to make provision for leisure as a social service, but it stops short of declaring access to leisure facilities and services as a right.

SPORTING RIGHTS

Various bodies have declared the practice of sport to be a right (see Box 4.3), including the International Olympic Committee, UNESCO and the Council of Europe. As with the WLO charter, these declarations envisage a major role for governments in coordinating, planning and providing for sport. The *Sport for All Charter* has received the formal endorsement of the member governments of the Council of Europe, and individual member countries have generally adopted Sport for All policies which the Council of Europe monitors through a permanent committee. The idea of the *general right* to participate in sport has not been the subject of much attention in the scholarly literature: attention in the area of sport and human rights has been concentrated on racial, ethnic and gender discrimination, primarily in relation to elite level sport (Taylor, 1999). However, if denial of access to sporting opportunity for particular social groups is considered an infringement of human rights, this implies the acceptance of a general right for everyone to participate.

ARTISTIC AND CULTURAL RIGHTS

The *arts* are explicitly recognized in Article 27 of the Universal Declaration in the reference to the right to 'participation in the cultural life of the community' and to 'enjoy the arts'. Donald Horne, in *The Public Culture* (1986: 232–237), produced a 'declaration of 'cultural rights'', consisting of rights to access to the human cultural heritage, rights to new art and rights to community art participation.

Box 4.2. World Leisure Organization: Charter for Leisure.

Introduction

Consistent with the Universal Declaration of Human Rights (Article 27), all cultures and societies recognize to some extent the right to rest and leisure. Here, because personal freedom and choice are central elements of leisure, individuals can freely choose their activities and experiences, many of them leading to substantial benefits for person and community.

Articles

1. All people have a basic human right to leisure activities that are in harmony with the norms and social values of their compatriots. All governments are obliged to recognize and protect this right of its citizens.

2. Provisions for leisure for the quality of life are as important as those for health and education. Governments should ensure their citizens a variety of accessible leisure and recreational opportunities of the highest quality.

3. The individual is his/her best leisure and recreational resource. Thus, governments should ensure the means for acquiring those skills and understandings necessary to optimize leisure experiences.

4. Individuals can use leisure opportunities for self-fulfilment, developing personal relationships, improving social integration, developing communities and cultural identity as well as promoting international understanding and co-operation and enhancing quality of life.

5. Governments should ensure the future availability of fulfilling leisure experiences by maintaining the quality of their country's physical, social and cultural environment.

6. Governments should ensure the training of professionals to help individuals acquire personal skills, discover and develop their talents and to broaden their range of leisure and recreational opportunities.

7. Citizens must have access to all forms of leisure information about the nature of leisure and its opportunities, using it to enhance their knowledge and inform decisions on local and national policy.

8. Educational institutions must make every effort to teach the nature and importance of leisure and how to integrate this knowledge into personal lifestyle.

Approved by the World Leisure Board of Directors, July 2000. The original version was adopted by the International Recreation Association in 1970, and subsequently revised by its successor, the World Leisure and Recreation Association in 1979. The organization is now known as the World Leisure Organization (WLO) – see: http://www.worldleisure.org

---

Statements about the right to participate 'freely in the cultural life of the community' and the right to 'enjoy the arts' are even more vague than those relating to leisure. If 'culture' includes 'popular culture' then the statement is hardly worth making since popular culture is, by definition, enjoyed by the mass of the population. If 'culture' and 'the arts' refers to high culture then, as Harvey suggests, most countries could be said to violate these rights on a wide scale, since such participation and enjoyment is generally highly skewed in favour of the better-off groups in society. Most governments would point to programmes of subsidy and free services, such as public broadcasting, but the result is often still a pattern of minority participation and enjoyment. As 'user pays' policies are pursued in public services, this becomes more and more pronounced. Again, such situations are rarely spoken of in terms of violation of human rights.

Box 4.3. Declarations on the right to sport.

The Olympic Charter

Article 1: The practice of sport is a human right. Every individual must have the possibility of practising sport in accordance with his or her needs (International Olympic Committee, 2004: 1, and at: http://www.olympic.org).

1978: UNESCO International Charter of Physical Education and Sport (source: UNESCO, 1982)

Article 1: The practice of physical education and sport is a fundamental right for all.
Article 2: Physical education and sport form an essential element of lifelong education in the overall education system.
Article 3: Physical education and sport programmes must meet individual and social needs.
Article 4: Teaching, coaching and administration of physical education and sport should be performed by qualified personnel.
Article 5: Adequate facilities and equipment are essential to physical education and sport.
Article 6: Research and evaluation are indispensable components of the development of physical education and sport.
Article 7: Information and documentation help to promote physical education and sport.
Article 8: The mass media should exert a positive influence on physical education and sport.
Article 9: National institutions play a major role in physical education and sport.
Article 10: International cooperation is a prerequisite for the universal and well-balanced promotion of physical education and sport.

1976: European Sport for All Charter

Article I: Every individual shall have the right to participate in sport.

1992: European Sports Charter

Article 1: Aim of the Charter
Governments, with a view to the promotion of sport as an important factor in human development, shall take the steps necessary to apply the provisions of this charter in accordance with the principles set out in the Code of Sports Ethics in order:
1. to enable every individual to participate in sport and notably:
    (a) to ensure that all young people should have the opportunity to receive physical education instruction and the opportunity to acquire basic sports skills;
    (b) to ensure that everyone should have the opportunity to take part in sport and physical recreation in a safe and healthy environment; and, in co-operation with the appropriate sports organisations:
    (c) to ensure that everyone with the interest and ability should have the opportunity to improve their standard of performance in sport and reach levels of personal achievement and/or publicly recognised levels of excellence;
2. to protect and develop the moral and ethical bases of sport, and the human dignity and safety of those involved in sport, by safeguarding sport, sportsmen and women from

(Continued)

Box 4.3. Continued.

exploitation from political, commercial and financial gain, and from practices that are abusive or debasing, including the abuse of drugs.

Article 3: The Sports Movement

1. The role of the public authorities is primarily complementary to the action of the sports movement. Therefore, close co-operation with non-governmental sports organisations is essential in order to ensure the fulfilment of the aims of this Charter, including where necessary the establishment of machinery for the development and co-ordination of sport.
2. The development of the voluntary ethos and movement in sport shall be encouraged, particularly through support for the work of voluntary sports organisations.
3. Voluntary sports organisations have the right to establish autonomous decision-making processes within the law. Both governments and sports organisations shall recognise the need for a mutual respect of their decisions.
4. The implementation of some of the provisions of this Charter may be entrusted to governmental or non-governmental sports authorities or sports organisations.
5. Sports organisations should be encouraged to establish mutually beneficial arrangements with each other and with potential partners, such as the commercial sector, the media, etc, while ensuring that exploitation of sport or sports people is avoided.

Article 4: Facilities and Activities

1. No discrimination on the grounds of sex, race, colour, language, religion, political or other opinion, national or social origin, association with a national minority, property, birth or other status, shall be permitted in the access to sports facilities or to sports activities.
2. Measures shall be taken to ensure that all citizens have opportunities to take part in sport and, where necessary, additional measures shall be taken aimed at enabling both young gifted people, but also disadvantaged or disabled individuals or groups to be able to exercise such opportunities effectively.
3. Since the scale of participation in sport is dependent in part on the extent, the variety and the accessibility of facilities, their overall planning shall be accepted as a matter for public authorities. The range of facilities to be provided shall take account of public, private, commercial and other facilities which are available. Those responsible shall take account of national, regional and local requirements, and incorporate measures designed to ensure good management and their safe and full use.
4. Appropriate steps should be taken by the owners of sports facilities to enable disadvantaged persons including those with physical or mental disabilities to have access to such facilities.

Article 5: Building the Foundation

Appropriate steps shall be taken to develop physical fitness and the acquisition of basic sports skills and to encourage the practice of sport by young people, notably:

1. by ensuring that programmes of and, facilities for, sport, recreation and physical education are made available to all pupils and that appropriate time is set aside for this;
2. by ensuring the training of qualified teachers in this area at all schools;
3. by ensuring that appropriate opportunities exist for continuing the practice of sport after compulsory education.

(Continued)

Box 4.3. Continued.

Article 6: Developing Participation

The practice of sport, whether it be for the purpose of leisure and recreation, of health promotion, or of improving performance, shall be promoted for all parts of the population through the provision of appropriate facilities and programmes of all kinds and of qualified instructors, leaders or 'animateurs'.

Sources: UN: http://www.un.org/rights; Sport for All Charter (Council of Europe, 1978); Council of Europe: http://www.coe.int

TOURISM AND TRAVEL RIGHTS

In the area of *tourism* the right to holidays with pay and the right to freedom of travel, for any purpose, are enshrined in the Universal Declaration and reiterated in a number of subsequent declarations, as indicated in Box 4.4. Of particular note is the *Global Code of Ethics for Tourism* promulgated by the World Tourism Organization in 1998, which extends the idea of rights in this area to: 'the discovery and enjoyment of the planet's resources'; conditions of work in the tourism industry; and the right of host communities not to be exploited by tourism.

The right to holidays with pay illustrates the moral rights/positive rights distinction. Even among the most highly developed economies holiday entitlements vary substantially – workers in the USA and Japan, for example, enjoy only about half the entitlements of workers in Europe. But there are no claims that American and Japanese workers' human rights are therefore being violated. As noted in Chapter 1, the study of tourism has been less public-sector-orientated than the study of leisure, so the idea of the holiday as a right, which might parallel the idea of leisure services as a right, is not a significant feature of debates in the tourism literature. An exception among tourism researchers is Krippendorf, who states:

> What our society offers routine-weary people is tourism, a variety of holidays outside the everyday world, extolling them as escape-aids, problem-solvers, suppliers of strength, energy, new lifeblood and happiness. The get-away offer should be accessible to everyone. After the 'right to holidays', the 'right to holiday travel' has now become a socio-political issue: tourism for all social classes.

> (Krippendorf, 1987: 17)

He does not, however, indicate where or with whom these matters have become a 'socio-political issue'.

A further exception to the rule is the idea of 'social tourism'. While the term is occasionally used in a different sense, here it refers to the practice of social security organizations providing for people in various disadvantaged situations to take a holiday away from home. This practice, less common than it once was, can be seen as extending the 'right' to a holiday to those who would otherwise be denied. It merits a passing mention in the *Global Code of Ethics for Tourism*, but only as something which 'should be developed'. The concept is discussed further in Chapter 14.

Box 4.4. Declarations on rights to travel, holidays and tourism.

1948: The Universal Declaration of Human Rights

Article 13: Everyone has the right to leave any country, including his own, and to return to his country.

Article 24: Everyone has the right to rest and leisure, including reasonable limitation of working hours and periodic holidays with pay.

1998: Global Code of Ethics for Tourism

We, members of the World Tourism Organization (WTO) representatives of the world tourism industry, delegates of States, territories, enterprises, institutions and bodies that are gathered for the General Assembly at Santiago, Chile on this first day of October 1999, … affirm the right to tourism and the freedom of tourist movements …

Article 7: Right to tourism

1. The prospect of direct and personal access to the discovery and enjoyment of the planet's resources constitutes a right equally open to all the world's inhabitants; the increasingly extensive participation in national and international tourism should be regarded as one of the best possible expressions of the sustained growth of free time, and obstacles should not be placed in its way.

2. The universal right to tourism must be regarded as the corollary of the right to rest and leisure, including reasonable limitation of working hours and periodic holidays with pay, guaranteed by Article 24 of the Universal Declaration of Human Rights and Article 7.d of the International Covenant on Economic, Social and Cultural Rights.

3. Social tourism, and in particular associative tourism, which facilitates widespread access to leisure, travel and holidays, should be developed with the support of the public authorities.

4. Family, youth, student and senior tourism and tourism for people with disabilities, should be encouraged and facilitated.

Article 8: Liberty of tourist movements

1. Tourists and visitors should benefit, in compliance with international law and national legislation, from the liberty to move within their countries and from one State to another, in accordance with Article 13 of the Universal Declaration of Human Rights; they should have access to places of transit and stay and to tourism and cultural sites without being subject to excessive formalities or discrimination.

2. Tourists and visitors should have access to all available forms of communication, internal or external; they should benefit from prompt and easy access to local administrative, legal and health services; they should be free to contact the consular representatives of their countries of origin in compliance with the diplomatic conventions in force.

3. Tourists and visitors should benefit from the same rights as the citizens of the country visited concerning the confidentiality of the personal data and information concerning them, especially when these are stored electronically.

4. Administrative procedures relating to border crossings, whether they fall within the competence of States or result from international agreements, such as visas or health and customs formalities, should be adapted, so far as possible, so as to facilitate to the maximum

(Continued)

Box 4.4. Continued.

freedom of travel and widespread access to international tourism; agreements between groups of countries to harmonize and simplify these procedures should be encouraged; specific taxes and levies penalizing the tourism industry and undermining its competitiveness should be gradually phased out or corrected.

5. So far as the economic situation of the countries from which they come permits, travellers should have access to allowances of convertible currencies needed for their travels.

Article 9: Rights of the workers and entrepreneurs in the tourism industry

1. The fundamental rights of salaried and self-employed workers in the tourism industry and related activities, should be guaranteed under the supervision of the national and local administrations, both of their States of origin and of the host countries with particular care, given the specific constraints linked in particular to the seasonality of their activity, the global dimension of their industry and the flexibility often required of them by the nature of their work.

2. Salaried and self-employed workers in the tourism industry and related activities have the right and the duty to acquire appropriate initial and continuous training; they should be given adequate social protection; job insecurity should be limited so far as possible; and a specific status, with particular regard to their social welfare, should be offered to seasonal workers in the sector.

3. Any natural or legal person, provided he, she or it has the necessary abilities and skills, should be entitled to develop a professional activity in the field of tourism under existing national laws; entrepreneurs and investors – especially in the area of small and medium-sized enterprises – should be entitled to free access to the tourism sector with a minimum of legal or administrative restrictions.

4. As an irreplaceable factor of solidarity in the development and dynamic growth of international exchanges, multinational enterprises of the tourism industry should not exploit the dominant positions they sometimes occupy; they should avoid becoming the vehicles of cultural and social models artificially imposed on the host communities; in exchange for their freedom to invest and trade which should be fully recognized, they should involve themselves in local development, avoiding, by the excessive repatriation of their profits or their induced imports, a reduction of their contribution to the economies in which they are established.

Source: World Tourism Organization, at: http://www.world-tourism.org

GROUP RIGHTS

Campaigns for equal or special rights have been mounted by or on behalf of numerous social groups with varying degrees of success, a number having been the subject of UN declarations, as shown in Box 4.1. In this section we consider rights as they relate to children, women, people with disabilities and ethnic minorities and indigenous peoples.

The 19th century campaigns for reduced working hours initially related to children and women, and such campaigns continue today in relation to certain Third World countries which exploit child labour. Others who have sought to assert their rights include the aged, people with disabilities and ethnic minorities and indigenous peoples. Planning for leisure in general for these various groups is discussed in Chapter 14; here the question of leisure rights in relation to each group is briefly discussed.

Disabled persons

The rights of *disabled persons* were the subject of a 1975 UN declaration, but that document makes no specific reference to the *leisure* of disabled people, just to the right to 'enjoy a decent life' and for disabled people to have their needs taken into account in social planning. In many countries these rights have been enshrined in legislation but, as Darcy (1999) points out, declarations of rights, and even legislation, do not ensure suitable provision; this requires a change in the mindset of the community and decision makers.

Children

The statements in regard to *children's* cultural rights and the right to play suffer from many of the same defects of vagueness as the general statements of the Universal Declaration. However, they do assert that governments should 'encourage the provision of appropriate and equal opportunities'. Again, the term 'appropriate' is undefined and it is certainly arguable that these rights are being widely violated. One of the most graphic examples of such rights being violated was the scenes of gross neglect of orphans in Rumania, revealed with the fall of the communist regime in 1990. The effects of the denial of any opportunity for play and exercise, along with denial of education and human affection, were all too plain to see on television screens throughout the world. But the perpetrators of such human rights violations were not apparently pursued and brought to justice by the international community. Similarly, campaigns against child labour, which is widespread in many countries, are generally conducted by voluntary/charitable bodies rather than by governments.

Women

Campaigns for the rights of *women* are part of the platform of feminist movements, discussed in Chapter 2. As Box 4.1 indicates, the 1979 *Convention on the Elimination of All Forms of Discrimination Against Women* contains references to 'recreational activities, sports and all aspects of cultural life'. In the feminist leisure studies literature, however, there is little mention of the idea of rights – the exception being a brief reference by Horna (1994: 25) to a report of Lenskyj (1991) on Canadian women's use of human rights legislation in the area of sport. It is notable that Article 24 of the Universal Declaration, which is concerned with hours of work and holidays with pay, is entirely addressed to those in paid employment and, in reality, those in *full-time* paid employment. Thus there is an implicit bias towards men since, certainly in 1948 when the Universal Declaration was drawn up, only a minority of women were in full-time paid employment. The idea that people not in paid employment might also have leisure rights is thus ignored. It is curious that this has not been taken up in discussion of women's rights to leisure.

Ethnic minorities and indigenous peoples

The rights of *ethnic minorities and indigenous peoples* have been the subject of more recent UN declarations. Here, as well as issues of discrimination and access to mainstream activities, there is an emphasis on cultural pluralism, with the declarations asserting the rights of minority groups to practise their own culture. This has implications for planning and provision, which are discussed in Chapter 7.

MEANINGFULNESS OF RIGHTS DECLARATIONS

Are these declarations of rights of assistance in determining the appropriate role of governments in relation to leisure? Yes and no. An analysis of the United Nations statements raises some doubts about the nature, scope and meaningfulness of the declared rights. Article 24 of the Universal Declaration refers to the right to 'rest and leisure', but these concepts are not defined, let alone quantified. Rest and leisure are, however, said to *include* 'reasonable limitation of working hours and periodic holidays with pay'. As *moral* statements, the declarations of human rights indicate a broad consensus that governments should be concerned about leisure but, with many more pressing matters engaging governments in the international arena, such statements about leisure rarely translate into *positive* rights. They therefore provide little guidance on the nature or extent of government involvement necessary to secure such rights.

Rights and freedoms

The upholding of some rights involves the denial of others, giving rise to dilemmas for defenders of civil rights and often to much political conflict. For example, upholding the right of people not to be abused on racial grounds involves denial of some people's right to freedom of expression, but where such discrimination has been outlawed it is generally accepted that the former right is more important. In the area of leisure and tourism, examples of curtailment of freedom can be seen in relation to taxation, in relation to direct controls over activities with moral implications and in the area of national sovereignty.

Taxation

Where rights involve the provision of goods or services – for example education or housing – any public provision must generally be funded from taxation. The compulsory nature of taxation can be seen as an infringement of individuals' right to spend their money as they please. Thus those on the right of the political spectrum, as discussed in Chapter 2, often oppose increased levels of public service provision, even if based on a reasonable claim of rights, because they see this leading to increased levels of taxation and hence to increased infringement of individual financial rights. For some right-wing political adherents, the accumulation of public expenditure, and the extension of legal controls on all sorts of activity, have given rise to 'big government' which, of its very nature, is seen as a threat to human rights and freedoms.

Moral concerns

There are many instances where leisure activities are strictly controlled, are subject to punitive levels of taxation or are outlawed, for moral or health reasons – a phenomenon which has been termed 'morality policy' (Mooney, 1999). Such controls are often opposed, by either individuals or organized groups. Regardless of the motive for the controls, they can be seen as an infringement on the rights of the individuals involved. Examples generally fall into the category of activity traditionally known as 'vices', namely gambling, prostitution and recreational drugs, including alcohol. In some cases controls or outright prohibition can be seen as the imposition of one group's moral or religious values on others and hence the denial of the latter's rights. An example is the period of alcohol prohibition in the USA in the 1920s. In tourism the process may involve a culture clash between visitors' and residents' values and norms of behaviour. It is not possible to pursue this complex area of public policy further here, but it is a subject which merits further research attention. Only limited examination of these contentious areas has appeared in the research literature, including, for example, the area of gambling (Dombrink, 1996; Veal and Lynch, 1999). The outlawing of leisure activities involving cruelty to animals, as discussed below, is another case where rights of some individuals are claimed to be infringed.

National sovereignty

Declarations of rights are often international in nature. Individual nations sign agreements or treaties which commit them to uphold the declarations – they become, in effect, international law. In some cases there are enforcement mechanisms, or at least monitoring systems, for example the International Court of Human Rights in The Hague. In signing treaties and accepting the jurisdiction of such entities, nations surrender a part of their sovereignty, which can be seen as a loss of freedom. This loss of sovereignty provides political ammunition for those opposed to the treaties in the first place.

OTHER RIGHTS

A number of ideas about rights have developed in recent years, some of which have implications for leisure and tourism, including the idea of the rights of future generations and the rights of animals.

Future generations

Sustainable development has become a significant theme in tourism following the publication in 1987 of the report of the World Commission on Environment and Development (WCED), *Our Common Future* (the Brundtland Report). Sustainable development was defined in the report as: 'development that meets the needs of the present without compromising the ability of future generations to meet their own needs' (WCED, 1990: 43). Thus the principle was established that development should respect the rights of *future generations*. It is not proposed to explore this issue in detail here – suffice it to say that it introduces a whole new dimension to the discussion of rights and imposes potentially highly significant constraints on development.

Animal rights

Another type of right which has been increasingly recognized and has had implications for leisure and tourism is *animal rights*. In the Coliseum in ancient Rome animals were slaughtered by the thousand for public entertainment. Part of the history of leisure in many countries has been the gradual outlawing of leisure activities involving cruelty to animals, including bear-baiting, cock-fighting and many forms of hunting, although they continue in many parts of the world. Bull-fighting in Spain and fox-hunting in the UK are examples of violation of animal rights for leisure and tourism purposes; the former continues today, although the latter was banned in Scotland in 2002 and throughout the UK in 2004. The banning of these forms of activity can, of course, be seen as an infringement of the rights of those who wish to participate, and such arguments are used by participants when the activity is threatened. The resolution of the conflict of interest between defenders of the right, for example to hunt, and the defenders of the rights of the animal to live, or at least to be killed humanely, becomes a matter of politics, a matter of which group has more political power. Less extreme examples include performing animals in circuses, unsuitable caging of animals in zoos, and often illegal capture of wild and endangered species for pets.

THE RIGHTS OF THE CITIZEN

Human rights, as discussed above, are intended to be universal in nature, which perhaps makes the link with leisure and tourism provision somewhat tenuous for most people. The idea of rights arising from *citizenship* is arguably more tangible, since citizenship applies to a particular country with a responsible government. Citizenship has been defined as: ... a bundle of entitlements and obligations which constitute individuals as fully fledged members of a socio-political community, providing them with access to scarce resources' (Turner, 1994: xv).

The idea of citizenship has a long history stretching back at least to the ancient Greek and Roman civilizations, but its modern form has developed over the last 300 years. In work originally published in the 1950s and 1960s, T.H. Marshall divided the rights of the citizen into three groups: civil, political and social (Marshall, 1994):

- *Civil*, or legal, rights concern the 'liberty of the person, freedom of speech, thought and faith, the right to own property and to conclude valid contracts and the right to justice'.
- *Political* rights concern the right to take part in the democratic process of electing governments.
- *Social* rights include the right to 'a modicum of economic welfare and security . . . the right to share to the full in the social heritage and to live the life of a civilized being according to the standards prevailing in that society' (Marshall, 1999: 9).

The last of these categories, social rights, is the most controversial because of its link with the welfare state. Critics from the radical left have attacked the idea because of claims that equality of social rights can overcome or ameliorate class-based inequality (Hindess, 1993). The guarantee of a minimum income or a minimum level of provision of certain services may, if effectively administered, eliminate the worst excesses of inequality but, it is argued, this does not eliminate inequality. The idea of citizenship has traditionally been defended by those on the right of the political spectrum, since it appears to accommodate the principles of the free individual and a compassionate market system (Saunders, 1994). However, the 20th century rise of 'social rights' in the form of the welfare state has been the focus of criticism from the political New Right, which has wished to see a 'rolling back' of the welfare state.

Citizenship implies not only rights but also duties or obligations. In earlier eras, obligations were often numerous – for example, duties owed to the local church or to the lord of the manor or, less formally, to neighbours. As the rights of citizenship became formalized, so did the obligations. In the civil/legal area citizens are expected to observe the law and, for example, to pay taxes, serve on juries and, if called upon, to bear arms to defend the state. In the political arena, citizens are expected to take part in the democratic process by voting, a duty enforced by law in a few countries, for example Australia. In the social area, the right to education is matched by the legal obligation of parents to send children to school. The right to social security is matched by the obligation to work when work is available. The right to a retirement pension is linked with the expectation of having worked for a living. Unemployment benefit is matched by an expectation that the unemployed will actively search for paid work and undertake required training. However, as Roche (1992: 159) argues, there is also an expectation of a 'right to work' and high levels of unemployment undermine this social contract. In general, however, as the idea of social rights developed during the 20th century, there was no commensurate increase in citizen obligations, except the obligation to continue to pay taxes to meet the increasing cost of the welfare state.

While rights to leisure *time*, including holidays with pay, can be said to arise from civil rights, any rights to leisure *services* arise as a social right. The idea is implicit in the concept of *standards* of provision, as discussed in Chapter 7. This principle, applied in areas such as education, housing and public health as well as in leisure services, suggests that people have a right to expect a certain minimum standard of public services regardless of where they live in a country, and that government should ensure that right. This is not an uncontested view: a free market perspective would be that people who are not satisfied with services in one area should simply move to an area where the combination of service level and taxation suits their needs and that those (local government) areas which wish to attract and retain residents should ensure that they maintain an appropriate level of services. For 'basic services' the standards approach is probably more widely accepted – but the question arises as to whether leisure services are included among those 'basic services' which are seen as 'social rights'.

In a number of contributions, Fred Coalter (1988: 31–32; 1998) has critically discussed the relationship between citizens' (social) rights and leisure services. His concern is primarily with the way interest in this nexus has exerted an undue influence on the theoretical study of leisure, resulting in an overemphasis on the role of public sector provision. The bulk of leisure services in Western countries is provided by the market, which is therefore likely to be satisfying *some* citizens' rights in regard to leisure provision. It is therefore not necessarily the case that only publicly provided leisure services are capable of contributing to the satisfaction of social rights.

Coalter suggests that the idea of 'citizens' rights' was an accepted basis of government policy in the UK, at least until the 1970s. In fact, the evidence for this is quite thin; his sources are primarily other academics who hold similar views. Wilson (1988: 10) makes a similar claim, that 'the right to leisure' is included among the social rights of citizenship, but without providing any evidence that this is in fact recognized by governments. In the 1970s the UK Labour government of the day produced a White Paper on *Sport and Recreation* (Department of the Environment, 1975), which accepted the view of an earlier parliamentary inquiry that recreation should be regarded as part of the 'general fabric of the social services' (see p. 54). Coalter states merely that this *implies* that leisure services had been recognized as rights of citizenship. The Marshallian schema outlined above would lead to the conclusion that something which is declared to be part of the social services must therefore be regarded as social right of citizenship, but it is notable that the final step, of explicitly declaring leisure provision as a right, has never been taken by a UK government. It is notable that, even with a Labour government in power, the 1975 White Paper was not followed by an Act of Parliament. And it is notable that a government which, in the international sphere, endorsed the Council of Europe's 'Sport for All' policy and the accompanying charter, did not explicitly declare sport, or access to sport facilities, as a right of citizenship. It had long been the wish of the leisure management profession in the UK that a statutory obligation be placed on local government to provide leisure facilities, but such provision has remained discretionary – hardly a ringing endorsement of a right of citizenship.

A similar reticence has existed in Australia, where a 1985 Labour government policy document on recreation spoke of the valuable contribution that various forms of leisure activity could make to a 'healthy lifestyle' (Brown, 1985), but stopped short of declaring any right of access to leisure services. In an Australian policy statement on culture, again from a Labour government, the recommendation of a panel of experts that the government commit itself to a 'Charter of Cultural Rights' was reproduced as a 'Preamble' to the policy document, but ignored in the main body of the document (Commonwealth of Australia, 1994).

In the UK, the philosophy of the Conservative government, which came to power in 1979 under Margaret Thatcher, was to 'roll back' the welfare state rather than extend it, so earlier talk of leisure as a social service was soon abandoned. In the early 1990s, however, under the leadership of John Major, the Conservative government enshrined the idea of citizenship in the *The Citizen's Charter: Raising the Standard* (Prime Minister, 1991). The Charter, however, involved a quite limited conceptualization of 'the citizen' as a consumer of public services, although principles were set out for areas such as health services, transport, social services, the police and postal services. With its emphasis on delivery of public services, the Charter was more of a 'political administrative initiative' than a 'full rights-orientated constitutional approach' (Doern, 1993). With its emphasis on 'choice' and 'value for money', it could be seen as a stalking horse for privatization of public services which failed to measure up to expectations. The opening paragraphs of the Charter stated:

> Choice can . . . be extended within the public sector. When the public sector remains responsible for a function it can introduce competition and pressure for efficiency by contracting with the private sector for its provision. . . . choice can be restored by alternative forms of provision, and creating a wider range of options wherever that is cost-effective. . . . Through the Citizen's Charter the Government is now determined to drive reforms further into the core of the public services, extending the benefits of choice, competition and commitment to service more widely.
>
> (Prime Minister, 1991: 4)

Thus *The Citizen's Charter* could be said to be focused more on the right of individuals as *customers* than their rights as citizens.

Local authorities' responses to the Charter in a range of service areas were assessed through 'performance indicators' developed by the Audit Commission. As Lentell (1996) points out, the limited attempts of the Audit Commission to achieve this in relation to leisure services raised as many questions as they answered.

With another change of government, to 'New Labour' in 1997, this particular approach was not abandoned, but modified. 'Charters' mushroomed under Labour: a total of 30 from different government agencies is listed on the Cabinet Office (2001) 'Service First' website. However, as with the former Conservative government's initiative, the rights enshrined in these charters are *consumer* rights: they are concerned with the efficient and fair administration of services rather than with consideration of the overall range and quantum of services to which the individual might be entitled.

With the change of government to New Labour, came the 'Third Way' in politics, as discussed in Chapter 2. Third Way politics, as outlined by Anthony Giddens, involves a re-examination of the relationship between rights and obligations:

> Having abandoned collectivism, third way politics looks for a new relationship between the individual and the community, a redefinition of rights and obligations. One might suggest as a prime motto for the new politics, *no rights without responsibilities*. Government has a whole cluster of responsibilities for its citizens and others, including the protection of the vulnerable. Old-style social democracy, however, was inclined to treat rights as unconditional claims. With expanding individualism should come an extension of individual obligations. Unemployment benefits, for example, should carry the obligation to actively look for work, and it is up to governments to ensure that welfare systems do not discourage active search. As an ethical principle, 'no rights without responsibilities' must apply not only to welfare recipients, but to everyone. It is highly important for social democrats to stress this, because otherwise the precept can be held to apply only to the poor or to the needy – as tends to be the case with the political right.
>
> (Giddens, 1998: 65)

The nature of the obligations of non-welfare recipients is not, however, spelled out. It is a sign of the confusing politics of our times that, while these principles were expounded by a Labour government in the UK, on the other side of the world, in Australia, a right-wing conservative government, under John Howard, was expounding a similar principle, using the term 'mutual obligation', under which unemployed people can be required to 'work for dole' and could lose benefits if they fail to fill a prescribed quota of job interviews.

While informal leisure-related obligations exist for the citizen – for example, to support various charitable fund-raising efforts, to serve on committees or act as sports officials, to attend social functions and, in smaller communities, to 'turn out' for sporting or celebratory events – obligations in regard to state-provided services have traditionally been virtually non-existent. The nearest to an 'obligation' is the notion of 'user pays', in whole or part. This increasingly common feature of public leisure services reflects the idea that the state should not bear the full cost of leisure services, but just that proportion which produces 'social' benefits for the community, while the individual bears the cost of the 'private' benefits (see Chapter 3).

Social rights arising from the idea of citizenship may be seen as more meaningful and practical and less contentious than the idea of human rights, but along with the possibility of implementation goes political dispute and uncertainty. Despite the rhetoric, it would seem that government practice implicitly reflects the view of Roberts, that leisure demands are so numerous, diverse and 'capable of indefinite extension' that servicing them 'cannot be made into a right of citizenship' (Roberts, 1978: 155).

SUMMARY: RIGHTS AND PUBLIC POLICY

- Declarations of human rights and of citizens' rights, including certain rights in the area of leisure and tourism, while they may have a philosophical or biological basis, are clearly political in nature. Declarations of rights are not scientific statements, they are values-based and reflect political commitment. Thus international rights declarations and covenants achieve legitimacy only when they have been formally ratified by governments. Once ratified the declarations have a status similar to an international treaty and become part of international law. Subsequent failure of governments to observe such statements become the focus of political protest and/or legal proceedings. By contrast, attempts have been made, particularly in the leisure studies literature, to imbue statements of need with a scientific status.
- The discussion in this chapter leads to the conclusion that, if they are to form the basis for public policy, statements of need must also be seen as values-based and political in nature. Thus rights and needs, in this context, are one and the same thing. It follows that public policy must inevitably be about values and politics.

RESOURCES

Human rights: Cranston (1973); Kamenka and Tay (1978); MacFarlane (1985); Brownlie (1992); Donnelly (1994); Villiers (2001).

Human rights and tourism: Edgell (1990) reproduces a number of international agreements and declarations as appendices.

Social tourism: Haulot (1981); McCabe (2009); Minnaert et al. (2009).

People with disabilities: Darcy and Taylor (2009).

Citizenship: Roche (1992); Doern (1993); Saunders (1993); Turner and Hamilton (1994); Lentell (1996); Coalter (1998); Houlihan (2001).
Sport: Kidd and Donnelly (2000).

QUESTIONS/EXERCISES

1. What is the difference between a 'right' and a 'need'?

2. In what ways are the right to: (i) travel; and (ii) leisure infringed by governments?

3. Marshall outlines three types of rights of the citizen: what are they and how is each defined?

4. If individuals have 'obligations' as well as 'rights', what obligations are there in: (i) leisure; and (ii) tourism?

5. In what way can declarations of rights be seen as potential threats to freedom?

6. Examine any one of the declarations in Boxes 4.1–4.4 and discuss the implications for public leisure and tourism policy at: (i) national level; and (ii) local level.

chapter 5

The Market Versus the State

INTRODUCTION

In a book on public policy, it is important to examine, theoretically as well as practically, the role of the state. In Chapter 2 this issue was considered from a number of political ideological perspectives. Here the issue is considered using the perspective of academic disciplines, although the two types of perspective involved cannot always be easily separated. For example, Marxism is both a political ideology and a mode of academic analysis. At the other end of the political spectrum, neo-liberalism is generally associated with mainstream economics. The rest of this chapter is divided into four sections:

- a brief discussion of the current worldwide triumph of capitalism;
- an outline of the approach of *mainstream economics* in analysing the role of the state within capitalism;
- a summary of *market failure* arguments for state activity arising from the branch of mainstream economics known as *welfare economics*;
- discussion of social/political arguments for state intervention not arising from mainstream economics;
- a number of *further issues* concerning the role of the state, including: (i) the question of facilitating versus direct provision; and (ii) the effects of globalization;
- an outline of recent history in the role of the state, particularly in the UK and Australia.

THE TRIUMPH OF CAPITALISM

The first half of the 20th century saw two World Wars, which cost tens of millions of lives, and the Great Depression, which saw unemployment rates of 30 per cent and untold suffering. This did not provide a good case for the capitalist system. The idea that some alternative system might offer the chance of a better world was entirely plausible. The main alternative at the time was the communist system of the Soviet Union and Eastern Europe. But these regimes failed to deliver democratic rights or economic prosperity and collapsed at the end of the 1980s. Most of the world, with the partial exception of China and a handful of minor states, now operates, or is attempting to operate, under a 'capitalist' or 'market' economic system. In this system the process of organizing the production and distribution of goods and services is largely in the hands of a mass of private enterprise organizations operating through market processes, with governments playing a restricted role. China is attempting the difficult balancing act of operating a capitalist economic system while maintaining a communist political system.

By the 1990s, therefore, there seemed to be a worldwide consensus which saw market capitalism as a basically acceptable system for running economic affairs. Nevertheless, in most countries, about a third of all economic activity was accounted for by government activities (Hodge, 2000: 3). Some wanted to see less state activity and some more, but few seem to wished to see the system changed fundamentally, to the extent that the society would no longer be basically 'capitalist'. Capitalism was 'triumphant' around the world: it had its critics but no apparent realistic alternatives.

The global financial crisis that struck in 2008 and at the time if writing was thought by some to threaten another global depression similar to that experienced in the 1930s, raised some doubts about 'extreme capitalism', as discussed in Chapter 2, but the remedy has been seen as a tightening of regulations and, for some, a shift towards social democratic-style reforms rather than replacement of the system.

Thus the economic rationalist perspective, even if subject to greater oversight and state intervention, still holds political sway in most of the world at present. It is therefore important that anyone studying the public policy process should understand its basis, which lies in *mainstream economics*, sometimes referred to as *orthodox economics*. This is the basic approach to economics taught in business and economics courses in most Western universities.

MAINSTREAM ECONOMICS

Introduction

The idea that the market mechanism is the 'norm' and government activity is appropriate only in certain specified circumstances is the basis of *mainstream* economics. It is referred to here as *mainstream* economics to distinguish it from various forms of Marxist, socialist or radical economics, which reject the market system on ideological grounds, and from other critics, such as Galbraith (1973) and Hirsch (1977), who questioned aspects of mainstream economics on more technical grounds.

Taken as a whole, mainstream economics should perhaps be referred to as *political economy*, the area of social theory which spans politics and economics. When interpreted in its most extreme form this framework is referred to as 'economic rationalism', and it takes on ideological overtones associated with the neo-liberal beliefs outlined in Chapter 2. What is often neglected is that mainstream economics, while primarily concerned with market processes, also includes a well-developed theory of the role of the state, which identifies situations in which the state might, and even should, 'intervene' in a basically capitalist market economy, but which is still consistent with the continuation of the market system, indeed in some cases is fundamental to its continued viability. This body of theory, sometimes referred to as *welfare economics*, provides a useful framework for examining the role of the state within the market system and can, and is, used by those of more left-leaning political persuasions to successfully *justify* state activity within a market environment.

The review below includes few references to sources since what is presented is 'standard' economic theory, widely accepted among economists, but references to texts which outline the theory in more depth are given in the Resources section at the end of the chapter. The review is divided into four sections, dealing in turn with:

- the workings of the market in general;
- the role of the state;
- types of market failure.

The workings of the market

The free, unregulated market mechanism should, according to mainstream economic theory, be the best means of organizing the delivery of goods and services to meet people's needs. In the 'marketplace' people indicate their desires, preferences and priorities for goods and services by their willingness to pay, or not to pay, for the goods and services on offer. Entrepreneurs note this willingness-to-pay and this justifies them in hiring the labour and investing in the capital necessary to provide the goods or services in demand. Entrepreneurs bid in the 'marketplace' to buy the labour and other resources, such as land, buildings, raw materials and equipment, which are necessary to produce the goods and services which people demand. Things that people want are successfully sold; things people do not want stay on the supermarket shelves. The entrepreneurs use this information about what people want and are willing and able to pay for, and what they do not want and/or are not willing or able to pay for, to adjust their production schedules so that supply is brought into line with demand.

No central body is needed to organize this – the market mechanism brings the resources, the supplier and the consumer together: the consumer pays and the consumer is believed to be 'sovereign' because he or she decides whether or not to buy. Fully articulated, the economic theory is, of course, more complex than this, and includes explanations of how consumers with different tastes and preferences balance their purchases within their income constraints, how firms respond to market information and seek to maximize profits, and how capital and labour markets work. Some economic theory involves the development of mathematical models to replicate these various market processes.

There are some stringent conditions attached to the analysis, the most important of which is that there must be competition among suppliers – monopoly negates the whole analysis.

The role of the state

The mainstream economic theory concludes that, in a competitive market situation, state activity should be kept to a minimum, because governments are *less* effective, efficient and responsive in meeting people's needs than the market. In fact, it is argued, the state, through its coercive powers, such as regulation and taxation, is a potential threat to the freedom of operation of the market and *distorts* market processes. Government activity should therefore be permitted only where it is unavoidable, for example in providing a framework of law and order and enforceable contracts, and all efforts should be made to keep the activities of government to a minimum.

American economist Milton Friedman, who was a 'guru' of economic rationalists in the 1970s and a staunch advocate of the market system, quotes approvingly the 18th century political economist Adam Smith, who outlined three essential duties of government:

> . . . first, the duty of protecting the society from the violence and invasion of other independent societies; secondly, the duty of protecting, as far as possible, every member of the society from the injustice or oppression of every other member of it, or the duty of establishing an exact administration of justice; and, thirdly, the duty of erecting and maintaining certain public works and certain public institutions, which it can never be for the interest of any individual, or small number of individuals, to erect and maintain; because the profit could never repay the expense to any individual or small number of individuals, though it may frequently do much more than repay it to a great society.

(Adam Smith, quoted in Friedman and Friedman, 1979: 49)

Thus national defence, maintenance of the rule of law and 'public works' are seen as necessary and legitimate activities for government. Friedman adds a fourth, namely 'the duty to protect members of the community who cannot be regarded as 'responsible' individuals' (Friedman and Friedman, 1979: 53). These include children and the mentally ill or handicapped. In the discussion below, Friedman's category of 'public works' has been subsumed under the category of 'market failure', and his fourth argument is widened somewhat to include other social/political arguments for government activity.

According to this argument, four broad functions of government within a primarily market system can be identified:

- national defence;
- provision of a system of law and order;
- correcting market failure;
- social/political arguments.

Each of these, and its relation with leisure sport and tourism, is discussed in turn below.

National defence

Leisure and tourism have some indirect connections with national defence. Certain sporting activities, such as equestrian activities, fencing and archery, have a military history and these and other sports are seen as valuable for training and maintaining fitness of military personnel. Sport has long been promoted as a means of maintaining physical fitness for military preparedness for the general (male) population. For example, in the *Book of Sports*, a declaration made by King James I of England in 1618, the King ordered that the prohibition on the playing of sports imposed by Puritan local authorities be lifted because, among other things: 'this prohibition barreth the common and meaner sort of people from using such exercises as may make their bodies more able for war, when His Majesty or his successors shall have occasion to use them'.

More recently, concerns about the lack of fitness of young men in times of war prompted the enactment of the Physical Training and Recreation Act and establishment of the National Fitness Council in the UK between the two World Wars (Hill, 2002: 152; Beavan, 2005: 163) and, in Australia, the passing of the National Fitness Act in 1941 (Bloomfield, 2003: 34). So, in an indirect way, national defence provides some justification for government involvement in sport. The military are also, incidentally, direct providers of leisure and tourism attractions, in the form of military bands and tattoos, air shows, monuments and museums and, in the UK, such rituals as the Changing of the Guard at Buckingham Palace and the institution of the Yeomen of the Guard at the Tower of London.

National defence also gives rise to government *restrictions* on leisure activity – for example, the military often occupy substantial areas of land and water that would be ideal for recreation. And international travel restrictions, such as visa requirements, are often, at least partly related to national security considerations.

Law and order

The impact on leisure, sport and tourism of the government activity of maintaining a framework of law and enforcement is largely restrictive:

- Legal restrictions apply to activities that are seen to have anti-social and/or moral implications, such as gambling, the sale of alcohol and use of recreational drugs.
- In some cases, government assumes ownership of certain assets and regulates them to prevent a 'free for all' – for example, airspace, radio and television broadcast channels and coastal waterways and fisheries.
- Some regulatory activities are designed to protect economic interests, for example copyright laws.
- Others are designed for public safety, for example fire and safety regulations in places of entertainment or in transport.
- Gun laws are a particularly controversial area where the recreational activity of hunting is affected by the demands of law and order.
- In a more positive sense, public leisure provision for young people is often justified on the grounds that if socially acceptable outlets are not available then young people are more likely to engage in anti-social, delinquent behaviour (Nichols, 2007).

Correcting market failure

Friedman sees the third role, 'of erecting and maintaining certain public works and certain public institutions' as raising the 'most troublesome issue', because it can be 'interpreted to justify unlimited extensions of government power'. Much of the 'economics of the state' is aimed at analysing this third, 'troublesome', category – that is, attempting to analyse those situations where an activity is not profitable for the private sector to undertake, but is beneficial to society at large. In general such situations are referred to as cases of *market failure*.

Market failure refers to situations where the market mechanism does not work very well or at all. Another term used in this context is *inefficiency*. Perfectly operating markets are seen as an *efficient* way of distributing goods and services, ensuring maximum output at minimum cost. Market failure is said to produce inefficiencies, involving the allocation of resources (land, capital, labour) which is less than optimal. Measures taken to correct the market failure are therefore said to produce an increase in the efficiency of the economy. A number of different types of market failure have been identified by economists; eight of these are discussed in turn in the following section. The types of market failure considered below are:

- public goods and services;
- externalities/neighbourhood effects;
- mixed goods;
- merit goods;
- option demand;
- infant industries;
- size of project;
- natural monopoly.

These ideas have for some time been widely accepted in the economics literature, albeit with slightly varying terminology, interpretation and emphasis. While each criterion/phenomenon is discussed separately, it should be noted that more than one criterion usually applies to a particular case of state provision.

Social/political arguments for government involvement

A number of arguments for government involvement might, in some circumstances, find favour with mainstream economists; they are in fact less 'technical' in nature and so have been treated separately below. They are:

- equity/humanitarian arguments;
- economic management and development;
- incidental enterprise; and
- tradition.

Types of market failure

Public goods and services

In economic jargon, *public* goods, or services, have two characteristics: they are *non-excludable* and *non-rival*. Non-excludable means that it is not technically possible to exclude anyone from enjoying the benefits of the good or service. Non-rival means that one person's enjoyment of the good or service does not preclude others from enjoying it also. The classic examples of public goods and services are national defence and the maintenance of law and order – two of Adam Smith's basic functions of government, as discussed above. Another example is the provision of street lighting. These services are *non-excludable* because people in the areas affected cannot be excluded from benefiting from the service, and they are *non-rival* because the provision of the service to one person does not affect its provision to others.

In these circumstances the usual market mechanism, where consumers pay the provider for the service they individually receive, cannot function effectively: there is 'market failure'. The market system, left to its own devices, will not, in these circumstances, produce what people want or would benefit from. Government intervention to provide the service and recoup the costs via taxation is therefore seen as a solution. Examples of public services in this sense in the field of leisure and tourism or relevant to it include:

- free-to-air broadcasting;
- public pride in the success of local or national athletes;
- open public events, such as firework displays or street parades;
- street signs and street lighting that facilitate access to leisure venues;
- major scenic amenities, such as a conserved historic or natural environment.

In the case of broadcasting, the product is 'free to air' and is therefore a public good/service; the fact that some governments choose to finance this by means of a licence to operate a television set and some by taxation, and commercial organizations finance it by selling advertising space, does not alter its intrinsic 'public good' nature.

In some cases the public good dimension of a facility or service is directly enjoyed by the general public – as in a firework display or broadcasting. In other cases the enjoyment is more indirect – for example, the general satisfaction and pride people might obtain from knowledge that the nation's, or even the world's, natural or cultural heritage is being preserved. People do not need to visit such places as the Tower of London, the Lake District, the Parthenon or the Great Barrier Reef to obtain some satisfaction from the knowledge that they exist and are being protected from damage. This satisfaction is worth something to people who experience it. These non-users or non-visitors are sometimes described as 'vicarious' consumers, and their enjoyment is sometimes referred to as 'psychic' benefit, in contrast to financial or material benefit. Governments feel entitled to contribute to the upkeep and preservation of these phenomena on behalf of these vicarious consumers.

The maintenance of law and order and street lighting were mentioned above as examples of 'classic' public services, but such services also have important implications specifically for urban leisure and tourism. If city streets are poorly lit and considered unsafe, then certain groups in the community are discriminated against in terms of their access to leisure at night, including the elderly, women and young people and those without access to private transport. In addition, such areas are not attractive to tourists. Law and order and street lighting can therefore be seen as important leisure-related public services.

In the case of the 'pure' public good, which fully meets the non-excludable and non-rival criteria, it is technically impossible to charge the consumer for the service. In other cases it is possible to conceive of a charge being made, but the cost of collecting the charge would be likely to exceed the revenue, for example a public open space with many access points. In this case the facility becomes, de facto, a public good.

It could be argued that people could contribute voluntarily for their enjoyment of public goods and services, but this would give rise to the problem of the *free rider* – the person who enjoys the good or service in question but does not pay, assuming that others will bear the cost. Contributions via the taxation system are seen as a fair and efficient means of collecting payment. It might be argued that this can result in some people contributing who have not seen or did not enjoy the goods or services involved but, in fact, taxation is levied on the basis of ability to pay, rather than services rendered to the individual taxpayer.

Externalities/neighbourhood effects

Externalities, sometimes referred to as *neighbourhood effects* or *third party effects*, arise when identifiable third parties are affected by transactions between providers and consumers. Externalities can be 'negative' or 'positive'.

The classic example of a *negative externality* is pollution: for example, smoke pollution from a factory or noise pollution from an airport. The factory or airport is the *first* party and its customers are the *second* party, and they are involved in the transaction of producing and buying the products of the factory or airport; the residents adversely affected by pollution are the *third* party; they are affected by negative externalities. There is market failure here because the producers and consumers are not taking account of all the costs involved in producing the product in question: they are ignoring the costs imposed on the third party. This is a distortion of the market. To overcome this market failure, either the producer should be required (by law) to install equipment to eliminate the pollution or the third party should be compensated, by the government making a levy on the factory or airport owners on behalf of the third party or by the third party suing the polluter in court. Either way the costs of the factory or airport would rise (external costs would be 'internalized'); and the prices it would have to charge the users would rise. Current moves to establish *carbon emissions trading schemes* to counteract global warming are examples of this process at work.

In the extreme case, costs would rise so much that the product would be priced out of the market and the factory or airport would be forced to close down. This would be accepted as right and proper by the economist because, in the initial situation the market is seen as distorted because the factory or airport – and the buyers of their services – are not meeting all their costs, and the product or service is artificially cheap: it is said to be *overproducing*.

This all sounds perfectly rational and reasonable. In practice of course, such an issue could become very controversial and would focus on what minimal level of pollution is considered acceptable before the polluter is required to do something about it. It should be noted that the 'offender' in situations of externality is not always an organization – it can be an individual. A classic example is road congestion. Every additional vehicle which uses a road increases congestion and imposes a cost on other road users, in terms of delays and increased fuel consumption, not to mention pollution costs imposed on the community at large.

In the leisure and tourism area, examples of negative externalities arise when facilities, such as pubs, nightclubs or resorts, or tourist traffic impose noise or congestion costs on neighbouring properties.

Positive externalities work in the opposite direction. The third party can gain *benefits* which they do not pay for. In that situation the producer is receiving a lower income than is justified (that is, not getting income from the third party beneficiaries); and it *underproduces* because the product or service is more expensive than it should be. In this case we talk of *positive externalities*.

An example might be the private golf course which preserves pleasant views for surrounding residents. The latter pay in terms of the higher cost of real estate, but not to the golf course owner. In fact many 'resort'-style developments attempt to recoup this externality by developing the golf course *and* the surrounding homes. When Walt Disney built Disneyland in California in the 1950s, the resultant tourism provided enormous gains for landowners in the area, who sold land to hoteliers to service the theme park. When Disneyworld was built in Florida in the 1970s the Disney organization bought up much of the surrounding land – ensuring that it 'internalized' the externality.

In the case of tourism, the basic attraction of a destination area may be publicly owned – for example, beaches, mountains, lakes or an historic town centre. The whole of the private sector tourist industry in the area may nevertheless be dependent on this resource. The resources are de facto public goods enjoyed by the public, but part of the benefit is gained by identifiable enterprises in the tourism industry and might be termed externalities. Valuing these externalities may become an issue when questions arise as to the cost of maintaining the basic attractions and the contributions which the tourist industry is asked to make. This idea of the tourist industry being dependent on a common public attraction is known as the *asset theory* of tourism (Gray, 1982).

A further example of positive externalities – or the prevention of negative externalities – is the question of provision of leisure facilities for youth. It is widely believed that young people in particular are liable to engage in antisocial activities in their leisure time – that is activities which impose external cost on others. Such externalities may be short term and immediate – for example, vandalism and hooliganism, or long term – for example, becoming involved with criminal subcultures or harmful drugs. The private sector provides some of the leisure facilities used by young people, but since it receives no financial benefit from the externalities produced (for example, the reduction in vandalism and hooliganism), it will tend to underprovide. State provision or subsidy of suitable leisure facilities for young people is therefore seen as justified (Nichols, 2007).

Mixed goods

The economists Baumol and Bowen (1976) coined the term 'mixed goods' to refer to those goods or services which combine public good and private good characteristics, applying the idea particularly to the performing arts. For example, when a person attends an arts perform-ance, they argued:

- First, the person gains a personal benefit (the enjoyment of the performance), which he or she might be expected to pay for – a standard market process.
- Second, the person subsequently becomes a conveyor and supporter of *culture*: a contribu-tor to a more civilized community – a form of public good.
- Third, cultural industries are supported and this is believed to benefit communities in a number of ways, such as improvement in 'quality of life', 'creativity' and spin-off in economic areas such as tourism, design, the attraction of industry and commerce and a lively media sector – a form of externality.
- Finally, arts facilities and organizations can be a source of 'civic pride' even to those who do not use them – a public good.

(Baumol and Bowen, 1976)

Therefore it is believed that the state should pay for part of the cost of the public arts performance, in recognition of these wider social benefits that are partly public goods and partly positive externalities. This is then a justification for a *subsidized* theatre/opera/concert seat rather than either a totally free one or a fully commercially priced one. A similar argument could be applied to an urban park:

- A person entering the park obtains a certain amount of enjoyment, which he or she might be expected to pay for.
- The park also offers externality benefits to the owners of the buildings that overlook it. These benefits are reflected in the value of the land, which in turn is reflected in the rates levied on the properties, so some payment returns to the public provider of the park – the council – for the benefit received.
- A further group of beneficiaries of the park are those people who walk or drive past and benefit from viewing a green space rather than a built-up area – the benefit may be very small per person, but many thousands, or even millions, may enjoy this benefit in the course of the year.
- Finally, parks produce a benefit in cities by dispersing pollution and thus contributing to cleaner air.

Thus a public park produces a mixture of public and private benefits. In practice, as discussed above, few parks charge users for the 'private' element of the visit by means of an entrance fee, because of the likely cost of collecting the fees.

Rural public open spaces, such as public forests, country parks and national parks, are also mixed goods, in that they are enjoyed by: (i) the users directly (private good); (ii) in some cases by vicarious users, as discussed above (public good); (iii) owners of property overlooking the open space (externality); and (iv) the general public who visit or live in the area and benefit from pleasant views (public good). This last phenomenon also occurs in relation to the benefit produced by the exercise of general planning powers by councils to prevent unsightly develop-ment in rural or heritage areas: the resultant amenity which people enjoy in their leisure time can be seen as a public good.

Participation in sport or physical recreation can also be viewed as a mixed good:

- Individuals engaging in physical exercise gain some private benefit from the experience, in the form of increased fitness and enjoyment of the experience.
- An individual who is inactive, and at risk of deteriorating health, and who is persuaded to take exercise resulting in improved health, produces benefits for others, including the person's family, his or her employer and either taxpayers or other payers of health insurance, depending on how the costs of illness are normally met.

Thus, it is argued, the state, on behalf of these beneficiaries (family, employer, taxpayer, health insurance subscribers), is justified in subsidizing sport and exercise programmes and facilities or providing the individual with the means to buy such services. It might be argued that the direct beneficiaries from a person's good health should pay rather than the community at large through the state. This is recognized by those employers who provide exercise facilities at the place of work; some even *require* their employees to take exercise, and health insurance companies also become involved in sport and fitness in various ways. However, because the benefits may be spread over a number of beneficiaries, including government organizations such as the health service, subsidization and promotion of sport and exercise is accepted as an area of legitimate state involvement.

Sable and Kling (2001) extend the concept and use the term 'double public good' to draw attention to the proposition that private consumption itself may also have externality qualities.

Merit goods

In some cases 'society' may decide that certain goods or services are highly desirable for the individual but that individuals require time, experience/exposure or even education in order to come to appreciate them; individuals are incapable immediately of appreciating their value. In this case, it is argued, the state is justified in intervening to provide that exposure to the good or service, by making direct provision or subsidizing others to do so. The most common example of a merit good is education; however, as with many merit goods, it is difficult to disengage the 'merit good' argument from the 'public good' and 'externality' aspects.

The merit good argument can be criticized for being elitist or paternalistic. Who is to decide what is meritorious? The idea that the general public is incapable of appreciating the 'finer things of life' unaided and that certain well-informed groups are capable of identifying these oversights and correcting for them can be a difficult proposition to defend. However, the process of deciding on what are and are not merit goods need not be elitist. In the same way that the smoker may agree that he or she should give up and may be happy to see public funds used to conduct anti-smoking campaigns, so many people might be willing to see public funds devoted to the support of the 'finer things of life', aware that they themselves might benefit in due course from such a move.

In the leisure area, examples of merit goods include environmentally based outdoor recreation resources that may be deemed to require education and interpretation to develop public appreciation, and the more demanding art forms. Generally, the merit good argument can be used to justify educationally orientated programmes, for either children or adults.

Option demand

Another idea put forward to support public sector provision is the concept of *option demand* – sometimes referred to as *existence value* and sometimes as *bequest value*. This involves the proposition that there may be certain goods or services which groups of individuals do not at present use and may have no specific plans to use, but which they feel should be maintained so that the option to use them is always there, for themselves or for their children or grandchildren. This applies particularly when the loss of the phenomenon in question would be irreversible. In this case people might wish the government to intervene to ensure the preservation of the option. The idea is similar to the vicarious consumer in relation to public goods, but in this case the vicarious consumption is concerned with something which *may* happen in the future.

This argument could apply to virtually all leisure facilities or heritage resources that individuals do not currently use, but of whose existence they approve.

Infant industries

If a country, state or city sets out to establish a new industry where well-established outside competitors already exist, the industry may find difficult in getting started. In such an instance it is argued that governments may be justified in intervening for a period to protect the new, *infant industry* from its competitors until it is well established and can survive without help. Such intervention could include subsidies of various kinds, such as cash grants, tax breaks and low rents, or tariffs or controls placed on the competitors.

This idea is, however, not accepted by all mainstream economists because it involves governments trying to 'pick winners' – that is, deciding which new industries should be supported and which should not – and governments are thought by many to be very bad at this (although some point out that certain governments, such as Japan, appear to have been quite successful at it). It can also be seen as featherbedding and preventing the new industry from becoming efficient in order to compete in the marketplace. It is argued that if the industry experiences a loss-making period while establishing itself, these losses should be borne by the investor as part of the set-up/investment costs, not by the taxpayer.

The infant industry argument applies particularly to tourism ventures, and particularly in developing countries or less developed areas of developed countries. The argument can also be applied in modified form in the cultural sector, such as film and the local content of television programmes. In these instances, the industry is generally seen as permanently infant, in relation to the size and power of the American industry in particular.

Size of project

It has been argued that certain investment projects are too large and have too long a development timescale to be taken on by the private sector, and can only be handled by government. This argument has however now become somewhat outmoded as we see private sector financing of such mammoth projects as Disneyland Paris, the Alaska oil pipeline and the Channel Tunnel (although not in every case without substantial losses and emergency government involvement).

Natural monopoly

The mainstream economic scenario of the market system producing the optimum range of goods and services depends on the market being perfectly competitive – that is, no single or small group of firms being able to dominate a market situation. Once the number of firms becomes small (oligopoly), or even singular (monopoly), excess profits are made and the consumer loses out. Governments in capitalist economies therefore generally have powers to regulate, and even break up, monopolies.

In leisure and tourism, however, there are often 'natural' monopolies. For example, there is only one Tower of London, only one Grand Canyon and only one Great Barrier Reef. Some natural monopolies are social or economic in nature – for example, major transport infrastructure or sewerage systems, where it makes sense to have only one operator. In these instances, the argument goes, government is justified in intervening to prevent private operators exploiting monopolistic advantage, particularly by charging extortionate prices. Such government intervention may take the form of regulatory intervention – for example, the regulation of air fares – or complete public ownership and/or control, as is the case with the national heritage.

Market failure in summary

A summary of the main features of the above arguments is provided in Table 5.1. Each of the arguments is fairly technical in approach. They attempt to establish that there are things which people want and would probably be prepared to pay for but, for technical reasons, the potential consumers and potential producers are unable to interact effectively and/or efficiently through the normal market mechanisms. Government is therefore seen as the main means of overcoming the problem, by regulation, by levying taxes and paying for the goods or services to be produced, or by subsidizing their production so that the price is reduced and more are consumed.

The question of how governments assess the *extent* of the various forms of demand, and how they might therefore determine just what scale of public funds to devote to the public provision of leisure services, is addressed in Chapter 12.

Types of social/political argument

Equity/humanitarian arguments

Equity means fairness. It impinges on leisure, sport and tourism because of the belief that certain goods and services – a certain quality of life – should be available to all regardless of their ability to pay, and that some leisure goods and services are among the minimal package required for a satisfactory quality of life. This focuses attention on people who are unable to pay for leisure/sport/tourism services, which is in contrast to all the arguments considered so far, which apply to *everyone* regardless of their ability to pay.

The equity argument is the most appealing of arguments because it is not technical in nature, it appeals to people's sense of fairness and everyone likes to think of themselves as fair (Cushman and Hamilton-Smith, 1980). It is at the heart of the difference between the left and the right in politics, since the right believes that a considerable degree of inequality is equitable, because it reflects the rewards given for effort and risk taking, whereas the left thinks that the level of inequality we generally see in Western societies is inequitable and therefore unacceptable. The question is very complex, involving consideration of such issues as the distribution of income, payments in cash or in kind and universal versus targeted benefits.

There is nothing in mainstream economics which suggests that everyone, in a market economy, will be able to earn a 'living wage', since not everyone has skills that command a living wage in the labour marketplace. However, in most societies it is accepted that there is a basic minimum subsistence below which no one should be allowed to fall – hence most societies have introduced 'welfare' payments such as unemployment pay, age and disability pensions and child allowances. There is also 'progressive' taxation, which means that the well-off contribute a greater proportion of their income towards

Table 5.1. Mainstream economics and the role of the state: summary.

Type of service	Characteristics	Leisure, sport, tourism examples
National defence	Protecting the nation/maintaining peace: a public good (see below)	Some sporting activities promoted to maintain physical fitness for military preparedness, e.g. Ancient Greek games and archery in medieval England, 1930s Australia National Fitness campaign. (Hamilton-Smith and Robertson, 1977: 178)
Law and order	Providing a legal framework for society, protection of life and property	Gambling; sale and consumption of alcohol; access to radio and television channels; copyright laws; fire and safety regulations in places of entertainment
Market failure		
Public goods and services	Non-excludable: not practically possible to exclude anyone from enjoying the good or service – so difficult to charge the user Non-rival – one person's enjoyment or consumption does not preclude consumption or enjoyment by others – so extra users do not cost more	Parks: amenity enjoyed by passers-by Pride from national sporting success Firework displays Public broadcasting Public sculpture Heritage conservation (e.g. national parks)
Externalities/ neighbourhood effects	Third parties are affected, positively or negatively, by transactions between providers and consumers: market is distorted by third parties not paying	Negative example: airport noise pollution or pub/club noise disturbance – need for government regulation/rules and/ or levy on polluters Positive example: community health benefits of sport participation – government may subsidize sport to encourage participation and produce social benefits
Mixed goods	Both public good/service and private dimensions (Baumol and Bowen, 1976)	Attendance at an arts event (patrons enjoy personal private benefit; general cultural development of society is a public benefit) – government subsidizes in recognition of public benefit Urban parks (visitors enjoy personal private benefit, but passers-by and neighbours enjoy 'neighbourhood' benefit)

(Continued)

Table 5.1. Continued.

Type of service	Characteristics	Leisure, sport, tourism examples
Merit goods	Goods and services considered beneficial, but with high learning threshold	Subsidy and education for some art forms Cultural heritage Environmental/heritage appreciation education
Option demand	Goods and services that people want to maintain in case they or their successors want to use them in future	Significant environmental, cultural and heritage items
Infant industries	Industries where it is difficult for new entrants to get started because of power of existing companies	Local film industry Local publishing industry Airlines
Size of project	Projects too large for private sector to invest	Few examples today – possibly major resort development, Olympic Games
Natural monopoly	Services where only one supplier is technically required	Unique heritage attractions or environmental resources
Socio-political arguments for governmental involvement		
Equity/ humanitarian arguments	Facilities or services considered essential for a minimum standard of living or quality of life, so must be provided for all (Cushman and Hamilton-Smith, 1980)	Access to play facilities for all children. Access to open space and physical recreation facilities for all – government provision or subsidy
Economic management/ development	Development of facilities or programmes that provide jobs and incomes	Tourism developments – e.g. resorts – government may provide land, tax 'holidays', infrastructure
		Major sports facilities – e.g. Olympic facilities – government may provide land, funds, infrastructure or direct provision
Incidental enterprise	Trading activities that are incidental to a public facility or service	Restaurants/cafes in museums, leisure centres Gift shops in visitor information centres
Tradition	Facilities/services that are valued because they have been provided for many years	Swimming pools in areas where population has declined or use patterns have changed

government costs by way of taxes. In short there is a 'redistribution of income' from rich to poor.

This process, while widely accepted as necessary or desirable, is nevertheless controversial in application. Some argue that taxation of the well-off or rich is too high, resulting in 'disincentives' to work or invest, and that unemployment and pension payments are too high, producing disincentives to seek work. Others argue exactly the opposite. Despite the controversy, the idea of the 'welfare' state is that everyone should have a sufficient minimum income to buy the necessities of life.

If everyone is deemed to have been provided with a minimum income sufficient to provide for the necessities of life, then why are certain additional 'necessities' provided 'in kind' by the state? Why are people not able, with the incomes provided, to pay for their own housing, education, health services – and leisure services?

Suppose that one of the services considered to be a necessity is access to a swimming pool or some similar form of physical recreation. Suppose that the full-cost recovery price for entry to a public pool is £2 and that the average user might be expected to visit once a week. If swimming is considered a necessity of life then welfare payments, such as pensions and unemployment benefit, should include £2 per week to enable everybody to attend – in the same way that such benefits are designed to cover essentials such as food. Instead, it would appear that we have the situation where, say, £1 is included in the pension for such purposes, but the visit to the pool is subsidized by £1. There are many of these sorts of concessions and subsidies. To gain full benefit from them a pensioner must go swimming, live in public housing, be ill periodically, attend an adult education course and so on. Suppose the average pensioner benefits to the extent of £25 a week from such subsidies. One view is that it would be easier, and arguably more respectful of the dignity of the recipient, to increase the benefits by £25 a week and let the pensioner or other beneficiary decide how to spend the money.

One fear might be that the recipients of such a payment might not spend the money on the intended leisure services but might choose to spend it on 'basics', such as food or clothing. This would imply that the pension or other benefit is not adequate to meet basic needs, and that therefore the provision of certain leisure facilities or services is not a priority. Another possibility is that benefit recipients might not spend the money on approved leisure *or* on food or clothing but might 'fritter' it away on 'undesirable' items such as gambling or alcoholic drink. In this case, the argument seems to be: we should subsidize the swimming pool – to provide benefits 'in kind' – because we cannot trust poor people to spend money wisely. This of course is a paternalistic attitude which flies in the face of the values held by proponents of the market system, who believe that individuals are the best judges of their own needs, and indeed is at variance with the values of critics of the market who would advocate self-determination and freedom from bureaucratic regulation.

Thus we can see that the equity-driven concern, that 'the poor cannot afford to pay', can also be seen as an argument which says: 'pay them in kind because you cannot trust them to do the right thing with the money'. Some have advocated a 'voucher' system for leisure along the lines of the American welfare food stamps (Sears, 1975), but this again implies that people cannot be trusted with money. A substantial proportion of the support for public provision and subsidy of leisure services is probably based on the 'poor cannot afford to pay' argument, but few appear to accept that such an argument can also be seen as a form of paternalism reflecting 19th century attitudes towards the 'undeserving' poor.

One of the reasons for the widespread use of the equity approach is that payment in kind is the only means open for some levels of government to make a contribution to the needs of the less well-off sections of the community. Thus a local council cannot give cash handouts to its pensioners but it can give concessions at its various facilities. Further, it could be argued that the *marginal* cost of this sort of assistance is small, especially if facilities have spare capacity, so that the in-kind payment is a cheaper option for the public sector than the cash payment option.

If it is accepted that equity is to be pursued through the provision of in-kind benefits, then the question arises as to how this should be done. In the example discussed above, the pensioner was subsidized by means of a concessionary charge. But some argue that such a targeted approach carries a stigma and that therefore the free or reduced charge should be available for everybody – a universal approach. Subsidizing everybody for the sake of a small number of poor users is, however, costly and could be seen as a wasteful and irresponsible use of public funds.

This does not mean that public leisure facilities should not be subsidized for the general user for market failure reasons as discussed above. But if the aim is to give *particular* benefits to the poor, then arguably some means of targeting that group should ideally be found.

Children and young people merit a special mention under the heading of equity. It might be argued that children and young people are still dependent on their parents and that their parents should therefore provide them with leisure resources. In practice, however, there is a feeling that children and young people should be treated more generously than adults and that children's opportunities should not be entirely dependent on their parents' means. This is shown for example in attempts to provide equal educational opportunity, but also extends to leisure – and in some cases to tourism. Here, the cash versus in-kind argument and paternalistic attitudes (i.e. not trusting the kids with the money) are probably more justified and there is less problem about stigma in offering concessions to young people. However, the problem still arises that some young people have well-off parents, so targeting is not very precise.

Economic management/development

It is widely accepted that governments have a role in overall economic management of market economies – although neo-liberal and committed free-market theorists claim that the ability of government to manage the economy is exaggerated, they have a poor track record in 'picking winners' and they often do more harm than good, so their role should be minimized. Nevertheless, most governments feel responsible for trying to ensure high levels of material prosperity, high levels of employment, a favourable balance of payments and so on. To achieve this they often feel justified in intervening directly to assist industries that can provide jobs or income. Such concerns can be felt at national, state or local level, although the lower levels of government have less power in this area.

Tourism is often seen as a suitable industry for such attention, so this justifies direct provision or indirect support for amenities and enterprises seen as tourist attractions, and encouragement and facilitating of related infrastructure such as transport and accommodation.

Other leisure provision is also seen to be an increasingly important part of the economic infrastructure. Some leisure facilities, for example, golf courses or theatres, are seen as key elements in the local quality-of-life necessary to attract general industrial and commercial investors to an area. Industries are attracted to areas that are attractive to potential employees, thus helping them to recruit and retain staff. Others, such as sports stadia and major events and cultural institutions and events are increasingly seen as industries in themselves. Thus what were previously seen as 'the arts' are now seen as 'cultural industries' or 'creative industries' (Zukin, 1995; Caves, 2000) and sport is increasingly seen as a tool for economic development (Gratton and Henry, 2001).

Incidental enterprise

Often governments find themselves involved in certain areas of service provision, almost by accident, because the provision is incidental to some other activity. For example, governmental bodies that own theatres also find themselves running bars and restaurants which happen to be part of the theatre complex. Museums often include restaurants and gift shops. Public broadcasting bodies become publishers of books, records and videos.

The difference between these and other sorts of public service is that there is no reason why they should be run any differently from commercial enterprises: they generally seek to make a profit. In fact, if the government body is competent at running them, they can be used to generate income to cross-subsidize the public activities of the organization.

Sometimes an organization, such as a large council or a government agency, finds itself running a number of such outlets and sets up an organization – such as a catering section – to run them. In other situations the operation is leased to private operators.

Tradition

It is clear that many publicly provided services are maintained because of tradition; there may have been a rational basis for their provision originally, but not at present. They are maintained, or free or subsidized entry is continued, because it is politically difficult to change.

The reason why it is politically difficult to change such situations is that there is often a lobby or interest group that would be offended by the change. The enjoyment which the members of such groups gain from the continued existence of the public service/facility in question may well be a public good or a mixed good as described above, but, as with all such provisions, there is still the question of balancing the cost of provision with the value of the benefits being received by the users; and over time the benefits may have been eroded, for example by falling population or use levels, while the costs may have risen. Nevertheless, the service is continued because of political expediency.

THE MARKET VERSUS THE STATE: ISSUES

A number of further issues affecting the role of the state are discussed below, namely:

- the question of profit-making versus loss-making in government;
- government size and government failure;
- government as provider or facilitator;
- the context of globalization.

Profit-making or loss-making?

Various combinations of the above arguments give rise to the provision of a wide range of public sector leisure, sport and tourism activity. It is clear that most of the arguments show that the costs of making the provision should be borne by the community at large through taxation, rather than by the immediate consumer of the service. This means that such public provision must, by definition, be *loss-making*, in commercial terms. If this were not the case then there would be no reason for government to be involved in the first place: if a profit could be made from the service provided at the level required, then a private company could provide it – there would be no market failure. It could therefore be argued that a profit-making public enterprise is a contradiction in terms. Thus criticisms of public services for making a loss are entirely misplaced.

This is not to say that public services cannot often be criticised for being *inefficient*. It is often possible to run things more cheaply or to obtain a better service from the resources employed. But if a service can be run profitably and still achieve the social objectives required, then in general there is no need for the state to become involved. The state becomes involved only when a level of service deemed to be necessary cannot be provided by the market – that is it *cannot* be provided at a profit.

This does not mean that if profits can be made from a service there is no need for *any* government intervention. For example, if there were no public provision of swimming pools, some commercial swimming pool operations would be profitable, but probably only in certain central locations where a sufficient market exists. If it was considered by the appropriate government body that more swimming pools should be provided so that more people could swim more often, then those additional pools would almost inevitably be loss-making. Thus a decision to intervene on the part of the state inevitably costs money.

It should be noted that, in this context, profitability means not just covering running costs but also providing a return on *capital investment* (land and buildings) comparable to expectations in the commercial sector – that is a rate of return sufficient to attract investment funds, given the level of perceived risk. Often, when public services are described as being profitable, this component is ignored.

Government failure/government size

Many of the arguments for government activity advanced above are in the realm of market failure – that is, they recognize the imperfections or failure of the market mechanism and the need to correct this with government intervention. However, the demands on government are seemingly endless and all lobby groups can no doubt quote one or more of the above arguments in support of their own particular pet project. This then raises the question of the size of government.

Neo-liberals would argue that the size of government should be limited for two reasons. First, government organizations are generally seen as innately less efficient than private organizations, so the larger the government sector the less efficient the economy is overall – this notion of generalized inefficiency of the public sector is sometimes referred to as *X-inefficiency*. Secondly, it is argued that the taxation required to finance government distorts the market, reduces incentives – such as the incentive to work – and reduces personal freedom, particularly people's freedom to spend their income as they wish.

The neo-liberal view is that government has become too big under post-Second World War governments of both left and right. Others of course dispute such a view and argue that state organizations are not necessarily less efficient than private organizations and that a substantial government is necessary to provide vital services and to preserve a humane and civilized society.

Provider or facilitator?

One response to the charge of excessive growth in the size of government is for governments, particularly at local level, to seek to play a *facilitating* role rather than a direct provision role.

Glover and Burton (1999) use the term *enabling state*. Facilitating and enabling generally refers to giving assistance and encouragement to the non-profit sector and the commercial sector to provide services and facilities formerly provided by the local council, but the discussion in Chapter 6 of *urban growth regimes*, which involve alliances of public and private interests, raises the issue of just how proactive a local authority should be in facilitating or enabling the activities of the private sector.

While, in practice, most local councils will continue to play both direct provider roles and facilitating/enabling roles, a preference for one or the other would affect strategic direction, in terms of the development of new programmes and facilities.

The context of globalization

The basic features of globalization and opposition to it are outlined in Chapter 2. Here we are concerned particularly with the implications of the phenomenon for the role of governments. In the same way that 19th century liberal advocates of the market system promoted free trade and new approaches to national government and economic management, so their 20th and 21st century successors have promoted the further freeing-up of international restrictions on trade and commerce. Advocates of a truly international, deregulated market system see it delivering rapid growth in international trade and an increase in wealth for all – a win–win situation – pointing to the economic success of the Asian 'tiger' economies and economic liberalization in China in support of their arguments (Ma, 2001).

Opponents see a decline in national sovereignty and many losers left by the wayside, as unaccountable multinational enterprises and international financial and market processes shift resources, investment and jobs around the world to maximize profits. And they point to massive disruption and unemployment in communities in Western industrial countries, and exploitative employment practices and undermining of traditional economies in developing countries, while national governments are helpless to intervene because of the commitments to unfettered free trade and competition entered into under World Trade Organization (WTO) agreements. Questions about the 'decline of the nation state' are further complicated in Europe by the growing influence of the European Union and other multilateral agreements, and the consequent loss of national sovereignty.

These trends can have an impact on policymaking and planning in the field of leisure, sport and tourism in cultural and economic terms.

Global factors clearly have an influence at the cultural level. In particular, the influence of American culture, in film, television, popular music and fashion, is very apparent worldwide and raises questions about national cultural identity. Governments have reacted in various ways: for example, in film, funds to support the maintenance of a local film industry have been established in many countries and many also have regulations concerning 'local content' in television. Such policies have, however, been successful in stemming the American 'juggernaut' in only a few countries. There seems to be little or no governmental concern about American domination of youth culture in music and fashion.

It is curious to note that, while American companies dominate the sports clothing and fashion markets (e.g. Nike, Reebok), the insular nature of much sport in the USA has meant that world sport itself has not become dominated by American capital.

These trends, while noticeable at local level, have not generally had much impact on leisure policies and provision by local authorities. It is, however, possible that some of the limited successes of American sports, such as basketball or baseball, can have significant local impacts. A successfully managed local league can lead to increased local demand for facilities for such sports, even if they are making little impact at national level. In the arts and cultural area an exception was the Greater London Council which, before its abolition in 1986, was actively pursuing programmes to stimulate local cultural industries (Garnham, 1987), and it has been suggested that such programmes will be increasingly necessary in post-industrial cities.

The more immediate impact of globalization is being felt economically. For example, as manufacturing activity has shifted to other parts of the world, Western countries such as the UK have experienced substantial unemployment in particular communities, resulting from the demise of such industries as steel-making, shipbuilding, coal-mining and now vehicle manufacture. This has resulted in two types of response from national and local governments. First, there has been the attempt to replace old industries with new. Some of the new industries have been leisure-based, including the development of tourism, events, entertainments, arts, sports and exhibition facilities. Secondly, local leisure providers have had to take particular note of the unemployed as a major client group (Glyptis, 1989).

OUT OF THE MAINSTREAM

The concentration on mainstream or orthodox economics in this chapter was deliberate, for the reasons outlined in the introduction. There are, however, numerous non-mainstream or non-orthodox forms of economics which have been put forward from time to time, but invariably these have only a minority following.

- *Marxist economics*, as indicated in Chapter 2, sees the state in capitalist society as propping up the exploitative market system.
- *Institutional economics* is of significance to leisure because one of its founders was Thorstein Veblen, author, in 1899, of *The Theory of the Leisure Class*, who saw the market as being subject to the interaction of human institutions, including classes, firms, unions, professions and governments, rather than as disembodied, rational utility-maximizing consumers or firms.
- *Humanistic economics* is also of significance to leisure and tourism because it is based on Maslow's ideas of human needs (see Chapter 3).

With few exceptions, these or other alternative perspectives do not feature in the literature on the economics of leisure, sport and tourism. The exceptions include:

- Jim Butterfield (1989), in a paper entitled *The economics of leisure: blue and green challenges to orthodoxy*, discusses the *Austrian School* and *green economics* and their application to leisure.
- Thea Sinclair and Mike Stabler (1997), in *The Economics of Tourism*, refer to the *structure, conduct and performance* (SCP) paradigm used in industrial economics to explain the behaviour of firms, and also to the *Austrian School*, and *behavioural, evolutionary, institutional* and *psychological economics*.
- Chris Gratton and Peter Taylor (2000), in *Economics of Sport and Recreation*, refer to *psychological economics* in relation to consumer behaviour.
- John Tribe (2005), in *The Economics of Recreation, Leisure and Tourism*, includes a final chapter entitled 'Critique, alternative paradigms and change', which summarizes *Marxist economics* and refers to the London-based think tank, *New Economics Foundation*.

SUMMARY

- While mainstream, market economics is not without its critics, in the context of the current 'triumph of capitalism' it seems appropriate to consider the economic arguments for the role of the state in a primarily market economy.
- Four broad functions of government are discussed: national defence; maintenance of law and order; market failure; and social/political arguments. Most of the chapter is devoted to discussing the last two of these.
- Market failure is discussed in terms of: public goods and services; externalities/neighbourhood effects; mixed goods; merit goods; option demand; infant industries; size of project; and natural monopoly.
- Social and political arguments are discussed under the headings: equity/humanitarian arguments; economic management/development; incidental enterprise; and tradition.
- A number of further issues on the role of the state is discussed, including the question of profit- and loss-making enterprise; 'government failure' related to government size; the question of whether governments should be providers or facilitators; and the effects of globalization.
- Many of the principles discussed here are operationalized in the cost–benefit analysis process discussed in Chapter 11.

RESOURCES

Discussion of mainstream/orthodox economics and its analysis of the role of the state in general: Musgrave and Musgrave (1980);
- and leisure: Gratton and Taylor (1991, 2000); Tribe (2005); Veal (2006a);
- and tourism: Bull (1991); Tribe (2005); Sinclair and Stabler (2007);
- and the arts: Baumol and Bowen (1966; 1976); Pearce (1991); Throsby (2001); Frey (2003).
Changing relationship between the state and the market in leisure: Clarke (1995); Ravenscroft (1996, 1998); Henry (1999); Coalter (2000).
Globalization generally: Bauman (1998); Beck (2000); Hutton and Giddens (2000); Keller (2000); Langhorne (2001).
Globalization and culture: Barnet and Cavanagh (1996); Craik *et al.* (2000).
Globalization and sport: Maguire (1999), Miller *et al.* (2001).
Sport/leisure and youth crime reduction: Coalter (2007); Nichols (2007).
Critics of capitalism and globalization: Korten (1996); Mander and Goldsmith (1996); Klein (1999).
Privatization/compulsory competitive tendering (CCT): Ott and Hartley (1991); Coalter (1995); Nichols (1996); Ravenscroft (1998); Hodge (2000).
Cultural industries: Landry and Bianchini (1995); Zukin (1995); Caves (2000).
Sport and economic development: Gratton and Henry (2001).
Recent history: Henry (2001).

QUESTIONS/EXERCISES

1. Is the 'triumph of capitalism' actually 'mythic', as Korten (1996) suggests?
2. In what ways are leisure and tourism involved in the governmental roles of: (i) national defence; and (ii) maintenance of law and order?

3. What, in general terms, is 'market failure'?

4. What is the difference between the principle of the 'public good or service', in the economist's sense, and externalities or neighbourhood effects?

5. Why is the concept of the 'mixed good' particularly associated with the arts?

6. What is the difference between a 'merit good' and 'option demand?

7. Why is the concept of 'infant industry' particularly relevant to tourism?

8. Why are equity/humanitarian arguments for government activity ideologically controversial?

9. Should publicly owned enterprises make profits?

10. What are the potential problems associated with 'big government'? How can they be overcome?

11. In what ways can globalization be said to be threatening the role of governments? Are there examples in the leisure/tourism sector?

PART II

Planning Frameworks

This part of the book is concerned with the overall methodologies and approaches used in policymaking and planning for leisure, sport and tourism. It comprises three chapters:

- Chapter 6, *Public Policy-making*, considers formal governmental constitutions and models of public decision-making.
- Chapter 7, *Leisure, Sport and Tourism: Plans and Planning*, examines the concept of strategic planning and values, mission/vision, goals and objectives and then evaluates eight alternative approaches to planning for leisure.
- Chapter 8, *U-Plan: a Participation-based Approach to Planning for Leisure, Sport and Tourism*, outlines a particular approach to planning, based on the setting of participation targets.

chapter 6

Public Policymaking

INTRODUCTION

The first five chapters of the book are concerned with theoretical ideas and the social, economic and political context of public policymaking and planning; in this chapter the variety of ways in which public policy is actually made is considered in more detail. In an increasingly complex world, the question of just how organizations make, or should make, decisions to best fulfil their commitments and meet their objectives has been the subject of much debate among practitioners and theorists. For public bodies there is a formal decision-making mechanism, usually underpinned by a constitution or other legal framework, which indicates how decisions are *intended* to be made. In the real world, however, things rarely work exactly as intended. In this chapter the following are discussed:

- international dimensions;
- formal national constitutions;
- decision-making: theoretical models and approaches;
- urban growth regimes and their application to leisure, sport and tourism.

INTERNATIONAL DIMENSIONS

International dimensions of public policy are becoming increasingly important, particularly in Europe, as the powers of the European Union increase. Two dimensions of this phenomenon are highlighted in the discussion of globalization and of human rights in Chapters 2 and 4. In general, international policymaking and planning is conducted via agreements and treaties to which member states become a party if they see it as being in their national interests to do so. Most of these operate under the auspices of the United Nations, which uses a variety of terms to describe different stages and statuses of agreements, as shown in Table 6.1. At the time of writing, the most high profile of these agreements is the series relating to climate change, beginning with the 1997 Kyoto Protocol. Typically, draft agreements are determined at a series of meetings and conferences: government representatives sign the agreement and they must

Table 6.1. Types of international agreement.

Type	Definition	Examples
Treaty[a]	Agreements on 'matters of some gravity that require more solemn agreements, typically requiring ratification'	Treaty of Rome, 1957: the origin of the EU
Agreement[a]	Usually less formal and deals with a 'narrower range of subject matter than "treaties"'; generally involves a limited number of states and often 'of a technical or administrative character' and 'not subject to ratification'	General Agreement on Tarrffs and Trade (GATT): predecessor to WTO agreements
Convention[a]	'Instruments negotiated under the auspices of an international organization'	Convention on the Rights of the Child, 1989 (UNICEF) World Heritage Convention, 1972 (UNESCO)
Charter	'Particularly formal and solemn instrument, such as the constituent treaty of an international organization … has an emotive content that goes back to the Magna Carta of 1215'	The United Nations Charter, 1948 The Olympic Charter (IOC)
Protocol	An instrument 'subsidiary to a treaty' or 'framework'	The Kyoto Protocol, 1997, to the UN Framework Convention on Climate Change, 1992
Declaration	'The term is often deliberately chosen to indicate that the parties do not intend to create binding obligations but merely want to declare certain aspirations'; however, some declarations are legally binding	Rio Declaration on Environment and Development, 1992

[a] These terms are also used generically to refer to a wide range of agreements, as well as for the specific uses indicated. Quotations from United Nations Treaty Collection (Treaty Reference Guide) at http://untreaty.un.org/English/guide.asp

then be formally *ratified* by national parliaments; only when a specified number of states have ratified the agreement does it come into force. States which break the terms of an agreement or voluntarily withdraw from the agreement may be subject to sanctions, such as trade restrictions, by other states still abiding by the agreement. For the most part such agreements apply to *states*, but in some cases they apply to individuals, for example, in the case of some human rights violations and sport doping offences.

While agreements are typically developed and administered by an organization established as part of the United Nations, a few non-UN organizations exercise regulatory powers, for example, the Court of Arbitration for Sport and the World Anti-doping Agency established under the International Olympic Committee. Examples of international organizations involved in the areas of leisure, sport and tourism are shown in Table 6.2.

Table 6.2. International organizations involved in leisure, sport and tourism.

Organization		Responsibilities in leisure, sport, tourism
Regulatory		
IATA	International Air Transport Authority	Regulation of international airline routes
ITU	International Telecommunications Union	International telecommunications, including communication satellite orbits
WTO	World Trade Organization	Intellectual property rights in literary and artistic works: e.g. books, musical compositions, paintings, sculpture, computer programs, films
WHC	World Heritage Committee of UNESCO: UN Educational, Scientific and Cultural Organization	Designation of World Heritage Areas
CAS	Court of Arbitration for Sport	Adjudication of disputes in sport
WADA	World Anti-doping Agency	Designation and testing regarding illegal performance-enhancing drugs in sport
Advisory/independent/specialist		
WLO	World Leisure Organization	Leisure
IOC	International Olympic Committee	Olympic Games
IPC	International Paralympic Committee	Paralympic Games
IFS	International Federations of Sport	Administration of individual sports
CGF	Commonwealth Games Federation	Commonwealth Games
UNWTO	UN World Tourism Organization	Tourism
IUCN	International Union for the Conservation of Nature	Conservation

Of particular note is the advent of *supranational* organizations, the most prominent of which is the European Union. In this situation, member states cede some of their powers to the supranational organization. In the EU these powers relate particularly to economic activity; examples are shown in Box 6.1.

Box 6.1. Sport and competition in the European Union.

The European Union is a supranational organization in which, as a condition of membership, the 27 member countries cede their powers in certain areas to the governing body – the European Commission. One of these areas is commercial competition policy. Paradoxically, sporting competitions have some inherently uncompetitive characteristics. Although sporting clubs within a league compete like firms in a market, they are organized in a league that controls the competition – a phenomenon which, in any other industry, would be called a *cartel* and would be illegal. Typically certain rules have covered the method by which players (employees) may be recruited into the competition and between clubs, and the number of international players who can play in any one club. In the 'Bosman ruling' of 1991 the Court of Justice of the European Communities ruled that these practices were against EU laws on freedom of movement of labour and discrimination on grounds of nationality (European Commission, 2004: 9). This has had significant effects on the way football leagues and clubs have operated. European laws have also impinged on sports broadcasting, regarding the issue of whether states have the right to insist on certain sporting events being broadcast free-to-air and whether the European Broadcasting Union's purchasing of sports broadcasting rights on behalf of all European public broadcasters is anti-competitive (Jeanrenaud and Késenne, 2006).

Despite supposed threats to national sovereignty, from globalization and supranational organizations, the nation-state *is* still sovereign; thus, for the time being, the concentration of this chapter on national, regional and local government seems justified.

FORMAL NATIONAL CONSTITUTIONS

National constitutions can be broadly classified along two dimensions:

- *unitary* as opposed to *federal*;
- Westminster as opposed to presidential.

This gives four types in total: examples of countries with each of these four types of constitution are shown in Table 6.3, and the two dimensions are outlined in brief below.

Unitary versus federal systems

In *unitary* government systems, such as those in France and the Scandinavian countries, there are two tiers of elected government – central government and local government. In *federal*

Table 6.3. Examples of countries with different constitutions.

Constitution	Westminster	Presidential: US style	Presidential: French style
Unitary	UK, New Zealand, Ireland, Holland, Japan	Argentina, Kenya	France, Korea, Indonesia
Federal	Canada, Australia, India, Germany	USA, Brazil, South Africa,	Russia

systems, as in the USA, Canada, Australia, Germany and India, there are three levels: central or federal government, state or provincial governments and local government. The UK, with its Scottish, Welsh and Northern Ireland assemblies, now lies between the two systems, since the assemblies arise from law, which can be relatively easily changed, rather than from a constitution, which is not easy to change. In both unitary and federal systems, local government, while democratically elected, is very much controlled, in terms of powers and funding, by the higher tiers.

In some areas of the UK the local authority system is split into two tiers – county councils and district councils. In large urban areas there is only one 'unitary' tier – city or borough councils. County councils have some similarities to state/provincial governments in federal systems – for example in running schools, police forces and hospitals. But a fundamental difference is that counties do not have legislative powers – they cannot make laws; they are entirely subject to the national legal system. While leisure, sport and tourism functions are divided in a variety of ways in the two-tier county/district systems, in this book, 'local government' is dealt with as a single level.

Westminster versus presidential models

Modern governments consist of: (i) a head of state; (ii) a head of government and government ministers; and (iii) one or more elected assemblies – usually a 'lower house' with most power and an 'upper house' as a review body with limited powers. In both unitary and federal systems governments may be of the 'Westminster' type or 'presidential' type. The differences between these two systems are summarized in Table 6.4 and Figure 6.1.

Table 6.4. Westminster versus presidential government: features.

Function	Westminster	Presidential: USA style	Presidential: French style
Head of state	Ceremonial president or constitutional monarch	Executive president	Executive president but with prescribed powers (e.g. foreign relations, defence)
Head of government	Prime Minister (Germany: 'Chancellor')	Executive president	Prime Minister
Government	Ministers drawn from Members of Parliament	Ministers appointed by president – not Members of Congress	Ministers drawn from Members of Parliament
Elected assemblies	Parliament – usually two assemblies, e.g. House of Commons, House of Lords (UK); House of Representatives, Senate (Australia)	Congress – usually two assemblies, e.g. House of Representatives, Senate (USA)	Parliament – usually two assemblies
Government formed by	Party that can command a majority in the Parliament	President, elected by the people, who appoints ministers	Party that can command a majority in Parliament

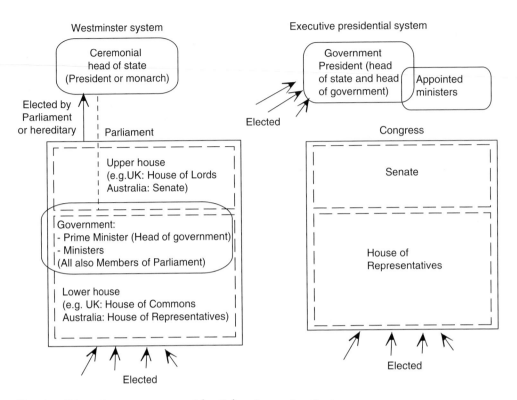

Fig. 6.1. Westminster versus presidential systems: structure.

In the Westminster system the *head of state* – a monarch or ceremonial president – is a formal, ceremonial position[1] and the *head of government* – the Prime Minister – and the rest of the government are members of the elected assembly or Parliament, which is known as the *legislature*. The head of state appoints a prime minister who is the leader of the party, or coalition of parties, that can command a majority in the elected assembly.

The presidential system can be divided into two types:

- *US model*: the roles of head of state and head of government are played by the same person, the elected, executive president, who appoints ministers to form a government; the president and government are entirely separate from the elected assembly.
- *French model*: the head of state is an elected executive president, but with prescribed powers, usually related to foreign relations and defence; as in the Westminster system, the president appoints a head of government/prime minister who is the leader of a party/parties that can command a majority within the elected assembly.

In both systems, while most of the laws and taxation measures are developed and proposed by the government, they must be passed by the elected assembly before being formally passed into law by the head of state[2]. In the Westminster system this process is controlled by the government because the party of government controls the elected assembly, but in the executive presidential system the political party of the president may or may not enjoy a majority in the assembly, so the process of legislation can involve negotiation between the president and the leaders of oppositional groups in the assembly.

In federal systems, the format of the national government is replicated at state/provincial level. Thus, in the USA, the states have executive *governors*, corresponding to the president, separate from their legislative assemblies, whereas in Australia and Canada, the states/provinces have a ceremonial governor, nominally representing the Queen, and the head of the state/provincial government, the Premier, is a member of the state legislature. This pattern even flows through to local government, with US cities having directly elected executive mayors, while British and Australian cities have mayors who are in most cases drawn from among the elected councillors.

The location of leisure and tourism

In federal systems the powers of the federal and state/provincial governments are generally laid out in a constitution. Typically, leisure and tourism responsibilities are shared between all levels, as indicated in Table 6.5. In some cases there is a clear demarcation – for example, in the case of broadcasting or dealing with unequivocally national institutions, such as a National Gallery or National Theatre. In other cases, historical accident has resulted in all levels of government being involved – for example in the provision of parks – even if one level is predominant.

Formal decision-making procedures

While principles discussed below apply in a broad sense to both the Westminster and the presidential type of government, for simplicity the Westminster model is assumed in the discussion. The formal procedure by democratic governments making decisions is as follows:

- Political parties are formed around an ideology or set of interests, as discussed in Chapter 2.
- At election time the parties present a *manifesto* of actions which they would undertake if elected, and endorse candidates to stand for election to the legislature.
- Following the election, the leader of the party that has a majority of seats in the lower house of the legislature is called on by the head of state to be Prime Minister and to form a government.
- If no single party has an absolute majority, the largest party might be invited to form a 'minority' government, or a coalition of parties might be formed.
- Subject to the constitutional *term* for a legislature (typically 3–5 years), the government will remain in power as long as it continues to command a majority in the legislature.
- Laws and taxation measures are enacted by the government to fulfil its election manifesto; this is done by presenting *Bills* to the legislature which, when approved by the legislature and formally endorsed by the head of state, become *Acts*.

The above outline presents only the very basic characteristics of the political and legislative system. Other procedures and institutions, such as a constitutional court, are also involved, but these are beyond the scope of this book.

It should be noted that in some situations, notably rural areas in the UK and smaller councils in Australia, parties are not a significant factor: individual councillors or groups of councillors designate themselves as 'independent'. They nevertheless have to present a manifesto or 'platform' to the electorate at election time and, if elected, have to make decisions in areas of policy not covered by their manifesto, in which case, at future elections, they are judged

Table 6.5. Leisure, sport, tourism and levels of government.

Area of involvement	Unitary system		Federal system		
	National	Local	National	State/provincial	Local
Leisure/culture					
Broadcasting	●		●		
National arts/cultural institutions	●		●		
Provincial arts/cultural institutions		●		●	
Local arts/cultural institutions		●			●
National parks	●		●	●	
Heritage conservation	●	●	●	●	●
Regional parks	●	●		●	
Local parks		●			●
Children's play facilities		●			●
Urban planning		●		●	●
Beaches		●		●	●
Community social/arts/recreation facilities/ programmes		●			●
Sport					
National sports teams/athlete support	●		●		
Doping control	●		●		
Major sport stadia	●	●		●	
Sport development	●	●	●	●	●
Community sport facilities/ programmes		●			●
Tourism					
International tourism promotion	●		●	●	
Air travel	●		●		
International travel	●		●		
Domestic tourism promotion		●		●	●
Road/rail travel	●		●	●	

on their records. Often, the manifesto and voting record of independent politicians will place them at some point on the political spectrum depicted in Fig. 2.1.

Quangos

Much of the policymaking and policy implementation in leisure, sport and tourism, particularly at national level, is undertaken by *quangos* (Quasi-autonomous Non-governmental Organizations). These are organizations established and funded by governments with Board members appointed by governments, but which are seen as, to some extent, separate from and independent of government. One rationale for the use of such an organizational device is referred to, in the arts in particular, as the *arm's length* principle. This is the idea that government should not be seen to be directly interfering with such matters as the arts or sport or heritage: policy should be in the hands of disinterested experts – government should be at arm's length. An alternative reasoning is that, in these specialized areas, a more flexible organizational structure is required than the traditional, bureaucratic government department; this argument is more likely to be applied in more commercially orientated areas such as tourism.

Thus in a number of leisure sectors the most important single public organization is usually the national quango – the sports council, the arts council, the countryside agency, the tourism commission and so on. Such organizations are extremely important to their field because of their connection with national government, the financial resources they command and their ability to conduct research, launch campaigns and generally influence the direction of the field. However, it should be borne in mind that quangos, however influential, are only one 'player' in the field. Often the collective importance of other organizations is greater, particularly in the financial sense; thus, for example, local authorities collectively spend far more money on sport, the arts and the countryside than do Sport England, the Arts Council and Natural England, respectively, and voluntary organizations are equally important in some areas. And in sport, tourism and broadcasting commercial organizations are generally much larger than the public sector quango. A further distancing of quangos in the UK in recent years has been the institution of funding by the National Lottery, as discussed in Box 6.2.

Box 6.2. Leisure and the proceeds of gambling.

A major change in the UK in recent years has been the advent of the National Lottery. The profits from the lottery now provide a substantial proportion of central government funding of leisure, through organizations such as Sport England and the Arts Council (Evans, 1995). This eases the political task of funding these areas because the funds do not appear to come from *taxation*. This is, of course, to a large extent an illusion, since the profits are generated only because of the governmental monopoly over this form of gambling – monopolies make *excess profits,* so the bonanza of the lottery is, in effect, a de facto tax.

This is illustrated by the practice in Australia, where gambling control is a state government rather than a federal government responsibility. The six Australian states and two territories, through taxation on licensed clubs (gaming machines), casinos, bookmakers and state lotteries, garner sums comparable to those of the British government, relative to population (A$4.8 billion in 2007 – Queensland Treasury, 2008). In this case, however, the funds come from taxation and are not separately administered: they go into state consolidated revenue. But regardless of the source of the funds, there remains the task of allocation of funds between competing projects within leisure, sport and tourism and between leisure, sport and tourism and other sectors.

The non-profit or voluntary sector

Trusts and non-profit organizations established as associations or corporate entities frequently play roles that might otherwise be played by governmental bodies, such as quangos or local councils.

Trusts may be established under appropriate legislation or, in the UK, under Royal Warrant and are overseen by Boards of Trustees. The trust format is common in the arts, where, even though they may be in receipt of substantial government funding, many theatres, museums and galleries operate in this way. This is partly for historical reasons: the institution may have been originally established by private benefactors. And it may be partly for taxation reasons, since there can, for example, be advantages in making bequests to organizations with charitable status. The National Trust is the most well-known example in the heritage area, holding natural and built heritage properties in trust for the nation.

In some countries – Germany for example – non-profit sporting organizations play a wide community role, often underpinned by substantial grants from the state. In the state of New South Wales in Australia, registered clubs, related to sport, veterans and ethnic groups, play a unique role as community centres and supporters of sport, partly as a result of benefiting from their, until recently, monopoly income from poker machines (Caldwell, 1985; Veal and Lynch, 1998). The International Olympic Committee is another high-profile organization in the sporting world which might be thought to be an intergovernmental organization, particularly in relation to its role in policing illicit drug use in sport, but is in fact part of the 'third sector' (Toohey and Veal, 2007).

In some contexts non-profit organizations can be seen as part of the public sector, in other instances they are closer to the private sector, and this varies from country to country and locally. In this book therefore, no attempt is made to deal systematically with the role of the voluntary or non-profit sector, but its existence should be borne in mind. It should be noted that these organizations are particularly relevant to the *pluralist* model of government discussed below.

Public–private partnerships

Finally, it should be noted that governments can enter into partnerships with the commercial or non-profit sectors and can even engage in profit-making enterprises. Local or regional tourism development organizations often include a mixture of public and private sector organizations, and may be established as a consultative body, with activities carried out on its behalf by a public body, such as the local council, or it may be established as a corporate entity in its own right, with public and private sector shareholders. In some city centre and harbourside developments, local councils or state governments may enter into a *joint venture* with private enterprise, setting up a company for the purpose, in which the public body and its private sector partners have shareholdings, or they may establish trading companies on their own. This sort of device is often used in the *urban growth regime* phenomenon, as discussed later in the chapter.

Models of Decision-making

In practice, the processes by which governmental decisions are made are much more complex than the above outline suggests. In particular, organizations and interests other than the legislature and government are involved to a greater or lesser extent, including business, non-profit organizations, trade unions, professional bodies, lobby groups, the media, the military, the judiciary, religious groups, public servants, other governments and international organizations. A variety of theories and models have been suggested involving different views on how these various interests interact to influence government decision-making. Parsons (1995) divides such theories and models into five groups, focused respectively on:

- *Power*, in which the main emphasis is on securing, exercising and maintaining political power.
- *Rationality*, which reflects the classic management approach of setting objectives and finding the best way of achieving them.
- *Public choice*, where decisions reflect sectoral community interests.
- *Institutions*, in which decisions are influenced more by formal non-governmental organizations.
- *Personality, cognition* and *information processing*, in which decisions are best explained in terms of the personal characteristics and processes of decision-makers.

These are discussed in turn below, with the main emphasis being on the first two.

Power-based models

Power-based models concentrate on economic, political, social and military power wielded by various groups in society in addition to elected governments. Parsons (1995) discusses six different forms of power-based model, referred to as elitism, pluralism, Marxism, corporatism, professionalism and technocracy models. These are discussed briefly in turn below. In addition, a model not included in Parsons' list, hallmark decision-making, is discussed.

Elitism

Elite models hold that power in society is wielded by a relatively small number of people and groups of people who form an elite who have direct contact with government ministers and legislators and, often behind closed doors, can influence them to act in their interests rather than in the interests of the wider community. Such groups might include leading business people or media owners, the 'military–industrial complex' involving the leaders of the armed forces and the suppliers of military hardware, religious groups or landed interests. It has been argued that such relationships exist, at least from time to time, in various sections of the leisure industries, such as the arts and sport, thus ensuring continued funding for elite art forms such as opera and ballet or for elite sport at the expense of mass participation. In the tourism sector it might be speculated that such phenomena as the continued anti-competitive control of international air routes and the bizarre practice of the duty-free trade may be partly explained by the elite model of government decision-making.

An example of the process at work can be found in the following quotation from the memoirs of Hugh Jenkins, a British Labour Minister for the Arts in the 1970s, which outlines the activities of the arts establishment in opposing proposals from the government of the time to introduce a Wealth Tax which threatened, among others, wealthy owners of valuable works of art:

Months before the Green Paper[3] was published the arts plutocrats and their minions sprang into action. The National Arts Collections Fund in the person of Sir Anthony Hornby was quickly off the mark, writing to Denis Healey [Chancellor of the Exchequer] on April 9. Simultaneously,

Ernle Money (Tory [Member of Parliament], Ipswich) was asking questions in the House [of Commons] and the Earl of Rosse, Chairman of the Standing Commission on Museums and Galleries was equally active. . . . Lord Perth . . . [Chairman of the Reviewing Committee on the Export of Works of Art] wrote . . . to the Chancellor. The Duke of Grafton raised the matter in the [House of] Lords . . . Letters to the press from Hugh Leggatt, a dealer, from George Levy, President of the British Antique Dealers Association, from Denis Mahon, a collector and Trustee of the National Gallery, and from sundry stately home owners continued throughout the summer of '74 and among others I received a *cri-de-coeur* from the Earl of Crawford and Balcarres. . . . I met Sir Geoffrey Agnew at the Hazlitt Gallery and I agreed that he should come in for a talk after the publication of the Green Paper. . . . One must admit that they [the plutocrats and their spokesmen] were remarkably successful in recruiting to their side thousands of people, perhaps millions, who would never pay the tax and who could only benefit from its application to the top group of property owners.

(Jenkins, 1979: 141, 143).

The government eventually withdrew its Wealth Tax proposals, wealthy art-owners no doubt being just one among many groups which had used their influence to oppose the tax. It is perhaps notable that the UK class and honours system provides such convenient labels to identify many members of the elite. Peers and knights of the realm are recruited to board membership and to preside over a range of public, voluntary and commercial organizations and are expected to use their status and influence in times like the above. In countries without such titles the membership of the elite is less obvious, but this does not mean that it does not exist.

Pluralism

Pluralist models see political decision-making as involving a much wider range of pressure groups and interest groups that influence government by direct lobbying, but also by use of publicity or by giving or withholding financial or political support to individual politicians or political parties. Some groups claim to represent significant numbers of voters, for example groups representing the retired, farmers or trade unions. Others use research, data and publicity to make their views known in the political arena – for example, groups concerned with welfare or health issues. As indicated in Fig. 6.2 therefore, in this model, political decision-makers, rather than making decisions solely on the basis of their election commitments, technical evaluations of proposals and debate, are believed to base their decisions on an assessment of the competing claims, promises and threats of a range of, possibly opposing, groups and the likely political consequences of favouring one group over another. There is a continuum, therefore, between the elite model, which depends on contacts and often on behind-the-scenes influence, and the pluralist model, with its more public political campaigning by known pressure groups.

Political pluralist models have been used particularly to describe the political system in the USA, where political lobbying has become an art form, election campaign funds donated by interest groups run into billions of dollars and lobby groups can represent millions of votes. One view is that such a pluralist system is democratic in nature because any group can form itself into a lobby group and have its say. But increasingly it has come to be seen as a distortion of democracy, since the system favours the groups with greater financial resources. However, the recent electoral success of Barack Obama was based on a different model, in which millions of supporters donated relatively small contributions via an Internet-based campaign. The arts example given above can also be said to illustrate the pluralist model in operation since, while many of the characters involved could be identified as part of the UK elite, and were able to use

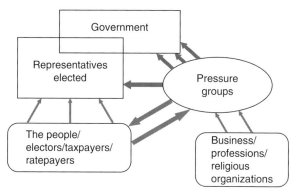

Fig. 6.2. Political pluralism.

their influence behind the scenes, it is also clear that representative bodies, such as the British Antique Dealers Association, and public processes, such as writing letters to newspapers, were also utilized in the campaign. It is also clear, however, that members of those groups that might have benefited from the proceeds of Wealth Tax proposals were probably less well organized and resourced.

It should be borne in mind that the pluralist model does not apply only to national and state/provincial politics. As the discussion in Chapter 2 suggests, international business interests also bring pressure to bear on governments – some would see organizations such as the World Trade Organization and the International Monetary Fund as the equivalent of pressure groups, although they and individual multinational enterprises also operate in the elite mode as discussed above and the corporate mode as discussed below. At local government level pressure groups are often vocal and influential, and are often associated with various forms of leisure, including sporting and arts organizations seeking funding from councils and environmental groups lobbying for open space and conservation.

Marxism

As discussed in Chapter 2, Marxism sees the contemporary state as propping up the capitalist system. Such a support process must operate in some practical way, and so this Marxist perspective can be seen as a particular form of the elitist or a non-democratic version of the pluralist model, where the dominating interests that influence or control government are those of capital.

Corporatism

Corporatist models involve governments working very closely with specified industrial or commercial organizations. They have some similarities with elitist and pluralist models but in this case, rather than being the hapless victim of the elites or lobby groups, the government is an active partner in the process and seeks to incorporate the non-governmental organizations involved. The classic example of the corporatist model in action is the relationship between the Nazi government in Germany in the 1930s and the military–industrial complex. At the urban level a few politicians and commercial interests might be able to, in effect, run the city – such a phenomenon is known as an urban growth regime and is discussed in more detail later in the chapter.

Professionalism

Long-established and well-organized professional bodies can have a significant influence on government, particularly when they are involved in a major area of public service delivery. Mention has already been made of the military and judiciary, but also of relevance are the education profession and unions and the medical profession, particularly where a socialized health system exists. The humorous UK television series *Yes Minister*! and *Yes Prime Minister*! illustrate this thesis in relation to the profession of public servant (Lynn and Jay, 1988, 1989). Such influence can be at all levels of government. Professions in general have been subject to a considerable critique for using their power to further their own interests at the expense of the wider community, for example by Ivan Illich in his book *Disabling Professions* (Illich *et al.*, 1977).

Many public servants have a personal, even emotional, commitment to the field in which they work and may have strongly held views about particular policies. Such commitment and opinions can be seen as political in nature, especially if the opinions differ from those of the political group in government. Nevertheless, it is widely accepted that, because of their basis in technical expertise and professional knowledge, the work of managers or administrators in the public sector is generally different from the activities of politicians. This expertise and knowledge is involved in the decision-making processes of public bodies – how influential it may be in those processes varies, according to the political environment, the level of expertise of the manager concerned and the innate nature of the field. Some studies of these influences at work in the leisure, sport and tourism sectors are referred to in the Resources section.

Technocracy

The technocracy model sees decision-making increasingly being taken out of the hands of 'ordinary people' and being usurped by technological experts. This envisages scenarios in which politicians are persuaded that society has 'no choice' but to invest in the form of – usually expensive – technology. In the Cold War period of the 1960s and 1970s, the model applied particularly to nuclear power, armaments and space exploration; in recent times it has applied to decisions on such matters as broadband broadcasting, biotechnology and global warming. While the increasingly significant role of economists in government in recent years might be seen as an example of professional influence, it can also be seen as a form of technocracy, as decisions have been based on increasingly complex economic models.

Hallmark decision-making

The leisure, sport and tourism sectors are particularly afflicted by a further alternative approach to decision-making that might be termed *hallmark decision-making*. The name seems appropriate because it generally arises in relation to what have come to be called *hallmark events* or projects (Syme *et al.*, 1989; Hall, 1992). Such phenomena include major events, such as the hosting of the Olympic Games, and major building and planning projects, like the building of a national theatre or developments such as the London Docklands or Sydney's Darling Harbour. Because of their high profile such projects usually involve politicians directly, there is a great deal of media attention, and normal planning, decision-making, budgeting and evaluation procedures are often by-passed, for example by means of special legislation. Cost over-runs and controversy tend to be the norm. The decision-making process involved appears to consist of making the decision to go ahead with the project first, and then seeking ways of justifying it. While all areas of the public sector are affected by hallmark decision-making, leisure seems to suffer particularly because so many non-experts either consider themselves to be expert in the area, or assume that no particular expertise is necessary. One researcher, having analysed the planning of a wide range of hallmark projects (centres for art, culture, exhibitions, sport and conferences) around the world, concluded that: '… decisions to go ahead were most often made before any data collection, analysis, evaluation, or constraint determination. Extra-rational factors such as whim, influence, creativity, intuition, vision and experience played large roles in the planning and/or decision to undertake the project' (Armstrong, quoted in Roche, 2000: 18).

The work of Peter Hall (1980) on *Great Planning Disasters*, Syme *et al.* (1989) on sporting events and Colin Michael Hall (1992: 219) on hallmark tourist events represents the beginnings of a literature on this phenomenon. In practice, there is an element of hallmark decision-making in nearly all public investment projects.

Rationality models

That policy decisions should be made on some rational basis is an attractive idea that most people would probably subscribe to. Much of the rest of this book is predicated on the idea that leisure, sport and tourism policy professionals should be equipped to contribute to such a rational ideal. The ideal is enshrined in the *rational-comprehensive* approach to decision-making, which seeks to base decisions on rational evaluation of all available information and all possible courses of action. One representation of such a model is presented in Fig. 6.3. It consists of ten steps or processes, beginning with establishment of the brief or terms of reference for a project, programme or organization and ending with an evaluation or feedback loop. At the heart of the process is the need to consider and evaluate all possible courses of action and choose the course of action that maximizes the likelihood of the organization achieving its goals.

It is widely believed that this approach, while it remains a model of perfection, is in fact impractical, and is rarely implemented in its pure form. The main problem is the time and effort needed to identify and evaluate all possible options, particularly in a large, complex project. The identification of *all* possible options may be theoretically possible but is invariably not practical. Even consideration of a large number of options is often impossible because of time and resource limitations. In recognition of this, in the 1950s Herbert Simon coined the term *bounded rationality* to describe the more limited scope of most decision-making exercises, in which the range of options to be considered is limited quite early in the process (Parsons, 1995).

Also in the 1950s, Lindblom (1959) argued that organizations, in practice, do not use the rational-comprehensive approach; they consider only a few alternatives, and often with only a limited amount of information to hand. When making decisions, rather than beginning 'from scratch' with the goals of the organization, the tendency is to start with consideration of where the organization is now – current policies, commitments and practices – and to consider only marginal changes from that status quo situation. This view suggests that only *incremental* change is considered; alternative courses of action are not identified on a rational-comprehensive basis, but in a somewhat haphazard, or disjointed manner. This style of decision-making Lindblom termed *disjointed incrementalism* or the *science of muddling through*. The advantage of disjointed incrementalism is that it is cheaper and quicker to implement than the ideal rational-comprehensive approach.

However, while disjointed incrementalism may reflect what goes on in many organizations in practice, it could hardly be recommended as an ideal way to proceed; in particular it favours

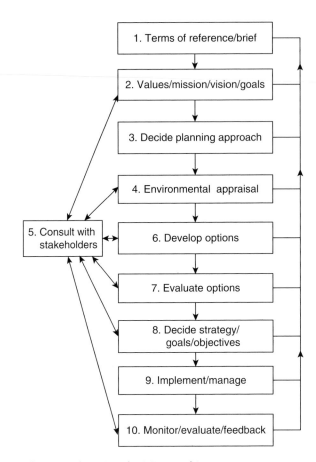

Fig. 6.3. The rational-comprehensive decision-making process.

the status quo, whether or not that is the best set of policies, and, in failing to consider all alternative courses of action, it is in danger of missing important opportunities for change. Etzioni (1967) proposed, as a compromise, the idea of *mixed scanning*, a two-stage process involving a broad review of a wide range of possible courses of action, followed by more detailed evaluation of just a few, selected alternatives. But this raises the question of how comprehensive the initial scan is to be and how the more limited list of options is to be selected.

It has been suggested that the debate between the rational-comprehensive approach on one hand and disjointed incrementalism/mixed scanning on the other is inappropriate because they are modelling different things (Smith and May, 1993). The rational-comprehensive model describes what *ought* to be while the disjointed incrementalism/mixed scanning model describes what *is*. When empirical studies are conducted to discover how decisions are made in organizations, most actors in the process would see themselves as engaged in a rational-comprehensive process, even if it appears to the observer that their practice is closer to the disjointed incrementalism/mixed scanning model.

Arguably, therefore the rational-comprehensive model remains an ideal against which alternatives and practice are assessed. Figure 6.3 therefore provides the basis for the discussion of strategic planning in Chapter 7.

Public choice

Public choice theory draws a parallel between market processes and political processes. In the market process, decisions on what goods and services to produce are made by firms on the basis of how self-motivated consumers, in effect, 'vote' with their money. If more consumers want, and are prepared to pay for, red apples rather than green apples, then more red apples will be produced and fewer green apples. In the political process, public choice theory argues, voters support, in a self-interested way, political parties that offer them more of what they want. In turn, political parties bid against each other to offer voters more of what they want – a sort of 'bread-and-circuses' scenario. Such a process invariably leads to an expansion of the role of government as parties seek to meet as many demands of as many groups as possible. Since much of government provision was therefore a quasi-market process, proponents of the theory have argued, why not privatize these services and so reduce taxation and the size of government? Thus the public choice model was used to support the 'rolling back of the state', which took place under New Right governments in the 1980s. Despite the connotations of 'bread and circuses', this model has generally not been pursued in the research literature in the context of leisure and tourism.

Institutional approaches

The decision-making models discussed above concentrate on processes, unlike the formal model of the governmental system initially outlined, which concentrated on institutions (legislature, government, party, etc.). The *institutional* approach to analysing decision-making explores this dimension in more detail, examining ways in which the structures and functions of political institutions and the structures and functions of the organizations to which they relate (e.g. private sector firms, trade unions) affect their decision-making practices. Verbal and diagrammatic presentation of formal structures tends to suggest that the system operates smoothly, but this is rarely the case in human affairs. The relationships between national, state/provincial and local tiers of government are more often than not in tension, if not open conflict, especially when different political parties control the various tiers.

The institutional model has not been extensively explored in relation to leisure and tourism and so is not pursued in detail here, but reference to general literature on the model can be found in Parsons (1995: 323–326).

Personality, cognition and information processing

Clearly, decisions in public organizations are made by *people* – elected representatives and paid officials. It makes sense, therefore, to explore the characteristics and behaviour of the individuals involved and the processes they use to assess information and arrive at decisions. Again, this is not an area that has been pursued in the leisure, sport and tourism research literature and is not discussed further here (see Parsons, 1995: 336–380).

URBAN GROWTH REGIMES AND THE GOVERNANCE OF THE LOCAL STATE

In the discussion of decision-making models above, reference was made to corporatism, in which a close relationship develops between government and business in relation to particular projects or policies, and to the idea of elites and their potential to influence government decision-making. The idea of *urban growth regimes* discussed here relates to both these models.

Much of the policymaking and planning for leisure, sport and tourism with which we are concerned in this book takes place at the local, urban or rural, level, making the functioning of the *local state* of particular importance. Since the majority of the populations of the developed world live in urban areas, the bulk of the policymaking, planning and provision takes place in towns and cities. Since classical Greek and Roman times and before, cities have been the focus of collective leisure, even when this has been a by-product of other functions, such as commerce (market days and fair days) and government (the activities of royal courts): cities provided the resources and the people to support collective leisure facilities, including theatres, orchestras, museums, stadia, parks and gardens.

In analyses of the local sate the term *governance* is often used to refer to the particular combination of formal and informal mechanisms by which local communities are run. These mechanisms involve a number of actors, including:

- elected members of local councils;
- paid council officials;
- political parties;
- other public sector/statutory bodies;
- higher levels of government: providing legal framework and, often, partial funding;
- trade unions: public sector and other;
- local businesses and their representative organizations;
- voluntary service organizations;
- special-interest pressure groups;
- local communications media: press, radio, television, Internet;
- citizens/ratepayers;
- clients for council services.

These are represented in Fig. 6.4. Of course membership of many of these groups overlaps considerably, which gives local governance its particular characteristics.

As discussed above, the classic view of how government operates is that candidates representing parties with particular political programmes present themselves for election and

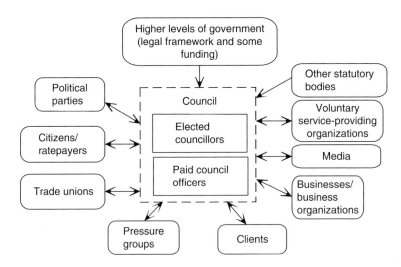

Fig. 6.4. The local state.

the successful party or coalition of parties forms the ruling group, which takes control of the government machinery and implements its programme in the interests of the electorate. But because of the role of pressure groups, entrenched interests, personal interests and external constraints, it is doubtful that this pattern ever operates in such a simple way. Patrick Dunleavy (1980: 135) has argued that such a portrayal is quite misleading. In the UK he notes that the terms of political debate are generally set at national level and local council elections have generally followed national political swings, suggesting that local policy platforms are largely irrelevant to the political process. At local level, parties gain and hold power as a result of national party endorsement rather than as a result of local democratic support for local policy platforms. Decision-making, he argues, does not take place through the formal process of open debate and voting in council chambers, but is controlled by the ruling party's leadership working outside the formal political process, in behind-the-scenes negotiations with party factions and other interests, with the council chamber acting as a 'rubber stamp'. This means that local governmental decision-making, rather than arising from a broadly based democratic process, is often in the hands of a small group of people who 'do deals' with party factions and local-interest groups, such as trade unions or business interests.

This style of governance has been referred to as an *urban regime* or *urban growth regime* (Harding, 1994). The ways the various actors and influences interact create a particular style or model of regime focused on achieving, for example: (i) general economic growth and development; (ii) development of a specific large-scale project; (iii) a reduction in the level of expenditure/taxation; (iv) privatization of services; or (v) a change in a city's image.

While this model of local government is widely viewed as common in Europe, doubts have been expressed as to whether it is still relevant in US cities, particularly when focused on growth. Clark (2000: 33–34) suggests that such regimes have been sidelined by the emergence of a 'new political climate' that involves anti-growth sentiments and a displacement of traditional concerns with production and jobs by a greater emphasis on 'consumption, amenity and lifestyle decisions such as the environment'.

The forces of globalization and post-industrialism have, however, made this approach to urban analysis particularly apposite, as leaders in Western cities, faced with de-industrialization, have searched for an understanding of the process of change and the role cities should play. The stage was therefore set for a rediscovery of leisure, sport and tourism as important functions of cities. Reflecting Castells' ideas on collective consumption (see also Dunleavy, 1980: 42–50), urban regime activity has increasingly turned to: (i) leisure and tourism-related developments, such as retail/leisure complexes (Stevenson, 2000); (ii) sport and cultural facilities as a focus for growth strategies (Noll and Zimbalist, 1977; Henry and Paramio Salcines, 1998); (iii) tourism (Greenwood, 1992); and (iv) major events, such as the Olympic Games (Burbank *et al.*, 2000). Many of these developments have been commercial in nature but Clark, in reviewing a wide range of international research on policy development in cities, detects a shift away from commercial intervention to more traditional public goods provision:

> Amenities are increasingly recognized as critical … Efforts to improve the 'quality of life', via festivals, bicycle paths, or culture, are recognized as central not just for consumption but for economic development, which is increasingly driven by consumption concerns. How? Amenities are … public goods; they do not disappear like a payment to a firm if the firm goes bankrupt. Amenities benefit all firms as well as citizens in the area. They often enhance the local distinctiveness (of architecture or a waterfront) by improving a locality, rather than just making it cheaper for one business. … the focus is less on the firm and its location and more on the citizen as consumer/tourist/workforce member.
>
> (Clark, 2000: 15–16)

SUMMARY

This chapter has been concerned with the process of decision-making in government. First the chapter includes brief accounts of some of the formal structures of democratic governments and their formal decision-making processes, including: (i) unitary versus federal systems; (ii) Westminster versus presidential models of government; and (iii) the roles of quangos, trusts and the non-profit sector. Alternative models of decision-making are reviewed, including: (i) power-based models; (ii) rationality models; (iii) public choice; (iv) institutional approaches; and (v) personality, cognition and information processing. While the rational-comprehensive model has been criticized as being unrealistic and unworkable in practice, it remains a useful framework for analysing and undertaking planning and policy development; the model presented in Fig. 6.3 is therefore used as a framework for some of the discussion in subsequent chapters in the book. Finally there is a brief introduction of the concept of urban regimes, seen as an increasingly common feature of governance of the local state and particularly relevant to leisure, sport and tourism policy-making.

NOTES

[1] In some of the Commonwealth countries, notably the former 'Dominions' (Canada, Australia, New Zealand), the Queen of the United Kingdom remains formally head of state and is represented by Governors General at national level and by a Governors in the states/provinces.

[2] In presidential systems the final stage of the legislative process is the signing of the Bill by the president. In executive presidential systems, the president has the power of veto over Bills that have passed through the legislative assembly without the approval of the government. In constitutional monarchies, such as those headed by the Queen of the UK, the equivalent process is known as the giving of the *Royal Assent*. In the UK the Royal Assent is still given in Norman French, the language of the court following the Norman Conquest in 1066: Bills become law with the words: *La Reyne le veult* – 'The Queen wishes it'.

[3] A *Green Paper* is a discussion paper outlining government proposals for a new policy and/or legislation. If the proposals survive the public discussion they are generally presented, possibly modified in light of the discussion, in a *White Paper*, and eventually, if legislation is involved, in a Bill to Parliament.

RESOURCES

Policymaking and decision-making generally: Parsons (1995).
Public choice theory: Self (1993).
Interest groups: in tourism: Hall and Jenkins (1995, Chapter 4).
Politicians and professionals: Henry (2001: Ch. 5); Yule (1997a, b); Coalter (1988).
Elite theory: Dye (1978: 25–28); Haralambos *et al.* (1996: 110–121).
The local state: Dunleavy (1980).
Urban growth regimes: Harvey (1989); Harding (1994); Clark (2000).
Leisure-related analyses of urban growth regimes at work: Henry and Paramio Salcines (1998, 1999); Long, P. (2000).

QUESTIONS/EXERCISES

1. What is the difference between a unitary and a federal system of government?

2. What is the difference between a Westminster and a presidential system of government?

3. What is a quango? Name an example in the area of: (i) sport; (ii) the arts; (iii) tourism.

4. Give examples of where the 'elitism' model of government decision-making might exist in the field of leisure and tourism.

5. Give examples of possible non-governmental participants in the 'pluralist' model of government.

6. What are the characteristics of hallmark decision-making?

7. On what grounds is the rational-comprehensive model of decision-making criticized?

8. What are the main alternatives to the rational-comprehensive model of decision-making?

9. Examine, using newspaper archives, a recent high-profile leisure/tourism event or planning/development decision and assess to what extent it involved hallmark decision-making and/or the activity of an urban growth regime.

chapter 7

Plans and Planning for Leisure, Sport and Tourism

INTRODUCTION

This chapter examines:

- types of plan;
- the strategic planning process;
- terms of reference/briefs for planning exercises;
- the concepts of mission, vision and goals;
- evaluating planning approaches for leisure, sport and tourism;
- town planning and its relationship to leisure, sport and tourism planning.

All except the last of these items revisit the rational-comprehensive model of decision-making depicted in Fig. 6.3.

The contents of the chapter are addressed primarily to the local government sector, since local government is the level of government which has a comprehensive range of powers and responsibilities with regard to leisure, sport and tourism services. Much of the book's content is also applicable to specialist agencies, such as tourism development or national parks organizations, trusts responsible for single services or facilities, in either the public or non-profit sector and, in federal systems, to state or provincial governments. In what follows reference is made to 'elected councils' as the source of authority and decision-making power, but for other types of agency this role is played by a board or committee or, in the case of state and provincial governments, by state or provincial governments and parliaments.

TYPES OF PLAN

Plans and policy statements come in many forms. One of these is the 'local cultural strategy' which the Department of Culture, Media and Sport (DCMS) requires British councils to prepare. But, as under DCMS guidelines, these strategies are linked to numerous other

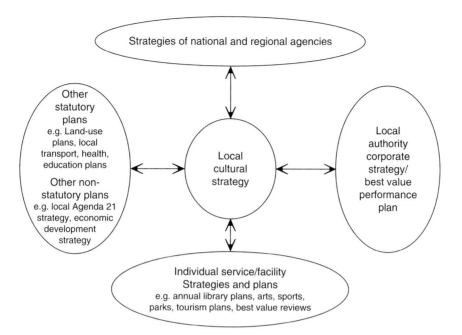

Fig. 7.1. Links between strategies/plans (from Department for Culture, Media and Sport, 1999: 25).

plans produced by the councils themselves and other agencies, as shown in Fig. 7.1. The diagram introduces some key generic and specific plan types, which are further explored in Table 7.1.

The discussions of planning that follow in this and the next two chapters in particular are focused on *strategic planning*, which is discussed in more detail below, and relate primarily, but not exclusively, to planning at the local level, that is plans related to a single local council area, a city, subregion or county. The most important plans at this level are the plans prepared as part of the statutory development planning process. These are concerned in the main with land uses, so their leisure, sport and tourism content is related primarily to open space and natural and heritage conservation. More detailed planning for leisure, sport and tourism deals with built facilities and services as well as open space, and will be required to specify, or provide the basis for specifying, numbers of facilities and locations. This is done in the context of the 'other plans' listed in Table 7.1: the local cultural strategies in the UK and the local leisure/sport/tourism strategies in Australia. These latter plans must, of course, be consistent with the statutory plans and may provide inputs into the latter.

STRATEGIC PLANNING: INTRODUCTION

The terms *strategic planning* and *strategic management* have been used to refer to an approach to planning and management which seeks to ensure that medium- to long-term goals are given

Table 7.1. Types of plan and related documents.

Type of plan	Description
Generic	
Development application	Application to the planning authority for permission to proceed with a specific development: e.g. one or more houses, factories, shops; in principle, must conform to the development plan
Development plan	Generic term for plans concerned with land use (housing, industry, transport, retail, open space, etc.), for example, for a city, county or suburb
Environmental impact assessment	Study undertaken as part of the process of seeking planning permission for major projects (e.g. new roads, mines), including effects on flora, fauna, landscape, cultural heritage, waterways, traffic, noise
Management plan	Detailed plan, generally for a specific site or facility (e.g. a national or urban park), often statutory; typically involves zoning, visitor access points and facilities and management treatments
Master plan	A detailed land-use plan for a specified area, usually in the form of a map and supporting documentation
Statutory plan	Plan mandated to be prepared by Act of Parliament and which, once approved, has the backing of law
Strategic plan	A plan concerned with broad principles and issues, not with detail, generally with a planning period of several years
UK statutory development planning system since 2004	
Regional spatial strategy	Statutory strategic plan at regional level to provide a framework for local development frameworks; includes regional transport strategy, subregional strategies
Local development framework	Statutory detailed land-use plan at the district council level, within the regional strategy; includes: local development scheme, statement of community involvement, annual monitoring
Other UK plans	
Local cultural strategy	Plan which UK government requires each local council to prepare (DCMS, 1999); may provide inputs into development plans
New South Wales statutory development planning system[a]	
Local environmental plan (LEP)	Statutory land-use plan for a single local government area
State environmental planning policy (SEPP)	Statutory plan/policy document which 'deals with issues significant to the state and people of New South Wales', e.g. (i) Western Sydney Parklands (2009); (ii) Kosciuszko National Park – Alpine Resorts (2007); (iii) Sydney Region Growth Centres (2006); and (iv) Coastal Protection (2002)

(Continued)

Table 7.1. Continued.

Type of plan	Description
Section 94 contributions plan	Statutory plan setting out levies which must be paid, per dwelling in new developments, to cover costs of infrastructure, such as roads, drainage and leisure facilities, under Section 94 of the Planning Act.
Other NSW plans[a]	
State plan	Ten-year strategic plan for all state activities; 2006 plan includes targets for participation in sport/physical recreation, cultural activities and tourist numbers and spending
Leisure/recreation/ tourism strategy	Non-statutory local council plans that vary in scope and content from council to council. May include management component and provide inputs to LEP; tourism strategy often undertaken at regional level

[a] Similar systems operate in the other five Australian states and two territories, each under its own state/ territory legislation.
Sources: UK: Cullingworth and Nadin (2006); NSW: http://www.planning.nsw.gov.au (under 'Planning System').

prominence, and day-to-day management is harnessed to the achievement of such goals rather than being distracted by ad hoc, short-term objectives. This approach has its origins in the private sector, but in recent decades public bodies have increasingly been required to behave much like private corporations, preparing strategic plans that are *rolled forward* annually and which integrate forward planning with budgeting, implementation strategies and performance or outcomes appraisal (Caret *et al.*, 1992: 5–24).

The terms *strategic planning* and *strategic management* are used interchangeably by some, but strategic *planning* is seen here as the initial process of preparing a direction and broad programme of activity for the organization. Strategic *management* on the other hand, is seen as comprising those aspects of management concerned with ensuring that the strategic plan is *implemented* and that the organization does not lose sight of its strategic directions because of day-to-day concerns.

Mintzberg (1994) recorded the *rise and fall* of strategic planning in 1994, but perusal of library catalogues and relevant websites will reveal that strategic plans in the area of leisure, sport and tourism continue to be produced in significant numbers. While strategic planning may change in format and context, it seems to be an unavoidable activity of public leisure, sport and tourism organizations and would appear to be here to stay.

We all make decisions all the time, as individuals and as part of social groupings, such as a household or a group of friends. Some of the decisions are short-term or day-to-day in nature, such as what brand of instant coffee to buy; others are more significant, often with a number of long-lasting consequences, for example buying a house, embarking on an educational course or getting married. These more significant decisions might be called *strategic* – they imply a *strategy* for the future with a range of factors and further decisions being dependent on them. More time and care is generally taken over these strategic decisions than over day-to-day decisions; often they involve complete appraisals of our lives, our values and our relationships. Leisure, sport and tourism organizations similarly make both day-to-day and *strategic* decisions. Examples of the range of decision-making, from the minor day-to-day level to the *strategic* level, in leisure organizations, are given in Table 7.2.

Personal strategic decision-making may be complicated enough, especially when it involves a number of other people, but when an organization makes strategic decisions thousands of people may need to be involved and millions may be affected by the decisions made. The more strategic the decision the more people are likely to be involved or affected. For example, if a large manufacturing company makes a strategic decision – such as to build a plant to produce a new product or to close down a plant and cease producing a particular product – hundreds or even thousands of staff and their families, local communities and possibly millions of customers may be affected. When an organization makes strategic decisions therefore, considerable care must be taken both in the *process* of making the decisions and in considering their *effects*.

The planning/decision-making process is similar at all levels of a management hierarchy, although it might be expected that the process would be less elaborate at lower levels. A 'nested' planning/decision-making process can therefore be envisaged, in which the basic strategic, rational decision-making process shown in Fig. 6.3 is replicated at lower levels. This is illustrated in Fig. 7.2, in which the overall plan breaks into four programme areas. Since, in a typical local council for example, a programme area might contain a number of sub-programmes or individual facilities, the process could be repeated yet again at a third or fourth tier. In the lower tiers the content of some of the components could be identical to the equivalent component in the higher tier – for example the organizational mission and some aspects of the environmental appraisal – some components would have different emphasis, with more detail in some areas and less on others, and some will have totally new content specific to the programme.

Table 7.2. Levels of decision-making.

Level	Indoor sports/leisure centre	Tourist Commission	National Park
▲ Day-to-day	Choose brand of floor cleaner	Decide what information to send to an inquirer	Close park for a day due to flooding
	Decide seasonal price increases	Commission a market research project	Appoint one ranger
	Employ new manager	Choose 3-year marketing theme	Designate a new National Park
	Reorganize staff structure	Open offices in target market locations	Adopt 'user pays' principle
Strategic ▼	Build large extension to centre	Determine target markets for next 5 years	Allow mining in National Parks

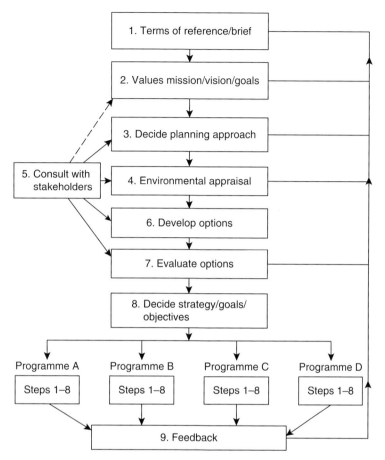

Fig. 7.2. Nested planning/decision-making processes.

TERMS OF REFERENCE/BRIEF

Any task must have a clear brief, or terms of reference, and producing a comprehensive or strategic leisure or tourism plan is no exception. Typical briefs for a team about to embark on such tasks might be:

- to determine the sport and other leisure requirements of the community over the following 10 years and prepare a feasible strategy to address those requirements;
- to determine the desirable scale and nature of tourism development and consequent tourism marketing activities for the community over the following 10 years.

In some strategic planning exercises the terms of reference may relate to the function of the whole organization – for example, a National Parks Commission or a Tourism Commission. Typically, such 'whole-of-organization' terms of reference are stated in the legislation or charter which established the organization. In other cases it refers to just one function of the organization – for example, a tourism strategy for a local council.

Two aspects of the brief need initial consideration, namely timescale and scope.

Timescale

The timescale for a strategy could be longer or shorter than 10 years, depending on the rate of change within the community or the market and, perhaps, on the political horizons of the organization. Different aspects of the strategy will relate to different timescales. For example, the *mission* of an organization, as discussed below, does not generally have a timescale, unless the organization has a specific task, such as the holding of a one-off event. By contrast, the *objectives* developed in a plan tend to be associated with specific time periods: for example, an objective might be to 'double the number of tourists visiting the city over a 10-year period'. Such an objective may be implemented in stages, for example, each year during the 10 years of the plan, a specific participation target would be set.

Scope

Whether a multi-purpose local council is left-leaning or right-leaning in its politics or more or less community-orientated in its approach to planning and decision-making, a decision has to be made about the scope of its responsibilities. One approach is a 'minimalist' one, where the council's activities are determined only by statutory obligations and obvious electoral demands. An alternative approach is to accept a broad-ranging responsibility for enhancement of the quality of life of the community, using statutory powers as tools to achieve this end. It is important, therefore, to clarify the *scope* of the plan. This has differing implications for leisure and tourism.

The question of scope is particularly important in the area of *leisure*, which means different things to different people. Governments at all levels are in the unique position of being able to take a comprehensive view of leisure in the community. In practice, however, this opportunity is rarely grasped. Since, for a variety of reasons, government is itself involved in direct provision of only a limited range of leisure facilities and services, public leisure plans often deal only with that particular restricted range. Frequently planning documents *begin* by considering leisure – or recreation – in its entirety, but then proceed to ignore major aspects of leisure, simply because the local council is not directly involved in their provision.

At the local level, examples of major aspects of leisure that are usually excluded from plans are: home-based leisure, entertainment, pubs and restaurants and holidays. Such aspects are ignored presumably because local authorities feel that, since they are not direct providers, they have no powers or rights to engage in planning in these areas. The commercial and the private sector are often deemed to be 'out of bounds'. This logic is, however, not applied in areas such as retailing and industrial and office space, where detailed planning activity is undertaken by councils, despite the fact that these are primarily commercial activities. In the past the leisure facilities which were 'in' and those which were 'out' of the planning process at least corresponded to broad sectors, but with increasing levels of private sector involvement in traditionally public sector areas, this will no longer be the case: as discussed in Chapter 1, almost all forms of leisure are served by a mixture of public and private sector organizations. The fact that the local council identifies certain requirements for the community and puts forward a plan to meet those requirements does not necessarily imply that it will be the agency which will be responsible for making the provision.

Because the inclusion of these particular areas of leisure in the public planning process is so rare, it is perhaps worth considering briefly just how they might be incorporated into plans and what relationship the plan and the local council might have with them.

Home-based leisure

It is known from leisure surveys that the home is the most important site for leisure for virtually everybody. It is sometimes noted in plans that people living in flats are likely to be in need of more out-of-home leisure provision because of lack of access to gardens, but such observations are rarely followed through into policies. In mainland Europe, allotments often take the form of 'leisure gardens' rather than as areas for simply growing food, but this has not generally happened in the UK. This may be because of differing cultural traditions, but it may also be because local authorities have not considered the question of home-based leisure in their planning, so the provision of leisure gardens has not arisen. It might also be suspected that the somewhat untidy collective appearance of leisure gardens, with their summer houses and sheds, and varying standards of upkeep, would not conform to the architect-planners' vision of the urban landscape.

Electronic forms of entertainment are generally accepted as being the most significant of the home-based leisure activities. One way in which the public sector has been involved with this area is that public libraries have for many years offered loans of recorded music. However, in considering the quality of *leisure* in a community, local councils could adopt a position on, for example, local broadcasting or, in contrast, on the need to encourage alternatives to television for young people.

Entertainment, pubs, restaurants

This area of what might be termed 'social leisure' could be said to be a major contributor to the quality of life of a community. The contribution which the quantity, quality and distribution of social facilities make to the character of an urban environment is often considered in plans – although not very systematically – in the context of visitors to an area, but rarely in relation to the needs of local residents. There is clearly a difference between a successful 'leisure precinct' in a town centre, whether it has been deliberately planned or not, and an unsuccessful one. In the successful precinct, transport systems, cinemas, bingo halls, theatres, pubs, restaurants, gardens, walking areas and associated retail activity all complement one another, and there is an appropriate 'ambience', so that the whole is greater than the sum of the parts, business booms and more investment in facilities is attracted. Such a scenario can be either facilitated or hindered by planning (Stansfield and Rickert, 1970; Jansen-Verbeke, 1985).

A more inclusive approach is often taken in planning for *tourism* because tourism is clearly primarily a private sector industry, so it would be absurd to ignore the role of the private sector in any plan. Local government and other public sector agencies are often responsible for key attractions, such as beaches, waterways, museums and galleries and heritage items, but hotels, restaurants and many attractions are commercially operated. Plans therefore often have a town planning and economic development perspective, with public and private sector development being considered together, often in the context of 'growth regime' politics, as discussed in Chapter 6. Local government in tourism areas is often also involved in tourism promotion, marketing and information services, usually in collaboration with private sector organizations and other councils, so forecasting demand and setting targets for visitor numbers also becomes part of the planning activity.

While the production of development and marketing strategies to attract tourists *to* their areas is common, local authorities tend not to consider the holiday needs of their own residents. And yet a holiday is, arguably, one of the most important forms of leisure to the individual. In the same way that variable, and inequitable, access to sporting facilities is examined in leisure plans, there is no reason why variable and inequitable access to holidays should not also be examined. National tourism organizations tend not to collect data on those who do go on holiday and are not generally interested in those who do not. The idea of 'social tourism' – assisting deprived groups, such as people with disabilities or carers, to take a holiday is not a new idea (Haulot, 1981). In this case, social services organizations would be more likely to be involved, and they tend not to be the responsibility of the lowest tier of government.

While the above is a plea for comprehensiveness, particular authorities or agencies may find themselves constrained in what they can include by legislation and/or by the responsibilities and activities of other bodies. For example, while health education might arise naturally in considering a sport and fitness plan, it might be inappropriate for a local council to launch a major education programme without consulting with relevant education authorities or health authorities. It would also make sense to take account of the existing plans and current planning activities of such bodies, as shown in Fig. 7.1. These might well already include health education programmes.

VALUES, MISSION/VISION, GOALS, OBJECTIVES

Whatever planning approach is used, an organization must have a mission that reflects the philosophical values of the organization and/or the people that established it, and is expressed in terms of goals and pursued via objectives.

- *Values* are the key features of the moral, philosophical or political principles underlying and guiding the activities of the organization; in the case of multi-purpose organizations these values will, of course, apply to all the organization's activities, not just its leisure/ sport/tourism activities.
- *Mission* is the organization's overall *purpose* or *raison d'être*, generally, if possible, summarized in a succinct phrase or two: the 'mission statement'. Sometimes the term *vision* is used – examples of *visioning* have been described in the literature (e.g. Ritchie, 1994a; White, 2000).
- *Goals* are more detailed statements of components of the mission/vision.
- *Objectives* are more specific, are generally linked to specific programmes or facilities and generally include a time dimension and quantification; the measured outcomes of policies designed to achieve objectives are sometimes referred to as *performance indicators*, as discussed in Chapter 12.

In effect there is a values/mission/goals/objectives hierarchy, as indicated in Fig. 7.3. Some illustrative mission statements, goals and objectives are set out in Boxes 7.1 and 7.2 (see also Web-box 1, available at http://www.leisuresource.net).

Mission statements attempt to provide an 'all-purpose' statement to which all members of the organization and its stakeholders might subscribe. However, the discussion in the opening chapters of this book suggests that different people and political groups hold different values and have differing views on the role of the state, in relation to leisure, sport and tourism as much as in relation to other areas such as education or defence. It might be expected therefore that differing values and philosophies would lead to differing missions or goals statements. Table 7.3 summarizes the main philosophical positions outlined in Chapters 2 to 4 and offers suggestions as to what effect such positions might have on the mission/goals of a public leisure, sport or tourism agency.

Mission/goals statements can be expected to reflect value positions, but they are often expressed in general terms so that they are acceptable to most shades of opinion, and consequently *differences* emerge only at later stages in the planning process. For example, a statement to the effect that a council aims to enhance health by promotion of participation in sport might have wide acceptance, but one group might wish to do this by making public sports

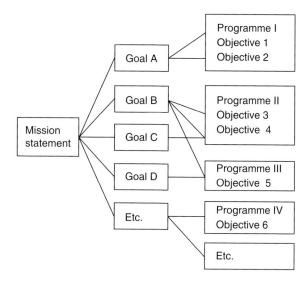

Fig. 7.3. Values, mission/goals, objectives: hierarchy.

facilities freely available to all, while another group might wish to facilitate a private enterprise approach. Or the council might declare a goal to develop tourism and only later does it emerge that one group envisages the development of high-rise, four-star hotels, while another group envisages chalets and backpacker hostels.

The mission statement and related statement of goals can perform a number of functions:

1. They are the lynchpin of the rest of the strategic planning process – all projects should be orientated towards the fulfilment of the mission and pursuit of the goals.
2. If well formulated, they can provide a common focus of attention for all members of an organization, including elected and staff members, whether or not they are directly engaged in the strategic planning process, and for others with an interest in the activities of the organization, particularly the public, as both electors and consumers of its services – the 'stakeholders'.
3. In appropriate format, they can also assist in establishing the 'corporate identity' of the organization.

The process of developing a mission/vision and goals cannot be entirely internal to the organization: it must have some relationship to other relevant bodies and their powers, responsibilities and policies. In particular, the organization must take account of those bodies which control or contribute to its budget. Thus local councils must have regard to state/provincial or national governments, the boards of quangos must have regard to the parent body responsible for their funds and departments within a council or government must have regard to the broader policies of the body of which they are a part. These considerations may strategically affect the shaping of mission/vision and goals. This regard for the organization's role with regard to other bodies is referred to as *positioning*. John Crompton of Texas A&M University has published a number of papers on this topic, suggesting that local leisure provision organizations (separate boards in the USA, but departments in the UK and Australia) should shape their mission/vision/goals entirely in these terms. For example, if the council is concerned with economic development and crime reduction, the leisure board/department should

Box 7.1. Strategic plans 1: Sport England Strategy, 2008–2011.

Vision: 'Our overarching aim is to build the foundations of sporting success through the creation of a world-leading community sport system'.

Key outcomes[a]	Overall impact[b]	Programmes	Key performance indicators
1. Excel: 'Developing and accelerating talent'	• Improved talent development systems in at least 25 sports	• Each sport's NGB 'Whole Sport Plan' provides basis for funding • Re. disabled athletes: 49 county-based athlete development centres plus Playground to Podium programme • 25% of Sport England funds	• Appropriate systemic and quantitative measures: e.g. size and quality of the talent pool immediately below the elite level • Re. disabled athletes, from 2007–2010: • 5000 participants directed to coaching • 2000 adults introduced to coaching • 8500 young disabled people have access to assessment/development
2. Sustain: 'Sustaining current participants in sport by ensuring that people have a high-quality experience and by taking action	• 25% reduction in post-16 'drop-off' in at least five sports by 2013 • Increase in satisfaction	• 5 sports to be selected for funding • 4000 new coaches engaged between 2009 and 2011 • 60% of Sport England funds	• For selected sports: 25% reduction in 'drop-off' by end of 2012–2013 (Active People survey) • 5% increase in sport satisfaction by 2013 (measured by new sport satisfaction survey)

to reduce the 'drop-off' in 16–18 sports participation			• As a result of the above, 200,000 increase in adult participation by 2013 (Active People survey)
3. Grow: 'Increasing regular participation in sport by 200,000 adults per annum'	• 1 m people doing more sport by 2013 • Contribution to the Five Hour Sport Offer (5HSO) for engaging more 15–19s	• Funding NGB Whole Sport Plans • Engaging with/'incentivizing' higher education sector • Engaging the third (voluntary) sector • Support Football Foundation and increase commercial sponsorship • Five Hour Sport Offer (5HSO) and other youth programmes • 15% of Sport England funds	• By 2013: increases in regular sport participation (three sessions of moderate-intensity sport each week (Active People survey): • 500,000 adults (NGB programmes) • 300,000 students (HE programmes) • 100,000 adults (voluntary sector) • 150,000 adults (commercial) • Various targets (5HSO, etc.)

Comment: Of the 'overall impact' measures, it is notable that the first and last items relate to inputs rather than measurable outcomes. The desired outcome of 'improved talent development systems' is the actual development of more talent (more talented people, talented people in more sports or higher levels of talent). Similarly, the outcome of the Five Hour Sport Offer is more 15–19-year-olds engaged in sport.

[a]Equivalent to goals; [b]equivalent to objectives; NGB, national governing body.

Source: http://www.sportengland.org/sport_england_strategy_2008-2011.pdf

Box 7.2. Strategic Plans 2: Australian Sports Commission (ASC): Strategic Plan, 2006–2009.

Values: 'In our relationship with our stakeholders, we will: be responsive to their needs; consult and endeavour to reach common understandings; be open and transparent; listen and communicate openly; and accept full responsibility for our decisions and actions.'

Vision: 'To continue to be recognised as the world leader in developing high performance and community sport.'

Mission: 'To enrich the lives of all Australians through sport.'

Goals (called 'objectives' in original document)[a]	Objectives (called 'critical result areas' in original document)
To secure an effective national sports system that offers improved participation in quality sports activities by Australians	• Growth in sports participation at the grassroots level, particularly by youth, indigenous Australians, women and disabled • Increased opportunities for children to be physically active • Best practice management and governance of sport within and through national sporting organizations • Adoption of values of fair play, self-improvement and achievement • Recruitment, retention and, where appropriate, accreditation of people within the sports sector • Enhance Australia's leadership in international sports
To secure excellence in sports performance by Australians	• Improved economic efficiency and commercial return to the Australian Sports Commission and national sporting organizations. • Sustained achievements in high-performance sport • A drug-free sporting environment • Recognition of the Australian Institute of Sport as a world centre of excellence for elite athletes and coaches

Comment: In relation to each objective/critical result area, the plan outlines 'strategies' and 'sub-strategies', but does not provide time-lines or quantified measures of outcomes. In some cases these items are included in Annual Reports. In the 2007–2008 Annual Report, the two goals are listed as 'Outcomes' in the chapter on 'Performance reports', but these are followed by 'Activities' and lists of 'Targets' rather than 'Critical result areas', and these do not correspond to the lists used in the Strategic Plan. Virtually all the information provided relates to inputs rather than outputs, that is to activities conducted by the ASC rather than their effects.

[a]Accompanied by the statement: 'These objectives flow from the statutory objects identified in the Australian Sports Commission Act 1989 and, in turn, become the outcomes that the Government expects the Australian Sports Commission to achieve.'

Source: http://www.ausport.gov.au/about/publications/corporate_documents

Table 7.3. Values, mission/vision, goals and objectives.

Term	Definition	Examples	Implementation
Values	Moral/political/ operational principles guiding all the activities of the organization	Commitment to: democratic practices, non-discrimination on grounds of race, gender, etc., efficient use of resources, environmental sustainability	Expressed through mission statement and goals
Mission/ vision goals	Over-riding purpose of the organization More detailed expression of the mission	Enhance the economic, environmental and cultural well-being of the community A healthy community An active community A prosperous community A low-crime community	Via goals and objectives Devise measures/ indicators of progress; develop programmes to address goals
Objectives	Specific targets reflecting the goals, to be achieved in a specified time period and often quantified	Short-term: complete construction and launch of leisure centre within 12 months Medium-term: increase physical activity participation by 5% in 3 years Long-term: double tourist numbers and income in 10 years	Set specific, measurable targets with completion dates and associated projects and resources

shape its mission/vision/goals to emphasize the role of leisure in contributing to economic development and preventing crime (Crompton, 2000, 2008).

In addition to considering external influences, most public organizations are faced with differences of outlook *within* their own ranks, both horizontally (across a range of services) and vertically (from top management via line management to the operational level). In practice the multipurpose organization is likely to have a hierarchy of mission/goals statements relating to different levels and sections of the organization, reflecting the nested system depicted in Fig. 7.2. The strategic planning and management process proceeds to ask: how might this mission and these goals be best pursued? The result is a set of policies, programmes and facilities, with an organizational and management structure to go with it. Each of the sections of the organization would then be expected to subscribe to the mission of the whole organization, with its own set of contributory goals and targets. Each section will engage in its own strategic management process – considering alternative ways of achieving the broad goals that arise from the overall strategic planning process.

For example, if a local council, as one of its goals, seeks to the enhance the health of the community, as discussed above, it might produce a plan to pursue that goal by means of the provision of a public swimming pool and the organization of an annual marathon. The pool manager is given the goal of maximizing health benefits through swimming participation, while the officer responsible for organizing the marathon is given the goal of maximizing health through marathon participation. Each of these managers now has a 'mini-strategic plan' to prepare; each has a range of possible courses of action which might be pursued.

Of particular note in the public sector, and leisure in particular, is the often very diverse nature of the organizational goals involved. By contrast, in the private sector there is generally a single main goal, to make the maximum possible profit. In practice it is more complicated than that, with short-term versus long-term considerations to be taken into account, which leads to consideration of such issues as growth, assets, liquidity and customer loyalty, as well as profit, but all the goals and indicators of success tend to be quantitative and can be relatively easily compared between different companies (Gratton and Taylor, 1988: 150). In the public sector goals are not only diverse, but often difficult to quantify – for example, goals related to excellence in the arts or to conservation of the environment or heritage. Furthermore, goals can often be conflicting – for example, conservation versus recreational or tourism access in natural areas and some conceptions of excellence versus popularity in the arts.

EVALUATING APPROACHES TO PLANNING FOR LEISURE, SPORT AND TOURISM

Over the years, numerous individuals and organizations, including academics and practition-ers, have given considerable thought to the question of how planning for leisure, sport, tourism and culture should be carried out at the local level. The results of many of these considera-tions have been published in sets of guidelines which have appeared in reports published by governments or professional organizations, generally for the guidance of local councils. Some guidelines have appeared in books as guidance for students and practitioners. A recent review identified almost 50 of such sets of guidelines from around the English-speaking world, but was generally critical of them for their lack of rigour and detail (Veal, 2009b). From this review a number of approaches to planning for leisure, sport and tourism were identified and these are summarized here. Nine approaches are identified, as follows:

- adopting fixed standards;
- providing opportunity;
- resource-based planning;
- meeting demand;
- meeting the requirements/requests of stakeholder groups;
- meeting unmet needs;
- providing benefits;
- equity;
- increasing participation.

A planning methodology should be consistent with the mission of the agency using it, it should be based on a plausible model of consumer motivation and behaviour and it should incorporate an operational model which indicates the nature and quantity of what is to be provided. Different approaches to planning for leisure, sport and tourism are based on different consumer motivation/behaviour and operational models. In the discussion below, therefore, each of the above planning approaches is evaluated in terms of:

- mission/goal implications: what is the approach seeking to achieve?
- consumer behaviour model: as discussed above;
- operational model: concerning what to provide and how much to provide, as discussed above;
- tourism implications;
- limitations of the approach.

Tourism is given special attention because of its nature as an economically focused area of policy, as discussed in Chapter 1.

Each planning approach is considered in isolation, in terms of its own rationale. In practice few of the methods are used alone: typical planning exercises involve a combination of methods. However, invariably this leads to what can be termed the *black box* syndrome, in which guidelines – and the plans that follow them – fail to make clear the process by which policy proposals arising from different planning approaches should be evaluated and prioritized to produce the final plan. Furthermore, the fact that some planning approaches require inputs from other approaches suggests that they each have weaknesses, indicating the need for a fully comprehensive approach, with the respective roles of its component parts and their relationships fully explained.

Adopting fixed standards of provision

Fixed standards of provision are prescriptions regarding the quantity of leisure facilities to be provided for a given level of population, as specified by an official or quasi-official organization external to the planning agency. This is one of five types of planning standard encountered in leisure planning, as shown in Table 7.4. This discussion is focused primarily on the first of these, *fixed* standards, although most of the criticisms of the approach also apply to the second and third type. The fixed standards approach is summarized in Fig. 7.4.

The most well-known example of fixed standards is the standard of 2.43 ha (6 acres) per 1000 population for playing fields and children's play space put forward by the UK organization Fields in Trust (previously National Playing Fields Association) (Fields in Trust, 2009), but many other examples have been produced over the years, particularly for sports facilities. Until the 1990s, the main professional body in the USA, the National Recreation and Park Association, also provided a set of fixed standards for use by its members and local planning agencies, but this was replaced by a set of largely demand-based guidelines published in 1996 (Mertes and Hall, 1996). This reflected a growing movement against the use of such standards among academics and practising recreation planners (see Veal, 2009b, c). Fields in Trust have, however, persisted with their standard, publishing an updated version as recently as 2008. A summary and critique of the standard is presented in Box 7.3.

Mission implications

The aim in this planning approach is to provide a quantum of facilities as specified in the standard. A planning agency using this approach therefore implicitly adopts the objectives of the agency promulgating the standard: therefore this should logically be articulated and defended in relation to the planning agency's own values/goals/mission. This has not generally been done: planning agencies that have used this approach in the past seem to have been happy to accept the authority of the promulgating organization, perhaps because it was 'quick and easy' to do so; or sometimes because the standard was declared to be 'widely accepted'. But if planning agencies had explored the basis of some of the most commonly used standards they would have found that these were variously based on: (i) conditions in the UK in the 1920s; (ii) conditions in the USA in the 1950s (but undocumented); or (iii) the views of various interest groups and pressure groups (such as single-sport bodies) with a variety of objectives (Veal, 2009b).

Consumer motivation model

The likely level of participation in a given activity within any community is assumed, in the standards approach, to be relatively fixed, and can therefore be accommodated in a nationally,

Table 7.4. Types of standard.

Standard	Definition	Source
Fixed standard	A prescribed level of provision of facilities or services related to some criterion, typically the level of population	National, governmental, professional or other authoritative body; for examples, see Torkildsen (2005: 239); Veal (2009b)
Area-percentage standard	A specified percentage of land to be reserved for open space	As above; for examples, see Veal (2009b)
Catchment area-based standard	Specification of the 'service area' of various categories of facilities, or maximum distances which residents should have to travel to access a facility	As above; for examples, see Veal (2009b)
Facility standards	Dimensions and other specifications for individual facilities – for example, size, markings and equipment for a soccer pitch	Sporting bodies; for examples, see OMCR (1976: 45–54); Daley (2000: 204)
Local standards	Standards of provision, specific to an area – based on local conditions and data	Locally determined

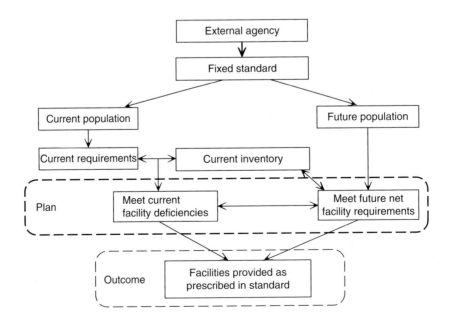

Fig. 7.4. Fixed standards-based planning approach.

Box 7.3. Fields in Trust standard: summary and critique.

The open space standard developed by the National Playing Fields Association (NPFA), now Fields in Trust (FiT), has a long history. It was first developed in 1925, based on the following premises: (i) for every 1000 population, 500 people were below the age of 40; (ii) of these it was assumed that 150 would either not want to play sport or would be unable to because of infirmity; (iii) a further 150 would use school facilities; and (iv) so 200 people in every 1000 would need to be catered for. Given the size of sports teams and frequency of play, it was estimated that the needs of these 200 people could be accommodated on: one senior football pitch; one junior football pitch; one cricket pitch; one three-rink bowling green; two tennis courts; one children's playground of 0.5 acres (0.2 ha); and one pavilion. The standard excluded: school playing fields; road verges; commons; golf courses; indoor facilities; military sports grounds; woodlands; gardens and parks; and large areas of water.

After a number of iterations, in 1938 the standard of 6 acres (2.4 ha) per 1000 population was promulgated and has remained at that level ever since, despite changes in age-structure, family size, mobility, incomes and other aspects of lifestyle among the UK population. Thus the original NPFA standard was based on an estimate of likely participation levels, which can be seen, for its time, as a demand-based approach. These demand estimates appear to have been made in the absence of formal survey data on participation but, although survey evidence has been available in the UK since the 1960s, the published reports of the revisions of the standards do not refer to such evidence.

In the most recent, 2008, review and restatement, the standards are referred to as 'benchmark standards' and variations are offered for urban and rural areas, as shown in Table 7.5.

Table 7.5. Fields in Trust (FiT) standards.

Type of open space	Hectares per 1000 population		
	Urban areas	**Rural areas**	**All areas**
Outdoor sport			
Playing pitches	1.15	1.72	1.20
Other outdoor sport	0.45	0.04	0.40
Total outdoor sport	1.60	1.76	1.60
Children's playing space			
Designated playing space	0.25	0.25	0.25
Informal playing space	0.55	0.55	0.55
Total children's playing space	0.80	0.80	0.80
Total	2.40	2.56	2.40
Maximum walking distance from home to playground (m)			
Local 'doorstep' provision			100
Local equipped play areas			400
Neighbourhood equipped play areas			1000

Source: Fields in Trust (2008); see also Veal (2009b).

(*Continued*)

Box 7.3. Continued.

The chapter of the report in which the standards are presented is entitled ' The New Approach – Benchmark Standards for Quantity, Quality and Accessibility'. They are portrayed as neither maximum nor minimum standards of provision, but: 'Fields in Trust does, however, recommend strongly that any moves to adopt standards below the appropriate 'Benchmark' could only be justified where full public participation and support for such a move can be robustly evidenced' (Fields in Trust, 2009: para. 4.1.4).

Thus, although the benchmark/standard is not a minimum, FiT basically advises against provision levels below the benchmark! In general usage a benchmark is usually seen as a minimum desirable performance level.

What is the *basis* of the FiT 2008 'benchmark standard'? First, it should be noted that, with the exception of the introduction of variations for urban and rural areas, the 2008 standard is identical to the 2002 standard and, basically, to all previous versions of the standard dating back at least to the 1930s. The report nevertheless gives the following information on how the 2008 standard was developed:

> In 2006, Fields in Trust commissioned a postal survey of local planning authorities throughout the United Kingdom and consultation with key stakeholder organisations, in relation to local and national standards of provision for outdoor provision for sport and play. . . . The purpose behind the survey was to provide an evidence-based framework for recommended Benchmark Standards, in the context of current policy and practice relating to the disciplines of planning, development, leisure, sport and play (para. 4.1.1). The 'Benchmark' … provides guidance, based on the use of median averages [sic] (para. 4.1.3). . . . [the survey and stakeholder consultations] have contributed significantly to the document and the recommended approach of using Benchmark Standards (para. 4.1.5).
>
> (Fields in Trust, 2008)

This is clearly an incomplete explanation. It is indicated that a survey of councils was conducted and this is described in Appendix C of the report. Responses from councils in Wales and Scotland were too few to be usable, so the analysis is based on English councils only. Of the 359 English councils only 147 (41%) responded, and only a little more than half of these provided information on provision of playing pitches and a third provided information on designated children's play space. The implied average level of provision of playing pitches per 1000 population was identical to the FiT standard, while that for children's play areas was significantly higher. It is of course no surprise that councils might be providing playing pitches at the NPFA/FiT recommended level, since it had been the only standard suggested for the previous 70 years. The report states that this is evidence that the standards are 'very relevant' and 'carry general value' (para. C14), and so they remained unchanged. But the standard for children's play areas was also not increased, even though councils were clearly providing at a higher level.

The ideal way to test the validity of a recommended standard would be to examine levels of use and assess levels of met and unmet demand and/or need in areas with differing levels of supply and differing socio-demographic and environmental conditions, but there is no evidence from the available documentation that this has been done in relation to the NPFA/ FiT standards.

or even internationally, specified quantum of facilities. Once this quantum of facilities has been provided, it is assumed that the implied level of activity will be automatically forthcoming, providing that the facilities are suitably located, designed and managed.

Operational model
- What to provide: the plan provides for those facilities and associated activities for which standards have been promulgated.
- How much to provide: a fixed quantum (typically related to the size of the population) is specified in the standard; in most cases planners are advised to 'take local conditions into account', but little guidance is offered on how this should be done.

Tourism implications
Provision standards are generally not used in tourism planning.

Limitations
There are misgivings about the original basis of some standards and it is now widely accepted among specialist recreation planners that planning should be based on local circumstances, not on a 'one-size-fits-all' formula.

Conclusion
It has long been argued and accepted in official, professional and academic pronouncements that this approach is no longer appropriate.

Providing opportunity

Providing opportunity is invariably part of the terminology used in the leisure planning process, and to some extent in the marketing of leisure services to the public. *Opportunities* are provided by the existence of facilities and services, but the concept, of itself, does not provide a basis for determining the types and level of provision of those facilities and services, which must be determined by some other means. Providing opportunity is therefore not a complete planning approach, so no diagrammatic representation is offered.

The term is often used in the phrase 'provision of a diverse range of opportunities', which can be seen as the public sector version of the marketing concept *market segmentation*, which in turn is based on the proposition that different groups of people have different tastes/demands/needs/lifestyles. In market segmentation as used in the private sector, the diversity (segmentation) of *products* is designed to match the diverse requirements of market segments, that is identifiable groups of consumers with distinct characteristics and tastes, in order to sell more of the product or brand in total. Market segmentation is therefore not an end in itself but a means to an end: selling more product. Its success is judged in terms of increased sales. Translated to public sector leisure provision, the success of a policy of 'provision of a diverse range of opportunities' should logically be judged in terms of increased levels of participation achieved, but often the policy is presented as an end in itself.

It should be noted that when this approach is applied in the public sector, target 'segments' are often selected on the basis of socio-economic deprivation criteria rather than maximum participation potential, so the criterion for success should not necessarily be maximization of participation overall, but increasing participation among targeted socio-economic groups. This is demonstrated in some of the performance criteria referred to in Chapter 12.

While market segmentation analysis may indicate *what* services to provide, determination of the *amount* of provision, while possibly related to the size of the various groups, requires the use of one of the other planning approaches.

Mission implications

The aim is to provide (a diversity of) opportunities as an end in itself or possibly as a means to increase participation.

Consumer motivation model

For diversity of opportunities: different consumers have different tastes and will make use of facilities/services that match their tastes.

Operational model

- What to provide: distinct groups are identified in the community ('market segments') and a range of facilities/services designed and provided to match the tastes of these groups.
- How much to provide: determined partly by the size of the groups concerned, but some other method is required to estimate the appropriate (increased) level of participation.

Tourism implications

As a primarily commercial activity, the demand and benefits (economic) approaches discussed below are most appropriate, but the concept of market segmentation is relevant.

Limitations

Goals and criteria for success are not intrinsic to the notion of 'provision of opportunities', but should involve demand or participation.

Conclusion

Provision of opportunity is not a planning approach in its own right, but a variation on demand-based or participation-based approaches.

Resource-based planning

Traditionally, planning involved the process: survey → analysis → plan. Contemporary versions tend to label the 'survey' stage *environmental appraisal* and sometimes as the production of a *position statement*. Certain leisure, sport and tourism planning approaches, some of which probably predate the use of standards, can be referred to collectively as *resource-based* planning. They concentrate almost entirely on the survey stage of the planning process. The generic model is shown in Fig. 7.5.

Four variations on the resource-based theme can be identified: (i) residual planning; (ii) opportunistic planning; (iii) conservation; and (iv) environmental spectrum planning. These are described in Tables 7.6 and 7.7.

Mission implications

These vary according to the type:

- *residual*: implications will depend on the methodology used to determine the quantum;
- *opportunistic*: often concerned with economic development/job creation;

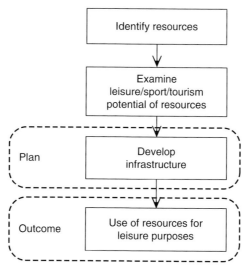

Fig. 7.5. Resource-based planning model.

- *conservation*: generally concerned primarily with conservation goals;
- *environmental spectrum*: may be concerned with conservation-related values, but may also be concerned with maximizing visitor satisfaction and hence visitor numbers, so is a version of demand-based or participation-based approaches.

Consumer motivation model
- *residual*: no discernible consumer model;
- *opportunistic*: feasibility studies are generally used and are demand-based;
- *conservation*: consumer model undefined;
- *environmental spectrum*: similar to the opportunities/market segmentation approach discussed above.

Operational model
What and how much to provide is determined by the characteristics of the resource, but feasibility studies may introduce other dimensions/criteria.

Tourism implications
Opportunistic: conservation versions are highly relevant to tourism planning.

Limitations
The approach is generally limited by the lack of explicit reference to the leisure user, who must be introduced using other planning approaches.

Conclusion
Resources, whether environmental, cultural, built, financial or human, must be considered in any planning process: *resource appraisal* can therefore be seen as a component of other planning approaches rather than a planning approach in its own right.

Table 7.6. Types of resource-based planning.

Type	Characteristics	Advantages	Limitations
Residual planning	Land is allocated for leisure purposes when it is not usable for other purposes: e.g. open space in residual flood-plains	Relatively cheap	May not be physically suitable for purpose (e.g. sloping, subject to flooding. May not be accessible to users
Opportunistic planning	Existing resources adapted for leisure purposes: e.g. natural, scenic, heritage and cultural resources for tourism products; obsolete docklands for waterfront leisure purposes (Craig-Smith and Fagence, 1995)	Unique architectural/ natural/ cultural features	Cost of conversion. Location may not be ideal in relation to markets
Conservation	Use of natural and heritage resources for leisure/tourism purposes: e.g. use of historic buildings as restaurants, community centres or sports facilities, or historic estates as parks	Making use of resources that must be preserved. Offsetting some of the costs of conservation	Cost of adaptation. Heritage considerations. Location may not be ideal in relation to markets
Environmental spectrum planning	Allocating land for various leisure purposes on the basis of a landscape classification scheme: e.g. the Recreation Opportunity Spectrum (ROS) (Clark and Stankey, 1979), as shown in Table 7.7	Provides a clear framework for land managers	Classification basis not always clear. Does not provide a basis for balancing recreational versus conservation values

Meeting demand

Demand-based planning models are based on the concept of demand, as discussed in Chapter 3. The format of the approach is shown in Fig. 7.6.

Current or existing, *met, satisfied* or *effective* demand results from the interaction of demand with the current level and quality of supply of facilities/services at a particular set of prices (including subsidized and zero prices). As discussed in Chapter 3, some demand analysis of the past has been criticized for using models dependent only on the socio-demographic characteristics of current participants and non-participants and then using such models, together with future population projections, to estimate future demand and the required level of facility provision. But, as pointed out in Chapter 3, more sophisticated models incorporate *supply conditions* (prices, facility quality, location, access) as variables, thus providing a means to explore how *unmet, potential* or *latent* demand might be revealed. The quantum of facility provision specified in such a demand-based plan depends on an understanding of how demand

Table 7.7. The Recreation Opportunity Spectrum.

Management/ on-site activities	Spectrum of settings			
	Modern	**Semi-modern**	**Semi-primitive**	**Primitive**
Access (roads, etc.)	Easy	Moderately difficult	Difficult	Very difficult
Non-recreation resource uses (e.g. forestry)	Compatible on large scale	Depends on circumstances	Depends on circumstances	Not compatible
Management site modification	Very extensive	Moderately extensive	Minimal	None
Social interaction (contact with other users)	Frequent	Moderately frequent	Infrequent	None
Visitor impact	High	Moderate	Minimal	None
Regimentation (overt visitor control)	Strict	Moderate	Minimal	None

Sources: Clark and Stankey (1979); Pigram (1983: 27).

is expected to respond to favourable changes in supply conditions. However, virtually ever-increasing demand could be achieved by ever more costly improvements in supply conditions (e.g. reducing the entry charge to zero, providing subsidized transport), so, in the absence of an externally imposed budget constraint or the use of cost–benefit analysis, the approach could result in virtually open-ended commitments. Cost–benefit analysis is discussed in Chapter 12.

Mission implications
The aim is to meet all currently unmet demand and future demand for a given activity.

Consumer motivation model
A demand model is used, relating levels of actual and projected demand to a range of variables, including *consumer characteristics* and *supply conditions*.

Operational model
- What to provide: private sector: determined by market processes; public sector: based on tradition or informal reference to those activities that generate benefits (thus related to the benefits approach discussed below).
- How much to provide: private sector: determined by market processes; public sector: *current unmet* demand is revealed by modelling of changes in supply conditions; *future demand* is estimated by population projections as well as supply variables.

Tourism implications
The demand approach is relevant to tourism, but invariably also involves the benefits (economic) approach.

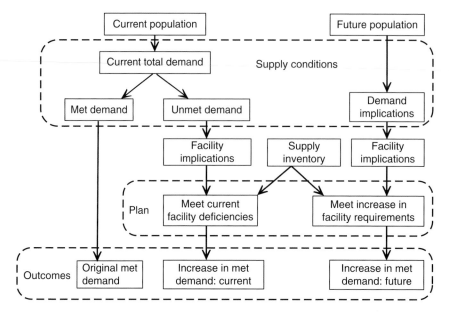

Fig. 7.6. Demand-based planning model.

Limitations

An external budget limitation or the use of cost–benefit analysis is required to place a limit on the level of provision to be made. Both demand modelling and cost–benefit analysis are relatively complex and expensive undertakings. There is considerable confusion among non-economists over the demand concept, especially the 'unmet demand' component, as discussed in Chapter 3.

Conclusion

In practical terms, the demand approach is limited by the complexity of demand modelling and the cost of implementing it. Given that cost–benefit analysis is required to determine the quantum of provision, the economics-based benefits approach, as discussed below, is arguably a more satisfactory approach to use, particularly in the case of tourism, which has primarily economic objectives. However, this does not solve the problem of cost and complexity.

Meeting the requirements/requests of stakeholders

While stakeholder consultation is an accepted component of most approaches to planning and, indeed, is a statutory component of many, in some planning guidelines it appears to be the only part of the process which is described in any detail, so it often becomes the mainstay. The approach is summarized in Fig. 7.7. Some planning approaches explicitly make stakeholder consultation the focus of the exercise: at a more strategic level, this has been termed the *issues approach*, while a more localized version has been termed the *community development approach* (see Chapter 9).

Representatives of organized groups, such as sports clubs, environmental groups or business groups, are typically consulted in any planning exercise and, assuming the

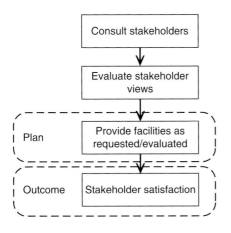

Fig. 7.7. Stakeholder consultation planning model.

representatives fully reflect the views of their organizations and their members, they can provide useful inputs to the process. However, there has been some research in the USA (Lord and Elmendorf, 2008) that indicates that, for some leisure activities at least, only a minority of participants belongs to relevant organizations and that members and representatives of such organizations, being above average in experience, commitment and enthusiasm, have different views from those of non-members, and the representatives have different views from the mass of the members. Futhermore, organization representatives may or may not be well informed about current non-participants who may be potential participants.

In situations where organizations are representative of participants, their inputs can provide ideas for further investigation and qualitative information (e.g. concerning design and management issues) and can advise on likely demand for some forms of organized activity. But they can rarely provide reliable information on the scale of future demand/participation – and hence on the quantum of facilities/services which might be justified – particularly for non-organized activity.

Some consultation processes also include groups of the general public who are not necessarily members of organized groups and may or may not be users of existing facilities/services – for example, young people or seniors. When this consultation is undertaken by means of a *sample survey*, this part of the stakeholder consultation process can be seen as an example of the Demand, Need or Participation approaches, depending on how the data are collected, analysed and utilized. When the consultation is conducted using only *focus groups* then, as with representatives of organized groups, the result may be the provision of useful qualitative information on how some individuals view leisure, sport and tourism provision, but it does not provide a basis for quantification – that is the likely future level of usage of suggested facilities/services.

Planning approaches which appear to rely virtually exclusively on stakeholder consultation must deploy some sort of decision-making process to determine which suggestions/requests arising from the consultation process are viable, in some sense, and to decide between competing demands. This implies the existence of a set of criteria/objectives upon which to base such decision-making, but this is rarely clear, certainly in the guidelines advocating this approach, and so the decision-making process actually used in such situations often appears to be a *black box*.

Mission implications
Provision is made in response to stakeholder requests/requirements.

Consumer motivation model
It is assumed that stakeholder representatives can be relied on to indicate the likely response of members of the community to proposed policy measures: that is, that any facilities/programmes provided will be used.

Operational model
- What to provide: determined by the advice of the stakeholders.
- How much to provide: determined by the advice of the stakeholders: in theory there is no upper limit; in practice the quantum is determined by 'black box' processes.

Tourism implications
As far as the general public is concerned, stakeholder consultation is generally concerned with environmental impacts of tourism. Stakeholders also include the tourism industry, but often relevant organizations (e.g. major investors) are not local, so local stakeholders may or may not provide relevant information.

Limitations
While stakeholder consultation clearly forms part of the decision-making process, it cannot form the major basis of planning because stakeholder representatives may not in fact be representative of their constituency and/or their constituency may be unknown or limited: furthermore they can rarely quantify likely demand/participation. In practice, stakeholder consultation is rarely the only basis of a plan: but if other inputs are involved, this raises the question of *how* stakeholder advice is evaluated against advice from other sources.

Conclusion
In general, stakeholder consultation provides qualitative inputs to the planning process and suggestions for provision, and may be involved in political decision-making processes, but it leaves open the question of how proposals are to be evaluated.

Meeting unmet needs
Needs-based planning, as represented in Fig. 7.8, has become one of the most common approaches in policymaking/planning for leisure. The concept of need is discussed in Chapter 3, where it is observed that public policy statements focused on need are rarely explicit about what is actually meant by a leisure need.

Mission implications
Once identified, a specific level of need should be met in full.

Consumer motivation model
People have an identifiable set of *needs*, including *unmet needs*, which, it is assumed, can be determined from survey responses. Since people have a basic human drive to satisfy their needs, they will make use of facility/service provision that offers to satisfy those needs.

Operational model
- What to provide: determined by the nature of needs identified via resident survey.
- How much to provide: determined by grossing up the above identified needs.

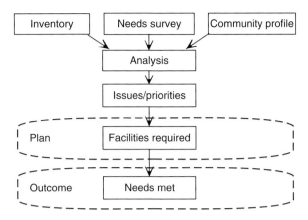

Fig. 7.8. Needs-based planning model.

Limitations

Based on the discussion of need in Chapter 3, five operational limitations should be noted:

1. It is almost impossible to conduct research that distinguishes unmet leisure *needs* from unmet *wants* or *obligations* and, in any case, this is rarely, if ever, attempted in practice.

2. It is virtually impossible for facility/programme managers to distinguish between:

- those would-be users of a facility/service who wish to satisfy their *needs*, and for whom, using the needs-based methodology, the facility/service has ostensibly been provided; and
- those who wish merely to satisfy their *wants* (or obligations) and who would therefore not have been taken into account in a needs-based plan.

3. The approach is based on the assumption that there is a specific level of 'need', for example for a given activity, which can be *technically* identified and should be provided for, whereas *values* must inevitably enter into any decision as to what does and does not constitute a need that should be met by public provision.

4. Even if it is accepted that the term *need* is used very loosely to encompass needs, wants and obligations, the typical approach used in leisure needs-based planning is to focus on discovering *felt needs*, which involves asking people, via surveys, focus groups, etc., what they want/need and acting on that information. This is based on the questionable assumption that people know, and can articulate, their needs/wants and can accurately predict their behaviour when policy measures have been taken to address those articulated needs/wants.

5. If the meeting of *all* identified needs is deemed to be *not possible*, then other criteria for determining priorities among competing needs are required, but such criteria are not clearly spelled out, if at all, in the various guidelines which advocate a 'needs-based' approach.

Tourism implications

Needs-based planning is not appropriate for tourism in the sense used above. As discussed in Chapter 3, some tourism marketers see need as a factor underlying demand, but here this would be subsumed in the demand approach.

Conclusion

The above limitations suggest that a needs-based approach to planning is difficult, if not impossible, to implement in practical terms.

PROVIDING BENEFITS

Participation and demand are concerns of public policy because of the *benefits* they generate. We should, in fact, speak of *net* benefits because the benefits arising from a policy should ideally be assessed in relation to the costs of securing them, and the benefits should exceed the costs – this may be assessed either entirely in monetary terms (cost–benefit analysis) or in terms of a combination of monetary and non-monetary criteria. As discussed above, the goals of an organization should ideally reflect its values, and it is in consideration of benefits that such values can be expected to come most fully into play.

Two main approaches to analysing benefits were discussed in Chapter 3: the economic approach and the Outcomes-Focused Management/Benefits-Based Management (OFM/BBM) approach: their respective planning models are presented in Fig. 7.9.

Benefits: economic approach

Mission implications

The aim is to increase the level of user and community benefits from leisure provision.

Consumer motivation model

Economic demand/'consumption function' models are used, which relate demand to a range of individual and supply variables.

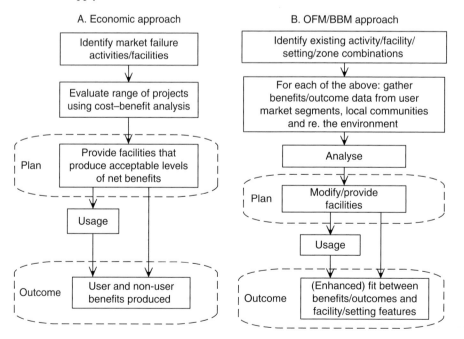

Fig. 7.9. Benefits-based planning models. (OFM/BBM, Outcomes-Focused Management/Benefits-Based Management).

Operational model
- What to provide: determined by market failure arguments (discussed in Chapter 3).
- How much to provide: determined by cost–benefit analysis (see Chapter 11).

Tourism implications
This approach is highly relevant to tourism planning, since public interest is based on economic impacts, as discussed in Chapter 11.

Limitations
A detailed assessment of costs and benefits of projects could provide a complete decision-making system for leisure planning, but to do this, covering *all* social, economic and environmental costs and benefits, is beyond the resources of most public leisure planning and provision agencies. Generic benefit values for different activities *could* be developed by state or national governments and utilized by local planning agencies – a procedure known a 'value transfer' – but the necessary research to operationalize this has not been carried out.

Conclusion
Use of this approach is theoretically possible, but operationally problematic in most planning situations because of the expertise required and the cost of data collection. The exception is tourism (including sport tourism), where economic impact (incomes and job creation) is a more significant component of decision-making. The difference between economic impact measurement and cost–benefit analysis is discussed in Chapter 11.

Benefits: Outcomes-Focused Management (OFM)/Benefits-Based Management (BBM)

Mission implications
Management of a setting should be guided by seeking the best possible fit between outcomes/benefits and setting characteristics.

Consumer motivation model
Matching user and other stakeholder assessments of benefits/outcomes with setting characteristics will enhance overall benefits/outcomes arising from the facilities/settings.

Operational model
- What to provide: activities/facilities that best match setting characteristics.
- How much to provide: the approach is not clear.

Limitations
As indicated in Chapter 3, there is a lack of guidance in the OFM/BBM literature on non-user data collection and analysis; it is not clear how new facilities are to be evaluated, and the amount of data to be collected is at least as great as for cost–benefit analysis.

Conclusion
Due to the lack of operational detail in regard to measurement and data analysis and its substantial data requirements, the OFM/BBM approach does not offer a practical approach to operational planning.

Increasing participation

Participation-based models of leisure planning are not presented in the planning guidelines literature but, as Boxes 7.1 and 7.2 and Web-box 1 illustrate, participation targets have begun to feature in the plans of state/province and national governments in recent years, but less at the local level. A planning approach focused on participation is illustrated in Fig. 7.10.

Participation can be measured by the percentage *participation rate*, or the average *volume of activity* per resident of a designated area, which takes account of frequency of participation and possibly of time spent.

Most, but not all, of the benefits arising from leisure result from *participation*. Typically, participation-based planning documents make reference to benefits, but do not attempt to measure benefits directly. In effect, participation is used as a proxy for benefits. In some cases the goals are expressed without quantification – to 'increase', 'enhance', 'encourage' participation – while in other cases specific targets are adopted. In some cases the goal relates to participation among the population generally, while in other cases specific groups are targeted – youth, women, underprivileged groups.

The question arises as to what targets to set. In some cases there may be a theoretical maximum that is widely accepted and at which policy could be directed. For example, if participation in physical recreation is being publicly supported primarily on health grounds, reference could be made to the commonly accepted ideal that everyone should participate in moderately intensive physical activity for at least 30 minutes at least three times a week. This may not be the ultimate level of participation which might be supported, but it presents a challenging interim target for most planning agencies for the typical planning period of up to 10 years. For other types of leisure activity there are no comparable maximum participation levels. Ultimately, the level of participation to be aimed at is a political one. In the U-Plan system presented in Chapter 8, initial target-setting is based on social and spatial equity criteria, on the principle that, in relation to broad categories of leisure, all groups and geographical areas within a community should be enabled to reach the current average: a process which, if successful, gradually increases the overall average participation rate.

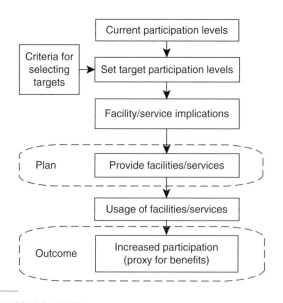

Fig. 7.10. Participation-based planning model.

Mission implications

The approach concentrates on the level of participation in leisure activity and therefore requires the setting of target participation levels.

Consumer motivation model

No specific model of consumer motivation is intrinsic to the approach: in most published examples the assumed model is far from clear. In the U-Plan system presented in Chapter 8, a simplified demand model is used, in which the probability of an individual participating is based on specified socio-demographic and facility access variables.

Operational model

- What to provide: support is given to those activities that produce benefits; the approach therefore rests on the theoretical underpinnings of the benefits approaches.
- How much to provide: in some cases, there may be (interim) maximum targets, but ultimately the decision on what level to aim for is political. A staged approach might be based on social and spatial equity criteria.

Limitations

Benefits that are not dependent on participation are not incorporated – this is accepted as a limitation, while noting that any such benefits over and above participation-based benefits can be acknowledged in a qualitative way, as is common in most planning approaches. Project proposals arising *primarily* from non-participation-based factors (e.g. wildlife conservation) should arise from other planning processes and could be incorporated at the Facility/Service Audit stage (Task 16, Chapter 8).

All forms of participation are not of equal value: some produce more benefits than others and should therefore be given more weight. These differences arise in regard to social groups, which can be taken care of in the target-setting process, or in regard to the existence of *non-user benefits* generated by some forms of participation but not by others – such benefits could be taken into account by some sort of weighting system. In practice, of the alternative planning approaches, only benefit-based approaches take this fully into account, while needs-based and stakeholder consultation approaches can reflect it but only in an informal way.

Tourism implications

The number of tourists visiting an area and their use of local leisure facilities correspond to the participation measure used in relation to residents (although it might more appropriately be referred to as *demand*), and could be used as a proxy for benefits in the same way; arguably the benefits of tourism – income and jobs – should be considered directly.

Conclusion

The participation-based approach overcomes a number of the limitations of the other approaches discussed above.

Planning approaches: conclusions

Figure 7.11 draws together the implications of some of the above analysis. It shows that each of the planning methods eventually finds expression in terms of benefits, and most via the phenomenon of participation. As illustrated in the diagram:

- The standards, opportunities and resource-based approaches are focused directly on facilities but, assuming that the facilities are duly used by participants, this *implies* a

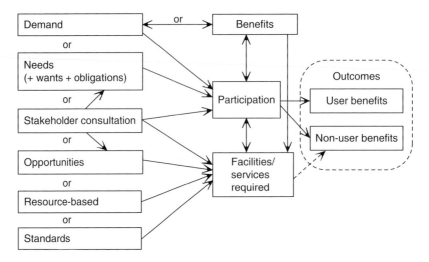

Fig. 7.11. Planning approaches: an overview.

level of participation to be accommodated in the facilities specified. Thus, for example, these approaches could be saying: 'We plan to provide this community with a facility/opportunity of such-and-such a size'. If this facility can accommodate, say, 250,000 visits a year, this is equivalent to saying: 'We are planning for a participation level of 250,000 visits a year in this community'.

- The aims of the stakeholder consultation process may be expressed via one or more of the other approaches.
- Needs-based, demand-based and benefits-based approaches are all realized through the medium of participation.
- Participation results in user benefits and some non-user benefits (identifiable third-party beneficiaries and the community at large).
- Some non-user benefits arise without the intermediary of participation (see dotted arrow, e.g. aesthetics-based real-estate value benefits of parks).

Thus all seven planning and provision processes are ultimately concerned with benefits, and an ideal planning system would be based on the analysis of benefits but, as we have seen, benefits analysis is either prohibitively complex or costly to administer (the economics approach) or has equally demanding data requirements but has not been fully operationalized (the OFM/BBM approach). It is therefore concluded that a planning approach based on *participation* overcomes many of the theoretical and/or practical limitations of the other approaches reviewed. Such an approach is outlined in the following chapter.

LAND-USE PLANNING

This chapter has been involved with strategic planning in relation to the specific fields of leisure, sport and tourism. We should also note the existence of *town planning*, which impacts on all social, economic and environmental activity at the local levels. Cullingworth and Nadin (2006: 2), in the standard UK reference for the subject, define land-use planning as: 'a process concerned with the determination of land uses, the general objectives of which are set out in legislation or in some document of legal or accepted standing'. The system has legal status, or the backing of statutes – hence it is often referred to as part of the system of *statutory planning*. Cullingworth and Nadin (2006) list over 90 Acts of Parliament relating to land-use, or environmental, planning in Britain, although the current basic system was outlined in the Town and Country Planning Act, 1968, modified by further Acts in 1990 and 1991 and reforms introduced in 2001. In federal systems, such as Australia, each state has its own planning legislation.

At the heart of the land-use planning process is the idea of *zoning* – legally designating the purpose to which land can be put. Thus land might be zoned for: residential, retail, entertainment, hotel accommodation, office, industrial, transport, education or open space use. The zoning system also includes matters such as height restrictions and parking controls. The zoning system is set out in a published *land-use plan* prepared by the local authority and endorsed by a government minister. Landowners who flout the zoning regulations may be prosecuted and will be required to desist from the 'non-conforming use', and may even be required to demolish unauthorized buildings. The land-use plan can relate to either newly developed areas or existing developed areas. Thus land-use planning involves two processes: the development of an appropriate land-use plan and the subsequent implementation and enforcement of the provisions of the plan, or *development control*.

While early planning approaches were fairly simplistic in their approach to zoning, later versions have become more sophisticated. Thus the 1968 UK Act established the idea of *structure plans*, in which zoning was to be based on a thorough understanding of the social, economic and environmental *structure* of the urban or rural area under consideration. This means that, in addition to such matters as transport, housing and industry, the role of leisure and tourism in a community must be taken into account and incorporated into the structure plan. Thus the sorts of planning activity described in this and the next chapter can provide inputs into the structure planning process.

Land-use planning is involved in a number of specialized areas, including demographic planning, transportation planning and housing. Of particular interest to the field of leisure and tourism are areas such as heritage and natural area conservation. There is a system of protection for ancient monuments, historic buildings and precincts, even when they are in private ownership. Similarly, the designation of World Heritage Areas, National Parks and Nature Reserves – and in Australia Aboriginal heritage sites – have statutory protection. Also important for outdoor recreation in the UK is the network of 'rights of way', such as public footpaths on private land, which are often hundreds of years old.

In general, the statutory land-use planning system, because of its statutory basis, remains the most powerful form of planning and one of the most effective means of securing and implementing policies. While leisure and tourism professionals are often preoccupied with management and development, it follows that they would be unwise to ignore the land-use planning process.

RESOURCES

Strategic planning/management: Wheelen and Hunger (1989); Certo and Peter (1991); Carter *et al.* (1992); Mintzberg (1994).
Visioning: Ritchie (1994a); White (2000); Walzer (1996); Helling (1998).
Decision-making: Lindblom (1959); Ham and Hall (1984); Parsons (1995).

Recreation Opportunity Spectrum: Clark and Stankey (1979); Driver *et al.* (1987); Stankey *et al.* (1999); as applied to tourism: Butler and Waldbrook (1991).

Tourism planning generally: Hall (2000).

Land-use planning: in the UK: Cullingworth and Nadin (2006); in Australia (NSW): Department of Environment and Planning (1987).

General approaches to leisure planning: Kelsey and Gray (1985); Ravenscroft (1992); Torkildsen (2005: 239).

Outdoor recreation: Lieber and Fesenmaier (1983); Williams (1995); Anderson *et al.* (2000).

Standards: Buechner (1971); Torkildsen (1999: 168); Fields in Trust (2008); Veal (2009b).

Resource-based planning: Jubenville and Twight (1993, Chapters 11 and 12); Craig-Smith and Fagence (1995).

Spatial methods: Coppock and Duffield (1975); Ewing (1983); Smith (1995: 150–173).

QUESTIONS/EXERCISES

1. Distinguish between mission, goals and objectives in relation to one of the following: (i) a local council park system; (ii) a national sport promotion agency; (iii) a regional tourism development organization.

2. Why does the definition of leisure and of tourism present difficulties with regard to the appropriate scope of a leisure/tourism plan?

3. Locate a local council, national park agency or tourism agency strategic plan or master plan document in a library or online and assess what it has to say about the organization's mission, goals and objectives.

4. Using the same document as identified in item 3, identify the approach or approaches to planning used in the document.

chapter 8

A Participation-based Approach to Planning for Leisure, Sport and Tourism

INTRODUCTION

This chapter describes a step-by-step approach to planning for leisure, sport and tourism focused on the concept of participation, as discussed in Chapter 7. The particular approach outlined here is the 'U-Plan system' developed at the University of Technology, Sydney. In this chapter a brief summary is presented. Information on access to the full details of the system, which provide guidance and resources to enable its full implementation, are provided in the Resources section.

U-Plan components and features

The U-Plan system comprises three *core modules* and 18 *tasks*, as shown in Fig. 8.1. The roles of the core modules are as follows:

- *Objectives/Outcomes Module*: in the context of the goals of the organization, to set participation targets in broad categories of leisure, such as 'exercise, recreation and sport' or 'cultural activity', and to monitor progress towards their achievement over time.
- *Participation Module*: to identify the individual activities that will be most suitable for achieving these targets and to quantify the required levels of participation in those activities.
- *Supply Module*: to estimate the facility/service supply implications of the adopted participation *targets*.

Some of the other key features of the system are as follows:

- *Focus*: the focus is on *participation*, as discussed in Chapter 7. This is based on the proposition that participation captures the bulk of the benefits of provision for leisure, sport or tourism and can therefore be used as a proxy for these benefits.

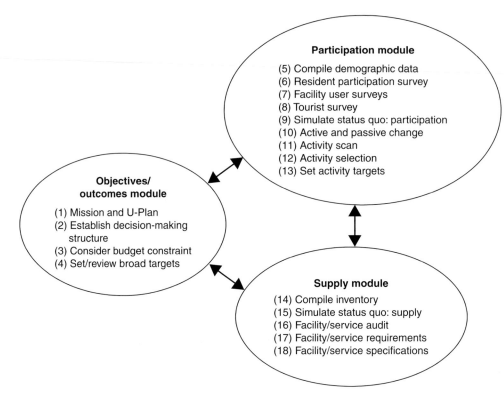

Fig. 8.1. The U-Plan system.

- *Planning area*: the U-Plan system is designed around a hypothetical *planning area*, referred to as *Area X*, which is assumed to be, typically, a local council area. But the system could be applied to groupings of such areas, forming a region or subregion, or a county, state or province. At whichever level Area X is located, the next level above is referred to as the *region* in which it is located, as shown in Table 8.1. Furthermore, Area X may itself be divided into a number of geographical subdivisions for some purposes, and these subdivisions are referred to as *planning zones*.

Table 8.1. Spatial hierarchy.

| U-Plan hierarchy | Examples | | | |
	UK-1	UK-2	Australia-1	Australia-2
Region	County	Region	State	State
Area X	Local council	County	Local council	Metropolitan area
Planning zones	Local planning zones	Local councils	Suburb/ postcodes	Local councils

- *Who decides?* In the full exposition of the system, consideration is given at each stage to the question of 'who decides?'. This addresses the respective roles of the elected or appointed body that constitutes the planning agency which has ultimate decision-making authority, its appointed technical officers, various stakeholder groups and organizations and the general public. In this summary, 'Who Decides?' is discussed separately when all the tasks have been reviewed.
- *Planning period*: policymaking and planning is concerned with appraising the present situation and setting goals to be achieved over some future period. In the U-Plan system, this period is referred to as the *planning period* and is assumed to be about 10 years in duration, although it could be more or less than this and could be broken down into a number of short-term, medium-term and long-term stages.
- *Spreadsheets*: since a comprehensive leisure, sport and tourism planning exercise involves a wide range of activities and facilities/programmes, much of the quantitative analysis is carried out using spreadsheets, as illustrated in Fig. 8.2.
- *Activities and facilities*: in Fig. 8.2, it can be seen that activities are grouped according to the type of facility which they tend to use. Some facilities, such as grass sports fields, arts centres, halls and parks, are multi-use: they can accommodate a number of activities. So switching from accommodating one activity to accommodating another is a short- or medium-term management task. Planning for this type of multi-purpose facility is therefore concerned with the aggregation of activities which it accommodates. Other facilities, such as squash courts, golf courses or bowling alleys, are single-purpose.
- *Programmes/services* such as art classes, coaching courses, environmental interpretation offerings or arts festivals can be viewed, and therefore planned for, as part of the demand for use of facilities. Programmes such as fun-runs or street parades that do not take place in leisure facilities can be taken into account by including streets, etc. as a special kind of facility.
- *Focus Modules*: ten Focus Modules provide additional guidance on specific topics:

A	B	C	D	E	F	G	I	J	N	O	
	Tasks	Facility type A			Facility type B			Facility type C			Total
		Act. 1	Act. 2	Etc.	Act. 1	Act. 2	Etc.	Act. 1	Act. 2	Act. 3	Etc.	
Objectives/ outcomes module	1											
	2											
	3											
Broad part'n targets	etc.											
Participation module	5											
	6											
Activity targets	etc.											
Supply module	14											
	15											
Facility requirements	etc.											

Fig. 8.2. U-Plan spreadsheet format.

1. Benefits of leisure.
2. Models of consumer behaviour.
3. Target-setting.
4. Data collection and analysis.
5. Forecasting.
6. Tourism.
7. Activity profiles.
8. Assets/resources.
9. Spatial analysis.
10. Participation database.

Details of some Focus Modules are discussed in later chapters of the book, while in other cases details are provided on the U-Plan website. A diagrammatic representation of the ways in which the modules and tasks are linked is shown in Fig. 8.3.

Before considering the U-Plan system in detail, we should note its relationship to the generic rational-comprehensive model (RCM) of planning and decision-making, as discussed in Chapter 6 and represented in Fig. 6.3. This relationship is summarized in Table 8.2, where it can be seen that all the items in Fig. 6.3, with the exception of item 9 (Implement/Manage), are accounted for in various ways in the U-Plan system.

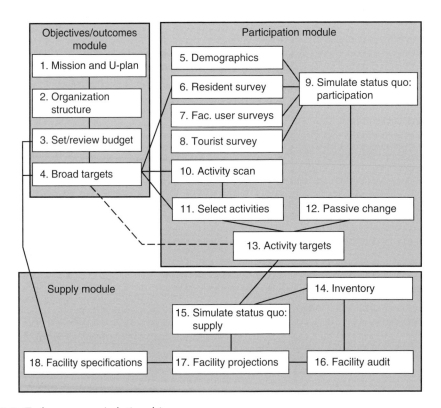

Fig. 8.3. Task sequence/relationships.

Table 8.2. Relationship between the rational-comprehensive model and the U-Plan system.

RCM[a] item	U-Plan Task	Comments
1. Terms of reference/brief	Terms of reference/brief	Terms of reference/brief for public bodies are generally provided by the legislation or charter under which they are established and regulated, and this generally finds expression in the organizational mission, as discussed at point 3
2. Mission/goals		The process of establishing the organizational mission and broad goals, as discussed in Chapter 7, is not outlined in detail in the U-Plan system since it is assumed that these will have been established in a broader context, particularly in regard to 1. above, but there may need to be some fine-tuning to make clear the link with participation/benefits, which is the basis of the U-Plan system
3. Decide planning approach	1. Organizational Mission and U-Plan	The decision taken to use the U-Plan system, based on participation/benefits, is taken in consideration of the organization's mission
4. Environmental appraisal	5–8. Surveys 10. Passive change 14. Facility/service inventory	Involves the collation of information, which, in the U-Plan system, is focused and itemized in a number of tasks concerned with surveys, examining passive change and establishing a facility/service inventory
5. Stakeholder consultation	2. Organizational structure + various	Some consultative mechanisms will be built into the organizational structure, then, as indicated in Fig. 6.3, stakeholder consultation takes place at various points during the planning process
6. Develop options	4. Setting/reviewing participation targets	Options are developed primarily in relation to the setting of broad participation targets
7. Evaluate options	11. Activity evaluation 16. Facility/service audit	This part of the process is divided into two stages, in relation to activities and facilities/services
8. Adopt strategy	12. Activity selection 13. Participation projections 17. Facility/service requirements 18. Facility/service specifications	A two-stage process, in regard to selection of activities and related participation targets and in regard to facilities/services
9. Implement/manage	–	This item is not part of the U-Plan system
10. Monitor/evaluate/feedback	3. Setting/reviewing budget constraint 4. Setting/reviewing participation targets	Tasks 3 and 4 are concerned not only with setting budgetary constraints and participation targets, but with periodically reviewing them at points during the planning period, and this involves periodic updating of the data collection

[a]RCM, Rational-comprehensive model.

The three core modules and their associated 18 tasks are discussed in turn below. The approach is illustrated with data on six activities: in practice a much larger number of leisure activities would be involved: at least 100 for a comprehensive leisure planning exercise.

OBJECTIVES/OUTCOMES MODULE

Task 1. Organizational Mission and the U-Plan system

Any planning organization considering using the U-Plan system must consider the alignment of its mission and goals, as discussed in Chapter 7, with the participation-based approach. In particular the system is based on two principles:

1. The benefits which are deemed to arise from leisure, sport and tourism can be attributed primarily to *participation*, as illustrated in Fig. 8.4.
2. The planning process involves the setting of *participation targets*.

Task 2. Establishing decision-making structures

Task 2 is concerned with ensuring that appropriate internal and external decision-making structures are in place. Ultimately, decisions are the responsibility of the legal entity which is responsible for the planning process: the elected members of a council, the appointed members of a board or the cabinet and legislature of a government. However, this agency may delegate certain decisions to others and may seek advice from a range of sources. Any decision-making structure is therefore likely to include a number of components, as suggested in Table 8.3. There are of course some overlaps in the membership of the groups/organizations shown.

A decision-making structure requires certain qualities that require careful consideration, including:

- efficiency of operation: it must not be so complex that decision-making gets bogged down by lengthy procedures;
- availability of appropriate professional skills, including recognition that planning for leisure/sport/tourism requires specialist knowledge and expertise;
- appropriate representativeness: appropriate representation for all stakeholder groups;
- availability of appropriate resources: particularly resources to gather, analyse and interpret data.

Task 3. Considering budget constraints

Budgetary constraints are often the key factor weighing on the collective minds of decision-makers in the policymaking process. In a multi-purpose organization, such as a local council, the overall budget for the leisure/sport/tourism function is ultimately decided in a

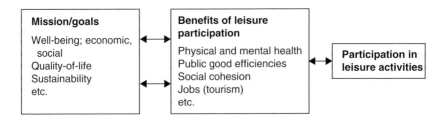

Fig. 8.4. Mission – benefits – participation.

Table 8.3. Decision-making structure: potential participants.

Component	Examples	Decision powers
Elected/appointed responsible body	Elected council	Ultimately: all decisions
Committees	Committees of council; steering committees; advisory committees	Delegated decisions and advice/recommendations
Appointed officers	CEO; Director of Leisure and Tourism	Delegated decisions and advice/recommendations
Consultants	Leisure planning consultants	Advice/recommendations
Stakeholder representatives/groups	Chamber of commerce; sports associations	Advice/recommendations
Residents	Voters; survey respondents	Opinions (and electoral power)
Facility/service users	Park visitors; library users	Opinions (via surveys, etc.)
Visitors	Day-visitors; tourists	Opinions (via surveys, etc.)

competitive political arena where other areas of public spending are also decided: a case must be made in competition with other areas of expenditure. This is invariably an iterative process, with each sector making ambit claims and the overall decision-making body deciding on final allocations of resources. This suggests the need for flexibility in the planning process and for the ability to develop a range of scenarios, depending on the budget constraints imposed at various points in the process.

The overall budget will also be affected by the revenue-raising components of the leisure/sport/tourism operations within the control of the planning organization. This will be a function of pricing policies, both for direct user-fees and leasing arrangements with other organizations.

Over a 10-year planning period, budget constraints can be estimated only approximately, and expressed in general terms. For example, it might be assumed that overall net expenditure will continue at prevailing rates in real terms (i.e. increasing in cash terms in line with inflation) or with a modest level of real growth, such as 2%/year; and/or, in both cases, increasing in line with population. In times of financial stringency or in conditions where a political commitment has been made to reduce public expenditure, it may be necessary to assume real reductions in expenditure, although this can still result in increasing levels of provision, but at a slower rate than in the past.

Task 4. Setting/reviewing broad targets

Task 4, the setting and reviewing of broad targets, involves examining current levels of leisure, sport and tourism participation in the community and setting participation targets for the planning period ahead. At this stage, targets are not set for individual activities but for broad categories of leisure activity, such as 'sport and physical recreation' and 'cultural activities'. In the case of tourism, the targets do not relate to the leisure activities of members of the community but to numbers of visitors and their expenditure and impacts.

The discussion here relates primarily to the initial setting of targets, but targets will also be subject to *review* in two contexts:

1. In each of the rounds of any planning exercise, as feasibility and budgetary constraints are negotiated.
2. At the end of the planning period and at various points during the planning period, when progress towards meeting the targets is monitored.

The decision-making strategy set out in Fig. 8.5 suggests criteria that might be used to determine suitable targets. It assumes the existence of baseline survey data on current leisure participation patterns in the community, which is discussed further in the Participation Module (Task 6). The strategy comprises seven steps, which are discussed in turn below.

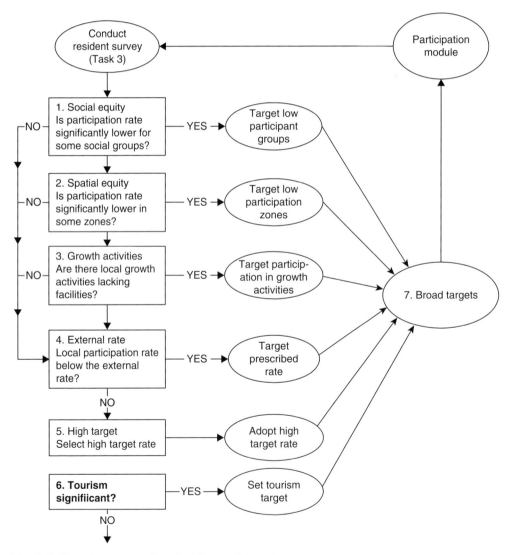

Fig. 8.5. Broad target-setting decision-making strategy.

Step 1. Social equity

This and the next step focus on the idea of *equity*, meaning fairness. Much has been written on the question of equity in leisure provision (e.g. Crompton and West, 2008). Here, given that the focus of policy is on participation, it is argued that an equitable outcome will be that all social groups and/or all areas of a community have, as far as possible, similar levels of participation in broad categories of leisure. Policy is aimed at achieving this outcome. This is likely to involve different mixes of activities and different mixes of public, private and non-profit sector provision, but this is explored in later stages in the system. Here the aim is to establish what increases in participation among different groups and areas would be implied by the above outcome.

A resident participation survey provides information regarding the current average Area X participation rate and the data are then examined to establish whether participation rates are significantly lower than average among certain *socio-demographic groups*. If so, one of the targets will be to aim to raise participation rates among those groups to at least the prevailing average for the planning area. This becomes one or more of the targets collated at Step 7. If the agency has a general policy to give priority to certain socio-demographic groups, this will be taken into account here: thus such groups might be included in the target groups even if their participation rates are not as far below the average as other groups selected.

A successfully implemented policy for increasing the participation rates of the targeted groups would, of course, increase the overall Area X participation rate.

Step 2. Spatial equity

The above process can be repeated in relation to *planning zones* within Area X, which may result in certain zones being targeted because of lower than average participation rates. Low participation rates in some zones may be related to socio-demographic characteristics of the population, so there might be a spatial dimension to the social inequity discussed in Step 1. Alternatively, low participation rates in some zones could be due to lack of facilities or poor-quality facilities. As with the social equity-based targets, a successfully implemented policy to increase the participation rates of the populations of the targeted zones would increase the overall participation rate of the Area X population.

Step 3. Growth activities

From time to time, local councils and other providers of leisure/sport facilities and services experience rapid growth in demand for some activities that is difficult to accommodate in existing facilities and which calls for a policy response. The social and spatial features of the demand may or may not align with the social or spatial priorities discussed in Steps 1 and 2, but if the planning agency has a policy to increase overall participation, there is logic in assisting spontaneous growth when it occurs and a certain growth target may be adopted for these activities – the precise target is discussed in the Participation Module.

Step 4. External rate

As we have noted, successful policy action arising from Steps 1–3 would, by increasing target group/zone participation levels, increase the overall participation by a predictable amount, so Step 4 may be conducted using as a starting point a revised, projected participation rate taking account of these other policies.

Step 4 refers to the possibility of adopting a participation rate prescribed by an external agency. The agency could be a government – see, for example, the increase in participation rates adopted by some governments as shown in Boxes 7.1, 7.2 and Web-box 1 – or a professional or scientific recommendation, such as the minimum level of participation in physical activity to achieve health benefits (Surgeon General, 1996). The planning agency would of course need to examine the recommendations and their rationale to ensure that they were aligned with its own goals and values. Such external rates will generally cover only a part of the full range of leisure activities being addressed in the planning exercise.

Step 5. High target

The decision-making process reaches Step 5 only if there are no social or spatial inequities still to be dealt with, or the actual or projected overall participation rate is above the prescribed rate. This can be expected to be quite rare. In such a situation, however, the agency could: (i) adopt a stand-still strategy; (ii) select an arbitrary target; or (iii) select a 'comparator' area or areas with a higher participation level to which it could aspire, e.g. the average for the top quarter of councils.

The last option assumes that data on participation levels in different council areas are known.

A further option is to proceed on the basis of cost–benefit analysis: that is, to continue providing facilities/services as long as all benefits generated by the increased participation levels continue to exceed the costs of provision. This of course assumes that appropriate 'transfer values' exist (see Chapter 3) and/or that resources are available to carry out the required research. Cost–benefit analysis is discussed in Chapter 12.

Step 6. Tourism

If tourism is not a significant phenomenon in Area X and there is no desire to boost tourism to the area to a significant level, then it is not necessary to set specific tourism targets: the limited amount of tourism and the leisure demand it generates in the area will be assumed to continue as indicated in data from facility user surveys and will be taken into account, along with the local demands of neighbours and commuters, as discussed under the Participation Module. If tourism *is* a significant phenomenon in Area X and/or there is a desire to boost tourism, then it will be necessary to set targets. This process is discussed in Box 8.1. It is possible that a tourism strategy will be developed as a separate exercise rather than as part of a leisure, sport and tourism strategy, but using the U-Plan system for both strategies enables the relationships between the two, notably in resident and tourist use of common facilities, to be recognized.

Box 8.1. U-Plan: tourism objectives/outcomes.

In the U-Plan system the objectives/outcomes for a leisure/sport planning exercise are expressed in terms of participation as a proxy for benefits. This approach, however, is based on a number of basic arguments which do not apply in the case of tourism:

- In leisure/sport the measurement of benefits on a routine basis is complex and costly, but the major positive benefits of tourism, in terms of income/jobs, are relatively easy to measure.
- In leisure/sport the costs and dis-benefits of facility/service provision are related solely to the leisure/sport facilities/services in the plan, but in the case of tourism the costs and potential dis-benefits are more significant because they concern not just the provision and impact of leisure facilities/services but also other infrastructure, notably accommodation and transport, associated additional environmental impacts and cultural impacts.
- Resident participation levels would be viewed by most people as an acceptable close proxy for the benefits of leisure/sport to the community but the equivalent in tourism, namely the number of tourist visits or tourist nights, is not necessarily a good proxy for benefits to the community because of the significance of non-leisure impacts as discussed above.

(Continued)

Box 8.1. Continued.

- An acceptable set of equity and other criteria can be devised to set leisure/sport targets on the basis of resident participation levels, as indicated in Fig. 8.5, but these are not applicable to tourism.

It is assumed here that the *rationale* for tourism development at the community level is the income and jobs it brings to the host community. There are, in some cases, other motives involved, for example communities hosting national or world cultural or natural heritage sites may feel an *obligation* to receive visitors and may indeed take a pride in doing so. But the primary focus is economic factors subject, of course, to environmental and cultural constraints, assessment of which is built into the planning process.

How should the scale of tourism to be planned for be determined? Figure 8.6 presents a suggested process, involving 15 components. The first seven components involve identification and analysis of types of constraint or opportunity, the results of which

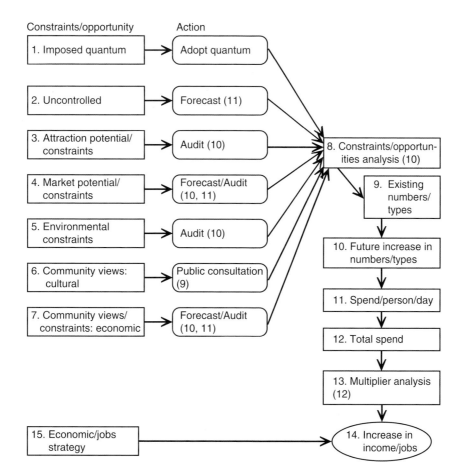

Fig. 8.6. U-Plan: tourism objectives/outcomes. Numbers in parentheses refer to the chapter in which the topic is discussed.

(Continued)

Box 8.1. Continued.

are considered together in component 8, the constraints analysis. The components are discussed in turn below:

1. *Imposed quantum*. In some planning environments it could be the case that the quantum of tourism to be accommodated in a planning area is given by a tourism strategy developed by a superior authority: for example, a national government strategy imposing a quantum on a provincial or regional planning organization. The local agency has no choice but to adopt the quantum given, although there is likely to be some scope for determining the type of tourism and possibly to challenge the quantum in light of further analysis.

2. *Uncontrolled*. Assuming the local planning agency has control over the development of accommodation, then it has broad control over tourism numbers, but this is not the case with day-trippers. These may be residents from population centres within day-trip reach or they may be tourists staying at locations within day-trip reach. Some control may be exercised through transport and parking controls (see Chapter 10, section on capacity), but this is not always possible. A forecasting exercise is required to quantify future day-tripper numbers.

3. *Attraction potential/constraints*. Existing and future possible attractions offer quantitative and qualitative constraints and opportunities and these will need to be evaluated, as discussed in Chapter 10.

4. *Market potential/constraints*. The markets from which the destination already draws visitors, and from which it might draw visitors in future, also have potential and constraints, related to, for example, growth of populations and level of incomes in those areas. This involves an audit and forecasting study.

5. *Environmental constraints*. Tourism growth may be limited by environmental constraints of natural ecosystems and/or by non-natural physical constraints such as transport, water supply and sewerage infrastructure, which require an audit.

6. *Community views: cultural*. There may be objections on social or cultural grounds to increased tourism numbers, which may be expressed through political processes and/or public consultation.

7. *Economic views/constraints*. There could be pressure to increase tourism numbers from businesses or workers in the industry, but there could be current or future constraints in the form of lack of available and suitably qualified labour; these factors should be assessed by audit and forecasting.

8. *Constraints analysis*. Analysis of the various constraints and opportunities is discussed in Chapter 10 in relation to tourism capacity. The result is a target number of tourists or tourist-days divided into types (accommodation type, transit, day-trippers, etc.).

9. *Existing numbers/types*. The existing numbers of tourists and types will have been established at Task 8 in the U-Plan process.

10. *Increase in numbers/types*. Comparing the outcome of components 8 and 9 gives the increase in tourist numbers to be planned for.

11. *Spend per person per day*. Expenditure per person per day types will have been established at Task 8 in the U-Plan process.

12. *Total spend*. Multiplying the increase in tourist numbers by the spend per person per day and then by the number of days in the season gives the total tourist expenditure.

(Continued)

Box 8.1. Continued.

13. *Multiplier analysis*. The initial tourist expenditure circulates within the local economy, creating an aggregate increase in income via the *multiplier process*, as outlined in Chapter 12.

14. *Increase in income/jobs*. The total additional income is divided by an average gross wage rate to provide an estimate of the increase in full-time-equivalent jobs.

15. *Economic/jobs strategy*. Component 15 indicates the possibility of a substantially different approach, in which the planning agency has adopted a broad economic development and/or jobs-creation strategy that specifies the number of jobs expected to be created in various sectors, including tourism. Thus the specification in component 15 determines, via components 14, 13 and 12, the number of tourists to be planned for. Components 1–8 then follow as part of a standard U-Plan process and may result in some modification of the initial specification. This sequence could also be followed by starting with component 14 and/or 10 and selecting an initial draft growth figure, perhaps based on a 'reasonable' rate of growth and proceeding with the various U-Plan tasks in the standard order. The constraints analysis would come later in the process and, if this resulted in a smaller increase in tourist numbers, the draft figure could be revised downwards.

Thus the objectives/outcomes process for tourism is potentially more involved and less self-contained than the equivalent process for leisure/sport, with a number of the tasks from the Participation and Supply Modules being activated earlier than in the standard system, unless the procedures in component 15 are used.

Step 7. Collation of targets

In this step the various targets are collated and are then considered in detail in the Participation Module. A simplified example is shown in Fig. 8.7.

PARTICIPATION MODULE

The Participation Module involves:

- conducting research to understand and simulate the status quo with regard to leisure/sport and tourism participation in Area X;
- using this understanding to identify the most appropriate means of achieving the targets established in the Objectives/Outcomes Module, in terms of specific activities;
- estimating the implications in terms of increased participation levels in specific activities to be catered for.

Framework

A framework for the Participation Module is described in Box 8.2. It follows a sequence from consideration of a resident population and its current patterns of leisure participation, to the distribution of that participation, together with participation by neighbours, commuters and tourists, in the leisure facilities within Area X. These facilities are either council-operated or operated by other public, non-profit or commercial organizations. Establishing such a picture of the status quo involves a programme of data collection indicated in Table 8.4 and described in more detail in Tasks 5–8.

	A	B	C
1		Participation rates in Area X	Target
2		% in year	
3	Area X average	77.9	
4	1. Social equity – age and gender		
5	Male 15 – 24	89.2	
6	Male 25 – 34	84.2	
7	Male 35 – 44	85.1	
8	Male 45 – 54	72.6	Increase by 5.3% to 77.9%
9	Male 55 – 64	73.6	Increase by 4.3% to 77.9%
10	Male 65+	69.5	Increase by 8.4% to 77.9%
11	Female 15 – 24	74.3	Increase by 3.6% to 77.9%
12	Female 25 – 34	81.9	
13	Female 35 – 44	79.6	
14	Female 45 – 54	77.6	
15	Female 55 – 64	78.0	
16	Female 65+	66.2	Increase by 11.7% to 77.9%
17	2. Spatial equity		
18	Zone A	77.9	No action–differences not significant
19	Zone B	77.3	
20	3. Growth activities		See participation and supply modules
21	4. External rate		
22	Region	79.4	
23	Area X	77.9	Raise to 79.4%

Fig. 8.7. Setting broad targets: simplified example – sport/physical recreation (covers all formal and informal sport/physical recreation, including walking).

Box 8.2. U-Plan Participation Module framework.

The framework for undertaking this module is outlined in Fig. 8.8, which indicates a local planning area, Area X, and the 'Rest of the world'.

The framework comprises the following components:

A. The resident population of Area X may be presented as a single figure relating to the whole population (A) or may be broken down into a number of different socio-demographic groups, such as age-groups (A1, A2, etc.).

B–E. Residents' leisure *participation* is based on the percentage of the population participating over the previous year (B) and, when combined with frequency of participation (C), length of season (D, where applicable) and the size of the population (A), can be expressed as a volume of weekly activity (E).

Unsatisfied wants, needs and obligations and market attitudes are included in the diagram: the unsatisfied needs/want/obligations component of this item is the focus of

(Continued)

Box 8.2. Continued.

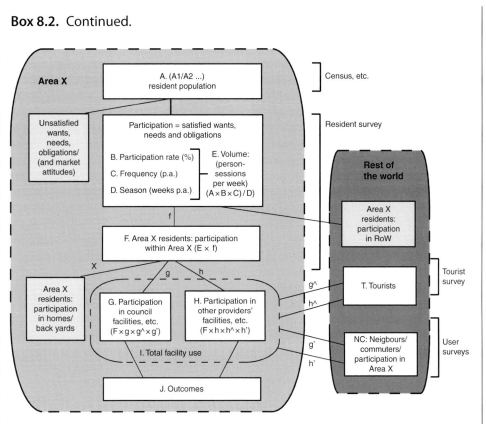

Fig. 8.8. Participation Module: framework.

needs-based planning methods, but it does not play a significant role in the U-Plan system; however, information on 'market attitudes' plays a role.

F. Residents' leisure participation takes place within Area X (F) and outside of Area X, in the 'Rest of the world' (RoW).

x. A proportion of residents' participation within Area X takes place in their homes (x).

G, H, I. Total participation (I) in Area X facilities takes place in council facilities/services (G) or in facilities/services provided by other organizations (H). This is made up of participation in council and non-council facilities/services by:

- residents (g, h);
- *neighbours*, who live outside of Area X and use facilities in Area X because of their quality and/or convenient location, but do not qualify as day-trippers because of the relatively short length of trip, in terms of time and distance; and *commuters* who work in Area X but live elsewhere (g', h'); and

(Continued)

Box 8.2. Continued.

- *tourists* (g^, h^), who comprise day-trippers and overnight staying visitors. If tourism is a significant phenomenon in the area and/or the intention is to boost tourism, as discussed above, more attention will be given to tourists and their requirements and impacts, as explained in Box 8.1.

J. The *ultimate outcomes* from the provision of facilities/services and their use, which are the net benefits generated. If a benefits-based approach were to be adopted J would be measured, but, as noted in Chapter 7, the data collection and measurement requirements of benefits approaches for leisure and sport are prohibitive, so the U-Plan system stops short of this and focuses on participation, I. The exception to this rule arises in relation to tourism. It would be possible to base tourism policy on the number of visits alone (T), but generally this is seen as inadequate: the focus of tourism development is on economic outcomes, involving the maximization of net incomes and job creation. This is explored further in Box 8.1.

The data items identified in Fig. 8.8 are listed in tabular form in Table 8.4, together with an indication of sources and an example of data for a single activity (soccer). There are 15 data items, of which ten must be collected from the various sources indicated, and five are calculated from the data collected.

Table 8.4. Participation Module: data items.

Item[a]	Description	Data source	Units	Data[b]
A	Resident population	Census	'000s	50
B	Participation rate	Resident survey	%	5.5
C	Frequency	Resident survey	Times pa	61.3
D	Season	Resident survey	No. of weeks	26
E	Volume	Calculated: $(A \times B \times C)/D$	Person-sessions/week	6501
f	% of activity within Area X	Resident survey	%	100
F	Resident participation in Area X	Calculated: $E \times f$	Person-sessions/week	6501
x	% of activity in private homes	Resident survey	%	0
g	% of activity in council facilities[c]	Resident survey	%	100
h	% in non-council facilities[c]	Resident survey	%	0
g'	Non-resident use of council facilities[c]	User surveys: council facilities[c]	Person-sessions/week	0
h'	Non-resident use in non-council facilities[c]	User surveys: non-council facilities	Person-sessions/week	0
T	Tourist numbers	Tourist surveys	Visits or bed-nights	0
g^	Tourist visits to council facilities[c]	Local tourist survey	Person-sessions/week	0

(Continued)

Box 8.2. Continued.

Table 8.4. Continued.

Item[a]	Description	Data source	Units	Data[b]
h^	Tourist visits to non-council facilities[c]	Local tourist survey	Person-sessions/week	0
G	Volume of use in council facilities[c]	Calculated: ($F^*g +$ $g' + g$^)	Person-games-visits/week	6501
H	Volume of use in non-council facilities[c]	Calculated: ($F^*h +$ $h' + g$^)	Person-games/visits/week	0
I	Total volume of use	Calculated: (G + H)	Person-games/visits/week	6501

[a]See Fig. 3.1.
[b]Items B, C based on Australian outdoor soccer data (via ERASS (Exercise, Recreation and Sport Survey)), modified by inclusion of ABS 5–14-year-old data and weighted to NSW age-structure; other data hypothetical.
[c]Facilities includes services/programmes.

Task 5. Collation of demographic data

The size of the resident population is obtainable from the latest population census and, for inter-census years, from the local or regional planning department. In addition to the whole population (A), information will be required on the size of various socio-demographic groups (A1, A2, etc.): at a minimum, an age/gender breakdown is likely to be required.

For the later tasks in the Participation Module, information will also be required on projections of these data over the planning period. Such projections are generally available from the local or regional planning department.

Task 6. Resident leisure participation survey

Tasks 6–8 are concerned with conducting surveys of the resident population, facility/services users and tourists, respectively. Some discussion of such surveys is included in Focus Module 4, but detailed guidelines on the conduct of surveys are not provided as part of the U-Plan system, since this information can be found in a number of texts, including Veal (2006b). A resident survey is required to gather data items B to h in Table 8.4.

Task 7. User surveys of facilities/services

User surveys of facilities/services are conducted to determine the proportion of visits to council and non-council facilities/services by residents and non-residents (neighbours, commuters and tourists). Such surveys would of course be likely to be used additionally to gather other information for management purposes.

Task 8. Tourist survey

A tourist survey is required only if tourism is already a significant feature of Area X or it is intended to boost tourism to the area. The survey would be used to establish the number and types of tourists visiting the area, their use of leisure and other infrastructure, notably accommodation, and their expenditure while in the area. In some cases such surveys are conducted at points of entry/exit, such as airports. Alternatives are interviewing tourists at their accommodation (but this excludes the visiting friends and relatives category) or at informal sites where it is known that most tourists gather (e.g. the beach at a seaside resort, Trafalgar Square in London, the Opera House forecourt in Sydney). National surveys of both international and domestic tourists are also a source of tourist numbers, but these often relate only to major destinations and subregions and do not provide information on smaller destinations.

Task 9. Simulation of status quo: participation

The 15 data items on soccer in Table 8.4 can be presented as one row of a spreadsheet. This is shown in Fig. 8.9, which also includes data for five additional activities for illustrative purposes. In the spreadsheet:

- The type of facility used for the activity is included.
- The shaded columns indicate data inputs from the sources shown in Table 8.4, and the unshaded columns indicate calculations which are carried out automatically by spreadsheet operations.
- A population of 50,000 aged 5 years and over is assumed.
- The final row gives the total weekly person-sessions taking place for the six activities: in a full version covering all sport/physical recreation, this row would provide a measure of total sport/physical recreation activity catered for in Area X.

In discussing the framework, it was noted that the population can be broken down into subgroups and this is, of course, necessary to pursue any social or spatial equity targets emerging from the Objectives/Outcomes Module. In Fig. 8.10 this principle is illustrated using gender and age, with item A broken down into 16 age/gender groups. Since this is the status quo, it makes no difference to the end result (columns B–I): it is the starting point for the activity target-setting process.

		Outdoor soccer	Indoor soccer	Aerobics/ fitness	Swimming	Golf	Netball
A	Population, '000s	50	50	50	50	50	50
B	% participation in year	5.5	1.7	17.7	12.9	4.8	3.9
C	Frequency (times pa)	61.3	46.7	132.0	66.1	47.4	58.3
D	Season (weeks)	26	26	50	50	45	26
E	Volume/week*	6,501	1,530	23,379	8,518	2,545	4,395
f	% in Area X	100	100	100	75	100	100
F	Volume in Area X*	6,501	1,530	23,379	6,389	2,545	4,395
x	% in home		0	50	20	0	0
g	Council %	100	100	25	100	0	100
g'	% Non-council	0	0	25	0	100	0
h	RoW:council ratio	1	1	1	1	1	1
h'	RoW:non-council ratio	1	1	1	1	1.25	1
G	Council volume/week*	6,501	1,530	5,845	6,389	0	4,395
H	Non-council volume/week*	0	0	5,845	0	3,181	0
I	Weekly volume, 2008*	6,501	1,530	11,690	6,389	3,181	4,395

*Person-sessions. Shaded items calculated.

Fig. 8.9. Participation: status quo spreadsheet.

		Popu-lation	Outdoor soccer	Indoor soccer	Aerobics/fitness	Swimming	Golf	Netball
A			50	50	50	50	50	50
			%	%	%	%	%	%
A1	Males	24,540	6.6	2.6	15.2	11.1	9.1	0.7
A2	Females	25,460	1.8	0.5	25.1	12.9	2.2	5.6
A3	Males 5–14	3,570	20.7	3.8	0.5	16.1	1.5	1.9
A4	Males 15–24	3,750	20.9	9.0	16.6	10.9	3.4	1.9
A5	Males 25–34	4,025	7.1	3.8	19.0	13.5	6.7	1.2
A6	Males 35–44	4,020	6.4	1.7	17.7	14.3	8.0	0.7
A7	Males 45–54	3,550	2.5	0.5	14.1	12.5	11.2	0.2
A8	Males 55–64	2,740	0.5	0.0	13.2	9.1	14.0	0.0
A9	Males 65+	2,885	0.2	0.0	9.7	5.4	12.8	0.0
A10	Females 5–14	3,370	5.7	0.7	0.9	18.7	0.4	14.9
A11	Females 15–24	3,655	5.7	1.7	27.5	12.7	0.8	15.2
A12	Females 25–34	4,155	1.9	0.7	31.3	15.7	1.6	9.6
A13	Females 35–44	4,160	1.8	0.3	29.2	16.7	1.9	5.4
A14	Females 45–54	3,685	0.7	0.1	23.2	14.5	2.7	1.4
A15	Females 55–64	2,745	0.1	0.0	21.9	10.5	3.4	0.2
A16	Females 65+	3,690	0.0	0.0	16.0	6.2	3.1	0.0
B	Total	50,000	5.5	1.7	17.7	12.9	4.8	3.9
C	Frequency p.a.		61.3	46.7	132.0	66.1	47.4	58.3
D	Season		26	26	50	50	45	26
E	Volume: p-s/week		6,501	1,530	23,379	8,518	2,545	4,395
f	% Area X		100	100	100	75	100	100
F	Volume Area X p-s/week		6,501	1,530	23,379	6,389	2,545	4,395
x	% in home		0	0	50	20	0	0
g	% council		100	100	25	100	0	100
g'	% non-council		0	0	25	0	100	0
h	RoW:council ratio		1	1	1	1	1	1
h'	RoW:non-council ratio		1	1	1	1	1.25	1
G	Council volume, p-s/week		6,501	1,530	5,845	6,389	0	4,395
H	Non-council volume, p-s/week		0	0	5,845	0	3,181	0
I	Total in volume, p-s/week		6,501	1,530	11,690	6,389	3,181	4,395

p-s, person-sessions; RoW, rest of world.

Fig. 8.10. Participation: status quo spreadsheet – age-/gender-related.

Active and passive change

Over the course of the planning period we can anticipate:

- *Passive change*: that is, change likely to take place regardless of the activities of the planning agency.
- *Active change*: that is, change arising from policy measures undertaken by the planning agency – this forms the bulk of the rest of the U-Plan exercise, but it takes place against the background of passive change, which is discussed in Task 10.

Task 10. Examination of passive change

Virtually all of the parameters indicated in Fig. 8.5 could change during the planning period as a result of local, regional and national – and indeed global – factors. This emphasizes the need to monitor the situation on a planned basis. Certain data, notably facility usage data, are available monthly, quarterly and/or annually while other data will, because of the cost of collection, be refreshed less often. Thus, for example, resident, facility users and tourist surveys might be conducted on a 3- or 5-year cycle.

A wide range of sources of change that might affect leisure participation could be considered, and a number of these are discussed in Chapter 11. The number of change factors that may be considered, and the detail with which they may be analysed, in a local planning context will vary, depending on time, resources and expertise available. Here we consider just one which is intrinsic to local planning, namely demographic change.

Demographic change, involving both the size of the population and its age-structure, is often the major source of change that needs to be taken into account in local planning. This is a phenomenon that can be readily addressed, since age-specific population projections are available – or should be – for all local council areas and projections are typically available for the planned population of greenfield sites. Furthermore, information on the relationship between leisure participation patterns and demographic characteristics is widely available, from local, regional and national participation surveys.

A relatively simple exercise is to examine the effects of demographic change (e.g. the ageing of the population) by projecting demand patterns based on demographic projections. This will not, of course, produce a *forecast*, since other change factors would need to be taken into account to achieve that. But if demographic change is as important as is often claimed, then it makes sense to examine the likely effect of this factor, even if examination of other factors is beyond the resources of the planning team.

The approach demonstrated here is an example of the cross-sectional method outlined in Chapter 11. Figure 8.11 examines the possible effects of anticipated demographic change over a 10-year planning period to the year 2020. The age-/gender-specific participation rates (and all the other parameters) are unchanged from Fig. 8.9 but the population figures have been changed, and the spreadsheet has been used to calculate the effects of this on levels of participation. It can be seen that:

- The population figures for 2020 show an increase of 4106 and some of the younger age-groups decline in absolute terms, while the older age-groups increase significantly.
- A new overall participation rate is calculated by multiplying the 2020 population of each age-group by its 2010 participation rate, which produces 14 new age-/gender-specific estimated numbers of participants, which are summed and presented as a percentage of the new total population – the new participation rate for soccer, for example is 5.1%, compared with the original 5.5%.
- It can be seen that the volume of participation is projected to increase by several hundred for aerobics/fitness, swimming and golf, but hardly at all for soccer and netball, reflecting the dependence of the latter two on younger age-groups.

Task 11. Activity scan

Task 11 examines individual leisure activities to assess their potential as vehicles to boost the participation rates of target groups.

Characteristics of leisure activities are examined in general terms and specifically in relation to the target groups identified in the Objectives/Outcomes Module. General characteristics include such things as participation trends over recent years, local variation from national/state/regional averages, land requirements and provision costs. The latter two relate to facilities

		Population 2010	Population 2020	Outdoor soccer	Indoor soccer	Aerobics /fitness	Swimming	Golf	Netball
A	Age:			54	54	54	54	54	54
A1	Males	24,540	26,546	6.6	2.6	15.2	11.1	9.1	0.7
A2	Females	25,460	27,560	1.8	0.5	25.1	12.9	2.2	5.6
A3	Males 5–14	3,570	3,491	20.7	3.8	0.5	16.1	1.5	1.9
A4	Males 15–24	3,750	3,720	20.9	9.0	16.6	10.9	3.4	1.9
A5	Males 25–34	4,025	4,347	7.1	3.8	19.0	13.5	6.7	1.2
A6	Males 35–44	4,020	4,147	6.4	1.7	17.7	14.3	8.0	0.7
A7	Males 45–54	3,550	3,698	2.5	0.5	14.1	12.5	11.2	0.2
A8	Males 55–64	2,740	3,182	0.5	0.0	13.2	9.1	14.0	0.0
A9	Males 65+	2,885	3,962	0.2	0.0	9.7	5.4	12.8	0.0
A10	Females 5–14	3,370	3,306	5.7	0.7	0.9	18.7	0.4	14.9
A11	Females 15–24	3,655	3,626	5.7	1.7	27.5	12.7	0.8	15.2
A12	Females 25–34	4,155	4,449	1.9	0.7	31.3	15.7	1.6	9.6
A13	Females 35–44	4,160	4,252	1.8	0.3	29.2	16.7	1.9	5.4
A14	Females 45–54	3,685	3,848	0.7	0.1	23.2	14.5	2.7	1.4
A15	Females 55–64	2,745	3,241	0.1	0.0	21.9	10.5	3.4	0.2
A16	Females 65+	3,690	4,837	0.0	0.0	16.0	6.2	3.1	0.0
B	Total population 2010/2020/% participation	50,000	54,106	5.1	1.6	17.7	12.6	5.0	3.7
C	Frequency p.a.			61.3	46.7	132.0	66.1	47.4	58.3
D	Season			26	26	50	50	45	26
E	Volume: p-s/week			6,548	1,550	25,235	8,988	2,870	4,452
f	% Area X			100	100	100	75	100	100
F	Volume Area X p-s/week			6,548	1,550	25,235	6,741	2,870	4,452
x	% in home			0	0	50	20	0	0
g	% council			100	100	25	100	0	100
g'	% non-council			0	0	25	0	100	0
h	RoW:council ratio			1	1	1	1	1	1
h'	RoW:non-council ratio			1	1	1	1	1.25	1
G	Council volume, p-s/week			6,548	1,550	6,309	6,741	0	4,452
H	Non-council volume, p-s/week			0	0	6,309	0	3,588	0
I 2020	2020 volume, p-s/week			6,548	1,550	12,617	6,741	3,588	4,452
I 2010	2010 volume			6,501	1,530	11,690	6,389	3,181	4,395
	Change			47	20	928	352	406	58

p-s, person-sessions; RoW, rest of world.

Fig. 8.11. Participation: passive change spreadsheet – demographic.

rather than the activities themselves, and so are addressed in the Supply Module: these are presented sequentially in this chapter but may, in part, be undertaken simultaneously. Target group-specific characteristics include those factors which are used to identify the target groups, such as demographics and market attitudes. Specific characteristics of activities that might be examined include the following:

- *Activity growth trends*: given that the aim is to stimulate or facilitate increased participation, then activities which are on a downward trend in popularity should be treated with caution, subject to the qualifications discussed earlier. 'Growth activities', should arise here if they have been identified as targets in Task 4, Step 3.
- *Comparison* of local participation rates with national, state and/or regional rates at the individual activity level is common in leisure planning. Clearly, as a basis for planning, this should be undertaken with care, since the aim of local planning is to reflect

local differences rather than seek to standardize participation patterns everywhere. Precautionary steps that might be taken include comparing local participation rates with national, as well as regional, rates, identifying known local traditions, and considering not only *statistically* significant but also *managerially* significant differences (small differences in participation rates – e.g. 0.5% – may be statistically significant if the data are based on large samples, but may not be significant in management or provision terms).

The relationship between *socio-demographic* (and other) characteristics of target groups and their leisure participation patterns will have been gathered via the resident participation survey discussed above. For example, the following conclusions can be drawn from the data for the simple case study of six activities and three target groups used in Fig. 8.10:

- Regarding *older men*: golf, aerobics/fitness and swimming are the activities most likely to be of relevance.
- Regarding *young women*: netball and swimming have the greatest potential.
- Regarding *older women*: aerobics/fitness offers the greatest potential, with swimming a second, but less promising, option.

Thus swimming is relevant to three of the groups, aerobics/fitness to two and golf and netball to one each. But according to the trend data, only aerobics/fitness is on a growth trajectory; the other three are in general decline.

Market attitude data, in the form of data on residents' aspirations as revealed by surveys, have often been used in traditional needs-based planning as the major basis of the planning process. However, marketers long ago concluded that aspirational responses given in questionnaire surveys are a poor guide to people's actual future behaviour. Use of such data is nevertheless suggested here, but in a more focused way. For example, if all existing national or regional data suggest that activity A is popular with group X, but the group has a low participation rate in the activity locally, there is a case for additional survey and/or other research to explore this apparent local anomaly. Thus surveys and other research might be undertaken in regard to the target groups to discover possible negative sentiments surrounding participation as much as, if not more than, positive sentiments.

In summary, the information from the above appraisals might be presented in a format as shown in Fig. 8.12.

Task 12. Activity selection

As a result of the Activity Evaluation, activities are selected which are most likely to attract members of the target groups or, if an overall participation increase is targeted, activities most likely to increase participation generally.

While a detailed procedure for making the selection has not been devised, a degree of transparency is achieved by indicating that the selection is based on the information in Fig. 8.12. For demonstration purposes, we will assume that the following are the selected activities for this exercise: (i) aerobics/fitness for older men and older women; (ii) swimming for older men and younger and older women; (iii) golf for older men; and (iv) netball for younger women.

Task 13. Activity targets

In this task, the targeted increases in overall participation for the target groups, as established in the Objectives/Outcomes Module, are distributed among the selected activities. Thus, for

Activity	Trends: Growing/ Declining/Static	Potential for:			Market attitude
		Males 45+	Females 16–24	Females 65+	
Outdoor soccer	Growing	–	–	–	
Indoor soccer	Growing	–	–	–	
Aerobics/fitness	Growing	Yes	–	Yes	Positive
Swimming	Declining	Yes	Yes	Yes	
Golf	Declining	Yes	–	–	
Netball	Declining	–	Yes	–	

Fig. 8.12. Activity scan: summary.

example, the aim is to achieve an increase of 5.3% overall for men aged 45–54, and this could be distributed as 2.1% in aerobics/keep fit and 1.6% each in swimming and golf. This process is based on informed judgement rather on than hard-and-fast rules: aerobics/fitness is given greater emphasis because, as shown in the activity evaluation, it is generally growing in popularity, whereas the other activities are in decline. It should be noted that the use of just six activities for illustrative purposes results in some unrealistic loading of expectations on to single activities. In practice it is possible that the +5.3% in this example would be spread across perhaps seven or eight activities. On the other hand, of course, if a 'stand out' activity emerged from the activity evaluation, it might be decided to concentrate efforts on just one or two activities.

Figure 8.13 shows the effects of adding these *active change* target figures to the *passive change* effects discussed earlier. The projected increases in volumes of activity arising from the active and passive change are now passed to the Supply Module for analysis.

In running the spreadsheet calculations to produce the final volume figure, one of parameters is changed: the 'rest of the world' ratio (h'): it is assumed that the active change will all take place within Area X. In our simplified case study this affects only golf, which, in the status quo had a net inflow of 25% of use from outside the area. In this case, this is assumed to fall to 20%.

The Participation Module and tourism

As noted in Box 8.1, in the case of tourism, a number of the Participation Module tasks may have been undertaken as part of the Objectives/Outcomes Module. Tourism enters the Participation Module process with Task 7, the facility surveys, which will identify the proportion of tourists using local leisure facilities. Task 8, the tourist survey, conducted if tourism is significant, will also gather this information but also information on types of tourists, length of stay and expenditure. Some of the resultant data are incorporated into the spreadsheet as part of Task 9, which simulates the status quo. Task 10, examination of passive change, includes forecasting of tourism trends, as discussed in Box 8.1 and Chapter 11. Tasks 11–13, discussed in terms of the activities above, apply to types of tourist, such as day-trippers, hotel users and backpackers, and would involve the selection of those tourist types most likely to achieve the overall tourism targets, and setting the appropriate detailed targets.

		Population 2020	Outdoor soccer	Indoor soccer	Aerobics/ fitness	Swimming	Golf	Netball	% increase over 2008
A	Total population, 2020	54,106	%	%	%	%	%	%	
A1	Total males	26,546	6.6	2.6	15.2	11.1	9.1	0.7	
A2	Total females	27,560	1.8	0.5	25.1	12.9	2.2	5.6	
A3	Males 5–14*	3,491	20.7	3.8	0.5	16.1	1.5	1.9	
A4	Males 15–24	3,720	20.9	9.0	16.6	10.9	3.4	1.9	
A5	Males 25–34	4,347	7.1	3.8	19.0	13.5	6.7	1.2	
A6	Males 35–44	4,147	6.4	1.7	17.7	14.3	8.0	0.7	
A7	Males 45–54*	3,698	2.5	0.5	16.2	14.1	12.8	0.2	+5.3
A8	Males 55–64*	3,182	0.5	0.0	15.1	10.3	15.2	0.0	+4.3
A9	Males 65+*	3,962	0.2	0.0	12.9	8.0	15.4	0.0	+8.4
A10	Females 5–14	3,306	5.7	0.7	0.9	18.7	0.4	14.9	
A11	Females 15–24*	3,626	5.7	1.7	27.5	14.5	0.8	17.0	+3.6
A12	Females 25–34	4,449	1.9	0.7	31.3	15.7	1.6	9.6	
A13	Females 35–44	4,252	1.8	0.3	29.2	16.7	1.9	5.4	
A14	Females 45–54	3,848	0.7	0.1	23.2	14.5	2.7	1.4	
A15	Females 55–64	3,241	0.1	0.0	21.9	10.5	3.4	0.2	
A16	Females 65+*	4,837	0.0	0.0	21.5	12.4	3.1	0.0	+11.7
B2018	Total: target % 2018		5.1	1.6	18.6	13.6	5.4	3.8	
C	Frequency pa		61.3	46.7	132.0	66.1	47.4	58.3	
D	Season (weeks)		26	26	50	50	45	26	
E	Volume/week		6,548	1,550	25,235	8,988	2,870	4,452	
f	% Area X		100	100	100	75	100	100	
F	Volume Area X		6,548	1,550	25,235	6,741	2,870	4,452	
x	% in home		0	0	50	20	0	0	
g	% Council		100	100	25	100	0	100	
g'	% non-council		0	0	25	0	100	0	
h	RoW: council ratio		1	1	1	1	1	1	
h'	RoW: non-council ratio		1	1	1	1	1.2	1	
G	Council volume/week		6,548	1,550	6,309	6,741	0	4,452	
H	Non-council volume/week		0	0	6,309	0	3,444	0	
I 2018	Target volume/week		6,548	1,550	12,617	6,741	3,444	4,452	
I 2008	2008 volume/week		6,501	1,530	11,690	6,389	3,181	4,395	
I incr	Change volume/week		+47	+20	+928	+352	+263	+58	

Shaded participation rates are target rates resulting from the target-setting process.

Fig. 8.13. Participation: active/passive change – projections.

SUPPLY MODULE

In the Supply Module the implications of current and projected participation for facility and programme provision and, to a limited extent, facility/programme management, are considered.

Framework

As with the Participation Module, the Supply Module is built around a framework and this is presented in Box 8.3. It begins with the participation projections (item J) from the Participation Module and works through the required facilities/services to accommodate that participation.

Task 14. Compilation of inventory of facilities/services

A key component of any planning exercise is a complete inventory of existing facilities and services. For the most part, as discussed above, services/programmes take place in facilities of one kind or another, so that the basic unit in an inventory is the facility.

Box 8.3. U-Plan Supply Module framework.

The Supply Module framework takes the current or projected participation data (I) from the Participation Module and works through the implications in terms of facility requirements which, in turn, can be translated into land requirements and costs. This sequence is shown diagrammatically in Fig. 8.14.

The process involves the following components:

I. Import the status quo participation data from the Participation Module (Fig. 8.8).

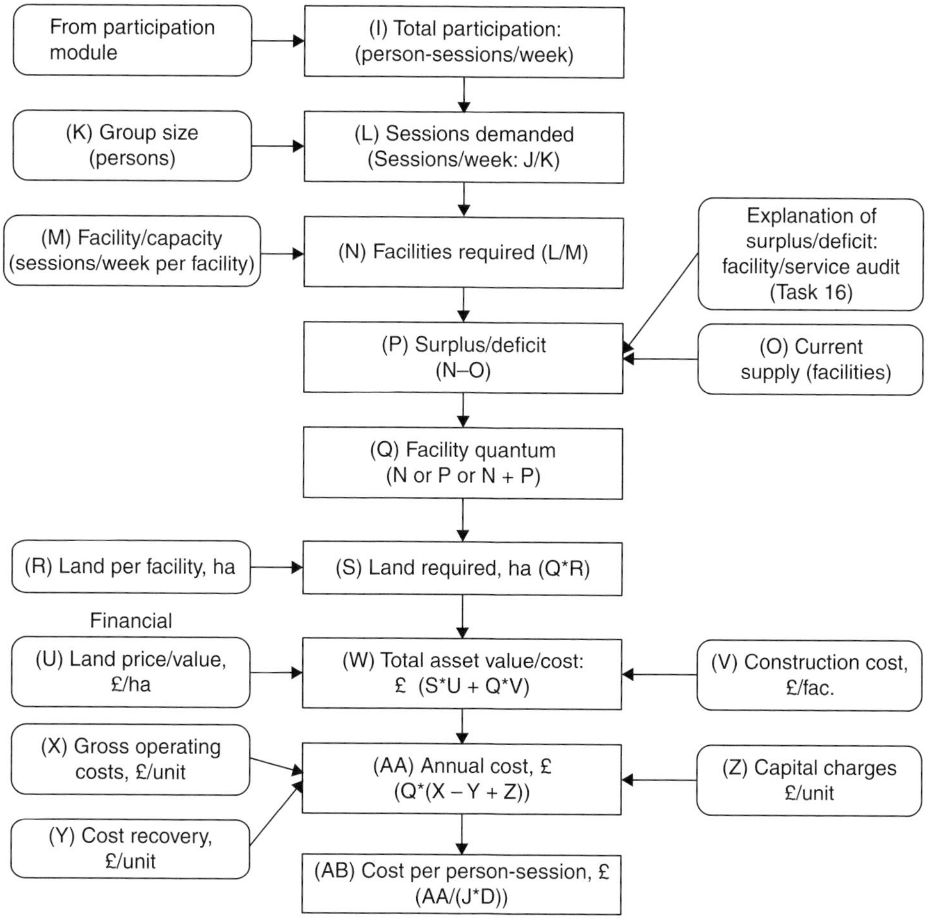

Fig. 8.14. Supply Module framework.

(Continued)

Box 8.3. Continued.

K. The 'group size' for each activity is inserted here – for example, a game of soccer involves 22 players, some reserves, a referee and two line judges, probably about 30 persons, whereas a squash game involves two people and a round of golf involves one person – for the various activities, these group sizes must be estimated from professional knowledge, but there is a need for some empirical work to be done to establish more precise figures for a number of activities, to ascertain the extent to which they vary among clubs and locations.

L. The number of 'sessions' demanded: calculated from demand divided by size of group, J/K.

M. Capacity of individual facilities, in terms of sessions per week – this is another item which must currently be estimated.

N. Facilities required, calculated from: L/M.

O. Current actual level of supply from the Inventory.

P. Current surplus (O > N), deficit (O < N) or par (O = N). In later rounds this will indicate the net additional facilities/services required. If, in the status quo round, a surplus or deficit is indicated, the reason for this is explored via Task 15, as discussed below.

The status quo exercise could end here, but it may be decided to continue with the following items/steps, which involve consideration of land requirements and costs.

Q. Facility/service quantum: different figures can be inserted here, depending on the purpose of the analysis:

- for simulating the status quo exercise, existing facility supply (O) would be inserted;
- in subsequent rounds, net additional facilities required (P) would be inserted;
- in subsequent rounds, inserting O + P would provide a picture of total supply at the end of the planning period.

R. Amount of land required or used per facility (ha) – from official sources.

S. Total amount of land used/required, calculated from Q*R.

T. The letter T is reserved for use in relation to tourism.

U. Value/price of land (£/ha).

V. Construction/development cost per facility (£/fac.): this will inevitably be a 'ballpark' figure, since construction costs can of course vary enormously, but at some stage in the planning process likely costs must be considered; as the process continues, cost estimates can be refined.

W. Value/cost of current/additional facilities (£), calculated from land costs plus construction costs (= S*U + Q*V).

X. Gross operating costs, £/unit/year.

Y. Cost recovery, typically from user fees, £/unit/year.

Z. Capital charges, where applicable, £/unit/year.

AA. Annual costs, £/unit/year: Q*(X − Y + Z).

AB. Cost per person-session, £ per person-session (= AA/(J*D)): can be used to compare cost differences between different activities.

As with the Participation Module, data sources are presented in tabular form, in Table 8.5, including information on sources and sample data for a single facility type.

(Continued)

Box 8.3. Continued.

Table 8.5. Supply Module data items; monetary units are in £.

Item	Description	Data source	Units	Data[a]
I	Total participation accommodated	Participation Module	Person-games/ visits/week	6,501
K	Group size[b]	Observation	Persons	30
L	Sessions demanded	Calculated (I/J)	Sessions/week	217
M	Facility capacity[b]	Management	Sessions/week	12
N	Facilities required	Calculated (K/L)	Number of facilities	18.1
O	Current supply[b]	Inventory	Number of facilities	17
P	Reconciliation: deficit/surplus	Facility/service audit	Number of facilities	1.1
Q	Additional facility requirements	N + P	Number of facilities	18
R	Land per facility[b]	Official, etc.	Ha per facility	0.9
S	Total land required	Q × R	Ha	16.2
U[c]	Land price/value[b]	Local valuer	£/ha	800,000
V	Construction/ development cost[b]	Architect	£/facility	200,000
W	Total value/cost	(S × T) + (Q × U)	£	16,613,000
X	Gross operating costs	Management department	£/unit	100,000
Y	Cost recovery	Management department	£/unit	20,000
Z	Capital charges	Finance dept.	£/unit	75,000
AA	Total annual net cost	Calc. Q(X − Y + Z)	£	2,799,000
AB	Net cost per person-session	Calc. AA/J	£/person-session	16.65

[a] Example data for netball.
[b] Dummy data for illustrative purposes only.
[c] Often not included for public facilities, because capital cost is historical and there is no actual debt to be serviced, but under current accounting regimes asset values should be available.
Letter T reserved for use in Focus Module 6: Tourism.

An important feature of facilities is their link with the activities which they accommodate, as discussed in relation to Fig. 8.2. The list of activities and facilities used in the development of the U-Plan system is presented in Fig. 8.15. For each facility, the inventory should include at least:

Facility			Activity	Facility			Activity
I	Physical activity/sport – outdoor			II	Physical activity/sport – indoor		
A	Urban parks	1	Events	K	Sports hall – large	1	Basketball (indoor)
		2	Jogging/running			2	Cricket (indoor)
		3	Picnic			3	Hockey (indoor)
		4	Walking (other)			4	Netball (indoor)
B	Trails	1	Walking			5	Soccer (indoor)
		2	Cycling			6	Volleyball
C	Sports fields–standard	1	Baseball	L	Hall – small	1	Aerobics/fitness
		2	Hockey (outdoor)			2	Boxing
		3	Rugby league			3	Carpet bowls
		4	Rugby union			4	Martial arts
		5	Soccer (outdoor)			5	Pilates
		6	Softball			6	Yoga
		7	Touch football	M	Specialist indoor	1	Dance
D	Sports fields – large	1	Aust. rules football			2	Squash
		2	Cricket (outdoor)			3	Tenpin bowling
E	Outdoor courts	1	Netball			4	Weight-training
		2	Basketball (outdoor)	III	Cultural activities		
		3	Tennis	N	Performing arts	1	Classical music concert
F	Specialist outdoor	1	Air sports			2	Pop music concert
		2	Athletics			3	Dance performance
		3	Bowls – lawn			4	Musical/opera
		4	Golf			5	Other performance
		5	Horse riding	O	Specialist arts/culture	1	Art gallery visiting
		6	Motor sports			2	Cinema visiting
		7	Roller sports			3	Library
		8	Sport spectating			4	Museum visiting
G	Pools	1	Aquarobics			5	Theatre going
		2	Swimming			6	Multi-arts festival
		3	Waterpolo	IV	Social activities		
H	Water-based	1	Fishing	P	Pubs/Licensed clubs	1	Drinking, socializing
		2	Sailing			2	Gambling
		3	Power-boating			3	Eating
		4	Other water sports	Q	Restaurants	1	Eating out
I	Natural areas	1	Bushwalking	R	Night club/disco	1	Dancing, socializing
	(National parks, beach/ocean)	2	Rock climbing	S	Pinball parlour	1	Play elect. games
		3	Ocean swimming	T	Shops/markets	1	Shopping for pleasure
		4	Surfing	U	Home-based activity		
J	Non-leisureresources	1	Cycling				
	(Mainly streets)	2	Walking				
		3	Roller sports				

Fig. 8.15. Supply: facilities and activities.

- category (indoor, outdoor, specialist, etc.);
- ownership/management (council, other public, non-profit, commercial);
- location (zone);
- activities accommodated;
- associated programmes;
- land area;
- capacity;
- usage.

Capacity and usage are measured in terms of the number of participation sessions which a facility of a given size and design can accommodate in a given period, such as a week. For a playing field this would be the number of games and/or practice sessions which can be accommodated, for a theatre it would be the number of performances, while for a museum it would be the number of individual admissions. Different types of facility raise different challenges in assessing capacity and use, and these are discussed in Chapter 10.

Task 15. Supply Module: simulating the status quo

As with the Participation Module, the status quo is simulated in spreadsheet format, as shown in Fig. 8.16.

Task 16. Facility/service audit

The facility/service audit is designed to analyse the capabilities of existing facilities/services in meeting current and projected participation targets. The task includes four components:

- *Confirmation of already indicated surpluses/deficits.* As noted above, in simulating the status quo, the audit will address item P, which indicates the difference between estimated facility requirements (N) based on existing participation and the actual stock of existing facilities (O). If P is a significant positive (deficit) or negative (surplus) figure, examination of individual facility capacities and use levels is required to confirm the figure or initiate a revision of the estimates.
- *Identification of other surpluses/deficits.* Even if the earlier analysis has not indicated the existence of current deficits or surpluses, there may be overuse or underuse of facilities that may be revealed by examination of the stock of facilities and their use.
- *Asset management.* Given a planning period of up to 10 years, physical examination of facilities is required to flag up requirements for major refurbishment or replacements: this information may be available from existing routine asset management procedures, and is discussed further in *Focus Module 8: Assets/resources.*

		Outdoor soccer	Indoor soccer	Aerobics fitness	Swimming	Golf	Netball
I	2008 volume (from Fig. 8.9)	6,501	1,530	11,690	6,389	3,181	4,395
K	Group size	30	14	20	100	1	16
L	Sessions/week	217	109	584	64	3,181	275
M	Facility capacity/week	12	70	70	70	1,000	25
N	Facilities required	18.1	1.6	8.3	0.9	3.2	11.0
O	Current supply (from inventory)	18	2	8	1	3	11
P	Surplus/deficit	−0.1	0.4	−0.3	0.1	−0.2	0.0
Q	Facilities quantum	18	2	8	1	3	11
R	Land per facility, ha	0.9	0.5	0.2	0.5	60	0.2
S	Land requirements, ha	16.2	1.0	1.6	0.5	180.0	2.2
U	Land price, £000/ha*	800	800	800	800	200	800
V	Constr. cost, £'000s	200	1,000	500	2,000	5,000	100
W	Cost/value, £'000s	16,560	2,800	5,280	2,400	51,000	2,860
X	Gross operating cost/unit, £000	75	150	75	500	500	10
Y	Cost recovery/unit, £000	20	100	30	300	1,500	5
Z	Capital charges/unit, £000*	50	120	75	240	500	80
AA	Total annual net cost, £000	2,610	740	1,440	1,040	7,500	1,045
AB	Net cost/person-session, £	15.44	18.60	2.46	3.26	52.39	9.15

*Land costs/value of existing facilities likely to be historical and annual capital charges may not apply.

Fig. 8.16. Supply Module status quo: spreadsheet.

- *Spatial equity*. In setting targets in regard to spatial equity (Task 4), it was noted that additional participation targets might emerge from the facility audit process based on analysis of facility catchment areas.

So, apart from the asset management item, discussed separately in *Focus Module 8*, the audit process involves assessment of the level of use of facilities in relation to their capacities and examination of their spatial pattern of use.

Task 17. Projection of facility/service requirements

In Task 17, projections of the increased provision for the activity targets established in the Participation Module are estimated. This is done by running Fig. 8.16 with the 2018 participation figures in row I or, perhaps more usefully, inserting the *increase* in participation in row I to indicate the increase in provision required. This is illustrated in Fig. 8.17.

A question arises in those cases where only a fraction of a facility is projected as required. Alternative solutions are:

- increase in capacity of existing leisure facilities: by physical extension; by management action: e.g. extended programming or opening hours;
- utilization/leasing/adaptation of capacity not previously used for leisure (e.g. education facilities);
- changing the projected increase in provision to a whole facility and adjusting other activities/facilities downwards to compensate – this involves going back to the Participation Module and changing the selections – a 'round 2' iteration.

		Outdoor soccer	Indoor soccer	Aerobics/ fitness	Swimming	Golf	Netball
I 2020	2020 volume	6,548	1,550	12,617	6,741	3,444	4,452
I 2010	2010 volume	6,501	1,530	11,690	6,389	3,181	4,395
I incr.	Change	47	20	928	352	263	58
K	Group size	30	14	20	100	1	16
L	Sessions/week required	218	111	631	67	3,444	278
M	Facility capacity/week	12	70	70	70	1,000	25
N	Facilities required 2020	18.2	1.6	9.0	1.0	3.4	11.1
O	Current supply 2010	18	2	8	1	3	11
P	Surplus/deficit	0.2	−0.4	1.0	0.0	0.4	0.1
Q	Additional facilities to be provided	0.5	0.0	1.0	0.0	0.5	0.0
R	Land per facility, ha	0.9	0.5	0.2	0.5	60	0.2
S	Land requirements, ha 2020	0.5	0.0	0.2	0.0	30.0	0.0
U	Land price, £000/ha	800	800	800	800	200	800
V	Constr. cost, £'000	200	1,000	500	2,000	5,000	100
W	Cost/value, £'000	460	0	668	0	8,500	0
X	Gross operating cost/unit, £000	75	150	75	500	500	10
Y	Cost recovery/unit, £000	20	100	30	300	1,000	5
Z	Capital charges/unit, £000	50	120	75	240	500	80
AA 2020	Total annual netcost 2020, £000	53	0	121	0	0	0
AB	Net cost/person-session, £	42.78	0.00	2.62	0.00	0.00	0.00

Fig. 8.17. Supply: projections of facility requirements.

Task 18. Facility/service specifications

Facility/service specifications takes the process closer to the implementation stage, including specifications of locations of facilities and capital and running costs. These details are not discussed here but can be found on the U-Plan website.

The Supply Module and tourism

The treatment of a significant tourism component will affect the conduct of the Supply Module in two ways. First, tourists may be the major, even the exclusive, users of some leisure facilities. Second, in addition to leisure facilities, the model would include types of accommodation, possibly other infrastructure requirements, such as transport and tourist information services.

THE SYSTEM AS A WHOLE

The Participation Module and the Supply Module tasks are processed using spreadsheets. Separate spreadsheets are presented above for the two modules, but the last row of the Participation Module spreadsheet forms the first row of the Supply Module spreadsheet. They do, therefore, form a single spreadsheet, as shown in Fig. 8.18. The highlighted rows indicate that the combined spreadsheet relates participation rates to final land requirements and, if the final eight rows are included, the cost implications. Once calibrated with relevant local data, the spreadsheet enables alternative participation scenarios to be explored.

WHO DECIDES?

Throughout the U-Plan process, there are points at which decisions must be made based on courses of action that must be based on judgement rather than analysis. In particular, the judgements will be related to the question of what will best serve the organization's mission. The decisions will ultimately all involve the responsible elected or appointed body, such as elected councillors, but the shaping of the decisions will generally involve other stakeholders at various points, depending on the decision-making structure established (Task 2). Key decisions are listed below.

It is appropriate that a number of key decisions must be made in the Objectives/Outcomes Module, since it sets the course for the rest of the process. Among these are:

- whether to adopt the U-Plan, as discussed above;
- budgetary parameters;
- what variables to include under the heading 'social equity';
- whether 'spatial equity' is to be considered and, if so, what zones to adopt;
- if social and/or spatial inequalities are identified:
  - the size of differences considered significant and therefore to be acted on – this affects which groups get included as targets (a final decision on this will probably be left until later, when cost implications of different decisions are known);
  - where action is decided on, the target participation levels to set;
- whether to adopt an external rate as a target;
- if Step 5 in the decision-making process is reached, whether to adopt a 'high target' and if so what it should be;
- whether to view tourism as a major component of local leisure and economic planning.

		Outdoor soccer	Indoor soccer	Aerobics/ fitness	Swimming	Golf	Netball
A	Population, '000	50	50	50	50	50	50
B	% participation in year	5.5	1.7	17.7	12.9	4.8	3.9
C	Frequency (times pa)	61.3	46.7	132.0	66.1	47.4	58.3
D	Season (weeks)	26	26	50	50	45	26
E	Volume/week	6,501	1,530	23,379	8,518	2,545	4,395
f	% in Area X	100	100	100	75	100	100
F	Volume in Area X	6,501	1,530	23,379	6,389	2,545	4,395
x	% in home	0	0	50	20	0	0
g	% council	100	100	25	100	0	100
g'	% non-council	0	0	25	0	100	0
h	RoW: council ratio	1	1	1	1	1	1
h'	RoW: Non-council ratio	1	1	1	1	1.25	1
G	Council volume/week	6,501	1,530	5,845	6,389	0	4,395
H	Non-council volume/week	0	0	5,845	0	3,181	0
I	2008 volume	6,501	1,530	11,690	6,389	3,181	4,395
K	Group size	30	14	20	100	1	16
L	Sessions/week	217	109	584	64	3,181	275
M	Facility capacity/week	12	70	70	70	1,000	25
N	Facilities required	18.1	1.6	8.3	0.9	3.2	11.0
O	Current supply (from inventory)	18	2	8	1	3	11
P	Surplus/deficit	−0.1	0.4	−0.3	0.1	−0.2	0.0
Q	Facilities quantum	18	2	8	1	3	11
R	Land per facility, ha	0.9	0.5	0.2	0.5	60	0.2
S	Land requirements, ha	16.2	1.0	1.6	0.5	180.0	2.2
U	Land price, $000/ha	800	800	800	800	200	800
V	Constr. cost, $'000	200	1,000	500	2,000	5,000	100
W	Cost/value, $'000	16,560	2,800	5,280	2,400	51,000	2,860
X	Gross operating cost/unit, $000	75	150	75	500	500	10
Y	Cost recovery/unit, $000	20	100	30	300	1,500	5
Z	Capital charges/unit, $000	50	120	75	240	500	80
AA	Total annual net cost, $000	2,610	740	1,440	1,040	7,500	1,045
AB	Net cost/person-session, $	15.44	18.60	2.46	3.26	52.39	9.15

Source: Figs 8.9 and 8.16.

Fig. 8.18. Combined Participation and Supply status quo spreadsheet.

In the Participation Module much of the activity is technical in nature concerning data gathering and analysis, but key decisions have to be made in regard to activity selection, since a number of options are likely to arise. In 'Round 1' it may be advisable for all the decisions to be taken by the technical team, since they are interim, and reversible, decisions, which will be affected by the Supply Module assessments. It would, however, be important to document the rationale for each decision. However, in later rounds, the responsible elected council, with or without wider consultation, would be involved in decisions on activity selection, particularly when costings are available from the Supply Module analysis.

The Supply Module consists largely of technical tasks, but it involves one decision that is likely to require political decision-making: to decide whether, if fractions of a facility are specified by the model, to increase capacity of existing facilities/programmes or to build a new facility, as discussed above.

GREENFIELD SITES

Applying the U-Plan system to a greenfield site is relatively simple. It can be done in two ways:

1. Total facility requirements for an area with a specified population – the age/gender population details of the proposed greenfield development area – are entered in the population row of Fig. 8.18, and it is assumed that the population of the development will have the same leisure participation rates as people with the same age/gender characteristics in the existing residential areas.

2. *Local* standards applying to a population of 1000, the age/gender population details of a typical 1000 residents of the proposed greenfield development area are entered in the population row of Fig. 8.18 – this makes the same assumption as above, but expresses provision in the form of a local per 1000 population standard rather than as a total.

The facility/service audit for a greenfield site will involve resource assessment involving the existing landscape, and possibly heritage items with leisure/tourism potential. This is discussed in Chapter 10.

SUMMARY

This chapter presents an outline of the U-Plan system, which is a participation-based leisure planning system arising from the evaluation of alternative planning approaches in Chapter 7. The system comprises three core modules: the Objectives/Outcomes Module, the Participation Module and the Supply Module. These are made up of 18 tasks supported by ten Focus Modules. The key component of the Objectives/Outcomes Module is to set broad participation targets for the community in regard to categories of leisure, such as 'sport and physical recreation' or 'cultural activities'. The Participation Module considers how these broad targets should be translated into targets for individual activities. Finally, the Supply Module translates individual activity participation targets into facility/service requirements.

RESOURCES

U-Plan

Appropriate reading for this chapter includes the preceding chapters in the book and the online working papers, which provide details of the system as a whole. Details are contained in the Reference list as Veal (2009b–i) and these papers, together with a set of spreadsheets, can be viewed at: http://www.leisuresource.net

National participation data

Sport: England: Active People survey: http://www.sportengland.org/research/active_people_survey.aspx; Australia: Exercise Recreation and Sport Survey: Standing Committee on Recreation and Sport: http://www.ausport.gov.au/information/scors

Arts: England: Active People survey, see above; Australia: Attendance at Selected Cultural Venues and Events: Australian Bureau of Statistics, available at http://www.abs.gov.au

Outdoor recreation – natural: England: 2005 England Leisure Visits Survey: Natural England (2005), available under 'publications' at: at: http://www.naturalengland.org.uk; Australia: no survey available;

Outdoor recreation – urban: Official/national data not available; see Veal (2006c) for review of data availability;

Tourism: UK: International Passenger Survey: http://www.statistics.gov.uk/ssd/surveys/international_passenger_survey.asp; domestic: see England Leisure Visits Survey under Outdoor recreation – natural; Australia: http://www.tra.australia.com/international.asp?sub=0038 and http://www.tra.australia.com/domestic.asp?sub=0031;

General: Cushman *et al.* (2006).

QUESTIONS/EXERCISES

There are no questions for this chapter, but an exercise using the U-Plan system is provided on the book's website (http://www.leisuresource.net).

PART III

Planning Tools

This part of the book presents various analytical tools that have been flagged in earlier chapters and are required to develop and evaluate policies and plans. It comprises three chapters:

- Chapter 9, *Planning Tools 1: Consultative*, considers the theory and practice of stakeholder consultation and its roles in the policy-making and planning process.
- Chapter 10, *Planning Tools 2: Facility/Service Audit*, outlines Task 16 of the U-Plan system, which involves consideration of facility capacities and catchment areas.
- Chapter 11, *Planning Tools 3: Forecasting*, examines change factors likely to affect the future of leisure, sport and tourism and a range of demand-forecasting techniques.

chapter 9

Planning Tools 1: Consultative

CONSULTATION IN THE POLICYMAKING/PLANNING PROCESS

Consultation with stakeholders – the general public, current and potential clients, other organizations, members of the planning agency itself – is widely seen as a vital component in the policymaking and planning process. There has been a growing movement for more direct community involvement over the last 40 years, with official recognition in the UK being marked by the publication of the *Skeffington Report* on public participation in 1969 (Ministry of Housing and Local Government, 1969). Nevertheless, public response to meetings and questionnaire surveys on broad planning policies are often minimal. Formal public inquiries are seen as inflexible and too expensive for all but the most well-resourced pressure groups to become involved in. At local level more success can be claimed: people can more readily understand and relate to problems and issues concerning their own neighbourhoods. Public participation has been most fully developed by the environmental planning profession, particularly because of statutory requirements, but has spread to all areas of public policy, including leisure, sport and tourism.

In the old model of planning, as shown in Fig. 9.1, technical inputs, such as demand or needs assessment and forecasting, held centre stage in the process; in the new model, public and stakeholder consultation and collaborative identification of issues intervene between the technical inputs and the development of the plan or strategy. Thus planning is often seen as less of a technical process and more of a collective community activity.

As with data collection, consultation can be a time-consuming process and it can easily be mishandled. If not undertaken competently, far from broadening the inputs to the planning process, it can have a narrowing effect, if sectional interests are permitted to hijack the process. In this chapter we consider:

- the characteristics of the consultation process;
- some specialist techniques involved in stakeholder consultation;
- examples of planning and policymaking approaches focused primarily on consultative processes;
- a critical appraisal of public consultation.

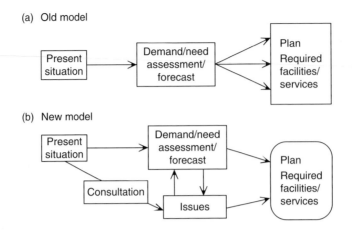

Fig. 9.1. Old and new models of planning.

CONSULTATION CHARACTERISTICS

Consultation can vary in its forms and functions, its timing, the range and types of people and organizations involved and its format. These issues are discussed in turn below.

Forms

As Sherry Arnstein pointed out in 1969, public participation can take many forms, from 'tokenism' to total citizen control of the policymaking process. The steps in Arnstein's 'ladder' of citizen participation are shown in Table 9.1 along with additional rungs, including a number offered by Zena Hoctor (Hoctor, 2003). In practice, most public consultation exercises involve a number of these forms, but very few venture up as far as the top third of the ladder.

Functions

Consultation may be undertaken for a variety of reasons, including:

- as a means of gathering information at an early stage in the policymaking process, for example issues of concern to particular groups and ideas for solutions;
- to obtain feedback in regard to specific proposals;
- as an integral part of a decision-making process covering all stages of the policymaking/ planning process.

Of particular importance in the area of leisure, sport and tourism, which are not public statutory services, is to produce a plan which is *implemented*. Implementation often involves organizations other than the planning agency, for example sporting organizations, businesses, landowners, service users or members of the general public. It is generally believed that this will be successfully achieved only if those who are expected to be affected and involved in the outcomes of a plan are also involved in its preparation: individuals and organizations must feel that they have some *ownership* of the plan.

Table 9.1. Ladder of citizen participation.

Rung	Type of participation	Source	Definition/comment
1.	Self-mobilization	H	People take initiatives independently of planning agencies: may or may not challenge power structure
2.	Citizen control	A	Full community engagement in policy formulation and decision-making
3.	Delegated power	A	Giving certain community groups decision-making power in specified limited areas
4.	Lobbying	–	Accepting inputs from lobbyists on behalf of the private, non-profit and public sectors
5.	Partnership	A	Developing proposals together
6.	Interactive participation	H	Joint analysis and ownership of decisions
7.	Functional participation	H	Participation seen by decision-makers as a means to achieve predetermined objectives
8.	Participation for material incentives	H	Participants are paid for their time: no commitment to outcomes
9.	Placation	A	Populist: giving the public what they are thought to want, but without genuine dialogue
10.	Consultation	A, H	Seeking comment on proposals already formulated
11.	Informing/passive	A, H	A one-way process
12.	Therapy	A	Using the process to reassure the public about decisions already taken
13.	Manipulation	A, H	A somewhat cynical use of the process by an organization

Sources: A, Arnstein (1969); H, Hoctor (2003), based on the work of Julian Pretty.

Timing

In the depiction of the rational-comprehensive planning process in Fig. 6.3, consultation is shown as 'step 5', but in fact it can take place at many stages in the whole policymaking/planning process. If the purpose is to generate ideas, consultation might take place at the beginning of the process; if it is to obtain reactions to proposals, it would take place later in the process. If the idea of consultation is fully embraced and its political role is recognized, then it is likely to take place in various forms throughout the process.

Parties involved

Consultation can involve: (i) the public at large; (ii) targeted groups of the public; (iii) existing clients of an organization; (iv) organizations and their representatives; and (v) the professional staff and elected or appointed members of the public organization doing the planning. Table 9.2 provides an indicative list of the range of individuals and organizations that might be involved in the consultation process for a leisure, sport or tourism plan.

Format

Consultation can take a variety of formats, using a variety of techniques, as listed in Table 9.3. It includes 31 different formats, divided into seven groups: (i) political/legal processes; (ii) information provision and requests for comment; (iii) meetings; (iv) social research methods; (v) activism; (vi) deliberative; and (vii) analytical.

Each of the formats/techniques has its merits and drawbacks. Some of these are related to the qualities highlighted in the table, namely: (i) the cost of administration; (ii) the quality of the information or other inputs obtained; and (iii) the representativeness of the participants and the contributions they offer. Typically, the lower the cost the poorer the quality of the outcomes and the lower the level of representativeness. These factors are discussed in more detail in the final section of the chapter. The following section presents comments on the seven groups of formats in the table.

SPECIFIC FORMATS

I. Political/legal processes

Voting

Voting is not often included in lists of public participation formats, but of course it is in some senses the ultimate form of participation. The item is divided into two parts: voting in elections and plebiscites/referenda.

Table 9.2. Individuals and organizations involved in consultation.

1. Public at large
2. Particular age/gender/ethnic/disability groups
3. Current users of facilities/services
4. Staff of Leisure/Sport/Tourism Departments
5. Elected members of council
6. Other departments of council
7. Neighbouring authorities
8. Regional/state/national governments/agencies
9. Sports/arts/environmental/special-interest clubs
10. Chambers of commerce
11. Owners/managers of private sector facilities
12. Professional/expert groups
13. Professional lobbyists representing any of groups 9–12

Table 9.3. Public participation formats.

Format	Description	Cost	Quality of information	Representativeness of respondents
I. Political/legal processes				
1. Voting				
Elections	Electors vote for representatives	High	High	May be reduced by low levels of participation where voting is voluntary (voting compulsory in Australia)
Plebiscites/referenda	Electors vote for policies	High	High	
2. Membership of a political party	Individual membership	Low	High	Membership in most democracies is low
3. Opinion polls	Voters surveyed usually by telephone	High	High	Generally carefully designed representative samples, typically of about 2000 voters
4. Lobbying	Representatives of organizations, including professional lobbyists, communicate with decision-makers directly	High	Variable	Representative of sectional interests
5. Statutory public notices	Notices of proposals placed by law in government gazette and/or commercial media	Low	Variable	Self-selected
6. Public inquiries/hearings	Formal governmental process: may be national or local	High	High	Bias towards organized/funded groups
II. Information and requests for comment				
7. Non-statutory media notices/requests for comment	Stakeholder written views invited by public announcement	Medium	Low	Possibly unrepresentative because respondents are self-selecting

(Continued)

Table 9.3. Continued.

Format	Description	Cost	Quality of information	Representativeness of respondents
8. Competitions	Often related to naming only; typically aimed at children	Medium	High for focused topics	Incentive boosts participation; respondents self-selecting, therefore probably unrepresentative
9. Letters inviting comment	Written communication with organized stakeholder groups	High: sending/processing responses	Medium	Wide distribution but probably unrepresentative
10. Letterbox drop	Production/distribution of printed material to residents	High/medium	Low	Usually low response, and therefore probably unrepresentative
11. Website information and comment	Information provided, and comment invited online	Low	Medium	Self-selected
12. Public exhibitions	Static or mobile exhibition with opportunity for comment	High/medium, especially if staffed	Medium	Distribution depends on distribution of exhibitions; respondents may be committed, self-interested, so may not be representative
III. Meetings				
13. One-on-one meetings/interviews	Officials interview stakeholders	High	High	Depends how meetings are arranged
14. Attendance at stakeholder meetings	Officials attend meetings of organized groups (e.g. sports clubs)	Medium	Mixed	Active members of groups not always representative of all participants
15. Public meetings	Officials and/or politicians speak and respond to questions/comments at public meetings	High/medium	Medium	As for exhibitions

16. Community dinners	Public meeting/discussion with full catering	High/medium	Medium	Low, due to self-selection
IV. Social research methods				
17. Focus groups	Groups of 6–12 individuals with discussion leader	Expensive	High	Dependent on selection process, but method not intended to be statistically representative
18. Organization surveys	Mail questionnaire survey of organizations	Medium	High if well-designed	Usually low response, and therefore probably unrepresentative
19. Community/resident/ client surveys	Mail questionnaire Other self-completion questionnaire Interviewer-administered questionnaire	Medium Low/medium High	Medium Medium High	Dependent on quality of the design of the survey process; can be low response and self-selecting
V. Activism				
20. Mass media involvement	Newspaper coverage/letters; talk-back radio	Low	Mixed	Low, due to self-selection
20. Internet-based activism	Emerging format	Low	Mixed	Low, due to self-selection.
21. Ad hoc campaigns	Ad hoc groups formed to campaign for or against a specific plan	Mixed	Mixed	May be locally representative but often low, due to self-selection
22. Demonstrations/rallies	Marches, rallies, lobbying public meetings and vigils	Low	Low	Self-selected
23. Civil disobedience	Attempts to invade premises, sit-downs, violence towards police, etc.	Low for participants, high for authorities, etc.	Low	Self-selected

(Continued)

Table 9.3. Continued

Format	Description	Cost	Quality of information	Representativeness of respondents
VI. Deliberative				
24. Working parties	Establishment of working parties of representatives/experts	Medium	High	Dependent on selection process
25. Citizen advisory committees/ panels/ community round tables/ planning cells	As for working parties, but may be more than one committee and may include representatives of general public	Medium	High	Dependent on selection process
26. Citizen juries	As above, but members randomly selected	High	High	Representativeness is a key feature of the approach
27. Delphi technique	A panel of experts provides views via questionnaire; aggregate results are fed back to the panel for review in additional 'rounds'	Low	High	Representative of experts in a field
28. Nominal Group Technique	Structured form of focus group	Medium	High	Dependent on selection process, as for focus groups
29. Adaptive Environmental Assessment and Management (AEAM)	Structured form of working party designed to reach consensus	High	High	Dependent on selection process
30. Interest-based negotiation (IBN)	Structured consensus-seeking process focused on competing and common interests	Medium	High	Dependent on selection process
VII. Analytical				
31. Stakeholder analysis	Collation of existing data on stakeholders	Low	Variable	Dependent on resources expended

Voting in elections is, for most people, their only formal participation in the political process. However, a significant proportion of the eligible population in most Western democracies do not avail themselves of this limited opportunity: in the UK about 60–70% of voters take part in national elections but only about 30% in local council elections; in the USA only just over 50% of voters take part in presidential elections. In Australia, one of the few countries where voting is compulsory at local, state and national level, the turnout is around 95%. However, apart from the level of voter participation, it is often thought that placing a tick in a box every few years does not constitute democracy in its full sense.

Plebiscites and referenda deal with specific items of policy, plebiscites being non-binding on governments while referenda are binding: that is, governments must implement the referendum decision. Typically, therefore, referenda relate to changes to the constitution. In the USA plebiscites and referenda at state level are referred to as *propositions* and may be initiated by citizens. They may seek to amend the state constitution or initiate legislation. At the local level, citizens vote not only for candidates for public office but also on proposals to issue bonds, that is to borrow money for specific projects. This level of public involvement in decision-making is less common in other democracies, with plebiscites and referenda being rare occurrences. Few if any plebiscites/referenda relate directly to leisure, sport or tourism but they may have indirect effects. Thus, for example, the famous Second Amendment of the United States refers to the right to bear arms and this affects not only the level of ownership of firearms for self-protection but also sport. One of the most famous state propositions, the 1978 Californian *Proposition 13*, placed a limit on the level of property taxes (rates) in the state, initiating a nationwide trend, which resulted in significant cuts in subsidies on local services, including leisure services.

Membership of political parties

Membership of political parties is part of the formal representative governmental system, as discussed in Chapter 6. Members of parties initiate and discuss policies and, in theory, determine the platform which the party takes to the election. In an ideal world, with a high proportion of citizens being members of a party, this would achieve a high level of public participation in a representative system. In practice, membership of political parties in most Western democracies is low. This may be because people in contemporary society are too busy, because they are simply complacent or because they are generally alienated from the political system. Part of the cause or the result may be the changes in parties themselves, with increased emphasis on the leader rather than the rank-and-file and, in democratic socialist and social democratic parties, the prominent role of unions which no longer represent the majority of workers. As noted in Chapter 2, political parties do have national policies on leisure, sport and tourism, and while these are important at national and state/provincial levels and in large cities, they are less relevant at local council level where 'independents' often dominate.

Opinion polls

Opinion polls are included because of their influence on the political process, even though politicians routinely say that 'the only poll that matters is the one that takes place on election day'. While sponsored by mass media organizations, the polls are generally conducted by reputable survey companies using small (typically about 2000) but demographically representative samples. Given the limited numbers involved, polls cannot be said to contribute to democratic involvement, but they are clearly a de facto part of the democratic scene and may have an influence on individual voters' voting intentions and attitudes towards the democratic process. At the local level the media-sponsored opinion poll is, in effect, and as far as leisure, sport and tourism are concerned, replaced by council-sponsored surveys (item 19).

Lobbying

Lobbying at national and state/provincial levels may involve stakeholder group members themselves or professional lobbyists employed on their behalf. Lobbying is so named because the place to meet and talk to politicians has traditionally been the lobby of the elected assembly; lobbyists play an increasingly significant role in influencing political decision-making in democratic, and not so democratic, states. Their role is similar to that of public relations consultants, but their role relates to politicians rather than to the public at large. Their function is to communicate with politicians, provide them with information to support the interests of their clients and, if possible, to arrange direct meetings between clients and politicians. At national and state/provincial level, political parties often facilitate this process by running 'fund-raising' events, such as dinners, where the entrance fee may be thousands of dollars in return for the opportunity to have direct discussions with ministers. This can, of course, be seen as undermining the democratic process by securing undue political influence for those who can afford to pay for it. While the phenomenon is legal and lobbyists and their clients are formally registered in many jurisdictions, it clearly opens up the possibility not only of undue influence but of corruption. The scale of lobbying activity is demonstrated by a recent study by the International Consortium of Investigative Journalists (2009), which showed that fossil fuel industries and other heavy carbon emitters were employing over 2800 lobbyists in the USA and hundreds more in other developed and developing countries, seeking to influence the national legislation and contributions to United Nations climate change agreements in their own favour.

Statutory public notices

Statutory public notices are one of the oldest conduits for public participation and are mandated by law. Many forms of legislation and administrative action are subject to this requirement, which involves placing a notice in the official government gazette and/or in major print media and giving the public a certain period of time to comment – usually with an indication as to where more detailed information can be found, such as council offices, libraries or a website. The most familiar of these is local building development proposals. In general, this formal approach, while fulfilling legal requirements, is not seen as effective in reaching the wider public, who do not read the official government gazette or the public notices section of the print media. However, these are scanned by the mass media and by stakeholder groups who may bring items to the broader public attention. Most of the other methods discussed below are seen as ways of overcoming the limitations.

Public inquiries/hearings

Public inquiries are divided into two groups: national (including the state/provincial level in federal systems) and local.

National public inquiries are established by governments or legislative assemblies to review an area of policy and produce recommendations for change. They may be established as a result of an event or train of events, such as a series of accidents resulting in an inquiry into air safety, as a response to an election commitment or public concern, or as a routine part of the legislative process, when they may be referred to as *hearings*, as in the US Senate hearings. The inquiry will be conducted by an eminent individual, often a judge if legal issues are involved, or by a specially established committee, including a *select committee* of a legislative assembly, or a standing committee. Typically there is a public call for written submissions to be submitted by organizations and individuals, and key individuals and organizations will be invited to give oral evidence. Some examples of committees of inquiry relevant to leisure sport and tourism are listed in Table 9.4. One of the most significant formative events in outdoor recreation

Table 9.4. Public inquiries: examples in leisure, sport and tourism.

Country	Date[a]	Name of inquiry	Establishing organization	Chair	Report reference
USA	1962	Outdoor Recreation for America – Outdoor Recreation Resources Review Commission (ORRRC)	President John F. Kennedy	Lawrance S. Rockefeller: businessman, philanthropist, conservationist	ORRRC (1962)
UK	1973	Select Committee on Sport and Leisure	House of Lords	Lord Cobham: former Worcestershire county cricketer	House of Lords Select Committee on Sport and Leisure (1973)
UK	1984	Recreation Management Training Committee	Secretaries of State for the Environment and for Education and Science	Anne Yates: member of Nottinghamshire County Council	Recreation Management Committee (1984)
UK	2000	Committee of Inquiry into Hunting with Dogs in England and Wales	Home Secretary	Lord Burns: economist, former Permanent Secretary to the Treasury	Committee of Inquiry into Hunting with Dogs in England and Wales (2000)
UK	2005	Review of National Sport Effort and Resources	Chancellor of the Exchequer and the Secretary of State for Culture, Media and Sport	Patrick Carter (Lord Carter of Coles): businessman, Chairman of Sport England	Carter (2005)
UK	2007–2008	London 2012 Olympic Games & Paralympic Games: funding & legacy / London 2012 Games: the next lap	House of Commons Select Committee on Culture, Media and Sport (HCSCCMS)	John Whittingdale, MP	HCSCCMS (2007) / HCSCCMS (2008)
UK	2008	Supporting Excellence in the Arts: from Measurement to Judgement	Secretary of State for Culture, Media and Sport	Sir Brian McMaster: arts administrator – Director of the Edinburgh International Festival, 1991–2006	McMaster (2008)

(Continued)

Table 9.4. Continued.

Country	Date[a]	Name of inquiry	Establishing organization	Chair	Report reference
Australia	1975	Report of the Australian Sports Institute Study Group	Minister for Tourism and Recreation	Allan Coles: Head of Dept of Human Movement Studies, Univ. of Queensland	Australian Sports Institute Study Group (1975)
Australia	1989	Going for Gold: the First Report of an Inquiry into Sports Funding and Administration	House of Representatives Standing Committee on Finance and Public Administration	Stephen P. Martin, MP	House of Representatives Standing Committee on Finance and Public Administration (1989)
Australia	1999	Shaping up: a Review of Commonwealth Involvement in Sport and Recreation in Australia	Australian government	Ross Oakley: CEO of Australian Football League	Sport 2000 Task Force (1999)
Australia	1999	Securing the Future: Major Performing Arts Inquiry	Minister for the Arts	Helen Nugent: company director; Deputy Chair of Australia Council for the Arts	Major Performing Arts Inquiry (1999)
Australia	2009	Steering Committee: Informing the National Long-term Tourism Strategy	Minister for Tourism	Margaret Jackson: former chair of Qantas Airways	Jackson (2009)
Australia	2009	The Future of Sport in Australia	Minister for Sport	David Crawford: Chairman of Foster's Group Ltd conducted reviews of the Australian Football League and of Australian Soccer	Independent Panel on Sport (2009)

[a] Year reported: most committees established 1–2 years before publication date.

development and research in the Western world was the first inquiry listed, the 1962 Outdoor Recreation Resources Review Commission.

At the time of writing (September 2009), the UK government website listed 29 departmental websites where consultation processes were in operation and sites for the Northern Ireland and Scottish governments and the Welsh Assembly; the Department for Culture, Media and Sport alone listed 15 consultations for 2009. On the Australian government web site ten current inquiries involving public consultation were listed, including three with some relevance to leisure, sport or tourism: an inquiry regarding free-to-air television broadcasting of national sporting events; an inquiry on intellectual property rights; and one regarding indigenous heritage protection.

Local public inquiries refer to the planning system in the UK. When an organization wishes to build a structure or make other significant changes to the environment a *planning or development application* must be submitted to the relevant local council, which evaluates and then approves or rejects it. A public inquiry into the proposed development, which takes the matter out of the hands of the council, may be established in two situations: (i) if the proposal has wider than local significance and is therefore 'called in' by the relevant minister; and (ii) if the applicant or other affected party wishes to appeal against the council's decision. The minister appoints an inspector, who reviews the application and receives written and oral submissions before making a recommendation to the minister, who makes the final decision.

II. Information provision and requests for comment

The second group of formats in Table 9.3, information provision and requests for comment, goes beyond the statutory public notice and seeks more engagement with the media, through more extensive advertising, articles and interviews and possibly competitions, mail-outs to organizations and individuals, an interactive website and public exhibitions. These media generally require a written response. The response is biased in favour of the individuals and/or organizations with the skills, time, application and level of interest to make such a response.

III. Meetings

Meetings of various sorts, with individuals or organizations and the general public, enable people to offer their comments orally. Bias still remains, of course, in favour of individuals with the time and levels of interest/commitment/involvement to turn up at meetings.

IV. Social research methods

Social research methods include focus groups and questionnaire-based surveys of organizations and individuals. Focus groups, by definition, provide qualitative rather than quantitative information – that is, they indicate a range of opinions, but not how many people hold which opinions. Questionnaire-based surveys produce data in a predetermined framework, but this can include open-ended information on opinions. Those conducted by mail are cheap but invariably suffer from a low – often very low – response rate, even from organizations, thus raising doubts as to the representativeness of the results. Similarly, surveys conducted by handing out questionnaires in an informal way without considering sampling methods also suffer from doubtful representativeness. Surveys conducted by interviewers, by telephone or face-to-face invariably provide better-quality data (fully completed questionnaires) and a more representative sample.

V. Activism

Whereas the rest of the formats discussed are conducted by the planning agency or other official body, activism happens *to* the agency, and is often unanticipated. The results, however, can often be more influential on public decision-making than many of the other formats.

Mass media

The mass communication media are not generally portrayed as part of the public participation process in leisure, sport and tourism planning, let alone as an aspect of political activism, but they are often influential in the political process. Newspapers and talk-back radio in particular often run their own campaigns on issues, either leading or following public opinion as they see it. The most long-established public participation component is the letter to the editor. The growth of talk-back radio over the last 40 years or so has arguably democratized the process, providing a public platform to groups who would be unlikely to write letters to newspapers. The eagerness of politicians to appear on talk-back radio shows is evidence of the level of influence of the medium. It is clear that specific media outlets, individual writers or presenters or the individuals who write letters to a particular newspaper or telephone, text or e-mail a particular radio station, are not representative of the wider community. Whether the many media outlets are collectively representative of the community on any one issue is an empirical question.

Internet-based methods

The Internet is a relatively new medium that has added a further level of democratization to the public participation process via websites, blogs and social networking sites such as Facebook and 'twittering'. The 2008 US presidential election campaign of Barack Obama used the Internet to engage millions of mainly young people who would not normally be involved in organized political processes. In Australia, the GetUp! campaign is an alternative political movement which uses the Internet to garner support on specific issues and generally act as a ginger group on the national political scene.

Ad hoc campaigns

Specific single-purpose campaigns established to oppose or support a particular policy or proposed development, typically with an appropriate acronym and slogan printed on colourful tee-shirts, are a common feature of modern life. In terms of the ladder of citizen participation shown in Table 9.1, this represents the top rung: self-mobilization. Members of such campaigns will utilize a number of the other formats/techniques listed in Table 9.3, particularly attendance at public meetings, letter-writing, use of the mass media, demonstrations and possibly civil disobedience.

Many such campaigns relate to leisure and tourism issues, including campaigns to save open space or coastline from housing or road development or to save historic buildings from demolition.

Single-site or single-event campaigns can develop into something more general and long-lasting. Belinda Wheaton (2007) describes the Surfers Against Sewage (SAS) campaign, which began as a protest about pollution on a single beach in Cornwall, UK, in 1990 and has developed into a global movement campaigning 'for clean, safe recreational water, free from sewage effluents, toxic chemicals, nuclear waste and marine litter' (SAS, undated).

Demonstrations

Another form of self-mobilization is the demonstration, which may involve mass marches, lobbying of meetings with placards, chanting, etc. and vigils. The aim is to draw public attention to issues, via media coverage, and also to directly influence governments. Few leisure-related issues prompt this type of activity, but two high-profile examples can be noted: (i) the demonstrations in Commonwealth countries in the 1960s and 1970s regarding sport and the apartheid regime of South Africa; and (ii) the campaigns against and in favour of fox-hunting in the UK in the early years of this century.

Civil disobedience

When people feel frustrated by 'normal' channels of political participation they may decide to break the law as a form of direct action regarding a specific cause or as a means of drawing attention to the cause. The idea of using peaceful, passive resistance as a political tool is associated historically with the campaign for voting rights for women in the UK in the early part of the 20th century, when some of the suffragettes chained themselves to the railings of the Houses of Parliament, and also with the campaign for Indian independence led by Mahatma Gandhi in the 1940s. During the Cold War the British Campaign for Nuclear Disarmament led sit-down demonstrations in Whitehall and attempts were made by some anti-nuclear demonstrators to invade nuclear defence sites. Recent examples of direct action are the animal rights activists who mount raids on factory farms to free caged birds and animals. Environmentalists have sought to protect natural sites from development by lying down in front of bulldozers or setting up camp high up in threatened trees.

Beyond civil disobedience lies *uncivil* disobedience, in the form of various acts of terrorism and military action.

VI. Deliberative

A number of the items listed in Table 9.3 seek to engage members of the public, stakeholders or invited experts in the process of generation or evaluation of proposals and resolving conflicts of interest.

Citizen advisory committees/panels/community round tables/planning panels/juries

The public inquiry is a quasi-judicial, 'top-down', 'arm's length' approach to public policy to which the public is invited to contribute, but the evaluation of the evidence and the resultant recommendations are the responsibility of the appointed committee or assessor. A number of approaches have been devised to engage members of the public in the process of discussion, appraisal of evidence and seeking of solutions. These can be seen as forms of *deliberative democracy*, which is designed to overcome the weaknesses of the standard representative democracy model and the traditional forms of public participation.

The first such approach is the appointment of a *working party* to advise the planning agency in regard to all or part of a policymaking/planning task. Such working parties tend to be focused on a single issue/project, have a fixed life and are made up of persons with expert and/or local knowledge. Variations on the working party model are *citizen advisory committees*, *citizen panels* and *planning cells*. These may have a similar membership to working parties, but will have wider terms of reference, for example being concerned with all environmental planning rather than a single project, and will have a longer-term or indefinite lifespan: they are established as a permanent part of the policymaking/planning machinery.

There may be a number of such bodies in a planning area, covering planning zones or particular policy areas.

This idea is taken a step further with the idea of the *citizen jury*, the members of which, rather than being selected on the basis of expertise or specific stakeholder status, are selected as broadly representative of the community, in some cases using a random selection process similar to that used in legal jury selection although, of course, participation is voluntary. Like legal juries, citizen juries listen to presentation of evidence and can call for additional evidence and witnesses, and they can play the lawyer's and judge's role of cross-examination. Meetings may therefore take several days. One suggestion has been made that membership of such juries should be open to all, using Internet technology, and that they should not be time-limited (Ward *et al.*, 2003). The method was developed in the USA by Ned Crosby of the Jefferson Institute, and has been used in that country, the UK and Germany (Smith and Wales, 2000), but no example is known of its use in relation to leisure, sport or tourism. Furthermore, the extent to which citizen juries achieve their aim of opening up political engagement to groups unrepresented by mainstream political processes has been queried (Sanders, 1997).

Delphi technique

The Delphi technique, named after the ancient Greek Delphic Oracle, involves asking a panel of experts, via a questionnaire, their views on likely consequences of policy actions. The results are aggregated and fed back to the participants, who may then revise their views in light of those of their peers in one or more additional rounds of questioning. The technique has been used in policymaking (e.g. Green, H. *et al.*, 1990) but is more commonly used in forecasting: it is therefore discussed in more detail in Chapter 11.

Nominal Group Technique

The Nominal Group Technique (NGT), developed by Andre Delbecq and Andrew Van de Ven in the late 1960s (Delbecq *et al.*, 1975), can be seen as a formalized version of the focus group technique. The term 'nominal' was used by early practitioners to refer to techniques which did allow individuals to communicate orally: 'Thus, the collection of individuals is a group 'in name only', or "nominally"' (Delbecq *et al.*, 1975: 7). While non-communication among participants remains an important component of the technique, it has developed to include oral communication, so the name is now somewhat misleading.

The technique involves one or more groups of up to about 15 selected stakeholders and is a formalized process for eliciting and ranking views in relation to an issue or policy/planning task. It can be divided into nine steps, as set out in Table 9.5.

Examples of the use of NGT in leisure/sport/tourism contexts can be found in the literature; these include:

- *Tourism*: Ritchie (1994a) summarizes a project conducted in the province of Alberta, Canada, to define 'priority issues and problems facing tourism in the province' as the initial input into the development of a strategic plan; in this case 16 NGT sessions were conducted involving a total of 288 tourism industry members of the Tourism Industry Association of Alberta.
- *Outdoor recreation* (including tourism and sporting components): Clark and Stein (2004) describe an exercise conducted for the Florida Fish and Wildlife Conservation Commission and comprising seven NGT sessions attended by a total of 111 representatives of recreational users groups, conservation groups, local government decision-makers, local landowners, 'active/concerned citizens', tourism development officials and local business owners.

Table 9.5. Nominal Group Technique: steps.

Task	Explanation
1. Specify issue/problem/task	–
2. Identify and assemble group	–
3. Present issue/problem/task to group	–
4. Silent generation of ideas in writing	Without discussion, individuals write down up to five suggestions/ideas in response to the issue/problem/task
5. Round-robin recording of ideas	In turn, each group member offers (and possibly explains briefly) one suggestion/idea, which is recorded on a flip chart/white board/butcher's paper/screen … going around the group several times until all suggestions exhausted
6. Serial discussion for clarification	Suggestions/ideas discussed in turn; may involve clarification of wording, elimination of duplication; each item given a code
7. Preliminary vote on item importance	Individuals rank or rate the items on the consolidated list; group averages calculated
8. Discussion of the preliminary vote	Optional step
9. Final vote	Required if step 8 implemented

In both these examples, collation of data from the individual sessions was quite straightforward, but consolidating the data from the 16 Alberta sessions or the seven Florida sessions into single prioritized lists of issues was a demanding process.

Because of its structured nature, the NGT has an advantage over the standard focus group in being less dependent on subjective interpretation of results by the facilitator, and ensures that all participants have relatively equal inputs and contributions to the outcomes. However, as with a number of the techniques available for stakeholder consultation, a weakness of the NGT is the uncertainty as to the representativeness of the participants. This is important because, despite its qualitative nature, the technique involves quantitative aspects in giving ranks or numerical ratings of importance to the issues identified and averaging of the ranks and indices of importance; thus the priorities determined are partly based on numerical strength of groups among the participants. For example, a numerically large user group is likely to have the same number of NGT representatives as a numerically small user group, or a user group that imposes significant impact on a resource and/or is costly to service may have the same input as one which has little impact and is cheap to service. The quasi-scientific nature of the NGT may therefore result in inappropriate weight being given to the outcomes in relation to other inputs to the policymaking/planning process. These issues are discussed further in the critique of stakeholder consultation in the final section of the chapter.

When the selected participants are experts widely dispersed geographically, the technique has some similarities to the Delphi technique of qualitative forecasting, as discussed in Chapter 11.

Adaptive Environmental Assessment Management (AEAM)

Adaptive Environmental Assessment Management (AEAM), developed in the 1970s by ecologist Crawford Holling and colleagues (Holling, 1978), is a consensus-seeking process involving stakeholders, managers and appropriate experts. It is typically conducted through a series of one-day workshops. The workshop participants work collectively to prepare a consensus report on the issue at hand, typically guided and serviced by consultants engaged to manage the process. Documentary and oral information from relevant experts is presented to the workshops, and discussions are recorded and fed back to participants between meetings. Rather than leaving conflicting views to be resolved entirely by the planning agency, stakeholder representatives and managers are required, where possible, to discuss compromises and reach agreement on a set of recommendations.

As with all consultation processes, the validity of AEAM is highly dependent on the selection of participants. It has the disadvantages of cost, in the time of the participants and in the cost of employing consultants to manage the process. However, since much of this cost is involved in recording stakeholder views and assembling and evaluating technical data, it is likely to be incurred in any planning exercise.

Interest-based negotiation (IBN)

Interest-based negotiation (IBN) includes features of both NGT and AEAM. The participants represent various stakeholders with different interests in a project or plan. The process involves initial statements of these interests from participants. These statements are analysed to identify issues, interests, common ground and options for agreement (Ritchie, 2000: 55), and the participants then work on expanding the common ground and options for agreement in order to reach a consensus.

VII. Analytical

Stakeholder analysis is a term used by Nancy Tague, in the *Quality Handbook* (2005) to describe a group of approaches in assessing the interest, influence and importance of stakeholders in order to 'change those assessments or work within them to ensure the success of the project or plan' (p. 477). The components of the process are summarized in Table 9.6.

The technique involves making a series of assessments of stakeholders concerning such things as the nature and degree of interest in the issue/project, their level of influence and their importance. Just how this is to be done is not made clear but, since Tague's description appears to be directed towards private sector organizations, subjective assessments are probably seen as acceptable. This would be less acceptable in a public sector context, so transparent methodologies would need to be devised. However, the technique does make explicit a dimension of the stakeholder consultation process that is often implicit or hidden in public planning: while stakeholder inputs are 'taken into account' in general, it is not always clear how the views of different stakeholders have been evaluated.

CONSULTATION-BASED METHODS OF PLANNING

In some policymaking/planning approaches, stakeholder consultation is not viewed as just another step in the process, but is the basis of the whole exercise. Two examples are discussed here: the *issues approach* and the *community development approach*.

Table 9.6. Stakeholder analysis: steps.

1. Issue	Identify the issue/proposal
2. Interest	List nature of each stakeholder's interest in the issue – classify as primary (directly affected) or secondary (intermediaries involved in implementing, funding, monitoring, etc.)
3. Attitude[a]	Rate the known attitude of each stakeholder towards the issue, from –2 (strongly opposed) to +2 (strongly supportive)
4. Influence	Rate the influence of each stakeholder in relation to the issue, from 1 to 5
5. Importance	Rate the importance of each stakeholder to the solution of the issues/ success of the project, from 1 to 5
6. Chart	Create a two-dimensional importance–influence chart and interpret
7. Strategies	Develop strategies for each stakeholder
8. Participation matrix[a]	Locates each stakeholder in a table indicating an Arnstein-type list of involvement across the top (inform, consult, partner, control) and stages of the project down the side (identification, planning, implementation, monitoring)

[a] Optional steps.
Source: Summary of Tague (2005: 476–481).

The issues approach

The issues approach to planning seeks to eliminate the lengthy, expensive and sometimes wasted research and preparatory work which is necessary for the more traditional rational-comprehensive approach. In terms of Arnstein's ladder, the approach can usually be seen as being located on the partnership rung. The origin of the approach in British leisure planning lies in the Department of the Environment (1977) circular containing guidelines for the Regional Councils of Sport and Recreation on the preparation of Regional Recreational Strategies, which suggested that the initial report in the strategy preparation process should be an Issues Report. The issues report would contain: (i) a brief statement of principles; (ii) a background review of the state of sport and recreation in the region; and (iii) an identification of issues and initial assessment of priorities. The final strategy was envisaged as a series of reports on each of the issues identified. This is in contrast to the rational-comprehensive approach discussed in Chapter 6, and is in effect a version of the 'mixed scanning' approach discussed there.

What is not always clear from the various guidelines suggesting the issues approach is just how the issues are to emerge. In general it is suggested that issues will emerge from the stakeholder consultation process, although the professionals in charge of the process usually have the responsibility to produce, from such an exercise, a list of issues which is 'manageable' and will avoid the expensive and time-consuming research and data collection of other planning exercises.

An early example of the use of the approach in the USA, which provided the basis for the Third Nationwide Outdoor Recreation Plan, illustrates how demanding, in terms of time and resources, the approach can be in practice, as shown in Box 9.1. Despite the widespread consultation involved, it can be seen that, at a number of points, it is not clear just how the particular list of issues was selected.

Box 9.1. Issues approach: US Third Nationwide Outdoor Recreation Strategy, 1979.

Phase 1. Involvement of Federal, State and local public agency and private sector participants in the identification of outdoor recreation issues of national significance.

Briefing 1: over 160 agency representatives attended a briefing in Washington, DC.

Consultation: over 5000 organizations contacted and asked to identify issues of national significance.

Response: responses from 3000 organizations and individuals received, identifying between them over 1000 separate recreation issues (not listed in the published report).

Phase 2. Correlation, evaluation and selection of outdoor recreation issues of national priority.

Classification: the 1000 issues were classified into 30 groups, following direct discussions with representative groups (not listed).

Briefing 2: a meeting of 125 organizational representatives discussed the list of 30.

Reduction: the 30 groups were reduced to 21 issues of 'national significance' (not listed), through discussion and analysis by Departmental Staff.

Submission: the 21 issues were submitted to the Secretary of the Interior for consideration.

Selection: the Secretary of the Interior selected 16 'priority issues' (criteria for selection not revealed):

- appropriate roles of:
    - federal, state and local governments;
    - private profit organizations; and
    - non-profit organizations.
- federal land acquisition programme;
- methods to protect significant open space and recreation resources;
- methods to protect coastal resources;
- evaluation of:
    - National Wild and Scenic Rivers System; and
    - National Trails System.
- federal water programmes and recreation;
- recreation needs of special populations;
- contribution of recreation to:
    - physical health;
    - mental health.
- federal role in urban recreation;
- federal agency research;
- outdoor recreation and:
    - energy conservation; and
    - environmental education.

Source: Heritage, Conservation and Recreation Service (1979: 86–87).

As with 'mixed scanning', the danger with the issues approach is that key issues will in fact be overlooked and that issues will be identified on the basis of the lobbying skills of various interest groups or the 'flavour of the month', rather than by any 'objective' evaluation. Against this, however, must be posed the various defects of rational-comprehensive planning as discussed in Chapter 6.

The community development approach

The essence of the community development approach to planning is public involvement and planning at the neighbourhood level. While the term *community* is used in a number of non-spatial contexts, for example the 'research community', it is mostly used to refer to the people who make up a defined geographical area, ranging from the international, via the nation state to the city and down to the village or neighbourhood scale. Community development could in theory apply at any of those levels, but for the most part is operates at the neighbourhood or district level. The ideal successful local community is seen as one which has *social capital*, where institutions such as sporting, cultural and social organizations and events have high levels of participation and where people are generally 'connected'. In developed countries community development programmes seek to enhance these qualities for their own sake, but in developing countries they may be, at least in part, a means to an end, such as economic development or public health improvement.

Leisure is seen as a component of such community development and this has resulted in the emergence of social development, sport development and arts/cultural development programmes, and also community-related tourism development programmes. These programmes may be specialist stand-alone projects or part of multi-sector community development programmes. In general, leisure-orientated community development is seen as an alternative to the traditional approach to leisure provision; it is designed to reach members of the community which the traditional approach has not been able to reach. Thus in the UK it has been associated with the government's *social inclusion* policy. The community development approach is community-orientated rather than facility orientated, as shown in Fig. 9.2. In the traditional approach the emphasis is on the provision and management of facilities; in the community development approach the team of community workers operates directly with groups in the community and the range of available facilities are utilized as required. In addition, the process may lead to the development of facilities which are campaigned for, and even built by, the community groups involved: a bottom-up as opposed to a top-down approach.

The community approach has also been put forward in relation to tourism, particularly in smaller communities, where the introduction of tourism may have a significant impact on

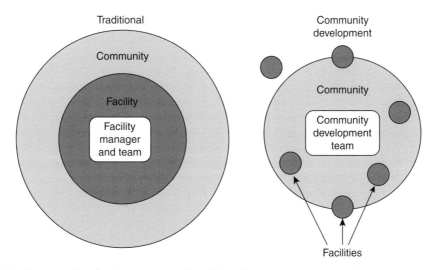

Fig. 9.2. Community development and traditional approach compared.

lifestyles, the environment and the economy. In such circumstances, it is argued, tourism can only survive and thrive if it is developed with community involvement. An early approach to community-based tourism planning was put forward by Murphy (1985) and, more recently, the idea has been pursued in relation to development of ecotourism (Wearing and McClean, 1997). Community involvement in tourism policymaking and planning is promoted for a mixture of reasons, some related to the needs of community members and some to the interests of the tourism developer or industry. Thus Van der Stoep (2000: 312–314) lists the following benefits of a community approach to tourism:

- community buy-in and empowerment;
- reduced potential of lawsuits being used to block projects;
- improved chances of long-term success;
- increasing community awareness of value of local historic, cultural and environmental attributes;
- increased sense of community identity;
- protection of 'sacred places' and sensitive resources;
- minimization of negative impacts of tourism developments;
- enhancement of community amenities for residents;
- opportunities for shared resources;
- keeping profits within the community.

CRITIQUE OF CONSULTATIVE METHODS

The theory and practice of stakeholder consultation in leisure, sport and tourism policymaking and planning can be critically examined on a number of grounds. Two issues are discussed here: (i) the relationship of the consultation to the democratic process; and (ii) the analysis of the outcomes.

Consultation and democracy

Arguably, public consultation can be seen as undermining the standard representative democratic government model. In the latter, in theory, issues are discussed in the political arena and sections of the voting public elect to the democratic assembly representatives who reflect their views on one or a range of issues. It is commonly accepted that this theory often does not work well in practice. Political parties have small and declining memberships and the general public participates, if at all, only in the process of voting once every few years. Hence the efforts to establish other methods to facilitate deliberative democracy, such as the citizens juries discussed above. However, in major policy areas, such as education, transport and health, there is at least public debate in the media. One of the difficulties in the case of leisure, sport and tourism is that they do not often feature in general political debate although, as established in Chapter 2, political philosophies and ideologies do have potential implications for the field. Furthermore, in the major policy areas inputs from professionals, pressure groups and think tanks involved in the area – the *policy community* (Homeshaw, 1995) – help stimulate and shape public political debate.

Public consultation is used to fine-tune the implementation of policies, but this is less common in the case of leisure, sport and tourism: as a consequence, governments and ruling groups, particularly at local level, often arrive in office without clear leisure, sport or tourism policy commitments, so the policymaking process often begins with a 'blank sheet of paper'. This may have a certain attraction for politicians, since it appears to be a democratic process: through public consultation they can be seen to be responding to public demands without being unduly constrained by professional principles or prior political commitments. Listening to what the people have to say is easier to understand than more technical information. Arguably, it could be said that there are also many professionals involved in leisure, sport and tourism planning/management who are content with this situation, leaving the bulk of policymaking/planning to be based on the public consultation process.

Acceptance of such a situation as desirable is to assume that: (i) professional principles and prior political analysis and commitments would not produce a better result; and (ii) the public consultation process is truly democratic. Clearly, the message of the whole of this book is that professionally based analysis and political debate of leisure, sport and tourism are a desirable input to policymaking and planning. But what of the democratic credentials of the public consultation process? Two issues might be identified: (i) the question of numbers; and (ii) the representativeness of representatives.

- *Numbers*: the question of numbers becomes a problem when the results of public consultation are treated as popularity polls. In the case of consultation with the wider public, for example via surveys, this assumes that people's responses in surveys about leisure requirements or intentions will be reflected in their later leisure behaviour and that basing policy on the most popular items on a 'wish list' will produce the greatest net public benefit; both of these assumptions are contestable. The popularity poll approach is even used when the consultees are organizations rather than individuals and no consideration is given to the relative size of the organizations.
- *Representativeness of representatives*: when consultation is conducted by means of surveys, assuming the sample has been appropriately selected, the results can be said to be representative of public opinion. But in other forms of consultation the representativeness of the consultees is often in question. As was noted in Chapter 7, research by Lord and Elmendorf (2008) indicates that representatives of some leisure organizations have different views from the mass of organization members, let alone participants in the activity who are not organization members. In his paper on the use of Interest-based negotiation, Ritchie (2000: 49) refers to a three-level structure of representative bodies: chair, committee, constituency: arguably this should be extended by splitting the constituency into a number of components, as shown in Fig. 9.3.

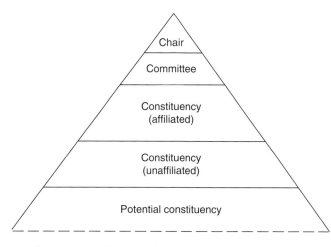

Fig. 9.3. Structure of representative organizations.

Analysis of outcomes

There are questions as to how the views of different, competing organizations should be weighed and evaluated, how the information gathered should be combined with other types of data gathered in the planning process and the relative importance of views coming out of the consultation process compared with those of the elected members of councils and governments. Invariably, planning guidelines emphasize that public consultation is just one input into the policymaking and planning process. However, it is often not clear just *how* the results of consultation are to be evaluated and combined with other data. All the data collected disappear into a 'black box' process and an acceptable plan appears, via some unspecified process, on the other side (see Veal, 2009c). This, of course, is not a fault of the consultation process itself, but a weakness of the various overall approaches to policymaking and planning, as discussed in Chapter 7.

Thus the information collected in stakeholder consultation processes may not always be valid, that is, it may not accurately represent what the planning organization believes it represents. But even if it did, there are questions as to the appropriate analysis and utilization of the information as a basis for policymaking and planning. These observations are not intended to dismiss the public consultation process but simply to raise questions about how it is conducted and how it is intended to relate to technical planning processes, political debate and decision making.

SUMMARY

This chapter reviews the process of stakeholder consultation within the policymaking and planning processes. Consultation processes vary in their functions, timing, parties involved and formats and range from tokenism to citizen control. Some 30 different formats are reviewed, grouped into seven groups: (i) political/legal processes; (ii) information provision and requests for comment; (iii) meetings; (iv) social research methods; (v) activism; (vi) deliberative; and (vii) analytical. Two planning approaches based specifically on consultative processes are discussed: the issues approach and the community development approach. The chapter concludes with a critical discussion of stakeholder consultation in the leisure, sport and tourism environment in relation to the formal representative process and professional/technical inputs.

RESOURCES

Websites

Committee of Inquiry into Hunting with Dogs: http://www.huntinginquiry.gov.uk/
GetUp! organization: http://www.getup.org.au
House of Commons Select Committee for Culture, Media and Sport, reports: http://www.publications. parliament.uk/pa/cm/cmcumeds.htm
International Association for Public Participation: http://www.iap2.org/
Surfers Against Sewage (SAS): http://www.sas.org.uk

Publications

Public participation: Arnstein (1969); Gittins (1993); Renn *et al.* (1995); Propst *et al.* (2000); Carr and Halvorsen (2001); Cullingworth and Nadin (2006: 431 ff.); in leisure: Limb (1986); Clark and Stein

(2004); in tourism planning: Simmons (1994); Bramwell and Sharman (1999); Sautter and Leisen (1999); Bramwell and Lane (2000); Hoctor (2003), Darcy and Wearing (2009).

Self-mobilization/activism: Wheaton (2007);

Community dinners: Carr and Halvorsen (2001);

Lobbying: Beauchamp (1985); International Consortium of Investigative Journalists (2009);

Stakeholder analysis: Tague (2005: 476–481);

Public inquiries, local: Cullingworth and Nadin (2006: 167–171, 443–446);

Campaigns, apartheid and sport: Payne (1993);

Citizen juries: Vari and Lee (1993); Smith and Wales (2000); Ward *et al.* (2003); critique: Sanders (1997);

Community round tables: Jamal and Getz (2000);

Delphi technique: Green, H. *et al.* (1990); see also Chapter 11;

Nominal Group Technique (NGT): general: Sample (1984); recreation: Clark and Stein (2004); tourism: Ritchie (1985, 1994a); Garrod and Fyall (2005);

Adaptive Environmental Assessment Management (AEAM): Holling (1978);

Interest-based negotiation (IBN): Ritchie (2000);

Critical perspectives: Day (1997);

Sport development: Hylton and Totten (2001); Bolton *et al.* (2008);

Cultural development: Braden (1979).

QUESTIONS/EXERCISES

1. Following Arnstein and Hoctor, approaches to citizen participation have often been arranged in a 'ladder': what does the ladder represent?

2. Name three stakeholder consultation formats and indicate their likely performance in relation to the quality of information they generate and their representativeness regarding the general public.

3. Locate a local authority leisure/sport plan or a National Park agency or tourism agency strategic plan or master plan document in a library or on the Internet and assess what it has to say about public consultation in relation to the categories in the ladder of citizen participation.

4. What are the advantages and limitations of the issues approach to planning?

5. What are the advantages and limitations of the community development approach to planning?

6. How does stakeholder consultation relate to the formal process of representative government?

Chapter 10

Planning Tools 2: Facility/Service Audit

INTRODUCTION

Policymaking and planning for leisure, sport or tourism invariably involves the provision of facilities or the services and programmes which take place in those facilities (Wagle, 2000). Even resources not specifically designed for leisure, sport or tourism – for example, streets used for walking or cycling or farms hosting farm-stay holidays – can be viewed as leisure facilities in this context, and natural and heritage resources may have potential – and limitations – as leisure facilities even if they are not currently used for that purpose. In all planning situations there is invariably an existing stock of facilities/services which accommodate current participation or have the potential to accommodate future participation and, clearly, planning for the future involves being informed about the capacity, use patterns, potential and limitations of these existing facilities/services and resources. In 'greenfield' sites yet to be developed, the land and topography represents a resource that will need to be evaluated for leisure as well as for other purposes.

In this chapter we consider the process by which this is achieved: namely the *facility/service audit*, which is Task 14 in the U-Plan system described in Chapter 8. This envisages stock being taken of existing facilities at the beginning of the planning process, as an input to the formulation of a plan. The facility/service audit is also part of the review and evaluation process – the *review* component of Task 2, which takes place at points throughout the planning period and at the end. It therefore provides part of the basis for the performance evaluation, which is discussed in Chapter 13.

First, the audit process is outlined in general terms, and this is followed by consideration of four major processes: capacity assessment, usage assessment, analysis of spatial patterns of use and resource assessment.

Most *services* or *programmes* take place in built or natural facilities, so they form part of the usage of a facility and are therefore included in the audit of that facility. For most of this chapter, therefore, the term facility will be assumed to include services or programmes that take place in facilities. However, large-scale programmes or events that use multiple facilities merit attention in their own right, so a section on *programmes and events* is included at the end of the chapter.

© A.J. Veal 2010. *Leisure, Sport and Tourism, Politics, Policy and Planning*, 3rd Edition (A.J. Veal)

THE FACILITY AUDIT PROCESS

Facility audit and policymaking/planning

The facility audit process is outlined in Box 10.1. It is a 12-step procedure which draws certain conclusions about the adequacy of the current supply of facilities, based on examination of their capacities, level of use and catchment areas and the nature of potential physical resources. It is centred on questions posed in four of the steps in the diagram:

- Are the facilities fully used (step 2)? To answer this question it is necessary to measure the current *levels of use* of facilities and their *capacity*.
- If facilities are underused, can management measures correct this (step 3)? To answer this question requires a management appraisal covering such issues as programming, staffing and marketing, which are beyond the scope of this book.
- In natural areas: if existing facilities are fully used and there is evidence of unmet demand, *assess the resource* in regard to its ability to accommodate increased use (step 10).

Box 10.1. Facility audit process.

The facility audit process plays a particular role in the U-Plan system (Task 14), but can be seen as relevant regardless of the planning system adopted. One approach to the process is summarized in Fig. 10.1. It involves 12 possible steps, which are outlined below.

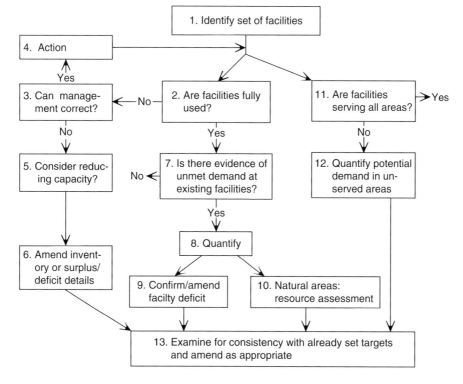

Fig. 10.1. Facility/service audit process.

(Continued)

Box 10.1. Continued.

1. Identify set of facilities. Typically, relatively homogenous sets of one or more facilities, such as swimming pools or playing fields, are examined together.

2. Are facilities fully used? To answer this question requires the measurement of capacity and use levels, as discussed later in the chapter.

3. If NO to Q.2, can management correct underuse? In some cases, underuse is a matter of management action, such as more active marketing, price changes or programming innovations.

4. If YES to Q3, implement management action to correct underuse. Proposed management actions are implemented and question 2 is posed again after a suitable period.

5. If NO to Q.3, consider reducing capacity. Reducing capacity could involve management measures, such as reducing opening hours, or it could mean decommissioning all or part of a facility.

6. Modify the inventory. The facility may be deleted entirely from the inventory or its recorded capacity modified.

7. If YES to Q.2, is there evidence, from existing facilities/services, of unmet demand? Evidence of unmet demand may include recorded evidence of people being turned away, booking requests being refused or observed overcrowding in some types of facility.

8. If YES to Q.7, quantify unmet demand. Quantification of unmet demand may be based on the evidence recorded under 7 (e.g. five football teams cannot be accommodated), or it may draw on catchment area data gathered at 10.

9. Record level of unmet demand. In the U-Plan system a deficit may confirm the findings of Task 14 or may have identified additional deficits, which may or may not conform with the targets set by the planning process as discussed at step 13.

10. Do the existing facilities serve all zones of the planning area (step 11)? To answer this question it is necessary to examine spatial patterns of use of each facility, that is to establish its catchment area, which is the geographical area from which the bulk of users are drawn. This, by implication, also identifies the areas where there are few if any users of the facilities, that is, unserved areas.

11. Are the available facilities serving all areas? Answering this question involves the establishment of the spatial coverage of the catchment areas of existing facilities, as discussed later in the chapter.

12. If NO to 11, quantify participation potential in unserved areas. Examination of the pattern of participation/use in existing catchment areas provides information on the potential participation that would be enabled if facilities were to be provided in currently unserved areas, as discussed later in the chapter.

13. Examine outcomes of items 6, 9 and 11 for consistency with goals and already-set targets and modify targets as appropriate. The possible outcomes of the three processes are:

- reduced capacity, including closure of facilities;
- unmet demand justifying increased provision/capacity in areas already served with facilities;
- unmet demand justifying provision of facilities in areas not already served.

In the context of U-Plan, the findings must be examined in light of the original target-setting process, which involves returning to Task 4, setting/reviewing targets and revising targets as necessary.

Before addressing capacity, use levels, spatial dimensions and resource assessment we consider the definition and typology of facilities.

WHAT IS A FACILITY?

In sport, a facility is generally a single playing area, such as a court or playing field. But such units often exist in groups: for example, a *squash centre* will have a number of courts. Furthermore, individual facilities and groups of facilities may be located in multipurpose centres, such as a leisure centre with sports halls, squash courts and a swimming pool. In a facility inventory, therefore, individual units may be classified at various levels: for example, a squash court may be identified, and audited, in its own right, as part of a group of squash courts and also as part of a multipurpose centre. The same approach may be used in a multipurpose arts facility, which may include a gallery, a theatre and a number of dance studios. Similarly, a hotel may contain conference, social and fitness facilities as well as accommodation.

FACILITY TYPES

Facilities can be classified along two dimensions: (i) formal and informal; and (ii) purpose-built and natural/heritage, as shown in Table 10.1. The more formal the facility the easier it is to define and measure use levels and capacity. For example, the capacity and use levels of a theatre, a formal facility, are defined by the number of seats, the number of shows and the number of tickets sold, but in the case of an urban park, an informal facility, none of these measures is available. In natural or heritage-based facilities use levels and capacities tend to be imposed by management actions related to conservation concerns. Thus, for example, the capacity of a national park may appear to be large, but is limited by, for example, the number of parking spaces available or designation of some areas as accessible by provision of paths and others as non-accessible by barriers imposed by management. The specific limits may be related to the availability of resources for investment in infrastructure or conservation considerations, or both.

Table 10.1. Facility types.

	Purpose-built	Natural/heritage
Formal		
User occupies a specified space and time and access is controlled by bookings and/or ticketing	(A) Examples: playing fields, squash courts, theatres	(B) Examples: organized activities at natural/heritage sites, e.g. safaris, whitewater rafting, guided tours of sacred sites
Informal		
User does not occupy a specified space and time and access may or may not be controlled	(C) Examples: urban parks, trails, museums, galleries	(D) Examples: non-organized use of national parks, forests, beaches, rivers, historic buildings/sites

CAPACITY

The capacity of a facility is the amount of leisure use that it can accommodate. In natural areas, and to some extent in tourism, the term *carrying capacity* is used, a concept carried over from the idea of the amount of livestock that grazing land can sustainably accommodate. It might be assumed that the capacity of a facility is easily measurable, but a few examples of the various facility categories identified in Table 10.1 will demonstrate that this is far from the case:

- *Category A: a squash court*. Squash courts are available for 45-minute bookings and there are 168 hours in a week so, allowing one booking a day for cleaning gives a weekly capacity per court of 217 bookings, or 434 person-sessions if singles are assumed. But, of course, some bookings are for doubles, which immediately introduces an element of uncertainty. Furthermore, although squash courts could, theoretically, be open 24 hours a day, 7 days a week, in practice they are not. And even when they are open, achieving 100% utilization is probably unrealistic. So, in the light of these uncertainties, what is a 'reasonable' number of hours/bookings for which a squash court should be open to provide a benchmark capacity measure?

- *Category A: a theatre* with 500 seats. An evening show on six nights a week and one matinee performance a week suggests a capacity of 3500 visits a week. But would it not be possible to put on another type of performance on the 'dark' evening, and other shows on the six empty afternoons? Perhaps the capacity is 5000 visits a week, or more. But the theatre could be used for other purposes during these times, for example conferences, so the capacity of the building might be measured in terms of theatre visits *and* other types of visit.

- *Category A: a grass playing field* suitable for such sports as soccer, rugby and hockey. These sports typically require a booking period of 2 hours for a training session or a match, so, given daylight hours of 8 hours a day, this implies a capacity of 28 sessions a week and, assuming 30 players/referees per session, 840 person-sessions per week. But a grass playing field, even of the highest quality, could not physically withstand 56 hours of play a week, particularly in very wet, or very dry, periods. Thus, although a grass playing field meets the criteria for Category A, it is subject to the natural constraints of turf characteristics, although these can be modified by design and maintenance practices. Thus it has certain of the characteristics of category B. In any case, the demand for weekday morning and late afternoon use is very limited. However, floodlighting can extend usage into the evenings. So what is the typical capacity of a playing field?

- *Category B: whitewater rafting* in a natural ravine. The capacity of such a service will depend on such concerns as: (i) the size of the craft used; (ii) daylight hours; (iii) weather conditions; (iv) safety issues determining the number of craft that can be permitted on the course at any one time; and (v) the area of land available for storage, services and parking that may be affected by ecological impact constraints. However, a US study of the capacity of a stretch of river used for whitewater boating could legitimately ignore ecological constraints because of the resilience of the short stretch of rocky canyon involved, and so was able to base estimates of optimum carrying capacity entirely on participants' perceptions of crowding levels (Tarrant and English, 1996).

- *Category C: an urban park*. On a summer Sunday afternoon: all the benches are full, the formal picnic shelters are all full, the boats on the lake are all leased out, the tennis courts are being fully used and there is an average of one person every metre on all the paths and a scattering of people on the grassed areas – a total of, say, 500 people. Is this the park's capacity? It may be, but what if another 100 people turned up, would they turn away because it looked too crowded, or would some of the existing visitors leave because the park had become too crowded for them? And what determines the number of benches, picnic shelters, boats for hire, tennis courts and length of pathways? If these were all doubled would the capacity double? Even if we could agree that 500 people was a reasonable capacity figure, how does this relate to the level of visits through the course of a week? Research suggests that half of urban park use is at weekends and 20% of that is at the peak period, that is, about 10% of all usage is at the peak period (Veal, 2006c). This would mean that the total weekly visit capacity of an urban park is about ten times the level of peak-period visits.

- *Category D: a national park* of 100,000 ha with two vehicular access points with a total of 1000 car parking spaces. Given a maximum vehicle occupancy rate of four, this apparently results in an maximum operational 'recreational carrying capacity' of 4000 people. But the park is also used by an unknown number of minibuses with a capacity of 12–15 persons, by pedestrian and cyclist visitors and, in busy periods, by additional car-borne visitors who park in various places outside the national park boundaries. However, the number of visitors admitted should be limited by their likely impact on the natural environment in the form of wear and tear on park infrastructure, littering and disturbance to flora and fauna, and this is also related to *cumulative* use numbers rather than just peak numbers. The 1000 parking spaces may be fully used on only a few days in the course of a year; so it may be during the rest of the year, when the parking area may be less than half full, that the bulk of the cumulative impact occurs, so it is an annual number of visits rather than the peak number which should be concerning us. But at both peak times and off-peak times, visitor impacts may be mitigated by suitable infrastructure design, signage, information/education and supervision/enforcement. So the actual level of use of the park, its temporal patterns and impacts and how visitors should be managed are all complex issues affecting the issue of use levels and capacity.

These brief examples highlight the complexity of measuring facility use and capacity, and the range of concepts and measures involved.

Contexts, concepts, measures and types of capacity

The examples discussed above suggest that the issue of capacity can be viewed in a range of *contexts* in which certain common parameters vary in importance, as shown in Fig. 10.2. The parameters are:

- the potential market – the population from which facility visitors/users are drawn;
- access controls – mechanisms controlling access to a facility, notably booking systems, where applicable, and travel arrangements (roads, flights/airports, parking facilities);
- the visitors – numbers, characteristics, behaviour, temporal distribution;
- the facilities – size, quality, etc.;
- the social and natural environment.

In context A in Fig. 10.2, contained, the social/natural environment is, to all intents and purposes, irrelevant. This could arise in purpose-built facilities in urban areas (squash courts, theatre) or at least where the location precludes significant interaction between the facility and the neighbouring social or physical environment – for example, playing fields surrounded by substantial physical buffers. In this context the question of capacity is entirely related to

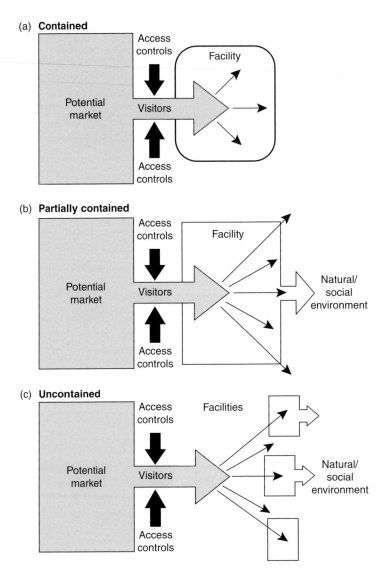

Fig. 10.2. Capacity contexts.

the characteristics of the facility. In context B, partially contained, a single facility has some interaction with the surrounding physical or social environment – for example, playing fields causing noise nuisance to neighbours or beach-goers affecting marine or terrestrial wildlife or vegetation. In context C, non-contained, there are multiple facilities and direct interaction between the visitors and the social or physical environment: this is typical of tourist areas in natural or historic areas. The range from contexts A to C reflects to some extent the Recreation Opportunity Spectrum typology discussed in Chapter 7.

Some of the complexity of the capacity concept is captured in the various concepts and measures listed in Table 10.2. Clearly, the level of use a facility can accommodate is affected by a wide range of factors, a number of which are listed in Table 10.3.

Table 10.2. Concepts and measures of capacity/use.

Concept	Definition	Measure
General concepts		
1. Theoretical capacity	The level of use that could be accommodated in the absence of any constraints on management	Any of measures 4–12 may be used
2. Operational capacity	Level of use that can be accommodated given current infrastructure/managerial constraints	Any of measures 4–12 may be used
3. Group size	Number of persons typically attending at a facility/event together	Number of persons per session/booking
Concepts/measures related to a period of time (e.g. a day, a week, a month, a year)		
4. Session	The typical event that takes place in a facility: for example, a booking, game or practice session on a playing field; a performance in a theatre	Number of sessions/bookings per time-period
5. Person-session or visit	One person attending a session or making a visit to a facility	Person-sessions/visits per time-period
6. Visitor-hour	One person visiting a facility for one hour	Number of visitor-hours per time-period
7. Peak period use	Number of visits during a peak period	Number of visitor-hours per time-period
8. Arrivals	Number of persons arriving/ entering over a given time period	Number of persons arriving in a given time-period
9. Beds/bed-nights	Number of persons that can be accommodated in tourist accommodation facility in any one night/the number of tourists staying in a destination for one night and up to 24 hours	Capacity: number of beds available in a destination; use: number of bed-nights spent in a destination in a given period
Concepts/measures related to a point in time		
10. Physical capacity	Maximum number of persons possible/permitted to be present at any point in time	Number of persons

(Continued)

Table 10.2. Continued.

Concept	Definition	Measure
11. Number present	Number of persons present at a given point in time	Actual number of persons present at a specified time
12. Peak use	Maximum number of persons present during peak periods	Maximum number of persons present at a point during a time-period

Table 10.3. Factors affecting facility capacity.

Factor	Definition	Examples
Physical		
Size: natural	Physical size when sport specifications do not apply	Size of a beach, river, lake, mountain area
Size: design	Non-sport: area set aside for the leisure facility	Area of an urban park; administrative boundaries of a national park
	Sport: size specifications and rules on team size and length of sessions	Specified size of a tennis court or soccer field, specified team sizes and time-periods for matches
Site design	Physical features that facilitate visitor use	Lighting and/or shelter from inclement weather; on-site pedestrian or vehicular traffic flow management
Infrastructure quality	The ability of infrastructure to withstand wear and tear	Quality of path surfaces, fencing, etc.
Sustainability of the resource	The point at which any additional use would result in significant, even irreversible, damage to flora and fauna or other natural or heritage features	Particularly natural and some sensitive heritage sites; playing fields
Regulation/Management		
Safety	Regulations relating to human safety	Building weight-bearing capabilities and fire exits; life-saving arrangements in pools
Management	Effect of management practices on use levels	Marketing; customer service, staffing, pricing, maintenance practices

(Continued)

Table 10.3. Continued.

Factor	Definition	Examples
User Attitudes/Behaviour		
On-site user activity	Nature of the leisure activity taking place on the site	Walking on trails versus motor vehicle use; imposed fishing catch limits
On-site user behaviour	Extent to which users (are permitted to) engage in impact-creating practices	Permitted or non-permitted fires, domestic pets, graffiti, noisiness
Social custom	Socially determined practices regarding participation in the activity	People's availability or willingness to visit at different times of the day, week or year
User perception of crowding	The point at which users' or potential users' perception of the level of crowding limits the number of users	Crowding at beaches, ski slopes; length of queues to enter/use facilities; noise, etc. from other users
Neighbours		
Neighbourhood impacts	1. Effects of neighbouring land uses on the facility use	Noise, pollution, access
	2. Limitations due to effects of facility use on neighbours	Noise, access

The interplay of these contexts, concepts, measures and factors has led to discussion in the literature of different types of carrying capacity, as shown in Table 10.4. Each of the capacity types mentioned merits some comment.

Physical capacity

The concept of physical capacity is relatively easy to apply to formal facilities where the space to be occupied by the user is specified – for example, a theatre or a sporting facility with fixed numbers of participants. But even then, some measures are inevitably operational: for example, a theatre may have a capacity dictated by its 500 seats, but the number of shows accommodated in a week or a year is an operational matter.

Operational capacity

The idea of operational capacity is illustrated by the squash court example discussed above: in *theory*, squash courts could be open 24 hours a day, but in practice – or *operationally* – this does not happen. A specification of the operational capacity of squash courts involves a judgement as to what is a normal period of time for which squash courts should be open and the level of bookings that industry 'best practice' suggests could be expected in a well-designed, well-located and well-managed centre (e.g. 75% capacity). The urban park example discussed above also illustrates this idea: in the medium term, and with sufficient resources, the capacities of the various components of a park infrastructure – benches,

Table 10.4. Types of capacity.

Type	Definition
Physical capacity	The number of people who can physically fit into the space available
Operational capacity	The number of people who can be accommodated, subject to the constraints of society, the organization, including such factors as safety considerations, staffing constraints (skills, numbers, hours), funding and design/equipment
Economic capacity	The level of use which either optimizes returns (in financial or cost–benefit terms) or maintains the operation within prescribed budgetary financial limits
Social/psychological capacity	Level of use that maximizes the aggregate enjoyment of visitors and/or, in the case of tourism destinations, considers economic and cultural costs and benefits to local residents
Ecological capacity	Level of use that maintains the ecological status of the resource at an acceptable level
Tourism capacity	In a multiple-facility destination: constraints on tourism numbers/types imposed by a combination of any or all of the above constraints

pathways, tennis courts, etc. – could be increased, so the theoretical capacity is higher than the current operational capacity.

Operational capacity is partly related to externally imposed constraints, for example restrictions on numbers of patrons permitted in a nightclub due to fire safety regulations, partly due to short-term management decisions, for example on opening hours, partly to medium-term management decisions, for example related to staffing and equipment, and partly to longer-term management decisions, for example related to significant structural investments.

Economic capacity

Pigram and Jenkins (2006: 126) see *economic capacity* as relating only to multiple-use situations, where a facility accommodates leisure activity in addition to some other commercial or quasi-commercial enterprise, for example a water supply reservoir with recreational access or a forest with timber-harvesting operations and recreation. In these situations recreation may be subject to the same economic performance requirements as the commercial enterprise and this will determine the optimum level of use. But this is too limiting. Any facility can have an economic capacity, which is the level of use that either optimizes returns, in financial or cost–benefit terms, or maintains the operation within prescribed budgetary financial limits (Patmore, 1983: 232).

Social/psychological capacity

Measurement of *social/psychological capacity*, sometimes referred to as *perceptual capacity*, presents challenges because it involves assessing people's perceptions. This is done in regard to two groups of people: facility users and, in the case of tourism destinations, the hosts. The latter is discussed in relation to tourism capacity, below.

It is generally believed that satisfaction with a leisure experience is related to the level of use of a facility. For some types of facility, the user may feel uncomfortable if there are, in his or her view, too few other users; then, as the number of users increases and the facility becomes more and more crowded, user satisfaction declines. But as the number of users increases, even though the level of satisfaction per person may be falling, the aggregate satisfaction level for all the people may be increasing, until it reaches a peak and starts to decline. One view is that the social/psychological capacity is reached at that peak point. This idea is illustrated in Fig. 10.3, with some hypothetical data for the use of a park. To obtain the data to produce such a graphic it would be necessary to conduct surveys of users at various times when the number of users present varies. The individual average level of satisfaction would be measured by use of a Likert-type scale, ranging from 1, unsatisfied, to 6, very satisfied. The aggregate score assumes that such scales can be added to obtain a total measure of satisfaction for the people present.

Ecological capacity

The concept of ecological capacity, sometimes referred to as biological capacity, and often with the word 'carrying' inserted, applies to natural area facilities, such as National Parks, and relates to the sustainability of the resource. There is a substantial research literature on this topic (see Resources section) discussing the ways in which environmental values should be used to determine the appropriate level of recreational use of natural areas. Making such judgements involves the input of technical data: for example, the impact of walkers on soil compaction or the effect of disturbance on wildlife. But recent contributions to the debate have emphasized

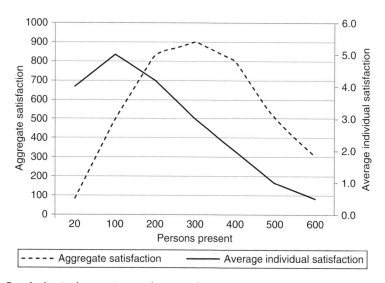

Fig. 10.3. Psychological capacity: park example.

that, ultimately, the decision is determined by political and values-related opinion as to what natural resources should be maintained in what condition. As can be seen in some of the high-profile conservation debates, such as the one regarding whale conservation or climate change, not only do differences exist in regard to economic importance as opposed to conservation factors, but such differences affect views on the importance and validity of technical/scientific data and their interpretation.

Tourism capacity

There is a considerable body of literature on the concept of tourism capacity, or tourism carrying capacity. Much of it refers to two of the concepts already discussed above, social/psychological capacity and ecological capacity. Two unique aspects of tourism capacity should, however, be highlighted. First is the idea of social/psychological capacity relating not just to facility users but also to the hosts or residents of a tourism destination. Second is the idea of the capacity of a tourism destination as a complex of a number of facilities and resources.

Residents of a tourism destination are stakeholders with varying relationships to the tourism phenomenon: they may be beneficiaries (jobs, incomes, improved services, lively social environment) or losers (increased cost of living and labour costs, congestion, pollution, culture clash). Subjective evaluations of the net effects of these gains and losses can be measured by survey methods and related to the number of visitors. A relationship similar to that in Fig. 10.3 may be discovered, where the evaluation relates to tourism in the destination as viewed by the host population while the 'persons present' become 'tourists present'. But conducting such an empirical study would be more difficult, because it would need to be done over a period of years, as the number of tourists increased. Furthermore, if the number of tourists passes the optimum point, there is not usually much that can be done to reverse the situation – certainly not with staying tourists, where investment will have been made in accommodation facilities, although it might be possible to reduce day-tripper numbers. However, it may be possible to increase capacity in some respects, without increasing numbers of tourists. This leads to the second feature of tourism capacity.

The tourism product is made up of a number of components: access transport, accommodation, major attractions and other amenities/infrastructure. Each of these components can be the subject of capacity – and use level – assessment. An ideal tourism development plan would achieve complementarity in all components and in all types of capacity measurement. This is possible in a purpose-built, self-contained resort, but is difficult to achieve in other situations, such as a seaside or historic town. Some examples of attempts to address these challenges are indicated in the next section.

Capacity estimation

In the light of the above discussion, approaches to estimating capacities of formal and informal facilities are discussed in turn below, divided into purpose-built and natural areas.

Capacity estimation: formal facilities

Examples of estimates of capacity for formal facilities are shown in Table 10.5. The actual figures given are based on a number of informed 'guesstimates' which may vary in practice, depending on some of the limiting factors discussed above. They are intended to illustrate an approach. The aim is to arrive at a capacity measure expressed in terms of person-sessions per week (as defined in Table 10.2) and involves six steps or data inputs:

Table 10.5. Formal facilities: capacities.

Facility type	(A) Time available (h/week)[a]	(B) Time utilized (%)[a]	(C) Length of session (h)[a]	(D) Group size (persons)[a]	(E) Capacity sessions/week (A × B/C/100)	(F) Capacity person-sessions/week (E × D)	Comments
Grass playing field							
Poor drainage, etc.: no lights	10	100	2	30	5	150	
Good drainage, etc.: no lights	28	50	2	30	7	210	Session includes playing and training sessions; group includes players, reserves, referees
Good drainage, etc.: with lights	28	80	2	30	11	330	
Bowling green	56	50	2	10	14	140	
Hard court: outdoor tennis: no lights	56	65	2	3	21	65	Group size: average between doubles and singles; group includes players, reserves umpires
Tennis: with lights	84	65	2	3	31	95	

(Continued)

Table 10.5. Continued.

Facility type	(A) Time available (h/week)[a]	(B) Time utilized (%)[a]	(C) Length of session (h)[a]	(D) Group size (persons)[a]	(E) Capacity sessions/ week (A × B/C/100)	(F) Capacity person-sessions/ week (E × D)	Comments
Netball/basketball/5-a-side: no lights	56	65	2	14	21	250	
Netball/basketball/5-a-side: with lights	84	65	2	14	31	370	
Squash court	91	75	0.75	2.2	91	180	Mix of badminton, netball, basketball,
Sports hall (≥ 2 courts)	91	75	1.5	20	45	900	
Sports/community hall (< 2 courts)	91	60	2	20	27	540	Mix of fitness, etc. and community/cultural
Athletics stadium	56	30	2	25	8	200	
Weights room	91	60	1	10	55	550	Group size (D), depends on size/ equipment
Golf course	56	65	0.05	1	730	730	Assume 1 person tees off every 3 min (C)
Theatre	98	50	2-3	500	20	10,000	

[a]'Guesstimates', which could vary in light of local conditions and data. For playing fields, numbers can be doubled for juniors if the field is divided in two.

1. Determination of the amount of time per week the facility is available, which will be affected by factors such as those listed in Table 10.3.

2. The proportion of this time for which the facility is available for use.

3. The length of a typical session or booking.

4. Group size per session: this is the number of people who are actively engaged in a session. The basis of this number varies among facilities/activities, as shown in Table 10.6. For the first four categories indicated in the table, some initial observational research will be required to establish the numbers of people present in a typical session. One approach would be to accept these observed group sizes as the norm and to use them throughout the planning period, although some checks should be made to ensure that the numbers are stable over time. Alternatively, particularly if group sizes vary significantly across different comparable facilities, it would be possible to adopt figures from the top of the range (e.g. the top quintile) as the norm. Thus, those facilities found to have lower use densities would be deemed to have spare capacity and there might be an expectation that management measures would be taken in those facilities to raise their intensity of use. The same considerations could apply to the '% of time utilized' (B in Table 10.5).

5. Calculate capacity in terms of sessions/bookings per week (= (a × b)/d).

6. Calculate capacity in terms of person-sessions per week (= e/d).

Capacities will, of course, vary from community to community, depending on local conditions, including the design of facilities and management practices.

Table 10.6. Assessing group sizes.

	Match/show/meet	**Training/tuition session**
Team games	No. of players + reserves + referees for a session	At least one team + reserves + coaches
Tennis/squash	A number between 2 and 4	May be a larger number
Sports/community halls	Depends on programming; team sports and tennis, as above	Depends on programming; team sports, as above; group sessions (keep fit, yoga) depend on size of group, but maximum may be specified by fire regulations
Athletics stadium	Depends on number of events and teams/competitors	Depends on club size
Weights room	na	Depends on number of pieces of equipment
Golf	A single person/round is used	
Theatre	Determined by the number of seats	

Capacity estimation: informal facilities – purpose-built

The most common purpose-built informal facilities are urban parks and trails which are, arguably, the most pervasive public leisure service in Western countries and, as shown in Table 1.3, one of the services upon which most public funds are spent. But what is the capacity of an urban park or trail?

The idea of *capacity* for an informal facility, such as a park, is almost a contradiction in terms, since there is almost no limit to the amount of open space that the individual can enjoy. Thus, for some types of experience the capacity of a 100-hectare park or a 10-kilometre trail could be one or two persons only. In urban areas such experiences may be possible at some times of the day, week or year and they may be routinely possible in non-urban contexts, but planning in urban areas must also be concerned with peak demand.

In practice, there is little or no published guidance available on this matter for informal purpose-built facilities. The various guidelines upon which open-space planning was based in the past almost universally failed to refer to the capacity of informal open space or adopted seemingly arbitrary provision standards based on no apparent research evidence (see Veal, 2009c). In fact, urban parks have been generally neglected in leisure research. The implications of this are presented in Box 10.2, which presents some information on the limited amount of research that has been carried out.

Box 10.2. Urban park capacity and use.

Urban park capacity is a neglected area of study and a neglected issue in policy and planning and practice. This is despite the significance of these facilities in public urban leisure provision, as shown in Table 1.3.

Almost 40 years ago, in a well-known paper, Seymour Gold (1972) concluded that neighbourhood parks in certain American cities were 'underused'. This was based on observations which showed that during peak periods only 10% of the resident population of park catchment areas were present in the parks and only 1% during off-peak periods, but no reference was made to capacity. Thus, by 'underused', Gold appeared to mean 'not very popular'. This conclusion has been widely and uncritically referred to, suggesting that it is accepted that Gold's data are accurate and appropriately interpreted and probably applicable in other areas and urban parks generally. A number of subsequent studies have demonstrated much higher levels of urban park use than indicated in Gold's observational studies: in particular, an analysis of park use in Sydney, Australia, indicated that 97% of the population made use of local and regional metropolitan parks during the course of a year and 55% in any one week (Veal, 2006c). Furthermore, the Sydney data suggest that about 8% of weekly visits to local parks took place in peak periods, between midday and 2.00 pm on weekends, and this was equivalent to about 10% of the population. Overall, it would appear that urban parks, far from being 'not very popular', might be viewed as 'very popular'.

A further consequence of the neglect of urban parks in leisure research generally is that a biased view is often presented of the social reach of public leisure provision generally. A typical comment comes from Michael Collins, who declares that 'overall leisure facilities and services, public and voluntary, are over-used by those with above average incomes' (Collins and Kay, 2003: 239), a statement supported by data on the social class bias of a range of public sector leisure participation, including sport participation generally and

(Continued)

Box 10.2. Continued.

visits to sports centres (p. 33), libraries, theatres and museums/galleries (p. 247), but not parks. The Sydney data again offer a different perspective, with all socio-economic groups showing similar high levels of use of urban parks (Veal, 2006c); given the large volume of urban park visits, inclusion of such data would be likely to have a significant effect on the overall pattern of use of public leisure facilities.

Thus, not only have urban parks been neglected as a research topic over the years, but they have suffered from the propagation of misleading myths about their level of use, and their neglect has resulted in a potentially biased picture of the use of public leisure facilities generally. Considerable research effort will be required to correct this situation. Because urban parks are free to the user, data on visit numbers are not routinely available from ticket sales or bookings as they are for other types of facility, but must be gathered by means of surveys of various types, as discussed in Table 10.8. Similarly, because of their informal nature, capacity is difficult to assess; possible approaches are discussed below.

1. Personal/social space. Turkish researchers Gedikli and Ozbilen (2004) based their analysis of park capacity on the proposition that for people using a park for informal purposes, such as picnicking or socializing, each person requires a personal 'social area' with a minimum radius (r) and each group of users requires a minimum distance (x), a 'social privacy limit', between themselves and other groups. Figure 10.4 illustrates this idea, with one group of four people and another of two people. From observational studies of park use, the researchers concluded that the value of r was about 0.4 metres and the value of x was about 7 metres. Mathematically this meant that the total space required for each person was 15.7 m², or 0.16 hectares for every 100 visitors present. This is, of course, based on data from one Turkish city: the parameters could be quite different in other countries.

2. Satisfaction and perceived crowding. Capacity estimates could be based on seeking to maximize total user satisfaction. We have already seen a hypothetical illustration of this in Fig. 10.3., which shows aggregate satisfaction peaking when the density is 500 persons per hectare, or 0.2 hectares per 100 visitors present. It has, however, been

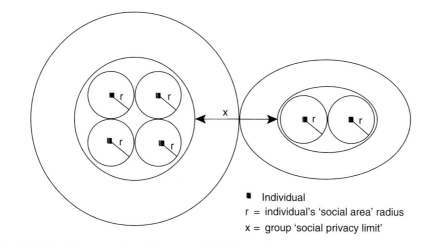

■   Individual
r = individual's 'social area' radius
x = group 'social privacy limit'

Fig. 10.4. Social area and social privacy limit in parks.

(Continued)

Box 10.2. Continued.

suggested that this peaking of aggregate satisfaction may not occur because of the phenomenon of *succession*: that is, as a facility becomes more crowded, some of those who find this unpleasant no longer attend, or shift their attendance to less crowded times, and are replaced by others who are more tolerant of crowding. As a result the satisfaction scores may not fall as much as might be have been expected as use levels increase. This is of course a well-known feature of the life cycle of some tourism destinations.

3. Equity. A third approach to determining the capacity of urban parks is to adopt the principle that people recreating in parks should have a similar level of provision of open space to people recreating in other forms of physical recreation. Thus, if the average capacity of other physical recreation areas was × visits per hectare, then the capacity of parks should be assumed to be the same. Since some other types of provision are capital intensive – for example, swimming pools – the exercise might be based initially on expenditure per visit. No examples are known of this approach being adopted in practice.

4. Cost–benefit analysis. A fourth approach would be to base the assessment on cost–benefit analysis, which is described in Chapter 12. The cost–benefit approach is based on the proposition that provision should be increased as long as the total benefits produced exceed the costs of provision. There would be a 'tipping point' at which costs would begin to exceed benefits produced. In this approach, in the assessment of capacity, the measure 'number of visits per hectare' is replaced by the notion of 'benefits produced per hectare'. As indicated in Chapter 12, only a few cost–benefit studies have been conducted on urban parks, for research rather than for practical planning purposes.

Conclusion

Of course, further investigation of all four approaches would be appropriate, but if we were to seek to operationalize one of the first two, it would be necessary to discover:

- the density of use of parks (D) at peak periods in an average park, or different types of park, in persons per hectare;
- the likely number of park visits (V), for activities such as walking, dog-walking, picnicking and children's play, for a given population in a week;
- the proportion of weekly park visits (P) which takes place at peak time (the Sydney research already referred to indicates that, for all urban parks (local and regional) about 9% takes place at a single peak period, on Saturday or Sunday, but this needs confirmation from other research).

Then, the amount of park space required for the given population = $(V \times P)/D$ hectares.

None of the options discussed above is in general use in practice; leisure planners and managers appear to operate without formally assessing park capacity. At the very least, therefore, there is scope for further research on this topic.

While this discussion relates to urban parks and trails as formal, purpose-built facilities, aspects of it are applicable to other settings, such as beaches and the more high-intensity use areas of national parks.

Increasing attention is being given to walking and cycling *trails* in urban areas, often created to exploit existing linear features, such as a canal towpaths or disused railway lines, and also to link existing parks. In capacity terms, walking trails can be considered as parks, which just happen to have a linear form. In the 1960s and 1970s some research was done in the UK on estimating capacities of 'major scenic routes' and 'minor scenic routes' for walkers, in terms of 'persons per mile' (Lavery, 1971: 46), but the design of such routes varies so much that capacity estimates do not have much credibility. In the case of cycle paths, capacity measures have been developed by traffic engineers (Rouphail *et al.*, 1998), in which, for paths of varying width and with exclusive (cyclists only) or shared (cyclists and walkers) use, increasing levels of use are related to increasing numbers of 'events' (passing, overtaking, etc.) that eventually lead to unsafe and/or unattractive conditions.

Museums and art galleries could be classified as heritage facilities discussed below but, in general, the heritage exhibits are sufficiently protected from the public that capacity is not related to impacts of visitors on the exhibits but to the physical capacity of the public circulation areas. In general, museums and galleries obtain some idea of maximum capacity when attendances rise for 'blockbuster' exhibitions or, in the case of zoos, high-profile 'new arrivals' attract the public interest. Organized queueing, deployment of staff to encourage visitors to 'keep moving', and increased opening hours are ways in which maximum throughput is ensured in such situations. But special exhibitions generally occupy just a portion of the museum/gallery, so the numbers of visitors involved would not necessarily present capacity problems if they were spread over the whole institution.

Capacity estimation: informal facilities – natural/heritage

Informal natural/heritage facilities include: (i) multiple-use outdoor areas, such as forests; (ii) protected natural areas, such as national parks or designated wilderness areas; (iii) beaches and lakes, which may or may not be part of protected areas; and (iv) historic sites. Most of the published theorizing and research on natural area capacity relates to the concept of *recreational carrying capacity*, as discussed above. In general, the discussions are conducted in regard to the management activities of a single agency, such as a National Parks authority or a forestry commission. Such agencies are generally concerned with management of a single site or a number of sites, with a remit to conserve the resource and cater for recreational access, but without any wider responsibility for a specific resident population.

The context for this type of planning is summarized in Fig. 10.5, which suggests that leisure is just one of five sectors that may have an interest in a natural or historic resource. In some countries, for example the USA and Australia, national parks are wholly owned by government and the pressures from agricultural, mining and development interests are generally experienced at the time of designation, when political battles are fought to have certain areas excluded from the designated national park area. But in the UK, designation as a National Park does not involve government ownership of the whole designated area: agricultural and other extractive industries may continue within park boundaries, as do whole towns and villages. While such activities are subject to strict controls, there is a continuing tension between them and the National Park functions of conservation and leisure provision. On the other hand *country parks* in the UK are

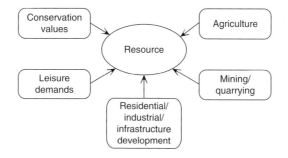

Fig. 10.5. Natural/heritage resource planning/management: context.

fully publicly owned and may be similar to a National Park with significant conservation values, or may be similar to a large urban park. In some natural areas commercial or semi-commercial dimensions are intrinsic to the site, for example land and natural water areas held by water supply organizations or public forests where plantation activity and timber harvesting both take place. Historic heritage sites are more likely to be wholly owned by the government or the National Trust, but this is not always the case and there are often pressures for adaptations for commercial uses, such as restaurants, and for selling off parts of estates.

Leisure activities for which capacity assessment is required in natural/heritage areas tend to fall into three groups:

- *Highly specialized activities*, such as fishing, water sports, hunting, rock climbing, skiing and bird watching: the demands of these activities are directly juxtaposed with the conservation of the resource: thus at some stage the number of rock climbers can cause significant damage to a rock face; and at some point the amount of fishing in a body of water will result in the disappearance of the fish stock. Judgements must be made on the maximum level of activity and how it will be controlled. It is clearly not possible to pursue this area in detail in a general text such as this.
- *Walkers*, sometimes including long-distance walking involving rustic camping, and general informal recreation: may not call for specialized facilities, and may be sufficiently few in number and sufficiently widely dispersed not to raise capacity issues, but at some point they may begin to have an impact judged to be unacceptable, so a capacity limit may have to be imposed and access rationed by a permit system.
- *Sightseer*s constitute the bulk of visits to most natural areas: assessment of capacity generally relates to designated *access areas*, which provide parking spaces, information and amenities and from which the bulk of visitors will rarely stray very far. Since the bulk of visitors are car-borne, capacity is therefore related primarily to the number of car parking spaces provided. Thus the technical task of assessing the capacity of existing access areas is relatively straightforward; the more significant challenge is to determine how many access points there should be and their size and location. This is concerned with the overall approach to planning, as discussed in Chapters 7 and 8.

Capacity estimation: informal facilities – tourism destinations

In the previous section the concept of tourism capacity was discussed and it was noted that, while many tourism facilities are just cases of the above formal and informal facilities, the multi-facility destination presents particular conceptual and measurement challenges. A number of empirical studies have addressed these challenges, including the following:

- An early study in County Donegal in north-western Ireland (McCarthy and Dower, 1967) measured the capacity of various types of infrastructure, including: overnight accommodation; indoor, wet-weather facilities; evening facilities; water supply; sewerage; public transport; and access roads. These could be assessed fairly objectively, but the capacities of outdoor recreation attractions/facilities were based on subjective assessment of reasonable visitor densities. On this basis, levels of car parking provision were recommended.
- A later study by Houghton-Evans and Miles (1970) of the Peak District National Park in northern England, however, showed that much higher visitor densities appeared to be tolerable near a large population centre (Leeds/Sheffield) than the subjective densities assumed in the Donegal study.
- A study of the daily visitor capacity of Venice, Italy conducted by Canestrelli and Costa (1991) is summarized in Box 10.3.

Box 10.3. Tourism capacity of Venice.

Venice is one of the most well-known heritage tourism destinations in the world, with 16.5 million visitors a year but a resident population of just 60,000 (Venice in Peril, 2009). Being an island connected to the mainland by a causeway, it presents a physically clearly defined entity for a capacity case study. Staying visitor numbers are limited by the amount of accommodation in the city, and day-tripper numbers only by the amount of designated car-parking space, which is located on the mainland, from where visitors take a water taxi to the city. The water transport system is also a constraint, but so is the capacity of the major heritage attractions, notably St Mark's Basilica. But because of its unique architecture and urban form, the city is an attraction in its own right. So in terms of the typology in Table 10.1, the city can be seen as an informal/heritage facility.

Elio Canestrelli and Paolo Costa conducted a study of the tourist capacity of the city, where they stated: 'It is … possible that the current quantity of visitors (a total of 6.04 million people in 1987) has already passed the tourist-carrying capacity of Venice' (Canestrelli and Costa, 1991: 296). Their estimate of the 'optimal' number of visitors was 22,000 a day or 8 million a year; with visitor numbers 20 years later at more than double this figure, the researchers' actual figures are of little consequence, but their methodology is of interest.

Canestrelli and Costa identified seven capacity constraints: three related to hospitality, two to transport, one to waste disposal and one to the major attraction, St Mark's. More could have been selected. These are listed in Table 10.7, together with the maximum capacity, their *aspirational* capacity (what we have called operational capacity) and the amount of daily use by different types of visitor. It should be noted that the maximum figure for St Mark's was under 'conditions of stress', but the aspirational level, as indicated by the officer in charge of maintenance would 'avoid excessive wear and tear to the monument (like the effects of excessive temperature and humidity on the golden mosaics induced by visitor congestion)' (pp. 305–306). In Table 10.7, the total number of tourists will be the sum of the hotel-based (TH), non-hotel-based (TNH) and day-trip (DT) visitors. It can be seen that different types of visitor place different levels of demand on the services and resources of the city. Thus, for example, because they are in the city for only one day, day-trippers have a far bigger average daily visit rate to St Mark's than the other two groups.

The authors seek to find an 'optimum' capacity – and level of daily expenditure – based on a balance of perceived benefits between residents of the city who benefit directly from tourism and those who do not, but still bear some of the costs. They use a 'fuzzy' linear programming methodology to derive their 'optimum solution', which is indicated in the table. Linear programming is a management tool used to optimize a phenomenon (in this case capacity/visits/expenditure) subject to constraints, but is too specialized to be explained here. It can be seen that the proposed solution maximizes the hotel-stayers and day-trippers and minimizes the non-hotel stayers.

(Continued)

Box 10.3. Continued.

Table 10.7. Tourism capacity constraints in Venice.

	Maximum		Aspirational (operational)	Consumption impact per visitor per day			Optimal solution
	No.	%	No.	TH	TNH	DT	Total
Hotel beds	11,000	80.0	9,000	1.0	–	–	9,780
Non-hotel beds	4,000	40.0	4,000	–	1.00	–	1,460
Lunches	40,000	62.5	25,000	1.0	0.75	0.5	10,875
Car parking (persons)	30,000	50.0	15,000	0.33	0.33	0.75	3,709
Water transport (trips)	40,000	75.0	30,000	1.0	1.00	2.00	11,240
Solid waste (kg)	60,000	50.0	30,000	2.3	2.00	1.50	25,414
St Mark's Basilica (visits)	15,000	66.7	10,000	0.4	0.30	0.70	4,350
Spend per day (lira[a])	–	–	–	221.00	85.40	149.00	
Optimal solution							
Visitors (no.)				9,780	1,460	10,857	22,097
Total expenditure (lire[a])							2,286,064

TH, tourist staying in hotel; TNH, tourist staying in non-hotel accommodation; DT, day-tripper.

[a] 1984 prices.

Source: data summarized from Canestrelli and Costa (1991). NB: Manipulable spreadsheet version of this table available on book website: http://www.leisuresource.net/service1.aspx

- The 2002 *New South Wales Tourism Masterplan* considered the expected impact of increasing tourist numbers on Sydney's city centre with the following words:

  On an average day in 2020, Sydney will be hosting almost 220,000 visitors. That represents 48,000, or 30 per cent more visitors than in 2001. On top of this, Sydney's projected population growth will add around 700,000 residents. Trends suggest that most of these visitors will be concentrated in and around the Sydney CBD [Central Business District]. If this is confirmed it would mean that by 2020 one in every four people in the CBD would be a visitor, compared to one in every five in 2001. To cope with such an influx, Sydney City would require effective growth management strategies. Some of the critical issues that must be addressed in the coming years include:

  ○ the need to handle substantially increased passenger flows at Sydney Airport;
  ○ provision of hotels, serviced apartments and other commercial accommodation in sufficient quantity and of sufficient quality to cater for increasing numbers;
  ○ essential visitor services, particularly inner-Sydney public transport and policing;
  ○ environmental protection measures capable of preserving the natural and social attractions that enhance a Sydney experience;
  ○ creation of a spread of visitor experiences and attractions;
  ○ fostering tourism awareness to ensure host city attitudes to visitors remains positive;
  ○ promoting and developing the tourist attraction infrastructure of Western Sydney tourism [away from the CBD]. (Tourism NSW (2002: 27)

- A more recent study of the Spanish Costa Brava by Sarda *et al.* (2009) demonstrates the complexity of such research: comparing the situation in a number of resorts over an 18-year period, it was found that, due to changing tourist behaviour patterns, user-density on the main attractions, the beaches, did not generally increase, despite increasing tourist numbers. So what might have been seen as a capacity constraint was not, in practice, during the period studied, a constraint.

FACILITY USE AND ITS MEASUREMENT

In this section we consider the challenges of measuring facility use levels which, in policymaking and planning, are analysed in relation to measures of facility capacity. Using the requirements of the U-Plan system set out in Chapter 8, the aim is to establish the level of use of facilities for a typical week, in seasons where that is applicable. Table 10.8 lists a range of data collection methods for assessing facility use levels, divided into three groups: administration-based methods, interview surveys and on-site counts. These are discussed in turn below.

Administrative

In some situations, data on facility use are generated automatically by the facility's administrative system. The obvious example is individual ticket sales. In some cases, such as the booking of a court or playing field, tickets are not issued to individuals: the administrative system records a booking for the facility. In this case, to turn session bookings data into person-sessions requires both the average group size and the number of persons present during a session, as discussed in relation to capacity assessment. This will generally be obtained by direct counts of a sample of sessions to arrive at an average group size.

In some cases, where all visitors arrive by car and must use a designated paying car park, these data can be used, but, similar to group size, a sample observation exercise will need to be established to estimate average vehicle occupancy.

Where usage is by members only, for example a fitness centre or lending library, the membership administration system can be utilized. A computerized system may be in place which records all member attendances. Where this is not available, a member survey could be conducted that would gather information on visit levels.

Interview surveys

A resident survey would operate by obtaining the proportion of residents who used a facility, and the average frequency in the course of a specified period, such as a year. For example, if 10% of a population of 50,000 visited a facility, on average 12 times a year, this would provide an estimate of 600,000 visits a year. If non-residents are a significant component of visits, on-site surveys would need to be conducted to establish the proportion of non-resident users (commuters, neighbours and tourists, as discussed in Chapter 8).

The resident survey is of course dependent on respondents being able to identify the facilities they have used over, say, the previous year. This seems a tall order, because of the amount of data involved, the problems of accuracy of recall and respondents' possible inability to identify specific facilities. However, against these challenges, must be set a number of features:

- The resident survey has the advantage of all, or most, of the information on facility use being gathered from one data source, including formal and informal facilities.
- If the planning agency is already committed to conducting a resident survey as a component of a participation-based planning exercise, then the costs of conducting the survey are already being incurred and reliance is already being placed on this data source.

Table 10.8. Usage data collection methods.

Method	Data available	Additional data	Visits per week
Administrative			
1. Individual ticket sales	Ticket sales per week (T)	–	$N = T$
2. Bookings data	Facility bookings per week (B)	Group size (by sample observation) (G)	$N = B \times G$
3. Season ticket/annual pass sales	Annual/season ticket sales (T)	No. of trips per week per ticket (by survey) (S)	$N = T \times S$
4. Membership records/ surveys	(a) If member visits automatically recorded – weekly average (V_m);	Number of members (M)	$N = M \times V_m$
	(b) if not: weekly average visits from member survey (V_m)		
5. Parking ticket sales data	Parking ticket sales per week (P)	Vehicle occupancy (by sample observation) (O)	$N = P \times O$
Interview surveys			
6. Resident interview surveys	Percentage visiting facility (V_r); average frequency per week (F_r)	Population (from census) (P)	$N_r = (V_r \times F_r \times P)/100$
7. Tourist surveys	Percentage visiting facility (V_t): no. of visits during stay (F_t)	No. of tourists (from national/regional tourist body or local research) (T) (see Table 10.9)	$N_t = (V_t \times F_t \times T)/100$
8. On-site visitor interview surveys	Percentage commuters, neighbours (C) (tourists could be included here instead of in bookings data)	–	$N_c = C \times N_r$
Total visits			$N = N_r + N_t + N_c$

On-site visitor counts

Automatic counts

9. Automatic vehicle counters	Number of vehicles per week (A)	Vehicle occupancy (by sample observations) (O)	$N_v = A \times O$
10. Automatic pedestrian counters	Number of persons per week (V_p)	–	$N_p = V_p$
11. Video/time-lapse cameras/aerial photography	Number of persons/vehicles/craft present: sampled times, gives person/vehicle/craft-hours (Y)	For vehicles/craft: vehicle occupancy (O) For all: average length of stay (by survey) (L)	$N = (O \times Y)/L$

Visual/manual counts

12. Entrance or exit flows	Number of visitors per week (N)	–	N
13. Spot-counts of numbers present	Number of persons present: sampled times, gives person-hours (Y)	Average length of stay (by survey) (L)	$N = Y/L$

- Survey respondents are already likely to be asked what activities they have participated in and how often, and whether it was within the planning area boundary or outside: all that is being added is to identify the facility used.
- While it is often observed that the public is not aware of the *ownership* of the leisure facilities they use, that is not an issue in this case since respondents would merely be asked to identify the facility, not the organization that owns or operates it, and the planning agency will generally already be committed to compiling a full inventory of facilities in the planning area, so it should be possible to overcome respondents' vagueness regarding the identity of facilities by cross-reference to the inventory.
- Most respondents to leisure surveys indicate participation in only a limited number of leisure activities outside the home: for example, in both the Sport England Taking Part surveys (2005–2007) and the annual Australian Exercise Recreation and Sport Survey, the average number of activities engaged in per person is less than two, although admittedly these surveys do not cover all leisure activities.
- If the number of activities per person makes the process unwieldy, it is possible to 'sample' among active individuals from whom additional information will be collected.
- The survey approach would:

    o overcome the difficulties arising from seeking to obtain usage data for private sector or non-profit facilities;
    o cover leisure activity taking place in small or informal areas (e.g. small beaches or areas of open space) where it may not be feasible to gather facility-based data;
    o have the advantage of facilitating analysis by socio-demographic characteristics – see the discussion of user characteristics, below.

It should be noted that on-site facility user questionnaire-based surveys are not suitable for estimating facility use levels, since they typically involve only a sample of users. When, in rare circumstances, such surveys involve all users in a given time-period the number of visits is, in effect, being counted by an on-site visitor count, as discussed below. Similarly, some survey designs involve interviewers interspersing periods of interviewing with periods conducting spot counts of the number of users present on site, as discussed below. The on-site user interview does, nevertheless, have a role to play in relation to the question of user characteristics, as discussed below, and in Chapter 8 under Task 7.

Tourists are, of course, not covered by resident surveys. A variety of methods exists to estimate tourist numbers, involving unique methods and variations and adaptations of the methods discussed below. These tourism-related methods are presented separately below.

On-site visitor counts

Direct, on-site counts of visitors are often conducted in parks, both urban and non-urban, where there are: no ticket sales or bookings; visitors may use a variety of transport modes; and there are multiple entrances and widely dispersed visitor origins. A variety of automated and manual techniques is available.

Automatic vehicle counters

Automatic vehicles counters consisting of a pressure tube laid across the road or an induction loop under the road surface, attached to a device for recording the number of vehicles crossing the tube or loop, are a long-established device, widely used by transport engineers.

More recently, infrared beams have been used and it has been possible for results to be transmitted wirelessly to a computer, thus eliminating the need for taking manual readings from the recording device. To obtain estimates of visit numbers it is necessary to multiply the vehicle count by the average vehicle occupancy, which must be assessed by an observational survey. Such a survey may also be used to estimate the proportion of non-vehicular numbers, including pedestrians and, in some locations, boat-users. Bicycles may be recorded by traffic counters, but some modern hi-tech bicycles are made of alloys which do not register; furthermore, it may be possible for cyclists to ride beyond the edge of the loop and groups of cyclists in a bunch may not be individually recorded. It may be necessary to estimate and exclude from the calculations:

- service or staff vehicles entering the site, which could distort the figures significantly in sites with low visitor numbers;
- vehicles accessing residential enclaves within or adjacent to sites;
- vehicles using the site as a transit route only – although it could be decided that such users are still enjoying the benefits of a park visit and so should be included.

Furthermore, there may be pedestrian and cyclist visitors using the site, as well as car-borne visitors.

The above factors are assessed by a *calibration* process, which involves sample periods of direct observation using manual methods, as discussed below, to establish ratios. The calibration exercise may be repeated periodically to check the stability of the ratios. This might be seasonally, then once every year or two years at the beginning, but could be less often if it is found that the ratios are relatively stable. Thus the number of visitors, N, to a facility would be:

$$N = O\,(V{-}sV) + pV + cV \tag{1}$$

where:

O is the average vehicle occupancy; V is the number of vehicles recorded by the counter; s is the proportion of service and residential (and transit if required) vehicles; p is the number of pedestrians as a proportion of the number of vehicles; and c is the number of cyclists as a proportion of the number of vehicles.

For facilities having multiple entrances, the calibration process can be used to determine the proportion of visitors using one entrance, so that traffic counters do not have to be placed permanently at all entrances. Thus, initially, it would be necessary to compile equation (1) for each entrance, but if it was known that total visits were always a certain multiple, m, of entrance 1 visit numbers, then equation (1) would be rewritten as:

$$N = m\,(O(V_1 - sV_1) + pV_1 + cV_1) \tag{2}$$

Some of these details for the counting of visitors to Yosemite National Park in the USA are provided on the book's website (http://www.leisuresource.net).

Automatic pedestrian counters

Automatic pedestrian traffic counters use an infrared beam across the pedestrian pathway, which records a visit when the beam is broken by a passing pedestrian. This is housed in a small (about $10 \times 10 \times 2$ cm) unit, which also stores the data for manual downloading or wireless transmission. Since pedestrians move in informal groups, the device may record only one break when two or three people break the beam together. In addition, some pedestrians may use the same pathway for entry and exit. These factors can be determined by a calibration process similar to that used for vehicle counters.

Video/time-lapse cameras/aerial photography

The use of standard CCTV to record site usage adds a visual dimension but is unlikely to be cost-effective because of the need for manual processing of the images. Hardware and software are used by traffic authorities for automatic recording of vehicle registration numbers on toll roads, but the cost is likely to preclude their use for assessing usage numbers of leisure facilities. Aerial photography can be used to present a static picture of usage, particularly in large areas with multiple access points and where on-site access may be difficult, such as lakes/ estuaries.

Manual/visual counts of entrance or exit flows

Numbers of vehicles and/or pedestrians entering or leaving a site can be counted directly by placing an observer at each entrance/exit. It is most unlikely that resources would be available for this to be done for all opening hours, so it would be expected to be undertaken on a sampling basis, covering a representative range of different times of the day, days of the week, seasons and public holidays. The number of sampling days required depends in part on the variability in usage levels; thus the number of sampling days required per year could be expected to fall over time once the patterns became known and the ratio between certain sampling days and total visit numbers became predictable.

This type of counting can be undertaken in conjunction with visitor interview surveys, with field workers alternating periods of counting and interviewing during the survey period.

Visual spot-counts of numbers present

In smaller sites, or sites where visitors congregate in specific areas, an observer can undertake a circuit and count the number of individuals present at any given time. This can be done periodically through the course of a day to provide an estimate of *visitor-hours*. Visitor-hours can be converted to number of visits by dividing by the average length of stay derived from survey evidence. As with counting of entrance/exit flows, sampling throughout the year is required to provide annual estimates. The method is not practicable for large sites with multiple entrances and scattered recreational use.

Tourists

Counting the number of tourist visits, particularly to a multi-facility resort, presents its own challenges. Table 10.9 summarizes ten available methods, including some that do not provide estimates of actual numbers but supply information on tourist characteristics and itinerary which can then be applied to visitor numbers derived from other sources.

User characteristics

The above discussion relates only to head counts of facility users. For most policymaking, planning and management purposes, head counts are only one of a number of indicators required. Thus, for example, in most cases socio-demographic characteristics and place of residence and, in the case of tourists, expenditure are required. The resident survey methodology provides this information and some of the other sources provide some limited data. For example,

Table 10.9. Counting tourist numbers.

Method	Nature	Visitors covered	A	B	C	D	E	Tourist numbers
Administrative								
Ports of entry short-term arrival/ departure data	All incoming passengers complete arrival cards, number of non-residents recorded (N)	All international visitors	•	•	•	•	•	N
Public transport data	In situations where all visitors arrive by one or more public transport modes (e.g. island destinations by boat); visits = ticket sales (S) (may need calibration for number of locals)	All visitors	–	–	–	–	–	N = S
Interview-/questionnaire-based surveys								
Road cordon survey: interview	On major entry roads: total vehicle numbers noted by camera/traffic counter (V); sample of vehicles stopped: vehicle occupancy noted (o); driver interviewed re. origin/destination, proportion of tourists noted (t)	All visitors arriving by major road	•	–	•	•	•	N = toV
Road cordon survey: questionnaire	As above, with additional self-completion mail-in questionnaire	All visitors arriving by major road	•	•	•	•	•	N = toV
International visitors survey	Interviews with sample of departing tourists at airports: provides characteristics, itinerary, etc., but dependent on ports-of-entry method for actual numbers	Sample of visitors departing by air	•	•	•	•	•	–

(Continued)

Table 10.9. Continued.

Domestic tourism survey	Survey of sample of residents on domestic tourism travel (e.g. ≥ 1 overnight stay and ≥ 40 km) over specified period: indicates proportion who have travelled in specified period (t)	Sample of domestic tourists	•	•	•	•	•	N = tP (P = pop'n)
On-site tourist survey	Interview a sample of tourists at known tourist gathering places; filter tourists only; dependent on other sources for actual numbers	Tourists who visit known gathering places	•	•	•	•		–
On-site facility visitor survey	Appropriate when one facility dominates the destination: e.g. a major national park; interview a sample of all visitors to a leisure/tourist attraction: identify tourist proportion (t); total visits to site available from other source (A)	All tourists who visit the attraction	•	•	•	•	•	N = tA
Accommodation survey	Survey of accommodation operators to ascertain number of guests over a particular period (G) (may need calibration for VFR (visiting friends and relatives))	Tourists staying in commercial accommodation		–	–	–		N = G
Direct counts								
Road cordon survey: automatic	Camera technology used to count all vehicles (V) and record origin state/county/country of vehicle registration: proportion of non-local vehicles noted (f)	All visitors arriving by major road	•	–	–	–		N = fV

*LOS = length of stay; A, origin; B, socio-demographic; C, purpose of visit; D, destination; E, length of stay.

administrative data may provide simple demographic data, such as gender and home location from a membership database, or broad age-group from ticket sales (child, adult, concession). But in the absence of a resident survey, additional on-site user surveys will be required to classify visits by these variables.

PUTTING CAPACITY AND USE TOGETHER

Policymaking and planning involves analysis of both capacity and use levels. This process is discussed in generic terms in the Supply Module section of Chapter 8; here a case-study is provided, which is not related to a comprehensive planning process but to a single issue: the potential community recreational use of schools. This is presented in Web-box 3, which can be accessed at the book's website (http://www.leisuresource.net).

SPATIAL DIMENSIONS

Much leisure activity takes place in the home, but our main focus is in activity outside the home. Thus the location of facilities, particularly in relation to where their potential users live, is an all-important factor in understanding actual and potential patterns of use and therefore in planning. In this section, we introduce the concept of the catchment area of a facility, then discuss ways of measuring catchments areas and the use of knowledge of catchment areas in planning.

The catchment area idea

A great deal of information has now been accumulated on the spatial aspects of leisure, sport and tourism facility use. The potential of this information has, however, not generally been fully exploited in the policymaking and planning process. The basic fact upon which spatial approaches are built is that each leisure facility has a *catchment area*, sometimes referred to as a *market area*. That is, there are generally identifiable areas from which most users travel to visit a facility. The size and nature of such catchment areas vary depending on the type of facility. Thus theatres generally have larger catchment areas than swimming pools; and, among swimming pools, larger, newer pools generally have larger catchment areas than smaller, older pools. In the case of tourism, the catchment area of a destination may be: (i) regional in a domestic context; (ii) national; (iii) regional in an international context; or (iv) global.

Catchment areas can be an important basis for planning. Figure 10.6 illustrates the catchment area idea, using two hypothetical facilities. The shaded areas are the areas from which the majority, say 75%, of the users of the two facilities, A and B, are drawn. It can therefore be seen that the facilities serve the populations living in the shaded areas but do not serve the populations living in the unshaded areas. There is a tendency for providers of leisure facilities to believe that, once they have provided a certain type of facility, their job is done – the community is served. But information of the type presented in Fig. 10.6 enables the *extent* to which the community is being served to be assessed.

The unshaded areas in Fig. 10.6 therefore become areas for further investigation. Provided there are people actually living in these areas then, assuming that the policy of the organization is to make the service available to all, the findings point to the need for additional provision to

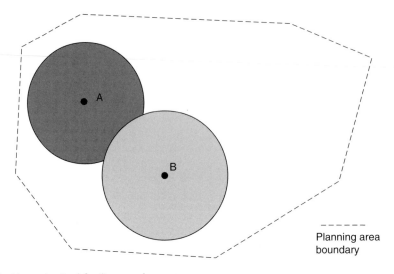

Fig. 10.6. Hypothetical facility catchment areas.

serve these areas. This is expressed in public service terms, but could equally well be expressed in market terms: an organization wishing to maximize usage and income would also be well advised to investigate the market potential of the unshaded areas in Fig. 10.6.

In a strategic sense, the smaller the catchment area of a typical facility, the larger the number of facilities required to serve an area. This is illustrated in Fig. 10.7 where, in situation B, the facility catchment area radius for each facility is half of that in situation A, resulting in four times as many facilities required to cover the same area in situation B.

Measuring catchment areas

It is possible to establish the catchment area of a facility by means of a user or visitor survey – interviewing users of existing facilities to discover where they have travelled from. Although a user survey is desirable it is not always necessary, at least for initial appraisals: it is possible to *infer* approximate catchment areas from user surveys carried out at similar facilities elsewhere.

In cases where membership schemes exist, membership records can be used as the basis for estimating catchment areas: this has, for example, traditionally been done in the case of libraries. The problem with membership records is that the spatial distribution of *membership* may not reflect the distribution of *users* – for example, people who live close to a facility may use it more frequently than people who live far away. This information would be captured in situations where records are kept of actual attendances of members rather than simply records of membership. It should also be noted that some people travel to use leisure facilities from their place of work or school rather than from their home address, so the spatial distribution of *home addresses* may not provide an accurate picture of the catchment area.

What do catchment areas look like? They are shaped by the distribution of the population surrounding the facility and transport routes and barriers. To reflect the population

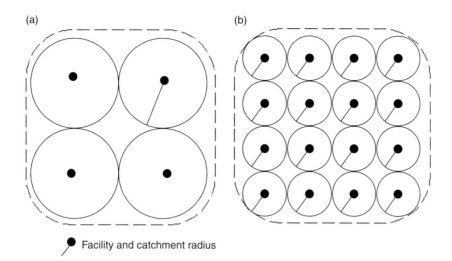

Facility and catchment radius

Fig. 10.7. Relationship between catchment radius and facility requirements.

distribution, catchment areas should be related to zones for which population data can be obtained, which involves the concept of *visit rates*.

Visit rates

The visit rate is the number of visits to a facility per 1000 population per time period from a given zone. This idea is illustrated in Fig. 10.8, which shows the visit rates around a leisure centre in terms of visits per week per 1000 population for 400 metre (quarter mile) grid squares. To produce this map a survey was conducted and interviewees were asked to indicate on a map which grid square they had travelled from. Thus, for example: if 3% of all visits in the survey period came from grid square X (from survey), the total visits per week were 800 (from centre records); and the population of grid square X was 500 (from population census: English census provides data at this level); then 24 visits a week would have come from grid square X (3% of 800); and the visit rate would be 48 visits per 1000 per week (24/(500/1000)).

Figure 10.8 illustrates a principle that holds in general terms for most leisure facilities, that is: visit rates decline with distance travelled, although this is only approximate because it is likely to be travel *time* rather than distance that is important, and the socio-demographic characteristics of the population also play a part. The relationship is illustrated very clearly in data from a major Sydney city centre park, as shown in Fig. 10.9.

Box 10.4 shows how such visit rates can be established in the case of three leisure facilities in a planning area and used to estimate the likely level of use of a new facility in a previously unserved area.

Social groups

Catchment areas have been discussed so far only in terms of 'people' and 'population' in general. In fact, catchment areas are likely to be different for different groups in the

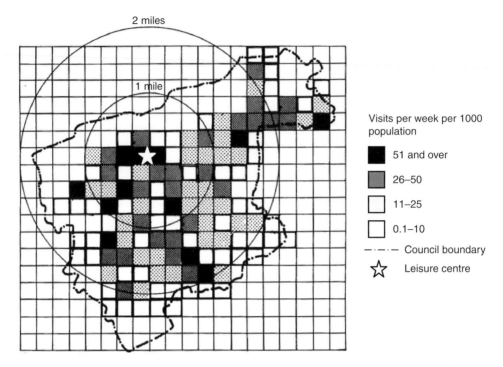

Fig. 10.8. Leisure centre visit rates (from Harlow leisure centre survey: BERG (1977)).

population. Thus car owners are likely to be able to travel greater distances than non-car owners and adults are likely to be able to travel greater distances than unaccompanied young children. Research has shown that in this respect the more deprived and less mobile groups of the community are less well served by facilities than the rest of the population – simply because they are not able to travel as far, as often or at all: their group-specific catchment areas are smaller than that of the population as a whole (Hillman and Whalley, 1977). Findings of this sort from user surveys could lead the planner to designate even larger areas as 'unserved' and requiring additional facilities if such groups were seen as a priority.

Catchment areas in a rural residential areas

So far it has been assumed that the setting for the spatial analysis is urban, with facilities located within substantial residential areas – as in Fig. 1.3(b). In rural areas the situation is different, with 'points' of population located in small settlements within a 'green fields' setting, as in Fig. 1.3(c). Catchment areas still apply, although rural residents generally have to travel further for their leisure than urban residents.

Knowledge of catchment areas of existing facilities can be just as useful in rural settings as in urban settings, but the approach to planning and provision is different, because of problems of access. In fact, the 'hierarchies of facilities' approach discussed below would be more appropriate than some of the methods described here. In addition, because of the rural tradition of community self-help, the community development approach discussed in Chapter 9 would also be more appropriate.

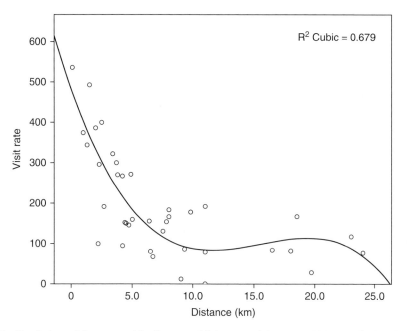

Fig. 10.9. Declining visit rates with distance. Visit rate, visits per 1000 population in 3 months; Distance, distance of local government area from city centre park; R^2 Cubic, the fitted line, indicating a strong relationship between distance and visit rate. Source: Sydney Royal Botanic Gardens data from special analysis of Sydney Parks Group community survey data (http://sydneyparksgroup.net.au).

Box 10.4. Catchment area planning.

This case-study illustrates the depiction of catchment areas using simple, concentric-distance circles. This loses the precision of grid squares, but data collection and analysis are easier. The data relate to one-mile (1.5 km) catchment zones surrounding three existing swimming pools, and are presented in a series of maps as follows:

- Fig. 10.10: visits per week – data from a user survey, which gives the percentage of users travelling from different distances; this is multiplied by the total number of visits per week (from the pools' own ticket sales data) to give the number of visits from each distance zone.
- Fig. 10.11: population of each zone – from the population census – information is generally available for the population within different distances of a point.
- Fig. 10.12: visit rates = visits per week divided by population divided by 1000. Thus, for example, for the inner zone of the top left-hand facility in the diagram: population/1000 is 13.3, so the visit rate = 1200/13.3 = 90 visits per 1000 population per week.
- Figure 10.12 shows that in the 1–2-mile rings the visit rates are only one-third or less of the visit rate within 1 mile from the facilities. Beyond 2 miles, the visit rate drops to only around one-tenth of the 0–1-mile rates.

(Continued)

Box 10.4. Continued.

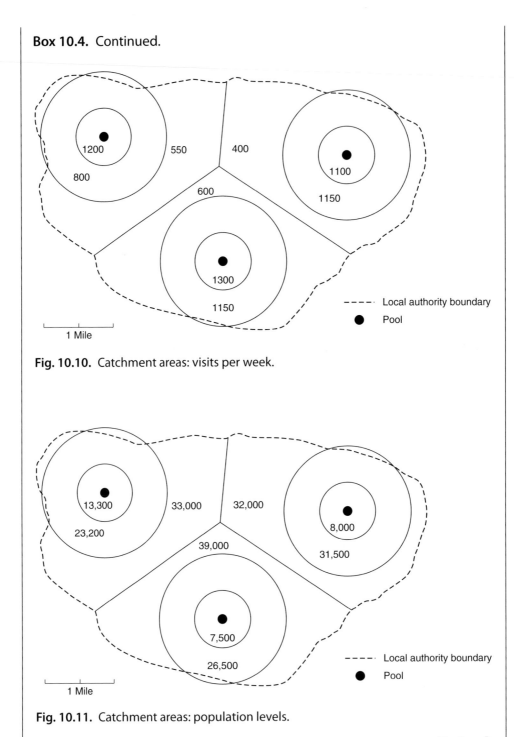

Fig. 10.10. Catchment areas: visits per week.

Fig. 10.11. Catchment areas: population levels.

(Continued)

Box 10.4. Continued.

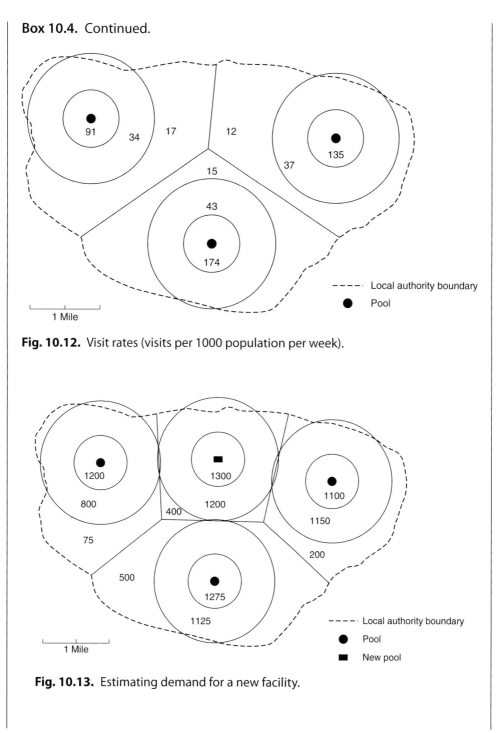

Fig. 10.12. Visit rates (visits per 1000 population per week).

Fig. 10.13. Estimating demand for a new facility.

(*Continued*)

Box 10.4. Continued.

In developing policy on this basis, it is necessary not only to identify unserved areas, but also to quantify the level of unmet demand in such areas. This is illustrated in Fig. 10.13. Demand for a hypothetical new facility is estimated using an average of the visit rates for the three existing pools applied to the population in the surrounding areas. Total visits to the new facility are estimated at 2900 per week. It should be noted that the new facility also affects the catchment area and level of use of the existing facilities, but the effect is minimal because the hypothetical new facility impinges only on the remote fringes of the existing catchment areas, where visit rates are low.

The example in Fig. 10.13 produced a 'viable' result – that is, the estimated level of demand in the unserved areas was sufficient to justify a new facility. But what if this were not the case? It is clear that, in the example in Fig. 10.3, even with the new facility there would remain areas which would still be poorly served, but the chances are that they would not generate enough demand to justify the provision of large facilities, such as a swimming pool.

The idea of 'viability' is a potentially contentious one. In a commercial context it is relatively unproblematical: if there are not enough customers to support a minimum-sized facility in a particular area, then such a facility will not be provided. Planners in companies such as Marks and Spencer, McDonald's Restaurants and cinema chains are fully aware of the minimum size of population necessary to support one of their facilities. In the public sector, however, things are not so simple: questions of equity have to be addressed. Thus, while the commercial organization could ignore the remaining unserved areas in the example shown in Fig. 10.13, public bodies must give them some consideration. Solutions could lie in the development of small-scale facilities which, while they may be costly to run per visit, may be acceptable in absolute terms. Alternatively, the form of the provision could be changed, involving, for example, dual use of education facilities, possibly at primary school level (Murphy and Veal, 1978), the development of multi-purpose facilities or the provision of other types of mobile facility.

Catchment areas and countryside recreation

In the case of countryside recreation the pattern is different again. In this case, recreation sites are dotted around the countryside and the bulk of the visitors come from urban centres, as in Fig. 1.3(d). If the urban centres are beyond day-trip distance, the activity becomes tourism rather than recreation and the area becomes a tourism destination, as in Fig. 1.3(e). In fact, the difference between tourism and non-tourism can become difficult to sustain in these situations. For example, a day-tripper from London to the Cotswolds would have the same *recreation* demands as someone from Edinburgh who may be staying overnight, and is thus classified as a tourist.

In the case of countryside recreation, planning must generally be examined at the regional rather than at the local level. Catchment area analysis makes it possible to identify those areas of the countryside which would come under increased demand pressure from population growth in adjacent urban areas. While the analysis could conceivably be achieved by means of a series of user surveys at recreation sites throughout the region, it is probably best done by means of a household survey throughout the region, including the major population centres from which most of the countryside recreation participants are drawn.

Knowledge of spatial patterns of recreation demand can be used as the basis for planning countryside recreation provision. Population growth is not currently a major feature of UK urban areas, but it is still a factor in other countries and could become so again in the UK. Catchment area analysis makes it possible to identify those areas of the countryside that would come under increased demand pressure from population growth in particular urban areas. Use of visit rates would enable the growth to be quantified.

Modelling

The descriptions of catchment areas and resultant planning approaches have been presented here in conceptual rather than highly quantified terms. However, the quantitative nature of the basic data lends itself to quantitative modelling – that is, using the catchment area data to simulate the spatial process mathematically. This process is, however, intimately bound up with the idea of forecasting, so is dealt with in the section of Chapter 11 on spatial models.

Hierarchies of facilities

The idea of hierarchies of facilities is a spatial phenomenon based on the idea that different sizes and types of facility have different catchment areas. A further principle is also invoked, in that different sizes and types of facility require different numbers of customers or clients to be viable and should therefore be related to different sizes and types of community.

Perhaps the most well-known example of the hierarchy approach is that developed for parks by the then Greater London Council (GLC), in the late 1960s. Surveys conducted by the GLC had established that people travelled different distances to visit different types of park with different functions. For example, people travelled relatively short distances to small parks to exercise the dog or to use children's play facilities, whereas they tended to travel longer distance to larger parks for family picnics or formal sporting activities. The GLC planners used this information to establish a parks hierarchy, as shown on the book's website (http://www.leisuresource.net). This became the basis for strategic parks planning by many of the London boroughs and by the GLC, until its abolition in 1986. The idea of a hierarchical parks system lives on in many local open-space plans.

Hierarchies can be applied to existing communities, but come into their own in the comprehensive planning of new communities – an activity which has been rare in the UK in recent years, because of the lack of growth in the population. In the 1960s and 1970s, however, numerous new towns were developed, including such places as Harlow, Stevenage, Telford and Milton Keynes. It was necessary to specify the whole range of facilities required in such communities. The new towns were themselves usually developed on a hierarchical basis, with neighbourhoods at the lowest level, a cluster of neighbourhoods forming some sort of district and, finally, a town or city level. Services of all kinds, including leisure, were planned within this framework, with education facilities often being the key organizing factor. In Australia, where the population of cities like Sydney and Brisbane is growing at more than 50,000 a year, the hierarchy idea is relevant to large new suburbs, in effect new towns, that are currently under construction.

Priority social area analysis

Social area analysis, sometimes called *factorial ecology*, is the process of analysing the socio-demographic characteristics of the populations of small areas of a city to identify areas with similar characteristics. This is generally based on data from census enumeration/collection areas (typically with populations of 300–400), using statistical computer packages and mapping software.

Priority social area analysis is a term coined in the previous edition of this book to describe the process of linking social area analysis with policy priorities, particularly in the area of leisure. As discussed in Chapter 3, needs-based planning may be based on the idea of giving priority for public leisure provision to those areas deemed to be in the greatest social need, as measured by census and other indicators. Direct measures of leisure facility provision can also be brought into play. Early experiments using this approach were conducted by the Greater London Council (Nicholls, 1975) and by the Tourism and Recreation Research Unit (TRRU: TRRU, 1982) in Scotland, while George Torkildsen (2005: 251–254), using the term *need index approach*, reports on an example from the 1990s for the same methodology. The GLC study is summarized on the book's website (http://www.leisiuresource.net).

The prerequisites for such analysis are small-area census data, which are now readily available to all local authorities, and a spatially identified facilities inventory. Modern computer technology makes the latter also relatively easy to assemble. Such census-inventory analysis was pioneered in Scotland by TRRU in their study for the Lothians Regional Council, which analysed particular social groups – such as youth and the elderly – in relation to a range of facilities (TRRU, 1982). By basing their analysis on kilometre-grid squares rather than wards, they were able to measure not just the number of facilities located within local areas but the distance to the nearest available facilities.

Variations on this approach are the various 'geo-demographic' analysis packages, the most well-known of which in the UK is ACORN (A Classification Of Residential Neighbourhoods). Data on the characteristics of residential areas are subject to multivariate analysis to produce residential area 'types'. While these tend to reflect the housing, socio-economic and demographic data upon which they are based, it is also believed that residents of the various area types will have distinctive leisure and consumption patterns – or lifestyles. Based on analysis of some 40 census variables covering age structure, mobility, socio-economic factors and housing, the ACORN analysis results in some five *categories*, eleven *groups* and 56 *types*, as shown in Table 10.10.

Any ward or census enumeration district can be classified according to one of the above types. The commercial company that produces ACORN has also inserted survey data on such variables as leisure interests, use of financial services, holidays, and Internet and telecommunications and media use, and can provide printouts and maps for any specified geographical area. Commercial and public sector organizations can therefore use ACORN to target neighbourhoods in which their priority client groups are concentrated – whether this be for the purposes of marketing or provision of services to alleviate deprivation.

The system distinguishes quite sharply between different groups/areas: for example, people in the top category in Table 10.10 are 'Wealthy mature professionals living in large houses' and, using an index of 100 for the UK average, members of this group score 344 for interest in snow-skiing, 167 for taking two or more holidays in a year, 21 for reading *The Sun* and 403 for reading the *Daily Telegraph*. By contrast, for 'Low-income, larger families

Table 10.10. ACORN categories.

ACORN Category	Groups	No. of types	UK population (%)
Wealth achievers	Wealthy executives	4	8.6
	Affluent greys (older people)	4	7.9
	Flourishing (well-off) families	4	9.0
Urban prosperity	Prosperous professionals	2	2.1
	Educated urbanites (young urban professionals)	5	5.5
	Aspiring singles (mainly students in urban areas)	4	3.8
Comfortably off	Starting out (young couples)	2	3.1
	Secure families	6	15.5
	Settled suburbia (older couples living in suburbs)	3	6.1
	Prudent pensioners	2	2.7
Moderate means	Asian communities	2	1.5
	Post-industrial families (older skilled)	2	4.7
	Blue-collar roots (manual workers)	3	7.5
Hard-pressed	Struggling (low-income) families	6	13.3
	Burdened singles (elderly and single parents)	3	4.2
	High-rise hardship	2	1.6
	Inner city adversity	2	2.1

Source: CACI (undated).

living in semi-detached houses', the corresponding indices are 45, 72, 161 and 33 (CACI, 2006).

The potential of ACORN has been explored in a number of leisure-orientated studies (Bickmore *et al.*, 1980; Nevill and Jenkins, 1986; Williams *et al.*, 1988; Jenkins *et al.*, 1989), and ACORN indicators are provided in the published results from the annual national Taking Part survey, conducted by the Department for Culture, Media and Sport (DCMS, annual).

GREENFIELD SITES

Most of the approaches discussed above assume an incremental planning situation that relates to a gradually changing population and builds on an existing supply of facilities within the planning area. But planning also takes place in *greenfield* sites, such as a major residential development on the edge of a city, or a tourist resort. Capacity, usage and catchment areas of existing facilities clearly do not apply. Adaptation of the participation approach to planning in greenfield sites in general is discussed in Chapter 8.

NATURAL AND HERITAGE RESOURCE ASSESSMENT

Assessment of natural and heritage resources brings several disciplines with expertise in such areas as natural ecosystems, including flora, fauna and water systems, cultural heritage of various types and landscape architecture, as well leisure and tourism planners. As noted in Chapter 7 in the discussion of resource-based planning, resource assessment has in the past been seen as the very basis of planning for leisure, but in recent decades it has come to be seen as one component of the planning process that varies in importance alongside leisure demand and need factors.

Natural and heritage resource assessments may be made in three situations:

- *environmental impact assessment*: conducted in relation to greenfield sites as part of the process of seeking planning permission for development – seen largely as identification of constraints to the proposed development (see Table 10.1);
- *site appraisal*: more detailed assessment of a greenfield site as part of the master-planning process (see Table 10.1);
- *tourism/cultural planning*: in countryside or coastal areas as an input for strategic planning for day-tripper and tourism development – concerned both with constraints and potential and is related to the concept of tourism capacity discussed above.

In the past, provided there were no major environmental or heritage constraints, the tendency was to bring in the bulldozers and impose the development plan on the landscape, with leisure activity sometimes being allocated arbitrarily to non-developable flood-prone areas. In recent years, there has been a change towards working *with* the existing landscape and ecosystem of a site, both for its own sake and to enhance the resultant development. Legislation provides for the protection of rare or threatened flora and fauna species and significant heritage items, and the resultant conserved areas may play a secondary role in education and recreation. Rather than being channelled into concrete culverts, waterways are often restored to their natural state with appropriate bank treatment and planting, thus attracting wildlife and becoming a focus for quiet recreation – and often coping more effectively with flood waters.

Similarly, disused industrial sites, once thought unremarkable, are now seen as *industrial heritage* and may be adapted for local use and become resources for education and even for tourism.

Cultural heritage, in the form of associations with past famous, or non-famous, residents or events, is researched and utilized in a similar way.

PROGRAMMES AND EVENTS

As noted at the beginning of the chapter, most programmes and events take place in facilities and so will be part of a facility audit. However, some programmes and events take place in a multiplicity of facilities and also in non-facilities, such as carnivals in the street. This format resembles the situation for destination tourism as discussed in relation to tourism capacity above, so the procedures discussed there would apply. Different facilities and other elements of infrastructure present different capacity constraints and, except for very large events, most will be beyond the influence of the event-organizing body. Where an event is an all-ticket affair, use data will arise from ticket sales, but where free events or events with free components are concerned, the situation again resembles destination tourism;

indeed, larger events are often organized specifically to attract tourists. Although resident attendance at programmes and events could be picked up in a resident participation survey, for tourists some sort of survey methodology will be required, as discussed in the use levels section above.

SUMMARY

This chapter outlines the facility/service audit process, particularly as required in the U-Plan system outlined in Chapter 8. It comprises three main parts: facility capacity, facility use and spatial dimensions. Six types of capacity are considered: physical capacity; operational capacity; economic capacity; social/psychological capacity; ecological capacity; and tourism capacity. Then the process of measuring capacity is examined for formal facilities and informal purpose-built and natural/heritage facilities. Facility use notes the significant difference between facilities for which usage data are readily available from ticket sales and other administrative processes and those facilities where use levels must be assessed by such techniques as surveys and on-site counts using manual or automatic methods. Spatial analysis is concerned with facility catchment areas, and the chapter considers how these might be measured and used in the planning process. Finally, the chapter gives some consideration to the contexts of greenfield sites, natural and heritage resource assessment and programmes and events.

RESOURCES

Websites

Venice in Peril: http://veniceinperil.org

Publications

Capacity studies: general: Veal (2009j); beaches: Sarda *et al.* (2009); countryside recreation/tourism: Houghton-Evans and Miles (1970); MCarthy and Dower (1967); pedestrian/cycling routes: Rouphail *et al.* (1988); tourist resorts: Saveriades (2000); Sarda *et al.* (2009); tourism: Venice: Canestrelli and Costa (1991); urban parks: Gedikli and Ozbilen (2004); white-water boating: Tarrant and English (1996).

Tourism capacity: Getz (1983).

Usage studies: Veal (2009j).

Social area analysis: Herbert and Johnston (1976).

Priority social area analysis applied to leisure: Nicholls (1975); Bickmore *et al.* (1980); TRRU (1982); Neville and Jenkins (1986); Williams *et al.* (1988); Jenkins *et al.* (1989); ACORN: CACI (2006); DCMS (annual).

QUESTIONS/EXERCISES

1. Discuss the challenges to be faced in measuring (i) the capacity; and (ii) the level of use of one of the following: an urban park; a tennis court; a beach; a theatre; a walking or cycling track; a skateboard facility; the historic/tourist core of a city.

2. Select a leisure, sport or tourism facility to which you have access and set up a project to estimate its capacity and current level of use.

3. Define the *catchment area* of a facility.

4. What is a *visit rate* and how can it be used in planning?

5. What is a facility *hierarchy*?

Notes

[1] The facility/audit process outlined here is an adaptation of the 'organic approach' to planning, as discussed in the previous edition of this book (Veal, 2002: 141–144).

chapter 11

Planning Tools 3: Forecasting

INTRODUCTION

All policies and plans are concerned with the future, whether the future extends over days, months or years. Typically, the policy and planning activity discussed in this book is focused on a planning period of several years, since plans generally take some time to implement and their consequences often remain with a community for decades. Admittedly, many policies and plans are concerned with meeting current deficiencies and solving current problems, but even in these situations, proposed solutions should ideally take account of the anticipated changing environment during the life of the facility. This is particularly important given the rapid rate at which social, environmental and technological change accelerates. Successful leisure, sport and tourism service organizations will surely be those which plan for the future rather than for the problems of the past – while of course learning from the past. In Chapter 8 reference is made to *passive* and *active* change, the former being change which, for the most part, the organization can do little if anything about and the latter being change that it seeks to bring about by its own actions. The discussion of forecasting in this chapter is largely concerned with passive change, but it is also concerned with ways in which the two might interact. Forecasting and planning can be seen to follow a sequence:

- Initial forecast: what will happen if we, the planning agency, do nothing?
- Analysis: are there undesirable outcomes that we can change or ameliorate?
- Policy development.
- New forecast taking account of policy measures.

An example of this sequence in operation would be:

- Initial forecast: significant ageing of the population.
- Analysis: ageing of the population will result in larger numbers with health problems resulting in increased health/care costs, which could be ameliorated if ageing people could be persuaded and assisted to adopt healthier lifestyles.

- Policy development: provide facilities and services to persuade and enable older people to adopt healthy lifestyles.
- New forecast of incidence of aged health problems and health/care costs taking account of estimated impact of the policy.

In this chapter the aim is to consider ways in which the future can be considered by policymaking and planning agencies. The techniques discussed vary considerably. They include highly technical approaches designed to produce quantified demand forecasts and less technical approaches concerned with qualitative issues and the 'big picture'. We will consider in turn:

- A brief history of forecasting in leisure, sport and tourism.
- The various ways in which leisure, sport and tourism demand might be measured.
- A range of social, economic and political factors that are likely to determine or affect leisure and tourism demand, and which therefore need to be taken into account in any forecasting exercise.
- Various techniques used in demand forecasting.

THE PAST OF THE FUTURE: A BRIEF HISTORY OF LEISURE, SPORT AND TOURISM FORECASTING

The origins of modern leisure demand forecasting lie in the early 1960s work of the American Outdoor Recreation Resources Review Commission (ORRRC, 1962). The umbrella term 'outdoor recreation' included a range of sporting activities and a considerable amount of natural area-based tourism. Data from the extensive research programme of the ORRRC were used to develop a quantitative modelling approach to demand forecasting using multiple regression equations that related levels of demand to demographic and socio-economic variables, such as age, race, income and level of education. This modelling approach was used extensively in outdoor recreation planning in the USA and, to some extent, in Europe. In the 1980s and 1990s, however, the approach fell out of favour with planners and policymakers, for technical reasons and because of the demonstrated inaccuracy of some of the early US forecasts. In other countries, such as the UK and Australia, researchers produced models that were statistically quite satisfactory, but their lifespan as the basis of planning and policy was, nevertheless, even more short-lived than in the USA. It is possible that, with more research, the technical limitations of the quantitative modelling experiment might have been overcome, but public sector policymakers in the leisure and sport area appeared to place much less emphasis on demand forecasting at national level after the 1970s. However, participation trends and their implications for the future have continued to be of interest in local planning.

Forecasting leisure demand, including sport participation, has generally been left to academics (e.g. Kelly and Warnick, 1999; Lynch and Veal, 2006: 44–45; Sport Industry Research Centre, annual) or the private sector (e.g. Miller and Asstes, annual). Tourism is particularly well provided for in terms of statistical trend data and forecasts. Internationally, the World Tourism Organization (WTO) produces regular demand forecasts: its current predictions are for international tourist arrivals to increase from the current (2009) figure of around 800 million to 1.6 billion in 2020 (WTO, undated). National governments, public tourism agencies and large tourism-related private companies, such as airlines, continue to commission demand forecasts, although for many, these have been thrown into disarray by such events as the attacks on the World Trade Center in New York in September 2001, the outbreak of foot-and-mouth disease in the UK in 2000–2001 and the 2008–2009 global financial crisis. In Australia, tourism forecasting merits its own quango, the Tourism Forecasting Committee, which updates domestic and international forecasts several times a year.

FORECASTING WHAT?

In Chapter 3 it is noted that, while the concept of *demand* has always been central to tourism analysis and policymaking, it has had a confused existence in the context of policymaking in leisure, and to a lesser extent in sport, but it has generally been accepted as an appropriate concept for forecasting.

Demand is what people consume in a given price/supply environment. When people take part in an activity they spend *time* and, often, *money* and this gives rise to a range of measures that are used in leisure demand analysis, as indicated in Table 3.3 in Chapter 3. Different measures are used in different policymaking situations.

In considering future demand we are dealing with demand that has not been and may never be realized: some of this may be consciously or unconsciously latent in the minds of the current population, but is frustrated in some way, and some may arise over time as a result of changes in the size or attributes of the population or in the supply side of the demand–supply equation. Furthermore, with the passage of time, leisure demand may switch from one facility to another or from one activity to another. Thus, in considering future demand we need to keep in mind different types of unmet demand in addition to existing – or expressed, current or effective – demand. Table 11.1 presents a demand typology drawing on earlier work by a number of commentators (e.g. Burton, 1971: 26; Gratton and Taylor, 1988: 99–100).

It is necessary to consider the various types of unmet or contingent demand because, for most people, the range of leisure goods and services they would like to have is constrained by, among other things, money and access to facilities. So what people *actually* do is not necessarily what they would *really* like to do if some of these constraints were removed. In particular, if prices for some activities were reduced, transport access improved or there was more capacity at peak periods or facilities were of a higher quality, effective demand would be higher than is currently observed. So, a statement such as: 'the demand for cinema visits in this community is 50,000 visits a year', should really be qualified to say: 'given current prices, availability of cinemas and quality of films offered, demand for cinema visits in this community is 50,000 visits a year'. This is true of any good or service in the economist's sense: the classic economic demand curve shows a particular level of *equilibrium* consumption/demand at the point where the demand and supply curve intersect, as shown in Fig. 3.6 in Chapter 3. The demand curve, which depicts only price and demand, extends to the right of this point, indicating that, if prices were lower, people would buy more.

In this classic economic model, *latent, induced, diverted* and *substituted* demand are not ignored – they all come into play when a shift occurs in the demand or supply curve. Thus effective demand increases if the supply curve moves downwards (there is an overall reduction in prices) or if it moves to the right (there is an increase in supply). Since a demand/supply curve for a particular leisure activity is only one of many which the consumer faces, for the many products and services available (it is one element in the economist's *general equilibrium system*), diversion and substitution are built into the system (e.g. in the form of the economist's *cross-elasticities*).

Table 11.1. Demand typology.

Type	Definition	Examples
Existing/expressed/ current/ effective demand	Activity currently taking place	Number of visits to a park
Unmet or latent demand	Activity frustrated by supply conditions or personal circumstances	Increased visits to parks that would take place if more parks were provided close to where people live (supply) and/or if more people owned cars which enabled them to visit existing parks (personal)
Supply induced/ generated demand	Activity materializing when supply conditions change	Increased visits to parks taking place when more parks are provided close to where people live
Diverted demand	Activity transferred from an existing facility to a new one	Portion of visits to a newly opened park that would have gone to an existing park
Substituted demand	Activity transferred from one activity to another when a new facility/service becomes available	Increase in skateboarding because of new facility in the newly opened park, by people who previously played basketball

As shown in using the Clawson method in Chapter 12 and in relation to various spatial planning techniques in Chapter 10, planning is very much about considering the extent to which these various forms of *unmet* demand might be transformed into *actual* demand in various supply scenarios.

DEMAND CHANGE FACTORS

Factors likely to influence leisure and tourism demand are endless; some are easily measured and incorporated into forecasting models while others are difficult, and sometimes impossible, to measure. The extent to which various factors can be taken into account also varies with the geographical level at which any forecasting exercise might be undertaken. Certain trends are applicable and measurable at national level, but at local level they may be inapplicable or there may simply be no locally based data. Further, at local level the considerable resources required to conduct research to fill data gaps may not be available. On the other hand, at the local level the impact of supply factors may be much more measurable and apparent. Even when data are lacking, however, an awareness of change factors and an informal, possibly qualitative, assessment of their likely impact can be valuable.

In the review of the 11 change factors below, the first four are relatively easily measurable and can be incorporated into a number of the forecasting techniques considered later in the chapter. As we move down the rest of the list, future trends in the factors become more unpredictable and their relationships with leisure behaviour more speculative. The 11 factors are:

- demography;
- income levels;
- supply: the activities of producers;
- leisure time and work time;
- transport;
- technology;
- the environment, including climate change;
- tastes and lifestyles;
- attitudes and values;
- the media;
- post-industrialism, postmodernity and globalization.

This is an indicative rather than an exhaustive list, and a number of factors are interconnected and overlapping. They can each be discussed only briefly here, but a guide to further reading is given in each case. Illustrative data are presented for a number of factors, typically relating to the UK, but in most cases comparable figures for Australia are included in the PowerPoint file for Chapter 11 on the book's website (http://www.leisuresource.net).

Demography

It is well known that the populations of advanced industrial nations are rapidly ageing. In the period 2005–2010 the first members of the *baby boomer* generation are reaching retirement age. The baby boomer generation was born between 1945 (the end of the Second World War) and the mid-1960s (introduction of the birth-control pill), and is so called because the period saw a particularly high birth rate. Because they experienced their formative years in the volatile 1960s, commentators often attribute particular cultural characteristics to this generation, but their significance in the forecasting context is their sheer numbers. In the 1960s and 1970s they were an exceptionally large cohort of teens and twenties; now, and for the next 20 years, they will form an exceptionally large cohort of retirees. Figure 11.1 shows the dramatic increases predicted in older age groups in the UK between 2007 and 2031; of the total increase in population of 10 million, more than 4 million will be accounted for by people over retirement age and a further 3 million by people aged between 45 and retirement age.

These changes are, on average, replicated at local level and are therefore highly significant for local leisure and sport planning, since the level of participation and the mix of activities vary markedly with age. In the case of tourism, national and international trends become relevant, since older people have different travel patterns and demands from younger age groups.

Apart from the uncertainties of migration and sudden changes in the birth rate, demographic forecasting is particularly reliable since, subject to a fairly predictable death rate, the group of people currently aged, for example, 55–59 will definitely be aged 60–64 in 5 years' time. Furthermore, there are clear and well-documented relationships between patterns of leisure participation and age, so demographic change is invariably a key feature of any leisure forecasting exercise. The use of this sort of information is demonstrated in the *cross-sectional analysis* forecasting technique discussed later in the chapter.

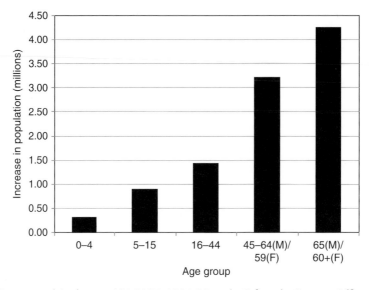

Fig. 11.1. Demographic change, UK, 2007–2031. M, male; F, female. Source: Office for National Statistics (2008); similar data can be found for Australia in Lynch and Veal (2006: 443).

Income

In the UK, between 1995–1996 and 2005–2006 total household expenditure grew by 13%, in real terms (that is, net of inflation). However, as Fig. 11.2 shows, expenditure on leisure *services* grew by almost 50%. Expenditure on leisure *goods*, on the other hand, grew by only 4.5%, probably a reflection of falling real prices of manufactured goods imported from

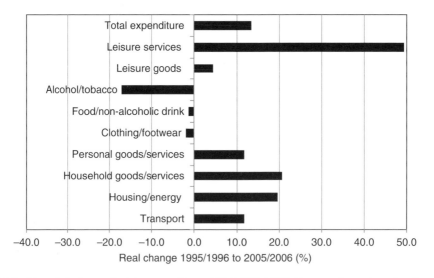

Fig. 11.2. Trends in household expenditure, UK, 1995–2006. Source: based on family expenditure survey, Office for National Statistics (2008).

China. These two items were partially offset by a fall in expenditure on alcohol and tobacco products, the latter due to the rapid decline in the proportion of people who smoke. The result was an overall increase of 21% in leisure goods and services. This indicates that expenditure on leisure goods and services increases at a significantly faster rate than overall expenditure.

While this trend is clearly significant for the commercial leisure sector, including tourism, it is less significant for planning of public sector facilities, which are generally offered at subsidized prices or free of charge.

Supply: the activities of producers

The suppliers of leisure goods and services provide the supply side of the demand–supply equation discussed in Chapter 3. Thus the future is partially determined by the activities of producers of goods and services: how they decide to research, invest, produce and market. This is true not only of the private sector but also of the public sector. For example, publicly funded campaigns, such as 'Sport for All' in the UK (McIntosh and Charlton, 1985) and 'Life. Be in it' in Australia (Watkins, 1981), are designed to influence people's behaviour – insofar as they are successful they influence the future. In the UK in the last 30 years of the 20th century, some 2500 indoor leisure centres were built by the public sector: if they had not been built in the way that they were, from public funds, it is most unlikely that the private or voluntary sector would have been able to build such centres on anything like that scale. Therefore it is highly unlikely, given the UK climate, that the millions of sporting and other leisure activities they now accommodate each year would be taking place. The activities of public providers *shaped* the future.

This is not to say that providers act without constraint: campaigns, products and facilities can fail. There are three groups involved in making decisions about future patterns of leisure behaviour and demand: the industry itself, the consumers and the people and organizations in between – the media, communicators, critics and 'culture brokers', which can be seen as an independent force with, arguably, a significant influence in determining the 'latest thing'. Consumer tastes and activities change as these forces interact in complex ways, as discussed below. It is arguable that providers keep their options by planning for and investing in multi-purpose *platforms* on which leisure activity can take place, but the precise products/services that come to dominate the platforms are determined by responses to consumer demand. Thus telecommunications companies provide mobile communication infrastructure, but which devices and uses of devices become successful is a more uncertain matter shaped by fickle consumer taste. Similarly, local councils provide multi-purpose leisure centres, which are indoor spaces for physical recreation, but the programming of such spaces, for badminton, keep-fit classes of various types, five-a-side soccer or netball, depends on changing demand. One lesson to be drawn from such an analysis then, is that planning should provide for flexibility.

Leisure time and work time

To engage in sport, tourism and other forms of leisure activity it is necessary to have available leisure *time*. This is often discussed as the complement of work time and, since annual working hours for full-time employees have fallen from over 3000 to less than 2000 since the beginning of the 20th century (Veal, 2004) and the amount of domestic labour time needed to maintain the average home has also fallen, it is generally accepted that leisure time has increased. However, whether it *continues* to increase in the 21st century is debatable.

In the early 1990s Juliet Schor (1991) observed that in the USA, in the 1970s and 1980s, there had been a reduction in leisure time, resulting in the emergence of the *Overworked*

American. This idea, that people in industrial nations are experiencing *less* leisure time, has become part of popular myth in recent years. Schor's own more recent research suggests that patterns differ between different countries, with many European countries in particular showing a different pattern from the USA (Schor, 2006). This is illustrated in Fig. 11.3, which shows a slow decline in weekly working hours in the UK and Australia since 1998. Furthermore, since it is sometimes said that the 'time squeeze' being experienced by many is at the household level, where there is often one full-time and one part-time paid employee, Fig. 11.3 also shows the trend in employed working hours for a 'household' (one full-time plus one part-time employee), which also shows a downward trend.

It is not only paid working hours that affect the amount of leisure time available to the individual: unpaid work, such as housework and childcare, education and personal care, including sleeping, are also variables. Time-use surveys measure these time allocations directly, but are expensive to conduct and so are conducted comparatively rarely, and not at all in some countries. Thus, for example, the UK has conducted only two official national time-use surveys, in 2000 and 2005 (Lader *et al.*, 2006), and similarly in Australia only two such surveys have been conducted, in 1997 and 2006 (ABS, 2008a). Three countries have conducted multiple time-use surveys across a number of decades: Canada, the Netherlands and the USA. Figure 11.4 shows data on free time from these surveys, indicating a different pattern from that suggested by Schor's work based on working hours data: that is, the USA is shown to have increasing leisure time, while the single European example, the Netherlands, has falling leisure time. Leisure time in Canada has been static since the 1980s. A more confused picture would be difficult to imagine.

Despite the common reference to 'increasing leisure time' in policy documents, the complexity of measurement, the cost, and therefore paucity, of data, the lack of research on the relationship between leisure time and leisure participation patterns and the lack of available forecasts of likely future trends in leisure time, means that leisure time is rarely, if ever, incorporated into forecasting models.

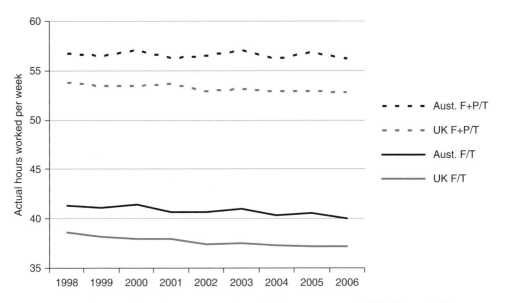

Fig. 11.3. Trends in working hours, Australia and UK, 1998–2006. F/T. full time; P/T, part time. Sources: Australia, ABS Social Trends; UK, Labour Market Trends.

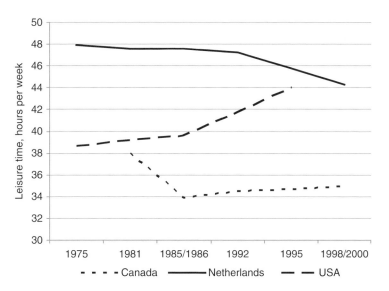

Fig. 11.4. Trends in leisure time, Canada, the Netherlands and the USA. Source: Cushman *et al.* (2005: 46, 167, 269).

Transport

There was a time when increasing levels of car ownership were a major influence on trends in leisure participation in Western nations, particularly informal recreation, such as day trips to the countryside. In recent years, however, this has changed. In the UK car ownership rose to 60 cars per 100 adults in 2005 and has been static ever since. Forecasting recreation trips can therefore no longer rely on predictions of car ownership as the major source of growth. As Fig. 11.5 suggests,

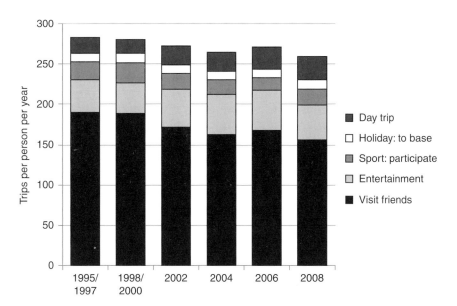

Fig. 11.5. UK leisure travel trends, 1995–2008. Source: National Travel Survey (Dept for Transport, available at http://www.dft.gov.uk).

more complex forces are at work; data on different trip types by all transport modes since the mid-1990s show a mixed picture, with different types of trip rising and falling at different times, but no clear consistent trend overall.

International tourism and longer-distance domestic tourism is affected by changes in the transport environment, with stimulus to demand coming from larger aircraft offering cheaper fares over time and, in recent years, the advent of budget airlines offering a further boost. World Tourism Organization data on international arrivals show a steady increase in the proportion of people travelling by air, from 39% in 1990 to 43% in 2004 (WTO, 2009).

Technology

Technological change is endemic to industrial economies, with significant proportions of national incomes being spent on research and development in industry, government and universities throughout the world. While relatively little of this research effort is aimed specifically at leisure and leisure products, its effects do inevitably have an impact on leisure. In the past, technology such as transistors and computers, lightweight materials, jet engines and satellites, often developed initially for military purposes, have become the basis of significant leisure industries.

New products, whether technological or cultural in origin, are not adopted instantaneously by consumers but are subject to a 'product life cycle', which generally involves a slow initial build-up, followed by a period of rapid growth and a peak, or 'saturation' level and then possibly a decline as the product is superseded by another innovation. This process takes several years. Indications of this at work can be seen in Fig. 11.6, which shows trends in the level of ownership of a number of durable goods in the UK.

One question that arises in examining technological change is the extent to which such change has an impact on leisure behaviour, as opposed to consumption. The advent of computer games, for example, created a totally new leisure activity, but quite significant technological advances in game technology may not affect the pattern of participation at all.

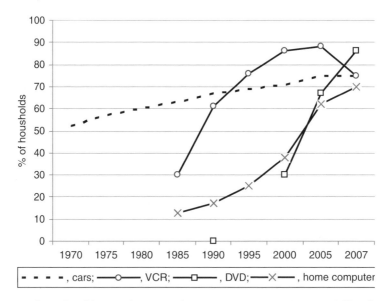

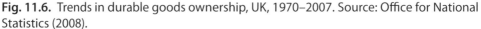

Fig. 11.6. Trends in durable goods ownership, UK, 1970–2007. Source: Office for National Statistics (2008).

Technological forecasting is an art in itself, generally undertaken using the Delphi method, as discussed below (Halal, 2000), but has not generally featured in leisure, sport and tourism forecasting.

The environment, including climate change

The growth of the global population and its leisure demands and the growth of international tourism both pose threats to the natural environment. The drive for development and growth places increasing pressure on already degraded resources and threatens others. The short-term and long-term effects of these pressures are well known and have been long debated (e.g. Ehrlich and Ehrlich, 1990). Governments have responded with a variety of policies and measures, from tree planting to clean air and waterways policies to the designation of protective National Parks and wilderness areas and declarations of commitment to 'sustainable development', that is development which 'meets the needs of the present without compromising the ability of future generations to meet their own needs' (World Commission on Environment and Development, 1990). While the connection between development and environmental damage is obvious for noxious industries and for urban development generally, it has been less obvious for seemingly innocent activities like recreation. But golf courses require water: many feet compact soil in natural areas and cause runoff and erosion; hotels and resorts generate sewage and litter; and all these activities take land which may be the habitat of other creatures. The future of leisure and tourism will depend partly on society coming to terms with these impacts and finding ways of ameliorating their worst effects. The question is whether human organizations, including leisure and tourism organizations, will respond by modifying their practices to achieve sustainability, or whether some sort of crisis will develop, leading to restrictions on activities.

These questions are particularly relevant to tourism. Local leisure demand is generally increasing but, in recent years, tourism has been the major leisure growth sector, and this can be expected to continue over the coming decade. The World Tourism Organization predicts that international tourist arrivals will more than double, to 1.6 billion by 2020 (World Tourism Organization, undated). This will clearly have a significant effect on the leisure industries, since tourists eat meals in restaurants and visit parks and beaches, museums and galleries, casinos and other attractions.

This additional demand has an economic impact on the providers of leisure services in tourist areas that is generally seen as positive, but it could also make public spaces, such as urban parks and National Parks, beaches, streets and shopping areas, overcrowded, particularly at peak periods. In some urban areas the effects may be insignificant or at least manageable by means of pedestrian and vehicle traffic controls – additional people can even give some urban areas an additional 'buzz' that adds to their attraction – but in some, such as central London, tourism levels may reach 'saturation' level, presenting challenges for city planners and managers. In many natural areas, increased visitor numbers are already presenting challenges to managers with conservation responsibilities, especially as the phenomenon of 'ecotourism' increases in popularity.

Climate change adds a new dimension to these factors. As well as their direct impact on the environment, many leisure activities have an indirect effect through their use of energy and production of carbon dioxide. The reactions of the leisure, sport and tourism industries and research communities fall into three groups involving consideration of:

1. Contributions which the industry sector could/should make to reduce its carbon footprint.
2. Possible effects of general emission abatement measures on the industry sector and its activities.
3. Possible effects of different climate change scenarios on the industry sector and its activities and possible adaptation measures.

The major leisure, sport and tourism carbon emission source relates to travel associated with such activities, especially tourism. General emission abatement measures are likely to increase fuel prices, and some airlines are offering carbon offset programmes, while others are experimenting with low-emission biofuels. Insofar as, even as abatement measures are put into place via international agreements, the climate is expected to continue to warm over the next few decades because of the existing levels of carbon dioxide in the atmosphere, so some change can be expected. The 2009 Copenhagen UN climate change meeting did not make substantial progress, but significant changes are taking place in individual countries. The leisure, sport and tourism industries have begun to consider the implications of climate change and some examples are shown in Box 11.1.

Box 11.1. Climate change and leisure, sport and tourism.

World Tourism Organization: Davos Declaration, October 2007 (quotation)

- Climate is a key resource for tourism and the sector is highly sensitive to the impacts of climate change and global warming, many elements of which are already being felt. It is estimated to contribute some 5% of global CO_2 emissions.
- Tourism – business and leisure – will continue to be a vital component of the global economy, an important contributor to the Millennium Development Goals and an integral, positive element in our society.
- Given tourism's importance in the global challenges of climate change and poverty reduction, there is a need to urgently adopt a range of policies that encourages truly sustainable tourism that reflects a 'quadruple bottom line' of environmental, social, economic and climate responsiveness.
- The tourism sector must rapidly respond to climate change, within the evolving UN framework and progressively reduce its greenhouse gas contribution if it is to grow in a sustainable manner; this will require action to:
  ° mitigate its greenhouse gas emissions, derived especially from transport and accommodation activities;
  ° adapt tourism businesses and destinations to changing climate conditions;
  ° apply existing and new technology to improve energy efficiency;
  ° secure financial resources to help poor regions and countries. (WTO, 2008: 2)

Climate Change and the Visitor Economy: Challenges and Opportunities for England's Northwest (McEvoy et al., 2006)

One view of the impact of climate change on tourism in temperate climate regions such as the northwest of England is that increasing temperatures will result in a 'Mediterranean climate', which will increase the attractiveness of the region to holidaymakers and increase the number of fine weather days that encourage day-trips. This study explores this proposition by applying climate change scenarios in a number of case studies. The case studies are:

(Continued)

Box 11.1. Continued.

- The Sefton coastal dune system containing golf courses and informal recreation areas – as well as playing a significant coastal defence and ecological role, it is found that increased temperatures would be likely to bring increased visitor numbers which would place increased pressures on the eco-system, while rising sea-levels could reduce the dune system and make it more unstable.
- Moorland wildfires in the Peak District National Park – handling the increased risk of fire would require additional resources for fire abatement management.
- Footpath erosion in the Lake District National Park – it is found that the climate change-induced loss of snow cover in winter (which protects paths from severe freezing) and higher rainfall in summer would result in increased erosion of footpaths which would also be under greater pressure from increased visitor numbers. Thus the cost of footpath maintenance would be increased.
- Public space in Manchester city centre – increased temperatures could 'supplement the trend towards 'outdoor lifestyles'', including the burgeoning café culture, but accommodating this growth would present a challenge to urban design and management.

Golf Participation in Toronto: Scott and Jones (2006)

This Canadian study examined the effect of weather patterns on the daily demand for golf at a golf course in the Toronto region over the period 2002–2003. The resultant statistical model was then used to predict the likely effects of two climate change scenarios for the 2020s, 2050s and 2080s. The warmer climate was predicted to result in an increase in rounds played of between 5% (2020s) and 28% (2080s) using current season lengths, but between 23% and 73% if playing seasons were extended to reflected changed weather conditions.

Snowmobiling in Canada: McBoyle *et al.* (2007)

This study, designed to estimate the likely effect of two alternative climate change scenarios, examined 13 non-mountainous snowmobiling regions in Canada. Using data from the period 1961–1990, a model was created relating weather factors to snowfall and the length of the season in a year. This model was then used to predict the likely effect of the two scenarios for the 2020s and the 2050s. The smallest effect was an 11% reduction in the length of the season for one of the Quebec regions in the 2020s, while the highest was a 100% reduction for two of the Prairie regions in the 2050s. The average reduction was 52% in the 2020s and 75% in the 2050s.

Changing tastes and lifestyles

Tastes are the most difficult of all the factors to predict (Bikchandani *et al.*, 1992) and few forecasting exercises attempt to do so. Some changes are long term, while others are short-term 'fads'. In some industries, such as fashion, regular changes in taste are institutionalized – led by the industry. Young people in particular seem to be susceptible to short-term fads or crazes – for example for skateboards or 'inline' skating (Davidson, 1985), partly because very often any activity or product would be new to them when passing through a certain age range, and there is no reason why they should adopt an established activity or product any more than a new one.

Since fads, fashions and crazes are, by definition, fickle, it is almost impossible to predict them, although they also tend to have 'product life cycles' like consumer goods, often extending over a number of years. But longer-term change in taste patterns may be mapped, monitored and even predicted. It might be thought that consumer taste and fashion is a private sector concern and therefore of little interest to the public sector. However, the private and public sectors are competing for the public's time and, to some extent, their money. The public sector has a range of 'products' that it wishes the public to 'consume'. Admittedly, in many cases the public sector product has its own unique image, and competition with the private sector is not an issue – for example, the traditional urban park. In other instances, for example leisure services for young people, the private sector tends to set the pace and the public sector must adapt accordingly if it is to stay 'competitive'.

Changing attitudes and values

More fundamental than changing tastes and lifestyles, although connected, is the idea of changing attitudes and values. Various commentators have argued that coping with the changing economic, technological and social environment will require significant changes in social attitudes.

In the 1930s, John Maynard Keynes, whose economic theories provided the basis for the post-World War II economic growth, anticipated the effects of technology and growing productivity and wealth, suggesting that the main challenge facing future societies would not be economic survival, but what to do with the resultant increase in free time:

> If the economic problem is solved mankind will be deprived of its traditional purpose ... I think with dread of the readjustments of the habits and instincts of the ordinary man, bred into him for countless generations, which he may be asked to discard within a few decades ... there is no country and no people, I think, who can look forward to the age of leisure and abundance without dread. For we have been trained too long to strive and not to enjoy.
>
> (Keynes, 1931: 328)

The idea of the Protestant work ethic is, it has been argued, deep seated in Western culture. The German sociologist Max Weber made the connection between Protestant teaching and the development of industrial capitalism, summarizing the puritan, Protestant view as follows: 'Not leisure and enjoyment, but only activity serves to increase the glory of God ... Waste of time is thus the first and in principle the deadliest of sins. Loss of time through sociability, idle talk, luxury, even more sleep than is necessary for health ... is worthy of absolute moral condemnation' (Weber, 1930: 157).

The extent to which the work ethic has been internalized among the mass of the populations of Western countries is debatable, but numerous commentators are sufficiently convinced that it is to call for major attitude changes to cope with the future. In the past, commentators have called for the development of alternatives to the work ethic, including a 'life ethic' (Clemitson and Rodgers, 1981: 13), a 'contribution ethic' (Clarke, 1982: 196), a 'non-work ethic' (Ritchie-Calder, 1982: 16) and a 'leisure ethic' (Argyle, 1996: 282). The call for changed values was also reflected in the manifesto of French Marxist sociologist André Gorz (1980a), who urged the working class to liberate themselves from the burden of wage labour, a call he reiterated in the 1990s (Gorz, 1999). But Marxist Ed Andrew (1981: 180) declared that 'Any demand for a change in values, whether a return to a work ethic or and advance to a socially involved leisure ethic ... is, for the Marxist, just empty chatter'.

There is, however, little evidence of significant changes in attitudes towards work having taken place in the 20 years since these calls were made. More recently, Juliet Schor (1991: 164) proposed that Americans should break the 'insidious cycle of work-and-spend', arguing that 'There will be more leisure only when people become convinced that they must have it'. Aronowitz *et al.* (1998) have proposed a 'Post-work Manifesto' and UK forecasters Bill Martin and Sandra Mason called for 'the emergence of new attitudes to paid work and free time', but noted that this would be difficult because 'the structure of work time is something that is ingrained in daily life' (Martin and Mason, 1998: 108). While these calls attract media attention from time to time, there is little sign of them making an impact on Western politics or culture, but it is nevertheless advisable for the forecaster to keep a watching brief on this issue.

The media

The modern mass communication media, particularly television, dominate modern leisure, but are frequently ignored in leisure forecasting – perhaps because they largely relate to home-based leisure. Cinema and radio invaded people's leisure in the 1920s and 1930s but, as with changes in leisure time and the growth of car ownership discussed above, television emerged as a major force in the 1960s and subsequently became far and away the major leisure activity of the majority of people. What changes in this phenomenon will affect leisure behaviour in future? The average individual already spends two or more hours a day watching television and it seems unlikely that there is scope for this to increase significantly. Increases in multiple television sets within the home, the proliferation of available channels, delivered by a variety of technologies, and the 'convergence' of television with Internet-linked technologies are all likely to have some effect on viewing habits and will no doubt result in higher levels of expenditure on 'niche market' products, but, in terms of broad patterns of leisure behaviour, the effects are unlikely to be major.

Post-industrialism, postmodernism and globalization

The Industrial Revolution in Europe in the 18th and 19th centuries ushered in the *industrial* era, with its unprecedented levels of economic growth and development. From around the 1970s a number of commentators began to suggest that the economically developed part of the world was entering a *post-industrial* era, in view of the decline in the importance of manufacturing in highly developed economies and the growth in the importance of services, particularly in such areas as information technology, leisure and tourism (Bell, 1974; Jones, 1995), although some argue that the observed changes are merely a further stage in the development of the industrial era (Veal, 1987: 46–62; Kumar, 1995). Whether the economic and industrial changes that have taken place since the 1980s, and are still taking place, represent a new type of economy or merely a new stage in the development of industrial economies, they are certainly highly significant. In particular they are significant in moving more and more economic activity into the services sector. Typically in developed economies, less than 5% of the workforce is engaged in primary industries (agriculture, mining) and less than 20% in manufacturing, leaving over 70% in services. Within the services sector, leisure and tourism are becoming increasingly significant, as the expenditure trends discussed under 'income', above, indicate.

In cultural terms, the 19th and much of the 20th century has been seen as the culmination of the *modern* era, characterized in particular by the increasing secularization and 'rationalization' of the Western world and the associated ideas of continuous technical, economic and social 'progress'. *Postmodernism* implies the end of the modernist era. The idea of a *postmodern* era has particular implications for the cultural world and is clearly seen in areas such as architecture and literature, where the notions of 'progress' and a 'hierarchy' of excellence have been challenged. Further, postmodernism suggests that cultural phenomena, such as fashion, popular music, mass communications media, advertising and individual consumption, now *determine* the fundamental nature of society, rather than simply reflecting underlying economic, production-based relationships (Tomlinson, 1990; Featherstone, 1991; Docker, 1994; Rojek, 1995: 129–145).

Linked with these ideas is the concept of *globalization*, a concept discussed in Chapter 2 in relation to the role of the state. Here we consider the phenomenon as a force for change affecting the future. Anthony Giddens identifies four defining features of globalization: (i) the worldwide communications revolution; (ii) the growth of the 'weightless economy' or the 'knowledge economy' – financial markets being the most important, but including services such as entertainment, tourism and sport; (iii) the collapse of the Soviet Union and its communist allies, leading to an unchallenged worldwide capitalist system; and (iv) social change, for example the growing equality between men and women (Giddens and Hutton, 2000: 1–2).

One feature of globalization that is not captured by these four dimensions is the role of the multinational firm, or transnational corporation (Gratton, 1996). While many of these organizations, such as Time Warner and News Limited, are involved with the first of Giddens' features, the communications revolution, others are involved in traditional activities like manufacturing and are centrally involved in the shift of such activities from the developed countries to the developing or newly industrialized countries. Further, many of these companies – Nike being the most notable – are part of the leisure industry sector. A related theme is that, because of the activities and the financial 'muscle' of such companies, as well as the activities of stock and currency markets, there is a 'loss of sovereignty' of the nation-state, an issue discussed in Chapter 2.

These developments are clearly relevant to any consideration of the future of leisure, and can be related to developments in such areas as: (i) the organization of work and leisure; (ii) developments in urban leisure and tourism, such as the growth of theme parks and leisure/retail complexes; (iii) changes in electronic home entertainment; and (iv) the growing economic and cultural significance of events, such as major sporting events and film and arts festivals.

FORECASTING TECHNIQUES

A selection of nine forecasting techniques, as summarized in Table 11.2, is outlined below. Techniques are often divided into 'qualitative' and 'quantitative' groups, with informed speculation, the Delphi method, scenario writing and comparative analysis being seen as qualitative, asking the public and composite methods as both quantitative and qualitative, and the rest quantitative. While it is true that the so-called qualitative techniques can handle qualitative data, they are also capable of including quantitative data, and many of the quantitative techniques can take account of non-quantitative data, often using 'dummy' variables. The quantitative/qualitative divide is therefore more complex than most reviews suggest.

Informed speculation

In the 1920s and 1930s, and later in the 1960s, many commentators, noting the decline in paid working hours since the beginning of the century, speculated about the possibility of a future 'leisure society'. One of most famous, and earliest of these speculations was the famous essay *In Praise of Idleness* by the UK philosopher Bertrand Russell, who argued:

Table 11.2. Forecasting techniques.

Informed speculation	Researchers'/commentators' own ideas: no specific methodology
Asking the public	Surveys asking people about their participation intentions
Asking the experts (Delphi technique)	A panel of experts each identifies future events and the likely timing or probability of their happening; results are circulated to panel members and reassessed in two or more rounds
Scenario writing	Alternative future conditions are identified in relation to one or more major factors (e.g. high or low economic growth) and the leisure/sport/tourism implications explored
Time series analysis	Patterns of participation over recent years are extrapolated into the future, directly or based on 'structural equations'
Spatial models	Future participation patterns in different supply scenarios are based on spatial models of demand, as discussed in Chapter 10
Cross-sectional analysis	Relationships between participation and key socio-economic variables (e.g. age, income) are studied using current survey information, and predictions of future participation levels are based on forecasts of the key variables
Comparative analysis	Certain communities (nations, cities, regions) are identified as leaders ('bellwether communities') and provide an indication of where other communities will follow in future
Composite methods	A combination of two or more of the above techniques

> If every man and woman worked for four hours a day at necessary work, we could all have enough; … it should be the remaining hours that would be regarded as important – hours which could be devoted to enjoyment of art or study, to affection and woodland and sunshine in green fields … Man's true life does not consist in the business of filling his belly and clothing his body, but in art and thought and love, in the creation and contemplation of beauty and in the scientific understanding of the world.
>
> (Russell and Russell, 1923: 50)

The leisure society idea has had a chequered existence in the subsequent eight decades, having been generally dismissed by more recent leisure scholars, but never fully disappearing (Veal, 2009a).

Nevertheless, many essays and concluding chapters of leisure texts consist of less ambitious speculation about what leisure will be or should be in future. They tend not to present forecasts as such, but a broad overview of current and future social trends and how they might impact on leisure and leisure services. For example, in his book *Leisure in Your Life*, Geoffrey Godbey includes a final chapter entitled 'The Future of Leisure', in which he states that, in future, 'the portion of life spent at paid work is likely to decrease still further, while the amount of time spent learning will increase. There is, then, the potential for life to be centred around leisure' (Godbey, 2008: 429). In some cases, speculation is published not as personal prognostications but as statements arising from conferences or workshops, an informal version of the Delphi technique discussed below (see Kraus, 1998: 397–399 for a synopsis of examples of these).

Such speculations are not necessarily based on any specific techniques or analysis, but represent a distillation of the thoughts and impressions of the authors. Their value therefore arises from the wisdom and experience of the writer. Often they are intended to open up issues for thought and discussion.

Asking the public

Many leisure participation surveys go beyond asking what people currently do in their leisure time and ask what they would like to do or are planning to do in future, or would like to do in the absence of constraints. Responses to such questions cannot be relied on as even approximate indicators of the scale of future demand, since they often reflect wishful thinking that may never be acted upon. But they can be seen as indicators of sentiment, of what people may be drawn to do in favourable conditions, and what the popular and unpopular activities currently are. This point is illustrated in Box 11.2.

Box 11.2. Predicting trends by asking the public.

A survey of leisure participation in Australia in the early 1990s asked what leisure activities respondents would like to participate in, but had not been able to, in the survey period (DASETT, 1991). The most commonly mentioned activities were:

- men: golf: 7%; fishing: 7%;
- women: tennis: 5%; aerobics/keep fit: 5%.

Such information is useful market intelligence and can in some circumstances be an indicator of possible future trends in behaviour, but cannot necessarily be taken at face value.

In each case the most common reason given by respondents for not participating was lack of time. It is notable that, of the four desired activities mentioned, participation in three (golf, fishing and tennis) takes a considerable amount of time. By contrast, aerobics and general fitness activities can be undertaken in short periods of time of an hour or less. More recent Australian data show that, between 2001 and 2007, participation levels in golf, fishing and tennis declined, but participation in aerobics/fitness increased by more than 50% (SCORS, 2009).

This analysis suggests that, in considering future trends in participation, there is some value in studying people's stated aspirations and intentions, but also in taking into account actual and perceived constraints.

A national survey conducted 15 years later (ABS, 2007: 32) showed that lack of time was still the most common reason given for lack of participation in sport and physical activities.

Asking the experts: the Delphi technique

The Delphi technique exploits the fact that experts of various sorts are likely to have particular insights into future developments in their field of expertise. The term 'Delphi' relates to the Delphic Oracle of ancient Greece, a priestly entity who, in return for petitioning and often generous payment, could be persuaded to foretell people's future fortunes – often expressed in cryptic manner.

The modern Delphi technique involves asking a panel of experts to express their views of the future and distilling this information into forecasts. The number of experts involved could be as few as a dozen or so, or could number several hundred. They can be contacted when they are assembled together in one place, typically at a conference (e.g, Seely *et al.*, 1980; Jones, S., 1990) or, more commonly, they can be contacted by mail. In a questionnaire, the experts are asked a series of questions that can be in various forms, for example:

- What are the major changes you expect to see in your field of expertise over the next 5/10/20, etc. years?
- When, if ever, do you expect the following events to take place?
- What is the likelihood of each of the following events happening in the next 5/10/20, etc. years?

The first question format produces responses in the form of lists of events and the number of times they are mentioned by members of the panel. The second produces a range of dates and a mean or median date attached to a predetermined list of events. The third produces a range of probabilities and a mean or median likelihood score attached to a predetermined list of events.

The results of the first round of the survey are compiled and summary results are fed back to the participants, who are invited to modify their responses, if they wish, in light of the results from the rest of the panel. Typically, only one or two rounds are implemented, but additional rounds may be added until a stable situation is achieved – that is, panel members are no longer changing their views. The collated views of the panel from the final round then provide the basis of the forecast. The technique is commonly used in tourism research, but not often for forecasting: typically, it is used as a means of stakeholder consultation to seek views on issues such as the environmental impact of tourism (e.g. Green, H. *et al.*, 1990). Summary results from a sample of Delphi studies in the leisure, sport and tourism areas are presented in Box 11.3.

In some cases a 'quasi-Delphi' method is employed in forecasting, involving informal consultation with experts, but not involving the scaling of responses and rounds of consultation discussed above. An example is the World Tourism Organization Business Council (1999) international study of *Changes in Leisure Time: The Impact on Tourism*.

Scenario writing

Scenario writing is a technique that involves the devising of alternative pictures of the future, as characterized by alternative values of key variables and the relationships between them. The initial task in drawing up scenarios is to decide the key variables to be used to characterize the future. For example, a simple approach for an exercise at national level might select politics and the level of unemployment as two key variables. Alternative political scenarios for a country for the year 2020 might envisage either a right-wing conservative government or a left/centrist social democratic government. And there could be high unemployment or low unemployment. These two dimensions offer four alternative 'scenarios', as indicated in Fig. 11.7.

Box 11.3. Delphi studies in leisure, sport and tourism.

Future leisure environments: Shafer _et al_. (1975)

One of the earliest uses of the technique in the leisure area was by Shafer _et al_. (1975), who asked a panel of 400 American recreation professionals and academics to indicate the most significant future events likely to take place in the area of outdoor recreation. Among those predicted were:

- by 1985: most people work a four-day, thirty-two-hour week;
- by 1990: US Census of population includes questions on recreation; most homes have video-tape systems;
- by 2000: small recreational submarines common; average age of retirement 50 years;
- 2050+: first park established on the moon; average worker has three months annual vacation.

Clearly the experts do not always get it right! However, much of the value of the technique could be said to lie in its ability to open up debate and promote thought, rather than in the precise accuracy of its predictions.

Environmental impacts: Green, H. _et al_. (1990)

Green and colleagues used the Delphi technique to elicit the views of planners and other professionals on the likely environmental impact of a proposed development of an industrial heritage site for tourism in the north of England. This study can arguably be more appropriately viewed as an example of the use of the technique in stakeholder consultation, as discussed in Chapter 9, than as an example of forecasting as such, but is included here because of the methodological critique offered by Wheeler _et al_. (1990), who noted two problems with the study. First, there was a significant drop-out of panel members, from 40 to 21, between the first and second rounds: this is quite common. But it is pointed out that the final results are biased by the unevenness of the drop-out among the different groups: planners and economic and tourism development officers stayed the course, while residents and traders dropped out. Secondly, it is argued that the literature search appeared to offer a better overview of expert opinion than the Delphi survey, thus raising doubts about the value of Delphi in such a situation, particularly in light of the first methodological problem.

International Expo visits: Lee _et al_. (2008)

Lee and colleagues used three forecasting techniques to predict the number of visits to an International Marine Expo to be held in South Korea in 2012. A quantitative forecast was based on 'willingness-to visit' surveys of Korean residents and international visitors (which is a version of the 'asking the public' method), together with a trend analysis ARIMA model (discussed in this chapter) of total tourist numbers, and a qualitatively based forecast used the Delphi technique. The latter involved 29 experts chosen from tourism academics, the Korean National Tourism Organization, the tourism research institute and event managers. The numbers of Expo visitors predicted from the two methods were: quantitative forecast, 8.9 million; Delphi forecast, 6.8 million. The numbers are subject to margins of error but are remarkably close, given that the difference in cost and complexity of the two approaches: the quantitative model involved a survey of 2500 residents and 500 international tourists, while the Delphi method involved two rounds of questionnaire survey of 29 experts.

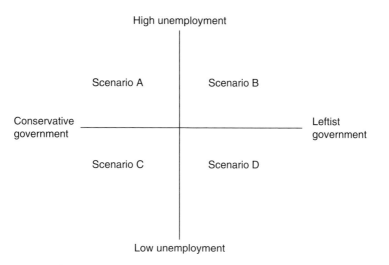

Fig. 11.7. Scenarios for the year 2020: two-dimensional illustration.

Scenario A, with high unemployment and a conservative government, could be characterized by low public sector spending and minimal unemployment benefits, whereas Scenario B, with a leftist government, might be characterized by higher government spending and more generous unemployment allowances, but possibly more economic crises as government attempted to solve the unemployment problem by spending money. Scenario C would be characterized by a prosperous private enterprise culture, with low taxes and low government spending, whereas Scenario D would probably involve a more substantial role for public enterprise, with higher taxes and government spending.

Once the general social and economic implications of the scenarios had been worked out, any more detailed forecasting of leisure or tourism demand would now be undertaken in the context of the scenarios, so that four sets of alternative forecasts would be produced instead of one. The commissioning agency would then be aware of the range of possible demand scenarios, depending on future political and unemployment outcomes. The detailed forecasts might use any of the other techniques discussed here.

The development of scenarios need not be restricted to two variables and two dimensions. For example, a third variable could be introduced into the above example: growth in leisure time might be proposed as zero, moderate or substantial. The resultant 12 scenarios would then be as shown in Fig. 11.8. It would become unmanageable to produce 12 sets of forecasts, so in practice just a selection of scenarios would be chosen for more detailed study, representing the widest range of possibilities and/or those considered to be most likely. Thus, for example, in Fig. 11.8, only the scenarios in bold might be selected for detailed study. In the case of inbound international tourism it would, of course, be necessary to develop either international scenarios or a series of scenarios for the markets from which tourists were generated.

An early example of the use of scenarios with leisure implications was produced by Miles *et al.* (1978) in their *World Futures* study. Later, Martin and Mason (1998: 89) developed forecasts on leisure in the UK using four scenarios based on the dimensions of economic growth (high/low) and social attitudes (conventional/transformed). They selected two scenarios for detailed work: 'conventional success', which involves continuing current trends, and 'transformed growth', a less materialistic and more sustainable course.

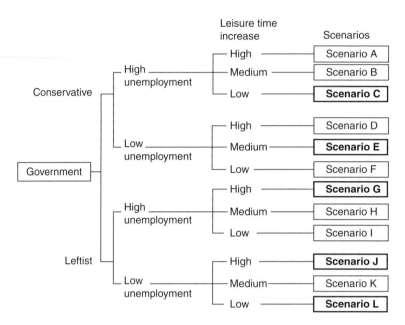

Fig. 11.8. Scenarios for the year 2020: three-dimensional illustration.

Time series analysis

Time series analysis is the most commonly used technique in tourism forecasting. It is a quantitative technique in which the future is predicted on the basis of trends in the phenomenon being studied. A prerequisite of the technique is the availability of data extending over a substantial time period. It is therefore most well developed in the area of international tourism, because information on tourist arrivals and departures is available extending back over many years. This cannot be said of many other forms of leisure activity.

Time series analysis has become very sophisticated, involving complex mathematical formulae and specialist computer software. The Resources section indicates sources for such techniques but, in the discussion here, quite simple approaches are presented to illustrate the underlying principles. The more sophisticated methods are appropriate when good data are available and the processes driving changes in demand are well understood; if these conditions are not met then some of the simpler methods might just as well be used to provide 'ball park' forecasts.

At its simplest the technique can be seen as the visual extension of a trend line, as shown in Fig. 11.9. The diagram uses data on net gambling expenditure in Australia, for which there is an annual data series extending back 25 years, expressed in 2006 prices: the 'actual' figures in the diagram. Two simple methods are used to extent the trend to 2020. The 'moving average' line is based on taking the average of the previous four years, so almost immediately levels off because there was virtually no change in the period 2003–2006. The 'long-term trend' line is created by applying the annual average 1981–2006 growth rate of about 5% from 2007 onwards and it can be seen that, at this rate, expenditure would double again by 2020.

In the case of tourism it has been found that the best predictor of tourist numbers, over the short term, is the last available figure, so that the forecast of tourist arrivals in year X is based on an equation involving the number of arrivals in year $X − 1$. It is possible to build equations

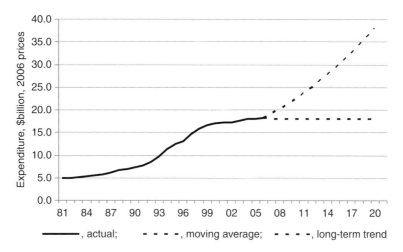

Fig. 11.9. Simple trend analysis: gambling expenditure in Australia (in Au$). Source: Queensland Treasury (2008).

that simulate such cycles, by taking account not just of the previous year's figure, but, say, the previous ten years' figures. Sophisticated modelling techniques, such as the ARIMA (Auto-Regressive Integrated Moving Average) technique, have been developed to capture these trends, in both annual and more frequent time series, such as quarterly and monthly arrivals, and to produce forecasts based on them. These techniques are described by Athiyaman and Robertson (1992), Witt and Witt (1992), Archer (1994) and Frechtling (1996) and computer packages are available, for example within SPSS, to carry them out.

An alternative time series approach is to explore the possibility that the past trend in demand is related to some underlying factor, such as trends in real incomes, prices or exchange rates. Such a 'model' is referred to as 'structural', because it reflects an understanding of the underlying structure of relationships between the phenomenon and causal factors. For example, the hypothetical data in Fig. 11.10 show a demand trend following the trend in real incomes, but lagged by a couple of years. An equation is developed with income as the independent variable and leisure or tourism demand as the dependent variable, and forecasts of demand are based on forecasts of real income. The technique therefore requires access to time series data and forecasts for the independent variable. In fact, such a structural model need not be restricted to a single independent variable. Crouch and Shaw (1991), for example, review a wide range of international tourism forecasting studies, involving as many as 25 different structural variables.

Spatial analysis

The idea of spatial models of leisure demand is explored as a planning technique in Chapter 10 and in the Clawson technique of cost–benefit analysis outlined in Chapter 12. These techniques rely on the observation that, where specific facilities or attractions are involved, patterns of leisure or tourism demand are influenced by the locations of those facilities or attractions in relation to where people live and to transport routes. These patterns are not random but are often sufficiently systematic to provide the basis for prediction. It has been observed in a wide range of facilities and attractions that the further people live from the facility or attraction, the less likely they are to visit it, as illustrated in Fig. 10.9 in Chapter 10.

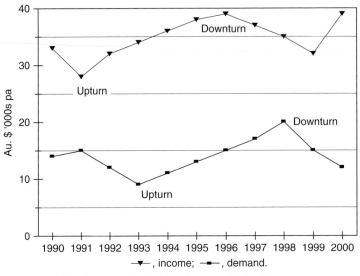

Demand line changes direction 1 or 2 years after the income line changes

Fig. 11.10. Structural trend line.

Visitation falls off with increased distance, either because of the additional cost and effort in travelling or because of leisure time availability compared with the time needed to undertake the visit and associated travel.

This principle and its use for prediction is illustrated in Box 10.4 in Chapter 10. The data depicted in Figs 10.10–10.12 are used to predict the effect of the hypothetical facility shown in Fig 10.13. But they could also be used to predict the effect on participation of:

- changes in the population distribution within the catchment area;
- changes in transport infrastructure (for example new roads that make travel to the site cheaper and/or faster);
- provision of additional facilities in the study area.

As indicated in Chapter 10, this lends itself to quantitative modelling, which is discussed in Box 11.4.

Cross-sectional analysis

The cross-sectional technique is based on analysis of the variation in leisure participation within – or across – the community, and is used particularly when time series data are not available. Cross-sectional analysis can be based on a single survey at a point in time. Participation in most leisure activities is known to vary according to certain factors, such as age, occupation, level of education and income. As the structure of the population changes with regard to these underlying factors or variables (for example, the ageing of the population or increasing levels of education and professionalization) so, it might be expected, will leisure participation. The method therefore relies on forecasts of the underlying factors/variables being available from other sources. Such sources include: (i) government agencies, which produce, for example,

Box 11.4. Spatial modelling of demand and supply.

The spatial patterns illustrated on Figs 10.8–10.13 are based on the relationship between visit rates (visits per 1000 population per week) from residential zones or areas to a facility and the distances between the facility and the residential areas. Typically, it is found that the visit rate declines with distance. This relationship is observed widely in natural and human situations, most famously in the case of gravitational force between two bodies in space. Hence, models that seek to simulate the relationship between leisure facilities and population centres have sometimes been referred to as 'gravity models', with the 'force' between the two bodies being the flow of visits and the respective 'masses' being the size and attractiveness of the leisure facility and the size of the population of the residential area. A simple model for one facility and residential area and i would be depicted as:

$$V/P = a + bD^c \qquad (1)$$

where: V = no. of visits per week from population centre;
P = population of the residential area in 1000s; therefore visit rate = V/P;
D = distance from facility to population centre;
a, b and c are *parameters* that would be found from empirical research.

Multiplying both sides of equation (1) by P provides the formula for the number of visits:

$$V = P(a + bD^c) \qquad (2)$$

The facility attracts visits from a number of residential areas, say 1 – n, so the total of visits to the facility is the total visits, V_t, from all residential areas:

$$V_t = \Sigma\, P_i(a + bD_i^c) \text{ for } i = 1 \text{ to } n \qquad \text{(where } \Sigma \text{ means 'the sum of'.)} \qquad (3)$$

For the park data in Fig. 10.9, if c is set at 2, regression analysis produces values for a of +23.0 and b of –0.04, giving a version of equation (2) as follows:

$$V = P(23.0 - 0.04D^2) \qquad (4)$$

This model could be used to estimate the level of visits to the facility as the populations of the residential areas change in future. The model could be extended in a number of ways, including:

- replacing distance with travel time or travel cost, as discussed in relation to the Clawson method in Chapter 12;
- extending the model to cover many facilities in the planning area, in which case there would be an equation for each of the facilities in the system;
- an additional variable could be included to indicate the intrinsic attractiveness of each facility, made up of such measures as area and facilities available;
- breaking down the visits and population figures into socio-demographic groups, for example, age groups.

(Continued)

> **Box 11.4.** Continued.
>
> These developments are beyond the scope of this book, but examples can be found in the research literature. Early pioneering examples of the approach include Coppock and Duffield (1975) in relation to countryside recreation in Scotland, and Milstein and Reid (1966) in relation to outdoor recreation in the USA. More recent work in relation to outdoor recreation appears in Hanley *et al.* (2003).

demographic forecasts and short-term economic forecasts; (ii) academic and independent research organizations; and, possibly, (iii) Delphi and scenario-drawing exercises.

Two approaches can be used in cross-sectional analysis: the 'cohort' method; and regression-based techniques. These are discussed in turn below.

Cohort method

The cohort method can best be demonstrated by an example, as shown in Table 11.3. The table gives data from a hypothetical community:

- Column A provides data from a survey showing that activity X is participated in primarily by young people.
- Column B shows the age cohorts of the current population.
- Column C shows the effect of applying the survey participation rates to the age cohorts, giving an estimate of the current total numbers of participants in the community by age group.
- Column D shows the projected population for the age cohorts for the year 2020, showing a fall in population numbers for the young, active age groups and an increase in the older, less active age groups.

Table 11.3. Cohort method example.

	Current year				Prediction: year 2020		
	Participation rate (%)[a]	Population	%	Estimated partici-pants (n)	Population[c]	%	Predicted partici-pants (n)
Age group	A Survey[b]	B Census	%	C (A × B)/100	D	%	E (A × D)/100
14–19	14.9	15,600	19.5	2,324	12,000	14.9	1,788
20–24	11.5	15,200	19.0	1,748	12,100	15.0	1,392
25–29	7.4	11,360	14.2	841	10,000	12.4	740
30–39	5.2	16,880	21.1	878	17,100	21.2	889
40–49	4.8	7,200	9.0	346	10,300	12.8	494
50–59	3.5	6,160	7.7	216	9,200	11.4	322
60+	2.5	7,600	9.5	190	9,800	12.2	245
Total	8.2	80,000	100.0	6,543	80,500	100.0	5,870

[a]Weekly, but in tourism more likely to be per year.
[b]Can be a local survey or regional/national data.
[c]Planning Department.

- Column E applies the same participation rates to the population forecasts to give an estimate of future participation numbers, which show an overall fall in numbers of participants in activity X, even though there is a slight increase in the total population.

If the activity had been one with high participation among older age groups, the analysis would of course have shown an increase in number of participants. Thus the predicted participation level depends on the *cross-sectional* pattern of participation and the predicted pattern of cross-sectional change in the underlying variable, in this case age.

One weakness of the approach is that the basic cohort-specific participation rates (column A) are not assumed to change, but this is not in fact intrinsic to the method. If different participation rates can be established using other methodologies, for example time series analysis, then such rates could be used for the prediction.

Underlying, or 'predictor' variables in addition to age could be used – for example, occupation or incomes. However, predictions of such variables are less readily available than for age, particularly for local communities. The technique could be used in combination with the scenario method, where hypothetical projections of the underlying variables could be used. For example, the impact of alternative income growth and distribution scenarios on participation could be explored.

Ideally, more than one underlying variable should be examined. For example, it might be predicted that, not only will there be more older people in a community, but that they will be relatively better off financially, because of improved superannuation provisions. Age-income cohorts would therefore reflect these changes. However, while current participation rates for such cohorts may be readily obtained from surveys, forecasts would be difficult to obtain, although, as discussed above, hypothetical predictions could be utilized for scenario purposes. But clearly, as the number of variables increases the number of separate cohorts increases, making the method unwieldy.

When used in tourism demand forecasting, the cohort method needs to consider the tourist origin communities, including countries, rather than the host community. This becomes difficult if the number of origin communities is high. But in many cases the bulk of tourist visits comes from just a handful of sources, so the task is manageable. Another difference is that age structure is not the most obvious variable to start with, unless the interest is in particular age-related market sectors, such as backpackers or retirement travellers. Typically, the more relevant variable is personal incomes. In general, however, tourism forecasters favour regression-based techniques, as discussed below.

Regression-based techniques

Regression-based techniques can cope more readily with a number of underlying variables, because the activity forecasts are based on predictions of mean values of variables rather on the size of multi-variable cohorts. Furthermore, the technique is not limited to the personal characteristics of the population: variables such as travel costs can be more easily incorporated. The technique involves two steps:

1. A *regression equation* is established using the available cross-sectional data, in which the *dependent* variable is a measure of leisure or tourism demand and the *independent* variables are the factors influencing demand, such as age or income.
2. The equation, together with forecasts of the independent variables obtained from elsewhere, is used to provide a forecast of demand.

In the typical regression-based model the unit of analysis is the individual, using data from surveys. The regression equation is of the form:

$$P = a + bVAR1 + cVAR2 + dVAR3 + \text{etc.} \tag{1}$$

where P = participation, VAR1, VAR2, etc. are independent, influencing, variables and a, b, c, etc. are coefficients determined by the regression analysis. The participation variable for each individual may be:

- a 'yes–no' variable, with the individual scoring one if he or she has participated in the activity and zero if not;
- the frequency of participation in a given time period, with zero for those who have not participated at all; or
- the level of expenditure on the activity – often used in the case of tourism.

A wide range of independent variables may be used, although the more variables used the more complex the technical statistical considerations become, and the more variables must be predicted eventually to obtain forecasts. Examples of regression-based studies using US and Australian data are shown on the book's website (http://www.leisuresource.net).

Comparative method

Joffre Dumazedier (1974: 187–205) argued that a given society might consider alternative futures for itself by examining the experiences of more economically advanced societies. In particular, societies approaching the 'post-industrial' phase of development could examine the impact of post-industrialism and ways of coping with it, as experienced by the most economically and technologically advanced countries, particularly the USA. Such an approach to considering the future has certain similarities to scenario writing, with the scenarios being provided by the experiences of existing countries rather than having to be devised hypothetically. The approach was not developed in detail by Dumazedier, and such factors as cultural and climatic conditions would seem to raise considerable problems in its application, but the approach is used informally by forecasters, and may offer potential for developing countries wishing to consider alternative models of development.

Dumazedier proposed the comparative method in an international context, but its most acclaimed application was intranational in *Megatrends*, by the American researcher John Naisbitt (Naisbitt, 1982; Naisbitt and Aburdene, 1990). Naisbitt's technique involved examination of social trends in different parts of the USA, via content analysis of local media. Certain states were identified as 'bellwether' states, which set the pace for social change, which other states then followed. While Naisbitt's 'megatrends' for the 1980s virtually ignored leisure, his 1990s version included 'Renaissance in the Arts' as one of ten 'megatrends', prompting the following assertion: 'In the final years before the millennium there will be a fundamental and revolutionary shift in leisure time and spending priorities. During the 1990s the arts will gradually replace sport as society's primary leisure activity' (Naisbitt and Aburdene, 1990: 53). The basis of the claim that sport was currently society's 'primary leisure activity' is not clear, but, with the passing of the millennium, it would seem safe to say that this particular prediction has not been realized.

Composite approaches

Many leisure forecasters tend, in practice, to utilize a combination of techniques rather than rely on any one. One method can be used to complement or to overcome the weaknesses of another. Thus the mechanical nature of some of the more quantitative techniques can be modified by results of Delphi exercises, and the broad-brush results of national forecasts can be combined with spatial analysis for application at local level. Martin and Mason (1998) used a combination of time series, cross-sectional and scenario-writing techniques in their forecasting of UK leisure patterns, and in his studies of recreation trends in the USA John Kelly utilized cross-sectional 'cohort' methods, time series analysis and consideration of trends in lifestyles and 'leisure styles' (Kelly and Warnick, 1999).

SUMMARY

This chapter examines the forecasting of leisure, sport and tourism demand, which is seen as one of the key inputs to the planning process. Forecasting has its origins in the early development of leisure and tourism research in the 1960s. While interest in tourism demand forecasts has been consistent, static populations in some countries and levelling off of some demand factors have resulted in fluctuating levels of interest in leisure forecasts in recent years.

Demand for leisure and tourism can be measured in a number of ways, including participation rates, trip volume and expenditure.

Changes in demand for leisure and tourism are affected by many factors, all of which are not equally susceptible to prediction. Among the *change factors* reviewed in this chapter are: (i) demographic change; (ii) income levels; (iii) the activities of producers; (iv) leisure and work time; (v) transport; (vi) technological change; (vii) the environment; (viii) tastes and lifestyles; (ix) attitudes and values; (x) the media; and (xi) post-industrialism, postmodernism and globalization.

A range of forecasting techniques is reviewed in the chapter, namely: (i) informed speculation; (ii) asking the public; (iii) asking the experts (the Delphi technique); (iv) scenario writing; (v) time series analysis; (vi) spatial models; (vii) cross-sectional analysis; (viii) comparative analysis; and (ix) composite methods. In tourism forecasting the time series method has been most common, because of the ready availability of time series data. In leisure/sport forecasting, cross-sectional methods have been the most common but are now being replaced by composite methods, which draw on a number of techniques and data sources.

RESOURCES

Websites

Richard K. Miller and Associates produce annual reports on trends in: sport, travels and tourism and leisure: http://www.rkma.com

The Sport Industry Research Centre at Sheffield Hallam University (UK) produces two annual publications, *Leisure Forecasts* and *Sport Market Forecasts*: http://www.shu.ac.uk/research/sirc/

(Australian) Tourism Forecasting Committee: http://www.tourism.australia.com/Research.asp?sub=0408&al=979

World Tourism Organization climate solutions website: http://www.climatesolutions.travel/Pages/default.aspx

Publications

Forecasting techniques: Makridakia *et al.* (1998).

History of leisure demand forecasting: Coppock and Duffield (1975); Settle (1977); Brown and Hutson (1979); Veal (1999: 146–154).

Leisure demand forecasting techniques: Brown and Hutson (1979); Gratton and Taylor (1988: 99–114); Field and MacGregor (1987); Veal (1987); Zalatan (1994).

Leisure futures and trends: Godbey (1997); Martin and Mason (1998); Kelly and Warnick (1999); Lynch and Veal (2006: Ch. 14).

The idea of of a 'leisure society': Veal (2009a).

Climate change: McEvoy *et al.* (2006); Scott and Jones (2006); Becken and Hay (2007); McBoyle *et al.* (2007); WTO (2008).

Changing tastes/lifestyles: Tomlinson (1990); Featherstone (1991).

Tourism forecasting techniques: Witt and Witt (1992); Var and Lee (1993); Archer (1994); Lundberg *et al.* (1995: 149–165); Smith (1995: 116 ff); Frechtling (1996).

Technological forecasting: Rhodes (1999); Halal (2000); PriceWaterhouseCoopers (2001).

Time-pressure: Zuzanek and Veal (1999).

Informed speculation: Asimov (1976); Kelly and Godbey (1992: 479–512).

Asking the people: Coppock and Duffield (1975: 84).

Asking the experts: Delphi: Chai (1977); Linstone (1978); Moeller and Shafer (1983, 1994); Ng *et al.* (1983); Kaynak and Macaulay (1984); Green, H. *et al.* (1990); Jones, S. (1990); Donohoe and Needham (2009).

Time series analysis: Hill (1978); Stynes (1983); Athiyaman and Robertson (1992).

Scenarios: Miles *et al.* (1978); Henry (1988); Martin and Mason (1998).

Spatial techniques: Coppock and Duffield (1975); Ewing (1983); Smith (1995).

Cross-sectional technique: Young and Willmott (1973); Coppock and Duffield (1975); Veal (1980).

Econometric methods: Ewing (1983); Hanley *et al.* (2003).

Comparative method: Dumazedier (1974); Naisbitt (1982).

Composite techniques: Martin and Mason (1998); Kelly and Warnick (1999).

QUESTIONS/EXERCISES

1. Of the various demand change factors discussed, which are most likely to affect the following over the next 10 years: (i) domestic tourism demand in a coastal resort; (ii) international tourism demand in a large capital city; (iii) demand for youth sport facilities; (iv) demand for the performing arts; (v) demand for countryside recreation close to a large city.

2. What is the difference between time series and cross-sectional forecasting methods?

3. What are the respective advantages and disadvantages of quantitative and qualitative forecasting methods?

4. Using library or Internet sources, locate a time series leisure or tourism demand data set in an area of interest and produce a simple trend forecast.

5. Conduct a Delphi exercise on a topic of your choice among the class members with whom you are studying.

6. Replicate the exercise in Table 11.3 for a local area, region or country for which population forecasts are available.

NOTES

[1] The trends for other Western countries are similar. For example, a similar diagram for Australia can be found in Lynch and Veal (2006: 387).

PART IV

Evaluation

This section contains two chapters concerned with evaluation of outcomes of the planning and development process:

- Chapter 12, *Economic Evaluation*, provides outlines of two economics-based evaluation processes; cost–benefit analysis and economic impact analysis.
- Chapter 13, *Performance Evaluation*, considers mainly non-economic evaluation processes, providing a link between the policy-making/planning process and management of facilities and services.

Economic Evaluation

INTRODUCTION

In this chapter two forms of economic evaluation are considered: cost–benefit analysis and economic impact analysis.

- Cost–benefit analysis seeks to replicate for public sector investment projects or services the sort of financial evaluation usually undertaken in the private sector. But in addition to the financial outlays and incomes that are taken into account in evaluating a private sector investment, the public enterprise must consider the many additional, non-market, costs and benefits of the sort discussed in Chapter 5.
- Economic impact analysis relates particularly to the 'economic management/development criterion for government activity (see Chapter 5); governments at all levels feel justified in becoming involved with various projects if they will create jobs and incomes – economic impact analysis seeks to quantify the impact of a project on the host community, in terms of jobs and incomes.

Both techniques are concerned with the public sector but they assume the acceptability of the predominantly capitalist market framework for analysis – that is, that the state exists alongside the market, the market process is considered to be a broadly acceptable way of ordering economic affairs, that wages and prices are determined in the market sector and are considered to be valid measures of economic costs and values. For those who believe that the market system is fundamentally flawed or, for instance, that the distribution of after-tax incomes and welfare payments is fundamentally unjust, the techniques are largely irrelevant. However, for those who believe that the market system is flawed but capable of being reformed, the techniques can be useful tools, because they use market-based thinking and analysis to justify non-market government activity, and so can be used to achieve shifts in resources away from the market in favour of the public sector – a move which many reformists would see as beneficial.

Both techniques can be used to evaluate projects in advance, as part of a feasibility study designed to consider whether a project should go ahead, or when a project is up and running, or has been completed, to examine whether it has fulfilled its promised potential and/or to provide guidance when considering decisions on similar projects in future.

It should be noted that, whereas economic analysis is very often scorned or viewed suspiciously by enthusiasts for such areas as the arts, heritage, the environment or sport, because they feel that their area of interest is thereby threatened, it is usually the case that analyses are carried out by economists who are also enthusiasts for that particular area. Economists who specialize in studies of the arts, sport or the environment are often personally committed to the field. And more often than not the analysis demonstrates that the benefits or impacts from the leisure phenomenon being studied are currently being grossly undervalued by decision-makers. It is rare for a cost–benefit or economic impact study of a public leisure project to find that a project is poor value for the community. Such economic analyses have invariably been *supportive* of public enterprise rather than a threat to it.

It cannot be stressed too much that the techniques described here are *inputs* to decision-making processes rather than complete decision-making procedures in their own right. Apart from the innate limitations of the procedures, as outlined in the discussions below, it should be borne in mind that any public sector leisure or tourism project exists in the context of other calls on public sector resources, including such areas as health, education, transport and defence. While some economic decision-making procedures enable a degree of comparison to be made between projects in different sectors, in the end decisions will be influenced by political and moral values, with economic factors playing, possibly, only a minor role.

COST–BENEFIT ANALYSIS

Introduction

Cost–benefit analysis is a technique designed to estimate and compare *all* the costs and *all* the benefits of a project in money terms. This sounds straightforward enough, but is far from it. Actual financial outlays and incomes can generally be estimated fairly readily, but in the case of public sector projects other factors need to be taken into consideration. Many public services are free to the user – for example, a public park, beach or library. So how can the value of such usage – the benefits – be quantified and compared with the cost of provision? Conversely, a project may have negative impacts – such as noise from a city-based Grand Prix motor race or loss of an informal play space to development. How are such negative impacts – costs – to be quantified?

Cost–benefit analysis has had a chequered career in leisure research. In the early days of leisure research, it was a key feature of the quantification and modelling school of research, exemplified by the work of Clawson and Knetsch (1962) and Lieber and Fesenmaier (1983) in the USA and Coppock and Duffield (1975) in the UK. Subsequently, in the late 1970s and early 1980s, it fell out of favour, along with quantification generally. But in later years there has been increasing interest in the technique as economic policy based on neo-liberal principles sought to cut back the size of the public sector, and it became necessary to account for public investment in economic terms. Thus cost–benefit analysis has been used to evaluate, for example, sporting and cultural events and environmental and heritage projects. There are, however, also objections to the use of the technique.

There are those who object to the use of economic criteria in certain areas, on the grounds that the value of certain things is 'beyond measure', 'intangible' or 'priceless'. In fact the public does put a value on 'priceless' things when, for example, money is raised by public appeal to buy a major painting for the public collection, to prevent it being sold overseas. Occasionally the required amount of money is *not* raised for such purchases, implying that the price asked for the 'priceless' painting is too high and that there is a limit to the price people are prepared to pay for such a 'priceless' item. At a more mundane level, when local councils decide on the specific level of grant to give to the local repertory theatre or on the budget for the municipal museum, they are indicating some sort of monetary valuation of those services to the community. Private individuals also make decisions on what to spend on 'intangible' things such as the enjoyment of a Beethoven symphony, when they decide whether or not to pay the required price for a recording or to attend a concert. It could be argued that, in such circumstances, the community or the individual is not *placing a value* on the intangible item but simply indicating what they can afford. The argument then becomes semantic: the economist's definition of *value* is what someone, or some organization, will pay for something.

This is somewhat different to, for example, the 'value' an individual might place on a personal relationship or the 'value' of a human life. These two senses of value are, however, not entirely distinct. For example, massive savings of lives could be made if all country roads were lit, but the cost would be huge. No community is prepared to spend such sums, indicating a sort of limit to the value of (saving) human life. Therefore the meaning of the term value, as used in the discussions below, is: the amount the community, or individual, is willing or able to pay (see Peterson and Loomis (2000) for an extended discussion of the concept of value).

Cost–benefit analyses can be used in three different situations: (i) study of a single proposed project; (ii) comparison between alternative proposed projects; and (iii) evaluation of an existing project or projects. There is a great deal of literature giving examples of applications of type (iii) cost–benefit analysis to leisure, sport and tourism, especially to outdoor recreation/tourism (see Resources section), but relatively few of the other two types. This is in contrast to other fields, notably transport, where the technique *is* actively used in this way. New roads produce savings in terms of travel time savings and reductions in accidents (the costs of which can be measured). These savings can be compared with the costs of construction and maintenance of the road, and various road development proposals can then be ranked in order of the levels of net benefits they are expected to produce. Many highway authorities in the Western world adopt this approach, but there is no comparable use of the techniques in the leisure area. While cost–benefit analysis is sometimes used for investment appraisal where leisure is an adjunct to an economic product, such as in recreational use of reservoirs or forests, generally the examples of its use in leisure are *post hoc*.

Measurables and unmeasurables

Defenders of cost–benefit analysis accept that there are limitations to the technique, pointing out that in practice there are often costs and benefits which, for various reasons, *cannot* be measured. The technique seeks to put money values on those things that *can* be measured, so that decision-making of a more qualitative kind can concentrate on those elements which cannot be valued in money terms. The process can thus be an aid to clarifying decision-making procedures by distinguishing between those aspects of a project that can be quantified and valued in money terms and those that cannot. Four types of cost and benefit are therefore involved in any project, as shown in Table 12.1.

Cost–benefit analysis involves *identifying* and listing all costs and benefits, but it concentrates on *quantifying* the measurable aspects, A and C, only. Decision-makers must then concentrate on whether the measurable net costs (A–C) or net benefits (C–A) outweigh the non-measurables, B and D.

Table 12.1. Measurable/non-measurable costs and benefits.

	Costs	Benefits
Measurable	A	C
Non-measurable	B	D

The cost–benefit approach

Cost–benefit analysis seeks to replicate private sector investment appraisal methods in the public sector, so we should briefly consider the latter. In the private sector the main criterion generally used to determine whether an operation or project is viable – that is, profitable – is whether it can generate sufficient income to pay its costs and provide an acceptable return on the capital employed. In the planning phase the projected income and expenditure streams must be estimated and, if they do not result in an acceptable surplus, then the facility or service will not be provided. If an acceptable surplus is envisaged and the project is proceeded with, the projected figures may or may not turn out to be correct. If they are wrong in an unfavourable way (costs higher than expected or income lower than expected, or both) then, sooner or later, the facility or service will be closed or will be sold at a loss to another owner who may be able to run it at a profit because of reduced capital costs.[1]

The investment market in the private sector is competitive, so that entrepreneurs only put their money into projects they think will produce profits that are expected to be at least equal to the 'going rate of return' on capital invested. The precise level of this rate of return will vary depending on current bank lending rates and the degree of risk associated with the project, and must be higher than the rate of interest investors would obtain by placing their money in very low-risk investments – for example, depositing their money in a bank or in government bonds. The combination of perceived risk and expected level of return must be acceptable to the investment market. Generally, leisure and tourism projects are seen as *high*-risk areas (compared with, say, retailing or food manufacture), so the rate of return demanded is comparatively high.

In the public sector different criteria apply – generally facilities or services do not produce a financial surplus. With few exceptions, there is generally a subsidy to the users of the service. This makes sense in terms of the various non-market social benefits which public services are believed to provide, as discussed in Chapter 5. If a public service can be run profitably, *and still achieve the objectives of the public agency concerned*, then it might be expected that a private sector operator could and would run it. There are very few truly financially profitable public sector operations that cover all their operating costs *and* provide a return on *realistically valued* capital resources. The question then arises as to how to decide which proposed projects in the public sector are worthwhile. How can alternative projects be compared and the best selected? How can we ensure that the money spent in one area of public expenditure, say roads, is as effective in producing benefits as money spent in another sector, such as parks? If less benefits are being obtained per pound or dollar spent in one area then, as in the market situation, it would seem sensible to transfer resources into other areas that can produce benefits until some sort of balance is achieved. Indeed, it should also be possible to demonstrate that money spent in the public sector is producing benefits at least as great as would be obtained from returning the subsidy moneys to taxpayers' pockets and allowing them to spend the money themselves in the marketplace.

In the private sector, a firm assesses a project's viability in terms of *expenditure versus income*. In the public sector, the corresponding terms are *costs versus benefits*.

In the private sector income must exceed expenditure by the required amount for the project to be viable; in the public sector benefits must exceed costs by the required amount. The two systems are compared for a hypothetical £10 million project in Table 12.2.[2] In the public sector project, the capital is assumed to be entirely borrowed money, so there are interest and repayment charges (capital charges). In the private sector case it is assumed that half the capital is provided by a bank loan and half by the risk-taking investors.[3]

Table 12.2. Private sector versus public sector project evaluation.

Private sector	£'000	Public sector	£'000
Capital cost		**Capital cost**	
(a) Investor	5,000	(a) Public agency funds	5,000
(b) Bank loan	5,000	(b) Borrowings[a]	5,000
(c) Total capital (a + b)	10,000	(c) Total capital (a + b)	10,000
Annual expenditure		**Annual costs**	
(d) Bank interest (10% of b)	500	(d) Capital charges (8% of b)	400
(e) Running costs	3,500	(e) Running costs	3,500
(f) Total (d + e)	4,000	(f) Total costs (d + e)	3,900
Annual income		**Annual income**	
(g) Sales	5,000	(g) Fees and charges	1,500
Annual profit		**Annual deficit/subsidy**	
(h) Profits (g − f)	1,000	(h) Net cost/loss (g − f)	−2,400
(i) % Return on investors' capital (100 × h/a)	20.0	(i) Net social benefits	?

[a] May be from a bank or bonds.

In the private sector case the investor would assess the anticipated 20% return in the light of the level of risk involved and decide whether to invest. In the public sector case, the income is less, resulting in a cash deficit of £2.4 million. For the project to go ahead, the net social benefits (social benefits minus social costs) must be deemed to be at least worth this amount. The task of cost–benefit analysis is to identify and quantify as many of the social benefits as possible and to assess whether they are worth the £2.4 million each year. Quantification involves expressing them in the same terms as the tangible costs and benefits, namely in money terms. This process is described in the next four sections, which deal with: (i) identifying and measuring costs; (ii) identifying and measuring benefits in general; (iii) comparing the costs and benefits; and (iv) measuring private benefits.

Identifying and measuring costs

The question of identifying and measuring costs would seem to be straightforward and, indeed, it is more straightforward than measuring benefits. In fact, many studies in the literature involve only benefit measurement because the measurement of costs is seen as unproblematical or because, when comparative studies are being conducted, the costs of two or more projects may be similar and the study is then concerned only with identifying which project produces the most benefits. Costs can be of four types:

- capital costs;
- running costs;
- externalities as costs;
- opportunity costs.

These are discussed in turn below. Although, as mentioned above, the analysis can be undertaken to evaluate a project when it is up and running, the discussion is couched in terms appropriate for assessing a proposed new project.

Capital costs

Capital costs are those costs necessary for purchase, construction and equipping a project and generally getting it started – the investment. These costs can be measured in two ways: as a lump sum or as an annual cost. The lump sum is easy enough to understand: if a project costs a million pounds to start up then that is its capital cost. But if, to set up the project, a million pounds is borrowed at an interest rate of 10% per annum, the annual cost will be £100,000 in interest payments. Since it will also be necessary to pay back the million pounds over, say, 20 years – a mortgage – then the annual costs will be somewhat more than £100,000 a year. In conducting the cost–benefit analysis, it is this total annual capital charge that is generally used.

The capital charge may be partially offset by the increasing value of the asset, but more commonly an asset falls in value over time and therefore an annual *depreciation* charge must be included. Until recently this was ignored in public sector accounting, but it is now commonly included.

Running costs

Running costs are a relatively simple concept. The costs of staffing, materials, heating, lighting, transport and so on are easily envisaged and often quite easy to estimate.

Externalities as costs

While there is much theory on negative externalities – costs borne by a third party not directly involved in the project, as discussed in Chapter 5 – there are few empirical data. This is largely because most public projects are aimed primarily at producing benefits, so externalities of a negative type are generally seen as insignificant or ignored. A study of the Adelaide Grand Prix is a rare example of research on such negative externalities as traffic congestion (Dunstan, 1986), noise and property damage (McKay, 1986) and accident costs (Fischer *et al.*, 1986), as shown in Box 12.1. Three specific examples of negative externalities are discussed in turn below; they are: traffic congestion, noise and accidents.

Traffic congestion is an inevitable consequence of some leisure phenomena, such as special events or tourism. A new project can increase traffic congestion in its vicinity. This imposes costs on local residents, who now take longer to get from A to B. Surveys can be conducted to establish just how many vehicles are involved and the time delays suffered. A hypothetical example is shown in Table 12.4, showing how time lost and extra vehicle fuel costs might be valued. In addition to time loss, congestion causes vehicles to use more fuel; however, if each vehicle used, say, an extra 5 pence worth of fuel per trip because of the delays, this would amount to only £12,500 – a small sum compared with the time costs.

Noise is another negative externality that may be caused by leisure facilities and events. One way of valuing the cost of noise to the sufferers is to estimate the cost of soundproofing their homes. This is done in cost–benefit studies of, for instance, airports, in relation to houses under the flight path. It may, however, be only a partial solution in that people are still inconvenienced in the use of their gardens and in not being able to leave their windows open. In this instance some estimate of the compensation for loss of amenity might be assessed, of the sort that might be awarded by a court. One way in which the monetary value of the cost of noise pollution might be assessed is by examining property prices. The difference between the price or rent of identical houses under and not under a flight path indicates the value that house buyers or renters place on peace and quiet. Note that, in this case, the cost is a

---

Box 12.1. Adelaide Grand Prix study.

A study of the 1985 Formula One Grand Prix held in Adelaide, South Australia (SA): the project included studies of tourism, the transport sector, the accommodation sector, the restaurant industry, residents' reactions, road accidents, the promotion of entrepreneurship and exports in SA and public sector finance. Some of the key findings are summarized in Table 12.3.

Table 12.3. Adelaide Grand Prix study: costs and benefits.

Benefits/Costs	Amount (AU$ million)[a]
Tangible benefits: visitor expenditure (including multiplier effects)	9.9
Tangible benefits: event costs funded from outside SA (including multiplier effects)	13.7–14.9
Social benefits: psychic income (general excitement, etc.)	28.0
Total benefits	51.6–52.8
Tangible costs: event and capital costs funded from SA sources	6.6–7.5
Social costs: traffic congestion	6.2
Social costs: property damage	0.03
Social costs: accidents	3.2–5.8
Total costs	16.3–19.8
Benefit:cost ratio	2.7–3.2

[a] A$1 = £0.55 at the time of writing (2009). Source: Burns *et al.* (1986).

Of particular interest is the psychic income/benefits included in the listed benefits. This item was estimated in the following way:

1. Proportion of population who experienced extra travel costs: 20% (one fifth).
2. Total extra travel costs: AU$6.2 m.
3. Proportion of group 1 who were *still* in favour of the Grand Prix being held: 90%.
4. Total extra travel costs of group 3 (90% of AU$6.2 million): $5.6 m.
5. Psychic value of Grand Prix to group 3: at least AU$5.6 m.
6. Psychic value of Grand Prix for whole population (group 5 × 5): AU$28.0 m.

For group 3 the enjoyment of the Grand Prix must at least have compensated for the extra travel costs. So this was seen as a minimum measure of the psychic benefit for that group. It was argued that the 80% of the population who did not experience extra travel costs would have enjoyed a similar level of psychic benefit. The study concludes that, since '… one fifth of the population had benefits of $5.6 million then, extrapolating to the total population, … total benefits are at least $28 million' (Burns *et al.* 1986: 26).

one-off cost imposed on the owner at the time the airport is built. When the house is sold, the new owners are already compensated for the noise by the fact that they have bought a cheaper house. Interview surveys of affected people may also be used to assess the extent of noise inconvenience.

Table 12.4. Estimating costs of traffic congestion (hypothetical data).

(a) No. of vehicles experiencing delays (data from a survey)	1,000,000
(b) Average increase in journey time (data from a survey)	0.25 hours
(c) Aggregate delay time (a x b)	250,000 hours
(d) Value of time per hour (average wage rate)[a]	£8.00
(e) Value of time lost (c x d)	£2,000,000
(f) Average fuel costs per vehicle per hour (from motoring organization)	£2.00
(g) Aggregate fuel costs of congestion (c x f)	£500,000
(h) Total costs of congestion (e + g)	£2,500,000

[a]If, as is likely, some of the travel time is lost by people not working in paid jobs, the valuation of their time is more complex, and this is discussed in more detail in Table 12.5 under benefits.

Accidents may increase as a result of increased traffic generated by major events and tourism. As with the congestion example above, some assessment must initially be made of the amount of additional traffic likely to be generated and the corresponding likely numbers and types of accident. Such assessments can be made by reference to similar events in the same community or elsewhere, and in discussion with local transport authorities. An estimated cost per accident is then multiplied by the anticipated number of accidents to establish the accident costs of the event. How is the 'cost of an accident' assessed? Although, in one sense, a money cost cannot be put on death and injury caused to humans by accidents, people nevertheless do frequently associate such phenomena with money. The courts for instance award financial damages for everything from death to minor injury. There is a 'going rate' in insurance cases for such things as loss of limbs, macabre though it may seem. Two inputs are made into assessment of these costs: medical costs and loss of income/output by the victim. Distress to victims and families is more difficult to assess in money terms, although again, compensation ordered by the courts can give some guide. Since cost–benefit studies are routinely carried out for road projects and saving of accidents is one of the major benefits from new or improved roads, transport authorities are able to provide up-to-date valuations of accident costs.

Opportunity costs

The *opportunity cost* of something is measured by the value of that something in its best possible alternative use. It is a measure of *benefits forgone* and underlies the concept of cost throughout economic theory. It is particularly important in cost–benefit analysis and perhaps particularly so in leisure and tourism. The idea is best explained by an example.

Large city-centre parks are dedicated to recreational use, but the opportunity cost of the decision to dedicate that land to recreation can be measured by considering the value of the land in its next best alternative use. For example, the land occupied by Central Park in New York or Hyde Park in London would be worth billions of dollars or pounds if sold on the open market for development. The community is *forgoing* that income as the price of providing the open space. Thus if the going rate of interest is 10% per annum then a park which could, in theory, be sold for £100 million is costing £10 million a year in income foregone – £10 million is its annual *opportunity cost*.

The opportunity cost of resources, especially land, arises frequently in the case of leisure, sport and tourism because such phenomena as urban parks, playing fields, national parks, coastline and prestige city sites tend to feature prominently. Since these resources have often been in the public domain from time immemorial and have not recently involved any cash outlay, they are popularly considered to be costless. But the economist would argue that it is wrong to consider them so. Even when it would be 'impossible' to sell the land, for example because of legal constraints, the decision to impose such constraints is made by the society and has a cost.

Even where cash costs have been incurred, for instance in recently acquired land, there may be a temptation to ignore such 'sunk' costs if they were met from reserves or grants. Again the economist would say this is erroneous. If opportunity cost is ignored then projects that have real cash capital costs rather than opportunity costs are disadvantaged.

Identifying and measuring benefits

Social, or non-market, costs and benefits generally correspond to the examples of market failure discussed in Chapter 5. The first five forms of market failure identified in Chapter 5 were public goods, externalities, mixed goods/services, merit goods and option demand. Each of these implies some sort of benefit (or cost) accruing to the community at large or to particular third-party groups in the community, with externalities also being capable of imposing costs on third parties, as indicated above. These five benefit types are discussed below, but first we should consider the other benefit types mentioned in Chapter 5.

Among the other arguments for government involvement in leisure and tourism discussed in Chapter 5 were infant industries, size of project, natural monopolies, economic management/development, incidental enterprise and tradition. If a project is justified on these grounds, then *economic impact* rather than cost–benefit analysis would be the appropriate technique for evaluation, as discussed in the second half of the chapter. The 'traditional' argument for government involvement is not easily susceptible to economic analysis unless the sense of tradition is itself seen as a public good.

The remaining argument discussed in Chapter 5 was equity. Equity issues are not intrinsic to cost–benefit analysis since, in mainstream economic analysis of markets, no distinction is generally made between groups of consumers, it being assumed that the question of equitable income distribution is dealt with through taxation and welfare policies. However, *distributional effects* of projects can be taken into account in the process of undertaking a cost–benefit study – that is, it is possible to indicate which groups will reap the benefits of a project and which groups will bear the costs. These factors can then be taken into account by decision-makers.

Public goods

The classic type of public provision is the public good – which is non-rival and non-excludable. Examples include firework displays, public broadcasting, preservation of the landscape and provision of marine navigational assistance, such as marker buoys. The fireworks display is the easiest of these to examine. Suppose it costs £100,000 to mount a firework display: how do we know this is worth it to the community? The benefits are enjoyed by the people who watch the display. If the display is in a public area, such as the Thames Embankment, then these people are unable to actually pay for the experience, but they are obtaining a benefit.

How do we find out what the value of this benefit is to them and therefore whether the total value of the benefits enjoyed is greater than the £100,000 spent? A common approach to measuring such benefits is the *willingness to pay* or *contingency* method. A social survey could be mounted, after the event, which would ask people whether they had seen it, and how much they would have been prepared to pay if asked. If it is found that, say 200,000 people had seen the event and would, on average have been prepared to pay £1 each, then the valuation of the users, at £200,000, is greater than the £100,000 cost, so the display is justified. If the research exercise was being done before the event, people could be asked whether they intended to watch and if so what they would, in theory, be prepared to pay.

There are problems with the willingness-to-pay approach because, if people thought they might *actually* be charged for such displays in some way, they might be tempted, in their response to the survey, to deliberately underestimate the amount they would be prepared to pay, so that any charge imposed would be small. In the case of a purely public event, like a firework display, where imposing a charge would be almost impossible, this tendency can be expected to be small. On the other hand, if respondents to the survey thought that there was no prospect of being charged and the question was entirely hypothetical, they might exaggerate the amount they would be willing to pay in order to ensure that the event continued in future. It is possible that these two tendencies cancel each other out to some extent in willingness-to-pay surveys, thus giving, on average, a true indication of the public's view. But there is some doubt about the validity of the technique generally, given its hypothetical nature.

A similar approach can be used to place a value on the public good dimension of maintenance of heritage, where *vicarious enjoyment, psychic benefit* or *national pride* are involved. The general public could be asked what they would be prepared to pay per annum, for example, to preserve the Lake District, or the Parthenon or the Pyramids.

An alternative valuation method is to base the valuation on the amounts that people pay for similar events or services for which are charged. This would not be suitable for the psychic income example, but it might be possible for the firework display example.

Burns *et al.* (1986) came up with an ingenious inferential method of measuring the psychic income that the residents of Adelaide gained from having the Formula One Grand Prix in their city, as shown in Box 12.1 above.

Where the public good involves direct enjoyment by users and the users have to travel to a specific site or area, as in the case of a public event or visiting a park, it is possible to assess valuations on the basis of travel patterns and costs. This methodology is discussed below under 'Measuring private benefits'.

Externalities as benefits

Externalities are one of the most important types of benefit associated with public leisure facilities; they are similar to public goods, except that the beneficiaries are identifiable third parties, rather than the public at large.

The existence of a public leisure facility can often give rise to increased tourist trade for neighbouring businesses – for example, nearby pubs and restaurants benefiting from the presence of a theatre. The value of this externality would be reflected in property values or rents or in the turnover of these businesses. The expenditure, the increased business and the increased property values or rents are all indicators of the same thing; so in a cost–benefit study care must be taken to count this phenomenon only once.

A further factor to be considered in relation to this type of externality is whether it represents a real net benefit of the project, or whether it results from a transfer of activity from elsewhere in the community. For example, if the increased business of restaurants and pubs is counterbalanced by a decrease in the business of restaurants and pubs elsewhere in the city, then there is no net benefit to the city as a whole. On the other hand, if the concentration of facilities causes an overall increase in pub and restaurant spending by residents or attracts more visitors from outside of the city and boosts jobs in the city, then there can be said to be a net increase in economic activity and therefore a net benefit to the community.

A large public organization can provide externality benefits to smaller organizations in an industry. For example, a large public cultural organization such as a national theatre or opera or broadcasting organization will often provide training and professional experience for workers in the industry, and will underpin a technical support industry of which others can make use. While the training costs and benefits of such organizations can be estimated, the value of the other externalities they produce can be difficult to estimate.

Mixed goods/services

In nearly all cases of public leisure provision, there are private consumer benefits involved in a project as well as public benefits: they are mixed goods. Very often the private benefit is not reflected in the price paid by the consumer of the service – as it would be in the private sector – because the price has been reduced, sometimes to zero, in order to achieve other social objectives. Reducing the price of something means that more people are able or willing to buy more of it. In addition to the wider social benefits (e.g. public good aspects enjoyed by non-users, externalities, merit goods or economic aspects), the users are obtaining an individual, private benefit which should also be taken into account. Examples are outlined in Table 12.5. In these instances the public and the private benefits must be measured for the purposes of the cost–benefit analysis. The public or social benefits are all examples of public goods, externalities, merit goods, etc., which are discussed under appropriate headings. The measurement of private benefits is a major issue that is discussed later in the chapter.

Table 12.5. Benefits from mixed goods/services.

Example	Public good and other social benefits	Private benefits
Performing arts	Cultural spin-off to community; tourist attraction and economic benefits	Enjoyment of performance by audience
Urban parks	Amenity for local properties and passers-by; pollution dispersal	Enjoyment of the park by users
National parks	Merit good, option demand, vicarious enjoyment, amenity for properties and passers-by	Enjoyment of the park
Sports facilities	Health effects reduce public or insurance health costs; public enjoyment of national sporting success	Enjoyment of participation; health benefit to participants
Youth facilities	Reduction of anti-social behaviour	Enjoyment of facilities
Facilities for the elderly	Physical and mental health effects reduce public or insurance health costs	Enjoyment of facilities by users; health benefit to users

Merit goods

Merit good arguments outlined in Chapter 5 would appear to be unquantifiable. It is not the general public or the leisure facility user who makes the judgements of merit but professional groups, pressure groups or politicians. However, in a democratic society, it might be expected that such decisions would be approved of by a majority of the general public. The value of the merit good dimension of a service might therefore be assessed in a similar manner to public goods, primarily by means of the willingness-to-pay or contingency method.

Option demand

Option demand, or existence value – where people are willing to see government expenditure on something to ensure its availability for possible future use – can be evaluated by surveys using the willingness-to-pay or contingency method.

Comparing costs and benefits

The results of a cost–benefit analysis exercise must be drawn together in a summary table, as shown in the hypothetical example in Table 12.6. This extends the public sector example given in Table 12.2: both the costs and the benefits increase as a result of the cost–benefit analysis, but the result is a surplus of £350,000 a year rather than the former £2.4 million deficit. Of course, the cash situation remains the same, but the analysis shows that the cash deficit is exceeded by the net social benefits.

In Table 12.6, the data are presented in terms of annual amounts. This is suitable for a project where the annual costs and benefits are relatively constant, but this is not often the case. Very often costs are high early on, but fall over time, and benefits are initially low, but increase over time. Rather than a single annual cost and annual benefit figure, therefore, it is

Table 12.6. Summary cost–benefit analysis (annual flows).

	Cash assessment[a]	Cost–benefit analysis
Costs (£'000 pa)		
Capital charges	400	400
Opportunity costs	–	300
Running costs	3500	3500
Externalities	–	450
Total costs	3900	4650
Benefits (£'000 pa)		
Private/user benefits paid for in fees and charges	1500	1500
Private/user benefits not paid for (consumer surplus, etc.)	–	1000
Non-user benefits (e.g. public good, option demand, externalities)	–	2500
Total benefits	1500	5000
Surplus/deficit	–2400	+350

[a] As in Table 12.2.

necessary to examine the *flow* of annual costs and benefits over the life of the project – that is, over a reasonable time period, by which time major replacement or rebuilding might be expected.

The simple solution to this would be to add the flows for, say, 20 years and compare the two totals. However, two projects could have the same aggregates arising from very different sequences of costs and benefits. For example, in Table 12.7 and Fig. 12.1 it can be seen that, although both projects have the same aggregate net benefits, Project A has more net benefits early on in its life, but Project B's net benefits are not produced until later. Project A would therefore be preferred because, generally, other things being equal, people would prefer to obtain benefits earlier rather than later. This is reflected in the realities of interest payments which must be paid on borrowed money. Project A is 'in the black' from year 2, when the £1 million first-year deficit has been paid off. But Project B is 'in the red' until year 7, when the net benefits cancel out the accumulated deficits. This sort of consideration is applied by accountants to projects in the private sector. Even though, in a public sector cost–benefit analysis, all the costs and benefits may not represent cash, but a combination of estimated cash and *social* costs and benefits, economists argue that they should be treated in the same way when evaluating projects.

Accountants overcome the problem of uneven flows of income and expenditure (costs and benefits) over the life of the project by use of a *discount rate*, which can be seen as the other side of the coin to interest rates. If the current rate of interest is 10%, then £100 invested for a year will be worth £110 in a year's time. Looked at another way, £110 in a year's time is worth £100 at present. The flow of net benefits can be *discounted* to the present to give the *net present value* (NPV) of the project. At an interest rate of 10%, the NPV of project A is £11.3 million, whereas the NPV for project B is £7.6 million.

Table 12.7. Two projects compared over 10 years. Figures are given in £ million.

Year	Project A			Project B		
	Costs	Benefits	Net benefits	Costs	Benefits	Net benefits
1	10	9	−1	11	8	−3
2	8	9	+1	10	8	−2
3	7	10	+3	9	7	−2
4	7	10	+3	9	8	−1
5	6	11	+5	9	9	0
6	8	12	+4	8	12	+3
7	9	11	+2	7	12	+6
8	10	10	0	7	14	+7
9	9	9	0	7	13	+6
10	8	9	+1	8	12	+4
Total	82	100	+18	85	103	+18
NPV[a]			11.3			7.6

[a] Net present value at a 10% discount rate: see text.

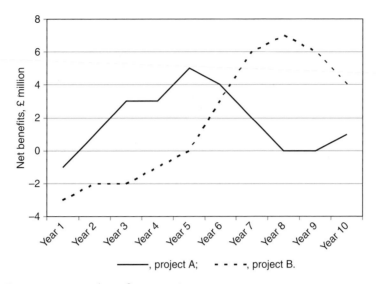

Fig. 12.1. Two projects: net benefits over 10 years.

Measuring private benefits: travel cost and other methods

In private sector leisure facilities, and in a few public sector facilities, the market price for the service is charged to the user and, in economic terms, this is seen as an indicator of the minimum value of the benefits enjoyed by the user. For example, if 100,000 people a year pay £5 each to visit a leisure facility then they can be said to be placing a collective value of at least £500,000 on the experience. In the case of public leisure facilities that are mixed goods or public goods, the price of entry is either zero or subsidized, in recognition of the public good or externality benefits generated, so the price paid for entry is not a reflection of the value the user attaches to the experience. How are the user benefits to be measured in such cases? Three alternatives are discussed here: (i) willingness-to-pay; (ii) the travel cost or 'Clawson' method; and (iii) the idea of 'switching values'.

Willingness-to-pay

The willingness-to-pay approach is considered above in the discussion of public goods. As discussed, this survey-based approach clearly has limitations because survey respondents may exaggerate or understate the amount they would be willing to pay for a service, or simply not be able to answer such a hypothetical question. Nevertheless, it is widely used in cost–benefits studies.

The travel cost or Clawson method

The *travel cost, revealed preference* or *Clawson method* of valuing individual recreation benefits is based on measurement of the *consumer surplus*. This concept is explained in Chapter 3 (see Fig. 3.5). Table 12.8 and Fig. 12.2 demonstrate how, if the demand curve is known, the consumer surplus (CS) can be estimated.

Table 12.8. Estimate of consumer surplus.

Group	(a) Number of customers (n)	(b) Price range would have paid (£)	(c) Price actually paid (£)	(d) Average price would have paid (£)	(e) Difference (d − c; £)	Consumer surplus (a × e; £)
A	30	15.00–16.99	5	16.00	11.00	330
B	70	10.00–14.99	5	12.50	7.50	525
C	100	7.00–9.99	5	8.50	3.50	350
D	80	5.00–6.99	5	6.00	1.00	80
Total	280					1285
E	220	0–4.99	0	2.00	−3.00	–

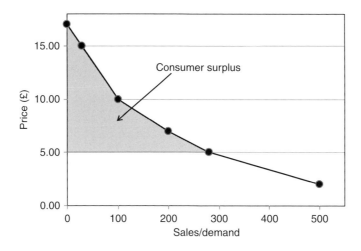

Fig. 12.2. Consumer surplus.

In this example:

- The price charged for the service is £5 and total sales are then 280.
- Ideally, information on every consumer represented in the demand curve would be available, but an approximate calculation can be based on the observations/groups indicated in the example.
- There are 220 potential customers (Group E), who would have been prepared to pay only between £2.00 and £4.99, and so do not buy.
- The 280 customers who actually buy are all charged £5, but:

  ○ Group A (n = 30) would have been prepared to pay between £15.00 and £16.99, say £16.00 on average, so they receive an average consumer surplus of £11.00 each.
  ○ Group B (n = 70) would have paid £10.00–£14.99 (average £12.50, CS £7.50).

    ○ Group C (*n* = 100) would have paid £7.00–£9.99 (average £8.50, CS £3.50).
    ○ Group D (*n* = 80) would have paid £5.00–£6.99 (average £6.00, CS £1).

  • The total consumer surplus enjoyed by the 280 customers can therefore be estimated as £1285.

  The total consumer surplus is a measure of the benefit that the buyers are getting over and above what they paid, and is represented diagrammatically as the shaded area in Fig. 12.2. The consumer surplus is seen as a useful measure of the benefit users obtain from a leisure service. If, as is the case with many public facilities, the price charged was reduced to zero, it would still be possible to estimate the consumer surplus because it is based on what various groups of users would be *prepared* to pay. The question is, how can the list of prices and quantities – the demand curve – be established in practice?

  The travel cost or Clawson method, first applied in the leisure context in the 1960s by American researchers Clawson and Knetsch (1962), was developed particularly in the context of outdoor leisure/tourism trips and is based on the idea of deriving a demand curve, and hence the consumer surplus, from a study of the costs that users of a leisure/tourism site incur in travelling to a leisure/tourism site. This is outlined in Box 12.2.

Box 12.2. Travel cost/Clawson method.

Suppose that the travel catchment area of a site can be divided into four zones, A, B, C and D, as shown in Fig. 12.3. For each zone there are different travel costs to the site. A user survey could establish how many people travelled from each zone, and the population census could be used to find out the resident population of each zone, to produce data of the sort given in Table 12.9.

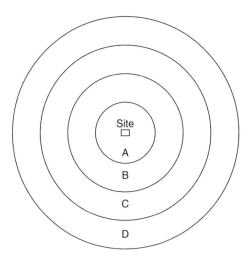

Fig. 12.3. Leisure site with travel zones.

(Continued)

Box 12.2. Continued.

Table 12.9. Hypothetical leisure/tourism site.

	Source of information	Zone				
		A	B	C	D	Total
(a) Travel costs/ head (£)	Survey	5	10	15	20	
(b) Total no of visits to site pa	Survey/counts	40,000	60,000	25,000	0	125,000
(c) Zone population	Census	20,000	40,000	50,000	60,000	170,000
(d) Visit rate[a]	Calculated (b/c)	2,000	1,500	500	0	

[a]Visits per 1000 population per annum.

It can be seen that the visit rate (a concept discussed in Chapter 10), falls as the travel costs increase, as shown in Fig. 12.4. It is assumed that entry to the site at present is free. How do we use this information to estimate the level of use for different price levels – that is, determine a demand curve?

The process proposed by the Clawson method is set out in Table 12.10. It uses the information on how people react to changes in *travel costs* to infer how they would react to changes in *entry charges*. The effects of a range of hypothetical entry charges are explored.

For example, if an entry fee of £5 were to be introduced, people living in zone A would be faced with total costs of £10 (£5 travel and £5 entry). This is the same as the travel costs for Zone B. If people react to entry charges as they do to travel

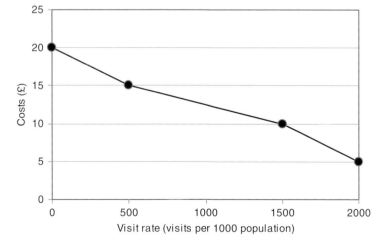

Fig. 12.4. Costs versus visit rates.

(Continued)

Box 12.2. Continued.

Table 12.10. Travel cost analysis.

	Source of information	Zone A	Zone B	Zone C	Total visits
(a) Population ('000s)	Census	20	40	50	
Entry charge nil: actual situation, as in Table 12. 9					
(b) Total cost (£)	Survey	5	10	15	
(c) Total visits	Survey/counts	40,000	60,000	25,000	125,000
(d) Visit rate[a]	c/a	2,000	1,500	500	
Hypothetical entry charge £5					
(e) Total cost (£)	b + 5	£10	15	20	
(f) Visit rate[a]	d	1,500	500	0	
(g) Estimated no. of visits	f × a	30,000	20,000	0	50,000
Hypothetical entry charge £10					
(h) Total cost (£)	b + 10	15	20	25	
(i) Visit rate[a]	d	500	0	0	
(j) Estimated no. of visits	i × a	10,000	0	0	10,000
Hypothetical entry charge £15					
(k) Total cost (£)	b + 15	20	25	30	0
(l) Visit rate[a]	d	0	0	0	
(m) Estimated no. of visits	l × a	0	0	0	

[a]Visits per 1000 population.

costs – that is, if Fig. 12.4 could be said to relate to aggregate travel and entry costs, rather than to just travel costs – then it might be expected that the *visit rate* for Zone A would fall to 1500 per 1000, the level that Zone B residents produced when faced with total costs of £10.

Similarly, with an entry charge of £5, Zone B costs would rise to £15 and the visit rate would fall to 500 (the visit rate which Zone C originally had). Zone C costs would rise to £20 and their visit rate to zero, since Zone D had zero visits when faced with costs of £20. A similar analysis could be done for a £10 and £15 entry fee, as shown in Table 12.9 (Zone D is omitted because it generates no trips).

The resultant price/visits schedule is as shown in Table 12.11, from which a demand curve could be drawn and consumer surplus estimated. This shows that the 125,000 visitors to the site are obtaining £612,500 of benefits, even though they

(Continued)

Box 12.2. Continued.

are not paying for them. Such a sum could be entered on the benefit side of a cost–benefit analysis.

The travel cost/Clawson method is not without its critics, since it makes a key, challengeable, assumption that people would react to entry charges as they react to travel costs. Nevertheless, it is one of the few alternatives to the 'willingness-to-pay' method.

Table 12.11. Price/visit (demand) schedule and consumer surplus.

Entry price (£)[a]	Total estimated visits (demand)[a]	Price range would pay (£)	Visits added at this price range	Average price would be prepared to pay (£)	Consumer surplus (£)
0	125,000	0 – 4.99	75,000	2.50	187,000
5	50,000	5.00 – 9.99	40,000	7.50	300,000
10	10,000	10.00 – 14.99	10,000	12.50	125,000
15	0	–		–	–
Total					612,500

[a] From Table 12.

Switching values

The switching values approach avoids the problem of direct measurement of user benefits. Rather than measuring benefits it suggests to decision-makers the minimum value that the benefits would have to be if a project is to be approved. This is illustrated by the example in Table 12.12. In this case the net annual costs of the project are £800,000 and the number of visits is 400,000, so that each visit costs £2 in subsidy. The decision-makers (e.g. councillors) make the decision as to whether visits are worth that level of subsidy (Manidis, 1994). The subsidy per visit, or switching value, is the focus of attention; decision-makers could, for instance, say that a subsidy of £1 only is acceptable – the project officers would then need to see if a viable plan could be devised at such a level of subsidy – if not, the project would be abandoned.

Table 12.12. Switching values (hypothetical).

Annual costs of project	£3 million
Annual income of project	£2.2 million
Net annual costs	£800,000
Number of visits per annum	400,000
Cost per visit: switching value	£2

The value of time

A type of benefit that arises in mixed goods situations is the saving of leisure time. This arises particularly when recreation or tourist traffic is a significant factor in new road schemes. It can also be incorporated into the travel costs element of the Clawson method – that is, total travel costs can incorporate *time costs* as well as such things as fuel and vehicle wear and tear.

In cost–benefit studies of road developments the value of time savings by travellers is usually the major benefit arising. Thus, for example, if a proposed road scheme saves 15 minutes of travel time for 2 million motorists a year (i.e. 500,000 hours), and if time is worth £10 an hour, the time saved would be worth £5 million a year.

Leisure enters into the road cost–benefit analysis, since a proportion of the motorists using the road will be at leisure or on holiday. Is their time worth anything? For someone involved in paid work – truck drivers or couriers, for example – their time savings can be valued at their wage rate. This, incidentally, means that the value of time savings of highly paid workers is higher than that of lower-paid workers; so road schemes that save more time of the former will produce more savings and more economic benefits. It can be argued that leisure time should also be valued at the wage rate because, at the margin, workers can be said to value their leisure time at the wage rate. If they valued it less they should, in theory, work longer hours; if they valued it more, it would make sense for them to work shorter hours. But this sort of analysis suggests that it should be the *overtime* rate rather than the normal hourly pay rate that should be used. Or it could be pointed out that the existence of collective bargaining and fixed working hours means that the individual has little choice about working hours, so this is not a useful basis for valuation.

There are, however, instances where individuals can be seen to pay to save their own leisure time. In such situations people appear to put a value on their leisure time for themselves. An example of where this can be observed is in the choice of travel mode: people fly rather than drive to a holiday destination to save time, but they pay more to do so, thus putting a value on the time saved. People also pay tolls on motorways and bridges rather than take the slow road or the long way round. Studies have been conducted in such situations and have usually come up with leisure time valuations somewhat less than the wage rate – usually between half and two-thirds of the wage rate in fact.

This raises an important equity issue. Wealthy people are able to place a higher monetary value on their leisure time than poor people. The leisure time savings of a road scheme that affects residents of a wealthy area would therefore be valued more highly than the leisure time savings from a road scheme serving residents of a poor area; so the former scheme would be favoured. But it is generally accepted that this would not be equitable, so all leisure time savings tend to be valued at an average rate.

Value transfer

As noted in Chapter 3, the cost of gathering and analysing the necessary data for cost–benefit analysis is too high to be used in routine local leisure, sport or tourism planning exercises because of the variety of facilities and services involved, although it may be used in relation to large investment projects. Even in sectors where cost–benefit analysis is routinely used, such as transport planning, a database of sets of values from a wide range of studies is generally available that can be utilized in specific studies as, for example, in the case of the value of time discussed above. This technique is known as *value transfer*. While some work has been done on this possibility for non-urban outdoor recreation in the USA (Rosenberger and Loomis, 2001), it is far from being developed as a practical planning tool, although it remains a possibility for the future (see Resources section).

Conclusion

Overall, cost–benefit analysis is a rigorous methodology that is consistent with neo-liberal market thinking, but is also clearly focused on establishing a legitimate role for the public sector. The rigour of the method is also, however, a limitation, because thorough applications of the method quickly generate into economic jargon, statistical complexity and substantial data collection costs. This is perhaps why less rigorous, more limited and less expensive techniques tend to find favour with leisure managers – for example, techniques concentrating on customer satisfaction or on benefits only. Examples of these are discussed in Chapter 13.

ECONOMIC IMPACT ANALYSIS

Introduction

While cost–benefit analysis is concerned with the overall viability of an investment project, economic impact analysis is more limited in scope, being concerned mainly with the extent to which the project generates jobs and incomes in an area, and not with other benefits or with detailed examination of costs. Thus giving everybody £100 cash from council coffers to spend as they please is unlikely to be seen as wise use of funds in cost–benefit terms, but *would* have a measurable *economic impact*.

In terms of the economic arguments for state involvement in leisure, as discussed in Chapter 5, economic impact analysis is linked to the *economic development* argument, where government activity is justified in terms of its impact on jobs and incomes, in contrast to cost–benefit analysis, which is related to the *market failure* arguments, such as public goods and externalities.

If government activity is to be justified in terms of economic development, then the main criterion for decision-making should be to obtain the maximum impact in terms of increased incomes and employment per pound or dollar of government expenditure. Economic impact studies are therefore designed to produce statements of the form: 'The outlay of X pounds of government money on this project will produce Y pounds of increased income and/or Z new jobs'.

Economic impact studies may be undertaken:

- before initiating a project, as an aid to decision-making;
- after completion of the project, as a form of evaluation;
- after a single event (e.g. a festival) in order to persuade government to continue to support future events;
- in relation to whole sectors of industry to establish its economic significance (e.g. sport or the arts).

Studies may be undertaken by government for its own needs, or by an interest group or organization (including a quango, such as the Arts Council) to persuade government and/or the community of the worth of a project or sector. The form of economic impact study that examines the economic impact of a whole sector, such as the arts or sport, on the economy might be better termed *economic significance* studies, and is discussed separately below.

Often, an economic impact study is concerned primarily with a private sector development – for example, studies of tourism development in a host community or of a privately run sporting event – the motivation for doing the study is invariably related to government and its role. The private sector does not generally undertake economic impact studies for its own use. Economic impact studies are undertaken to convince *government*, from an economic management point of view, to support a project. Often, an event cannot run profitably and requires a subsidy from government: the subsidy is justified by demonstrating the amount of additional income that the event generates for the host community. For example, a report on the Adelaide Grand Prix study (as described in Box 12.1), states that the Grand Prix '… regularly makes a financial operating loss of from £1m to £2.6m, but generates over £20m in extra income in South Australia' (Burgan and Mules, 1992: 708).

The outline of economic impact studies below considers first the principles and practice of identifying and quantifying the expenditure associated with the project whose impact is being assessed; secondly, the phenomenon of the *multiplier* is considered; and, finally, studies of economic significance to leisure and tourism sectors are examined.

Counting the cost

The initial stage in economic impact analysis is to specify the area to which the analysis is to relate and to identify and quantify the expenditure items to be counted.

The definition of study area is of key importance for the analyses. The net economic impact of a project is affected by the flows of money it generates, into and out of the study area. Thus, if the study area is small, such as a local government area, the impact of a project is diminished by the considerable sums of money generated by the project that will inevitably flow *outside* the area to non-local firms, organizations and individuals. The larger the area the less chance there is of these 'leakages' occurring, since a project will be able to source its supplies and labour needs from within the area. The extent to which an area can do this, and therefore retain the maximum proportion of the income generated, depends not only on its size but also on its overall economic structure. Thus an area with a furniture manufacturing industry, or high-tech design capabilities, would not need to import these goods and services and so would retain the benefit from expenditure on such items.

The smaller the study area the greater the proportion of money generated by a project that *leaks*. For example, if the study area is a single city the leakages are likely to be substantial; if it is a region the leaks will be less because more supplies will be sourced from within the region. If the study area is a whole country, the leakages include only international imports and overseas holiday expenditure. The level of leaks is also affected by the diversity of the economy. For example, an area with very little manufacturing will, in effect, import most of its material supplies. At national level, small countries are likely to need to import more supplies than large countries.

To conduct an economic impact study, data must be gathered to track the expenditure arising from a project, so it is necessary to know something about the structure of the local economy, particularly how the recipients of money from a project (firms and other organizations and private individuals) spend their incomes – for example, how much private individuals save, spend on food, housing and so on, and how much firms spend on wages, materials and rent. In the study area, surveys of organizations and private individuals may be conducted to discover this, or use can be made of existing data, for example national surveys of consumer and industry expenditure patterns. In small study areas the vital information on how much expenditure is allocated locally can generally only be gathered by local surveys. In the case of firms, they might be divided into different sectors, such as construction, services, retailing, and so on, which have different expenditure patterns.

The multiplier

The multiplier idea applies to any form of expenditure, but is usually applied to expenditures that represent net increases in demand for goods and services within an economy. Thus it is usually applied to any increase in expenditure from *outside* the area of study – for example, export income, visitor expenditure, investment by firms from outside the area, or expenditure by a higher tier of government. However, it can also be applied to new investment expenditure by local firms or increased expenditure by the local tier of government, as long as it is not funded by increased taxation, since the latter would cancel out the project expenditure. In the area of leisure, the main area where this sort of analysis would apply is in the area of tourism, since tourism brings expenditure into an area from outside. Non-tourism examples do, however, exist. For example day-visitors from outside the study area have the same effect as tourists; this applies to coastal and rural areas that attract day-visitors from urban settlements, and also to urban centres that attract visitors from suburban and rural hinterlands for cultural, sporting and entertainment purposes. Investment by private firms or governments in leisure projects, such as sports or entertainment facilities, also has multiplier effects.

The multiplier idea is that the initial expenditure of a sum of money is just the start of a process, not the end. For example, an investor who spends £1 million on building a leisure complex spends that money on wages of construction workers and suppliers of building materials and equipment. The construction workers spend their money on food, transport, housing and so on, and the suppliers of building materials and equipment spend the money they receive on wages for their workers, further supplies and so on. And so the process continues, with more and more rounds of expenditure spreading throughout the economy, so that the effect is potentially much greater than the original £1 million.

So does the original £1 million multiply endlessly, to produce an *infinite* 'multiplier'? The answer is 'no', because of the phenomenon of *leakages*. The firms and workers who receive payments in the various expenditure rounds do not spend all the money they receive in the local area – much of it *leaks* out. Some is spent directly outside the study area, for example by construction firms, equipment suppliers and retailers buying in supplies from outside the area and workers and their families going on holiday or buying on the Internet. Some of the money is not *spent* at all, but is deducted as income tax or sales tax, or is retained as savings. So, on each round of expenditure the amount of money circulating within the local economy is reduced.

The aim of multiplier analysis is to quantify these effects so that the overall net local impact of project expenditure can be quantified. There are basically two ways in which this is done in economic impact studies. One is by special surveys and the other is by means of an economic technique known as input–output analysis. We consider the use of special surveys first.

To simplify the explanation we will assume that surveys have established that the various firms in the area are fairly similar in their patterns of local and non-local expenditure. Suppose the survey reveals that firms, on average, spend 25% of their income with other local firms, 40% on wages for employees and payments of profits to local residents, and 35% outside the study area, in terms of imported supplies and taxes. And suppose that a resident survey establishes that the average resident spends 50% of their income locally and 50% goes in non-local expenditure, taxes or savings. We are now in a position to trace what happens to project expenditure, and this is shown in Fig. 12.5. The analysis is done in relation to a 'typical' £1000 of expenditure – for a project costing, say, £500,000 the figures would need to be multiplied by 500. These calculations can be relatively easily done by computer using a spreadsheet, a copy of which is provided on the book's website (http://www.leisuresource.net).

After 15 'rounds', the sums involved become very small, so the analysis has been terminated at that stage. It shows that, as a result of the initial £1000 expenditure:

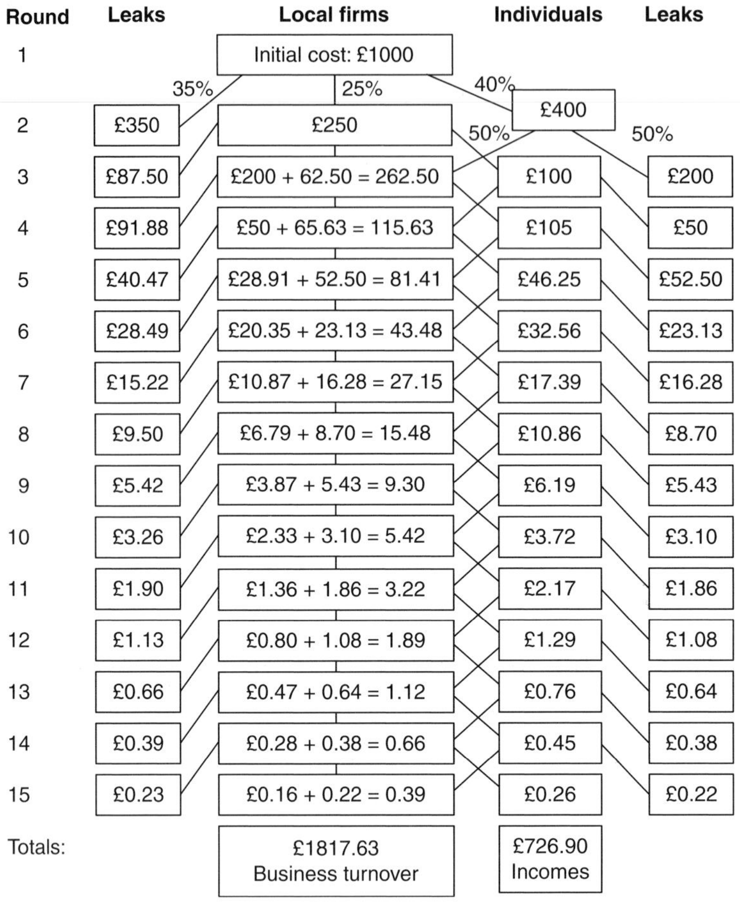

Round	Leaks	Local firms	Individuals	Leaks
1		Initial cost: £1000		
	35%	25%	40%	
2	£350	£250	£400 50%	50%
3	£87.50	£200 + 62.50 = 262.50	£100	£200
4	£91.88	£50 + 65.63 = 115.63	£105	£50
5	£40.47	£28.91 + 52.50 = 81.41	£46.25	£52.50
6	£28.49	£20.35 + 23.13 = 43.48	£32.56	£23.13
7	£15.22	£10.87 + 16.28 = 27.15	£17.39	£16.28
8	£9.50	£6.79 + 8.70 = 15.48	£10.86	£8.70
9	£5.42	£3.87 + 5.43 = 9.30	£6.19	£5.43
10	£3.26	£2.33 + 3.10 = 5.42	£3.72	£3.10
11	£1.90	£1.36 + 1.86 = 3.22	£2.17	£1.86
12	£1.13	£0.80 + 1.08 = 1.89	£1.29	£1.08
13	£0.66	£0.47 + 0.64 = 1.12	£0.76	£0.64
14	£0.39	£0.28 + 0.38 = 0.66	£0.45	£0.38
15	£0.23	£0.16 + 0.22 = 0.39	£0.26	£0.22
Totals:		£1817.63 Business turnover	£726.90 Incomes	

Fig. 12.5. Multiplier analysis.

- Local businesses experience an increase in turnover of £1817.63, including the initial £1000.
- Private individuals – wage-earners and business shareholders – experience an income increase of £726.90.

The business turnover figure calculated in this way should be treated with some caution. It does not, in the economist's terms, represent *value added* – there is a certain amount of 'double counting' in the figure. For example, if a leisure centre cafe buys pre-cooked meals from a catering company, which has in turn bought supplies from a retailer in the area, who in turn bought them from a wholesaler in the area, the value of the original supplies is counted three times (including the final sale to the customer); only the *mark-up* at each sale constitutes value added (this is the principle enshrined in the levying of Value Added Tax (VAT) in the UK and Goods and Services Tax (GST) in Australia). The totals in Fig. 12.5 nevertheless mean that an investment project of, say, £1 million, would generate an estimated £1,817,640 of business turnover in the area and £726,900 of personal incomes.

Multipliers are ratios relating the initial rounds of expenditure to aggregate effects. There are various types of multiplier that can be calculated:

- The *business turnover* multiplier relates the total business turnover to the initial business turnover: 1817.64 ÷ 1000 = 1.82.
- The more important *income* multiplier or *orthodox income multiplier* relates the overall income effect to the initial income figure in round 2: 726.90 ÷ 400 = 1.82.
- The *unorthodox income multiplier* relates the increase in income to the initial, round 1, expenditure: 726.90 ÷ 1000 = 0.73.

The multiplier can be used to calculate the effect of projects of various size; thus, the impact of a £15 million project would be:

- Business turnover impact: £15,000,000 × 1.82 = £27,300,000.
- Income impact: £15,000,000 × 0.73 = £10,950,000.

The calculations illustrated in Fig. 12.4 can be repeated with varying levels of 'leakage' to show the effects of an economy with low leakage as opposed to one with high leakages, as shown in Table 12.13.

Often, the interest in the economic impact of a project is in its job-generating effect. The income effect can be translated into a measure of the employment effect by use of an average wage or income rate. Thus, in the example given above, where a £15 million project produced a total increase in local incomes of £10,950,000, if the average income is £20,000 per annum, the number of full-time equivalent jobs created is 10,950,000 ÷ 20,000 = 547 full-time equivalent jobs.

The use of the term *full-time equivalent* jobs reflects the fact that such estimates rarely translate directly into *full-time* jobs. For some businesses the effect of the project will be very small and will not justify employing additional staff; it might result in increased overtime for existing staff or, if there is spare capacity, an increase in profits for the owners of the firm. Often, the additional employment will be in the form of short-term or part-time jobs. The estimate of the employment effect is therefore very approximate.

An alternative method of calculating multipliers, especially for large projects, is via an economic technique known as *input–output* analysis. This is a form of economic modelling that seeks to emulate the interrelationships among the various sectors of the economy.

Table 12.13. High-leakage and low-leakage multipliers.

		Proportion of expenditure	
	Expenditure item	High-leakage situation	Low-leakage situation
Firms	Wages, etc.	0.3	0.4
	Local suppliers	0.2	0.4
	Leakage	0.5	0.2
Private individuals	Local firms	0.4	0.7
	Leakage	0.6	0.3
Business turnover multiplier		1.5	3.1
Income multiplier		0.4	1.2

This procedure is quite technical and is beyond the scope of this book, but a discussion of the use of input-output analysis in tourism can be found in Fletcher (1989), and further examples are given in the Resources section.

Economic significance studies

In times when economic rationalism is guiding overall policy for many governments, representatives of certain industry sectors feel compelled to justify their existence in economic terms. This is especially true of areas of leisure which have, in the past, been viewed primarily as a *cost* to the community – a consumption item viewed as non-essential or simply not recognized as a significant industry sector. To some extent all service industries in modern developed countries suffer from this problem of perception. Despite the fact that services constitute as much as three-quarters of a modern economy, including a significant proportion of international trade, the perception seems to persist in the community that the *real* business of the economy lies in such activities as agriculture, mining and manufacturing. Service industries suffer from an image problem. Organizations representing sport and the arts in particular have seen it as necessary to draw the attention of government, and the rest of the community, to the dimensions of these areas *as industries*.

Such studies involve collation of statistics on turnover of relevant sectors of the economy, and of relevant departments of government and categories of consumer expenditure. This often entails considerable effort, since official statistics do not always identify leisure expenditure as such. For example, a considerable proportion of transport and clothing expenditure is for leisure purposes.

Recent studies of this sort have included British reviews by Casey *et al.* (1996) on the arts and by Rotherham *et al.* (2005) on countryside recreation and sport. The most recent equivalent studies in Australia were conducted over 20 years ago (DASETT, 1988a, b).

SUMMARY

This chapter reviews two economic evaluation methods: cost–benefit analysis and economic impact analysis. Both can be seen as aids to decision-making at the planning stage or part of the evaluation of projects when they are up and running or completed.

Cost–benefit analysis seeks to measure *all* the costs and benefits associated with a project, whether or not they fall directly on the promoters of the project or its users. In that sense the method tries to capture some of the public good dimensions and externalities associated with public projects, as discussed in Chapter 5. It is noted that some costs and benefits may not be measurable and convertible into monetary quantities, and these are identified in any cost–benefit study.

Among the approaches explored in measuring benefits are the willingness-to-pay or contingency method, the travel-cost or Clawson method and switching values.

Economic impact studies are not concerned with the costs of a project, but only in its effects in terms of income and jobs in an area. The approach can therefore also be used to assess the importance to an economy of an industry sector, such the arts, tourism or sport.

Of particular interest in economic impact studies is the idea of the *multiplier*, which is explored in the chapter.

RESOURCES

Websites

Multipliers, value transfer: a compilation of leisure, sport and tourism benefit values from published research can be found on the book website (http://www.leisuresource.net) and in Veal (2009g: Appendix 1).

Publications

Economics of sport and leisure/recreation: Cooke (1994); Gratton and Taylor (2000).

Economics of leisure and tourism: Tribe (2005).

Willingness-to-pay: Peterson *et al.* (1988); Garrod *et al.* (1993).

Cost–benefit analysis and tourism: Smith (1995: 284–295).

Travel cost/Clawson method: Clawson and Knetsch (1962); Garrod *et al.* (1993).

Value transfer: Rosenberger and Loomis (2001).

Economic value/scale: countryside recreation and sport: Rotherham *et al.* (2005); arts: Casey *et al.* (1996).

Input–output analysis: a simple exposition in relation to sport: Hefner (1990); a technical presentation in relation to tourism: Fletcher (1989); in relation to tourism and including a discussion of tourism 'satellite accounts': Smith (2000); in relation to a theme park: Sasaki *et al.* (1997).

Tourism impacts: Mathieson and Wall (1982); Faulkner (1993); Frechtling (1994a, b); Erkkila (2000).

The arts: Baumol and Bowen (1976); Throsby and O'Shea (1980).

Parks and gardens: Garrod *et al.* (1993).

Sport: in Europe: Jones (1990); in Australia: DASETT (1988a, b).

Sporting events: Burgan and Mules (1992); Gratton *et al.* (2000).

Sports stadia and teams: Noll and Zimbalist (1997).

Outdoor/countryside recreation: Rotherham *et al.* (2005); including a discussion of the concept of value: Peterson and Loomis (2000).

QUESTIONS/EXERCISES

1. What is the difference between cost–benefit analysis and economic impact analysis?
2. How does cost–benefit analysis deal with costs and benefits that cannot be measured?
3. What are the equivalent terms to *cost* and *benefit* used in the private sector?
4. Name three types of cost that might be included in a cost–benefit study.
5. What is the basic measure of benefit that the travel-cost or Clawson method seeks to measure?
6. What is another term for the 'contingency' method and what are its drawbacks as a way of measuring benefits?
7. Provide a brief description of the way the *multiplier* works.
8. What is 'leakage' in multiplier analysis?
9. List the costs and benefits that might arise in a local community from: (i) building a sports and leisure centre; (ii) building a museum; or (iii) holding an arts festival.

NOTES

[1]The on-selling of loss-making projects is quite common and can ensure the survival of a project. For example, a project that cost £100 million to set up will have to generate about £12 million a year (12%) to 'service the capital' – that is, to pay interest to banks and/or dividends to shareholders. This is in addition to covering running costs. If the project is unprofitable, the owner might sell it for, say £50 million, taking a £50 million loss. The new owner now has to generate only £6 million a year (12% of £50 million) to service the capital. In such circumstances the project may be profitable.

[2]In a number of cases in this chapter the generic term 'project' is used. In each case the reader may find it useful to imagine a specific type of project with which she or he is familiar, for example, a museum, a swimming pool, a park, a resort or a hotel.

[3]In this example the private sector operation involves the investors' own capital of £5 million and £5 million borrowed from the bank; the interest on the borrowed money is fixed at 10% and is therefore a running cost. The profit is therefore seen as a return on the money put up by the investors. The public sector may also involve money that is not borrowed (e.g. a grant from a higher level of government, or cash from reserves), as shown here, or the whole capital cost could be borrowed.

chapter 13

Performance Evaluation

INTRODUCTION

The logic of formal models of the planning/management process is that outcomes of programmes or projects should be *evaluated*. That is, they should be examined to assess the extent to which they are achieving what they were intended to achieve (effectiveness), and whether they are doing so at an acceptable cost (efficiency). Evaluation is clearly an important part of the rational-comprehensive model of decision-making, as illustrated in Fig. 6.3, but also of less formal models. Regardless of the decision-making model used, decisions on future policies and project initiatives are made to a large extent on the basis of experience of current and past policies and their outcomes; this evaluation feeds into subsequent rounds of decision-making.

In this chapter, the aim is to explore the evaluation stage of the policy and planning process. As Fig. 6.3 indicates, evaluation is concerned with the *implementation* of a plan, policy, project or programme and therefore engages with its ongoing *management*. The management of a project involves a range of processes and skills not covered in this book, including human resource management, promotion and sales and financial management. The outcomes of a project to be evaluated clearly depend intimately on the effectiveness of these management processes. In this chapter, while performance indicators which bear directly on these management processes are considered, the management processes themselves are not considered; other texts, such as Torkildsen (2005), deal with these aspects.

The rest of the chapter is divided into four sections. First, there is broad-ranging discussion of the context of evaluation. Second, the steps in a typical evaluation process are outlined. This is followed by an outline of some examples of evaluation systems, including the Comprehensive Area Assessment performance framework recently introduced in England and Wales, customer service approaches and importance–performance analysis. This is followed by examples of applications of evaluation systems in community recreation, arts, cultural venues and events, sports facilities and tourism. Finally there is a discussion of the overall relationship between corporate goals and the evaluation process.

EVALUATION IN CONTEXT

Before examining evaluation processes in detail, we consider some contextual and conceptual issues: (i) the role of economic evaluation, as discussed in Chapter 12; (ii) managerialism and privatization; (iii) forms of evaluation; (iv) sustainability/carbon footprint/water conservation; (v) triple bottom line accounting; and (vi) effectiveness and efficiency.

Economic evaluation

One key method of evaluation is economic evaluation, and two economics-based techniques, cost–benefit and economic impact analysis, are examined in Chapter 12. As indicated in Chapter 12, these techniques can be used to evaluate projects *before* they happen, when they might be viewed as part of the planning process, or they can be used to evaluate projects *after* they have been implemented or partially implemented, when they become part of the evaluation process. However, in most areas of public policy these techniques tend to be used for major, high-cost, high-profile projects and tend to be treated as research or special-inquiry techniques rather than routine tools of management. For day-to-day, or year-on-year, decision-making, public organizations tend to use less formalized and less expensive techniques.

Managerialism and privatization

Most observers would agree that, in the Western world, there will continue to be pressure on public sector organizations to evaluate their activities in a formal manner, and leisure and tourism service organizations will not be exempt from this pressure. The pressures will come from outside of leisure and tourism service organizations – mainly from elected governments that provide the money – and also from inside these organizations, as staff with professional management skills, who are familiar with the processes involved and see them as a legitimate part of professional management, gain ascendancy. The use of rationalized management practices similar to those used in the private sector is sometimes referred to as *managerialism.*

It might be thought that privatization and competitive tendering have simplified the evaluation process by reducing it to primarily financial considerations. But this is not the case. While financial dimensions are invariably part of the evaluation process, other quantitative and qualitative considerations must also come into play, including the following.

- If the management of a service is contracted out to a commercial operator, then the public body doing the contracting-out must decide just what terms to include in the management contract and still has the responsibility to decide, on behalf of taxpayers and ratepayers, whether or not the resultant service is effective as well as being worth the management fee.
- Even where a contracted-out service is apparently financially self-sufficient, it is rarely the case that capital or opportunity costs are covered; thus the authority still has to decide whether the nature and quality of the service provided is worth the allocation of land, buildings and other resources.
- In the case of tourism development policies, while the ultimate objectives of public policy are generally financial/commercial, the results are widely dispersed among tourism and other businesses and impacts are experienced more widely in the community, so evaluation of outcomes generally involves a wide range of considerations.

- The decision to leave all or the bulk of leisure, sport and tourism provision to the private sector is itself a policy decision, the outcomes of which should, logically, be monitored and evaluated. If a local council is concerned about the quality-of-life of the community as a whole,[1] then such monitoring and evaluating could be quite complex.
- The same argument can be applied in the case of a single-sector agency, such as an arts, sports or tourism commission. If the agency has responsibilities in relation the sector as a whole – for example, boosting participation – then it will need to monitor and evaluate beyond its own immediate programmes.
- In fact, as pointed out in Chapter 6, competitive tendering, if anything, focused the attention of public agencies on the process of clarifying objectives and the related process of evaluation. In the UK, this focus has been reinforced by the Best Value system and its successors, which replaced compulsory competitive tendering.

Forms of evaluation

Evaluation exercises can take a variety of forms, including the following:

- *Routine internal.* These may be a routinized element in the organization's internal management information system, with the performance of particular programmes or departments being evaluated on a regular and frequent basis, perhaps weekly or monthly – this is comparable to the regular financial reports that managers receive on *profit centres* in private sector organizations.
- *Strategic.* These may be reports forming part of the organization's corporate planning cycle, following the conventional management/planning model, involving the setting of objectives and evaluation of outcomes on an annual basis and/or over a set planning cycle period – for example, 3 years.
- *Accountability.* They may be designed primarily to appear in the organization's official annual report, which most public organizations are required to produce. Whereas in the past such annual reports were primarily 'window dressing' (and many still are), they are increasingly structured around evaluative information, linked to strategic corporate plans.
- *Ad hoc.* These may be one-off policy or programme reviews in the form of reports commissioned by senior management or external authorities, as required.

Evaluation can be seen as either *internal* or *comparative. Internal evaluation* is designed to assess the performance of a programme or project in its own terms: it is a self-contained exercise. For example, if an organization establishes a programme designed to increase the numbers of a certain category of visitor to a site by 25% in a given time period at a cost of £5 million, the programme can be evaluated in those terms: that is, whether it has resulted in the targeted increase in visitors in the time period specified and has stayed within budget, without any reference to other criteria that might indicate that this was an efficient expenditure of resources. Internal evaluation has the advantage that the criteria for success are decided by the organization or section of the organization responsible for establishing the programme and which should therefore be most familiar with it. This feature can, however, be abused by those individuals or organizations who choose unambitious targets or criteria, so that, in effect, they cannot fail. This is overcome to some extent by comparative evaluation.

Comparative evaluation is more difficult to implement because it involves deciding how one programme is performing compared with another. This involves comparing similar types of programme/facility with similar objectives – for example, comparing the performance of two or more outdoor swimming pools. It can be implemented internally, for example when one organization operates two or more similar facilities; high-performing facilities set the standard for low-performing facilities. The process becomes more demanding when comparisons are made with facilities operated by other organizations, perhaps with the whole industry sector. The process is sometimes referred to as *benchmarking*, a process by which external benchmark performance measures are established for certain types of management unit. In the commercial sector a range of largely financial comparators is used, such as the rate of return on capital and share price/earnings ratio. Internally, non-financial measures are also used – for example, because of waterfront labour disputes in the past, one of the most well-known benchmarks in industry is the number of shipping containers that a port can load or unload from a ship in an hour. In the public sector some financial measures can be used as part of the evaluation process, but because many of the objectives tend to be non-financial, performance measures must also be non-financial. A public example of this is the information published about universities, which includes such things as student/staff ratios, the proportion of academic staff with PhDs, the proportion of graduates who gain employment and the evaluation of teaching quality by students (Ashenden and Milligan, annual). Of course, in applying this idea to leisure facilities and programmes, differences between facilities – for example in their age, building quality and design, transport access or the nature of the catchment population – may produce differences that make comparisons of performance difficult, or at least very complex.

At a higher level, government may seek to evaluate across different sectors; for example, they may wish to decide whether a museum service is performing as well as a national parks service, or how arts programmes compare with health programmes in terms of value for money. It is at these levels that the pressure to use economics-based methods comes to the fore, since such methods reduce all factors involved to the common denominator of money, based on consumer preference and costs. However, the loss of detail and of qualitative differences between the measures of performance, or outcomes, used often causes such an approach to be resisted.

Sustainability/carbon footprint/water conservation

Among the non-financial performance measures that have become increasingly important in recent years are the ideas of sustainability and the carbon footprint and water conservation capabilities of a development.

The idea of sustainability has been a particular concern in recreation and tourism development in ecologically and culturally sensitive areas. A sustainable development is one that does not degrade the resource upon which it depends, thus ensuring that the recreation/tourism activity can continue indefinitely. Ecological sustainability is relatively easy to understand and is another way of looking at the concept of ecological capacity discussed in Chapter 10. Thus, in natural areas, issues such as water supply, sewerage, soil compaction/erosion and disturbance to flora and fauna can be understood and regular measurements can be taken to monitor impacts. Assessing impacts on host communities in tourism areas presents a different set of challenges. Economic impacts are relatively easy to assess (incomes, jobs, local ownership of businesses), but social impacts (effects of lifestyle, family structure, cultural practices) are difficult to measure and evaluate.

More recently, the idea that all human activity, including what takes place in urban areas, has environmental consequences, has come to the fore as a result of the discovery of anthropogenic climate change. The net amount of carbon dioxide generated by a facility is sometimes referred to its *carbon footprint*, and this can be measured and compared with other like facilities.

Because in some areas global warming is expected to result in reduced rainfall, conservation and re-use of rainwater and waste water has also become a concern and this can clearly be measured and compared. The potential for this in leisure facilities is substantial because of their relative size. Not only can these areas capture waste water, but irrigation is a cost-effective use for recycled waste water.

At the time of writing most activity in this area is voluntary rather than mandatory, and often costly: individuals and organizations have incorporated carbon footprint limitation an water conservation processes into their activities because of their concern for the environment. Increasingly, it is expected that pricing regimes imposed on carbon emission and water use will accelerate this trend.

Triple bottom-line accounting

In the private sector evaluation has traditionally been based almost entirely on financial criteria as implemented through the accounting process, with profit, the *bottom line*, being the most important indicator. The idea that social and environmental indicators should also be considered was popularized by the concept of *triple bottom-line* accounting (Elkington, 1997; Davidson, 2006). The idea can, of course, also be applied in the public sector. However, while triple bottom-line accounting has its supporters, it is a long way from becoming the norm.

Effectiveness and efficiency

Two similar-sounding terms are used continually in evaluation, and the difference between them should be clearly understood; they are: *effectiveness* and *efficiency*. *Effectiveness* is the extent to which a project has achieved what it was intended to achieve. *Efficiency* is the cost per unit of output. It is here where evaluation often becomes particularly threatening to the public service, because, even if measures of effectiveness can be agreed upon and a programme or project is evaluated as being very successful in terms of its effectiveness, it can still be seen as inefficient.

The public sector professional is often motivated by professional values concerned with quality of output and standards appropriate to the culture of the service involved; so talk of efficiency, particularly when associated with cost-cutting, can be seen as a threat to all that – indeed, as a threat to the very substance of the professional's judgement. By contrast, in the commercial sector, where making profit is the main aim, cost-cutting is more likely to be seen in a positive light, especially if things are arranged so that the person or department achieving the savings is seen to get the credit for doing so. This however does not preclude problems in the private sector where certain groups in an organization may be less profit orientated and more 'quality' orientated than others – for example, the design, engineering or research sections of a manufacturing company or the creative workers in the broadcasting or entertainment sector.

Despite fears and misgivings, the pressure is on to measure efficiency as well as effectiveness. This requires public organizations to measure *outputs* as well as *inputs*. In Fig. 13.1, as output (effectiveness) increases, an organization would expect to move along a

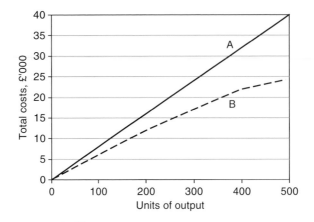

Fig. 13.1. Effectiveness and efficiency.

line such as A – that is, costs would rise proportionately, so if outputs double, costs would double. This, however, means that efficiency – costs per unit of output – remains constant. Increasing efficiency involves moving on to a lower line, such as B. While the proponents of corporate management and evaluation would claim to be attempting to move organizations on to a more efficient line such as B, others would claim that often the effect of reducing costs per unit of output is simply cost cutting, which can only be achieved by moving the organization back down along line A – thus reducing costs, but also reducing output, and therefore effectiveness.

STEPS IN THE EVALUATION PROCESS

In essence the evaluation process involves, for every policy, facility, service, programme or sub-programme, 12 steps, as listed in Table 13.1. Ideally, steps 1 and 2 will already have been established as part of the policy-making and planning process, but this is not always the case. When particular programmes, projects or facilities are being evaluated, it may be that the corporate, strategic planning process has provided only some very broad terms of reference or none at all, and a *post hoc* formal rationalization of the project must be devised.

The heart of the process is the specification of *performance indicators*, generally quantified measures of effectiveness or efficiency of the outcomes of a project that will indicate the extent to which objectives are being met. Performance indicators (PIs) are common in the private sector in the form of the basic measures, such as profit rate, sales growth and price/earnings ratios. Gratton and Taylor (1988: 150, 152) list a number of ratios commonly used in the private sector generally, and Huan and O'Leary (1999) review a wide range of indices used in the tourism industry to monitor performance in individual firms and whole industry sectors. In the public sector, the use of PIs appears at an earlier stage of development and, because of the diverse nature of public sector goals, the process of developing PIs is more complex than in the private sector, where financial ratios predominate.

In some cases the specification of a PI follows simply and logically from a stated goal and objective. In other cases, the process will be more complex. Hypothetical examples are given in Table 13.2, relating to increasing leisure participation among residents and tourism development.

Table 13.1. Steps in the evaluation process.

1. Identify goals
2. Specify objectives
3. Devise measures of effectiveness: performance indicators (PIs)
4. Devise measures of efficiency: PIs
5. Specify data collection methods
6. Collect baseline PI data
7. Set targets
8. Collect PI data collection at specified times (e.g. weekly, quarterly, annually)
9. Identify and obtain external benchmark data
10. Compare baseline values of PIs with current values, targets and external benchmark data
11. Deliver verdict
12. Consider implications

Table 13.2. Strategic goals/objectives – performance indicators (PIs) – targets: examples.

	Participation[a]	Tourism development[a]
Goal	Increase participation	Stimulate employment growth through tourism
Objective(s)	Increase participation to target levels among specified socio-demographic groups and in specified planning zones	Increase number of tourists and tourist expenditure to create additional specified number of jobs in tourism and related sectors
Effectiveness PIs	Level of participation for target groups (A, B) and zones (C)	Number of additional tourists; number of jobs created
Efficiency PIs	Cost per additional participant	Public sector cost per job created; total cost per job created
Environmental PIs/benchmarks	Amount of carbon emitted per 1000 customers	Amount of carbon emitted per 1000 tourists
Data collection methods	Resident survey Administrative Special audit	Tourist survey and industry survey Tourist survey, industry survey and administrative Special audit
Baseline PI value: current year	Overall participation: 30.0% Participation group A: 22.0% Participation group B: 18.0% Participation in zone C: 15.0% Average net cost per participant-session: £2.00 Carbon emitted per participant-session: 1.5 kg	Number of tourists: 100,000 Total tourist expenditure: £25 million Number of jobs in tourism and related sectors: 500 Council annual spend per tourism job: £100 Carbon emitted per tourist bed-night: 15.0 kg

(Continued)

Table 13.2. Continued.

	Participation[a]	Tourism development[a]
Targets: year x	Overall participation: 32.0% Participation group A: 30.0% Participation group B: 30.0% Participation in zone C: 30.0% Average net cost per participant-session: £2.00 Carbon emitted per participant-session: 1.2 kg	Number of tourists: 120,000 Total tourist expenditure: £30 million Number of jobs in tourism and related sectors: 600 Council annual spend per tourism job: £100 Carbon emitted per tourist bed-night: 13.0 kg

[a] As in the U-Plan system described in Chapter 8.

APPROACHES

In this section various examples of performance evaluation are considered, including overall systems of evaluation: the English Comprehensive Area Assessment performance framework, marketing-based customer service approaches and importance–performance analysis.[2] In the subsequent section, applications in various sectors are considered.

Comprehensive Area Assessment (CAA)

The Comprehensive Area Assessment (CAA) performance framework for local authorities was introduced by the government for local councils in England and Wales in 2008, replacing the earlier Comprehensive Performance Assessment system and the Best Value Performance Indicator system, which had been operating since the late 1990s, and which itself had replaced the system associated with Compulsory Competitive Tendering operated by the previous Conservative government. Details are provided in Box 13.1.

Box 13.1. Comprehensive Area Assessment.

The Comprehensive Area Assessment (CAA) framework is operated by the Department of Communities and Local Government (DCLG) and is based on almost 200 National Indicators (NIs) on which English local councils must report annually and which form the basis for some of the funding that councils receive from central government (Performance Reward Grants). Of the 200 NIs, 18 are 'statutory', relating to education and childcare. For each council, a maximum of a further 35 NIs are designated as priorities through negotiation of a *Local Area Agreement* (LAA) with central government.

Table 13.3 lists four NIs directly concerned with leisure/sport (there are none specifically related to tourism), and a further 14 with some relevance to the leisure area.

(Continued)

Box 13.1. Continued.

Table 13.3. Comprehensive Area Assessment (CAA): selected National Indicators (NIs).

Stronger and Safer Communities (total indicators 49)

(3) Civic participation in the local area

(4) Percentage of people who feel they can influence decisions in their locality

(5) Overall/general satisfaction with local area

(6) Participation in regular volunteering

(7) Environment for a thriving third sector

(8) Adult participation in sport and active recreation[a]

(9) Use of public libraries[a]

(10) Visits to museums and galleries[a]

(11) Engagement in the arts[a]

(38) Drug-related offending rate

(39) Rate of hospital admissions per 100,000 for alcohol-related harm

(40) Number of drug users recorded as being in effective treatment

(41) Perceptions of drunk or rowdy behaviour as a problem

(42) Perceptions of drug use or drug dealing as a problem

Children and Young People (total indicators 67)

Indicators concerned with health, education and safety

Adult Health and Well-being, Tackling Exclusion and Promoting Equality (total indicators 29)

Indicators concerned with health, welfare/care, disability and ex-prisoner services

Local Economy and Environmental Sustainability (total indicators 39)

(175) Access to services and facilities by public transport, walking and cycling

(188) Planning to adapt to climate change

(189) Flood and coastal erosion risk management

(197) Improved local biodiversity: proportion of local sites where positive conservation management has been or is being implemented

[a]Directly relevant to leisure.
Source: Department of Communities and Local Government (DCLG) (2007).

The *Handbook of Definitions* (Department of Communities and Local Government (DCLG), 2007) provides a commentary on the rationale for their inclusion and how they are to be measured. Table 13.4 provides a summary of this commentary for the four main leisure indicators.

(Continued)

Box 13.1. Continued.

Table 13.4. Comprehensive Area Assessment (CAA): selected National Indicators (NIs) – rationale, etc.

Indicator	NI 8: Participation in sport and active recreation
Rationale	Participation in sport and active recreation is an important part of a full and fulfilling life and provides unique personal and intrinsic benefits
	They also have wide-ranging impacts, so increased levels of participation will impact on other local priority outcomes such as community cohesion and improved health
	The measure will focus on participation amongst the whole target population, including those whose opportunities are limited. Evidence shows that there are inequities in levels of participation amongst some groups: lower socio-economic groups, women, older people, black and other ethnic minority populations and people with a limiting, long-standing illness or disability have particularly low levels of participation
Policy ref.	This indicator relates to the Department for Culture, Media and Sport (DCMS)'s broad Departmental Strategic Objectives both to encourage more widespread enjoyment of culture and sport and support talent and excellence
Definition	The percentage of the adult population (16+) in a local area who participate in sport and active recreation, at moderate intensity, for at least 30 minutes on at least 12 days out of the last 4 weeks (equivalent to 30 minutes on 3 or more days a week)
Data source	The annual Active People Survey is undertaken by Sport England; reporting coordinated by DCMS
Indicator	**NI 9: Use of public libraries**
Rationale	Public libraries can make an important contribution to a full and fulfilling life and provide unique personal and intrinsic benefits
	The services they provide are capable of giving positive outcomes for a wide variety of enquiries and purposes, including promotion of community cohesion, education and well-being
	The measure will focus on engagement by the whole adult resident population, including those whose opportunities are limited
	As for NI 8
Policy ref.	The percentage of the adult population who say they have used a public library service at least once in the last 12 months
Definition	
Data source	As for NI 8

(Continued)

Box 13.1. Continued.
Table 13.4. Continued.

Indicator	NI 10: Visits to museums and galleries
Rationale	Museums and galleries can make an important contribution to a full and fulfilling life and provide unique personal and intrinsic benefits They also have a range of local impacts, including promotion of education and well-being and a sense of identification with their locality The measure will focus on attendance by the whole adult resident population, including those whose opportunities are limited. Evidence shows that there are inequities in levels of participation amongst some groups – lower socio-economic groups, older people, black and other ethnic minority populations and people with a disability have particularly low levels of participation.
Policy ref.	As for NI 8
Definition	The percentage of the adult (16+) population who say they have attended a museum or gallery at least once in the last 12 months in leisure time
Data source	As for NI 8
Indicator	**NI 11: Engagement with the arts**
Rationale	As for NI 10
Definition	The percentage of the adult (16+) population that have attended an arts event or participated in arts activity at least three times in the past 12 months
Data source	As for NI 8

Source: Department for Culture, Media and Sport (DCLG) (2007).

For these indicators, annual performance data are collected via the centrally administered Sport England 'Active People' survey. Details of this annual survey series are as follows:

- It was first conducted in 2005 for sport only, before the establishment of the CAA, but it was deemed to be the ideal vehicle for the leisure-related National Indicator data collection, so the culture items were added at the instigation of the Department for Culture, Media and Sport (DCMS).
- It currently has a sample size of 190,000 adults (16+), providing a minimum sample size of 500 for each council.
- The cost, born primarily by Sport England, is approximately £3 million a year, an average of just around £9000 per local authority (but this should be seen in the context of total national annual spending on sports and arts programmes of several billions of pounds – see Table 1.3).

(Continued)

Box 13.1. Continued.

Table 13.5 shows the highest and lowest scores for these indicators for the early surveys. At the time of writing (2009), results from two surveys are available for NI 8, sport and recreation, but only for one survey for the other indicators. Clearly, the intention is to track change over time but, for most councils, with samples of around 500, the margins of statistical error on the results are substantial, so very fine comparisons between councils or for the same council from year to year are not possible. For example, a participation rate of 30% in a leisure activity based on a sample of 500 persons is subject to an margin of error of plus or minus 4% (i.e. the population value is estimated to lie within the range 26–34%). So, only differences of 4.1% and above are significant, and survey results from year to year are likely to fluctuate within this range for a variety of reasons. It therefore seems likely that the real value of this unprecedented data collection exercise will be realized only after several years, after which clear trends will be discernible.[3]

One feature of Table 13.5 should be noted in passing: by far the highest level of visits to museums/galleries is in the London Borough of Camden, home to the British Museum, thus dramatically demonstrating the effect of proximity of facilities on participation, as discussed in Chapter 10.

Table 13.5. Comprehensive Area Assessment (CAA): selected National Indicator (NI) results, 2007/09.

National Indicator	Area of interest	Year	Result	Local authority	%
NI 8	Sport and recreation	2008/09	Highest	Richmond-upon-Thames	26.6
		2008/09	Lowest	Newham	13.1
NI 8	Libraries	2007/08	Highest	Rugby	60.1
		2007/08	Lowest	Boston	32.6
NI 10	Museums/galleries	2007/08	Highest	Camden[a]	78.2
		2007/08	Lowest	Boston	35.5
NI 11	Arts	2007/08	Highest	Kensington and Chelsea	65.5
		2007/08	Lowest	Bolsover	29.6

[a] The London Borough of Camden is home to the British Museum.
Source: Sport England (website: http://www.sportengland.org/research/active_people_survey.aspx)

The CAA framework is concerned largely with annual operational management, implemented through 3-year Local Area Agreements (LAAs) between councils and central government. In drawing up their LAAs, councils must designate certain NIs as priorities for which their performance is expected to improve over the course of the agreement. If a council selects leisure NIs and sets specific targets for these NIs, the process resembles the

Objectives/Outcomes Module of the participation-based planning approach outlined in Chapter 8, Box 13.2.

The CAA system and associated National Indicators represent a significant advance for performance evaluation in leisure services in England, offering uniform indicators for over 300 local councils and indicating a recognition that national leisure policies are largely dependent on local implementation. However, a single indicator for sport/physical

---

Box 13.2. The Comprehensive Area Assessment framework in practice: leisure objectives in Birmingham, UK.

The Comprehensive Area Assessment (CAA) in England is implemented by means of Local Area Agreements (LAAs) between local councils and central government. An example of such a LAA is that of Birmingham City Council, the council area with the largest population (over one million) in the country. In its 2008–2011 LAA document, the city designates 33 non-statutory National Indicators (NIs) in 19 groups, each with an overall goal. The 17th group relates to leisure, with the following goal: 'Raise Birmingham's profile and attract more people, trade and opportunities through renowned facilities and events across the cultural, sport and creative sectors, and ensure residents have access to high quality facilities, programmes and activities locally' (Birmingham City Council, 2007: 39).

Thus leisure is seen as primarily an aspect of economic development. This is emphasized in the accompanying explanation of why this is seen as a priority for the city, although part of the rationale also refers to the direct contribution of leisure to residents' quality of life:

> Top-quality cultural, leisure and sporting assets and facilities are a vital ingredient in Birmingham's development and growth into a world city. Their presence makes the city a great place to live but also attractive to visit, with numerous opportunities to enjoy, learn and participate in events and activities. One of Birmingham's core strengths is its rich and diverse cultural offering (including a strong and growing creative industries sector), which brings great economic and other benefits to the city and needs to be promoted more strongly. This is one of the key factors in drawing tourists to the city and is also of vital importance in attracting people, especially young skilled professionals, to move to Birmingham. High-quality, easily accessible cultural, sport and leisure facilities at a neighbourhood level also play a major contribution [sic] to residents' overall quality of life through provision of enjoyable, healthy, safe and positive activities. A key aspect of this is increasing engagement in sport and leisure amongst people at risk of poor health outcomes.
>
> (Birmingham City Council, 2007: 39)

These statements are followed by a set of three indicators, as shown in Table 13.6:

- National Indicator 8 is concerned with participation in sport and active recreation: targets are set to increase this from 17.2% to 20.2% over 3 years.
- Local Indicator 1 refers to positive tourist attitudes towards Birmingham as a destination and is not part of the National Indicators system. This is targeted to increase from 65% to 69%.

(Continued)

Box 13.2. Continued.

- Local Indicator 2 appears to be a combination of NI 8 and NI 11 (concerned with the arts) and is applied to four low-participant suburbs, targets being set to bring non-participation rates down to the city average. Assuming the data source is the Active People survey, it should be noted that this suburb-based analysis is made possible by the fact that Birmingham's Active People sample size is 5000, rather than the 500 available to most councils.

Table 13.6. Birmingham City Council: Local Area Agreement (LAA) leisure performance indicators (PIs).

Indicator	Area of interest	Baseline (%)	Targets (%)		
			2008/09	2009/10	2010/11
NI 8	Adult participation in sport and active recreation	17.2[a]	18.2	19.2	20.2
Local Indicator 1	Tourists who think Birmingham is a good place to visit	65.0[b]	66.0	67.5	69.0
Local Indicator 2	Reduce the percentage of residents in Erdington, Hodge Hill, Ladywood and Perry Barr who have not used any cultural facilities (sports and leisure, library, museum and gallery or theatre and concert hall) in the past 12 months	33.5[c]			31.6[g]
		41.3[d]			37.5
		35.7[e]			31.6
		33.4[f]			31.6

[a]Sport England (undated); [b]telephone survey; [c]Erdington; [d]Hodge Hill; [e]Ladywood; [f]Perry Barr; [g]31.6% is current city average.

recreation is clearly not adequate for most local planning exercises, and even the three indicators for arts/culture are not much of an improvement. Most local planning would also require data on the socio-demographic characteristics of participants and details of individual activities. This information is, however, collected as part of the Active People survey, as Table 13.7 indicates, and is available for analysis at the single council level. Thus councils can develop more finely tuned analysis and targets for local use. For the majority of councils, however, the sample size is only around 500 and this is a severe limitation. Using the above example of a 30% participation rate in a leisure activity, if the sample of 500 is split into two subsamples of 250 (e.g. for gender comparison) the findings for each subsample would be subject to a margin of error of plus or minus 5.7% and, for four groups of 125 (e.g. for income-group comparisons), the error would be plus or minus 8.1%.[3]

Table 13.7. Active People survey data items.

Participation data items	Socio-demographic data items
Sport and recreational physical activity	Gender
Walking participation of at least 30 minutes (frequency in last 4 weeks, pace)	Age
	Ethnic group
Cycling: as for walking	Age completed full-time education
Other types of 'sport and recreational physical activity': for each activity, as for walking	Highest qualification
	Accommodation type
Sports club membership	No. of children in household
Competitive sports participation	Car/van availability
Instruction/coaching in sport	Disability
Overall satisfaction with sports provision	Current work status
Likelihood of doing more sport: name one activity	
Change in participation in last 12 months: reason for doing less	
Cultural	Socio-economic status (ten questions)
Museum/gallery attendance in last 12 months	Main income-earner occupation
Public library use in last 12 months	Postcode
Attendance at creative, artistic, theatrical or musical events in last 12 months: number attended	
Actually doing creative, artistic, theatrical or musical activities in last 12 months: frequency	

Source: Department for Culture, Media and Sport (DCMS) (website: http://www.culture.gov.uk/images/research/Active_People_Survey_questionnaire.pdf).

Service quality

The CAA system concentrates on strategic goals/objectives. The quality of customer service *could* be a strategic goal/objective in its own right for some types of organization at some times, but here we see it as an operational matter, subservient to overall social (effectiveness) goals/objectives, as shown in Fig. 13.2, which also shows similar relationships between the strategic and the operational in the area of financial and environmental factors. The operational activities relate to the facilities and services put in place in order to achieve the strategic goals/objectives. Any failure to achieve the operational goals/objectives can be due to lack of performance at the operational level. Therefore, in addition to being subject to the strategic performance indicators, the managers of facilities and services have their own performance indicators related to the operational objectives. Customer service can be seen as one component of this.

Customer service models derive from market research, the most well-known model being the SERVQUAL system developed by Parasuraman and his colleagues (Parasuraman *et al.*, 1988).

Fig. 13.2. Strategic and operational goals/objectives/indicators.

The main focus of SERVQUAL is to assess service quality by comparing customers' expectations of service quality with the level of service quality actually received. Service quality is broken down into components, and scores for these components can be seen as performance indicators. Scores are obtained from customers via a standardized survey instrument comprising mainly Likert-style rating scales covering:

- reliability;
- empathy (of staff);
- responsiveness (of staff and management system);
- assurance;
- tangibles (physical features of the facility).

Customer service approaches to evaluation, such as SERVQUAL, have been applied in a number of leisure contexts (e.g. Williams, 1998 a, b). The advantages in conducting customer surveys are their comparatively low cost and efficiency and the fact that facility managers are often motivated to ensure that they take place. There is therefore a case for performance monitoring to 'coat-tail' on customer surveys for some of its data requirements. The system outlined in Chapter 8 and the related facility audit process discussed in Chapter 10 require facility-based surveys in addition to resident surveys. The interest of facility managers in conducting customer surveys is such that research/consultancies offer an advice and analysis service using a standardized system and, because they deal with a range of facilities and organizations, can offer benchmarking against average data from other comparable facilities. Two such services are summarized below: the Australian CERM system and the British National Benchmarking Service. It should be noted that neither of these services is exclusively concerned with service quality.

The CERM PI system

The CERM PI system (Centre for Environmental and Recreation Management Performance Indicators) was developed by Gary Crilley, Gary Howat and associates at the University of South Australia, Adelaide, and has been tested in a range of mainly Australian leisure centres. Details are presented in Box 13.3.

Box 13.3. The CERM PI customer service data items.

The CERM PI (Centre for Environmental and Recreation Management Performance Indicators) system offers a performance appraisal service to leisure facility managers and has been applied at 200 leisure facilities in Australia and New Zealand, notably aquatic centres, but also at indoor sports centres and golf courses. Related research has been carried out at campgrounds and caravan parks, zoos and botanical gardens, residential outdoor recreation centres and skating parks.

Subscribing leisure facilities conduct annual user surveys using a standard questionnaire; the completed questionnaires, along with operational data, are submitted to the CERM unit, which then analyses the data and provides performance indicators compared with averages for comparable facilities on the database.

In addition to customer service measures, the CERM PI system includes 'organizational performance' indicators relating to the strategic, financial and environmental indicators. Examples of performance indicators are shown in Table 13.8.

Numerous papers on the CERM PI system have been published in the research literature (see Table 13.8 for CERM website). The version of the system including organizational performance indicators is presented in Howat and Crilley (2007), and analysis of data from these indicators is presented in Howat and Crilley (2005).

Table 13.8. Centre for Environmental and Recreation Management Performance Indicators (CERM PIs).

Customer service: expectation and performance: examples
Safe and secure parking facility cleanliness
Value for money
Suitable food and drink
Staff friendliness
Pool water cleanliness
Behaviour of others
Problem resolution
Overall satisfaction
Behavioural intentions

Organizational: examples
Expense recovery of operations (fee income as percentage of expenditure)
Promotion/marketing cost share
Total visits per year
Visits per square metre
Water costs per visit
Fit of socio-demographic profile of centre users to that of the local community

Source: Howat *et al.* (2005); CERM website (http://www.unisa.edu.au/cermpi).

National Benchmarking Service (NBS)

During the era of the Best Value process, in the late 1990s and early 2000s, Sport England commissioned the Leisure Industries Research Centre (LIRC) of the University of Sheffield to devise a set of performance indicators for sports halls and swimming pools and to survey 155 such facilities to gather data for benchmarking purposes. The list of PIs developed is reproduced in Table 13.9. The project established the range of values in the 155 facilities for each of the indicators, so that each facility could be classified into a *quartile*, that is the top 25% to the bottom 25%.

This system has developed into the Sport England-sponsored National Benchmarking Service, as outlined in Box 13.4.

Analysis: importance–performance

One way in which service quality data of the sort included in the CERM and NBS systems can be analysed is by using the *importance–performance* technique. This was developed in relation to individual consumer choice (Martilla and James, 1977) and can be utilized in a variety of contexts, including: (i) organizational decision-making, as indicated by Harper and Balmer (1989); (ii) in relation to perceived benefits of public leisure services, as a form of consumer consultation (Sieganthaler, 1994); (iii) to measure customer satisfaction (Langer, 1997: 147); and (iv) to analyse performance data.

For a single facility, the results of a customer service survey will be in the form of: (i) a set of Likert-type average scores indicating customers' evaluations of their experience of service items; and (ii) a corresponding set of scores measuring either the importance of each of the items to the customer or their expected level of service. These scores can be plotted on a graph, as shown in Fig. 13.3. The service items in the top right corner of the graph (C, F) are ideal because they are performing well and also have high customer importance/expectations. Those in the bottom right corner (A, H) are a cause for concern because they have high customer importance/expectations but are not performing well, while those on the top left (G) may represent wasted resources because they have low customer importance/expectations but are performing very well. In this case, the management would concentrate on improving the performance of items A and H and see if resources could be saved on item G.

If management is successful in the above measures, the result should be happier customers, but would it result in improving the achievement of the strategic goals/objectives – for example, increased numbers of visits? In general terms: do happier customers result in more customers? This could be analysed by tracking change over time and/or comparing facilities with similar characteristics. This is demonstrated in Table 13.11. Four cases are presented, which could be four similar facilities or the same facility in different years, with the same eight customer service items as in Fig. 13.3. It is assumed that the importance/expectation scores are constant over the four cases – this a plausible scenario, but different scores could be found. The performance scores change across the four courses. Following the Fig. 13.3 example, items A and H show increases, while item G declines somewhat. By multiplying each importance/expectation and performance score together and adding the total, we obtain an overall customer satisfaction score for each case (if expectation is measured rather than importance, the two scores could be subtracted rather than multiplied). Attendances are shown across the bottom of the table showing that, in this example, for every 1% increase in the satisfaction score there is a 0.5% increase in attendances.

This sort of analysis could be taken further. For example, if visit levels for certain target socio-demographic groups were a feature of the organization's objectives, Table 13.11 could be replicated for each of the target groups, with their own service quality ratings, thus management efforts to increase attendances by those groups could be focused on improving the particular services items that are of concern to them.

Table 13.9. Performance Indicators (PIs) and benchmarks for sports halls and swimming pools.

Groups	Policy	Performance Indicator	Data source
Access (effectiveness)	Access for youth[a]	% of visits by 11–19-year-olds ÷ % of cp aged 11–19 years	US + census
	Access for disadvantaged groups[a]	% of visits by SEG DE ÷ % of cp in SEG DE	US + census
	Access for ethnic minorities[a]	% of visits by black, Asian and other (minority) ethnic groups ÷ % black/Asian/other ethnic groups in catchment population (cp)	US + census
	Access for adults	% of visits by 20–59-year-olds ÷ % of cp aged 20–59 years	US + census
	Access for older people	% of visits by 60+ year-olds ÷ % of cp aged 60+ years	US + census
	First visits	% of visits that are first visits	US
	Use of discount card	% of visits using discount card	US and/or TS
	Use of discount card by 'disadvantaged' groups	% of visits using discount card for 'disadvantaged'	US and/or TS
	Use by females	% of visits by females	US
	Use by disabled people < 60 years	% of visits by disabled people aged < 60 years	US
	Use by disabled people 60+ years	% of visits by disabled people aged 60+ years	US
	Use by unemployed	% of visits by unemployed	US
Financial (efficiency)	Cost recovery[a]	Annual income as % of annual operating costs	Acc
	Subsidy per visit[a]	(Annual operating costs – annual income) ÷ no. of visits pa	Acc, TS
	Subsidy per square metre	(Annual operating costs – annual income) ÷ area of facility	Acc, area
	Subsidy per opening hour	(Annual operating costs – annual income) ÷ no. of hours open pa	Acc, PR
	Subsidy per catchment resident	(Annual operating costs – annual income) ÷ cp	Acc, census
	Operating cost per visit	Annual operating costs ÷ no. of visits pa	Acc, TS

(Continued)

Table 13.9. Continued.

	Operating cost per square metre	Annual operating costs ÷ area of facility	Acc, area
	Operating cost per opening hour	Annual operating costs ÷ no. of hours open pa	Acc, PR
	Maintenance/repair costs per m²	Annual maintenance/repair costs ÷ area of facility	Acc, area
	Energy costs per square metre	Annual energy costs ÷ area of facility	Acc, area
	Income per visit	Annual income ÷ no. of visits pa	Acc, TS
	Income per square metre	Annual income ÷ area of facility	Acc, area
	Income per opening hour	Annual income ÷ no. of hours open pa	Acc, PR
	Direct income per visit	Annual user fees ÷ no. of visits pa	Acc, TS
	Secondary income per visit	Annual subsidies, grants, etc. ÷ no. of visits pa	Acc, TS
Utilization (effectiveness and efficiency)	Visit level[a]	Annual visits ÷ area of facility	TS, area
	Visits per opening hour	Annual visits ÷ no. of hours open pa	TS, PR
	Casual visits	No. of casual visits as % of total visits pa (casual + organized)	TS
	Unused programme time	% of programmed time not used	PR
	Unused usable programme time	% of programmed time available for use but unused	PR
	No of people visiting halls	Weekly no. of people visiting halls as % of cp	TS, census
	No. of people visiting pools	Weekly no. of people visiting pools as % of cp	TS, census
	No. of users who visit other facilities	Weekly no. of users who visit other facilities as % of cp	US, census

cp, catchment population (data obtained from census: see Chapter 10 for discussion of catchment area); SEG, socio-economic group; DE, semi-skilled and un-skilled occupations; pa, per annum; US, user survey; TS, ticket sales (usually a computerized system capable of capturing data on bookings and numbers and types of ticket sold/used – but, NB, must be programmed to calculate no. of users for team, etc. game bookings); Acc, accounts; PR, programme/booking system; area, area of facility (m²).

[a] 'Key' indicators: the rest are 'Other' indicators.

Source: adapted from Sport England (2000: 18–24).

Box 13.4. National Benchmarking Service.

The National Benchmarking Service (NBS) is a service for indoor sports centres containing one or more sports halls and swimming pools. It is sponsored by Sport England and operated via:

- pmpgenesis Consultancy;
- Sports Industry Research Centre (SIRC), Sheffield Hallam University, which succeeded the Leisure Industry Research Centre (data analysis);
- Ipsos/MORI (survey conduct if required).

Centre managers compile two sets of data, completed questionnaires from a user survey and a financial report. These are submitted to SIRC, who then analyse the data and provide a report.

User survey

The conduct of the survey is organized directly by the centre management or by Ipsos/MORI. At least 350 standard user survey questionnaires are completed over a 9-day period, including data as listed in Table 13.10. It can be seen that service quality data (customer satisfaction) are expressed in SERVQUAL format.

Table 13.10. National Benchmarking Service (NBS): data items.

User survey
Usage patterns: frequency of use, main activity
Travel patterns: postcode, mode of transport, length of journey
Respondent profile: gender, age, employment status, ethnicity, socio-economic group
Customer satisfaction/perceived importance of service attributes: access, availability of facilities, quality of facilities/services cleanliness, value for money

Financial return
Facilities included
Size of facility
Total annual attendances
Total annual income
Total annual expenditure etc.

Source: NBS website (http://www.questnbs.info/).

Report

The report from SIRC provides:

- the centre's scores for the access, financial and utilization performance indicators compared with the 25%, 50% and 75% benchmark scores for comparable centres held on the NBS database, selected to represent similar type and size of facility and similar management type and catchment area socio-economically;
- importance–satisfaction gap scores for 19 service attributes, including accessibility, cleanliness, quality, staff and value for money;

(Continued)

Box 13.4. Continued.

- a catchment area map for the centre, for the area within which the centre is the dominant supplier;
- frequency distributions for all the questions in the user survey.

Source: National Benchmarking Survey website (http://www.questnbs.info/).

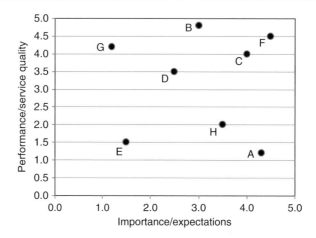

Fig. 13.3. Importance–performance analysis.

Table 13.11. Importance–performance evaluation: an example.

Service quality item	(a) Importance/ expectation score[a]	(b) Performance score[a]			
		Case 1	Case 2	Case 3	Case 4
A	4.3	1.2	2.0	2.7	4.5
B	3.0	4.8	4.8	4.8	4.9
C	4.0	4.0	4.0	4.2	4.3
D	2.5	3.5	3.5	3.7	3.7
E	1.5	1.5	1.6	1.7	1.9
F	4.5	4.5	4.5	4.5	4.5
G	1.2	4.2	4.0	3.5	3.5
H	3.5	2.0	2.5	3.0	4.7
Total score (sum of a × b)		78.9	84.0	89.6	104.3
Change (%)			+6.4	+6.7	+16.1
Attendances ('000)		50	51.5	53.3	57.5
Change (%)			+3.0	+3.5	+7.9

[a]Customer assessment: 1 = low, 5 = high. Data source: hypothetical.

Arts, cultural venues and events

There has been growing interest in performance appraisal in the area of the arts for some years. More than in most sectors, however, this field presents difficulties in handling the question of 'quality' versus 'popularity', since the general public may have different tastes from those of the arts aficionados, as discussed in Chapter 14 (Cohen and Pate, 2000). This is illustrated by an episode in Australia in 1989/90, when, following a national review of museums, the federal Department of Finance produced a report, entitled *What Price Heritage?* (Department of Finance, 1989), which proposed performance indicators for museums, relying largely on cost per visit and cost per square metre. This provoked considerable criticism from the museums sector and the arts industry in general, including, unusually, a critical response from the federal Department of the Arts, entitled *What Value Heritage?* (DASETT, 1990), and a specially convened conference (Skates, 1990). Little has been heard about performance indicators for Australian museums since then.

As indicated above, in England and Wales four National Performance Indicators (PIs) are included in the government's Comprehensive Area Assessment (CAA) system for local councils, namely overall participation in the arts and attendance at libraries, museums and galleries, and additional data are gathered in the Active People survey which provides the monitoring data for the PIs (see Table 13.7). During the era of Competitive Compulsory Tendering in the UK, the Audit Commission produced a study titled *Local Authorities, Entertainment and the Arts* (Audit Commission, 1991), which set out a wider range of possible performance indicators, as summarized in Table 13.12. The summary list is compiled from three different tables in the report and so consists of a mixture of objectives, policies and targets. There is just one attempt here to tackle the artistic quality issue, in the inclusion of newspaper reviews of productions as one of the PIs. Relatively few items (A2a, A3a, C5a) cover the strategic social goals/objectives as outlined above and in Fig. 13.2.

Examples of arts participation targets with clear implications for performance indicators can also be found on the book's website (http://www.leisuresource.net).

Sport

An example of objectives and explicit indicators at the national policy level can be found in the *Sport England Strategy, 2008-11*, summarized in Box 7.1 and in the New South Wales Department of Arts, Sport and Recreation plan summarized on the book's website (see above).

Tourism

Tourism New South Wales is a state government agency with responsibility for promotion of tourism in Sydney and the rest of New South Wales, Australia. As Table 13.13 shows, its 2002 *Masterplan* includes 35 operational performance measures divided into five groups concerned with: (i) Sydney's market position; (ii) sustainable management; (iii) investment climate; (iv) the promotion of regional and rural NSW (i.e. non-Sydney) tourism; and (v) overall success measures. Because Tourism NSW is a coordination and promotion organization, the success of its actions must be inferred from the success of the tourism industry as a whole, and the indicators therefore rely extensively on surveys of visitors, host communities and the tourism industry.

GOALS AND PERFORMANCE INDICES

In the course of this book a wide variety of goals and objectives for leisure facilities have been alluded to. Some arise from political philosophies and some are implicit in the planning and evaluation techniques discussed. Table 13.14 summarizes these various goals and objectives and relates them to appropriate measures of effectiveness and efficiency. This appears to be

Table 13.12. Performance Indicators for arts, cultural venues and events

Objective/ function	Performance Indicators	Data source[c]
A. Entertainment and the Arts		
1. Foster artistic excellence	(a) No. of performers supported	Own records
	(b) No. of engagements/recording contracts by supported performers	Survey of supported performers
	(c) Newspaper reviews of performances	Clippings service
	(d) No. of groups applying for grant aid	Own records
	(e) No. of groups receiving grant aid	Own records
2. Improve quality of life	(a) Use made by local population of supported facilities	Community or user surveys + census
	(b) No. of performances by type (eg. cultural, popular) in supported facilities	Facility records
	(c) Use made of supported facilities by people from different groups	Community or user surveys + census
3. Promote equity of access	(a) Breakdown of audiences by social background	User surveys
4. Foster a sense of community	(a) % of residents aware of the supported facilities	Community survey
	(b) No. of hires of supported facilities by local groups	Booking system
5. Conservation of cultural buildings	(a) Trading profit/loss on promotions[a]	Own financial records
	(b) Cost of building maintenance[a]	Own financial records
6. Increase participation in the arts by supporting local groups	(a) No. of groups supported	Own records
	(b) No. of groups using council facilities	Booking system
B. Venues and Events		
1. Council's own programme	(c) Number of events (performances/ hirings)	Own records
	(d) Number of different productions/ presentations	Own records
	(e) Mix of events (number and percentage of different types)	Own records
2. Pricing	(a) Admission prices charged	Own records
	(b) Average ticket price	Own records

(Continued)

Table 13.12. Continued.

Objective/ function	Performance Indicators	Data source[c]
	(c) Discounts offered to target groups	Own records
	(d) Take-up by target groups	Box office records, or user survey
3. Attendance	(a) Total number of attendances	Box office records
	(b) Frequency of attendance by different segments of the population	User surveys
	(c) % of seats sold	Box office records
4. Financial	(a) Average ticket yield	Box office records
	(b) Subsidy per attendance[a]	Box office + financial records
	(c) Subsidy per paid attendance[a]	Box office + financial records

C. Multi-purpose Venues	Targets[b]	
1. Performances	(a) Minimum number of evening performances a year	Own records
	(b) Minimum number of different performances a year	Own records
	(c) Minimum number of times any one production is to be performed	Own records
2. Financial arrangements with performers, managers, etc.	(a) Minimum and maximum share of hire, box office etc. income	Own records
	(b) Minimum hire fee	Own records
3. Programme	(a) Max/min. no. of events of different types - eg. rock, orchestral concerts.	Own records
4. Pricing	(b) Maximum prices to charge	Own records
	(c) Policy on discounts for target/ disadvantaged groups (eg. retired, students)	Own records
5. Audience	(a) Proportions of audience from particular sectors of society (eg. young people, ethnic minorities)	User surveys
6. Attendance	(a) Minimum percentage of seats to be sold	Box office
7. Subsidy	(b) Maximum average subsidy per seat sold[a]	Box office + financial records

[a]Efficiency indicators, the rest are effectiveness indicators; [b]this list is a mixture of targets, performance indicators and policies; [c]not in the original.

Source: adapted from Audit Commission (1991: 30, 34, 37).

Table 13.13. Towards 2020, the Tourism New South Wales Masterplan: operational performance measures.

Sydney's market position as Australia's premier tourist destination is maintained
Customer satisfaction
Share of Australian visitation: visitors, visitor nights, visitor experience, length of stay
Index of Sydney's attractiveness as a destination amongst potential customers: domestic, international
Share of cruise ship visits
Share of meetings, incentives, conference/exhibitions (MICE) visitation to Australia: count, visitor nights, experiences
Index of repeat holiday visitation to Australia by international visitors
Index of loyalty amongst domestic visitors
Tourism destinations in New South Wales are managed sustainably
Variation (seasonality) in visitation over the year: domestic, international
Index of host community: attitude towards tourism, acceptance of tourists
Percentage of operators with recognized environmental accreditation (e.g. Green Globe)
Index of NSW Government agency plans that incorporate tourism projections
Index of Regional Tourism Development Plans that reflect capacity issues
Index of environmental health
A positive climate for tourism investment and enterprises in New South Wales
Level of investment in tourism
Index of perceptions of tourism as an attractive area for investment: among brokers, investors
Count of qualified potential investors
Stock Exchange indices
Index of reinvestment opportunities
Tourism in regional and rural New South Wales is strengthened
Variation (seasonality) in visitation over the year: domestic, international
Count of tourism businesses operating in regional NSW
Lifespan of tourism businesses in regional NSW
Level of regional visitation: visitors, visitor nights, visitor experience, length of stay
Index of attitude to reinvestment
Count of tourism products in selected classes
Index of loyalty amongst domestic visitors
Index of awareness of and intention to visit NSW regional destinations
Overall success measures for Towards 2020
Index of affordability
Index of repeat holiday visitation
Value of investment decision-making information available to investors
Index of government tourism development/investment incentives
NSW share of government plans/programmes that support/facilitate tourism development/ investment

Source: Tourism New South Wales (2002).

a very daunting list but many, such as the political values, are alternatives and others, such as economic development or the encouragement of infant industries, only apply in special circumstances.

Table 13.14 points to a need for substantial data collection on a regular basis. The performance appraisal process suggests that, rather than being one-off exercises for the purpose of establishing a plan or strategy, routinized, ongoing data collection systems are required if policies are to be fully evaluated. This involves establishing reliable management

Table 13.14. Goals and measures of effectiveness and efficiency.

Goal	Measures of effectiveness/efficiency	Data sources[a]
Access to facilities for chosen leisure activities for all	Effectiveness: % of population participating % of population within reach of facilities % of population satisfied with service Efficiency: net cost per visit/participant	A A, E, H A, B C, D, F
Provision for need for all	Effectiveness: extent to which needs are met Efficiency: net cost per visit/participant	A, B F
Maintain existing provision	Effectiveness: qualitative measures Efficiency: cost per facility	E –
Promote excellence	Effectiveness: excellence: medals, awards, records, etc. Efficiency: costs per medal, etc.	I F
Minimize state role	Effectiveness: short-term: extent of privatization long-term: quantity and quality of service Efficiency: public/private service costs	G A F, G
Extend state role	Effectiveness: growth of facilities/staff/user numbers Efficiency: costs per visit/participant	E, G C, D, F
Promote equality of opportunity	Effectiveness: proportion of different social groups participating Efficiency: costs per visit by target group	A, B, H A, B, F
Promote democratization	Effectiveness: representation on governing bodies Efficiency: n/a	I –
Provide facilities and opportunities that counter commercial exploitation	Effectiveness: qualitative measures Efficiency: cost per facility	I –
Provide facilities/ programmes that counter patriarchy	Effectiveness: qualitative indicators of change Efficiency: cost per facility	A, B, I
Promote access to facilities for women	Effectiveness: number of facilities/programmes; female participation levels Efficiency: cost per visit/female participant	A, B, C, D, E B, C, D, F

(Continued)

Table 13.14. Continued.

Goal	Measures of effectiveness/efficiency	Data sources[a]
Provide childcare	Effectiveness: number of childcare places and utilization	C, E
	Efficiency: cost per child place/visit	C, E, F
Promote environmentally friendly activities	Effectiveness: 'environmental audit' of programmes	I
	Efficiency: cost per user compared with others	I
Protect the natural environment	Effectiveness: area protected qualitative review	E, I
	Efficiency: overall cost	G
Provide services that provide public good, externality, mixed good, merit good and option demand benefits	Effectiveness: willingness-to-pay surveys	A, B, H, I
	measure health, etc. benefits	A, B, I
	Clawson method	A, I
	Efficiency: costs per visit/rate of return	C, D, F
Promote economic activity through leisure	Effectiveness: profit	G, I
	economic impact: jobs, incomes	I
	Efficiency: cost per job created	F, I
Promote equity	Effectiveness: visits by deprived groups	A, B, H, I
	Efficiency: costs per visit	A, B, G, I
Meet standards (various)	Effectiveness: facility inventory	E
	Efficiency: cost per facility	G
Raise demand at least to the national/regional average	Effectiveness: participation levels	A, H
	Efficiency: costs per visit/participant	F
Serve all areas	Effectiveness: catchment areas, access, usage by area	A, B
	Efficiency: costs per visit in different areas	A, B, F
Ensure full range of facilities	Effectiveness: facility inventory for each community level	E
	Efficiency: overall cost	G
Meet needs of target groups in specified areas	Effectiveness: access and facilities in target areas	A, B
	Efficiency: costs per visit/target participant	A, B, F, I
Provide full range of experiences	Effectiveness: inventory of facility/resource types	E, G
	consumer reaction	A, B,
	Efficiency: cost per visit/experience type	A, B, C, D, E, F
Appropriate provision for all groups	Effectiveness: participation levels by all groups	A, B, G
	Efficiency: costs per visit/target participant	A, B, C, D, F

(Continued)

Table 13.14. Continued.

Goal	Measures of effectiveness/efficiency	Data sources[a]
Serve all areas	Effectiveness: facility catchment areas	B
	Efficiency: costs per visit/different areas	C, D, F
Maximize utilization of facilities	Effectiveness: facility utilization	C, D, E, H, I
	Efficiency: costs per unit of capacity	I
Meet community wishes	Effectiveness: community satisfaction	A, I
	Efficiency: overall cost	G

[a] A, community survey; B, user/visitor surveys; C, ticket sales; D, user counts; E, inventory; F, service costs; G, own records; H, census; I, special study.

information systems comprising: (i) routine ticket sale data (and user counts when these are not available); (ii) disaggregated financial data; (iii) booking records; (iv) regular user/visitor surveys; (v) community surveys; (vi) business surveys; and (vii) local population census analysis. In practice, however, the cost of collecting some of the data specified may be considered excessive and may be ignored or undertaken only rarely – this applies particularly to those items requiring research. Public sector agencies tend to see evaluative and market research as major, exceptional, undertakings, whereas many private sector organizations see continuous user and market research (for example, annual market surveys) as a normal activity. Public sector bodies will increasingly find it necessary to view such matters in a similar light if they are to justify their roles and respond to the demands increasingly being placed upon them.

Performance evaluation in the public sector of leisure, sport and tourism is still in its infancy, although considerable advances have been made in recent years. This is due partly to the history of public services and partly to the complexity of the policies and services involved. In the private sector, the goal generally is to maximize profits; the performance indicator – the rate of profit – is easily measured and there is a consensus among accountants, and even a legal specification, as to how it should be measured. The indicator provides a direct measure of the achievement of the goal. In the public sector, goals are generally more complex, concerned with issues such as community well-being, the quality of life or protection of the environment. Performance indicators in such situations are just that – indicators. Often, a number of indicators is required to give even an approximation of movement towards goal achievement. In practice, most public agencies are a long way from assessing performance and outcomes with this degree of sophistication, but the skills and infrastructure are being developed to make it possible in future.

SUMMARY

- This chapter addresses step 10 in the rational-comprehensive model presented in Chapter 6 (Fig. 6.3).
- The steps involved in performance evaluation are outlined and, in particular, it is emphasized that performance evaluation must be linked to goals and objectives.

- At the heart of modern performance evaluation is the Performance Indicator (PI) – generally a quantified measure of a specific aspect of performance.
- In the case of *internal* evaluation, PIs are measured against baseline and target values; in the case of *comparative* evaluation, PIs are *benchmarked* against the same PIs from a number of similar facilities or programmes.
- The chapter outlines the difference between strategic and operational and social, financial and environmental goals/objectives and performance indicators, including the idea of 'triple bottom-line' accounting.
- The chapter reviews a number of frameworks that have emerged in recent years to systematize evaluation, including the Comprehensive Area Assessment (CAA) framework operating for English local councils, services that focus on service quality (but include other PIs also), namely the CERM PI system (Australia) and the National Benchmarking Service (UK).
- In relation to customer service measures, the chapter considers importance–performance analysis and shows how it may be related to strategic goals/objectives, and considers applications of these and other evaluation exercises.
- The chapter concludes by noting that a major implication of performance evaluation is that its implementation requires a reliable information system comprising: (i) routine ticket sale data (and user counts when these are not available); (ii) disaggregated financial data; (iii) booking records; (iv) regular user/visitor surveys; (v) community surveys; (vi) business surveys; and (vii) local populations census analysis.

RESOURCES

Websites

Comprehensive Area Assessment (CAA) framework: http://www.communities.gov.uk/local government

CAA National Indicators 'Oneplace' site: http://oneplace.direct.gov.uk (at time of writing, December 2009, leisure indicators NIs 8–11 not provided on this site: see Active People survey site).

Active People survey: http://www.sportengland.org/research/active_people_survey.aspx

CERM Performance Indicators project: http://www.unisa.edu.au/cermpi

National Benchmarking Service: http://www.questnbs.info/

Sport Industry Research Centre (SIRC), Sheffield Hallam University: http://www.shu.ac.uk/ research/ sirc/index.html

Publications

Programme evaluation in general: Shadish *et al.* (1991);

Leisure programme evaluation: Bovaird (1992); Torkildsen (1993: Guide 13); Robinson (1997); Rossman (1999); Ogden and Wilson (2001); Henderson and Bialeschki (2002); Rossman and Schlatter (2008: Chapter 20);

Benchmarking: Ogden and Wilson (2001);

Managerialism: Gramberg and Teicher (2000);

Comprehensive Area Assessment: DCLG (2006, 2007); Central Council for Physical Recreation (2008); Active People Survey: Rowe (2009);

SERVQUAL: Langer (1997); Williams (1998a, b); Alexandris (2008); CERM: Howat *et al.* (2005); Howat and Crilley (2007);

Tourism: Hall and Jenkins (1995: Chapter 6); Langer (1997);

The arts: Department of Finance (1989); DASETT (1990); Skates (1990); Jackson (1991); Cohen and Pate (2000);

Sports facilities: Robinson and Taylor (2003); Taylor and Godfrey (2003);

Triple bottom-line: Elkington (1997); Norman and MacDonald (2004); Davidson (2006);

Importance–performance analysis: Martilla and James (1977); Guadagnolo (1985); Hollenhorst *et al.* (1992); Claxton (1994); Siegenthaler (1994); Langer (1997); Hudson and Shephard (1998); Rossman and Schlatter (2008: 397–403); Rial *et al.* (2008).

QUESTIONS/EXERCISES

1. What is the difference between efficiency and effectiveness?

2. What is a performance indicator and what role does it play in the evaluation process?

3. What is the difference between *internal* and *comparative* evaluation? What is another term for comparative evaluation?

3. Outline the features and limitations of the Comprehensive Area Assessment (CAA) framework operating in England.

4. Select two English councils and compare their Local Area Agreements (available on council websites) in regard to their treatment of leisure.

5. Select a recent Annual Report (most are available on organizational websites) of a leisure or tourism agency and assess its approach to performance evaluation.

6. Discuss the problems of assessing *quality* in leisure service performance evaluation.

7. For tourism agencies, the outcomes of policies and programmes are often widely dispersed in the industry, making evaluation difficult. Give examples of this problem and discuss ways of addressing it in the evaluation process.

8. Select a leisure or tourism facility, service or programme known to you and either obtain a copy of its goals/objectives or devise a suitable list of goals/objectives yourself. Now suggest a list of performance indicators based on these goals/objectives, indicating the data source for each PI.

9. Devise a list of five service performance indicators for a university/college course. Either as an individual or a group, grade your current course on the five indicators, in terms of importance and performance, and plot the results on a graph. What would be the priority areas for attention by the course providers on the basis of this assessment?

NOTES

[1]In England and Wales the Local Government Act 2000 requires local authorities to 'promote the social, economic and environmental well-being of their area, and … work with partners to prepare a community strategy'.

[2]In the second edition of the book, the American Benefits Approach to Leisure was included here. Later versions of this approach, as discussed in Chapter 3, indicate that the system has not, in my view, developed into a viable evaluation system for widespread application; this is discussed further in Veal (2009g).

[3]For details on sample error margins, or 'confidence intervals', see Veal (2006b: 288).

PART V

Sectors and Groups

Most of the book is generic in nature, dealing with leisure, sport and tourism as a whole and with people as a whole. The common elements among the various sectors of leisure, sport and tourism have been stressed: in this final part of the book their diversity is emphasized, the implications of that diversity for policy and planning are examined and the differing requirements of various social groups within the community are considered. The examination is necessarily brief, so more specialized and detailed sources are listed in the Resources sections of the chapters:

- Chapter 14, *Policy and Planning in Particular Sectors*, discusses five sectors of leisure, namely: sport and physical recreation; the arts and entertainment; outdoor recreation in natural areas; urban outdoor recreation; and tourism.
- Chapter 15, *Policy and Planning for Particular Groups*, discusses six social groups, namely: women; ethnic groups; people with disabilities; children; youth; and the elderly.

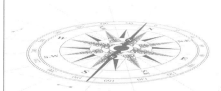

chapter 14

Policy and Planning in Particular Sectors

INTRODUCTION

This chapter is divided into five sections dealing with: (i) sport and other forms of physical recreation; (ii) the arts and entertainment; (iii) outdoor recreation in natural areas; (iv) urban outdoor recreation; and (v) tourism. The discussion of each sector is under five headings:

- the scope of the sector;
- the rationale and goals of policy within the sector;
- measurement of participation;
- institutional factors;
- planning.

Rationales

The rationale for public involvement in the sector and the consequent goals and planning activities generally pursued relate directly to many of the issues addressed in the earlier chapters of the book. A recurring feature is the multiple competing, and sometimes conflicting, goals that public policy seeks to pursue in each of the sectors, typically related to excellence as opposed to mass access or participation. This often gives rise to actual or potential tension between different professional groups working in the same sector. These issues are highlighted in the sector-specific discussions below, but are summarized in Table 14.1 to draw attention to the commonalities.

Measurement of participation

Given the emphasis in earlier chapters on planning for participation, the chapter provides information and brief comment on the measurement of participation in each sector for the UK and Australia. This information is summarized in Table 14.2. A guide to accessing data sources is provided in the Resources section.

Table 14.1. Multiple goals in public leisure policy.

	Excellence goal		Participation goal	
	Description	Associated professionals/ performers	Description	Associated professionals/ performers
Sport/physical recreation	High levels of sport performance	Coaches, professional and/or elite athletes	Grass-roots 'Sport for All'	Public sports facility managers
Arts and entertainment	Excellence in the arts Heritage conservation	Artists, performers directors, producers Curators, archaeologists	Audiences Visitors Amateur participation	Facility managers/ marketers Facility managers/ marketers Community arts workers
Outdoor recreation: natural	Conservation of flora/fauna	Biologists, ecologists	Public access	Natural area/ facility managers
Outdoor recreation: urban Tourism	Horticultural excellence Any of the above but main emphasis on participation goal	Horticulturalists Any of the above	Public recreation Tourist numbers/ income	Urban park managers Tourism managers/ marketers

SPORT AND OTHER FORMS OF PHYSICAL RECREATION

Scope

Sport can be defined as competitive or challenging physical, playful activity that takes a variety of forms, ranging from informal individual, family or community-based activity to highly competitive and commercialized phenomena of worldwide significance. *Physical recreation* is sometimes bracketed with sport and encompasses those activities which are physical in nature and leisure-orientated, but not necessarily competitive or organized – typical examples being walking, non-competitive cycling and some forms of water-based recreation. In Australia, one of the main data sets on grass-roots participation in this sector uses the inclusive term 'activities for exercise, recreation and sport' (SCORS, annual), while the Active People survey in England uses the term 'sport and active recreation' (Sport England, undated).

Table 14.2. Measurement of participation in leisure sectors.

	Sport/Physical recreation	Arts	Outdoor recreation[a]	Tourism (International)[b]
England				
Survey	Active People Survey	Active People survey	England Leisure Visits Survey	International Passenger Survey (IPS)
Organization	Sport England	Sport England	Natural England	Office for National Statistics
Frequency	Annual	Annual	Last: 2005	Annual
Sample size	190,000	190,000	23,500	250,000
Age range	16+	16+	16+	
Participation data	In last 4 weeks: participation in sport/active recreation to specified level + individual activities	In last year: visits to public library, museum/gallery, arts venues + actual participation in arts	All one-day leisure trips, urban and rural	Includes o/seas visitors to UK and UK residents' o/seas trips: nights, destination, expenditure, etc.
Socio-demographic data	Yes	Yes	Yes	Yes
Website[c]	http://www.sportengland.org	http://www.sportengland.org	http://naturalengland.org.uk	www.statistics.gov.uk/
Australia				
Survey	Exercise, Recreation & Sport Survey (ERASS)	Attendance at Cultural Venues and Events	No known official survey	International Visitor Survey
Organization	Standing Committee on Recreation & Sport	Australian Bureau of Statistics		Tourism Research Australia
Frequency conducted	Annual	5-yearly (last in 2006)		Annual

(Continued)

Table 14.2. Continued.

	Sport/Physical recreation	Arts	Outdoor recreation[a]	Tourism (International)[b]
Sample size	14,000	13,000		40,000
Age range	16+	16+		15+
Participation data	In last year: participation in ERAS and individual activities; in last 2 weeks: in ERAS to specified level	In last year: visits to list of venue/event types		No. of nights spent in Aust.; travel mode; reasons for visiting; places visited; info. sources; impressions; exp.
Socio-demographic data	Yes	Yes		Yes
Website[c]	http://www.ausport.gov.au	http://www.abs.gov.au		http://www.tra.australia.com

[a] Urban outdoor recreation: no known national data in either country.
[b] Domestic: see Chapter 8, Resources section.
[c] For more details see Chapter 8, Resources section.

Public policy rationale and goals

In general, public policy in sport has two goals:

1. *Mass participation*: to maximize participation in sport and physical recreation among the general population, encapsulated in the widely supported Sport for All campaign.

2. *Elite success*: to promote maximum high-level achievement in competitive sport, both locally and internationally.

Individual participants and groups of enthusiasts engage in sporting activity for its own sake, and for a variety of personal reasons, but public support, particularly in the form of funds raised from taxation or specially sanctioned measures, such as lotteries, requires a rationale. In this case support for the goals is widely seen as justified because of:

- the health benefits that participation can bring;
- the fostering of community cohesiveness and pride that can come from sporting success;
- economic development factors, such as the attraction of industry or tourists to a community or the economic benefits expected from the hosting of major events, such as the Olympic or Commonwealth Games.

Those involved in sport and physical recreation organizations tend to enjoy the activity for its own sake and may be somewhat bemused at others' need to justify public support in instrumental terms. As a result, much political support for sport can be said to arise as a result of the self-interested lobbying activity of sporting organizations and their supporters – the public-choice model discussed in Chapter 6 – rather than from some appraisal of the benefit of sport to the wider community (such as the public good arguments discussed in Chapter 5). This lack of understanding of the nature of public policy is exemplified by the following quotation from a report by the Central Council for Physical Recreation, the representative body for sporting organizations in England:

> The recent announcement of Sport England's new three-year strategy heralded a firm commitment to funding sport for sport's sake. This contrasts with much of what has gone before. For the last decade or so, an emphasis on the instrumental value of sport – its presumed contribution to health, crime, employment and education, for example – has reflected a government agenda of developing communities through sport, rather than developing sport in the community. In 2003, at CCPR's annual conference, Richard Caborn, the then Minister for Sport, stated that the Government would 'not accept simplistic assertions that sport is good as sufficient reason to back sport'. Contrast this with the speech made by James Purnell, the then Secretary of State for Culture, Media and Sport, who initiated this latest policy shift in 2007: 'Sport matters in itself … too often sport is justified on the basis of its spill-over benefits'.
>
> (CCPR, 2008: 4)

The two goals of sports policy, high-level performance and Sport for All – are to some extent complementary and to some extent in competition, even contradiction. One view is that sport thrives on a sort of pyramid or *trickle-down* model, as shown in Fig. 14.1. A strong, broad, mass participation base should, it is argued, provide the breeding ground for talent to produce the elite athletes for national and international competition. Conversely, a successful elite and a strong local and national competitive structure should provide inspiration and a suitable environment to encourage grass-roots participation. There is, however, some doubt about the extent to which the trickle-down effect works in practice (Veal and Frawley, 2009).

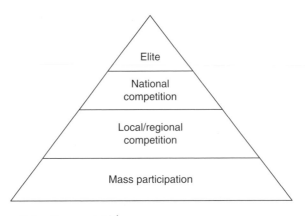

Fig. 14.1. Sports participation pyramid.

An alternative view is that the trickle-down effect simply does not work: that the dynamics of mass participation are governed by local culture and infrastructure and other lifestyle trends, rather than by any inspiration coming from the elite (Roche, 1993). It can be argued that, for many sporting activities, the relationship between the mass, grass-roots level is not pyramid-shaped at all, but more like the situation portrayed in Fig. 14.2, with what might be called a 'selective elitism' process beginning quite low in the system.

A third view is that, even if the trickle-down effect does work in theory, it is frustrated in practice because government resources inevitably flow to the elite level at the expense of the less glamorous mass participation level, as a result of the lobbying activity of sporting organizations and the profile association which elite sport can give politicians. Often, however, this conclusion is based on analysis of national government expenditure patterns alone, ignoring expenditure on the grass roots by lower tiers of government.

Measurement of participation

Measuring participation in sport has a long history, but is still evolving. We have noted in Chapter 13 that in England official participation figures from Sport England's large-scale annual Active People survey, as summarized in Table 14.2, form the basis of a nationwide Comprehensive Area Assessment (CAA) performance evaluation framework for local

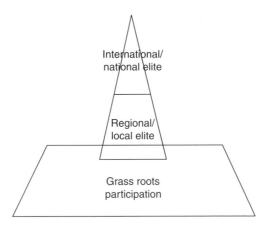

Fig. 14.2. Sport and selective elitism.

authorities, with a sample size large enough to provide data for all 330 council areas in England. In addition to the single measure of participation used for the CAA, the Active People survey also includes data for each local council area on individual activities and socio-demographic variables. Whereas in the past, participation measures were based on whether or not survey respondents had participated in a sporting or physical recreation activity at least once in the year prior to interview, more recently, policymakers have heeded the advice of health professionals and now identify people who participate on a regular basis for a specified minimum period of time, thus generating health benefits.

In Australia, the annual Exercise Recreation and Sport Survey still emphasizes the 'at least once' measure, but the health-related measures are also included. However, the sample size is such that the data are available only at national and state level.

From the planning point of view it is desirable to identify infrequent participants who do not meet the specified minimum as well as those who do, for two reasons. First, infrequent participants are a potential market for increased participation to increase the number of people securing health benefits. Second, infrequent participants still take up capacity in facilities, so should be taken into account in planning provision if they form a significant proportion of total participation.

Institutional factors

While the pyramid scenario may indeed work, or may be a goal to aim at, the planning and management of organizational structures to achieve it can be complex. Each level of sport organization involves public, private and commercial organizations, with different sets of goals and different modes of operation, as indicated in Table 14.3. Those professional and voluntary managers and policy-makers involved at opposite ends of the pyramid may not subscribe to, or even understand, the pyramid or trickle-down philosophy: they may have their own, differing perspectives. Indeed, someone involved in elite sports competition may have a low opinion of recreational sport and resent the public resources devoted to it, while someone involved in community recreation may be philosophically antagonistic towards the very concept of elitism, and resent the public resources being devoted to the support of elite sport.

At the community level in the pyramid, the distinction between sport, physical recreation and social recreation becomes blurred: the manager of a community sports and leisure centre may feel that it is just as useful, or even more useful, to provide opportunities to enable elderly people to get out of the house for a game of bingo at the leisure centre, or to encourage teenagers to engage in exercise through attendance at a discotheque, as it is to provide for formal competitive sports activities. On the other hand, management's desire to reach as wide a cross-section of the community as possible and to maximize attendances at leisure facilities may, in the view of some, lead to superficial dabbling in a wide range of sporting activities and neglect of facilities, resources and organizational structures for those who wish to progress or improve and take sport seriously.

At the elite level, questions can arise over just how far individuals should push themselves, or be pushed, to excel and win for the benefit of national pride, if this is at the expense of their own long-term physical and mental health. The concept of elitism raises issues concerning the relationship between public policy, amateurism, professionalism and commercialism. While public resources are provided to support the development of athletes in the context of an amateur ethos, increasing commercialization and professionalization of sport often results, ultimately, in great personal financial rewards for some, raising questions of 'who pays?' or 'who should pay?'

Table 14.3. Sport organizational structure.

Sport organizations	Government	Commerce
International		
International Federations of Sport (individual sports)International multi-sport organizations (Olympics, Paralympics, Commonwealth Games, etc.) World Anti-doping Agency Professional sports organizations	European Union	Multinational leisure clothing, media corporations, sport management agencies, sponsors
National		
National governing bodies of sport/franchises	Ministries of Sport	National leisure clothing, media corporations, sport management agencies, sponsors
National Olympic and Paralympic Committees	Sports commissions Universities (in USA)	
State/Provincial/Regional		
State/Provincial/Regional sports organizations	State/Provincial governments: ministries of sport and recreation, sports commissions	State/Provincial media, sports businesses and sponsors
Local		
Sporting clubs	Local government parks, sports, etc. departments	Local sport businesses and sponsors

In sport, professionalism usually implies financial self-sufficiency, that is, those sectors where the athletes are paid professionals do not generally look to the public sector for subsidy; they derive their income from spectators, television fees and sponsorship. In traditional sports, different relationships have grown up between the publicly funded amateur sector of the sport and the commercially funded, professional sector, although the relationship has not always been amicable, as witness the relationship between Rugby League (professional) and Rugby Union (traditionally amateur). Different sports have had different relationships with the public sector, for a mix of historical, cultural and technical reasons. For example:

- Boxing requires only modest facilities for training, which has enabled the sport, even at amateur level, to be fairly self-sufficient.
- Tennis has relied on private clubs, sometimes helped by public funds and sometimes using public facilities.
- In the case of golf, amateurs pay their way and often use the same facilities as the professionals, while publicly provided facilities also tend to be financially self-sufficient.

- Soccer is among the most commercialized and professionalized sports at the elite level, but the amateur game is extensively supported through subsidized access to publicly provided playing pitches.

A common feature of sport policy is the short-term project or programme using special funds, usually from central government. Such programmes are typically aimed at 'difficult to reach' young people who do not make use of mainstream provision. They can be seen as a genuine attempt to overcome the barriers to participation and assist young people's social development through sport or they may be viewed as somewhat opportunistic: if the government has money available for youth, the sport sector develops programmes for youth; if it has money for countering urban deprivation, the sport sector has urban programmes, and so on. They can also be viewed as politically convenient for the politicians providing the funds, because programmes with a limited time scale relieve governments of providing permanent funding and, by the time the programmes have been established, operated and evaluated, the world has changed, politicians have moved on and new priorities have emerged.

Collins and Kay (2003: 242), in their study of *Sport and Social Exclusion*, call for typical programmes to at least be extended to 7 to 10 years to enable assessment of longer-term impacts, although they admit that this would be a challenge for the political system. One of the key difficulties with such programmes is evaluating their effectiveness. Nichols, in his study of *Sport and Crime Reduction* (2007: 193), reviews a number of programmes and suggests that the 'gold standard' of scientifically rigorous research may not be possible in such contexts. In his wide-ranging review, *A Wider Role for Sport,* Coalter (2007: 1–2), notes the almost universal conceptual and methodological weakness of evaluative research in the area.

Increasingly, one view of sport, even within the public sector, is as an industry, particularly through its links with events and sports tourism. This is seen in the perspective of Birmingham City Council, summarized in Box 13.2, and in the former Australian Liberal government's sports industry policy statement *End Goal 2006* (Department of Industry, Science and Resources, 1999). In this case government support faces issues similar to those faced in regard to any other industry, in particular whether government is able to 'pick winners' – that is economically viable projects – in the marketplace.

Planning

As noted in Chapter 7, planning for sport facilities for the community was for many years focused on standards of provision for playing fields prescribed by such organizations as the National Playing Fields Association (now Fields in Trust) in the UK and the National Recreation and Parks Association in the USA. In recent decades, efforts have been made to widen the scope of planning to include facilities other than playing fields and to move away from externally prescribed standards. From its establishment in the early 1970s, the British Sports Council was instrumental in widening the scope of public planning to include such facilities as indoor sports and leisure centres and swimming pools and dual use of education facilities, utilizing relatively sophisticated demand-based planning techniques and the development of interlinked national, regional and local planning strategies for the provision of facilities (Sports Council, 1972, 1991, 1992, 1993). This has also been developed by the Scottish Sports Council (1996).

Planning for the promotion of mass participation by means other than the provision of facilities is a less certain process. Direct promotion through publicity campaigns have been difficult to evaluate, as have educational programmes (Watkins, 1981; McIntosh and Charlton, 1985).

Planning for the top part of the pyramid is complicated by the involvement of numerous national and international governing bodies of sport, commercial promoters, professional players' organizations, media interests and, in the pubic sector, a range of quangos, often with ministers looking closely over their shoulders, despite the supposed existence of the 'arm's length' principle. The core of planning at this level is the formal strategic plan of the governing body; such a plan is a necessity if the aspirations of the sport are to be supported by public funds (Elvin, 1990: 73).

THE ARTS AND ENTERTAINMENT

Scope

The arts cover a wide spectrum of human activity, including the performing arts (drama, music, opera and dance), painting and sculpture, craft activities, literature, poetry, architecture and design, film, television and radio. The arts industries cover the various activities and institutions that facilitate or conserve these activities and their outputs, including theatres and theatre companies, opera houses and opera companies, concert halls and orchestras and dance companies, art galleries, museums, heritage conservation, libraries and the various public and private bodies that provide financial support to the sector.

Rationale and goals

Public subsidy of the arts has traditionally been justified on the grounds of market failure arguments of the sort discussed in Chapter 5 (Frey, 2003). Other arguments relate to their growing importance in the economy (Casey *et al.*, 1996) and, especially in relation to galleries, museums and libraries, their educational value (Baumol and Bowen, 1976). More recently the arts have been viewed as an industry sector – the 'cultural industries' (Caves, 2000; Florida, 2003; Hartley, 2005) – and this is also frequently used as an argument for public support.

The arts have certain similarities with sport and certain stark differences. The similarities lie in the duality of objectives: excellence versus mass involvement. The differences lie in the structure of the industry and its relationship with the public.

Unlike sport, where the publicly subsidized sector and the commercial sector are both considered, unequivocally, to be sport, in the arts those elements of the industry that are financially self-sufficient, such as commercial film and theatre, recorded music and commercial television and publishing, tend to be classified as *entertainment* or *popular culture* rather than part of *the arts*. Thus it would seem that, to exaggerate just a little, only if an activity does not make money is it classified as *art*.

A further contrast between sport and the arts is that, whereas in sport public resources are largely devoted to enabling *direct participation in sport by members of the public*, and professionals are largely financially self-supporting, in the case of the arts, public resources are required to support *professionals*, with the public role being largely that of audience only. The area of the arts corresponding to grass-roots sports participation is 'amateur theatre', 'amateur music'; and whereas the 'amateur' is a celebrated phenomenon in sport, in the arts such activity is generally looked down upon or largely ignored. Active participation in the arts is left to voluntary effort (for example, amateur music and drama), to the public or commercial *education* sector (for example, adult education classes in painting or pottery, or commercial dance studios), or to self-help (for example, amateur rock and jazz bands). When the arts community itself ventures into the area or participation – in the form of *community arts* – it is often controversial (Kelly, 1984; Hawkins, 1993).

There is a further difference between sport and the arts which is notable because it leads to a particular difficulty in arts policy and management that does not arise in sports policy and management. This is that, in the arts, the concept of *excellence* is often disputed, whereas it is not in sport. There is generally no dispute about who is the number one-ranking tennis player, or what team won the World Cup. In particular, there is a consensus among athletes, sports administrators and the general public about what excellence is – even if there is lively debate from time to time as to which team or player is currently demonstrating such qualities. This is not the case in the arts: what artists or administrators think of as *excellence* is often at variance with the tastes of the general public. While there are of course exceptions, in general the public will flock to performances of the familiar and the 'unchallenging', but will stay away in droves from productions that are new or 'difficult'. Hence arts managers are continually being faced with the task of balancing artistic challenge and integrity with the commercial 'realities' of getting 'bums on seats'. All this, of course, makes application of traditional, rationalist, decision-making and performance evaluation difficult.

Libraries are often neglected in discussion of the arts, and yet they are the most pervasive and significant of the publicly funded arts/cultural services. Of course libraries have an educational and information-providing role that may well be the primary basis of their political support, but most of their use is for leisure purposes (Taylor and Johnson, 1973). While it is, no doubt, their educational and information roles that provide much of the basis for their continued political support as free public services, the leisure function of libraries offers an interesting case study of public provision. Lending libraries are obviously socially desirable and make efficient use of resources, since several hundred people can read one library book compared with only a few in the case of private ownership. But why should the borrower not pay? Private lending libraries existed into the 1950s, where people paid a small sum to borrow books, in the same way that people currently hire videos. But they were eventually undermined by the arrival of the cheap paperback. The free public lending library has the advantage of making a wider range of titles available to the reader (not all books are available in cheap paperback editions) and makes books available to those for whom even paperback prices would be a deterrent.

As a leisure service, therefore, the public lending library is both efficient and equitable. Against this must be balanced the financial interests of publishers and authors, who would no doubt prefer people to buy books rather than borrow them for free from libraries. But this has been addressed to a certain extent by the Public Lending Right Act, 1979, which requires public libraries to pay into a central fund which compensates authors and publishers for library use of their work.

Similar arguments apply to art galleries and museums: an infinite number of people may enjoy works of art and heritage items in galleries, compared with just a few if they were privately owned. To this extent galleries and museums meet the *non-rival*, although not strictly the *non-excludable*, criterion for public goods, as discussed in Chapter 3. In addition, the *natural monopoly* criterion applies in relation to single works of art, or collections of national, or even world, cultural importance. In the case of galleries and museums, however, the *mixed good* concept has prevailed in recent years and there has been a trend towards charging an entrance fee – albeit one that only partially covers costs. As with libraries, however, it is likely that the broader cultural heritage and educational role of galleries and museums is the basis of their political support, rather than their purely leisure functions. Increasingly, such institutions are also being seen as worthy of support because of their role as part of the infrastructure of tourism and potential for urban economic regeneration (Voase, 1997).

Broadcasting is a quintessential public good, even if provided entirely for leisure purposes and even if commercially supported through advertising. It is likely, however, that public broadcasting bodies, such as the BBC in the UK and the ABC in Australia, generally receive their political support not because of their leisure role but because of their educational, information and national cultural identity role.

Measurement of participation

As with sport, and noted in Chapter 13, in England official participation figures on arts participation are included in Sport England's large-scale annual Active People survey, as indicated in Table 14.2, and form the basis of a nationwide Comprehensive Area Assessment (CAA) performance evaluation framework for local authorities. However, while the CAA uses only a single indicator for sport, for the arts three indicators are included: use of public libraries, visiting museums and galleries and participation in the arts generally. The Active People survey also includes information on 'actually doing any creative, artistic, theatrical or musical activities', as well as socio-demographic variables.

In Australia the Australian Bureau of Statistics gathers survey data every 5 years on visiting selected cultural venues and events, but the sample size is such that the data are available only at national and state level.

Institutional factors

Because of the high cost of supporting professional performers in a subsidized environment, the central preoccupation of much of the arts management community would appear to be *funding*. While a large proportion of funding in the performing arts is generated from the box office and other entrepreneurial activities, the balance is sought in the form of grants from local, state or central governments. It is the latter that attracts the most debate and controversy. Clearly, if governments were to provide more money for the arts then directors, writers and performers would have more freedom to pursue their artistic aims, and would be less constrained by the discipline of the box office. The controllers of the public purse strings might, however, look askance at such a proposition: surely 'less dependence on the box office' could mean less people attending performances – surely that would not be achieving the public objective of bringing the arts to the people! Of course the arts organizations *could* be saying: if we had more money we could mount more lavish productions, provide more variety and put on more performances in more locations – this would bring the arts to more people. Insofar as the public funding bodies are suspicious of the earlier argument but are sympathetic to the latter, they have an interest in knowing just how any additional funding will be used. It is not uncommon, therefore, for governments to offer additional funds earmarked for specific activities, such as regional touring.

In the case of other art forms, notably galleries and museums, the preoccupation with funding is equally prevalent. While 'blockbuster', money-making exhibitions and entrance fees are becoming more common, galleries and museums are usually even more dependent on public subsidy than are the performing arts. This has traditionally been justified on the educational grounds discussed above. The demand for additional funding is nevertheless endemic. Museum and gallery trustees and managements always need money for acquisitions, for expansion to exhibit the artefacts they have stored away, or for staff to pursue research and conservation activities.

Planning

With the exception of libraries, planning for the arts can best be described as an ad hoc process. There is no apparent national strategic planning in the UK comparable to the then Sports Council's detailed plans for the provision of sports facilities. At local level, again with the possible exception of libraries, planning for the arts would appear to be more a matter of municipal pride than assessment of community requirements. The principle seems to be that any urban authority of any size feels that it should have a civic theatre, a museum and, possibly, an arts centre – indeed, the philosophy might well have been summed up by the title of one of the early, and few, books on arts centres, which was: *Every Town Should Have One* (Lane, 1978).

A feature of recent guidelines for planning in this sector has been the use of the term *culture* rather than the arts. Typically, such guidelines define culture widely, to include way-of-life generally and to cover such cultural expressions as sport and urban design. This sets up a challenge which it is virtually impossible to meet, since it implies the planning of social life generally. Invariably, the detail reverts to planning in the traditional arts sectors (see Veal, 2009c).

Before its abolition by the Thatcher government in 1980, the Greater London Council pioneered attempts at developing a strategic approach to local cultural planning. In subsequent years, a number of researchers kept alive the idea that *cultural industries* might be taken seriously as a key feature of urban life and an important economic sector, and that local strategies might be produced to address the development of such an industry and to secure community benefits from it (e.g. Garnham, 1987; Bianchini *et al.*, 1991; Landry and Bianchini, 1995; Zukin, 1995). In the UK, the establishment of a Department of *Culture*, Media and Sport has brought responsibility for the arts and sport into one government department, which has resulted, in turn, in nationally promulgated guidelines for the production of local *cultural* strategies (Department for Culture, Media and Sport, 1999). This recognizes that local authorities have responsibilities across the whole range of leisure and tourism, including outdoor recreation, sport, tourism, heritage and the arts.

It is notable that, during the brief period at the end of the 1980s and early 1990s, the Australian federal government included a similarly broad department, with the unwieldy title of the Department of the Arts, Sport, the Environment, Tourism and Territories (DASETT). A forward-looking national cultural policy document emerged, dealing with the arts (Commonwealth of Australia, 1994), but the various junior portfolios within the ministry remained separate, as they do at state level, and no local planning guidance emerged. In the UK then, it is possible that, with central government support, more planning for the arts, alongside planning for other aspects of culture, will be seen in local government in future.

OUTDOOR RECREATION: NATURAL AREAS

Scope

Outdoor recreation in natural areas takes place in national parks and country parks, in forests, on the coast and on footpaths and, through the phenomenon of 'driving for pleasure', throughout the countryside. The visiting of heritage and other attractions in the rural environment is also included.

Rationale and goals

As with sport and the arts, public policy with regard to outdoor recreation in the natural environment – in national parks, country parks and the coast – is faced with two potentially conflicting goals: conservation and recreational access. Conservation of flora, fauna, landscape, ecosystems and heritage seems a clear enough mandate, until it is realized that, in the case of the UK, hardly any area of the country has been untouched by human activity over the centuries. Before human beings made their mark the whole of the UK was covered in forest, but now even the national parks are grazed by sheep! Even in the supposedly pristine environment of the Australian bush, the landscape we see today results from tens of thousands of years of management by human beings through hunting and gathering activities and the use of fire (Flannery, 1994).

So what is *natural* and to be *conserved*? In some areas, phenomena such as abandoned mines, which would, in modern times, be seen as a desecration of the natural landscape, have now become a part of the cultural heritage. But the real problems arise when considering recreational access. For virtually any ecosystem, human activity – certainly on any scale – poses a threat. Walking tracks, car parks, toilet blocks and campsites usurp space that might have been used by flora and fauna, and their use inevitably disturbs the flora and fauna: ultimately, conservation implies the exclusion of the species *Homo sapiens* in its modern form.

And yet national parks authorities are required by law to facilitate recreational access as well as conserving the environment; and facilitating such access is a necessary part of their continued community and political support. But as a result of the dual goals, the sort of overt promotional and marketing activity we see in the sports and arts sectors is not part of the countryside recreation scene. In natural areas, a balance has to be struck between recreational access and conservation.

Measurement of participation

Natural England last conducted a survey of countryside visits in 2005 with the England Leisure Visits Survey, as indicated in Table 14.2. In fact the survey covers all leisure trips that begin and end at home and do not involve an overnight stay. Included are the following destinations: inland towns/cities, seaside towns/cities, countryside and the coast, and additional subcategories of woods and forests, inland waters with boats, inland waters without boats, national parks and open-access land.

There is no known comparable official survey in Australia.

Institutional factors

A unique feature of countryside recreation – particularly in the UK – is that much of it takes place on private property, with the public role being to ensure and to manage rights of access. This is true of large parts of the UK's national parks, and of footpaths and coastal access (although actual beaches are in the public domain). While initial campaigns for public access were organized by voluntary effort (Glyptis, 1991: 28), today the public interest in recreational access to the countryside is represented by elected councils and quangos (such as national parks agencies and Natural England, formerly the Countryside Agency), although non-profit sector organizations such as the National Trust remain important.

Providing for countryside recreation faces the further special problem that, typically, the population being planned for is not the resident rural population, but the nearby and distant urban population (see Fig. 1.3c and d). Consequently, rural communities can be seen to be providing for the recreational needs of urban residents. Of course this could be viewed as a balance to the cultural and other services provided by urban centres to rural residents, but things are rarely seen in such a light, especially given that the rural population is generally smaller in numbers and less wealthy than the urban population. This demographic and financial imbalance is of course an argument for national and regional government providing financial support for local rural councils and for national park organizations, and this is generally what happens in practice. In federal systems the problem is partly solved by state governments having responsibilities for natural areas.

Planning

One way in which policy-makers seek to balance the demands of conservation and recreational demand is by designation and zoning processes. Thus at one end of the spectrum nature reserves and, in some countries, wilderness areas, are established, from which humans are virtually excluded. Within national parks, efforts are made to concentrate high-volume visitation in limited areas where services can be provided and the impact on the natural environment can be contained. At the other extreme, in the UK, country parks were created, which are primarily devoted to recreation and can sometimes be indistinguishable from larger urban parks. The Recreation Opportunity Spectrum idea, as outlined in Chapter 7, is one way in which this 'spectrum' approach is formalized.

The fact that the clients for countryside recreation are urban residents, as discussed above, is a key feature of planning for countryside recreation. This means that, ideally, planning should be undertaken on a regional rather than local basis. Thus, for example, planning for outdoor recreation in the various counties in the south-east of England is dominated by the demands of the population of London; any one individual county cannot be expected to encompass this process in its entirety – researching and planning for the phenomenon must be a cooperative, regional, process. A similar situation exists along the south-east coast of Australia, dominated by the major cities of Melbourne, Sydney and Brisbane. However, in the UK, the need for this sort of approach to planning has become less urgent as static or declining populations and economic recession have slowed the rate of growth of recreation demand and, in some cases, put it into reverse (Rodgers, 1993; Natural England, 2005). Planning for outdoor recreation, in a no-growth situation, can become more 'resource-based' and less concerned with demand pressures.

URBAN OUTDOOR RECREATION

Scope

Urban outdoor recreation takes place primarily in parks, playing fields, playgrounds, squares and plazas. The provision of open space in urban areas constitutes the largest single public leisure service sector, in terms of expenditure, the value of land allocation and staff, and is the longest established. Parks include formal and informal landscaped areas for walking and relaxation and specific-purpose facilities designed for more physically active recreation, including boating facilities, playgrounds, hard sports areas such as tennis courts, and grass playing pitches. And they may contain catering facilities and performance spaces. Parks accommodate events, such as music performances, sports matches, demonstrations and rallies, and peripatetic phenomena such as funfairs and circuses. Other forms of urban public open space should not be ignored, including public squares and plazas, harbour and riverside areas, seaside promenades, marketplaces and village greens and, indeed, streets, especially where they have been pedestrianized.

Rationale and goals

This sector does not face the conflicting goals of recreational access versus conservation to anything like the extent that they are faced by its countryside counterpart. Urban parks can, however, extend to the urban fringe, where environmentally sensitive areas can be involved and, even within urban areas, parks may encompass areas that are valued for their nature conservation aspect rather than for their direct recreational facilities. In addition, parks can include natural or built items of heritage value, such as mature trees, or monuments and buildings, the conservation of which may conflict with some recreational objectives. In general, however, parks have been planned, designed and developed by human beings specifically for recreational purposes.

Nevertheless, there is an 'excellence' factor in park management that parallels that in sport or the arts, namely horticultural and landscape values. The horticulturalist or landscape planner has a set of professional values which may or may not be compatible with the demands of the recreational user of an area of open space. In general, the horticulturalist or landscaper wants to 'do things with plants' or with the aesthetics of the landscape. This is not necessarily in conflict with recreational requirements – for example, elaborate floral displays are generally popular with the public, although expensive to maintain.

Parks for informal recreation offer the same sorts of community benefits as natural areas, in the form of opportunities to relax, 'commune with nature' and take exercise. Generally the aim of the providers of such facilities is to 'provide opportunity' rather than to actively promote or maximize participation. Insofar as parks contain sports facilities, the goals should, logically, be similar to those discussed under sport and physical recreation, and areas developed in relation to cultural and entertainment, such as the recent growth of harbour-side developments, have a promotional ethos similar to commercial enterprises – 'the more the merrier' – and therefore a more proactive approach to promotion of participation is appropriate. There should therefore be a difference between the *resource-based* focus of 'green' open space recreation area management and the *people-based*, promotional orientation of sports and entertainment-related facilities.

Measurement of participation

Despite the significance of urban parks as a public leisure service and land-user, governments generally do not gather data on their use. As noted in Box 10.2, such data as are available from local surveys suggest that urban parks are more used by a higher proportion of the population than other public leisure facilities and usage is not socio-economically skewed as with arts and sports facilities.

Institutional factors

Generally, urban open space is in the ownership and control of local government. In large urban centres, however, other agencies may be involved, such as the Royal Parks in London, run by the Royal Parks Agency responsible to the Department for Culture, Media and Sport. In federal systems the state government may have responsibility for national parks and some major urban parks. Often, local government parks are administered separately from other leisure services, so the resource-based, facility maintenance approach has tended to be dominant.

Planning

As indicated in Chapter 7, planning for open space in urban areas was one of the earliest forms of leisure planning. While this activity was traditionally based on externally prescribed fixed standards of provision that have now been superseded, many of the alternative methods have their basis in open-space planning. In the UK the opportunity to develop new parks, even in areas with very low levels of provision, is very limited. In fact it is in the areas of greatest relative deprivation, in the centres of large cities, that the opportunities are most rare, because of the price of land. Planning of these areas today is therefore much closer to management – the task is to determine how to make the best use of the facilities available. Optimizing use can involve management practices (for example, increasing staff patrols in areas where usage is limited because of safety fears) or development work (e.g. improving drainage of pitches or providing artificial surfaces). However, in growing cities, such as those in Australia and in developing countries, the challenge of providing suitable open space for a growing population is significant.

TOURISM

Scope

Tourism is defined differently by different writers and agencies. Definitions of 'a tourist' generally involve an overnight stay away from home in a place other than the person's normal place of residence. Some definitions distinguish between those who travel for leisure purposes and those who travel for non-leisure purposes, such as business, and yet the business traveller's requirements overlap considerably with those of the leisure traveller. Similarly, day-trippers to holiday areas are not normally included in the strict definition of 'tourist', but many of their requirements and activities are similar to those of the staying tourist in all respects, except for the requirement for accommodation. While the high-profile sector of tourism is international travel, in most developed countries *domestic* tourism – people taking holidays in their own country – is larger in both the number of trips and financial turnover.

Tourism is often viewed and analysed in terms of the *industry* rather than the *tourist*. The tourism industry is fragmented, not only in terms of the dominance of small businesses (such as hotels and camping sites, restaurants and gift shops), but also in terms of the variety of subsectors involved, including travel agents, transport operators of all modes, the accommodation sector, cafes and restaurants and natural environment and built attractions. As with leisure generally, many sectors of the so-called tourism industry are only *partly* in the tourism industry – for example, transport, catering and many of the attractions (when they are used by locals as well as visitors).

Tourism is increasingly being seen as consisting of 'mass' tourism and a series of specialist tourism markets – although in practice one tourist might be involved in a number of markets in any one trip. Among the specialist areas are: (i) ecotourism or nature-based tourism; (ii) cultural tourism; (iii) the meetings, incentives, conventions and events sector (MICE); (iv) urban tourism; (v) wine tourism; (vi) the backpacker market; (vii) sports tourism; and (viii) the short breaks market. Each of these areas is developing its own body of research and expertise.

Rationale and goals

Public policy and planning for tourism have in common with countryside recreation planning the characteristic that the customers for the product are *not* local residents but people from outside the area. Thus, insofar as the public agency responsible for policy and planning is democratically elected or answerable to a democratically elected body, policy and planning are not directed at meeting the holidaymaking needs and demands of the electorate, rather, they are generally aimed at maximizing the benefits that local residents might obtain from *other people's* holidaymaking and minimizing the negative effects that they might impose. The benefits are seen almost exclusively as economic – the generation of jobs and incomes – and the negative effects are almost exclusively seen as environmental.

Parallelling the ambivalence of the dual goals of countryside recreation, tourism policy is generally juggling with two contradictory goals: the *maximization* of tourist numbers and their expenditure in a destination and the *minimization* of their environmental impact on the destination. The *maximization* part of the equation is generally much stronger. The conflict between the two goals is often resolved – or permitted to remain unresolved – by separating them institutionally, as discussed below.

A key feature of tourism policy is the way public bodies intervene in what is essentially a private sector industry. Public bodies, such as local councils, regional joint tourism boards or state or national tourism commissions, generally undertake a marketing and promotional role on behalf of the industry. Public money is spent generating customers for private industry with a view to reaping social benefits in the from of increased jobs and incomes (and tax income). Often, the main resource around which tourism develops is publicly owned and managed – for example, lakes, mountains and beaches or museums, galleries and historic buildings. Why does this sort of intervention happen in tourism and not in other industries, such as car manufacturing? Two factors would seem to explain it: one is the fragmentary nature of the industry, as discussed above. The other is the fact that the markets that must be addressed are, by definition, not local, so marketing and promotion costs are high and, although they can be justified and effective for the industry as a whole, they are too costly for many of the small individual commercial organizations involved. So government bodies step in as the promotional arm of the industry while claiming to represent the economic interests of the host community.

A form of state involvement in tourism not given a great deal of prominence in tourism policy or the literature is the idea of 'social tourism' (Haulot, 1981; McCabe, 2009), a process by which deprived groups in the community are assisted to go on holiday, usually via some form of subsidy, but also by direct provision. The idea is particularly appropriate for 'carers' – generally family members who take care of people with severe disability or chronic illness. Provision of relief for such individuals, in the form of a holiday, is a humanitarian gesture, but can also be very cost-effective for the state, the provision of periodic relief helping the carer to continue in that role, rather than the burden of care falling on the state.

Measurement of participation

Tourism is generally better served in terms of participation data than other sectors. This may be to do with the involvement of the private sector and the marketing emphasis of the public sector role, and it may be related to the comparative singularity of tourism policy objectives, as illustrated in Table 14.1.

International tourism (international visitors to the UK and UK residents' overseas trips) is monitored in the UK by the International Passenger Survey (IPS), which involves a sample of 250,000 passengers entering and leaving the UK by air, sea or the Channel Tunnel, as indicated in Table 14.2.

In Australia, data collection is coordinated by Tourism Research Australia, within the Australian Tourist Commission. Two major ongoing surveys are conducted: the International

Visitor Survey (IVS) as shown in Table 14.2, and the National Visitor Survey (NVS). The IVS is conducted throughout the year and samples 40,000 departing, short-term international travellers in the departure lounges of the eight major international airports, using computer-assisted personal interviewing (CAPI). The NVS is also conducted throughout the year and has an annual sample of 120,000 Australian residents interviewed using a computer-assisted telephone interviewing (CATI) system. It collects details about respondents' recent travel, for day trips, trips involving overnight stays and overseas travel.

Institutional factors

The contradiction between the maximization of tourist numbers and minimization of environmental impacts is often avoided as a result of the fact that the responsibility for tourism development and promotion is in the hands of the private sector and regional and national public marketing bodies such as tourism commissions and associations, while the responsibility for local environmental planning, protection and conservation lies with local planning authorities. Thus the option of reducing or stabilizing tourist numbers is not really available to the environmental planners – all they can do is seek to influence where developers and tourists are allowed to go and what they are allowed to do.

Planning

Planning for tourism is, like planning for countryside recreation, characterized by the fact that demand comes from outside the area. Planning activity is influenced by the institutional factors discussed above. Unlike many other fields of leisure planning, demand forecasting has played a significant role in tourism planning, but mainly at the national level. National tourism commissions and ministries produce tourism demand forecasts and targets, as discussed in Chapter 11. On the basis of such forecasts and targets, attention is then given to the question of future accommodation and airport capacity, but little attention is given to the capacity of the leisure environments and attractions that tourists come to see. That this is a problem is to some extent recognized in attempts by national and regional tourist bodies to spread the tourist load, both spatially and temporally – that is, it is recognized that certain places (e.g. London) become overcrowded at certain times of the year. At the regional and local level the tourism planning task is to cope with a level of demand that is seen as more or less an external 'given'. As tourism is a relative newcomer to the local planning scene, its integration into local planning is less fully developed than other sectors (Dredge and Moore, 1992; Long, 1994).

The concept that has caught the imagination of tourism researchers, policy-makers and planners in recent years is *sustainability*. The output of literature concerned with 'sustainability' and 'tourism' in the last couple of decades has been extraordinary. As indicated in Chapter 2, the concept arose from the environmental movement, and thus the tourism industry and its academic community can be said to have effected a clever move in adopting the concept as its own, since tourism development in natural areas has traditionally been seen as one of the bêtes noires of environmental conservationists. The term has been cemented into place in tourism planning by the suggestion that sustainability not only refers to environmental sustainability, but also to economic and social sustainability, in the sense of acceptability to the host community. In urban areas the natural environment is replaced by the built heritage as the focus of sustainability concerns (Fyall and Garrod, 1998).

Thus the potential wolf of tourism development is 'packaged' within sheep's clothing of 'sustainable development' strategies and made to appear less threatening. Meanwhile, as the plan unfolds in practice, as in any industry, the developers and operators of tourism facilities – and the often associated 'urban growth regimes', as discussed in Chapter 5 – follow their natural bent, which is to maximize profits, and there is little evidence to suggest that members of the community do not also wish to maximize their incomes from tourism. Thus environmentally sustainable development, with the best possible credentials, can lead to unintended 'creeping urbanization' in rural areas (Craik, 1987) or marketing and development that is culturally inappropriate, or contested (Hale, 2001).

SUMMARY

This chapter is concerned with leisure and tourism *sectors*. It includes brief discussions of five sectors: (i) sport and physical recreation; (ii) the arts and entertainment; (iii) outdoor recreation in natural areas; (iv) urban outdoor recreation; and (v) tourism.

The sectors are discussed in terms of: (i) the scope of the sector; (ii) the rationale and goals of policy within the sector; (iii) measurement of participation; (iv) institutional factors; and (v) planning.

RESOURCES

Participation data sources

See Chapter 8, Resources section.

Publications

Sport and physical recreation: Department of the Environment (1975, 1991); McIntosh and Charlton (1985); Kamphorst and Roberts (1989); Gratton and Taylor (1991, 2000); Roberts and Brodie (1992); Houlihan (1997); and various publications from Sports Council and Sport England.

The arts: Baumol and Bowen (1966, 1976); Draper (1977); Lane (1978); Braden (1979); Kelly (1984); Hantrais and Kamphorst (1987); Waters (1989); Hawkins (1993); Schouten (1998); Evans (1999); Stevenson (2000); Throsby (2001).

Outdoor recreation in natural areas: Coppock and Duffield (1975); Patmore (1983); Pigram (1983); Glyptis (1991, 1993); Groome (1993); Cordell (1999); Gartner and Lime (2000); Pigram and Jenkins (2006).

Urban outdoor recreation/urban parks: Jackson (1986); Welch (1991); Ravenscroft (1992); Jones and Wills (2005); Low *et al.* (2005).

Tourism: Mathieson and Wall (1982); Bull (1991); Dredge and Moore (1992); Johnson and Thomas (1992); Hall and Jenkins (1995); Smith (1995); Leslie and Hughes (1997); Faulkner *et al.* (2000).

Social tourism: Haulot (1981); McCabe (2009); Minnaert *et al.* (2009).

Ecotourism: Wearing and McLean (1997); Wearing and Neil (1999).

QUESTIONS/EXERCISES

1. How do the rationales for government involvement in the arts and sport differ?

2. A number of the sectors of leisure and tourism have two or more key goals that are potentially contradictory: identify these goals and why they are potentially contradictory in relation to: sport, the arts, natural area recreation and tourism.

3. How does planning for urban leisure differ from planning for leisure in the countryside or natural areas?

4. In what ways can the idea of sustainable tourism development be considered a contradiction in terms?

chapter 15

Policy and Planning for Particular Groups

INTRODUCTION

This chapter considers leisure, sport or tourism policy issues raised by five socio-demographic dimensions: gender, socio-economic status, disability, ethnicity, and age. Every individual is unique and so could be said to have unique leisure, sport and tourism preferences and requirements. In family settings and some organizational settings this uniqueness can be catered for, but human beings are also social animals with interests, demands and requirements in common. *Common* or shared experiences can be as important as individual experiences – people want to belong and to share. Classifying people into groups and considering their common character-istics, needs and preferences is not therefore to deny their individuality; in fact it has been the *failure* of providers to consider the common needs of some groups that has, in the past, denied members of such groups their individuality. As a result of campaigns, regulations, research and the spread of ideas such as affirmative action, market segmentation and niche marketing, some of these problems are now beginning to be overcome.

Four perspectives can be considered in examining social groups and their needs and demands:

1. The *welfare perspective* has dominated thinking about disadvantaged groups, such as people with disabilities and the elderly, in the past, but is rapidly being replaced by the concept of *inclusion*: the idea of ensuring that all groups are able to engage with society in a variety of ways. Furthermore, the traditional idea that disadvantaged individuals should be viewed as relatively passive recipients of assistance from the rest of the community is being replaced by the more active, subject-centred perspectives, as discussed below.

2. The *rights perspective* reflects the discussion of human rights and citizens' rights in Chapter 4 and is based on the premise that all individuals have the same rights of access to services and participation in the social, political and economic life of the community. Following the various international declarations referred to in Chapter 4, many of these rights are enshrined in national constitutions and legislation. Thus equal opportunity and anti-discrimination legislation designed to protect the rights of various minority or traditionally disadvantaged

© A.J. Veal 2010. *Leisure, Sport and Tourism, Politics, Policy and Planning,* 3rd Edition (A.J. Veal)

groups is now common. This in turn means that individuals or organizations that infringe the legislation can be sued or prosecuted. Such changes have, however, often only been brought about by a considerable amount of campaigning by members of the groups concerned and their supporters. Often, the campaign continues after legislation and regulations are in place, to ensure compliance through such measures as publicity and bringing test cases to court.

3. The *market perspective* draws attention to the power of particular groups as consumers in the marketplace, suggesting that it is in the commercial interest of manufacturers, retailers and service providers to consider the preferences of such 'market segments'. While this has traditionally been part of commercial thinking in relation to the youth market or women as consumers, more recently the tourism market has come to realize the value of the retired market, the gay and lesbian 'pink' pound or dollar has been recognized, and others, such as minority ethnic groups and people with disabilities, have begun to quantify their market power.

4. The *diversity perspective*: rather than thinking of society as a mainstream mass and various additional special groups with special needs, it is suggested that society as a whole be considered to consist of a host of groups with a variety of common and special demands – there is no mainstream, but rather a kaleidoscope of diversity (Dattilo and Williams, 1999; Patterson and Taylor, 2001). This reflects social change brought about by immigration, changed family and household structures and globalization, and reflects thinking in the commercial sector, which increasingly sees the market in terms of a wide range of overlapping lifestyle groups and market segments.

The five dimensions of gender, class, ethnicity, disability and age and the various groups they define are discussed in turn below.

GENDER

The issue of gender in leisure and sport policy was raised in the 1980s in the UK and in the 1970s in Australia (see Lynch and Veal, 2006: 373 pp.) as a counter to the 'gender-blindness' and male bias in research, policies and provision. As indicated below, the issue of leisure and sport for women and girls subsequently attracted considerable research and policy attention. It was not until the end of the 1990s that some researchers began to observe that specific attention might be paid specifically to some of the particular requirements of men and boys. Around the same time, attention also began to be paid to the requirements of gay and lesbian individuals. These three groups are therefore considered in turn.

Women and girls

Women comprise more than half the population, but early leisure and tourism research, policy and planning often gave the impression that women were at best a minority and at worst non-existent. In Chapter 2 the way women's leisure and tourism needs are viewed from feminist perspectives was considered. Here we consider the question: how should policy and planning for leisure and tourism in contemporary society seek to reflect the particular requirements of women and girls? Such an approach is avowedly reformist in feminist terms since, in a society of full equality between men and women there would be few particularly 'women's needs' – all would be human needs. Thus, if childcare were shared equally, childcare services at leisure facilities would be demanded by 'parents' rather than 'mothers'. If male violence were to be eliminated then travel after dark for leisure or any other purpose would not be a problem experienced by women or men. If all sports were open to both sexes – for mixed or single-sex competition – then particular provision for 'women's sports' would not be necessary: access would be available to all. But society is not equal and it is shaped by the practices of the past, so it is appropriate in the interests of equity to devise policies to redress the imbalances that exist and to put in place 'transitional arrangements', few of which would be necessary in a fully equal society.

The main problem area in leisure policy and planning for women would appear to be the area of sport. This is reflected in the substantial literature on women and sport; even in general discussions of leisure, sport is often the form of leisure used as an example to demonstrate existing inequalities. Women's comparatively low level of participation in sport and the reasons for it are discussed in terms of cultural expectations and constraints (e.g. Scraton, 1993), male organizational power (McKay, 1998), media sports coverage (e.g. Brown, 1993) and lack of facilities (Mowbray, 1993). Participation by women and girls is also often recognized as a specific target in policy documents, but it is notable that, while earlier Sport England strategic plans highlighted increased women's participation as a key policy (e.g. Sport England, 1997), the most recent strategy does not (Sport England, 2008).

Participation statistics suggest that, in most other areas women's participation levels are greater than or equal to those of men. It is rarely suggested that the arts or entertainment sectors discriminate against female audiences, or that libraries, parks or countryside recreation facilities do not cater to the needs of women.

While women participate in tourism to the same extent as men, there is concern that women are not free to travel alone or unaccompanied by men, partly because of safety concerns. Research on the gendered nature of tourism has begun to address this issue (Kinnaird and Hall, 1994; Swain, 1995; Pritchard, 2001).

Increased access and provision for women's leisure has implications for men. Some of the difficulties women face in gaining access to resources is explained by the fact that resources, for example of land, are limited, and men's sporting organizations may be required to give up some of the facilities they have hitherto enjoyed exclusively by default. In theory, to meet equal demand for women, provision of facilities and services in some areas would need to be almost doubled – and men would have to share the cost through taxation and/or other revenue-raising methods, in the same way that women have shared the burden of funding men's public leisure provision to date.

Men and boys

As far as boys are concerned, leisure policy issues arise as to whether activities in schools and play centres designed to suit both girls and boys and increased organizational concerns about public liability result in inadequate opportunities for boys to express physically boisterous, competitive and risk-taking behaviour. Aspects of this are sometimes related to the absence of male role models in single-parent families where the mother takes the major care role, and the trend for primary schools to have fewer male teachers.

A topic that combines concerns for both boys and girls, and men, is fathering, which has begun to attract some research attention (Kay, 2006). Fathers' interactions with their children are often dominated by leisure contexts. While issues arise in this context regarding equality between men and women and their respective roles, there are few direct impacts on public leisure policy. Ironically, a key policy issue that has arisen in relation to parents and leisure facilities is the provision of childcare facilities but, ironically, this becomes less of an issue for fathers since the priority for fathers accompanying their children to leisure facilities is generally to spend time *with* their children rather than in separate activities.

Particular issues arise with separated parents and the question of custody arrangements. In the majority of these situations, custody of the children is awarded by courts to the mother and the father has prescribed minimum contact rights. It has been pointed out that this results in increased association of 'father' with 'leisure activity', suggesting the need to facilitate a more balanced role (Jenkins and Lyons, 2006). This can be seen as an approach looking to both fathers' and children's rights.

A society with more equality between the sexes could lead to qualitative changes in men's leisure, especially in the area of sport, and such ideas are already being addressed in literature on the topic of 'masculinity' (e.g. Miller, 1990; Lynch, 1993; Webb, 1998).

Gays/lesbians

Gender awareness has also led to the development of research on the leisure and tourism experiences of gay men and lesbians (e.g. Markwell, 1998; Pritchard *et al.*, 2000; Waitt and Markwell, 2006). While there are clear public policy issues related to the recognition of same-sex couples, the implications for leisure, sport and tourism public policy appear to be limited. Much of the research is focused on cultural attitudes rather than on specific issues of policy and provision.

SOCIO-ECONOMIC STATUS

Socio-economic status refers to the occupational status of a person and his or her dependents, sometimes referred to as 'class' or 'social class'. Essentially, this is a measure of relative income or wealth arising from, and associated with, a wide range of socio-economic factors. Income is best considered in terms of the basic living unit, the household. Table 15.1 shows the expenditure patterns of UK households in the bottom 10% or *decile* of households, in terms of expenditure, and of the average and the top decile. It can be seen that households in the top decile spend seven times the amount of those in the bottom decile. But the latter are dominated by older persons in one- or two-person households (average household size 1.2 persons), with many dependent on the state pension. The households in the top decile are larger (average size 3.1 persons) and will include at least one person earning a high salary, but may include two or even more with paid jobs. The bottom part of the table therefore shows expenditure per person, which shows that those in the bottom decile exist on just over £140 a week per person. Not shown in the table is the fact that the second and third deciles from the bottom have marginally less to spend per person, because these groups will include more families with children, including single-parent families.

Policy in leisure and sport has traditionally been concerned about people with low incomes; in fact, the needs of the urban poor can be said to be the main motivation behind the instigation of modern public sport and leisure provision programmes in the 19th century. This is the essence of the welfare approach to policy, but its implementation has more recently been portrayed as part of a 'diversity and inclusion' approach to policy. Because of the practical difficulty in assessing incomes, policy has typically relied on indicators of relative poverty, such as being in receipt of welfare payments, including the state old-age pension or unemployment, disability or single-parent benefit payments. Thus at facilities having an entrance fee there are typically reduced concessionary fees for people who are able to demonstrate their status. This practice is

Table 15.1. Household expenditure, UK, 2007.

	Bottom 10%	Average household	Top 10%	Ratio of top to bottom
Household expenditure (£/week)	138.10	459.20	986.70	7.1
Size of household (persons)	1.2	2.4	3.1	2.6
Expenditure item (£/person/week)				
Leisure[a]	28.08	44.08	73.61	2.6
Food/drink (non-alcoholic)	20.42	20.04	23.58	1.2
Clothing/footwear	5.25	9.17	16.23	3.1
Housing/household	43.33	34.38	42.29	1.0
Transport/ communication	17.83	30.67	57.87	3.2
Other[b]	26.25	52.96	104.71	4.0
Total	141.16	191.30	318.29	2.2

[a]Leisure includes: recreation/culture, restaurants/hotels and alcohol/tobacco.
[b]Other includes: health, education, miscellaneous goods/services and mortgage interest.
Source: Office of National Statistics (2008); for similar information on Australia see Lynch and Veal (2006: 147–148).

also adopted by non-profit and some private sector organizations. Planning is also sometimes undertaken with these groups in mind, by locating facilities in areas with high concentrations of relatively deprived groups. Such approaches are widespread, but exclusive reliance on them can be criticized on a number of grounds:

- They are a blunt tool, in that not all the individuals in the identified categories have low incomes (for example, retired people who also have superannuation income or a single parent on a high salary).
- An area with a high proportion of people in deprived categories may not have a majority in such categories, and a majority of the people in deprived categories may live in other areas with low concentrations of deprivation.
- As noted in Chapter 13, the available evidence on whether such policies actually result in additional leisure/sport participation by members of the relevant groups is limited.
- Arguably, people on low incomes might prefer, as a priority, to have their incomes supplemented rather than have money spent on leisure/sport provision.
- Basing policy exclusively on services for deprived groups could result in the neglect of services that have public good characteristics which justify provision for all.

Except for the relatively rare phenomenon of social tourism referred to elsewhere in the book, tourism policy is not generally concerned with disadvantaged groups. Quite the contrary – if the aim is to maximize tourist numbers and/or expenditure, the tendency will be to concentrate on people with higher incomes and money to spend on holidays, although there are, of course, some tourism operators and facilities catering to lower-income groups. However, one low-income group, the impecunious young backpacker, is viewed as an attractive market segment because costs of provision are relatively low and, while they may spend much less per day than wealthier tourists, they stay much longer and therefore often spend more in total.

ETHNICITY

Ethnic groups are groups of people with a common culture – so everyone belongs to an ethnic group, whether it be a majority or minority in a particular society. While ethnicity is often associated with race, this need not be the case, as the experience of Northern Ireland illustrates. In general, minority ethnic and racial groups are at a disadvantage, in leisure and tourism as in other spheres of life. The challenge in contemporary societies is to achieve racial and ethnic equality and to gain the positive cultural benefits that *ethnic diversity* can offer. As discussed above and in Chapter 4, policies for equity and inclusion can also be seen in terms of the rights of citizenship. Leisure service providers are at the forefront of these processes and, indeed, face the dilemmas which these objectives can bring. For example, is it wise to encourage ethnically based sports teams to bring different groups together in friendly competition, or will the rivalry actually damage community relations? Will ethnically based cultural festivals result in the sharing of cultural experiences or greater separation among groups?

In the UK, most ethnic minority groups have their origins in immigration from various parts of the British Commonwealth/Empire. Often, immigrants were recruited by UK employers specifically as cheap labour in periods of labour shortage. Whole groups of migrants therefore suffered from low incomes and, as a result of this and racial discrimination, also suffered from poor housing and a 'cycle of deprivation'. Public policy for ethnic minority groups, including leisure policy, has tended to be orientated towards alleviating or compensating for general social deprivation. Such policies need to be handled sensitively, whether aimed specifically at ethnic minority groups or deprived groups in general since, while public leisure services may be provided with the aim of achieving equity, as discussed in Chapter 7, such provision can be viewed as a cynical exercise in placation if other services and opportunities, such as housing, health and education, not to mention jobs, are not being attended to at the same time.

In general, there is concern that participation in activities promoted by the state, notably sport and the arts, is lower than average among various ethnic minority groups, and policies are directed at facilitating increased participation, not only on grounds of equity and inclusion, but also because low participation among any social group lowers the overall average. While low participation rates among various ethnic minority groups in England are confirmed overall by the data in Tables 15.2 and 15.3, a mixed picture is also presented, with some activities and groups showing lower than average participation and some showing a higher than average rate.

Another dimension of policy in regard to ethnic groups relates not to deprivation but to differences in social customs and values. In particular, as discussed by Green, E. *et al.* (1990: 70–81), women and girls from Moslem or conservative Christian communities are restricted in terms of permitted public recreation behaviour. Such restrictions have slowly been recognized by public leisure providers and catered for by special programmes.

In many countries, notably the Americas and Australia, but also parts of Asia, descendants of the original inhabitants, indigenous peoples, form a distinct ethnic minority often suffering

Table 15.2. Sport participation among ethnic minority groups, England, 1999–2000.[a]

	Black Caribbean	Black African	Black other	Indian	Pakistani	Bangladeshi	Chinese	General population
All sports[b] (%)	39	44	60	39	31	30	45	46
Walking (%)	34	37	36	31	24	19	28	44
Swimming (%)	6	7	10	11	7	8	8	15
Keep-fit (%)	19	17	24	13	9	7	15	12
Football (%)	9	12	16	7	9	8	5	5
Cycling (%)	8	5	15	5	3	1	7	12
Snooker (%)	9	10	18	10	6	11	5	12
Sample size (%)	269	148	86	447	262	81	61	13,000[c]

[a]Percentage of persons aged 16 and over participating in a 4-week period before interview.
[b]At least one activity, including walking.
[c]Household survey (Rowe and Champion, 2000).
Source: Office for National Statistics Labour Force Survey and its monthly Omnibus Survey and General Household Survey.

Table 15.3. Arts/culture participation by ethnic groups, England, 2006–2007.[a]

	White	Mixed	Asian	Black	Chinese/ other
Arts attendance (%)	67.5	53.0	42.4	44.9	71.6
Arts participation (%)	70.1	63.8	45.8	58.9	56.7
Museum/gallery (%)	54.7	40.9	30.5	57.4	46.7
Public library (%)	56.9	47.7	27.2	55.8	40.8
Historic site (%)	50.9	46.5	44.2	53.3	59.0

[a]Percentage of persons aged ≥16 years participating at least once per year.
Source: Taking Part Survey: DCMS (annual).

from socio-economic deprivation and discrimination. In Chapter 4 (Box 4.1) it is noted that the United Nations Convention Concerning Indigenous and Tribal Peoples promotes the rights of such groups to maintain their social, cultural, religious and spiritual values and practices. Leisure, sport and tourism are relevant to such groups not only for reasons of equity and inclusion, but also because part of their identity is expressed in leisure-related forms, such as distinctive music, dance, art and storytelling, generally with spiritual significance, and they may be owners or custodians of areas of land with natural and heritage features that are attractive for domestic and/or international tourism.

DISABILITY

Disabilities come in a variety of forms and degrees of severity and affect a substantial proportion of the population. Included are mental illness and physical disability, either suffered from birth or as a result of illness or accident, and including deafness, dumbness, blindness, disabilities related to the nervous and the musculo-skeletal systems, and chronic conditions such as diabetes and asthma. Such a wide range of conditions calls for a correspondingly wide range of policy responses. Since a number of disabilities arise with ageing, there is considerable overlap between people with disabilities and the elderly population.

When the majority of people with severe disabilities lived in institutions, the question of access to leisure provision was seen as largely an institutional issue. Over the past 30 years a process of de-institutionalization has been taking place, in the belief that people with disabilities can live more dignified lives in the community. Leisure services have a clear role to play in such a process, since leisure activities can not only be therapeutic for the individual, but also a direct means of engagement with the wider community.

Provision of leisure and tourism services for people with disabilities was traditionally viewed in welfare terms, but is increasingly being seen in terms of rights, market power and inclusive diversity. Attitudes towards people with disabilities and the policies and practices of public and private sector agencies in regard to people with disabilities as clients, customers or users have often been shaped by a medical perspective that serves to marginalize and exclude people with disabilities from mainstream society. In the days of institutionalization, the result was that people with disabilities were largely 'out of sight, out of mind' to members of the wider community. Within this perspective, people with disabilities were seen as 'difficult' and requiring 'special' facilities and arrangements, viewed as causing trouble and expense for the provider.

This resulted in buildings, transport facilities and infrastructure and many services being designed in ways that deter or prevent people with various disabilities from using them. While modifications can be expensive once buildings and facilities have been constructed, suitable designs adopted from the very beginning can be relatively cheap or even costless – for example, the width of doorways, design of kerbless showers in hotel rooms, elimination of steps, positioning of light switches and the size of lettering in print and on computer screens. Following legislation to uphold the rights of people with disabilities – such as the UK Disability Discrimination Act, 1995 and the Australian Disability Discrimination Act, 1992 – building codes and regulations for access have been promulgated in many countries, but are not always willingly or fully observed.

Darcy and Taylor (2009) illustrate the human rights approach to access to leisure by people with disabilities by examining a sample of cases brought before the Australian Human Rights and Equal Opportunities Commission relating to organizations not meeting their obligations under the Disability Discrimination Act. They show that even when rights are enshrined in law, their observation is not automatically universally realized in design and management practice. Burns *et al.* (2009) use UK experience to show that understanding can be limited, with countryside recreation providers making provision for wheelchair users but generally ignoring other forms of disability.

Tourism opportunities for people with disabilities have attracted research and policy attention in recent years (Murray and Sproats, 1990; Burnett and Bender Baker, 2001; Darcy and Taylor, 2009). This research has focused particularly on the market perspective, drawing attention to the actual and potential size of the market and, in particular, that people with disabilities are generally accompanied by family and friends, so accommodation and hospitality facilities and attractions that cannot accommodate people with disabilities also lose the custom of their companions.

AGE

Age is arguably the most significant variable in shaping leisure behaviour. The idea of leisure being associated with a 'life cycle', related to the various roles that people take on and cast aside at various stages in their lives, has a long tradition (Rapoport and Rapoport, 1975). Research and policy in leisure, sport and tourism have, to varying degrees, focused on three groups: children, youth (from the teens to the early twenties) and the elderly. These three groups are discussed below.

Children

The origins of public leisure services can be traced to the early development of play facilities for young people (Kraus, 1998: 197–198), and children constitute a significant proportion, in some cases the majority, of the customers of public leisure facilities. Two policy areas are significant in relation to children: provision of outdoor play facilities and levels of physical activity.

The significance of Fields in Trust (FiT, formerly the National Playing Fields Association) in the specification of requirements for children's play is noted in Box 7.3, which also indicates the lack of publicly available research evidence to support the standards recommended. And while recommended standards differ for urban and rural areas, there is no guidance available on how provision might vary for different levels of child population. There is considerable guidance from FiT and other agencies (see Resources section) on the *design* of children's play areas and equipment, but comparatively little on planning.

The policy concern for children's participation in sport and physical activity generally has intensified in recent years as a result of increased child obesity believed to be caused, in part, by increasingly sedentary lifestyles brought about by such factors as: (i) a decline in walking and cycling as a means of transport to and from school and other destinations; (ii) the decline of physical education and sport in the school curriculum; and (iii) the attraction of physically inactive, screen-based leisure activity (Friedman, 2000). One of the challenges in this, as in other policy areas, is to separate anecdotal evidence from more reliable and appropriate sources. Thus, for example, the data presented in Table 15.4 suggest that, between 1994 and 2002, there was no decline in sports participation among children aged 6–16 in England, with pluses exceeding the minuses and the average number of sports played increasing. However, it is noticeable from the 1999 figures that: (i) participation rates fluctuate (and small fluctuations

Table 15.4. Young people and sports participation, England, 1994–2002.[a]

	1994	1999	2002	Change (1994–2002)
Football (including 5-a-side) (%)	60	67	63	+3
Netball (%)	17	18	17	0
Hockey (%)	14	15	14	0
Rugby (%)	17	19	15	−2
Basketball (%)	29	34	34	+5
Cricket (%)	40	43	37	−3
Rounders (%)	39	41	40	+1
Baseball/softball (%)	15	13	12	−3
Volleyball (%)	13	14	14	+1
Tennis (%)	53	51	55	+2
Badminton (%)	31	30	29	−2
Squash (%)	11	8	8	−3
Table tennis (%)	29	24	30	+1
Golf (%)	29	30	30	+1
Bowls (carpet/lawn) (%)	9	10	12	+3
Tenpin bowling (%)	38	35	50	+12
Snooker, pool (%)	55	48	48	−7
Darts (%)	37	32	33	−4
Swimming, diving (%)	82	79	80	−2
Dance classes (%)	15	14	18	+3
Ice skating (%)	30	27	28	−2
Sum				+32/−28
Average no. of sports (%)	10.0	10.3	11.2	

[a] Percentage of young people aged 6–16 participating (not in school lessons) at least once per year.
Source: Sport England (2003: 40); equivalent data for Australia can be found in ABS (2009).

may in any case be due to statistical error); (ii) a large part of the increase is due to one sport (tenpin bowling); and (iii) the measure refers only to participation at least once in the previous year, not to regular participation, so static or increasing participation rates could hide declines in frequency of participation.

There are signs of an emerging wider agenda for research on children's leisure and tourism. For example, the research of Malkin *et al.* (2000) reflects increasing concerns about child abuse and safety consciousness. Turley (2001) has recently presented research on children and zoos, and Cullingford (1995) on children and holidays.

Youth

The category 'youth' covers young people from the teenage years to the early twenties. Much of the political sentiment behind the support for public leisure services in general would appear to be based on the belief that approved leisure provision should be available for young people. Indeed, the very origins of modern public leisure services are often traced to the 19th century provision of 'Mechanics' Institutes' (Cunningham, 1980) for young people.

One belief is that provision of suitable leisure facilities will prevent juvenile crime. The 1975 White Paper on *Sport and Recreation* stated: 'By reducing boredom and urban frustration, participation in active recreation contributes to the reduction of delinquency among young people' (Department of the Environment, 1975: 3). The topic has been explored recently by Geoff Nichols (2007).

One of the concerns in youth and leisure has been the 'post-school gap', the tendency for young people who leave school at the minimum age to drop out of active pursuits, notably sport, without access to the structures and networks offered by the school, but being too young to engage with adult networks. Quantitatively, this has become less of a problem over time as more and more young people continue in full-time education until 18 and beyond.

Arguably, policy concern in the area of youth and leisure has focused less on levels of participation in mainstream activities such as sport and the arts, and more on the nature of leisure activities engaged in, particularly the use of legal and illegal recreational drugs (Parker *et al.*, 1998; Hadfield, 2006) and excessive use of passive screen-based entertainment.

Youth and their leisure and subcultures have been the subject of considerable research over recent decades (e.g. Rapoport and Rapoport, 1975; Brake, 1980; Roberts, 1983; Miles, 2000; Blackshaw, 2003). As with research on any social group in a changing society, this work can become dated as the economic and social environment of young people changes. In the 1960s and 1970s young people were 'affluent'. In the 1980s they bore the brunt of unemployment, so that most young people in their late teens were either in the education/training system or unemployed: relatively few were employed and 'affluent'. And yet new research focusing on lifestyle suggests that a creative and vibrant youth culture can exist without the underpinning of affluence (McRobbie, 1994; Miles, 2000), although there continues to be debate as to the influence of social class in determining lifestyles (Hendry *et al.*, 1993; Roberts and Parsell, 1994; Blackshaw, 2003). There is therefore a need for continual updating of research on youth and the policies that flow from it.

For many public leisure services, young people are simply one of a number of user groups or market segments. Designing programmes to meet the needs and demands of young people is therefore a challenge and opportunity for the management of existing facilities and services. 'Multiple use' is not always ideal of course. Facilities designed and managed exclusively or mainly for young people – for example, ice-skating rinks – have a very different atmosphere from those where other user groups must also be catered for. The commercial sector is generally highly successful at providing facilities that tap straight into youth culture and its styles, but most money is to be made among those in the older half of the youth category who can used licensed premises such as pubs and clubs and travel independently, as in the backpacker market.

The leisure facility traditionally provided by the public sector exclusively for youth has been the *youth club*. In fact, the status of the UK youth club as a *leisure* facility has been in question, since the youth service has traditionally been an arm of the education service rather than of the leisure service. The youth club, while using leisure as a *medium*, has therefore had other objectives, such as education or welfare work for 'at-risk' youth, which may explain why its relative popularity has declined in favour of general community leisure facilities and commercial outlets.

The elderly

The ageing of Western societies is a phenomenon with which most are now familiar (see Chapter 11). Much research has been done over the last two decades to remedy the neglect of the particular leisure needs and demands of older age groups. As with research on youth, there is a tendency for such research to become outdated in the light of changing social conditions. The elderly as a category are becoming more numerous, but also fitter and more affluent. They are also becoming younger because of a tendency for earlier retirement, and often the definition of 'the elderly' includes 'the retired'. They are becoming physically fitter as a result of improvements in diet and advances in medicine and also, possibly, because of a different outlook that encourages older people to be more active and to be more conscious of preventive 'lifestyle' factors. They are becoming more wealthy because of inheritance (particularly related to increasing levels of home ownership) and superannuation. While a significant proportion of the elderly still suffer from financial and health/mobility problems, an increasing proportion, particularly the 'younger elderly', suffer from none of these things: they present themselves to leisure providers as a market segment like any other, but one with a great deal of leisure time.

It might be said that, if the elderly are just another market segment, then the market can meet all their leisure needs, but this would be an inappropriate conclusion. Younger age groups also constitute market segments but, while commercial provision plays its part for all age groups, the state still has a role to play. As argued in the early parts of this book, equity, deprivation and 'need' are only *part* of the argument for state provision – net community benefits can also arise even if services are provided for relatively affluent people. And in some cases – for example, the provision of parks or swimming pools – the state has a virtual monopoly of supply, so being in that situation it has an obligation to provide for all, regardless of socio-economic situation, even if the service involves a significant element of 'user pays'.

The net benefits to the community from providing leisure opportunities for the elderly are likely to be even greater than in providing for younger age groups. For both the 'young' elderly and 'old' elderly, the mental and physical benefits to the individual and to the wider community of staying active are obvious. The challenge is therefore very much one for management and it is one that has been widely taken up. Often, the facilities are available: the task is to provide programmes at the right time, in the right place and at the right price to attract this 'market segment'. Fortunately many of the elderly demand and can use services at times when facilities are relatively underused, such as during the weekday daytime.

Similarly, retired people are able to go on holiday during off-peak periods, making them an attractive market segment for the tourism industry. While international tourism companies specializing in the elderly are a relatively new phenomenon, the public sector and traditional domestic tourism operators have been aware of the market for many years. Many English coastal resorts became retirement resorts long ago (Karn, 1977), resulting in the provision of infrastructure and services that can be attractive to older holiday-makers.

The 'continuity theory' suggests that the proportion of the elderly who take up new activities upon retirement is relatively low (Atchley, 1989). The implications of this are either that people must be attracted to the particular activity *before* retirement or that new ways of marketing the idea of experimentation to retired people must be found. Thus the challenge of leisure for the elderly may begin with the establishment of a leisure-orientated lifestyle earlier in life (Carpenter, 1997).

FINALLY

Each of the leisure sectors and social groups discussed in the last two chapters merits a book in its own right. Each could be examined in terms of the philosophical, ideological, economic, planning and demand issues raised in the bulk of the book. While public policies are developed for *leisure, sport* and *tourism* or for *the community*, in practice they relate to specific types of activity for specific groups of people. The challenge for the policy-maker and planner is to enhance the quality of life of real people by seeking to understand their leisure, sport and tourism needs and demands in the context of an understanding of the economic, political and social processes controlling the distribution of community resources.

SUMMARY

This chapter is concerned with social groups and their involvement with leisure, sport and tourism. It includes brief discussions of seven social groups defined by: gender; socio-economic status ethnicity; disability; and age – children, youth and the elderly. Four perspectives for viewing the needs and demands of different social groups are discussed: a welfare perspective; a human and citizens' rights perspective; a market perspective; and a diversity and inclusion perspective.

RESOURCES

Websites

Play England: http://www.playengland.org.uk/Page.asp

Children's Play Information Service: http://www.ncb.org.uk/cpis/home.aspx

Australian Bureau of Statistics: children's play: http://www.abs.gov.au (search for document no. 4901.0)

Standing Committee on Recreation and Sport (Australia): sport, etc. participation by age/gender: http://www.ausport.gov.au/information/scors

Sport England: sport participation: http://www.sportengland.gov.uk (go to Research, then Active People Survey).

Publications

Groups with special needs: Thompson (1999); Allison and Schneider (2000); Patterson and Taylor (2001).

Women: and leisure: Deem (1986a, b); Wimbush and Talbot (1988); Henderson *et al.* (1989); Green, E. *et al.* (1990); Wearing (1990, 1998); Scraton (1993, 1999); Yule (1997a, b); Henderson (2000); Aitchison (2003); and tourism: Kinnaird and Hall (1994); Swain (1995).

Men: Blackshaw (2003); Kay (2006).

Gay and lesbian leisure: Markwell (1998a, b); Clift and Forrest (1999); Pritchard *et al.* 2000); Patterson and Taylor (2001: Chapter 3); tourism: Waitt and Markwell (2006).

Ethnic groups: Khan (1976); Kew (1979); Pryce (1979); Green, E. *et al.* (1990: 70–81); Kraus (1994); Lashley and Hylton (1997); Hibbins (1998); Long (2000); Ravenscroft and Markwell (2000) Patterson and Taylor (2001: Chapter 10); Aboriginal people: Lynch and Veal (2006: Chapters 2 and 14).

People with disabilities: Stein and Sessoms (1977); Austin (1987); Kennedy *et al.* (1991); Levitt (1991); Aitchison (2000); French and Hainsworth (2001); Patterson and Taylor (2001: Chapters 6, 7 and 8); countryside recreation: Burns *et al.* (2009); tourism: Darcy and Dickson (2009); Darcy and Taylor (2009).

Children: Ellis (1973); Barnett (1991); Malkin *et al.* (2000).

Youth: Brake (1980); Roberts (1983, 1997); Hendry *et al.* (1993); McRobbie (1994); Roberts and Parsell (1994); Miles (2000); Blackshaw (2003).

The elderly: Rapoport and Rapoport (1975); Atchley (1989); Green, E. *et al.* (1990: 82–84); Collins *et al.* (1993); Wearing (1995); Patterson and Taylor (2001: Chapter 8).

QUESTIONS/EXERCISES

1. The traditional, mainstream pattern of provision of leisure facilities has tended to exclude or marginalize members of a number of the social groups discussed in this chapter. Select two groups and contrast the ways in which this tendency operates.

2. Discuss any two of the groups discussed in this chapter and consider their likely particular needs or demands as a tourism market segment.

3. Many public agencies produce sector-specific or group-specific plans and strategies – for example, strategies for sport or the arts or policies for ethnic diversity or for leisure provision for youth. Identify two different strategy documents from public or academic library or internet sources and contrast the approaches used for policy-making and planning.

REFERENCES

Aitchison, C.C. (2000) Young disabled people, leisure and everyday life: reviewing conventional definitions for leisure studies. *Annals of Leisure Research* 3, 1–21.

Aitchison, C.C. (2003) *Gender and Leisure: Social and Cultural Perspectives*. Routledge, London.

Alexandris, K. (2008) Special edition – performance measurement and leisure management. *Managing Leisure*, 13(3/4).

Allen, J. (1992) Post-industrialism and post-Fordism. In: Hall, S., Held, D. and McGrew, T. (eds) *Modernity and its Futures*. Polity Press, Cambridge, UK, pp. 169–220.

Allison, M.T., and Schneider, I.E. (eds) (2000) *Diversity and the Recreation Professions: Organizational Perspectives*. Venture, State College, Pennsylvania.

Alt, J. (1979) Beyond class: the decline of industrial labor and leisure. *Telos* (12), 55–80.

Anderson, D.H., Nickerson, R., Stein, T.V. and Lee, M.E. (2000) Planning to provide community and visitor benefits from public lands. In: Gartner, W.C. and Lime, D.W. (eds) *Trends in Outdoor Recreation, Leisure and Tourism*. CAB International, Wallingford, UK, pp. 197–211.

Andrew, E. (1981) *Closing the Iron Cage: the Scientific Management of Work and Leisure*. Black Rose Books, Montreal, Canada.

Archer, B. (1994) Demand forecasting and estimation. In: Ritchie, J.R.B. and Goeldner, C.R (eds) *Travel, Tourism and Hospitality Research, 2nd edition*, John Wiley, New York, pp. 105–114.

Argyle, M. (1996) *The Social Psychology of Leisure*. Penguin, London.

Armitage, J. (1977) *Man at Play: Nine Centuries of Pleasure Making*. Frederick Warne, London.

Arnstein, S. (1969) A ladder of citizen participation. *Journal of the American Institute of Planning* 35(1), 216–224.

Aronowitz, S. and DiFazio, W. (1994) *The Jobless Future*. University of Minnesota Press, Minneapolis, Minnesota.

Aronowitz, S., Esposito, D., DiFazio, W. and Yard, M. (1998) The post-work manifesto. In: Aronowitz, S. and Cutler, J. (eds) *Post-Work*. Routledge, New York, pp. 31–80.

Asimov, I. (1976) Future fun. In: Asimov, I. *Today and Tomorrow and …* Scientific Book Club, London, pp. 199–209.

Atchley, R. (1989) A continuity theory of normal aging. *The Gerontologist* 29(1), 183–190.

Athiyaman, A. and Robertson, R.W. (1992) Time series forecasting techniques: short-term planning in tourism. *International Journal of Contemporary Hospitality Management*, 4(1), 8–11.

Audit Commission (1989) *Sport for Whom? Clarifying the Local Authority Role in Sport and Recreation*. HMSO, London.

Audit Commission (1991) *Local Authorities, Entertainment and the Arts.* Audit Commission, London.

Austin, D.R. (1987) Recreation and persons with physical disabilities: a literature synthesis. *Therapeutic Recreation Journal* 17(1), 38–43.

Australia Institute (undated) *The Wellbeing Manifesto.* Australia Institute, Canberra (available at http://www.wellbeingmanifesto.net/index.htm).

Australian Bureau of Statistics (ABS) (1978) *How Australians Use Their Time.* Cat. No. 4153.0, ABS, Canberra.

Australian Bureau of Statistics (ABS) (2002) *Sport and Recreation Funding by Government, 2000–01.* Cat. No. 4147.0, ABS, Canberra.

Australian Bureau of Statistics (ABS) (2007) *Participation in Sport and Physical Activities.* Cat. No. 4177.0, ABS, Canberra (available at: http://www.abs.gov.au).

Australian Bureau of Statistics (ABS) (2008a) *How Australians Use their Time, 2006.* Cat. No. 4153.0, ABS, Canberra (tables available at: http://www.abs.gov.au).

Australian Bureau of Statistics (ABS) (2008b) *Cultural Funding by Government.* Cat. No. 4183.0, ABS, Canberra (available at: http://www.abs.gov.au).

Australian Bureau of Statistics (ABS) (2009) *Children's Participation in Cultural and Leisure Activities.* Cat. No. 4901.0, ABS, Canberra (available at: http://www.abs.gov.au).

Australian Government (2001) *Backing Australia's Sporting Ability: a More Active Australia.* Australian Government, Canberra.

Australian Sports Institute Study Group (1975) *Report of the Australian Sports Institute Study Group.* Dept of Tourism and Recreation/AGPS, Canberra.

Bacon, W. (1989) The development of the leisure profession in the United Kingdom; a comparative analysis of development and change. *Society and Leisure* 12(1), 233–246.

Bailey, P. (1979) *Leisure and Class in Victorian England.* Routledge and Kegan Paul, London.

Baldry, H.C. (1976) Community Arts. In: Haworth, J.T. and Veal, A.J. (eds) *Leisure and the Community.* Conference Papers, Leisure Studies Association, London, pp. 2.1–2.6.

Banks, R. (1985) *New Jobs from Pleasure: a Strategy for Creating New Jobs in the Tourist Industry.* Conservative Party, London.

Baric, A., Stevenson, Y. and van der Veen, L. (1997) Community involvement in tourism development for the Southern Highlands. In: Hall, C.M., Jenkins, J.M. and Kearsley, G. (eds) *Tourism Planning and Policy in Australia and New Zealand: Cases, Issues and Practice.* Irwin, Sydney, pp. 154–167.

Barnet, R. and Cavanagh, J. (1996) Homogenization of global culture. In: Mander, J. and Goldsmith, E. (eds) *The Case Against the Global Economy and for a Turn Toward the Local.* Sierra Club, San Francisco, California, pp. 71–77.

Barnett, L.A. (1991) Developmental benefits of play for children. In: Driver, B.L, Brown, P.J. and Peterson, G.L. (eds) *Benefits of Leisure.* Venture, State College, Pennsylvania, pp. 215–248.

Bauman, Z. (1998) *Globalization: The Human Consequences.* Polity Press, Cambridge, UK.

Baumol, W.J. and Bowen, W.G. (1966) *Performing Arts: the Economic Dilemma.* MIT Press, Cambridge, Massachusetts.

Baumol W.J. and Bowen W.G. (1976) Arguments for public support of the performing arts. In: Blaug, M. (ed.) *The Economics of the Arts.* Martin Robertson, London, pp. 42–57.

Beard, J.G. and Ragheb, M. (1980) Measuring leisure satisfaction. *Journal of Leisure Research* 12(1), 20–33.

Beauchamp, K. (1985) *Fixing the Government: Everybody's Guide to Lobbying in Australia.* Penguin, Ringwood, Victoria, Australia.

Beavan, B. (2005) *Leisure, Citizenship and Working Class Men in Britain, 1850–1945.* Manchester University Press, Manchester, UK.

Beck, U. (2000) *The Brave New World of Work.* Polity Press, Cambridge, UK.

Becken, S. and Hay, J.E. (eds) (2007) *Tourism and Climate Change: Risks and Opportunities.* Channel View Publications, Clevedon, UK.

Beeson, M. and Firth, A. (1998) Neoliberalism as a political rationality: Australian public policy since the 1980s. *Journal of Sociology* 34(3), 215–231.

Bell, D. (1974) *The Coming of the Post-Industrial Society*. Heinemann, London.

BERG (Built Environment Research Group) (1977) *The Changing Indoor Sports Centre*. Sports Council, London.

Bianchini, F., Fisher, M., Montgomery, J. and Worpole, K. (1991) *City Centres, City Cultures*. Centre for Local Economic Strategies, Manchester, UK.

Bickmore D., Shaw, M.G. and Tulloch, T. (1980) Lifestyles on maps. *Geographical Magazine* 52(11), 763–769.

Bikhchandani, S., Hirshleifer, D. and Welch, I. (1992) A theory of fads, fashion, custom and cultural change as informational cascades. *Journal of Political Economy* 100(4), 992–1026.

Birmingham City Council (2007) *Birmingham LAA 2008/11: Working Together for A Better Birmingham*. Birmingham City Council, Birmingham, UK.

Blackshaw, T. (2003) *Leisure Life: Myth, Masculinity and Modernity*. Routledge, London.

Blair, T. (1998) *The Third Way: New Politics for A New Century*. Fabian Pamphlet 588, Fabian Society, London.

Blond, P. (2009) Rise of the red Tories. *Prospect Magazine* 155, February: available at http://www.prospect–magazine.co.uk (accessed July 2009).

Bloomfield, J. (2003) *Australia's Sporting Success: the Inside Story*. UNSW Press, Sydney, Australia.

Bolton, N., Fleming, S. and Elias, B. (2008) The experience of community sport development: a case study of Blaenau Gwent. *Managing Leisure* 13(2), 92–103.

Bovaird, T. (1992) Evaluation, performance measurement and achievement of objectives in the public sector. In: Sugden, J. and Knox, C. (eds) *Leisure in the 1990s: Rolling Back the Welfare State*. Conference Papers, Leisure Studies Association, Eastbourne, UK, pp. 145–166.

Bowker, J.M., English, D.B.K. and Cordell, H.K. (1999) Projections of outdoor recreation participation to 2050. In: Cordell, H.K. (ed.) *Outdoor Recreation in American Life: a National Assessment of Demand and Supply Trends*. Sagamore Publishing, Champaign, Illinois, pp. 323–350.

Braden, S. (1979) *Artists and People*. Routledge, London.

Bradshaw, J. (1972) The concept of social need. *New Society* 496, 30 March, 640–643.

Brake, M. (1980) *The Sociology of Youth Culture and Youth Sub-Cultures*. Routledge, London.

Bramham, P. and Henry, I. (1985) Political ideology and leisure policy in the United Kingdom. *Leisure Studies* 4(1), 1–20.

Bramham, P., Henry, I., Mommaas, H. and Van Der Poel, H. (eds) (1993) *Leisure Policies in Europe*. CAB International, Wallingford, UK.

Bramwell, B. and Lane, B. (eds) (2000) *Tourism Collaboration and Partnerships: Politics, Practice and Sustainability*. Channel View Publications, Clevedon, UK.

Bramwell, B. and Sharman, A. (1999) Collaboration in local tourism policymaking. *Annals of Tourism Research* 26(2), 392–415.

British Government (2001) *A Sporting Future for All*. Departments of Culture, Media and Sport, London, available at: http://www.culture.gov.uk/Reference_library/Publications/archive_2000/sporting_ future_for_all.htm

Brohm, J-M. (1978) *Sport: a Prison of Measured Time*. Ink Links, London.

Brown, J. (1985) *Towards the Development of a Commonwealth Policy on Recreation*. Department of Sport, Recreation and Tourism, Canberra.

Brown, P. (1993) Women, the media and equity in sport. In: Veal, A. J. *et al.*, pp. 160–163.

Brown, T.L. and Hutson, D.L. (1979) Evaluation of the ORRRC projections. In: Heritage, Conservation and Recreation Service *Third Nationwide Recreation Plan: Appendix 2, Survey Technical Report 4*. US Govt Printing Office, Washington, DC, pp. 259–276.

Brownlie, I. (ed.) (1992) *Basic Documents on Human Rights*. Clarendon Press, Oxford, UK.

Buechner, R.D. (1971) *National Park Recreation and Open Space Standards*. National Recreation and Park Association, Washington, DC.

Bull, A. (1991) *The Economics of Travel and Tourism*. Pitman, Melbourne, Australia.

Burbank, M.J., Heying, C.H. and Adranovich, G. (2000) Antigrowth politics or piecemeal resistance? Citizen opposition to Olympic-related economic growth. *Urban Affairs Quarterly* 35(3), 334–357.

Burgan, B. and Mules, T. (1992) Economic impacts of sporting events. *Annals of Tourism Research* 19(3), 700–710.

Burnett, J.J. and Bender Baker, H. (2001) Assessing the travel-related behaviors of the mobility-disabled consumer. *Journal of Travel Research* 40(3), 4–11.

Burns, J.P.A. *et al.* (eds) (1986) *The Adelaide Grand Prix: the Impact of a Special Event*. Centre for South Australian Economics Studies, Adelaide, Australia.

Burns, N., Paterson, K. and Watson, N. (2009) An inclusive outdoors? Disabled people's experiences of countryside leisure services. *Leisure Studies* 28(4), 387–402.

Burns, P.M. and Novelli, M. (eds) (2007) *Tourism and Politics: Global Frameworks and Local Realities*. Elsevier, Amsterdam.

Burton, T.L. (1970) The shape of things to come. In: Burton, T.L. (ed.) *Recreation Research and Planning*. Allen and Unwin, London, pp. 242–268.

Burton, T.L. (1971) *Experiments in Recreation Research*. Allen and Unwin, London.

Butler, R.W. and Waldbrook, L.A. (1991) A new planning tool: the Tourism Opportunity Spectrum. *Journal of Tourism Studies* 2(1), 2–14.

Butterfield, J. (1989) The economics of leisure: blue and green challenges to orthodoxy. In: Parker, S.R. (ed.) *Work, Leisure and Lifestyles (Part 2)*. Publication 34, Leisure Studies Association, Eastbourne, UK.

Cabinet Office (2001) *Service First: the New Charter Programme*. Cabinet Office, London, available at: http://www.cabinet–office.gov.uk/service/index.list.htm (accessed January 2001).

Cabinet Office Enterprise Unit (1986) *Pleasure, Leisure – and Jobs: the Business of Tourism*. HMSO, London.

CACI Ltd (2006) *ACORN User Guide*. CACI, London, available at: http://www.caci.co.uk/index.html (accessed October 2009).

Caldwell, G. (1985) Poker machine playing in NSW and ACT clubs. In: Caldwell, G., Haig, B., Dickerson, M. and Sylvan, L. (eds) *Gambling in Australia*. Croom Helm, Sydney, Australia, pp. 261–268.

Callinicos, A. (2001) *Against the Third Way*. Polity Press, Cambridge, UK.

Canadian Parks and Recreation Association (CPRA) (1997) *The Benefits Catalogue: Summarizing Why Recreation, Fitness, Arts, Culture, and Parks are Essential to Personal, Social, Economic, and Environmental Well-being*. CPRA, Ottawa.

Canestrelli, E. and Costa, P. (1991) Tourist carrying capacity: a fuzzy approach. *Annals of Tourism Research* 18(2), 295–311.

Caret, N., Klein, R. and Day, P. (1992) *How Organisations Measure Success: the Use of Performance Indicators in Government*. Routledge, London.

Carpenter, G. (1997) A longitudinal investigation of mid-life men who hold leisure in higher regard than work. *Society and Leisure* 20(1), 189–211.

Carr, D.S. and Halvorsen, K. (2001) An evaluation of three democratic, community-based approaches to citizen participation: surveys, conversations with community groups, and community dinners. *Society and Natural Resources* 14(1), 107–126.

Carter, P. (2005) *Review of National Sport Effort and Resources* (2 Vols). Department for Culture, Media and Sport, London, available at: http://www.culture.gov.uk/images/publications/Carter_report.pdf

Casey, B., Dunlop, R. and Selwood, S. (1996) *Culture as Commodity? The Economics of the Arts and Built Heritage in the UK*. Policy Studies Institute, London.

Cassidy, J. (1997) Why Karl Marx was right. *Weekend Australia* 20 December, pp. 21, 24 (reprinted from *The New Yorker*).

Castells, M. (1977) *The Urban Question*. Edward Arnold, London.

Caves, R.E. (2000) *Creative Industries: Contracts Between Art and Commerce*. Harvard University Press, Cambridge, Massachusetts.

Central Council for Physical Recreation (CCPR) (2008) *Getting the Ball Rolling: Sports Contribution to the 2008–2011 Public Service Agreements*. CCPR, London, available at: http://www.ccpr.org.uk

Certo, S.C. and Peter, J.P. (1991) *Strategic Management: Concepts and Applications.* McGraw-Hill, New York.

Chai, D.A. (1977) Future of leisure: a Delphi application. *Research Quarterly* 48(3), 518–524.

Clark, J.K. and Stein, T.V. (2004) Applying the Nominal Group Technique to recreation planning on public natural areas. *Journal of Park and Recreation Administration* 22 (Winter), pp. 1–22.

Clark, R. and Stankey, G. (1979) *The Recreation Opportunity Spectrum: a Framework for Planning, Management and Research.* General Technical Report PNW–98, US Dept of Agriculture Forest Service, Seattle, Washington.

Clark, T.N. (2000) Old and new paradigms for urban research: globalization and the Fiscal Austerity and Urban Innovation Project. *Urban Affairs Review* 36(1), 3–45.

Clarke, A. (1995) Farewell to welfare? The changing rationales for leisure and tourism policies in Europe. In: Leslie, D. (ed.) *Tourism and Leisure – Perspectives on Provision.* LSA Publication No. 52, Leisure Studies Association, Eastbourne, UK, pp. 211–222.

Clarke, J. and Critcher, C. (1985) *The Devil Makes Work: Leisure in Capitalist Britain.* Macmillan, London.

Clarke, R. (1982) *Work in Crisis.* St Andrews Press, Edinburgh, UK.

Clawson, M. and Knetsch, J.L. (1966) *Economics of Outdoor Recreation.* Johns Hopkins University Press, Baltimore, Maryland.

Claxton, J.D. (1994) Conjoint analysis in travel research: a manager's guide. In: Ritchie, J.R.B. and Goeldner, C.R. (eds) *Travel, Tourism and Hospitality Research.* John Wiley, New York, pp. 513–522.

Clemitson, I. and Rodgers, G. (1981) *A Life to Live.* Junction Books, London.

Clift, S. and Forrest, S. (1999) Gay men and tourism: destinations and holiday motivation. *Tourism Management* 20(3), 615–625.

Coalter, F. (with Long, J. and Duffield, B.) (1988) *Recreational Welfare.* Avebury/Gower, Aldershot, UK.

Coalter, F. (1990) Analysing leisure policy. In: Henry, I.P. (ed.) *Management and Planning in the Leisure Industries.* Macmillan, Basingstoke, UK, pp. 149–178.

Coalter, F. (1995) Compulsory competitive tendering for sport and leisure management: a lost opportunity? *Leisure Studies* 1(1), 3–15.

Coalter, F. (1998) Leisure studies, leisure policy and social citizenship: the failure of welfare or the limits of welfare? *Leisure Studies* 17(1), 21–36.

Coalter, F. (2000) Public and commercial leisure provision: active citizens and passive consumers? *Leisure Studies* 19(3), 163–182.

Coalter, F. (2007) *A Wider Role for Sport: Who's Keeping the Score?* Routledge, London.

Cohen, C. and Pate, M. (2000) Making a meal of arts evaluation: can social audit offer a more balanced approach? *Managing Leisure* 5(3), 103–120.

Collins, M.F. (ed.) (1996) *Leisure in Industrial and Post-Industrial Societies.* Leisure Studies Association, Eastbourne, UK.

Collins, M.F. (1997) Does a new philosophy change the structures? Compulsory competitive tendering and local government leisure services in midland England. *Managing Leisure* 2(4), 204–216.

Collins, M.F. (with Kay, T.) (2003) *Sport and Social Exclusion.* Routledge, London.

Collins, M.F. and Cooper, I.S. (eds) (1998) *Leisure Management: Issues and Applications.* CAB International, Wallingford, UK.

Collins, S.M., Wacker, R.R. and Blanding, C. (1993) *Leisure, Recreation and Aging: A Selected, Annotated Bibliography.* National Recreation and Park Association, Ashburn, Victoria, Australia.

Committee of Inquiry into Hunting with Dogs in England and Wales (2000) *Report (Burns Report).* Stationery Office, London.

Commonwealth of Australia (1994) *Creative Nation: Commonwealth Cultural Policy.* Department of Communication and the Arts, Canberra.

Cooke, A. (1994) *The Economics of Leisure and Sport.* Routledge, London.

Cooper, W.E. (1999) Some philosophical aspects of leisure theory. In: Jackson, E.L. and Burton, T.L. (eds) *Leisure Studies: Prospects for the Twenty-First Century.* Venture, State College, Pennsylvania, pp. 3–15.

Coppock, J.T. and Duffield, B.S. (1975) *Recreation in the Countryside: a Spatial Analysis*. Macmillan, London.

Cordell, H. (ed.) (1999) *Outdoor Recreation in American Life: a National Assessment of Demand and Supply Trends*. Sagamore Publishing, Champaign, Illinois.

Council of Europe (1978) *Sport for All Charter*. Council of Europe, Strasbourg, France.

Cox, E. (1995) *A Truly Civil Society: The 1995 Boyer Lectures*. ABC Books, Sydney, Australia.

Craig-Smith, S.J. and Fagence, M. (eds) (1995) *Recreation and Tourism as a Catalyst for Urban Waterfront Redevelopment: an International Survey*. Praeger, Westport, Connecticut.

Craik, J. (1987) From cows to croissants: creating communities around leisure and pleasure. *Social Alternatives* 6(3), 21–27.

Craik, J., Davis, G. and Sunderland, N. (2000) Cultural policy and national identity. In: Davis, G. and Keating, M. (eds) *The Future of Governance: Policy Choices*. Allen and Unwin, Sydney, Australia, pp. 177–202.

Cranston, M. (1973) *What are Human Rights?* The Bodley Head, London.

Crompton, J.L. (2000) Repositioning leisure services. *Managing Leisure* 5(2), 65–76.

Crompton, J.L. (2004) *The Proximate Principle: the Impact of Parks, Open Space and Water Features on Residential Property Values and the Property Tax Base*. National Recreation and Park Association, Ashburn, Virginia.

Crompton, J.L. (2008) Evolution and implications of a paradigm shift in the marketing of leisure services in the USA. *Leisure Studies* 27(2), 181–206.

Crompton, J.L. and West, S.T. (2008) The role of moral philosophies, operational criteria and operational strategies in determining equitable allocation of resources for leisure services in the United States. *Leisure Studies* 27(1), 35–58.

Cross, G. (1990) *A Social History of Leisure Since 1600*. Venture, State College, Pennsylvania.

Crouch, G.I. and Shaw, R.N. (1991) *International Tourism Demand: a Meta-Analytical Integration of Research Findings*. Management Paper No. 36, Monash University Graduate School of Management, Clayton, Virginia.

Csikszentmihalyi, M. (1990) *Flow: the Psychology of Optimal Experience*. Harper & Row, New York.

Cullingford, C. (1995) Children's attitudes to holidays overseas. *Tourism Management* 16(2), 121–127.

Cullingworth, J.B. and Nadin, V. (2006) *Town and Country Planning in the UK, 14th edn*. Routledge, London.

Cunningham, H. (1980) *Leisure in the Industrial Revolution*. Croom Helm, London.

Cushman, G. and Hamilton-Smith, E. (1980) Equity issues in urban recreation services. In: Mercer, D. and Hamilton-Smith, E. (eds) *Recreation Planning and Social Change in Urban Australia*. Sorrett, Malvern, Victoria, Australia, pp 167–179.

Cushman, G., Veal, A.J. and Zuzanek, J. (eds) (2005) *Free Time and Leisure: International Perspectives*. CAB International, Wallingford, UK.

Daley, J. (2000) *Recreation and Sport Planning and Design, 2nd edn*. Human Kinetics, Champaign, Illinois.

Darcy, S. (1999) Access all areas? How the leisure industry provides for people with disabilities. *Australian Leisure Management* 15, 68–70.

Darcy, S. and Dickson, T. (2009) A whole-of-life approach to tourism: the case for accessible tourism experiences. *Journal of Hospitality and Tourism Management* 16(1), 32–44.

Darcy, S. and Taylor, T. (2009) Disability citizenship: an Australian human rights analysis of the cultural industries. *Leisure Studies*, 28(4), 419–441.

Darcy, S. and Wearing, S. (2009) Public–private partnerships and contested cultural heritage tourism in national parks: a case study of the stakeholder views of the North Head Quarantine Station (Sydney, Australia). *Journal of Heritage Tourism* 4(3), 181–199.

Dare, B., Welton, G. and Coe, W. (1987) *Concepts of Leisure in Western Thought*. Kendall Hunt, Dubuque, Iowa.

DASETT: see Department of the Arts, Sport, the Environment, Tourism and Territories

Dattilo, J. and Williams, R. (1999) Inclusion and leisure service delivery. In: Jackson, E.L. and Burton, T.L. (eds) *Leisure Studies: Prospects for the Twenty-First Century*. Venture, State College, Pennsylvania, pp. 451–463.

Davidson, J.A. (1985) Sport and modern technology: the rise of skateboarding, 1963–1978. *Journal of Popular Culture* 18(4), 145–157.

Davidson, P. (2006) A triple bottom-line analysis of the parks and recreation sector. *Australasian Parks and Leisure* 9(3), 15.

Davis, G. and Keating, M. (eds) (2000) *The Future of Governance: Policy Choices*. Allen and Unwin, Sydney, Australia.

Day, D. (1997) Citizen participation in the planning process: an essentially contested concept? *Journal of Planning Literature* 11(3), 421–434.

Deem, R. (1986a) *All Work and No Play? The Sociology of Women's Leisure*. Open University Press, Milton Keynes, UK.

Deem, R. (1986b) The politics of women's leisure. In: Coalter, F. (ed.) *The Politics of Leisure*. Publication 24, Leisure Studies Association, Eastbourne, UK, pp. 68–81.

Delbecq, A.L., Van de Ven, A.H. and Gustafson, D.H. (1975) *Group Techniques for Program Planning: a Guide to Nominal Group and Delphi Processes*. Scott, Foresman, Glenview, Illinois.

Dempsey, K. (1989) Women's leisure, men's leisure: a study in subordination and exploitation. *Australian and New Zealand Journal of Sociology* 25(1), 27–45.

Department of the Arts, Sport, the Environment, Tourism and Territories (1988a) *The Economic Impact of Sport and Recreation: Household Expenditure*. Technical Paper No. 1, AGPS, Canberra.

Department of the Arts, Sport, the Environment, Tourism and Territories (1988b) *The Economic Impact of Sport and Recreation: Regular Physical Activity*. Technical Paper No. 2, AGPS, Canberra.

Department of the Arts, Sport, the Environment, Tourism and Territories (1990) *What Value Heritage? Issues for Discussion*. AGPS, Canberra.

Department of the Arts, Sport, the Environment, Tourism and Territories (1991) *Recreation Participation Survey, February 1991*. DASETT, Canberra.

Department of Communities and Local Government (DCLG) (2006) *Strong and Prosperous Communities: the Local Government White Paper*. Cmnd 6939, DCLG, London, available at: http://www.communities.gov.uk

Department of Communities and Local Government (DCLG) (2007) *National Indicators for Local Authorities and Local Authority Partnerships: Handbook of Definitions, Annex 1: Stronger and Safer Communities*. DCLG, London, available at: http://www.communities.gov.uk

Department for Culture, Media and Sport (DCMS) (1999) *Local Cultural Strategies: Draft Guidance for Local Authorities in England*. DCMS, London, available at: http://www.culture.gov.uk

Department for Culture, Media and Sport (DCMS) (2000) *Comprehensive, Efficient and Modern Public Libraries – Standards and Assessment*. DCMS, Information and Archives Division, London, available at: http://www.culture.gov.uk

Department for Culture, Media and Sport (DCMS)/Strategy Unit (2002) *Game Plan: a Strategy for Delivering the Government's Sport and Physical Activity Objectives*. Strategy Unit, Cabinet Office, London.

Department for Culture, Media and Sport (DCMS) (2006) *Time for Play*. DCMS, London.

Department for Culture, Media and Sport (DCMS) (annual) *Taking Part: England's Survey of Culture, Leisure and Sport*. DCMS, London, available at: http://www.culture.gov.uk

Department of the Environment (1975) *Sport and Recreation*. Cmnd 6200, HMSO, London.

Department of the Environment (1977) *Recreation and Deprivation in Inner Urban Areas*. HMSO, London.

Department of the Environment (1991) *Sport and Recreation, Planning Policy Guidance Note* 17. HMSO, London.

Department of the Environment and Department of Education and Science (1977) *Leisure and the Quality of Life: a Report on Four Local Experiments* (2 Vols). HMSO, London.

Department of Environment and Planning (1987) *The N.S.W. Environmental Planning and Assessment Act 1979: a Guide for Local Government*. Department of Environment and Planning, Sydney, Australia.

Department of Finance (1989) *What Price Heritage? The Museums Review and the Measurement of Museum Performance*. Dept. of Finance, Canberra.

Department of Industry, Science and Resources (DISR) (1999) *End Goal 2006: Moving the Sport and Recreation Industry to a Higher Growth Path – Discussion Paper*. Sport and Tourism Division, Department of Industry, Science and Resources, Canberra.

Department of Planning (1992) *Outdoor Recreation and Open Place: Planning Guidelines for Local Councils*. Department of Planning, Sydney, Australia.

Dexter Lord, G. and Lord, B. (eds) (1999) *The Manual of Museum Planning, 2nd edn*. Stationery Office, London.

Diener, E. and Seligman, E.P. (2004) Beyond money: toward an economy of well-being. *Psychological Science in the Public Interest* 5(1), 1–31.

Docker, J. (1994) *Postmodernism and Popular Culture*. Cambridge University Press, Melbourne, Australia.

Doern, G.B. (1993) The UK Citizen's Charter: origins and implementation in three agencies. *Policy and Politics* 21(1), 17–29.

Dombrink, J. (1996) Gambling and the legalisation of vice: social movements, public health and public policy in the United States. In: McMillen, J. (ed.) *Gambling Cultures: Studies in History and Interpretation*. Routledge, London, pp. 43–64.

Donnelly, J. (1989) *Universal Human Rights in Theory and Practice*. Cornell University Press, Ithaca, New York.

Donohoe, H.M. and Needham, R.D. (2009) Moving best practice forward: Delphi characteristics, advantages, potential problems, and solutions. *International Journal of Tourism Research* 11(4), 415–437.

Dow, G. (1993) What do we know about social democracy? *Economic and Industrial Democracy* 14(1), 11–48.

Dower, M., Rapoport, R., Strelitz, Z. and Kew, S. (1981) *Leisure Provision and People's Needs*. HMSO, London.

Doyal, L. and Gough, I. (1991) *A Theory of Human Needs*. Macmillan, London.

Doyle, T. (2000) *Green Politics: the Environment Movement in Australia*. UNSW Press, Sydney, Australia.

Draper, L. (ed.) (1977) *The Visitor and the Museum*. American Association of Museums, Seattle, Washington.

Dredge, D. and Jenkins, J. (2007) *Tourism Planning and Policy*. John Wiley Australia, Milton, Queensland, Australia.

Dredge, D. and Moore, S. (1992) A methodology for the integration of tourism planning in town planning. *Journal of Tourism Studies* 3(1), 8–21.

Driver, B.L. (ed.) (2008) *Managing to Optimize the Beneficial Outcomes of Recreation*. Venture, State College, Pennsylvania.

Driver, B.L. and Bruns, D.H. (1999) Concepts and uses of the benefits approach to leisure. In: Jackson, E.L. and Burton, T.L. (eds) *Leisure Studies: Prospects for the Twenty-First Century*. Venture, State College, Pennsylvania, pp. 349–369.

Driver, B.L. and Bruns, D.H. (2008) Implementing OFM on public nature-based recreation and related amenity resources. In: Driver, B.L. (ed.) *Managing to Optimize the Beneficial Outcomes of Recreation*. Venture, State College, Pennsylvania, pp. 39–73.

Driver, B.L., Brown, P.J., Stankey, G. and Gregoire, T. (1987) The ROS planning system: evaluation, basic concepts, and research needed. *Leisure Sciences* 9(2), 201–212.

Driver, B.L., Brown, P.J. and Peterson, G.L. (eds) (1991a) *Benefits of Leisure*. Venture, State College, Pennsylvania.

Driver, B.L., Tinsley, H.E.A. and Manfredo, M.J. (1991b) The paragraphs about leisure and recreation experience preference scales: results from two inventories designed to assess the breadth of the perceived psychological benefits of leisure. In: Driver, B.L., Brown, P.J. and Paterson, G.L. (eds) *Benefits of Leisure*. Venture, State College, Pennsylvania, pp. 263–286.

Driver, B.L., Bruns, D. and Booth, K. (2000) Status and some misunderstandings of the net benefits approach to leisure. Paper to the *5th Outdoor Recreation and Tourism Trends Symposium*,

Michigan State University, Lansing, Michigan, September (available at: http://www.prr.msu.edu/trends2000/).

Dulles, F.R. (1965) *A History of Recreation: America Learns to Play*. Appleton-Century-Crofts, New York.

Dumazedier, J. (1967) *Toward a Society of Leisure*. Free Press, New York.

Dumazedier, J. (1971) Leisure and post-industrial societies. In: Kaplan, M. and Bosserman, P. (eds) *Technology, Human Values, and Leisure*. Abingdon Press, Nashville, Tennessee, pp. 191–220.

Dumazedier, J. (1974) *The Sociology of Leisure*. Elsevier, The Hague.

Dunleavy, P. (1980) *Urban Political Analysis: the Politics of Collective Consumption*. Macmillan, London.

Dunstan, G. (1986) Living with the Grand Prix: good or bad? In: Burns, J.P.A. *et al.* (eds) *The Adelaide Grand Prix: the Impact of a Special Event*. Centre for South Australian Economics Studies, Adelaide, Australia, pp. 105–123.

Dye, T.R. (1978) *Understanding Public Policy*. Prentice Hall, Englewood Cliffs, New Jersey.

Edgell, D.L. (1990) *International Tourism Policy*. Van Nostrand Reinhold, New York.

Ehrlich, P. and Ehrlich, A. (1990) *The Population Explosion*. Hutchinson, London.

Elkington, J. (1997) *Cannibals with Forks: the Triple Bottom Line of the 21st Century*. Capstone, Oxford, UK.

Ellis, M.J. (1973) *Why People Play*. Prentice Hall, Englewood Cliffs, New Jersey.

Elvin, I.T. (1990) *Sport and Physical Recreation*. Longman, Harlow, UK.

Erkkila, D.L. (2000) Trends in tourism economic impact estimation methods. In: Gartner, W.C. and Lime, D.W. (eds) *Trends in Outdoor Recreation, Leisure and Tourism*. CAB International, Wallingford, UK, pp. 235–244.

Etzioni, A. (1967) Mixed scanning: a 'third' approach to decision-making. *Public Administration Review* 46(1), 385–392.

Etzioni, A. (ed.) (1995) *New Communitarian Thinking: Persons, Virtues, Institutions, and Communities*. University Press of Virginia, Charlottesville, Virginia.

European Commission (2004) The Bosman case, a turning point for European sport. *The Magazine: Education and Culture in Europe* 23, 8–9.

Evans, G. (1995) The National Lottery: planning for leisure or pay up and play the game? *Leisure Studies* 14(4), 225–244.

Evans, G. (1999) The economics of the national performing arts – exploiting consumer surplus and willingness-to-pay: a case of cultural policy failure? *Leisure Studies* 18(2), 97–118.

Ewing, G.O. (1983) Forecasting recreation trip distribution behaviour. In: Lieber, S.R. and Fesenmaier, D.R. (eds) *Recreation Planning and Management*. E. & F.N. Spon, London, pp. 120–140.

Fain, G.S. (ed.) (1991) *Leisure and Ethics*. American Alliance for Health, Physical Education, Recreation and Dance, Reston, Virginia.

Faulkner, B. (2003) Evaluating the tourism impacts of hallmark events. In: Fredline, L., Jago, L. and Cooper, C. (eds) *Progressing Tourism Research: Bill Faulkner*. Channel View Publications, Clevedon, UK, pp. 93–113.

Faulkner, B., Moscardo, G. and Laws, E. (eds) (2000) *Tourism in the 21st Century: Lessons from Experience*. Continuum, London.

Featherstone, M. (1990) Global culture: an introduction. *Theory, Culture and Society* 7(3), 1–14.

Featherstone, M. (1991) *Consumer Culture and Postmodernism*. Sage, London.

Field, B.G. and MacGregor, B.D. (1987) *Forecasting Techniques for Urban and Regional Planning*. Hutchinson, London, pp. 159–231.

Fields in Trust (2009) *Planning and Design for Outdoor Sport and Play*. Fields in Trust, London.

Filipcova, B. (ed.) (1972) Special issue on socialist life style, *Society and Leisure* No.3.

Fischer, A. *et al.* (1986) Road accidents and the Grand Prix. In: Burns, J.P.A. *et al.* (eds) *The Adelaide Grand Prix: the Impact of a Special Event*. Centre for South Australian Economics Studies, Adelaide, Australia, pp 151–168.

Fitzgerald, R. (1977) Abraham Maslow's hierarchy of needs – an exposition and evaluation. In: Fitzgerald, R. (ed.) *Human Needs and Politics*. Pergamon, Sydney, Australia, pp. 36–51.

Flannery, T. (1994) *The Future Eaters: an Ecological History of the Australasian Lands and People*. Reed Books, Kew, Victoria, Australia.

Fletcher, J.E. (1989) Input–output analysis and tourism impact studies. *Annals of Tourism Research* 16(2), 514–529.

Florida, R. (2003) *The Rise of the Creative Class*. Pluto, North Melbourne, Australia.

Frechtling, D.C. (1994a) Assessing the impacts of travel and tourism – measuring economic benefits. In: Ritchie, J.R.B. and Goeldner, C.R. (eds) *Travel, Tourism, and Hospitality Research, 2nd edn*. John Wiley, New York, pp. 367–392.

Frechtling, D.C. (1994b) Assessing the impacts of travel and tourism – measuring economic costs. In: Ritchie, J.R.B. and Goeldner, C.R. (eds) *Travel, Tourism, and Hospitality Research, 2nd edn*. John Wiley, New York, pp. 393–402.

Frechtling, D.C. (1996) *Practical Tourism Forecasting*. Butterworth-Heinemann, Oxford, UK.

French, D. and Hainsworth, J. (2001) 'There aren't any buses and the swimming pool is always cold': obstacles and opportunities in the provision of sport for disabled people. *Managing Leisure* 6(1), 35–49.

Frey, B.S. (2003) Public support. In: Towse, R. (ed.) *A Handbook of Cultural Economics*. Edward Elgar, Cheltenham, UK, pp. 389–398.

Friedman, M. and Friedman, R. (1979) The role of government. In: *Free to Choose*, Penguin, Harmondsworth, UK, pp. 47–58.

Friedman, S.J. (2000) *Children of the World Wide Web: Tool or Trap?* University Press of America, Lanham, Maryland.

Fyall, A. and Garrod, B. (1998) Heritage tourism: at what price? *Managing Leisure* 3(4), 213–228.

Galbraith, J.K. (1973) *Economics and the Public Purpose*. Penguin, Harmondsworth, UK.

Garnham, N. (1987) Concepts of culture: public policy and the cultural industries. *Cultural Studies* 1(1), 24–37.

Garrod, B. and Fyall, A. (2005) Revisiting Delphi: the Delphi technique in tourism research. In: Ritchie, B.W., Burns, P. and Palmer, C. (eds) *Tourism Research Methods: Integrating Theory with Practice*. CAB International, Wallingford, UK, pp. 85–98.

Garrod, G., Pickering, A. and Willis, K. (1993) The economic value of botanic gardens: a recreational perspective. *Geoform* 24 (2), 215–224.

Gartner, W.C. and Lime, D.W. (eds) (2000) *Trends in Outdoor Recreation, Leisure and Tourism*. CAB International, Wallingford, UK.

Gedikli, R. and Ozbilen, A. (2004) A mathematical model to determine unit area size per person needed in a neighbourhood park: a case study in Trabzon city (Turkey). *Building and Environment* 39(4), 1365–1378.

Getz, D. (1983) Capacity to absorb tourism: concepts and implications for strategic planning. *Annals of Tourism Research* 10(2), 239–263.

Giddens, A. (1964) Notes on the concepts of play and leisure. *Sociological Review* 12(1), 73–89.

Giddens, A. (1998) *The Third Way: the Renewal of Social Democracy*. Polity Press, Cambridge, UK

Giddens, A. (2000) *The Third Way and its Critics*. Polity Press, Cambridge, UK.

Giddens, A. and Hutton, W. (2000) Anthony Giddens and Will Hutton in conversation. In: Hutton, W. and Giddens, A. (eds) *On the Edge: Living with Global Capitalism*. Jonathan Cape, London, pp. 1–51.

Gittins, J. (1993) Community involvement in environment and recreation. In: Glyptis, S. (ed.) *Leisure and the Environment*. Belhaven, London, pp. 183–194.

Glover, T.D. and Burton, T.L. (1999) Back to the future: leisure services and the reemergence of the enabling authority of the state. In: Jackson, E.L. and Burton, T.L. (eds) *Leisure Studies: Prospects for the Twenty-First Century*. Venture, State College, Pennsylvania, pp. 371–384.

Glyptis, S. (1989) *Leisure and Unemployment*. Open University Press, Milton Keynes, UK.

Glyptis, S. (1991) *Countryside Recreation*. Longman, Harlow, UK.

Glyptis, S. (ed.) (1993) *Leisure and the Environment*. Belhaven, London.

Godbey, G. (1989/1975) Anti-leisure and public recreation policy. In: Coalter, F. (ed.) *Freedom and Constraint: the Paradoxes of Leisure*. Comedia/Routledge, London, pp. 74–86 (originally delivered as a conference paper in 1975).

Godbey, G. (1997) *Leisure and Leisure Services in the 21st Century*. Venture, State College, Pennsylvania.

Godbey, G. (2008) *Leisure in Your Life: New Perspectives*. Venture, State College, Pennsylvania.

Gold, S.M. (1972) Nonuse of neighborhood parks. *Journal of the American Institute of Planners* 38 (November), 369–378.

Gold, S.M. (1973) *Urban Recreation Planning*. Lea and Febiger, Philadelphia, Pennsylvania.

Gold, S.M. (1980) *Recreation Planning and Design*. McGraw-Hill, New York.

Gorz, A. (1980a) *Farewell to the Working Class*. Pluto, London.

Gorz, A. (1980b) *Ecology as Politics*. South End Press, Boston, Massachusetts.

Gorz, A. (1999) *Reclaiming Work: Beyond the Wage-based Society*. Polity Press, Cambridge, UK.

Gramberg, B. and Teicher, J. (2000) Managerialism in local government. *International Journal of Public Sector Management* 13(5), 476–492.

Gratton, C. (1996) Transnational corporations and the leisure industry. In: Collins, M. (ed.) *Leisure in Industrial and Post-Industrial Societies*. Leisure Studies Association, Eastbourne, Sussex, UK, pp. 145–170.

Gratton, C. (2000) *COMPASS 1999: a Project Seeking the Co-ordinated Monitoring of Participation in Sports in Europe, Draft report*. Sheffield Hallam University, Sheffield, UK.

Gratton, C. and Henry, I.P. (eds) (2001) *Sport in the City: the Role of Sport in Economic and Social Regeneration*. Routledge, London.

Gratton, C. and Taylor, P. (1988) *Economics of Leisure Services Management*. Longman, Harlow, UK.

Gratton, C. and Taylor, P. (1991) *Government and the Economics of Sport*. Longman, Harlow, UK.

Gratton, C. and Taylor, P. (2000) *Economics of Sport and Recreation*. E. & F.N. Spon, London.

Gratton, C., Dobson, N. and Shibli, S. (2000) The economic importance of major sport events: a case-study of six events. *Managing Leisure* 5(1), 17–28.

Gray, H.P. (1982) The contributions of economics to tourism. *Annals of Tourism Research* 9(1), 105–125.

Gray, J. (1996) *After Social Democracy: Politics, Capitalism and the Common Life*. Demos, London.

Green, E., Hebron, S. and Woodward, D. (1990) *Women's Leisure, What Leisure?* Macmillan, Basingstoke, UK.

Green, H., Hunter, C. and Moore, B. (1990) Application of the Delphi technique in tourism. *Annals of Tourism Research* 17(2), 270–279.

Greenwood, J. (1992) Producer interest groups in tourism policy: case studies from Britain and the European Community. *American Behavioral Scientist* 36(2), 236–256.

Groome, D. (1993) *Planning and Rural Recreation in Britain*. Avebury, Aldershot, UK.

Gruneau, R. (1999) *Class, Sports, and Social Development*. Human Kinetics, Champaign, Illinois.

Guadagnolo, F. (1985) The importance–performance analysis: an evaluation and marketing tool. *Journal of Park and Recreation Administration* 3(2), 13–22.

Gunter, B.G. and Gunter, N.C. (1980) Leisure styles: a conceptual framework for modern leisure. *Sociological Quarterly* 21(2), 316–374.

Hadfield, P. (2006) *Bar Wars: Contesting the Night in Contemporary British Cities*. Oxford University Press, Oxford, UK.

Halal, W.E. (2000) The top 10 emerging technologies. *The Futurist* 34 (4), 1–10.

Hale, A. (2001) Representing the Cornish: contesting heritage interpretation in Cornwall. *Tourist Studies* 1(2), 185–196.

Hale, S., Leggett, W. and Martell, L. (eds) (2004) *The Third Way and Beyond: Criticisms, Futures, Alternatives*. Manchester University Press, Manchester, UK.

Hall, C.M. (1992) *Hallmark Tourist Events*. Belhaven, London.

Hall, C.M. (1994) *Politics and Tourism: Policy, Power and Place*. Wiley, Chichester, UK.

Hall, C.M. (2000) *Tourism Planning: Policies, Processes and Relationships*. Prentice Hall, Harlow, UK.

Hall, C.M. and Jenkins, J.M. (1995) *Tourism and Public Policy*. Routledge, London.

Hall. P. (1980) *Great Planning Disasters*. Weidenfeld and Nicolson, London.

Ham, C. and Hill, M. (1984) *The Policy Process in the Modern Capitalist State*. Wheatsheaf, Brighton, UK.

Hamilton-Smith, E. and Robertson, R.W. (1977) Recreation and government in Australia. In: Mercer, D. (ed.) *Leisure and Recreation in Australia*. Sorrett, Malvern, Victoria, Australia, pp. 75–189.

Hanley, N., Shaw, W.D. and Wright, R.E. (eds) (2003) *The New Economics of Outdoor Recreation*. Edward Elgar, Cheltenham, UK.

Hantrais, L. and Kamphorst, T.J. (eds) (1987) *Trends in the Arts: a Multinational Perspective*. Giordano Bruno Amersfoort, Voorthuizen, Netherlands.

Haralambos, M., Van Krieken, R., Smith, S. and Holborn, M. (1996) *Sociology: Themes and Perspectives*. Longman, Melbourne, Australia.

Harding, A. (1994) Urban regimes and growth machines: toward a cross-national research agenda. *Urban Affairs Quarterly* 29(3), 356–382.

Harper, J.A. and Balmer, K.R. (1989) The perceived benefits of public leisure services: an exploratory investigation. *Society and Leisure* 12(1), 171–188.

Hartley, J. (ed.) (2005) *Creative Industries*. Blackwell, Malden, Massachusetts.

Harvey, D. (1989) From managerialism to entrepreneurialism: the transformation in urban governance in late capitalism. *Geografiska Annaler* 71B(1), 3–17.

Harvey, D. (2000) *Spaces of Hope*. Edinburgh University Press, Edinburgh, UK.

Hatry, H.P. and Dunn, D.R. (1971) *Measuring the Effectiveness of Local Government Services: Recreation*. Urban Institute, Washington, DC.

Haulot, A. (1981) Social tourism: current dimensions and future developments. *International Journal of Tourism Management* 2(2), 207–212.

Hawkins, G. (1993) *From Nimbin to Mardi Gras: Constructing Community Arts*. Allen and Unwin, Sydney, Australia.

HCRS: see Heritage, Conservation and Recreation Service

Hefner, F.L. (1990) Using economic models to measure the impact of sports on local economies. *Journal of Sport and Social Issues* 14(1), 1–13.

Held, D. and McGrew, A. (2000) *The Global Transformations Reader*. Polity Press/Blackwell, Cambridge, UK.

Heller, A. (1976) *The Theory of Need in Marx*. Allison & Busby, London.

Helling, A. (1998) Collaborative visioning: proceed with caution! Results from evaluating Atlanta's Vision 2020 project. *Journal of the American Planning Association* 63(3), 335–349.

Hemingway, J.L. and Parr, M.G.W. (2000) Leisure research and leisure practice: three perspectives on constructing the research–practice relation. *Leisure Sciences* 22(1), 139–162.

Henderson, K.A. (2000) Gender inclusion as a recreation trend. In: Gartner, W.C. and Lime, D.W. (eds) *Trends in Outdoor Recreation, Leisure and Tourism*. CAB International, Wallingford, UK, pp. 17–28.

Henderson, K.M. and Bialeschki, D. (2002) *Evaluating Leisure Services: Making Enlightened Decisions*, 2nd edn. Venture, State College, Pennsylvania.

Henderson, K.M., Bialeschki, D., Shaw, S.M. and Freysinger, V.J. (1989) *A Time of One's Own: a Feminist Perspective on Women's Leisure*. Venture, State College, Pennsylvania.

Hendry, L.B., Shucksmith, J., Love, J.G. and Glendinning, A. (1993) *Young People's Leisure and Lifestyles*. Routledge, London.

Henry, I. (1984a) The politics of the New Right: consequences for leisure policy and management. *Leisure Management* 4(9), 10–11.

Henry, I. (1984b) Conservatism, socialism and leisure services. *Leisure Management* 4(11), 10–12.

Henry, I. (1985) Leisure management and the social democratic tradition. *Leisure Management* 5(2), 14–15.

Henry, I. (1988) Alternative futures for the public leisure service. In: Bennington, J. and White, J. (eds) *The Future of Leisure Services*. Longman, Harlow, UK, pp. 207–244.

Henry, I.P. (ed.) (1990) *Management and Planning in the Leisure Industries*. Macmillan, Basingstoke, UK.

Henry, I.P. (1993) *The Politics of Leisure Policy*. Macmillan, Basingstoke, UK.

Henry, I.P. (1999) Globalisation and the governance of leisure: the role of the nation-state, the European Union and the city in leisure policy in Britain. *Society and Leisure* 22(2), 355–380.

Henry, I.P. (2001) *The Politics of Leisure Policy, 2nd edn*. Palgrave, Basingstoke, UK, 199 pp.

Henry, I.P. and Paramio Salcines, J.L. (1998) Sport, culture and urban regimes: the case of Bilbao. In: Collins, M.F. and Cooper, I.S. (eds) *Leisure Management: Issues and Applications*. CAB International, Wallingford, UK, pp. 97–112.

Henry, I.P. and Paramio Salcines, J.L. (1999) Sport and the analysis of symbolic regimes: a case study of the City of Sheffield. *Urban Affairs Review* 34(5), 641–666.

Henry, I.P. and Spink, J. (1990a) Planning for leisure: the commercial and public sectors. In: Henry, I.P. (ed.) *Management and Planning in the Leisure Industries*. Macmillan, Basingstoke, UK, pp. 33–69.

Henry, I.P. and Spink, J. (1990b) Social theory, planning and management. In: Henry, I.P. (ed.) *Management and Planning in the Leisure Industries*. Macmillan, Basingstoke, UK, pp. 179–210.

Herbert, D.T., and Johnston, R.J. (eds) (1976) *Social Areas in Cities*. Wiley, New York.

Heritage, Conservation and Recreation Service (1979) *The Third Nationwide Outdoor Recreation Plan, Executive Report, Assessment and 4 Appendices* (United States Department of the Interior). US Govt. Printing Office, Washington, DC.

Hertz, N. (2001) *The Silent Takeover: Global Capitalism and the Death of Democracy*. William Heinemann, London.

Hibbins, R. (1998) Leisure and ethnic diversity in Australia. In: Rowe, D. and Lawrence, G. (eds) *Tourism, Leisure, Sport: Critical Perspectives*. Hodder Education, Rydalmere, NSW, Australia, pp. 100–111.

Hill, J. (2002) *Sport, Leisure and Culture in Twentieth-Century Britain*. Palgrave, Basingstoke, UK.

Hill, K.Q. (1978) Trend extrapolation. In: Fowles, J. (ed.) *Handbook of Futures Research*. Greenwood Press, Westport, Connecticut, pp. 249–272.

Hillman, M. and Whalley, A. (1977) *Fair Play for All*. PEP (now Centre for Policy Studies), London.

Hindess, B. (1993) Citizenship in the modern West. In: Turner, B.S. (ed.) *Citizenship and Social Theory*. Sage, London, pp. 19–35.

Hirsch, F. (1977) *Social Limits to Growth*. Routledge and Kegan Paul, London.

Hoctor, Z. (2003) Community participation in marine ecotourism development in West Clare, Ireland. In: Garrod, B. and Wilson, J. (eds) *Marine Ecotourism: Issues and Experiences*. Channel View Publications, Clevedon, UK, pp. 171–176.

Hodge, G.A. (2000) *Privatization: an International Review of Performance*. Westview, Boulder, Colorado.

Hollenhorst, S., Olson, D. and Forney, R. (1992) The use of importance–performance analysis to evaluate state park cabins. *Journal of Parks and Recreation Administration* 10(1), 1–11.

Holling, C.S. (ed.) (1978) *Adaptive Environmental Assessment and Management*. Wiley, Chichester, UK.

Homeshaw, J. (1995) Policy community, policy networks and science policy in Australia. *Australian Journal of Public Administration* 54(4), 520–532.

Horna, J. (1994) *The Study of Leisure: an Introduction*. Oxford University, Press, Toronto, Canada.

Horne, D. (1986) *The Public Culture*. Pluto, London.

Horner, S. and Swarbrooke, J. (2005) *Leisure Marketing: a Global Perspective*. Butterworth-Heinemann, Oxford, UK.

Houghton-Evans, W. and Miles, J.C. (1970) Environmental capacity in rural recreation areas. *Journal of the Royal Town Planning Institute* 56(10), 423–427.

Houlihan, B. (1997) *Sport Policy and Politics: a Comparative Analysis*. Routledge, London.

Houlihan, B. (2001) Citizenship, civil society and the sport and recreation professions. *Managing Leisure* 6(1), 1–14.

House of Commons Select Committee on Culture, Media and Sport (HCSCCMS) (2007) *London 2012 Olympic Games and Paralympic Games: Funding and Legacy*. House of Commons, London, available at: http://www.publications.parliament.uk/pa/cm/cmcumeds.htm.

House of Commons Select Committee on Culture, Media and Sport (HCSCCMS) (2008) *London 2012 Games: the Next Lap*. House of Commons, London, available at: http://www. publications.parliament.uk/pa/cm/cmcumeds.htm.

House of Lords Select Committee on Sport and Leisure (1973) *Second Report*. HMSO, London.

House of Representatives Standing Committee on Finance and Public Administration (1989) *Going for Gold: the First Report of an Inquiry into Sports Funding and Administration*. AGPS, Canberra.

Howat, G. and Crilley, G. (2007) Customer service quality, satisfaction and operational performance: a proposed model for Australian public aquatic centres. *Annals of Leisure Research* 10(2), 168–195.

Howat, G., Murray, D. and Crilley, G. (2005) Reducing measurement overload: rationalizing performance measures for public aquatic centres in Australia. *Managing Leisure* 10(2), 128–142.

Huan, T.C. and O'Leary, J.T. (1999) *Measuring Tourism Performance*. Sagamore, Champaign, Illinois.

Hudson, S. and Shephard, G.W.H. (1998) Measuring service quality at tourist destinations: an application of importance–performance analysis to an Alpine ski resort. *Journal of Travel and Tourism Marketing* 7(3), 61–77.

Hughes, H.L. (1984) Government support for tourism in the UK: a different perspective. *Tourism Management* 5(1), 13–19.

Hutton, W. and Giddens, A. (eds) (2000) *On the Edge: Living with Global Capitalism*. Jonathan Cape, London.

Hylton, K. and Totten, M. (2001) Community sports development. In: Hylton. K., Bramham, P., Jackson, D. and Nesti, M. (eds) *Sports Development: Policy, Process and Practice*. Routledge, London, pp. 66–98.

Illich, I., Zola, I.K., McKnight, J., Caplan, C. and Shaiken, H. (1977) *Disabling Professions*. Marion Boyars, London.

Independent Panel on Sport (2009) *The Future of Sport in Australia*. Australian Government, Canberra, available at: http://www.sportpanel.org.au

International Consortium of Investigative Journalists (2009) *The Global Climate Change Lobby*. Center for Public Integrity, Washington, DC, available at: http://www.publicintegrity. org/investigations/global_climate_change_lobby/

International Olympic Committee (IOC) (2004) *The Olympic Charter*. IOC, Lausanne, available at: http://www.olympic.org

Iso-Ahola, S. (1980) *The Social Psychology of Leisure and Recreation*. Wm C. Brown, Dubuque, Iowa.

Iwasaki, Y. (2006) Leisure and the quality of life and diversity: an international and multicultural perspective. In: Jackson, E. (ed.) *Leisure and the Quality of Life: Impacts on Social, Economic and Cultural Development: Hangzhou Consensus*. Zhejiang University Press/World Leisure Organisation, Hangzhou, China, pp. 25–39.

Jackson, E.L and Burton, T. L.(eds) (1999) *Leisure Studies: Prospects for the Twenty-First Century*. Venture, State College, Pennsylvania.

Jackson, M. (2009) *The Jackson Report: Informing the National Long-Term Tourism Strategy*. Commonwealth of Australia, Canberra, available at: http://www.ret.gov.au/tourism/Documents/Tourism%20Policy/jackson–report–july09.pdf.

Jackson, P.M. (1986) Adapting the R.O.S. technique to the urban setting. *Australian Parks and Recreation* 22(3), 26–28.

Jackson, P.M. (1991) Performance indicators: promises and pitfalls. In: Pearce, S (ed.) *Museum Economics and the Community*. Athlone Press, London, pp. 41–64.

Jamal, T. and Getz, D. (2000) Community roundtables for tourism-related conflicts: the dialectics of consensus and process structures. In: Bramwell, B. and Lane, B. (eds) *Tourism Collaboration and Partnerships: Politics, Practice and Sustainability*. Channel View Publications, Clevedon, UK, pp. 159–182.

Jansen-Verbeke, M. (1985) Inner city leisure resources. *Leisure Studies* 4(2), 141–158.

Jarvie, G. and Maguire, J. 1994, *Sport and Leisure in Social Thought*. Routledge, London.

Jeanrenaud, C. and Késenne, S. (eds) (2006) *The Economics of Sport and the Media*. Edward Elgar, Cheltenham, UK.

Jeffries, D. (2001) *Governments and Tourism*. Butterworth-Heinemann, Oxford, UK.

Jenkins, C. *et al.* (1989) Making waves: the structure of the catchment area of a leisure pool. In: Botterill, D. (ed.) *Leisure Participation and Experience: Models and Case Studies*. Conference Papers 37, Leisure Studies Association, Eastbourne, UK, pp. 137–168.

Jenkins, H. (1979) *The Culture Gap: an Experience of Government and the Arts.* Marion Boyars, London.

Jenkins, J. and Lyons, K. (2006) Non-resident fathers; leisure with their children. *Leisure Studies* 25(2), 219–232.

John Madin Design Group (1969) *Telford Development Proposals.* Telford Development Corporation, Telford, UK.

Johnson, P. and Thomas, B. (eds) (1992) *Perspectives on Tourism Policy.* Mansell, London.

Jones, B. (1995) *Sleepers Wake! Technology and the Future of Work, 2nd edn.* Oxford University Press, Melbourne, Australia.

Jones, H. (1990) The economic impact and importance of sport: a Council of Europe co-ordinated study. *Sport Science Review* 13, 26–31.

Jones, K.R. and Wills, J. (2005) *The Invention of the Parks: from the garden of Eden to Disney's Magic Kingdom.* Polity Press, Cambridge, UK.

Jones, S. (1990) The Australian tourism outlook forum Delphi. In: Horwath and Horwath Services Pty. (eds) *Australian Tourism Outlook Forum: Contributed Papers, Sydney, June 1990.* Bureau of Tourism Research, Canberra, pp. 51–55.

Jubenville, A. and Becker, R.H. (1983) Outdoor recreation management planning: contemporary schools of thought. In: Lieber, S.R. and Fesenmaier, D.R. (eds) *Recreation Planning and Management.* E. & F.N. Spon, London, pp. 303–322.

Jubenville, A. and Twight, B.W. (1993) *Outdoor Recreation Management: Theory and Application, 3rd edn.* Venture, State College, Pennsylvania.

Kamenka, E. and Tay, A.E. (eds) (1978) *Human Rights.* Edward Arnold, Port Melbourne, Victoria, Australia.

Kamphorst, T.J. and Roberts, K. (eds) (1989) *Trends in Sports: a Multinational Perspective.* Giordano Bruno Culemborg, Voorthuizen, the Netherlands.

Karn, V. (1977) *Retiring to the Seaside.* Routledge and Kegan Paul, London.

Kay, T. (ed.) (2006) Special issue on fathering through leisure. *Leisure Studies* 25(2).

Kaynak, E. and Macaulay, J.A. (1984) The Delphi technique in the measurement of tourism market potential. *Tourism Management* 4(1), 87–101.

Keller, P.F. (2000) Globalization and tourism. In: Gartner, W.C. and Lime, D.W. (eds) *Trends in Outdoor Recreation, Leisure and Tourism.* CAB International, Wallingford, UK, pp. 287–298.

Kelly, J.R. (1983) *Leisure Identities and Interactions.* Allen and Unwin, London.

Kelly, J.R. and Godbey, G. (1992) *Sociology of Leisure.* Venture, State College, Pennsylvania.

Kelly, J.R. and Warnick, R.B. (1999) *Recreation Trends and Markets: the 21st Century.* Sagamore, Champaign, Illinois.

Kelly, O. (1984) *Community, Art and the State: Storming the Citadels.* Comedia, London.

Kelsey, C. and Gray, H. (1985) *Master Plan Process for Parks.* American Alliance for Health, Physical Education, Recreation and Dance, Alexandria, Virginia.

Kennedy, D.W., Smith, R.W. and Austin, D.R. (1991) *Special Recreation: Opportunities for Persons with Disabilities.* Wm. C. Brown, Dubuque, Iowa.

Kenway, J. (1992) Feminist theories of the state: to be or not to be? In: Mueltzfeldt, M. (ed.) *Society, State and Politics.* Pluto, Leichhardt, NSW, Australia, pp. 108–142.

Kew, S. (1979) *Ethnic Groups and Leisure.* Sports Council/SSRC, London.

Keynes, J.M. (1931) Economic possibilities for our grand-children. In: *The Collected Writings of John Maynard Keynes, Vol. 9, Essays in Persuasion.* (1972 edn). Macmillan, London, pp. 321–332.

Khan, N. (1976) *The Arts Britain Ignores: the Arts of Ethnic Minorities.* Arts Council of Great Britain, London.

Kidd, B. and Donnelly, P. (2000) Human rights and sports. *International Review for the Sociology of Sport* 350 (2), 131–148.

Kinnaird, V., and Hall, D. (1994) *Tourism: a Gender Analysis.* John Wiley, Chichester, UK.

Klein, N. (1999) *No Logo: Taking Aim at the Brand Bullies.* Picador, New York.

Korten, D.C. (1996) The mythic victory of market capitalism. In: Mander, J. and Goldsmith, E. (eds) *The Case Against the Global Economy and for a Turn Toward the Local*. Sierra Club, San Francisco, California, pp. 183–191.

Kotler, P., Bowen, J.T. and Makens, J.C. (2006) *Marketing for Hospitality and Tourism, 4th edn*. Pearson Education, Upper Saddle River, New Jersey.

Kraus, R. (1994) *Leisure in a Changing America: Multicultural Perspectives*. Macmillan, New York.

Kraus, R. (1998) *Recreation and Leisure in Modern Society, 5th edn*. Jones and Bartlett, Sudbury, Massachusetts.

Krippendorf, J. (1987) *The Holiday Makers: Understanding the Impact of Leisure and Travel*. Heinemann, London.

Kumar, K. (1995) *From Post-Industrial to Post-Modern Society: New Theories of the Contemporary World*. Blackwell, Oxford, UK.

Lader, D., Short, S. and Gershuny, J. (2006) *The Time Use Survey, 2005*. HMSO, London, available via Office for National Statistics website: http://www.statistics.gov.uk

Lafargue, P. (1958) The right to be lazy. In: Larrabee, E. and Meyersohn, R. (eds) *Mass Leisure*. Free Press, Glencoe, Illinois, pp. 105–117 (paper originally published 1848).

Landry, C. and Bianchini, F. (1995) *The Creative City*. Demos/Comedia, London.

Lane, J. (1978) *Arts Centres: Every Town Should Have One*. Paul Elek, London.

Langer, M. (1997) *Service Quality in Tourism: Measurement Methods and Empirical Analysis*. Peter Lang, Frankfurt am Main, Germany.

Langhorne, R. (2001) *The Coming of Globalization: its Evolution and Contemporary Consequences*. Palgrave, Basingstoke, UK.

Lashley, H. and Hylton, K. (eds) (1997) Special issue: A Black Perspective. *Leisure Studies* 16(4).

Latham, M. (1998) Economic policy and the third way. *Australian Economic Review* 31(4), 384–398.

Lavery, P. (1971) The demand for recreation. In: Lavery, P. (ed.) *Recreational Geography*. David and Charles, Newton Abbot, UK, pp. 21–50.

Leach, R. (1993) *Political Ideologies*, 2nd edn. Macmillan, Melbourne, Australia.

Lee, C.-K., Song, H.-J. and Mjelde, J.W. (2008) The forecasting of International Expo tourism using quantitative and qualitative techniques. *Tourism Management* 29(6), 1084–1098.

Lenskyj, H. (1991) A new ball game? Historical and contemporary models of women's sport in Canada. *World Leisure and Recreation* 33(3), 15–18.

Lentell, B. (1996) Putting clothes on the invisible man: the Audit Commission, the Citizen's Charter and local authority leisure services. In: Collins, M. (ed.) *Leisure in Industrial and Post-industrial Societies*. Publication No. 49, Leisure Studies Association, Eastbourne, UK, pp. 269–286.

Lentell, B. (2001) Customers' views of the results of managing quality through ISO 9002 and Investors in People in leisure services. *Managing Leisure* 6(1), 15–34.

Leslie, D. and Hughes, G. (1997) Agenda 21, local authorities and tourism in the UK. *Managing Leisure* 2(3), 143–154.

Levitt, L. (1991) Recreation for the mentally ill. In: Driver, B.L., Brown, P.J. and Peterson, G.L. (eds) *Benefits of Leisure*. Venture, State College, Pennsylvania, pp. 161–178.

Lieber S.R. and Fesenmaier D.R. (eds) (1983) *Recreation Planning and Management*. E. & F.N. Spon, London.

Limb, M. (1986) Community involvement in leisure provision – private enterprise or public interest? In: Coalter, F. (ed.) *The Politics of Leisure*. Publication 24, Leisure Studies Association, Eastbourne, UK, pp. 90–110.

Lindblom, C.E. (1959) The science of 'muddling through'. *Public Administration Review* 19(2), 79–88.

Linstone, H.A. (1978) The Delphi technique. In: Fowles, J. (ed.) *Handbook of Futures Research*. Greenwood Press, Westport, Connecticut, pp. 273–300.

Long, J. (1994) Local authority tourism strategies – a British appraisal. *Journal of Tourism Studies* 5(2), 17–23.

Long, J. (2000) No racism here? A preliminary examination of sporting innocence. *Managing Leisure* 5(3), 121–134.

Long, P. (2000) Tourism development regimes in the inner city fringe: the case of Discover Islington, London. In: Bramwell, B. and Lane, B. (eds) *Tourism Collaboration and Partnerships: Politics, Practice and Sustainability*. Channel View Publications, Clevedon, UK, pp. 183–199.

Lord, B.E. and Elmendorf, W.F. (2008) Are recreation organizations representative of all participants? *Journal of Park and Recreation Administration* 26(1), 87–96.

Low, S., Taplin, D. and Scheld, S. (2005) *Rethinking Urban Parks: Public Space and Cultural Diversity*. University of Texas Press, Austin, Texas.

Lundberg, D.E., Krishnamoorthy, M. and Stevenga, M.H. (1995) *Tourism Economics*. John Wiley and Sons, New York.

Lynch, R. (1993) The cultural repositioning of rugby league football and its men. *ANZALS Leisure Research Series* 1, 105–119.

Lynch, R. and Veal, A.J. (2006) *Australian Leisure, 3rd edn*. Longman, Sydney, Australia.

Lynn, J. and Jay, A. (eds) (1988) *The Complete Yes Minister: the Diaries of a Cabinet Minister*. BBC Books, London.

Lynn, J. and Jay, A. (eds) (1989) *The Complete Yes Prime Minister: the Diaries of the Right Hon. James Hacker*. BBC Books, London.

Ma, J. (2001) From Shanghai to Davos. *Asian Wall Street Journal* 20 February, p. 6.

MacFarlane, L.J. (1985) *The Theory and Practice of Human Rights*. Maurice Temple Smith, London.

MacPherson, C.B. (1977) Needs and wants: an ontological or historical problem? In: Fitzgerald, R. (ed.) *Human Needs and Politics*. Pergamon, Sydney, Australia, pp. 26–46.

Magdalinski, T., Schimmel, K.S. and Chandler, T.J.L. (2005) Recapturing Olympic mystique: the corporate invasion of the classroom. In: Nauright, J. and Schimmel, K.S. (eds) *The Political Economy of Sport*. Palgrave Macmillan, Basingstoke, UK, pp. 38–56.

Maguire, J.A. (1999) *Global Sport: Identities, Societies, Civilizations*. Polity Press, Cambridge, UK.

Major Performing Arts Inquiry (1999) *Securing the Future: Major Performing Arts Inquiry Final Report*. Dept. of Communications, Information Technology and the Arts, Canberra.

Makridakis, S., Wheelwright, S.C. and Hyndman, R.J. (1998) *Forecasting Methods and Applications, 3rd edn*. John Wiley, New York.

Malkin, K., Johnston, L. and Brackenridge, C. (2000) A critical evaluation of training needs for child protection in UK sport. *Managing Leisure* 5(3), 151–160.

Mander, J. and Goldsmith, E. (eds) (1996) *The Case Against the Global Economy and for a Turn Toward the Local*. Sierra Club, San Francisco, California.

Manidis, P. (1994) Cost–benefit analysis in parks. In: *Royal Australian Institute of Parks and Recreation Seminar Proceedings: Who Pays – Open Space and Recreational Facilities*. RAIPR, Canberra, pp. 45–53.

Marcuse, H. (1964) *One Dimensional Man*. Routledge & Kegan Paul, London.

Markwell, K. (1998a) Playing queer: leisure in the lives of gay men. In: Rowe, D. and Lawrence, G. (eds) *Tourism, Leisure, Sport: Critical Perspectives*. Hodder Education, Rydalmere, NSW, Australia, pp. 112–123.

Markwell, K. (1998b) Space and place in gay men's leisure. *Annals of Leisure Research* 1, 19–36.

Marriott, K.L. (1990) *Recreation Planning: a Manual for Local Government*. South Australian Department of Recreation and Sport, Adelaide, Australia.

Marshall, T.H. (1994) Citizenship and social class. In: Turner, B. and Hamilton, P. (eds) *Citizenship: Critical Concepts, Vol. II*. Routledge, London, pp. 5–44.

Martilla, J.A. and James, J.C. (1977) Importance–performance analysis. *Journal of Marketing* 41(1), 77–79.

Martin, W.H. and Mason, S. (1998) *Transforming the Future: Rethinking Free Time and Work*. Leisure Consultants, Sudbury, UK.

Maslow, A. (1954/1987) *Motivation and Personality, 3rd edn*. Longman, New York.

Mathieson, A. and Wall, G. (1982) *Tourism: Economic, Physical and Social Impacts*. Longman, London.

Max-Neef, M. (1992) Development and human needs. In: Ekins, P. and Max-Neef, M. (eds) *Real-life Economics: Understanding Wealth Creation*. Routledge, London, pp. 197–214.

McBoyle, G., Scott, D. and Jones, B. (2007) Climate change and the future of snowmobiling in non-mountainous regions of Canada. *Managing Leisure* 12(4), 237–250.

McCabe, S. (2009) Who needs a holiday? Evaluating social tourism. *Annals of Tourism Research* 36(4), 667–688.

McCarthy, P.E. and Dower, M. (1967) Planning for conservation and development: an exercise in the process of decision-making. *Journal of the Royal Town Planning Institute* 53(1), 99–105.

McEvoy, D., Handley, J.F., Cavan, G., Aylen, J., Lindley, S., McMorrow, J. and Glynn, S. (2006) *Climate Change and the Visitor Economy: the Challenges and Opportunities for England's Northwest.* Sustainability Northwest, Manchester, and UK Climate Impacts Programme, Oxford, UK.

McIntosh, P. and Charlton, V. (1985) *The Impact of Sport for All Policy 1966–1984.* Study 26, Sports Council, London.

McKay, J. (1986) Some social impacts of the Grand Prix on residents closest to the circuit – noise and property damage. In: Burns, J.P.A. *et al.* (eds) *The Adelaide Grand Prix: the Impact of a Special Event.* Centre for South Australian Economics Studies, Adelaide, Australia, pp. 124–150.

McKay, J. (1998) Gender and organisational power in Australian sport. In: Rowe, D. and Lawrence, G. (eds) *Tourism, Leisure, Sport: Critical Perspectives.* Hodder Education, Rydalmere, NSW, Australia, pp. 180–193.

McMaster, B. (2008) *Supporting Excellence in the Arts: from Measurement to Judgement.* Department for Culture, Media and Sport, London, available at: http://www.culture.gov.uk/images/publications/supportingexcellenceinthearts.pdf

McRobbie, A. (1994) Shut up and dance: youth culture and changing modes of femininity. In: McRobbie, A., *Postmodernism and Popular Culture.* Routledge, London, pp. 155–176.

Mercer, D. (1973) The concept of recreational need. *Journal of Leisure Research* 5(1), 37–50.

Merritt, G. (1982) *World out of Work.* William Collins, London.

Mertes, J.D. and Hall, J.R. (1996) *Park, Recreation, Open Space and Greenway Guidelines.* National Recreation and Park Association, Ashburn, Victoria, Australia.

Miles, I., Cole, S. and Gershuny, J. (1978) Images of the future. In: Freeman, C. and Jahoda, M. (eds) *World Futures: the Great Debate.* Martin Robertson, London, pp. 279–342.

Miles, S. (2000) *Youth Lifestyles in a Changing World.* Open University Press, Milton Keynes, UK.

Mill, R.C. and Morrison, A.M. (2006) *The Tourism System, 5th edn.* Kendall/Hunt, Dubuque, Iowa.

Miller, R.K. and Associates (2007) *The 2007 Leisure Market Research Handbook.* Richard K. Miller and Associates, Loganville, Georgia, available at: http://www.rkma.com

Miller, T. (1990) Sport, media and masculinity. In: Rowe, D. and Lawrence, G. (eds) *Sport and Leisure: Trends in Australian Popular Culture.* Harcourt, Brace Jovanovich, Sydney, Australia, pp. 74–95.

Miller, T., Lawrence, G., McKay, J. and Rowe, D. (2001) *Globalization and Sport: Playing the World.* Sage, London.

Milstein, D.N. and Reid, L.M. (1966) *Michigan Outdoor Recreation Demand Study, Vol. 1, Methods and Models.* Michigan Depts of Conservation and Commerce, Lansing, Michigan.

Ministry of Housing and Local Government, Sociological Planning Research Unit (1966) *Open Space Survey: Assessing the Acreage Required for Sports Pitches.* MHLG, London.

Ministry of Housing and Local Government (1969) *People and Planning* (The 'Skeffington Report'). HMSO, London.

Minnaert, L., Maitland, R. and Miller, G. (2009) Tourism and social policy: the value of social tourism. *Annals of Tourism Research* 36(2), 316–334.

Mintzberg, H. (1994) *The Rise and Fall of Strategic Planning.* Prentice Hall, New York.

Moeller, G.H. and Shafer, E.L. (1983) The use and abuse of Delphi forecasting. In: Lieber, S.R. and Fesenmaier, D.R. (eds) *Recreation Planning and Management.* E. & F.N. Spon, London, pp. 96–104.

Moeller, G.H., and Shafer, E.L. (1994) The Delphi technique: a tool for long-range travel and tourism planning. In: Ritchie, J.R.B. and Goeldner, C.R. (eds) *Travel, Tourism, and Hospitality Research, 2nd edn.* John Wiley, New York, pp. 473–480.

Mooney, C.Z. (1999) The politics of morality policy: symposium editor's introduction. *Policy Studies Journal* 27(4), 657–680.

Moore, R.L. and Driver, B.L. (2005) *Introduction to Outdoor Recreation*. Venture, State College, Pennsylvania.

Mowbray, M. (1992) Local government recreation planning and equity. *Urban Policy and Research* 10(2), 17–23.

Mowbray, M. (1993) Sporting opportunity: equity in urban infrastructure and planning. *ANZALS Leisure Research Series* 1, 120–141.

Murphy, P.E. (1985) *Tourism: a Community Approach*. Methuen, New York.

Murray, M. and Sproats, J. (1990) The disabled traveller. *Journal of Tourism Studies* 1(1), 3–8.

Musgrave, R.A. and Musgrave, P.B. (1980) The theory of social goods. In: Musgrave, R.A. and Musgrave, P.B. (eds) *Public Finance in Theory and Practice*. McGraw-Hill, New York, pp. 54–95.

Naisbitt, J. (1982) *Megatrends: Ten New Directions Transforming our Lives*. Warner Books, New York.

Naisbitt, J. and Aburdene, P. (1990) *Megatrends 2000*. Pan Books, London.

National Park Service (2000) American *National Park Strategic Plan 2001–2005*. National Park Service/US Department of the Interior, Washington, DC., available at: http://www.planning.nps.gov/planning (accessed April 2009).

Natural England (2005) *England Leisure Visits: Summary of the 2005 Leisure Visits Survey*. Natural England, Sheffield, available under 'publications' at: http://www.naturalengland.org.uk

Nazareth, L. (2007) *The Leisure Economy*. John Wiley Canada, Mississauga, Ontario, Canada.

Nevill, A.M. and Jenkins, C. (1986) Social area influences on sports centre use, an investigation of the ACORN method of social area classification. In: Mangan, J.A. and Small, R.B. (eds) *Sports, Culture, Society, Proceedings of the VIII Commonwealth and International Conference on Sport, Physical Education, Dance, Recreation and Health*. E. & F.N. Spon, London.

Ng, D., Brown, B. and Knott, W. (1983) Qualified leisure services manpower requirements: a future perspective. *Recreation Research Review* 10(1), 13–19.

Nicholls, M. (1975) *Recreationally Disadvantaged Areas in Greater London. Report of an Analysis of Provision for Sports and Active Recreation*. RM 467, Policy Studies Unit, Greater London Council, London.

Nichols, G. (1996) The impact of compulsory competitive tendering on planning in leisure departments. *Managing Leisure* 1(2), 105–114.

Nichols, G. (2007) *Sport and Crime Reduction: the Role of Sports in Tackling Youth Crime*. Routledge, London.

Nichols, G. and Taylor, P. (1995) The impact on local authority leisure of CCT, financial cuts and changing attitudes. *Local Government Studies* 21(4), 607–622.

Noll, R.G. and Zimbalist, A. (eds) (1997) *Sports, Jobs and Taxes: the Economic Impact of Sports Teams and Stadiums*. Brookings Institution Press, Washington, DC.

Norman, W. and MacDonald, C. (2004) Getting to the bottom of 'triple bottom line'. *Business Ethics Quarterly* 14(2), 263–274.

NSW Arts/Dept of Local Government (NSWA/DLG) (2004) *Cultural Planning Guidelines*. Ministry for the Arts/Department of Local Government, Sydney, Australia, available at: http://www.dlg. nsw. gov.au/dlg/dlghome/documents/Information/CPG–final.pdf

NSW Department of the Arts, Sport and Recreation (DASR) (2007) *Corporate Plan 2007–2011*. DASR, Sydney, Australia.

Office for National Statistics (2008) *Family Spending, 2007*. ONS, London, available at: http://www.statistics.gov.uk

Office of the Deputy Prime Minister (2002) *Planning Policy Guidance 17: Planning for Open Space, Sport and Recreation*. ODPM, London.

Ogden, S.M. and Wilson, P. (2001) Beyond data benchmarking: the challenge of managing a benchmarking network in the UK public leisure sector. *Managing Leisure* 6(2), 95–108.

Ontario Ministry of Culture and Recreation (OMCR) (1976) *Guidelines for Developing Public Recreation Facility Standards*. Ministry of Culture and Recreation, Sports and Fitness Division, Toronto, Canada.

Ott, A.F. and Hartley, K. (1991) *Privatization and Economic Efficiency*. Edward Elgar, Cheltenham, UK.

Outdoor Recreation Resources Review Commission (ORRRC) (1962) *Outdoor Recreation for America*. ORRRC, Washington, DC.

Paddick, R.J. (1982) The concept of need in planning for recreation. In: Howell, M.L. and Brehaut, J.R. (eds) *Proceedings of the VII Commonwealth and International Conference on Sport, Physical Education, Recreation and Dance: 4 (Recreation)*. University of Queensland, Brisbane, Australia, pp. 39–47.

Papadakis, E. (1993) *Politics and the Environment*. Longman Cheshire, Melbourne, Australia.

Parasuraman, A., Zeithaml, V.A. and Berry, L.L. (1988) SERVQUAL: a multiple-item scale for measuring consumer perceptions of service quality. *Journal of Retailing* 64(1), 12–37.

Parker, H., Aldridge, J. and Measham, F. (1998) *Illegal Leisure: the Normalization of Adolescent Recreational Drug Use*. Routledge, London.

Parker, S. (1983) *Leisure and Work*. Allen & Unwin, London.

Parsons, W. (1995) *Public Policy*. Edward Elgar, Cheltenham, UK.

Patmore, A. (1983) *Recreation and Resources*. Basil Blackwell, Oxford, UK.

Patterson, I. and Taylor, T. (eds) (2001) *Celebrating Inclusion and Diversity in Leisure*. HM Publishing, Melbourne, Australia.

Payne, A. (1993) The Commonwealth and the politics of sporting contacts with South Africa. In: Binfield, J.C. and Stevenson, J. (eds) *Sport, Culture and Politics*. Sheffield Academic Press, Sheffield, UK, pp. 129–150.

Pearce, P.L. (2005) *Tourist Behaviour: Themes and Conceptual Issues*. Channel View Publications, Clevedon, UK.

Pearce, S. (ed.) (1991) *Museum Economics and the Community*. Athlone Press, London.

Peterson, G.L. and Loomis, J.B. (2000) Trends in leisure value and valuation. In: Gartner, W.C. and Lime, D.W. (eds) *Trends in Outdoor Recreation, Leisure and Tourism*. CAB International, Wallingford, UK, pp. 215–224.

Peterson, G.L., Driver, B.L. and Gregory, R. (eds) (1988) *Amenity Resource Valuation: Integrating Economics with Other Disciplines*. Venture, State College, Pennsylvania.

Pieper, J. (1965) *Leisure: the Basis of Culture*. Faber, London.

Pigram, J. (1983) *Outdoor Recreation and Resource Management*. Croom Helm, London.

Pigram, J.J. and Jenkins, J.M. (2006) *Outdoor Recreation Management, 2nd edn*. Routledge, London.

Porritt, J. (1984) *Seeing Green: the Politics of Ecology Explained*. Basil Blackwell, Oxford, UK.

President's Commission on Americans Outdoors (1986) *Report and Recommendations to the President of the United States*. US Government Printing Office, Washington, DC.

Price, M.E. and Dayan, D. (eds) (2008) *Owning the Olympics: Narratives of the New China*. University of Michigan Press, Ann Arbor, Michigan.

PriceWaterhouseCoopers (2001) *Technology Forecasts 2001–2003*, available at http://www.pricewaterhousecoopers.com (accessed May 2001).

Prime Minister (1991) *The Citizen's Charter: Raising the Standard*. Cmd 1599, HMSO, London.

Pritchard, A. (2001) Tourism and representations: a scale for measuring gendered portrayals. *Leisure Studies* 20(2), 79–94.

Pritchard, A., Morgan, N.J., Sedgley, D., Khan, E. and Jenkins, A. (2000) Sexuality and holiday choices: conversations with gay and lesbian tourists. *Leisure Studies* 19(2), 267–282.

Propst, D.B., Wellman, J.D., Campa, H. and McDonough, M.H. (2000) Citizen participation trends and their educational implications for natural resource professionals. In: Gartner, W.C. and Lime, D.W. (eds) *Trends in Outdoor Recreation, Leisure and Tourism*. CAB International, Wallingford, UK, pp. 383–392.

Pryce, K. (1979) *Endless Pressure: a Study of West Indian Life-Styles in Bristol*. Penguin, Harmondsworth, UK.

Queensland Treasury (2008) *Australian Gambling Statistics: 1981–82 to 2006–07*. Queensland Treasury, Brisbane, Australia.

Rapoport, R. and Rapoport, R.N. (1975) *Leisure and the Family Life Cycle*. Routledge, London.

Ravenscroft, N. (1992) *Recreation Planning and Development*. Macmillan, Basingstoke, UK.

Ravenscroft, N. (1993) Public leisure provision and the good citizen. *Leisure Studies* 12(1), 33–34.

Ravenscroft, N. (1996) Leisure, consumerism and active citizenship in the UK. *Managing Leisure* 1(3), 163–174.

Ravenscroft, N. (1998) The changing regulation of public leisure provision. *Leisure Studies* 17(2), 138–154.

Ravenscroft, N. and Markwell, S. (2000) Ethnicity and the integration of young people through urban park and recreation provision. *Managing Leisure* 5(3), 135–150.

Recreation Management Training Committee (1984) *Recreation Management Training Committee: Final Report*. Department of the Environment/HMSO, London.

Renn, O., Webler, T. and Wiedmann, P. (eds) (1995) *Fairness and Competence in Citizen Participation: Evaluation Models for Environmental Discourse*. Kluwer, Dordrecht, the Netherlands.

Rhodes, R. (ed.) (1999) *Visions of Technology: a Century of Debate about Machines, Systems and the Human World*. Simon and Schuster, New York.

Rial, A., Rial, J., Varela, J. and Real, E. (2008) An application of importance–performance analysis to the management of sports centres. *Managing Leisure* 13(3/4), 179–188.

Richter, L.K. (1989) *The Politics of Tourism in Asia*. University of Hawaii Press, Honolulu, Hawaii.

Riordan, J. (1980) *Soviet Sport: Background to the Olympics*. Basil Blackwell, Oxford, UK.

Ritchie, J.R.B. (1984) Assessing the impact of hallmark events: conceptual and research issues. *Journal of Travel Research* 23(10), 2–11.

Ritchie, J.R.B. (1985) The nominal group technique: an approach to consensus policy formulation in tourism. *Tourism Management* 6(2), 82–94.

Ritchie, J.R.B. (1994a) The nominal group technique: applications in tourism research. In: Ritchie, J.R.B. and Goeldner, C.R. (eds) *Travel, Tourism, and Hospitality Research, 2nd edn*. John Wiley, New York, pp. 493–502.

Ritchie, J.R.B. (1994b) Crafting a destination vision. In: Ritchie, J.R.B. and Goeldner, C.R. (eds) *Travel, Tourism, and Hospitality Research*, 2nd edn. John Wiley, New York, pp. 29–38.

Ritchie, J.R.B. (2000) Interest-based formulation of tourism policy for environmentally sensitive destinations. In: Bramwell, B. and Lane, B. (eds) *Tourism Collaboration and Partnerships: Politics, Practice and Sustainability*. Channel View Publications, Clevedon, UK, pp. 44–77.

Ritchie, J.R.B. and Goeldner, C.R. (eds) (1994) *Travel, Tourism, and Hospitality Research, 2nd edn*. John Wiley, New York.

Ritchie-Calder, Lord (1982) Education for the post-industrial society. In: Costello, N. and Richardson, M. (eds) *Continuing Education for the Post-Industrial Society*. Open University Press, Milton Keynes, UK, pp. 11–22.

Roberts, K. (1978) *Contemporary Society and the Growth of Leisure*. Longman, London.

Roberts, K. (1983) *Youth and Leisure*. Allen and Unwin, London.

Roberts, K. (1997) Same activities, different meanings: British youth cultures in the 1990s. *Leisure Studies* 16(1), 1–16.

Roberts, K. (1999) *Leisure in Contemporary Society*. CAB International, Wallingford, UK.

Roberts, K. (2006) *Leisure in Contemporary Society, 2nd edn*. CAB International, Wallingford, UK.

Roberts, K. and Brodie, D.A. (1992) *Inner-City Sport: Who Plays, and What are the Benefits?* Giordano Bruno Culemborg, Voorthuizen, Netherlands.

Roberts, K. and Parsell, G. (1994) Youth cultures in Britain: the middle-class take-over. *Leisure Studies* 13(1), 33–48.

Robinson, J.P. (1993) The time squeeze. *American Demographics* 12(1), 12–13.

Robinson, J.P. and Godbey, G. (1997) *Time for Life: the Surprising Ways Americans Use their Time*. Pennsylvania State University Press, University Park, Pennsylvania.

Robinson, L. (1997) Barriers to total quality management in public leisure services. *Managing Leisure* 2(1), 17–28.

Robinson, L. (1998) Quality management in public leisure services. In: Collins, M.F. and Cooper, I.S. (eds) *Leisure Management: Issues and Applications*. CAB International, Wallingford, UK, pp. 211–224.

Robinson, L. and Taylor, P.D. (2003) The performance of local authority sports halls and swimming pools in England. *Managing Leisure* 8(1), 1–16.

Robinson, N.A. (ed.) (1993) *Agenda 21: Earth's Action Plan, Annotated*. Oceana Publications, New York.

Roche, M. (1992) *Rethinking Citizenship: Welfare, Ideology and Change in Modern Society*. Polity Press, Cambridge, UK.

Roche, M. (1993) Sport and community: rhetoric and reality in the development of British sport policy. In: Binfield, J.C. and Stevenson, J. (eds) *Sport, Culture and Politics*. Sheffield Academic Press, Sheffield, UK, pp. 72–112.

Roche, M. (2000) *Mega-events and Modernity: Olympics and Expos in the Growth of Global Culture*. Routledge, London.

Rodgers, H.B. (1993) Estimating local leisure demand in the context of a regional planning strategy. In: Glyptis, S. (ed.) *Leisure and the Environment*. Belhaven Press, London, pp. 116–130.

Rojek, C. (1995) *Decentring Leisure: Rethinking Leisure Theory*. Sage, London.

Rosenberger, R.S. and Loomis, J.B. (2001) *Benefit Transfer of Outdoor Recreation Use Values*. Gen. Tech. Rep. RMRS-GTR-72, US Dept. of Agriculture, Forest Service, Rocky Mountain Research Station, Fort Collins, Colorado, available at: http://www.fs.fed.us/rm/pubs/rmrs_gtr72.pdf

Rossman, J.R. (1999) Assessing the leisure service delivery system. In: McLean, D.D., Bannon, J.J. and Gray, H.R. (eds) *Leisure Resources: its Comprehensive Planning*. Sagamore, Champaign, Illinois, pp. 211–250.

Rossman, J.R. and Schlatter, B.E. (2000) *Recreation Programming: Designing Leisure Experiences*, 3rd edn, Sagamore, Champaign, Illinois.

Rossman, J.R. and Schlatter, B.E. (2008) *Recreation Programming: Designing Leisure Experiences*, 5th edn. Sagamore, Champaign, Illinois.

Rotherham, I.D., Egan, D. and Egan, H. (2005) *A Review of the Economic Value of Countryside Recreation and Sports*. Central Council for Physical Recreation/Sport England, London.

Rouphail, N., Hummer, J., Milazzo, J. and Allen, P. (1998) *Capacity Analysis of Pedestrian and Bicycle Facilities: Recommended Procedures for the 'Bicycles' Chapter of the Highway Capacity Manual*. Federal Highway Administration, McLean, Virginia, available at: http://www.tfhrc.gov/safety/pedbike/pubs/98–108/cover.htm

Rowe, D. and Lawrence, G. (eds) (1998) *Tourism, Leisure, Sport: Critical Perspectives*. Hodder Education, Rydalmere, NSW, Australia.

Rowe, N. (2009) The Active People Survey: a catalyst for transforming evidence-based sport policy in England. *International Journal of Sport Policy* 191, 89–98.

Rowe, N. and Champion, R. (2000) *Sports Participation and Ethnicity in England: National Survey 1999/2000: Headline Findings*. Sport England, London, available at: http://www.sport england.org/research/tracking_trends.aspx

Rudd, K. (2009) The Global Financial Crisis. *The Monthly* 42 (February), available at: http://www.the-monthly.com.au

Rugman, A. (2000) *The End of Globalization*. Random House, London.

Rushton, M. (1999) Methodological individualism and cultural economics. *Journal of Cultural Economics* 23(1), 137–147.

Russell, B. and Russell, D. (1923) *In Praise of Idleness and Other Essays*. Allen and Unwin, London.

Sable, K.A. and Kling, R.W. (2001) The double public good: a conceptual framework for 'shared experience' values associated with heritage conservation. *Journal of Cultural Economics* 25(2), 77–89.

Sample, J.A. (1984) Nominal group technique: an alternative to brainstorming. *Journal of Extension* 22(2), accessed at: http://www.joe.org/joe/1984march/iw2.php

Sanders, L. (1997) Against deliberation. *Political Theory* 25(3), 347–376.

Sarda, R., Mora, J., Ariza, E., Avila, C. and Jimenez, J.A. (2009) Decadal shifts in beach user sand availability on the Costa Brava (Northwestern Mediterranean Coast). *Tourism Management* 30(2), 158–168.

Sasaki, K., Harad, M. and Morino, S. (1997) Economic impacts of theme-park development by input–output analysis: a process toward local industrialization of leisure services. *Managing Leisure* 2(1), 29–38.

Sassen, S. (1998) *Globalization and its Discontents*. New Press, New York.

Saunders, P. (1993) Citizenship in a liberal society. In: Turner, B.S. (ed.) *Citizenship and Social Theory*. Sage, London, pp. 57–90.

Sautter, E.T. and Leisen, B. (1999) Managing stakeholders: a tourism planning model. *Annals of Tourism Research* 26(2), 312–328.

Saveriades, A. (2000) Establishing the social tourism carrying capacity for the tourist resorts of the east coast of the Republic of Cyprus. *Tourism Management* 21(2), 147–156.

Schor, J.B. (1991) *The Overworked American: the Unexpected Decline of Leisure*. Basic Books, New York.

Schor, J.B. (2006) Overturning the modernist predictions: recent trends in work and leisure in the OECD. In: Rojek, C., Shaw, S. and Veal, A.J. (eds) *Handbook of Leisure Studies*. Palgrave, London, pp. 203–215.

Schouten, F. (1998) Access to museums as leisure providers: still a long way to go. In: Collins, M.F. and Cooper, I.S. (eds) *Leisure Management: Issues and Applications*. CAB International, Wallingford, UK, pp. 65–70.

SCORS: see Standing Committee on Recreation and Sport

Scott, D. and Jones, B. (2006) The impact of climate change on golf participation in the Greater Toronto area: a case study. *Journal of Leisure Research* 38(3), 363–380.

Scottish Sports Council (1996) *Facilities Planning Model*. Scottish Sports Council, Edinburgh, available at: http://www.sportscotland.org.uk

Scraton, S. (1993) Boys muscle in where angels fear to tread – girls' sub-cultures and physical activities. In: Horne, J., Jary, D. and Tomlinson, A. (eds) *Sport, Leisure and Social Relations*. Sociological Review, Keele, UK, pp. 160–186.

Scraton, S. (ed.) (1999) Special issue: The Big Ghetto: Gender, Sexuality and Leisure – 1998 LSA International Conference. *Leisure Studies* 18(3).

Sears D.W. (1975) The recreation voucher system: a proposal. *Journal of Leisure Research* 7(2), 141–145.

Seely, R.L., Iglarsh, H.J. and Edgell, D.J. (1980) Utilizing the Delphi technique at international conferences: a method for forecasting international tourism conditions. *Journal of Travel Research* 18(1), 30–34.

Self, P. (1993) *Government by the Market? The Politics of Public Choice*. Macmillan, Basingstoke, UK.

Settle, J.G. (1977) *Leisure in the North West: a Tool for Forecasting*. Study No. 11, Sports Council, London.

Shadish, W., Cook, T.D. and Leviton, L.C. (1991) *Foundations of Program Evaluation: Theories of Practice*. Sage, Newbury Park, California.

Shafer, E.L. (1994) A decision design for tourism CEOs. In: Ritchie, J.R.B. and Goeldner, C.R. (eds) *Travel, Tourism, and Hospitality Research*, 2nd edn. John Wiley, New York, pp. 23–25.

Shafer, E.L., Moeller, G.H. and Russell, E.G. (1975) Future leisure environments. *Ekistics* 40(236), 68–72.

Siegenthaler, K.L. (1994) Importance–performance analysis: application to seniors programs evaluation. *Journal of Park and Recreation Administration* 12(3), 57–70.

Simmons, D.G. (1994) Community participation in tourism planning. *Tourism Management* 15(2), 98–108.

Sinclair, M.T. and Stabler, M. (1997) *The Economics of Tourism*. Routledge, London.

Sirgy, M.J. (1986) A quality-of-life theory derived from Maslow's developmental perspective. *American Journal of Economics and Sociology* 45(3), 329–342.

Sirgy, M. J., Cole, D. and Kosenko, R. (1995) Developing a life satisfaction measure based on need hierarchy theory. In: Sirgy, M.J. and Samli, A.C. (eds) *New Dimensions in Marketing/Quality-of-Life Research*. Quorum Books, Westport, Connecticut, pp. 3–26.

Skates, A. (ed.) (1990) *Where are We Going? Evaluation in Scientific and Cultural Institutions Conference*. Australian Museum, Sydney, Australia.

Smith, G. and May, D. (1993) The artificial debate between rationalist and incrementalist models of decision making. In: Hill, M. (ed.) *The Policy Process: a Reader*. Harvester-Wheatsheaf, London, pp. 197–211 (originally published in *Policy and Politics* 1980, 8(1), 147–161).

Smith, G. and Wales, C. (2000) Citizens' juries and deliberative democracy. *Political Studies* 48(1), 51–65.

Smith, S.L.J. (1995) *Tourism Analysis, 2nd edn*. Pearson, Harlow, UK.

Smith, S.L.J. (2000) New developments in measuring tourism as an area of economic activity. In: Gartner, W. C. and Lime, D.W. (eds) *Trends in Outdoor Recreation, Leisure and Tourism*. CAB International, Wallingford, UK, pp. 225–234.

Sport 2000 Task Force (1999) *Shaping up: a Review of Commonwealth Involvement in Sport and Recreation in Australia*. Commonwealth of Australia, Canberra.

Sport England (1997) *England, The Sporting Nation: a Strategy*. Sport England, London.

Sport England (1999) *The Value of Sport*. Sport England, London.

Sport England (2000) *Performance Measurement for Local Authority Sports Halls and Swimming Pools*. Sport England, London.

Sport England (2003) *Young People and Sport in England: Trends in Participation, 1994–2002*. Sport England, London, available at: http://www.sportengland.org/research/tracking_trends.aspx

Sport England (2008) *Sport England Strategy 2008–2011*. Sport England, London, available at: http://www.sportengland.org/sport_england_strategy_2008–2011.pdf

Sport England (undated) *Active People survey*. Sport England, London, available at: http://www.sportengland.org/research/active_people_survey.aspx

Sport Industry Research Centre (2007) *The Economic Importance of Sport in England, 1985–2005*. Sport England, London.

Sport Industry Research Centre (annual) *Leisure Forecasts/Sport Market Forecasts*. Sport Industry Research Centre, Sheffield Hallam University, Sheffield, UK.

Sports Council (1968) *Planning for Sport*. Central Council for Physical Recreation, London.

Sports Council (1972) *Provision for Sport: Indoor Swimming Pools, Indoor Sports Centres, Golf Courses*. HMSO, London.

Sports Council (1991) *The Playing Pitch Strategy*. Sports Council, London.

Sports Council (1992) *Provision for Swimming* (one volume plus two technical reports). Sports Council, London.

Sports Council (1993) *Planning and Provision for Sport* (Facilities Factfile 2). Sports Council, London.

Spretnak, C. and Capra, F. (1985) *Green Politics*. Paladin, London.

Springborg, P. (1981) *The Problem of Human Needs and the Critique of Civilization*. Allen and Unwin, London.

Stabler, M. (1996) The emerging new world of leisure quality: does it matter and can it be measured? In: Collins, M. (ed.) *Leisure in Industrial and Post-Industrial Societies*. Leisure Studies Association, Eastbourne, UK, pp. 249–268.

Stabler, M. and Ravenscroft, N. (1993) *The Economic Evaluation of Output in Leisure Services*. Discussion Papers in Urban and Regional Economics No. 80, Department of Economics, University of Reading, Reading, UK.

Standing Committee on Recreation and Sport (SCORS) (2009) *Participation in Exercise, Recreation and Sport: Annual Report*. SCORS, Canberra, available at: http://www.ausport.gov.au/information/scors

Stankey, G., McCool, S., Clark, R.N. and Brown, P.J. (1999) Institutional and organizational challenges to managing natural resources for recreation: a social learning model. In: Jackson, E.L. and Burton, T.L. (eds) *Leisure Studies: Prospects for the Twenty-First Century*. Venture, State College, Pennsylvania, pp. 435–450.

Stansfield, C.A. and Rickert, J.E. (1970) The recreational business district. *Journal of Leisure Research* 2(4), 213–225.

Stein, T.A. and Sessoms, H.D. (1977) *Recreation and Special Populations*. Holbrook, Boston, Massachusetts.

Stevenson, D. (2000) *Art and Organisation: Making Australian Cultural Policy*. University of Queensland Press, St Lucia, Queensland, Australia.

Stewart, F. (1975) Opening address. In: Department of Tourism and Recreation *Leisure – a New Perspective: Papers Presented at a National Seminar in Canberra, 22–24 April, 1974*. AGPS, Canberra, pp. 3–6.

Stynes, D.J. (1983) Time series and structural models for forecasting recreation participation. In: Lieber, S.R. and Fesenmaier, D.R. (eds) *Recreation Planning and Management*. E. & F.N. Spon, London, pp. 105–119.

Surfers Against Sewage (SAS) (undated) *Surfers Against Sewage: Website*. St Agnes, Cornwall, available at: http://www.sas.org.uk

Surgeon General (1996) *Physical Activity and Health: a Report of the Surgeon General*. U.S. Department of Health and Human Services, Centers for Disease Control and Prevention, National Center for Chronic Disease Prevention and Health Promotion, Atlanta, Georgia.

Swain, M.B. (1995) Gender in tourism. *Annals of Tourism Research* 22(1), 247–266.

Sylvester, C. (1999) The Western idea of work and leisure: traditions, transformations, and the future. In: Jackson, E.L. and Burton, T.L. (eds) *Leisure Studies: Prospects for the Twenty-First Century*. Venture, State College, Pennsylvania, pp. 17–33.

Syme, G.J., Shaw, B.J., Fenton, D.M. and Mueller, W.S. (eds) (1989) *The Planning and Evaluation of Hallmark Events*. Avebury, Aldershot, UK.

Tague, N.R. (2005) *The Quality Handbook, 2nd edn*. ASQ Quality Press, Milwaukee, Wisconsin.

Tarrant, M.A. and English, D.B.K. (1996) A crowding-based model of social carrying capacity: applications for whitewater boating use. *Journal of Leisure Research* 28(3), 155–168.

Taylor, J.N. and Johnson, I. M. (1973) *Public Libraries and Their Use*. HMSO, London.

Taylor, P.D. and Godfrey, A. (2003) Performance measurement in English local authority sports facilities. *Public Productivity and Management Review* 26(3), 251–262.

Taylor, T. (ed.) (1999) *How You Play the Game: the Contribution of Sport to the Protection of Human Rights, Conference Proceedings*. University of Technology Sydney, Sydney, Australia.

Thompson, J.B. (1990) *Ideology and Modern Culture*. Polity Press, Cambridge, UK.

Thompson, P. (1999) Visitors with special needs. In: Dexter Lord, G. and Lord, B. (eds) *The Manual of Museum Planning*, 2nd edn. Stationery Office, London, pp. 69–84.

Throsby, C.D. (2001) *Economics and Culture*. Cambridge University Press, Cambridge, UK.

Throsby, C.D. and O'Shea, M. (1980) *The Regional Economic Impact of the Mildura Arts Centre*. Macquarie University, School of Economic and Social Studies, Sydney, Australia.

Tinsley, H.E., Barrett, T.C. and Kass, R.A. (1977) Leisure activities and need satisfaction. *Journal of Leisure Research* 9(2), 110–120.

Tomlinson, A. (ed.) (1990) *Consumption, Identity and Style*. Comedia/Routledge, London.

Toohey, K. and Veal, A.J. (2007) *The Olympic Games: a Social Science Perspective, 2nd edn*. CAB International, Wallingford, UK.

Torkildsen, G. (1993) *Torkildsen's Guides to Leisure Management*. Longman, Harlow, UK.

Torkildsen, G. (2005) *Leisure and Recreation Management*, 5th edn. Routledge, London.

Touraine, A. (1991) *Beyond Neoliberalism*. Polity Press, Cambridge, UK.

Tourism and Recreation Research Unit (1982) *Priority Groups and Access to Leisure Opportunity*. Dept. of Leisure Services, Lothian Regional Council, Edinburgh, UK.

Tourism New South Wales (2002) *Towards 2020: New South Wales Tourism Masterplan*. Tourism NSW, Sydney, Australia.

Tribe, J. (2005) *The Economics of Leisure and Tourism*, 3rd edn. Elsevier, Oxford, UK.

Turley, S.K. (2001) Children and the demand for recreational experiences: the case of zoos. *Leisure Studies* 20(1), 1–18.

Turner, B. (1994) General commentary. In: Turner, B. and Hamilton, P. (eds) *Citizenship: Critical Concepts, Vol. I*. Routledge, London, pp. xv–xxiv.

Turner, B. and Hamilton. P. (eds) (1994) *Citizenship: Critical Concepts*. Routledge, London.

UNESCO (United Nations Educational and Scientific Committee) (1982) UNESCO International Charter of Physical Education and Sport. *International Social Science Journal* 34, 303–306.

Urry, J. (2002) *The Tourist Gaze, 2nd edn*. Sage, London.

Van der Stoep, G. (2000) Community tourism development. In: Gartner, W.C. and Lime, D.W. (eds) *Trends in Outdoor Recreation, Leisure and Tourism*. CAB International, Wallingford, UK, pp. 309–321.

Var, T. and Lee, C. (1993) Tourism forecasting: state-of-the-art techniques. In: Khan, M.A., Olsen, M.D. and Var, T. (eds) *VNR's Encyclopedia of Hospitality and Tourism*. Van Nostrand Reinhold, New York, pp. 679–696.

Vari, A. (1995) Citizens' advisory committees as a model for public participation: a multiple-criteria evaluation. In: Renn, O., Webler, T. and Wiedmann, P. (eds) *Fairness and Competence in Citizen*

Participation: Evaluation Models for Environmental Discourse. Kluwer, Dordrecht, Netherlands, pp. 103–116.

Veal, A.J. (1975) *Recreation Planning in New Communities: a Review of British Experience*. Research Memo 46, Centre for Urban and Regional Studies, University of Birmingham, Birmingham, UK.

Veal, A.J. (1979a) *New Swimming Pools for Old*. Study 18, Sports Council, London.

Veal, A.J. (1979b) *Six Low Cost Indoor Sports Facilities*. Study 20, Sports Council, London.

Veal, A.J. (1980) *Trends in Leisure Participation and Problems of Forecasting*. Sports Council/SSRC, London.

Veal, A.J. (1982a) The future of leisure. *International Journal of Tourism Management* 1(1), 42–55.

Veal, A.J. (1982b) *Planning for Leisure: Alternative Approaches*. Papers in Leisure Studies No. 5, Polytechnic of North London, London.

Veal, A.J. (1984) Planning for leisure: alternative approaches. *World Leisure and Recreation* 26(5), 17–24.

Veal, A.J. (1986) Planning for leisure: alternative approaches. *The Planner* 72(6), 9–12.

Veal, A.J. (1987) *Leisure and the Future*, London, Allen and Unwin.

Veal, A.J. (1988) The concept of recreational need re-considered. Paper to the *World Leisure and Recreation Association Congress*, Lake Louise, Canada, July.

Veal, A.J. (1991) Lifestyle, leisure and neighbourhood. In: Veal, A.J., Jonson, P. and Cushman, G. (eds) *Leisure and Tourism: Social and Environmental Change, World Leisure and Recreation Association 1991 Congress Proceedings*. Centre for Leisure and Tourism Studies, University of Technology, Sydney, Lindfield, NSW, Australia, pp. 404–413.

Veal, A.J. (1993) Planning for leisure: past, present and future. In: Glyptis, S. (ed.) *Leisure and the Environment*. Belhaven, London, pp. 85–95.

Veal, A.J. (1994a) The future of outdoor recreation. In: Mercer, D. (ed.) *Perspectives on Australian Outdoor Recreation*. Hepper-Marriott, Melbourne, Australia, pp 153–159.

Veal, A.J. (1994b) *Leisure Policy and Planning*. Longman, Harlow, UK.

Veal, A.J. (1997) *Research Methods for Leisure and Tourism*. Financial Times-Pitman, London.

Veal, A.J. (1998) Leisure studies, pluralism and social democracy. *Leisure Studies* 17(4), 249–268.

Veal, A.J. (1999) Forecasting leisure and recreation. In: Jackson, E.L. and Burton, T.L. (eds) *Leisure Studies: Prospects for the Twenty-First Century*. Venture, State College, Pennsylvania, pp. 385–398.

Veal, A.J. (2004) A brief history of work and its relationship to leisure. In: Haworth, J.T. and Veal, A.J. (eds) *Work and Leisure*. Routledge, London, pp. 15–33.

Veal, A.J. (2006a) Economics. In: Rojek, C., Shaw, S. and Veal, A.J. (eds) *Handbook of Leisure Studies*. Palgrave, London, pp. 140–161.

Veal, A.J. (2006b) *Research Methods for Leisure and Tourism*, 3rd edn. Financial Times/Prentice Hall, Harlow, UK.

Veal, A.J. (2006c) The use of urban parks. *Annals of Leisure Research* 9(4), 245–277.

Veal, A.J. (2009a) *The Elusive Leisure Society*. School of Leisure, Sport and Tourism Working Paper 9, University of Technology, Sydney, Lindfield, NSW, Australia.[1]

Veal, A.J. (2009b) *Open Space Planning Standards in Australia: in Search of Origins: U–Plan Project Paper 1*. School of Leisure, Sport and Tourism Working Paper 11, University of Technology, Sydney, Lindfield, NSW, Australia.[1]

Veal, A.J. (2009c) *Alternatives to Standards: a Review of Leisure Planning Guidelines: U–Plan Project Paper 2*. School of Leisure, Sport and Tourism Working Paper 12, University of Technology, Sydney, Lindfield, NSW, Australia.[1]

Veal, A.J. (2009d) *Leisure Wants, Needs, Obligations, Participation, Demand, Preferences, Opportunities, Rights, Benefits and other Concepts: U-Plan Project Paper 3*. School of Leisure, Sport and Tourism Working Paper 13, University of Technology, Sydney, Lindfield, NSW, Australia.[1]

Veal, A.J. (2009e) *Leisure and the Concept of Need: U-Plan Project Paper 4*. School of Leisure, Sport and Tourism Working Paper 14, University of Technology, Sydney, Lindfield, NSW, Australia.[1]

Veal, A.J. (2009f) *Leisure and the Concept of Demand: U-Plan Project Paper 5*. School of Leisure, Sport and Tourism Working Paper 15, University of Technology, Sydney, Lindfield, NSW, Australia.[1]

Veal, A.J. (2009g) *Leisure and Benefits: U-Plan Project Paper 6*. School of Leisure, Sport and Tourism Working Paper 16, University of Technology, Sydney, Lindfield, NSW, Australia.[1]

Veal, A.J. (2009h) *Planning for Leisure: Approaches and Models: U-Plan Project Paper 7*. School of Leisure, Sport and Tourism Working Paper 17, University of Technology, Sydney, Lindfield, NSW, Australia.[1]

Veal, A.J. (2009i) *U-plan: a Participation-based Approach to Planning for Leisure: U-Plan Project Paper 8*. School of Leisure, Sport and Tourism Working Paper 18, University of Technology, Sydney, Lindfield, NSW, Australia.[1]

Veal, A.J. (2009j) U-plan: Focus Modules: U-Plan Project Paper 9. School of Leisure, Sport and Tourism Working Paper 19, University of Technology, Sydney, Lindfield, NSW, Australia.[1]

Veal, A.J. and Frawley, S. (2009) *'Sport For All' and Major Sporting Events: Trends in Sport Participation and the Sydney 2000 Olympic Games, the 2003 Rugby World Cup and the Melbourne 2006 Commonwealth Games*. School of Leisure, Sport and Tourism Working Paper 6, University of Technology, Sydney, Lindfield, NSW, Australia.[1]

Veal, A.J. and Lynch, R. (1998) Economics versus leisure in the development of gambling in Australia. *Annals of Leisure Research* 1, 67–84.

Veal, A.J., Jonson, P. and Cushman, G. (eds) (1993) *Leisure and Tourism: Social and Environmental Change, World Leisure and Recreation Association 1991 Congress Proceedings*. Centre for Leisure and Tourism Studies, University of Technology, Sydney, Lindfield, NSW, Australia.

Veblen, T. (1899) *The Theory of the Leisure Class*. Allen and Unwin, London (1970 edition).

Venice in Peril (2009) Website. Venice in Peril, London: available at: http://veniceinperil. org/

Villiers, P. (2001) *Human Rights: a Practical Guide for Managers*. Kogan Page, London.

Voase, R. (1997) The role of flagship cultural projects in urban regeneration: a case-study and commentary. *Managing Leisure* 2(4), 230–241.

Wagle, U. (2000) The policy science of democracy: the issues of methodology and citizen participation. *Policy Sciences* 33(2), 207–233.

Waitt, G. and Markwell, K. (2006) *Gay Tourism: Culture and Context*. Haworth, Binghamton, New York.

Wall, G. (1983) The economic value of cultural facilities: tourism in Toronto. In: Lieber, S.R. and Fesenmaier, D.R. (eds) *Recreation Planning and Management*. E. & F.N. Spon, London, pp. 15–25.

Walzer, M. (2005) *Politics and Passion: Toward More Egalitarian Liberalism*. Yale University Press, New Haven, Connecticut.

Walzer, N. (ed.) (1996) *Community Strategic Visioning Programs*. Praeger, Westport, Connecticut.

Ward, H., Norval, A., Landman, T. and Pretty, J. (2003) Open citizens' juries and the politics of sustainability. *Political Studies* 51(2), 282–299.

Waters, I. (1989) *Entertainment, Arts and Cultural Services*. Longman, Harlow, UK.

Watkins, G. (1981) Reflections on 'Life. Be in It': still searching for a soul. In: Heine, R. *et al.* (eds) Consolidation through integration – health, physical education, recreation, sport. Papers from the *13th ACHPER National Biennial Conference*, Melbourne, Australia, January. Australian Council for Health, Physical Education and Recreation, Canberra, pp. 113–122.

Wearing, B. (1990) Beyond the ideology of motherhood: leisure as resistance. *Australia and New Zealand Journal of Sociology* 26(1), 36–58.

Wearing, B. (1995) Leisure and resistance in an ageing society. *Leisure Studies* 14(4), 263–279.

Wearing, B. (1998) *Leisure and Feminist Theory*. Sage, London.

Wearing, S. and McLean, J. (1997) *Developing Ecotourism: a Community Based Approach*. HM Leisure Planning, Williamstown, Victoria, Australia.

Wearing, S. and Neil, J. (1999) *Ecotourism: Impacts, Potential and Possibilities*. Butterworth-Heinemann, Oxford, UK.

Webb, J. (1998) *Junk Male: Reflections on Australian Masculinity*. Harper Collins, Sydney, Australia.

Weber, M. (1930) *The Protestant Ethic and the Spirit of Capitalism* (1976 edn.). Allen and Unwin, London.

Weir, A. (1999) *Elizabeth the Queen*. Pimlico/Random House, London.

Welch, D. (1991) *The Management of Urban Parks*. Longman, Harlow, UK.

Wheaton, B. (2007) Identity, politics, and the beach: environmental activism in Surfers Against Sewage. *Leisure Studies* 26(3), 279–302.

Wheelen, T.L. and Hunger, J.D. (1989) *Strategic Management and Business Policy*. Addison-Wesley, Reading, Massachusetts.

Wheeller, B., Hart, T. and Whysall, P. (2000) Application of the Delphi technique: a reply to Green, Hunter and Moore. *Tourism Management* 17(3), 121–122.

White, G. (2000) Using a community vision to develop integrated plans. *Australian Parks and Leisure* 3(2), 20–25.

Whitson, D. (1987) Leisure and collective consumption: some issues for professionals. *World Leisure and Recreation* 29(3), 17–20.

Williams, C. (1998a) Is the SERVQUAL model an appropriate management tool for measuring service delivery quality in the UK leisure industry? *Managing Leisure* 3(2), 98–110.

Williams, C. (1998b) Application of the SERVQUAL model to the UK leisure industry: are they servicing the service rather than servicing the customer? In: Collins, M.F. and Cooper, I.S. (eds) *Leisure Management: Issues and Applications*. CAB International, Wallingford, UK, pp. 225–254.

Williams, E.A., Jenkins, C. and Nevill, A.M. (1988) Social area influences on leisure activity – an exploration of the ACORN classification with reference to sport. *Leisure Studies* 7(1), 81–94.

Williams, S. (1995) *Outdoor Recreation and the Urban Environment*. Routledge, London.

Wilson, J. (1988) *Politics and Leisure*. Unwin Hyman, London.

Wimbush, E. and Talbot, M. (eds) (1988) *Relative Freedoms: Women and Leisure*. Open University Press, Milton Keynes, UK.

Witt, S.F. and Witt, C.W. (1992) *Modelling and Forecasting Demand in Tourism*. Academic Press, London.

World Commission on Environment and Development (1990) *Our Common Future – Australian Edition (The Brundtland Report)*. Oxford University Press, Melbourne, Australia.

World Leisure Organization (WLO) (2000) *Charter for Leisure*. WLO, Okanagan Falls, BC, Canada, available at: http://www.worldleisure.org

World Tourism Organization (WTO) (1998) *Global Code of Ethics for Tourism*. WTO, Madrid, available at: http://www.world-tourism.org/statistics/index.htm (accessed October 2008).

World Tourism Organization (WTO) (2008) *From Davos to Bali: a Tourism Contribution to the Challenge of Climate Change*. WTO, Madrid, available at: http://www.world-tourism.org

World Tourism Organization (WTO) (2009) *Facts and Figures*. WTO, Madrid, available at: http://www.unwto.org/facts/menu.html

World Tourism Organization (WTO) (undated) *Tourism 2020 Vision*. WTO, Madrid, available at: http://www.unwto.org

World Tourism Organization Business Council (1999) *Changes in Leisure Time: the Impact on Tourism*. WTO, Madrid.

Young, M. and Willmott, P. (1973) *The Symmetrical Family*. Routledge, London.

Yule, J. (1997a) Engendered ideologies and leisure policy in the UK. Part 1: gendered ideologies. *Leisure Studies* 16(2), 61–84.

Yule, J. (1997b) Engendered ideologies and leisure policy in the UK. Part 2: professional ideologies. *Leisure Studies* 16(3), 139–154.

Zalatan, A. (1994) *Forecasting Methods in Sports and Recreation*. Thompson Educational Publishing, Toronto, Canada.

Zukin, S. (1995) *The Cultures of Cities*. Blackwell, Oxford, UK.

Zuzanek, J. and Veal, A.J. (1999) Trends in time pressure: two ends against the middle? *Loisir et Société* 21(2), 319–326.

[1] These items are available at: (i) the book's website (http://www.leisuresource.net); and (ii) the University of Technology, Sydney's website: (http://datasearch.uts.edu.au/business/publications/lst/index.cfm ?year=2009).

Subject Index

ACORN 282–283
Active People survey 214, 361, 376, 383, 386, 392
activism 230
Adaptive Environmental Assessment Management (AEAM) 234
Adelaide Grand Prix study 324, 325, 340
'Agenda 21' 38
American Declaration of Independence 82
anti-globalism 38–41
anti-leisure 57
art gallery performance indicators 357
arts, the 390–393
    funding 392
    participation indicators 357, 370–371
    performance appraisal 368–69
    professionals 4
asset theory of tourism 107
attitudes 300
Australian Bureau of Statistics (ABS) 383, 392
Australian Labor Party 27
Australian Sports Commission 158

bars 153
benefits 65–70
    Benefits Approach 66–69, 174
    economic approach 69–70
    Outcomes Focussed Method 67–68, 174, 175
    health-related 70
bequest value 109
Best Value 35, 363

Birmingham City Council CAA/LAA 359–360, 389
black box syndrome 161, 171
Blair, Tony 34
Book of Sports 103
bounded rationality 139
bourgeoisie 28
broadcasting 392
Brundtland Report 38, 94
budget constraint in U-Plan 186
Bush, George W. 24, 27

Cameron, David 24
capacity
    estimation of 254–265
    types of 249–254
capitalism 100–101
carbon footprint 350
catchment area 271–281
CERM-PI system 362–363, 376
change factors 290
Charter for Leisure 85, 86
Charter of Cultural Rights 96
children 410–412
China 30, 31
Christian Democrats 25
citizen advisory committees 231
citizen participation, *see* public consultation
Citizens' Charter 97
citizens' rights, *see* rights
civil society 34, 35

civil disobedience 231
class divisions 20
Clawson method, *see* cost-benefit analysis
climate change 38, 226, 297, 351
Clinton, Bill 34
Cold War 29, 138
collective consumption 76
commercial sector, *see* private sector
communism 28–31, 100
communitarian liberalism 36
communitarianism 36
community
    arts 390
    development approach 237
complementary leisure 57
Comprehensive Area Assessments 354–361,
    376, 386
compulsory competitive tendering (CCT) 28, 34, 35
conservation planning 166
conservatism 21–25
    compassionate 20
    progressive 24, 36
constitutions 128
consultation, *see* public consultation
consumer surplus 60, 333
contingency method, *see* cost-benefit analysis
contracting out 3
control/regulation 8, 15, 55
Convention Concerning Indigenous and Tribal
    Peoples 84, 92, 409
Convention on the Elimination of all Forms of
    Discrimination Against Women 83, 92
Convention on the Rights of the Child 82, 83
cost-benefit analysis 63, 320–339
    contingency method 63, 328
    Clawson method 63, 64, 332–337
    willingness-to-pay method 63, 328
    travel cost method 63, 64, 328
councils, *see* local councils
counting tourists 272–273
cultural strategies 50, 55, 146–147
culture, *see* arts
culture venues, *see* arts
cultural industries 390

day-trippers 5
decision-making 131
    levels of 150
    models of 134–141
    power-based 135
    structures 186

Declaration on the Rights of Disabled
    Persons 83, 92
Declaration on the Rights of Persons Belonging
    to National and Ethnic Minorities 84, 92
defence 103–104, 113
Delphi technique 232, 303, 305
demand 58–64
    based planning 168
    curve 59
    definition 58
    modelling 63–64
    and public policy 60–62
    theory 59–60
    typology of 289–90
democratic socialism 31–32
demographic
    change 291
    data 197
disability 409–410
disjointed incrementalism 139
Disney 107
durable goods ownership 296

East Germany 31
Eastern bloc 30, 100
economic
    development 111, 115
    evaluation 319–346
    impact analysis 339–344
    management 111, 115
    multiplier 340–344
    rationalism 26, 101
economics
    humanistic 119
    institutional 119
    Marxist 119
effectiveness 351
efficiency 351
elderly 413–414
elitism 24, 28, 32, 135
England Leisure visits survey 214, 383, 394
entertainment 153 and *see* arts
environmental appraisal 166
environmental spectrum planning 166
environmentalism 37–38
equity 69, 70, 112, 113
    social 189
    spatial 189
ethnicity 407–409
European Sport for All Charter 87–89, 96
European Union 128

events 284, 368
excellence 24
Exercise, Recreation and Sport Survey
(ERASS) 214, 383, 387
existence value 109
externalities 69, 70, 106, 113, 234

facility
capacity 246–265
types 245
facility/service audit 242–86
in U-Plan 209
use, measurement of 265–271
false consciousness 29
false needs 29, 30
feasibility study 5
feminism 13, 36–37
Fields in Trust 161, 163–164, 389, 410
flow 48
forecasting 287–316
asking the public 304
comparative 314
composite 314
cross-sectional 310
Delphi technique 306
informed speculation 302–303
scenario writing 305
spatial approach 311
techniques 303
time series 308
fox-hunting, see hunting
framework 11–12
functionalism 12–13

gambling revenues 133
gays/lesbians 405
GetUp! campaign 230, 240
global capital 40
Global Code of Ethics for Tourism
89–90
global warming, see climate change
globalization 38–41, 118, 301
goals 154, 373–375
government
bodies 3
expenditure 10
as facilitator 117
failure 117
levels of 7–9, 132
as provider 117

roles 7–10, 13
size 117
grand narratives 19
Greater London Council 119, 281, 393
green movement, see environmentalism
greenfield sites 213, 283
gross demand approach 16
gun lobby 53

hallmark decision-making 138
Hawke, Bob 27
Hawke/Keating government 35
health 70
hegemony 29
hierarchy of facilities 16, 281
history 14–15
home-based leisure 152–153
household expenditure 406
Howard, John 27
human rights, see rights
humanitarian measures 111, 112
hunting 94, 227, 231

ideology 18–43
definition 18
importance-performance analysis
364, 368
incidental enterprise 111, 116
infant industries 110, 111
input-output analysis 343
institutional leisure 57
interest-based negotiation (IBN) 234
international
agreements 126
organizations 127–128
International Association for Public
Participation 240
International Covenant on Economic
Social & Cultural Rights 82, 83
International Passenger Survey 204,
383, 398
International Visitor Survey 383, 399
National Visitor Survey 399
internet 230
inventory of facilities 205, 208
issues approach 235

Keating, Paul 27
Kennett, Jeff 28

ladder of citizen participation, *see* public consultation
land-use planning 178
law and order 104, 113
left-right spectrum 20–21
leisure
 definition 4
 expenditure 292
 participation 176
 time trends 293
Leisure Industries Research Centre, *see* Sport Industries Research Centre
liberalism 25–28
libraries performance 356
Life. Be in it! campaign 293
lifestyle 299
local
 area agreements 358
 authorities, *see* local councils
 councils 7
 cultural strategies 146–147
 state 142

mainstream economics 101–116
Major, John 28, 97
management
 day-to-day 14
 strategic 147
managerialism 348
market
 failure 104, 111, 113
 segmentation 76, 165
 system 102
Marxism 13, 28–31, 137
Maslow's hierarchy of need, *see* need
materialism 30
matrix approach 16
media in public participation 301
meetings, incentives, conventions and events (MICE) 397
men and boys 404–405
merit goods 109, 111, 330
mission 154, 186
 statements 154
mixed economy of leisure, sport and tourism 4
mixed goods 108, 113, 329
mixed scanning 140
muddling through 139
multi-national enterprises (MNEs) 39, 40
multiplier 340–44
museums performance indicators 357

National Benchmarking Service 363, 368, 376
National Indicators (NIs) 369, 354–357
National Lottery 133
national parks, capacity of 262
National Playing Fields Association (NPFA), *see* Fields in Trust
National Recreation and Parks Association (NRPA) 161
nationalization 33
Nationwide Outdoor Recreation Plan (USA) 235, 236
natural areas, *see* outdoor recreation
natural monopoly 110, 111
need 45–56
 based planning 172
 basic 48
 Bradshaw/Mercer typology 49, 51, 53
 comparative 51
 expressed 49
 false 29, 30, 52
 felt 49
 harm prevention 47
 marketing approach 48
 Maslow's hierarchy 45
 and motivation 55
 normative 51
 optimal arousal and incongruity 48
 and public policy 53, 54
 socio-economic deprivation 52–53
 universal 52–53
neighbourhood effect 106, 113
neo-conservatism 24
neo-liberalism 20, 25–28
neo-Marxism 29
net present value 331
New Labour 34, 97
New Right 24, 26, 29, 95
News Limited 39
Nike 39, 118
nominal group technique 232
not-for-profit sector, *see* voluntary sector

Obama, Barack 136, 230
objectives 154, 186
Office for National Statistics (ONS) 383
obligations 34, 36, 57–58, 95
Olympic
 Charter 87
 Games 31, 138, 227
 ideology 19
Olympism 19

open space standards 161
opinion polls 225
opportunistic planning 166
opportunities 75, 76, 165
opportunity cost 326
optimal arousal and incongruity, *see* need
option demand 109, 111, 330
organic approach 16
outdoor recreation
    in natural areas 393–345
    in urban areas 395–397
Outdoor Recreation Resources Review
    Commission (ORRRC) 227, 229

parks 258–260, 277, 395–397
participation 70–74
    citizen, *see* public participation
    based planning 176
    measurement of 72, 73–74, 383–384
    target-setting 186
    U-Plan module 193
partnerships 3, 134
patriarchy 36
pedestrian counters 269
performance-importance analysis,
        see importance-performance analysis
performance
    evaluation 347–377
    indicators (PIs) 352
planning
    definition 12
    scope 152
    juries 231
    panels 231
    strategic 147
    time-scale 152
    types of 148–149
pluralism 136
policy, definition 12
Policy Action Team Report 50
political
    behaviour 15
    ideology 18–43
    rationalities 20
position statements 166
post-Fordism 29
post-industrialism 301
postmodernism 13, 19, 301
presidential constitution 128–130
pressure groups 137
price 58–64

priority social area analysis 282
private sector 3
privatization 3, 33, 348
professionalism 138
professions 14
profit 116
programmes 284
project size 110
prohibition of activities 8, 94
public
    choice model 141
    consultation 218–41
    goods 69, 70, 105, 113, 327, 391
    inquiries 226
    lending rights 391
    ownership 33
    participation, *see* public consultation
    participation ladder 219
pubs 153

quality of life 75, 76
quangos 133

rational-comprehensive model 139, 185
rationality models 139
Reagan, Ronald 27
Recreation Management Training
    Committee 227
Recreation Opportunity Spectrum
    16, 168, 169, 248
recreational drugs 8, 28, 53
reformism 13
reformist socialism 31
Regional Councils of Sport and Recreation 235
Regional Recreation Strategies 235
residual planning 166
resource-based planning 16, 166–168
restaurants 153
rights 80–99
    animals' 94
    children's 92
    citizens' 95–98
    cultural 85
    declarations 93
    definitions 81
    disabled persons 92
    ethnic minorities' 92–93
    future generations 94
    group 91–92
    history 81

rights (*continued*)
    moral 85
    positive 85
    sporting 85
    tourism/travel 89–91
    women's 92
Royal Parks Agency 396

semi-leisure 57
service quality 361–68
SERVQUAL 361
size of project 110, 111
small government 28
Smith, Adam 103
social
    capital 35
    democracy 14, 32–35
    exclusion 389
    networks 230
    tourism 7, 55, 153, 398
socialism 28–32
    scientific 28
    democratic 31–32
socio-economic
    deprivation 52
    status 405–406
Sony 39
Soviet Union 31, 100
spatial
    dimensions 5–7, 271–283
    modelling 281
sport 382–390
    definition 4
    funding 228
    organizational structure 388
    participation indicator 356
    professionals 4
    pyramid 386
Sport England 156–157
Sport for All 293
    Charter 85, 87
Sport Industries Research Centre
    363, 376
sporting competition 128
Sports Council 389
sports hall performance indicators 365
spot counts 270
stakeholder
    analysis 234, 235
    planning 170
standards 16, 161

Standing Committee on Recreation
    and Sport (SCORS) 383
state, role of 3, 31, 102–116
statutory public notices 226
strategic management, *see* management
strategic planning, *see* planning
substitutability 13
supply module in U-Plan 204
supra-national organizations 127
Surfers Against Sewage 230, 240
surveys in U-Plan 197, 204
sustainability 350, 399
swimming pool performance indicators 365
switching values 337

Taking Part survey (UK) 409
target-setting 188, 202
tastes 299
technocracy 138
technological trends 296
terms of reference 151
Thatcher, Margaret 24, 26, 28, 35
Thatcherism 26, 29, 36
third party effects 106
Third Way politics 14, 20, 34–35
time valuation 338
timescale of planning 152
tourism 397–400
    business 4
    definition 4
    performance appraisal 369, 372
    planning objectives 190
    in U-Plan 190, 203
Tourism Research Australia 383
tourist
    counting 270, 272–273
    gaze 41
    rights 89–91
tradition in planning 111, 116
travel-cost method, *see* cost-benefit analysis
travel trends 295
trickle down effect 385
triple bottom-line accounting 351

UNESCO International Charter of PE
    and Sport 87
Universal Declaration of Human
    Rights 82, 83
U-Plan vii, 181–214
urban growth regimes 141

user-pays principle 28
utopian socialism, *see* democratic socialism

value transfer 338
values 18, 154, 300
vehicle counters 268
Venice
    capacity of 262
    in Peril 285
vision 154
visit rate 275
voluntary sector 3, 28, 134

wants 56
water conservation 350

welfare
    economics 101
    state 31, 95
well-being 77
Westminster system 128–130
willingness-to-pay method, *see* cost-benefit
    analysis
work ethic 300
work time trends 293
women, *see* feminism
women and girls 403–404
World Leisure Organization 86
World Trade Organization
    (WTO) 39, 118, 137

young people 412–413

Author Index

ABS, *see* Australian Bureau of Statistics
Aburdene, P. 314
Aitchison, C. 415
Alexandris, K. 376
Allen, J. 29
Allison, M. 415
Alt, J. 30
Anderson, D. 180
Andrew, E. 300
Archer, B. 309, 316
Argle, M. 300
Armitage, J. 81
Arnstein, S. 218, 219, 240
Aronowitz, S. 301
Asimov, I. 316
Atchley, R. 414, 415
Athiyaman, A. 309, 316
Audit Commission 369
Austin, D. 415
Australia Institute 77, 78
Australian Government 71
Australian Sports Commission 158
Australian Sports Institute Study Group 228
Australian Bureau of Statistics (ABS) 10, 58, 294, 414

Bacon, W. 17
Bailey, P. 17
Baldry, H.C.
Balmer, K. 364
Banks, R. 27

Barnet, R. 40, 120
Barnett, L. 415
Bauman, Z. 39
Baumol, W. 108, 113, 120, 345, 390, 400
Beard, J. 46, 49, 78
Beauchamp, K. 241
Beaven, B. 103
Beck, U. 120
Becker, R. 5
Becken, S. 316
Beeson, M. 20
Bell, D. 301
Bender Baker, H. 410
Bialeschki, D. 376
Bianchini, F. 393
Bickmore, D. 283, 285
Bikhchandani, S. 295
Birmingham City Council 360
Blackshaw, T. 412, 415
Blair, T. 42
Blond, P. 20, 24, 36
Bloomfield, J. 103
Bolton, N. 241
Bovaird, T. 376
Bowen W. 108, 113, 120, 345, 390, 400
Bowker, J. 400
Braden, S. 241, 400
Bradshaw, J. 46, 49, 78
Brake, M. 412, 415
Bramham, P. 17, 42
Bramwell, B. 241
British Government 75

Brodie, D. 400
Brohm, J.-M. 42
Brown, J. 65, 71, 75, 96
Brown, P. 404
Brown, T. 315
Brownlie, I. 98
Bruns, D. 67, 68, 78
Buechner, R. 180
Bull, A. 120, 400
Burbank, M. 143
Burgan, B. 143, 340, 345
Burnett, J. 410
Burns, P. 42
Burns, J. 325
Burns, N. 410, 415
Burton, T. 118, 289
Butler, R. 180
Butterfield, J. 119

Cabinet Office 97
Cabinet Office Enterprise Unit 27
CACI Ltd 283, 285
Caldwell, G. 134
Callinicos, A. 42
Canadian Parks and Recreation Association 67
Canastrelli, E. 262, 285
Capra, F. 42
Caret, N. 149
Carpenter, G. 414
Carr, D. 240, 241
Carter, P. 179
Casey, B. 344, 345, 390
Cassidy, J. 30
Castells, M. 76, 178, 143
Cavanagh, J. 40, 120
Caves, R. 116, 120, 390
Central Council for Physical Recreation 376, 385
Certo, S. 179
Chai, D. 316.
Charlton, V. 293, 389, 400
Children's Play Information Service 414
Clark, R. 166, 169, 180
Clark, T. 143, 144
Clarke, A. 120
Clarke, J. 30
Clarke, R. 300
Clawson, M. 58, 320, 334, 345
Claxton, J. 377
Clemitson, I. 300
Clift, S. 415
Coalter, F. 17, 42, 96, 99, 120, 144, 389

Cohen, C. 369, 377
Collins, S. 415
Collins, M. 258, 389
Committee of Inquiry into Hunting with
    Dogs 227, 240
Commonwealth of Australia 50, 96, 393
Commonwealth Department of Health
    and Family Services 66
Cooke, A. 345
Cooper, W. 42
Coppock, J. 70, 180, 315, 316, 320, 400
Cordell, H. 400
Costa, P. 262, 285
Council of Europe 85, 87
Cox, E. 35
Craig-Smith, S. 180
Craik, J. 120, 400
Cranston, M. 98
Crilley, G. 363, 376
Critcher, C. 30
Crompton, J. 70, 155, 159, 189
Cross, G. 82
Crouch, G., 310
Csikszentmihalyi, M. 48
Cullingford, C. 412
Cullingworth, B. 149, 178, 179, 180,
    240, 241
Cunningham, H. 17, 412
Cushman, G. 72, 78, 112, 113, 204, 295

Daley, J.
Darcy, S. 98, 241, 410
Dare, B. 42
DASETT (Department of the Arts, Sport, the
    Environment, Tourism and Territories)
Dattilo, J. 403
Davidson, P. 377
Davidson, J. 299.
Davis, G. 120
Day, D. 241
Dayan, D. 42
DCLG, see Department of Communities and
    Local Government
DCMS, see Department for Culture, Media
    and Sport
Dear, M.
Deem, R. 42, 415
Delbecq, A. 232
Dempsey, K. 57
Department of the Arts, Sport, the Environment,
    Tourism and Territories 70, 344, 369, 377

Department of Communities
    and Local Government 355, 376
Department for Culture, Media and Sport 50,
    51, 66, 71, 75, 283, 285, 357, 361, 393
Department of the Environment 46, 54, 75, 96,
    235, 400, 412
Department of Environment and Planning 180
Department of Finance 65, 369, 377
Department of Industry, Science
    and Resources 27, 389
Department of Planning 50
Dickson, T. 410
Diener, E. 77, 78
Dobson, N. 345
Docker, J. 302
Doern, G. 97, 99
Dombrink, J. 94
Donnelly, J. 81, 82, 98
Donnelly, P. 99
Donohue, H. 316
Dow, G. 42
Dower, M. 262, 285
Doyal, L. 46, 52, 78
Doyle, T. 42
Draper, L. 400
Dredge, D. 17, 399, 400
Driver, B. 46, 49, 67, 68, 78, 180
Duffield, B. 70, 180, 315, 316, 320, 400
Dulles, F. 81
Dumazedier, J. 57, 82, 314, 316
Dunleavy, P. 143, 144
Dunn, D. 75
Dunstan, G. 324
Dye, T. 144

Edgell, D. 98
Ehrlich, P. 297
Elkington, J. 377
Ellis, M. 415
Elmendorf, W. 171, 239
Elvin, I. 390
English, D. 246, 285
Erkkila, D. 345
Etzioni, A. 36, 42, 140
European Commission 128
Evans, G. 400
Ewing, G. 180, 316

Fagence, M. 180
Fain, G. 42

Faulkner, B. 345, 400
Featherstone, M. 40, 302, 316
Fesenmaier D. 180, 320
Field, B. 315
Fields in Trust 161, 163, 180
Filipcova, B.
Firth, A. 20
Fischer, A. 324
Fitzgerald, R. 78
Flannery, T. 394
Fletcher, J. 344, 345
Florida, R. 390
Forrest, S. 415
Frawley, S. 385
Frechtling, D. 309, 316, 345
French, D. 415
Frey, B. 120, 390
Friedman M. 102–103
Friedman, S. 411
Fyall, A. 241, 399

Galbraith, J. 101
Garnham, N. 101, 393
Garrod, B. 241, 345, 399
Gartner, W. 400
Gedikli, R. 259, 285
Getz, D. 241, 285
Giddens, A. 34, 35, 42, 57, 97,
    120, 302
Gittins, J. 240
Glover, T. 118
Glyptis, S. 119, 394, 400
Godbey, G. 57, 76, 304, 316
Godfrey, A. 377
Gold, S. 259
Goldsmith, E. 40, 42, 120
Gorz, A. 30, 38, 42, 300
Gough, I. 46, 52, 78
Gramberg, B. 376
Gratton, C. 116, 119, 120, 160, 289,
    302, 315, 345, 352, 400
Gray, H. 107, 180
Gray, J. 36, 42
Green, H. 232, 241, 305,
    306, 316
Green, E. 42, 407, 415
Greenwood, J. 143
Groome, D. 400
Gruneau, R. 42
Guadagnolo, F. 377
Gunter, B. 57

Hadfield, P. 412
Hainsworth, J. 415
Halal, W. 316
Hale, S. 42
Hale, A. 400
Hall, C.M. 17, 42, 138, 139, 144,
    180, 377, 400, 415
Hall, J. 161
Hall, D. 404
Hall. P. 139
Halvorsen, K. 240, 241
Ham, C. 179
Hamilton, P. 99
Hamilton-Smith, E. 112, 113
Hanley, N. 78, 316
Hantrais, L. 400
Haralambos, M. 144
Harding, A. 143, 144
Harper, J. 364
Hartley, J. 390
Hartley, K. 120
Harvey, D. 30, 84, 144
Hatry, H. 75
Haulot, A. 78, 98, 154, 397, 400
Hawkins, G. 391, 400
Hay, J. 316
HCRS, *see* Heritage, Conservation
    and Recreation Service
Hefner, F. 345
Held, D. 42
Heller, A.
Helling, A. 179
Hemingway, J. 14
Henderson, K. 42, 376, 415
Hendry, L. 412, 415
Henry, I. 17, 28, 29, 31, 33, 42,
    116, 120, 143, 144, 316
Herbert, D. 285
Heritage, Conservation
    and Recreation Service 61, 65
Hertz, N. 42
Hibbins, R. 415
Hill, J. 103
Hill, M. 179
Hill, K. 31, 276
Hillman, M. 276
Hindess, B. 95
Hirsch, F. 101
Hoctor, Z. 218, 219, 241
Hodge, G. 28, 101, 120
Hollenhorst, S. 377
Holling, C. 234, 241

Homeshaw, J. 238
Horna, J. 92
Horne, D. 85
Horner, S. 78
Houghton-Evans, W. 262, 285
Houlihan, B. 42, 99, 400
House of Lords Select Committee on Sport
    and Leisure 50, 227
House of Commons Select Committee
    on Culture, Media and Sport 240
House of Representative Standing Committee on
    Finance and Public Administration 228
Howat, G. 363, 376
Huan, T. 352
Hudson, T. 377
Hughes, G. 400
Hughes, H. 42
Hunger, J. 179
Hutson, D. 315
Hutton, W. 120, 302
Hylton, K. 241, 415

Illich, I. 138
Independent Panel on Sport 228
International Consortium
    of Investigative Journalists 226
Iso-Ahola, S. 46, 48, 49, 57, 78
Iwasaki, Y. 78

Jackson, E. 289
Jackson, M. 228
Jackson, P. 377, 400
Jamal, T. 241
James, J. 377
Jansen-Verbeke, M. 153
Jarvie, G. 13
Jay, A. 138
Jeanrenaud, C. 17, 128
Jeffries, D. 42
Jenkins, C. 283, 285
Jenkins, H. 135–136
Jenkins, J. 17, 144, 252, 377, 400, 405
Johnson, I. 391
Johnson, P. 400
Johnston, R. 285
Jones, B. 299, 301, 316
Jones, K. 400
Jones, H. 345
Jones, S. 305, 316
Jubenville, A. 5, 180

Kamenka, E. 98
Kamphorst, T. 400
Karn, V. 414
Kay, T. 258, 389, 404, 415
Kaynak, E. 316
Keating, M. 279
Keller, P. 120
Kelly, O. 391, 400
Kelly, J. 57, 288, 315, 316
Kelsey, C. 180
Kennedy, D. 415
Kenway, J. 42
Kesenne, S. 17, 128
Kew, S. 415
Keynes, J. 300
Khan, N. 415
Kidd, B. 99
Kinnaird, V. 404, 415
Klein, N. 40, 42, 120
Kling, R. 109
Knetsch, J. 58, 320, 334, 345
Korten, D. 120
Kotler, P. 47, 55
Kraus, R. 304, 410, 415
Krippendorf, J. 89
Kumar, K. 301

Lader, D. 294
Lafargue, P. 82
Lancaster, R.
Landry, C. 393
Lane, B. 241
Lane, J. 393, 400
Langer, M. 376, 377
Langhorne, R. 39, 120
Lashley, H. 415
Latham, M. 42
Lavery, P. 261
Lawrence, G. 120
Leach, R. 42
Lee, C. 241, 316
Lee, C.-K. 306
Leisen, B. 241
Lenskyj, H. 92
Lentell, B. 97, 99
Leslie, D. 400
Levitt, L. 415
Lieber S. 180, 320
Limb, M. 17, 240
Lime, D. 400
Lindblom, C. 139, 179

Linstone, H. 316
Long, J. 399, 415
Long, P. 144
Loomis, J. 70, 78, 321, 338, 345
Lord, B. 171, 239
Low, S. 400
Lundberg, D. 316
Lynch, R. 134, 288, 316, 403, 406, 415
Lynn, J. 138
Lyons, K. 405

Ma, J. 118
Macaulay, J. 316
MacDonald, C. 377
MacFarlane, L. 98
MacGregor, B. 315
MacPherson, C. 52
Magdalinski, T. 19
Maguire, J. 13, 40, 41, 120
Major Performing Arts Inquiry 228
Makridakis, S. 315
Malkin, K. 412, 415
Mander, J. 40, 42, 120
Manidis, P. 337
Marcuse, H. 46, 52
Markwell, K. 405, 415
Marriott, K. 75
Marshall, T. 95
Martilla, J. 377
Martin, W. 301, 307, 314, 316
Maslow, A. 45, 46, 48, 78
Mason, S. 301, 307, 314, 316
Mathieson, A. 4, 345, 400
Max-Neef, M. 46, 52, 78
May, D. 140
McBoyle, G. 299, 316
McCabe, S. 78, 98, 397, 400
McCarthy, P. 262, 285
McClean, J. 238, 400
McEvoy, D. 298, 316
McGrew, A. 42
McIntosh, P. 293, 389, 400
McKay J. 324, 404
McMaster, B. 227
McRobbie, A. 412, 415
Mercer, D. 46, 49, 51, 78
Mertes, J. 161
Miles, I. 307, 316
Miles, J. 262, 285
Miles, S. 412, 415
Mill, R. 47, 56

Miller, R. 288, 315
Miller, T. 120, 405
Milstein, D. 311
Ministry of Housing
    and Local Government 217
Minnaert, L. 78, 98, 400
Mintzberg, H. 12, 149, 179
Moeller, G. 316
Mommaas, H. 419
Mooney, C. 93
Moore, S. 399, 400
Morrison, A. 47, 56
Mowbray, M. 37, 404
Mules, T. 340, 345
Murphy, P. 238
Murray, M. 410
Musgrave, R. 120

Nadin, V. 149, 176, 177, 180,
    240, 241
Naisbitt, J. 314, 316
National Playing Fields Association,
    see Fields in Trust
Natural England 395
Nazareth, L. 17
Needham, R. 316
Neil, J. 400
Nevill, A. 283, 285
Ng, D. 316
Nicholls, M. 282, 285
Nichols, G. 104, 107, 120,
    389, 412
Noll, R. 17, 143, 345
Norman, W. 377
Novelli, M. 42
NSW Arts/Dept of Local Government 51
NSW Department of the Arts, Sport
    and Recreation 71, 75
NSW Department of Planning 61

O'Leary, J. 352
O'Shea, M. 345
Office of the Deputy Prime Minister 51
Office for National Statistics 237692, 406
Ogden, S. 376
Ontario Ministry of Culture and Recreation
Ott, A. 120
Outdoor Recreation Resources Review
    Commission (ORRRC) 61, 227, 288
Ozbilen, A. 259, 285

Paddick, R. 54, 78
Papadakis, E. 42
Paramio Salcenes, J. 143, 144
Parasuraman, A. 361
Parker, S. 57
Parker, H. 412
Parr, M. 14
Parsell, G. 412, 415
Parsons, W. 135, 139, 141, 144, 179
Pate, M. 369, 377
Patmore, A. 252, 400
Patterson, I. 415
Payne, A. 241
Pearce, P. 56
Pearce, S. 120
Peter, J.P. 179
Peterson, G. 321, 345
Pieper, J. 42
Pigram, J. 169, 252, 400
Porritt, J. 37, 42
President's Commission
    on Americans Outdoors 65
Price, M. 42
PriceWaterhouseCoopers 316
Prime Minister 97
Pritchard, A. 404, 405, 415
Propst, D. 240
Pryce, K. 415

Queensland Treasury 309

Ragheb, M. 46, 49, 78
Rapoport, R. 412, 415
Ravenscroft, N. 120, 180, 400, 415
Recreation Management Training
    Committee 227
Reid, L. 311
Renn, O. 240
Rhodes, R. 316
Rial, A. 377
Richter, L. 42
Rickert, J. 153
Riordan, J. 42
Ritchie, J. 31, 179, 232, 234, 239, 241
Ritchie-Calder, G. 300
Roberts, K. 4, 27, 98, 400, 412, 415
Robertson, R. 113, 309, 316
Robinson, L. 376, 377
Robinson, N. 42
Roche, M. 95, 99, 139, 386

Rodgers, H. 395
Rodgers, G. 300
Rojek, C. 302
Rosenberger, R. 70, 78, 338, 345
Rossman, J. 376, 377
Rotherham, I. 344, 345
Rouphail, N. 261, 285
Rowe, N. 376
Rowe, D. 434
Rudd, K. 20
Rugman, A. 40
Rushton, M. 42
Russell, B. 302

Sable, K. 109
Sample, J. 241
Sanders, L. 232, 241
Sarda, R. 264, 285
Sasaki, K. 345
Sassen, S. 40, 41
Saunders, P. 95, 99
Sautter, E. 241
Saveriades, A. 285
Schlatter, B. 376, 377
Schneider, I. 415
Schor, J. 293, 294, 301
Schouten, F. 400
SCORS, *see* Standing Committee
    on Recreation and Sport
Scott, D. 299, 316
Scottish Sports Council 389
Scraton, S. 404
Sears D. 114
Seely, R. 305
Self, P. 144
Seligman, E. 77, 78
Sessoms, H. 415
Settle, J. 315
Shadish, W. 376
Shafer, E. 306, 316
Sharman, A. 241
Shaw, R. 310
Shaw, M. 419
Shephard, G. 377
Shibli, S. 345
Siegenthaler, K. 377
Simmons, D. 241
Sinclair, M. 119, 120
Sirgy, M. 77, 78
Skates, A. 369, 377
Smith, G. 140, 232, 241

Smith, S. 78, 180, 316, 345, 400
Spink, J. 42
Sport 2000 Task Force 228
Sport England 357, 366, 400, 404, 411
Sport Industry Research Centre 288, 315
Sports Council 61, 389, 400
Spretnak, C. 42
Springborg, P. 78
Sproats, J. 410
Stabler, M. 119, 120
Standing Committee on Recreation
    and Sport 414
Stankey, G. 168, 169, 170
Stansfield, C. 153
Stein, T. 232, 240, 241, 415
Stevenson, D. 400
Stewart, F. 50, 54
Stynes, D. 316
Sunderland, N. 120
Surfers Against Sewage 230
Surgeon General 66
Swain, M. 404, 415
Swarbrooke, J. 78
Sylvester, C. 42
Syme, G. 138

Tague, N. 234, 235, 241
Talbot, M. 42, 415
Tarrant, M. 246, 285
Tay, A. 98
Taylor, J. 391
Taylor, P. 119, 120, 160, 289, 315,
    345, 352, 400
Taylor, P. D. 377
Taylor, T. 85, 98, 410, 415
Teicher, J. 376
Thomas, B. 400
Thompson, J. 19
Thompson, P. 415
Throsby, C. 120, 345, 400
Tinsley, H. 134
Tomlinson, A. 302, 316
Toohey, K. 134
Torkildsen, G. 180, 282, 376
Totten, M. 241
Touraine, A. 42
Tourism Forecasting Committee 315
Tourism NSW 264, 372
Tourism and Recreation Research
    Unit 282, 285
Tribe, J. 119, 120

Turley, S. 412, 345
Turner, B. 95, 99
Twight, B. 180

UNESCO 85, 87
United Nations 126
Urry, J. 41

Van der Stoep, G. 238
Var, T. 316
Vari, A. 241
Veal, A. vii, 14, 42, 64, 72, 78, 120, 134, 160, 161,
    180, 240, 255, 259, 285, 288, 293, 301, 303,
    315, 345, 385, 393, 403
Veblen, T. 119
Venice in Peril 285
Villiers, P. 98
Voase, R. 392

Wagle, U. 242
Waitt, G. 405, 415
Waldbrook, L. 180
Wales, C. 232, 241
Wall, G. 4, 345, 400
Walzer, N. 36, 42, 179
Ward, H. 232, 241
Warnick, R. 288, 315, 316
Waters, I. 400
Watkins, G. 293, 389
Wearing, B. 13, 37, 42
Wearing, S. 238, 241
Webb, J. 405

Weber, M. 300
Weir, A. 81
Welch, J. 400
West, S. 189
Whalley, A. 276
Wheaton, B. 230, 241
Wheelen, T. 179
White, G. 179
Whitson, D. 76, 78
Williams, C. 362, 376
Williams, E. 283, 285
Williams, R. 403
Williams, S. 180
Willis, M. 427
Willmott, P. 316
Wills, J. 400
Wilson, P. 376
Wilson, J. 42, 96
Wimbush, E. 42, 415
Witt, S. 309, 316
World Commission on Environment
    and Development (WCED) 38, 94, 297
World Leisure Organization 85, 86
World Tourism Organization 288, 296, 297, 298,
    305, 315, 316

Young, M. 316
Yule, J. 19, 144

Zalatan, A. 315
Zimbalist, A. 17, 143, 345
Zukin, S. 116, 120, 393
Zuzanek, J. 316, 423